8/13/91

Analyzing Strategic Nuclear Poli

D0143655

Analyzing Strategic Nuclear Policy

Charles L. Glaser

PRINCETON UNIVERSITY PRESS

PRINCETON, NEW JERSEY

Copyright © 1990 by Princeton University Press
Published by Princeton University Press, 41 William Street,
Princeton, New Jersey 08540
In the United Kingdom: Princeton University Press, Oxford

Library of Congress Cataloging-in-Publication Data

Glaser, Charles L. (Charles Louis), 1954–
Analyzing strategic nuclear policy / Charles L. Glaser.
p.   cm.
Includes index.
1. United States—Military policy. 2. Nuclear warfare.
3. Deterrence (Strategy) I. Title.
UA23.G636   1991   355.02'17—dc20   90-40844

ISBN 0-691-07828-9 (alk. paper)—ISBN 0-691-02312-3 (pbk. : alk. paper)

This book has been composed in Linotron Times Roman

Princeton University Press books are printed on acid-free paper,
and meet the guidelines for permanence and durability of the
Committee on Production Guidelines for Book Longevity of the
Council on Library Resources

Printed in the United States of America by Princeton University Press,
Princeton, New Jersey

10 9 8 7 6 5 4 3 2 1
10 9 8 7 6 5 4 3 2 1
(Pbk.)

TO MY PARENTS

Bernard Glaser and Harriet Shirley Treiber Glaser

Contents

Preface

SWEEPING CHANGES in the Soviet Union and East Europe have shaken the core assumptions of U.S. defense policy. By the end of 1989, the Cold War, which had characterized U.S.-Soviet relations since the dawn of the nuclear age, was commonly believed to have come to an end. In the three decades during which the United States developed its nuclear doctrine, and the wide array of arguments supporting it, the prevailing American view of the Soviet Union was far more hostile than it is today. Thus, basic questions about American nuclear strategy and force requirements must be reexamined.

For the foreseeable future, the United States must continue pursuing policies designed to avoid nuclear war while protecting its interests in a world of extreme vulnerability to nuclear attack. Even before recent changes in the Soviet Union, the probability of nuclear war between the Soviet Union and the United States was very small. Convincing scenarios in which the superpowers ended up in an all-out nuclear war were hard to develop. Superpower nuclear war warranted continuing attention not because it was likely, but rather because it would be so horrible. The end of the Cold War may further reduce the probability of nuclear war. Pessimists, however, believe that the coming dissolution of the NATO and Warsaw Pact alliances will increase political instability in Europe and, as a result, increase the number of paths by which the United States and the Soviet Union could find themselves in a large war. Either way, nuclear war will remain possible. Reduced superpower tensions may make the questions appear less urgent, but they are hardly less important.

Debate over the implications of radical changes in the Soviet Union for U.S. nuclear strategy has barely begun. Numerous recent proposals have called for the United States to forgo some modernization of its strategic nuclear triad. However, they are motivated primarily by the desire to reduce the U.S. defense budget and create a "peace dividend," not by a revised assessment of U.S. strategy and military requirements. Consequently, these proposals provide little insight into whether the United States can maintain its security without these new and more capable nuclear weapons systems.

Beyond raising questions about current nuclear strategy and force modernization, changes in the Soviet Union are likely to fuel interest in alternatives to our current nuclear world of mutual assured destruction capabilities (MAD). There are three basic alternatives—nuclear disarmament, mutual perfect defenses, and U.S. superiority. Much of the previous interest in alternatives to MAD was generated by the vulnerability of the U.S. population to nuclear incineration. This vulnerability remains a fact that is unaltered by the ending of the Cold War. Most obviously, nuclear disarmament is likely to receive increasing attention since improved superpower relations appear to make such extensive cooperation more feasible. In the coming decades, other alternatives might come to appear more feasible. For example, arms control agreements that drastically reduce American and Soviet nuclear forces could support calls for strategic defenses capable of defeating these smaller forces, but not much larger ones. Breakthroughs in strategic defense technology would lend additional weight to these arguments. If U.S.-Soviet relations take a turn for the worse and the Soviet economy remains in a shambles, drastically reduced nuclear forces might contribute to American confidence in the U.S. ability to win an arms race back to nuclear superiority.

This book analyzes which nuclear strategy and forces can provide the United States with the greatest security. To establish a solid foundation for this analysis, Part I identifies and evaluates the basic factual and theoretical disputes that underlie the ongoing debate over U.S. nuclear weapons policy. To assess which long-term goals should influence current policies, Part II compares U.S. security in our current nuclear world of mutual assured destruction capabilities to the basic alternatives. Part III draws on the earlier parts of the book to analyze key issues in MAD, including whether U.S. security requires the ability to destroy Soviet nuclear forces and what type of arms control agreements the United States should negotiate with the Soviet Union.

This book seeks to be comprehensive, offering a detailed analysis of the central questions of American nuclear strategy. It identifies where familiar beliefs about nuclear strategy and force requirements should be qualified and demonstrates how systematic analysis can lead to surprising and counterintuitive conclusions.

Changes in the Soviet Union help demonstrate the importance of the book's methodological argument: by beginning with an assessment of the basic facts and theories that underlie the nuclear debate, analysts can focus attention on the issues that really matter while avoiding the often passing and/or relatively unimportant details of competing policy options. Using this approach, the implications of the changing international environment for U.S. strategic nuclear policy are clear.

I conclude that the United States should revise its nuclear strategy, rejecting deterrent threats that require the ability to destroy Soviet nuclear forces—that is, that require extensive counterforce capabilities—and forgoing entirely efforts to limit the damage if all-out nuclear war occurs. This finding, however, is not the result of recent changes; the arguments supporting such a basic revision were strong even before the recent radical changes in the Soviet Union. Nonetheless, these arguments are stronger today, since the case for extensive counterforce capabilities is built partially on the need for the United States to extend deterrence to allies, most importantly to enhance deterrence of Soviet conventional and limited nuclear attacks against Western Europe. Changes in the Soviet Union, therefore, may be best viewed as improving the prospects for implementing changes that are more than twenty years overdue, not as requiring a new nuclear strategy. Further, there is some risk in focusing on changes in the Soviet Union, since the Soviet Union will retain large military capabilities and we cannot entirely rule out the possibility of a reversal in Soviet foreign policy. A case for not changing American nuclear strategy can be built on the need to hedge against the possibility that the Soviet Union will be more dangerous in the future. I believe, however, that this case is undermined by the weakness of the arguments that currently support American nuclear strategy.

Regarding the alternatives to MAD, I conclude that the United States is probably safer in MAD than any of the alternatives. Thus, although these alternatives are commonly presumed to be preferable to MAD, the United States should not pursue policies to increase the prospects of eventually reaching any of these alternative worlds.

Over many years of working on this book I have acquired numerous personal and intellectual debts. I have been unusually fortunate in receiving valuable advice and criticism from a large number of friends and colleagues. Al Carnesale and Tom Schelling provided me with a wonderful introduction to questions of nuclear strategy. I thank them, and Joseph Nye, for assistance with my dissertation, which Chapter Four draws on heavily. For comments on various chapters I thank Robert Art, Richard Betts, Albert Carnesale, Ashton Carter, Ted Hopf, Stuart Kaufman, Steven Miller, Michael Nacht, Barry O'Neill, Robert Powell, Philip Sabin, Scott Sagan, Jack Snyder, Frank Wayman, and many of my former colleagues at the Center for Science and International Affairs at Harvard. I thank George Downs, Lynn Eden, Matthew Evangelista, David Glaser, Donald Hafner, Donald Herzog, Paul Huth, Chaim Kaufman, John Mearsheimer, Robert Pape, Stephen Van Evera, Steven Walt, William Zimmerman, and an anonymous reviewer for helpful comments on the entire manuscript. I must admit that at moments so much help seemed like a mixed blessing, leaving me convinced that some of my colleagues would never be satisfied. It is to them, however, that I owe the greatest debt. My work has benefited enormously from their advice and from the high standards they set, even if I did not meet them entirely. For help with making the manuscript easier to read I would like to thank my friend Bradley Seeman, and my copyeditor Ron Twisdale.

A number of organizations provided financial support and office space while I worked on this book. In the early stages of the project I was affiliated with the Center for Science and International Affairs, John F. Kennedy School of Government, Harvard University; during this period I received financial support from the Institute for the Study of World Politics and the Avoiding

Nuclear War Project, which was funded by the Carnegie Corporation, as well as from the CSIA. The Defense and Arms Control Studies Program at the Center for International Studies, Massachusetts Institute of Technology, provided me with the critical opportunity to finish a draft of the manuscript before I began teaching. Numerous rounds of revisions were completed while I was at the University of Michigan, where the Program for International Peace & Security Research supported my work. I was a fellow at the United States Institute of Peace during the final stages of finishing the manuscript.

Chapter Two of this book appeared in a rather different form as a chapter in Lynn Eden and Steven E. Miller, eds., *Nuclear Arguments: Understanding the Strategic Nuclear Arms and Arms Control Debates* (Cornell University Press, 1989). Early versions of Chapters Four and Nine appeared as articles in *International Security*. Some of the arguments in Chapter Eight also appeared in an *International Security* article that I coauthored with Albert Carnesale. I thank Cornell University Press and *International Security* for granting me permission to include this material in my book.

My wife, Carol Carter, has been a loving companion through this project, and deserves thanks for being patient through years without weekends. I dedicate this book to my parents, who have always been a great source of encouragement and emotional support. From them I learned the importance of trying to contribute to society's well-being.

Analyzing Strategic Nuclear Policy

CHAPTER ONE

Introduction

THIS BOOK seeks to provide a comprehensive analysis of the basic issues of American nuclear strategy and force requirements. Strategic nuclear weapons play a central and controversial role in protecting U.S. interests. They are commonly believed to provide important benefits, by reducing the probability of superpower war,[1] while at the same time creating grave dangers, by providing the Soviet Union with the ability to destroy the United States. Beyond such broad judgments, however, lies a continuing debate over which nuclear strategy can most effectively deter the Soviet Union. Further, looking to the future, many analysts hope to find policies that eliminate American vulnerability to Soviet nuclear attack, but disagree about which alternatives are most promising and about how the United States should try to move toward them.

The analysis in this book proceeds through three stages. Part I, "The Questions behind the Questions," identifies and evaluates the basic factual and theoretical disputes that underlie disagreements about U.S. nuclear weapons policy. Among the key disputes are questions about the nature of the adversary (what are Soviet intentions?), about the nature of military capabilities (can the United States acquire capabilities required to reduce the damage from a Soviet nuclear attack?), and about the role of military policy in the U.S.-Soviet relationship (will competitive American policies generate unnecessary tensions or instead convince the Soviets to cooperate?). Since facts and theories are the essential building blocks of policy analysis, assessing these basic premises establishes a solid foundation from which to analyze U.S. nuclear policy. It also enables us to cut to the core of specific policy debates, since the major divisions between analysts are usually determined by fundamental disputes.

"Alternative Nuclear Worlds" compares our current nuclear world—in which both superpowers' societies are highly vulnerable to nuclear retaliation—to the basic alternatives: mutual perfect defenses, U.S. superiority, and nuclear disarmament. Neither superpower can today protect its society; instead, both maintain the capability to virtually destroy each other following an attack against their nuclear forces. This condition in which both superpowers have assured retaliatory capabilities is often described as one of "mutual assured destruction" capabilities, and referred to by its acronym—MAD.[2]

---

[1] An exception is John Mueller, *Retreat from Doomsday: The Obsolescence of Major War* (New York: Basic Books, 1989).

[2] An "assured destruction" capability was defined by Secretary of Defense McNamara as the ability to destroy, in a retaliatory attack, approximately 20–25 percent of the Soviet population

Would any of the basic alternatives be preferable to MAD? Technological and political constraints prevent either superpower from escaping MAD for the foreseeable future. Nevertheless, although currently infeasible, these alternatives need to be understood, since conclusions about U.S. nuclear strategy and force requirements should reflect long-term U.S. objectives.

"Decisions in MAD" draws on the earlier sections of the book to analyze key American choices in MAD. MAD is a condition, not a strategy; within MAD a spectrum of strategies and force postures are possible. The United States could maintain forces of moderate size or quite large ones. Probably more important are the kinds of forces the United States deploys. A key choice is between "counterforce" weapons designed to destroy Soviet nuclear forces and "countervalue" weapons that threaten primarily Soviet society. With a given nuclear force, the United States could plan only quite large attacks, or it could in addition plan an array of smaller nuclear attacks. And, in attempting to satisfy its force requirements, the United States could pursue more or less cooperative and competitive policies, which would influence the importance of arms control and unilateral restraint in American policy. Consequently, in MAD, basic questions remain: Which nuclear strategy can provide the United States with the greatest security? Closely related, which types of strategic nuclear weapons are required to support this strategy?

These questions are not new. Since the nuclear age began over 40 years ago, hundreds of books and articles have been written analyzing the implications of nuclear weapons for strategy and international politics. Although innovative ideas and approaches occasionally appear, the central issues raised by nuclear weapons were identified long ago. The broad outlines of the debate have been clear since the late 1940s[3] and the formative theoretical work on deterrence and nuclear strategy was completed in the late 1950s and early 1960s.[4] The terms of the debate—first strike and second strike capability,

---

and 50 percent of Soviet industry, which corresponded roughly to the ability to destroy the Soviet Union's largest cities. McNamara's criteria for assured destruction were heavily influenced by the diminishing damage potential of increasing the size of the U.S. attack—that is, once the United States could inflict this level of damage, large increases in U.S. forces were required to achieve relatively small increases in the damage the United States could inflict on the Soviet Union. Mc-Namara estimated that 200 "equivalent megatons" could inflict the level of damage required for assured destruction. Alain C. Enthoven and K. Wayne Smith, *How Much Is Enough?: Shaping the Defense Program, 1961–1969* (New York: Harper & Row, 1971), p. 207.

[3] Well ahead of its time was Bernard Brodie, ed., *The Absolute Weapon* (New York: Harcourt Brace, 1946). An opposing view is found in William Borden, *There Will Be No Time* (New York: Macmillan, 1946).

[4] Key works include William W. Kaufmann, ed., *Military Policy and National Security* (Princeton: Princeton University Press, 1956); Albert Wohlstetter, "The Delicate Balance of Terror," *Foreign Affairs* 37, no. 2 (January 1959); Thomas C. Schelling, *The Strategy of Conflict* (Cambridge: Harvard University Press, 1960); idem, *Arms and Influence* (New Haven: Yale University Press, 1966); Bernard Brodie, *Strategy in the Missile Age* (Princeton: Princeton University Press, 1959); Herman Kahn, *On Thermonuclear War* (Princeton: Princeton University Press,

counterforce and countervalue targeting, credibility of threats, crisis stability, and arms race stability—have not changed significantly. Since then scholars have explored the logic of U.S. nuclear doctrine in great detail,[5] improved our understanding of the history of U.S. nuclear doctrine and warplans,[6] identified important dangers that were not previously appreciated,[7] and provided valuable technical analysis of key policy issues.[8] Given the attention that this subject has received, to offer one more book may seem quixotic or superfluous.

I do not believe so. Despite the enormous attention that has been devoted to these issues, the existing literature suffers important weaknesses. First, underlying sources of policy disagreement are rarely explicit. As a result, why analysts actually disagree often remains obscure. The policy debate tends to focus on the details of specific options, while overlooking the more basic disagreements about the facts and theories on which the analyses are based. This burying of basic premises slows progress in resolving or at least narrow-

---

1960); and Glenn H. Snyder, *Deterrence and Defense* (Princeton: Princeton University Press, 1961). On early works on arms control see Chapter Ten. On the development of nuclear strategy see Lawrence Freedman, *The Evolution of Nuclear Strategy* (New York: St. Martin's, 1981), Fred Kaplan, *The Wizards of Armageddon* (New York: Simon and Schuster, 1983), and Marc Trachtenberg, ''Strategic Thought in America, 1952–1966,'' *Political Science Quarterly* 104, no. 2 (Summer 1989): 301–34..

[5] The key example is Robert Jervis, *The Illogic of American Nuclear Strategy* (Ithaca: Cornell University Press, 1984).

[6] The authoritative study of the earlier years is David Alan Rosenberg, ''The Origins of Overkill: Nuclear Weapons and American Strategy, 1945–1960,'' *International Security* 7, no. 4 (Spring 1983): 3–72. On later years see Desmond Ball, *Deja Vu: The Return of Counterforce under the Nixon Administration* (Los Angeles: California Seminar on Arms Control and Foreign Policy, 1975); idem, *Targeting for Strategic Deterrence*, Adelphi Paper No. 185 (London: IISS, 1983); idem, ''U.S. Strategic Forces: How Would They Be Used?'' *International Security* 7, no. 3 (Winter 1982/1983): 31–60; Desmond Ball and Robert C. Toth, ''Revising the SIOP: Taking War-Fighting to Dangerous Extremes,'' *International Security* 14, no. 2 (Spring 1990): 65–92; Aaron L. Friedberg, ''The Evolution of U.S. Strategic Doctrine, 1945–1980,'' in Samuel P. Huntington, ed., *The Strategic Imperative* (Cambridge, Mass.: Ballinger, 1982), pp. 53–100; Henry S. Rowen, ''The Evolution of Strategic Nuclear Doctrine,'' in Laurence Martin, ed., *Strategic Thought in the Nuclear Age* (Baltimore: Johns Hopkins University Press, 1979), pp. 131–56; Leon Sloss and Marc Dean Millot, ''U.S. Nuclear Strategy in Evolution,'' *Strategic Review* 12, no. 1 (Winter 1984): 19–28; and Scott D. Sagan, ''The Evolution of U.S. Nuclear Strategy,'' in his *Moving Targets: Nuclear Strategy and National Security* (Princeton: Princeton University Press, 1989).

[7] Comprising perhaps the most prominent example are the dangers that result from vulnerable command and control systems. See, for example, John D. Steinbruner, ''National Security and the Concept of Strategic Stability,'' *Journal of Conflict Resolution* 22, no. 3 (September 1978); for additional citations see Chapter Two.

[8] For example, on command and control see Bruce G. Blair, *Strategic Command and Control: Redefining the Nuclear Threat* (Washington, D.C.: Brookings Institution, 1985), and Ashton B. Carter, John D. Steinbruner, and Charles A. Zraket, eds., *Managing Nuclear Operations* (Washington, D.C.: Brookings Institution, 1987); on basing ICBMs see Office of Technology Assessment, *MX Missile Basing* (Washington, D.C.: GPO, 1981); and on ballistic missile defense see citations in Chapter Four.

ing debates, and increases the chances that the United States will pursue undesirable policies.

Second, alternatives to MAD are rarely analyzed.[9] Instead, they are presumed to be far preferable to MAD, and as a result exert influence on current policy. However, this lack of analysis leaves us with little insight into how much and what type of influence is justified.

Third, notwithstanding the large number of arguments and counterarguments, analysis of nuclear weapons policy is rarely systematic and complete. Although the basic concepts that have guided the field are essentially sound, analysts often use them incorrectly, overlooking the conditions that limit when and how they apply, and that lead to important qualifications. Consider, for example, the debate over nuclear weapons designed to destroy Soviet nuclear forces. The standard logic holds that these counterforce weapons can increase the probability of all-out war: if both superpowers can reduce the damage they might suffer in an all-out war by launching a preemptive first strike, then each may feel pressure in a time of crisis, when nuclear war appears likely, to start the nuclear war instead of suffering the other's first strike. Yet opponents of counterforce commonly argue both that counterforce *cannot* limit damage in MAD and, based on the logic of preemptive strikes, that counterforce is dangerous.

More surprising, some central questions about U.S. policy in MAD have not been thoroughly addressed. For example, is counterforce dangerous in MAD? As just noted, the most prominent argument against counterforce— that in times of crisis it generates pressures for preemptive attack, thus reducing "crisis stability"—does not apply if damage limitation is understood to be infeasible.[10] Additional possible dangers of counterforce, including other dimensions of the problem of preemptive incentives in MAD, have received far less attention. To take another example: Can arms control help reduce the probability of war when neither superpower can build its way out of MAD? Classic arms control theory focuses on the value of limiting forces that might jeopardize the superpowers' retaliatory capabilities, and therefore sheds little light on this question when retaliatory capabilities are assured.

Finally, scholars have left a gap at the intersection of theory and policy analysis. There are few analyses of key questions of U.S. strategic nuclear force requirements which lay out the full range of important competing argu-

[9] An exception is Stephen W. Van Evera, "Causes of War," (Ph.D. diss., University of California at Berkeley, 1984), Chapter 13. See also David C. Gompert, Michael Mandelbaum, Richard L. Garwin, and John H. Barton, *Nuclear Weapons and World Politics: Alternatives for the Future* (New York: McGraw-Hill, 1977), and relevant chapters in Joseph S. Nye, Jr., Graham T. Allison, and Albert Carnesale, *Fateful Visions: Avoiding Nuclear Catastrophe* (Cambridge, Mass.: Ballinger, 1988).

[10] Chapter Seven analyzes disagreements about the feasibility of damage limitation in MAD, reviews the dangers that have been identified, and suggests additional ones.

ments, evaluate their strengths in terms of broader theoretical and factual disputes, and reach overall assessments.

In short, therefore, this book has twin objectives. The first, and in the end the more important one, is to reach conclusions about U.S. nuclear strategy and force requirements. In addition, I have a primarily methodological objective: to demonstrate the power of rigorous analysis that starts from basic premises.

PART I: THE QUESTIONS BEHIND THE QUESTIONS

Analyzing U.S. National Security Policy

To better appreciate the significance of current weaknesses in the strategic nuclear debate, it is useful to briefly review the necessary elements of policy analysis. In principle, policy analysis has a neat logical structure. It matches means to ends while taking account of constraints.

The end we are interested in here is U.S. national security. U.S. security depends upon the probability of war and the costs if war occurs. It also depends upon the United States' ability to protect allies and other areas of "vital" interest. Some also include U.S. economic health among the factors determining national security.[11]

Strategic nuclear weapons are one of a variety of possible means for achieving U.S. security. Other military means include theater nuclear forces and conventional forces. Arms control, that is, cooperating with the Soviet Union over the size, type, and/or operation of the superpowers' arsenals is a closely related means of achieving security. In addition, the United States possesses important nonmilitary means: its foreign policy and international economic policy can play key roles in protecting its interests.

Theories play an integral part in policy analysis, providing the logical link between means and ends. They reflect beliefs and conclusions about how the world works. For example, without theories we could not judge whether, and how, the size and type of U.S. forces influence the probability of war. Deterrence theory provides the key link in most analyses of this relationship.

[11] Thoughtful discussions include Alexander L. George and Robert O. Keohane, "The Concept of National Interests: Uses and Limitations," in Alexander L. George, *Presidential Decisionmaking in Foreign Policy* (Boulder, Colo.: Westview Press, 1980); James N. Rosenau, "National Interest," *International Encyclopedia of Social Sciences*, Vol. 11 (1968); Richard H. Ullman, "Redefining Security," *International Security* 8, no. 1 (Summer 1983): 129–53; Bernard Brodie, *War & Politics* (New York: Macmillan, 1973), pp. 341–74; Stephen M. Walt, "The Case for Finite Containment: Analyzing U.S. Grand Strategy," Steven R. David, "Why the Third World Matters," and Michael C. Desch, "The Keys that Lock Up the World: Identifying American Interests in the Periphery," all in *International Security* 14, no. 1 (Summer 1989); and Stephen Van Evera, "American Strategic Interests: Why Europe Matters, Why the Third World Doesn't," *Journal of Strategic Studies*, (forthcoming).

Theories also play a role in determining constraints. For example, beliefs about Soviet reactions to a U.S. military buildup influence judgments about whether the United States can acquire certain military capabilities. To take a specific example, judgments about whether the United States could build an effective defense against Soviet missiles depend on one's beliefs about how the Soviet Union will respond to U.S. strategic defenses. Analysts who believe that the Soviet Union will place high priority on defeating U.S. missile defenses are more likely to find that the United States cannot protect itself against Soviet attack. In turn, beliefs about Soviet responses can be based on general beliefs about how superpowers react to military threats to their vital interests.

Thus, analysts holding different theoretical convictions are likely to reach divergent policy conclusions. They may disagree about which policies are desirable and which outcomes are feasible. Resolving these policy disputes requires first identifying the theoretical disagreements, and then determining which positions are strongest.

Given the central role of theory, it is odd that policy analysis is often believed to be atheoretical. Policy analysts are necessarily applying theories. They should be the most important consumers of theorists' work. Further, policy analysts can help to generate and focus important theoretical questions. By structuring complete analyses, they can identify theories that are underdeveloped.

Possibly more obvious than the role of theories is the role of facts. Facts determine the conditions under which the relevant theories are to be applied. They are especially important because theoretical predictions are usually conditional. For example, according to contending models of how to exert international influence, the choice between cooperative and competitive policies depends on one's view of the adversary: if one's adversary is bent on expansion, then competitive policies might be necessary; on the other hand, if the adversary is a status quo power, then competitive policies are likely to be self-defeating.

Facts also play a central role in determining constraints. Continuing with the example of the feasibility of strategic defenses, whether the United States can build a highly effective defense against Soviet missiles depends heavily on how the cost of building defenses compares to the cost of building offenses that can defeat them.

Ideally, analysts would make their analysis as "transparent" as possible. They would begin with a statement of the objectives of the policies being considered. For most strategic nuclear issues this may seem superfluous—the objective is understood to be reducing the probability of large superpower war, especially nuclear war. There are exceptions, however. Certain policies—for example, greatly increasing the U.S. ability to destroy Soviet forces—might be pursued partly to reduce the costs if war occurs; other strategic nuclear policies might be directed at influencing Soviet foreign policy; still others might be pursued to reduce the economic costs of maintaining U.S. security.

Next, analysts would establish the foundations of their analysis by providing their views on the relevant facts, theories, and constraints. Beyond these basics, they could provide valuable insights by laying out which theories and facts are disputed, by explaining why certain ones were chosen over competing alternatives, and by describing the uncertainties that will be incorporated into the analysis. Then the analyst's task is to apply theories under specific conditions, eventually identifying tradeoffs between competing options and conflicting objectives. In effect, the analyst would be providing an analytic road map in which theories provide the link between available means and ends, while the specific conditions determine which theories apply and their implications. The analysis of complicated issues will remain complex, but its logic should be readily accessible.

Reaching policy conclusions requires performing net assessments—comparisons of overall benefits and costs—which in turn demands that analysts strive for "completeness," that is, they must explore the full range of options and the full range of arguments over the cost and benefits of these options.[12] Partial analyses are easily biased and do not provide sufficient grounds for reaching an overall conclusion. When completeness is beyond their scope, analysts should explain what part of the overall issue they have explored and qualify their policy conclusions accordingly.

Among its many advantages, such transparent and complete analysis would make it relatively easy to determine where analysts disagree. They might have started from different facts and theories, have considered different options (i.e., different means and constraints), or have weighed the costs and benefits of competing options differently. With this type of analysis the policy debate could focus immediately on the points of divergence. Equally important, for a given analytic structure it would be relatively straightforward to determine the implications of different facts and theories.

Unfortunately, we see little of this type of analysis in the debate over strategic nuclear weapons. Analysts are, of course, applying theories; without them, drawing conclusions about the effects of policy would be impossible. The problem is that analysts frequently build theoretical beliefs into arguments without making them explicit and without laying out the conditions under

---

[12] In principle, this could be guaranteed by applying the full set of relevant theories to each option. In practice, a somewhat less fundamental, but no less complete, structure is more common. Specific arguments about costs and benefits will have already gained currency in the policy debate. These arguments are themselves the product of theories having been applied to the options in question. In this case, the analyst joins the debate by starting with existing arguments and then assessing them by identifying the theories on which they are based. If the existing arguments about costs and benefits are incomplete, then the analyst should offer additional arguments based upon relevant but still unapplied theories.

which they apply. As a result, theoretical and factual disputes tend to lie below the surface of the policy debate and disagreements appear to hinge on the details of policy options and not upon the more fundamental disputes.

Of course, the low visibility of fundamental disputes is not entirely inadvertent. Analysts who judge that their theoretical or factual convictions will not be politically persuasive can frame policy questions in ways that are likely to yield their desired outcome while minimizing attention to underlying questions. For example, some analysts oppose arms control primarily because they believe that cooperating with the Soviet Union will decrease U.S. security. Domestic and allied support for arms control makes this a politically unpopular position, however. By framing opposition to arms control in terms of the details of a proposal, for example, the verifiability of specific provisions, analysts can avoid raising pivotal theoretical and factual questions.

Basic Disputes in the Strategic Nuclear Debate

The two chapters in Part I identify basic factual and theoretical questions on which analysis of strategic nuclear policy should be built. In presenting this foundation, I divide the debate along two related dimensions—military requirements and international political consequences.

Chapter Two examines the debate over the military requirements of strategic nuclear deterrence: what military capabilities does the United States require to deter premeditated Soviet attacks and to maintain crisis stability? Key broad questions include: What are Soviet intentions and what risks are they willing to run to achieve their objectives? What military capabilities are feasible for the United States? What determines the credibility of U.S. threats? Because the debate on these questions is extensive, I have not answered them from scratch. Instead, I show how these questions arise in more specific forms in the current debate, assess the competing answers, and suggest which ones should guide U.S. policy.

Chapter Three examines the debate over the international political consequences of U.S. nuclear policy, focusing on the interaction between U.S. military policy and the sources of superpower conflict. Do U.S. forces and military policies influence Soviet objectives and/or generate superpower tensions and misperceptions of intentions, which in turn increase the probability of war? Some argue that competitive policies, built on forces that threaten Soviet military capabilities, will lead the Soviets to conclude that the United States has malign intentions, thereby encouraging more competitive Soviet policies, and a spiral of misperceived intentions and increasing conflict. Others hold that competitive U.S. policies play a constructive role, by convincing the Soviets that the United States is determined to protect its interests. According to these arguments, cooperative policies are risky, since they might mislead the Soviets into questioning U.S. resolve.

Identifying and assessing these basic disputes at the outset has a variety of advantages. Understanding basic disputes provides analytic leverage, since, as later chapters demonstrate, the basic questions play an important role across a range of key nuclear policy issues. Further, especially in an already extensive debate, laying out analytic foundations helps to insure that the debate is cumulative, requiring that we establish which arguments have been made and what we know about how strong they are. In addition, by emphasizing the importance of basic questions that cannot now be resolved, policy analysts can help identify research that might narrow fundamental disputes. Finally, close attention to the strength of basic premises can increase our ability to confront uncertainties. Especially in a heated policy debate, there is a tendency to ignore uncertainties about facts and theories. Starting with an assessment of basic questions encourages recognition of current uncertainties. When confronting uncertainties about the validity of competing positions, we should search for policies that balance the demands of the competing views, although such solutions may be unavailable.

Part II: Alternative Nuclear Worlds

Analysts' conclusions about current policy are often influenced by the belief that an alternative nuclear world would be preferable to MAD. Three alternatives are especially important: mutual perfect or near-perfect strategic defenses (both superpowers deploy systems capable of protecting their homelands from an all-out nuclear attack), U.S. superiority (the United States can protect itself from Soviet attack while holding the Soviet Union vulnerable), and nuclear disarmament (the United States and the Soviet Union agree to get rid of their nuclear weapons).

Although long-term objectives should influence near-term policy, gauging the proper extent of this influence requires understanding how much more secure the United States would be in the alternative world than in MAD.[13] For the most part, however, analysts simply assume that the alternatives are preferable to MAD. MAD is well known and extensively studied; it is considered dangerous because it leaves U.S. society completely vulnerable to Soviet attack. The alternatives are believed to be preferable because they would leave the United States far less vulnerable. Thus, the radical change required to reach these alternatives is considered the only barrier to increasing U.S. security. However, these judgments are incomplete since they do not compare the probability of war in the alternative worlds to the probability of war in

---

[13] We also need to consider: the probability of achieving that world; the near-term strategic, political, and economic costs of policies required to explore the feasibility of the alternative world; and the risks of what is commonly called the "transition," that is, actually moving from MAD to the preferred alternative.

MAD. If war would be more likely in the alternative worlds, then MAD could be preferable.

This failure in comparing alternative worlds to MAD is critical, because the central question is whether the alternatives are desirable. If the alternatives are not clearly preferable to MAD, then their feasibility hardly matters.

Nevertheless, the reputed desirability of alternative worlds continues to influence American strategic nuclear policy. Virtually all analysts believe the superpowers are stuck in MAD for the foreseeable future, but many believe that the United States should pursue policies that hold some prospect of eventually making an escape feasible. Analysts disagree about which alternative world is most desirable, so views about long-term U.S. objectives are a source of disagreement about current nuclear policy. Although much of the disagreement about the desirability of competing alternative worlds is best understood as a manifestation of the disagreements examined in Part I, some of it stems from disagreement about the special features of these worlds. Thus, conclusions about the alternative worlds both reflect more basic disputes and are a source of dispute themselves.

The connection between the presumed desirability of alternative worlds and current policy is most explicit in the case of perfect strategic defenses: support for ballistic missile defense and the Strategic Defense Initiative (SDI) stems from the presumed benefits of a new and different, non-MAD world. Even some who have grave doubts about the feasibility of such highly effective defenses believe that the potential benefits justify extensive research on strategic defense technologies.

The desire for military superiority also has real, if less obvious, influence on U.S. strategic nuclear policy. While some conservative analysts have been calling for the United States to regain superiority since at least the late 1970s, these arguments have not received broad public support. The United States, however, has continued to acquire much of the offensive force that superiority would require, albeit based upon different arguments. Moreover, the other half of the superiority equation, strategic defense, has received extensive support from conservative members of the national security community. Since President Reagan launched SDI, these supporters of strategic defense have rarely spelled out whether their preferred end point is mutual highly effective defenses or U.S. superiority. There are strong reasons for suspecting the latter, however.

The influence of the presumed desirability of disarmament on analysts' beliefs about the objectives of arms control is clear, but rarely explicit. Nuclear arms control could take a variety of forms, including changing the types of strategic nuclear forces the superpowers deploy as well as reducing their size. The arguments for limiting the type of forces deployed in MAD are better developed, and in the end more persuasive. Nevertheless, recent U.S. arms control policy has focused on reducing the size of superpower forces and, across the political spectrum, the success of arms control negotiations is frequently judged by this measure. Though analysts do not usually relate their support for negotiated reductions to the eventual goal of disarmament, it is reasonable to conclude that the strong belief that arms control should be directed toward reductions likely stems in part from the belief that living in a disarmed world would be safer than living in MAD.

Because none of the alternatives can be shown to be certainly infeasible, they will have continuing influence. In the coming decades, technological advances or changes in superpower relations may increase the prospects for achieving one of these alternatives. It is far more likely, however, that these worlds will remain beyond U.S. reach, though technical or political changes will be incorrectly understood to have increased their feasibility. Either way, the possibility of catastrophic nuclear war insures that interest in these alternative worlds will continue. Thus, it is especially important that we understand how they compare to MAD.

Part II devotes a chapter to each of the key alternatives to MAD. I present a framework for analyzing these alternative worlds which, paralleling the chapters in Part I, considers both their military and political dimensions. U.S. military capabilities influence the probability of war through their ability to deter premeditated Soviet attacks, to maintain crisis stability, and to maintain arms race stability (which I term "robustness"). Military capabilities may also influence the probability of war by influencing how the superpowers understand each other's intentions and the extent of conflict of interest between them. Because these alternative worlds have been analyzed so little, my analysis of them is more broad-gauge than the analysis of American policy options in MAD. These chapters provide a structure for analyzing the alternative worlds and provide basic arguments about nuclear deterrence far from the edges of MAD.

PART III: DECISIONS IN MAD

The third part of the book examines four controversial policy issues of long-standing importance. Decisions on these issues go a long way toward defining the broad outlines of U.S. strategy and forces in MAD. I devote a chapter to each of the following questions:

Should the United States continue to deploy counterforce weapons, that is, weapons designed to destroy Soviet nuclear forces?

Does the United States need land-based ballistic missiles, that is, ICBMs?

Should the United States deploy ballistic missile defense (BMD) capable of performing certain limited missions but incapable of reducing the vulnerability of U.S. cities?

What types of arms control agreements should the United States negotiate with the Soviet Union?

While the United States now faces specific decisions on each of these questions, the issues are neither new nor likely to be resolved in the foreseeable future. For this reason, I consider the questions in their most general form. For example, I am more interested in whether the United States should deploy counterforce than in the specific choices about the MX and Trident II missiles. Similarly, I focus on the types of arms limitations the United States might want to negotiate, and why these limits would increase U.S. security, not on specific levels at which various limits might be established.

Each chapter reviews the previous debate on its question and examines the important arguments on all sides of the issue. I assess the strength of these arguments based largely on my analysis of the underlying disagreements about facts, theories, and alternatives to MAD. Reaching a conclusion, however, often requires extending these basic arguments and examining them in greater detail in light of the specific policy issues. Further, I contribute new arguments where the debate appears incomplete.

These chapters demonstrate the value of working from a clear analytic foundation. Disagreements over the facts and theories reviewed in Part I, and over the alternative worlds explored in Part II, account for much of the divergence in the policy debate. Disagreements with my conclusions about the costs and benefits of a given policy option can be traced back to more basic disagreements studied in the first two parts of the book. Thus, beyond their own clarity, such analyses expose why analysts disagree and help to establish a research agenda for resolving ongoing policy debates.

In addition, these chapters in Part III complement each other. Although these four policy issues are often analyzed with little regard for one another, my analysis shows how conclusions about one issue are frequently important to analysis of another. For example, conclusions about counterforce influence conclusions about survivable ICBMs, limited BMD, and arms control; and conclusions about the dangers posed by vulnerable ICBMs play a central role in conclusions about limited BMD and arms control. Taken together, these chapters provide more coherent advice than is possible when key issues are examined individually.

POLICY CONCLUSIONS

This book supports two broad conclusions about U.S. nuclear strategy and force posture. First, the United States should explicitly reject efforts to escape from MAD. Even after making assumptions that favor the alternatives, thorough analysis suggests that the United States is probably more secure in MAD than it would be in any of the three basic alternatives—perfect (and near-perfect) strategic defenses, U.S. superiority, and nuclear disarmament. Considering what appear to be the more likely cases shows the alternatives to be even less desirable. Thus, the influence that each alternative exerts on current policy is unjustified. The United States should devote itself to living in MAD as safely as possible.

Second, having committed itself to MAD, the United States should reject strategies that depend on counterforce either for deterring Soviet attacks or limiting the damage of an all-out war. Counterforce adds little or nothing to the U.S. ability to deter Soviet attacks, including Soviet attacks against U.S. allies. The United States should be able to threaten a spectrum of attacks against Soviet society, but it does not require the capability to destroy Soviet nuclear forces. This flexible assured destruction capability would offer essentially all of the deterrent capability that strategic nuclear forces can provide in MAD. Contrary to common claims, forgoing counterforce does not require the United States to adopt a strategy that limits nuclear weapons to detering only Soviet nuclear attacks against the United States. Rather, a flexible assured destruction capability can support the current U.S. strategy of threatening strategic nuclear first use to extend deterrence to its allies, and therefore satisfies the strategic nuclear requirements of NATO's doctrine of flexible response. Many analysts believe that the United States no longer requires counterforce because the Soviet threat to Western Europe has greatly diminished, essentially eliminating the American requirement for extending deterrence. The more basic point, however, is that counterforce was unnecessary even before recent changes in the Soviet Union and Eastern Europe.

Further, whereas most opponents of counterforce have shown primarily that it is unnecessary, I conclude that counterforce is also dangerous. The United States' continuing interest in counterforce policies reflects a failure to fully appreciate the implications of the nuclear revolution. A variety of dangers results. Correctly understood, MAD makes both superpowers' first-strike incentives too small to warrant the risks of launching a preemptive attack. However, U.S. interest in counterforce partly reflects its continuing interest in damage limitation. Consequently, although preemption would never be the United States' best option, in a severe crisis U.S. decisionmakers may fail to fully recognize this. Counterforce is therefore dangerous because it both reflects and reinforces the continuing U.S. desire to be able to limit the costs of an all-out war, and could therefore reduce crisis stability. In addition, counterforce can generate unnecessary tensions between the superpowers, since each superpower sees the other's counterforce reflecting malign intentions, and increase the probability of accidental war during a superpower crisis.

Consequently, the United States should not buy additional counterforce systems and should consider reducing much of the counterforce it has already deployed. Counterforce ballistic missiles like the MX and Trident II are most worrisome because they combine high accuracy—which enhances their ability to destroy Soviet nuclear forces—with the ability to reach their targets promptly. For similar reasons, a new strategic bomber is unnecessary if its key purpose is to destroy Soviet nuclear forces or command and control; and it is dangerous if U.S. leaders conclude that it provides an enhanced damage-limitation capability. Further, since arguments for second-strike counterforce are weak, the United States should not increase the survivability of its ICBMs to provide this capability. In addition, the United States should not pursue strategic defenses that might contribute to a damage-limitation capability.

Having revised its policy along these lines, U.S. arms control efforts would give priority to limiting counterforce, not to reducing the size of superpower forces per se. Since the United States can maintain its necessary deterrent capabilities unilaterally, arms control that constrains Soviet counterforce is not required primarily to protect necessary American deterrent capabilities. Such agreements are valuable, however, since they can reduce the dangers noted above: they can help to diminish misunderstandings of MAD by reducing the role that counterforce plays in superpower doctrines, and they can moderate the military competition that is most likely to generate superpower tensions. Along these lines, the United States would strongly support the ABM Treaty to avoid a competition in strategic defenses that might appear useful for damage limitation. By comparison with limits on counterforce, reducing force size would do far less to reduce the dangers that exist in MAD. Thus, arms control proposals that focus on reducing the size of superpower arsenals misconstrue the real dangers and misdirect our attention.

PART I

The Questions behind the Questions

CHAPTER TWO

Disputes over the U.S. Military Requirements of Nuclear Deterrence

A RELATIVELY small number of disputes about facts and theories determine the broad outlines of the debate over U.S. nuclear policy. Analysts' positions on these disputes go a long way toward determining their policy conclusions. Consequently, identifying and assessing the competing positions on basic disputes enables us to cut quickly to the core of the strategic nuclear debate and provides a solid foundation from which to evaluate specific questions in greater detail.

I divide the overall strategic nuclear debate along two dimensions—the military requirements of deterrence and the broader international political consequences of the interaction between military policy and superpower politics. This chapter examines disputes in the debate over the military requirements of deterrence.[1] This debate implicitly assumes that U.S. military policy influences neither Soviet objectives and the value they place on achieving those objectives, nor superpower relations more generally. Chapter Three examines disputes over these assumptions, which are at the center of what I have termed the international political dimension of the debate.

The broad question in the debate over military requirements is: What capabilities does the United States require to deter given Soviet actions? Most of the strategic nuclear debate focuses on this question. Force deployments and arms control proposals are judged by their contribution to U.S. retaliatory capabilities and limited nuclear options, and their effect on first-strike advantages. Most analysts believe that relatively small numbers of survivable nuclear weapons are adequate to deter attacks against U.S. cities. Analysts disagree, however, about the requirements for deterring a large Soviet attack against U.S. strategic nuclear forces, that is, a "counterforce" attack. Probably even more important are disagreements about the strategic nuclear capabilities that the United States requires to extend deterrence to U.S. allies—that is, to deter Soviet conventional and nuclear attacks against Western Europe and other areas of vital interest by threatening to escalate to the use of strategic nuclear weapons. Some analysts stress that even in MAD, U.S. "counter-

---

[1] Here I focus on the logical foundations and have not tried to capture the texture of the actual debate. For a more detailed analysis of the debate since the early 1970s see my "Why Do Strategists Disagree about the Requirements of Strategic Nuclear Deterrence?" in Lynn Eden and Steven E. Miller, *Nuclear Arguments* (Ithaca: Cornell University Press, 1989).

value'' capabilities—forces targeted against Soviet cities and economic targets—are sufficient to deter Soviet counterforce attacks and to extend deterrence to U.S. allies. Others disagree, holding that the United States requires counterforce options to achieve these deterrent objectives.

This chapter begins by describing and assessing six areas of dispute in the debate over the military requirements of deterrence:

1. How do Soviet leaders view the costs of nuclear war?
2. How do Soviet leaders view the benefits of expansion?
3. Can the United States significantly limit damage to itself in an all-out war?
4. What determines advantages in credibility and capability between the nuclear superpowers?
5. How does the difficulty of limiting a nuclear war affect the requirements of deterrence?
6. What is required for crisis stability?

Looking across the above disputes, the closing section of the chapter identifies three broad schools of thought in the current nuclear debate and then, based on my assessment of the basic disputes, evaluates their overall arguments about U.S. nuclear strategy and force requirements. In later chapters, my analysis of military requirements begins from these positions and explores challenges and qualifications raised by specific policy issues.

It is important to recognize that disagreements about the military requirements of deterrence do not stem primarily from disagreements about the basic logic of deterrence. Before proceeding, I therefore briefly describe this logic, using the United States and the Soviet Union as examples. Most analysts agree, at a general level, that Soviet decisionmakers interested in pursuing a specific action will be deterred by the United States if they judge that the probable costs that will be imposed by the United States exceed the probable benefits of pursuing the action. Stated somewhat more precisely, Soviet leaders will be deterred from pursuing a specific action if they are confronted by a threat from the United States, and if they judge that the *probability* that the United States will carry out the threat combined with the *costs* if the threat is carried out is greater than the *probability* that the Soviet Union can accomplish the contemplated action combined with the *benefits* they expect to derive from it.[2]

---

[2] In simple symbolic terms, the Soviet leaders will be deterred if they judge that:

(Probability of U.S. carrying out threat × Costs if threat carried out) >
(Probability of accomplishing the action × Benefits of the action)

This formulation assumes that the country considering launching the attack does not see potential costs in continuing to accept the status quo, that is, refraining does not carry potential costs. More generally, this country should compare the expected costs of not acting to the net expected costs and benefits of acting. If its leaders judge that there may be costs to not acting, then deterrence could fail even if the expected costs of acting exceed the expected benefits. Such comparisons can, for example, lead to preemptive attacks.

The first consideration, the Soviets' assessment of the probability that the United States will carry out its threat, reflects their judgment of U.S. *credibility* and is particularly important in the debate over the military requirements of strategic nuclear deterrence. In theory, a rational decisionmaker who finds the expected costs of pursuing an action to exceed its expected benefits will be deterred.[3] Analysts disagree, however, about how to translate this general logic into a policy of strategic nuclear deterrence that adequately considers the facts and complexities of today's world.

The Disputes

How Do Soviet Leaders View the Costs of Nuclear War?

The difficulty of deterring the Soviet Union depends on the costs Soviet leaders expect from a nuclear war. Other things being equal, the Soviet Union will be harder to deter when its leaders see smaller costs.

This section examines three arguments which hold that the United States cannot inflict sufficiently high costs on the Soviet Union. The proposed solutions call for increasing the U.S. ability to damage Soviet society and to destroy the Soviet leadership and its military forces. However, persuasive counterarguments hold that U.S. forces can already inflict overwhelming costs since current U.S. retaliatory capabilities can destroy much of Soviet society.

---

[3] For a detailed discussion of the decisionmaker's deterrent calculus see Glenn H. Snyder, *Deterrence and Defense: Toward a Theory of National Strategy* (Princeton: Princeton University Press, 1961), pp. 12–30. For discussions of the evolution and current status of deterrence theory see Robert Jervis, "Deterrence Theory Revisited," *World Politics* 31, no. 2 (January 1979): 289–324; Alexander L. George and Richard Smoke, *Deterrence in American Foreign Policy: Theory and Practice* (New York: Columbia University Press, 1974), pp. 1–104, 501–88; Patrick M. Morgan, *Deterrence: A Conceptual Analysis*, 2d ed. (Beverly Hills: Sage Publications, 1983); and "The Rational Deterrence Debate: A Symposium," *World Politics* 41, no. 2 (January 1989). Other important discussions of the conditions under which deterrence is likely to succeed and the problems that a deterrence policy can generate include: John D. Steinbruner, "Beyond Rational Deterrence," *World Politics* 28, no. 2 (January 1976): 223–45; Robert Jervis, "Deterrence, the Spiral Model and Intentions of the Adversary," in his *Perception and Misperception in International Politics* (Princeton: Princeton University Press, 1976), pp. 58–113; George H. Quester, *Deterrence before Hiroshima: The Airpower Background of Modern Strategy*, rev. ed. (New Brunswick, N.J.: Transaction Books, 1986); John J. Mearsheimer, *Conventional Deterrence* (Ithaca: Cornell University Press, 1983); Paul Huth and Bruce Russett, "What Makes Deterrence Work? Cases from 1900 to 1980," *World Politics* 36, no. 4 (July 1984): 496–526; Paul Huth, *Extended Deterrence and the Prevention of War* (New Haven: Yale University Press, 1988); Robert Jervis, Richard Ned Lebow, and Janice Gross Stein, eds., *Psychology and Deterrence* (Baltimore: Johns Hopkins University Press, 1985); Richard Ned Lebow, *Between Peace and War: The Nature of International Crises* (Baltimore: Johns Hopkins University Press, 1981); John Orme, "Deterrence Failures: A Second Look," *International Security* 11, no. 4 (Spring 1987): 96–124; and Richard Ned Lebow, "Deterrence Failures Revisited," *International Security* 12, no. 1 (Summer 1987): 197–213.

SOVIET DAMAGE-LIMITATION AND CIVIL DEFENSE CAPABILITIES

Analysts have argued that Soviet investments in counterforce, strategic defenses, and civil defense might enable the Soviet Union to dramatically reduce the costs of a nuclear war and to recover quickly. Paul Nitze, for example, claimed that Soviet estimates that their civil defense program combined with a counterforce attack "should hold casualties to 3 per cent or 4 per cent of their population" were "not wholly out of the ball park."[4] T. K. Jones and W. Scott Thompson found that if the United States were to launch its entire surviving force against urban and industrial targets, civil defense would enable the "Soviets to return to their full prewar GNP . . . [in] about five years if they protected both population and industry."[5] Based on these estimates of the Soviet ability to withstand U.S. retaliation, analysts raise doubts about the U.S. ability to deter the Soviet Union and argue for substantial increases in the U.S. ability to damage Soviet society.

Contrary to these claims, available analyses suggest that Soviet efforts to limit the damage to their society would be far less effective. Following a full attack against its forces, the United States would be left with surviving forces that provide many times the destructive capability usually required for assured destruction of Soviet society.[6] Although a Soviet attack against U.S. command and control might reduce the U.S. ability to inflict damage, the U.S. retaliatory capability would almost certainly remain very large.[7] Similarly,

[4] Paul H. Nitze, "Deterring Our Deterrent," *Foreign Policy* no. 25 (Winter 1976–77): 204–6. In the same article he claims that the United States needs "something on the order of 3,000 deliverable megatons remaining in reserve after a counterforce exchange" to keep the Soviet population hostage to a countervalue attack (p. 209).

[5] T. K. Jones and W. Scott Thompson, "Central War and Civil Defense," *Orbis* 22, no. 3 (Fall 1978): 681. They conclude that the potential for protecting societies is sufficiently great that the United States should shift to a "survival-oriented" nuclear strategy (p. 711). See also Leon Goure, *War Survival in Soviet Strategy* (Coral Gables, Fla.: Center for Advanced International Studies, University of Miami, 1976), who finds Soviet war survival capability "putting into question the [deterrence and warfighting posture] of the U.S." (p. 3), and R. J. Rummel, "Will the Soviet Union Soon Have a First-Strike Capability?" *Orbis* 20 (Fall 1976): 579–94.

[6] See Michael Salman, Kevin J. Sullivan, and Stephen Van Evera, "Analysis or Propaganda? Measuring American Strategic Nuclear Capability, 1969–1988," in Eden and Miller, *Nuclear Arguments*; Joshua M. Epstein, *The 1988 Defense Budget* (Washington, D.C.: Brookings Institution, 1987), p. 22; and Michael M. May, George F. Bing, and John D. Steinbruner, "Strategic Arsenals after START: The Implications of Deep Cuts," *International Security* 13, no. 1 (Summer 1988): 90–133. For recent calculations of the damage to the Soviet Union as a function of equivalent megatonage see Barbara G. Levi, Frank N. von Hippel, and William H. Daugherty, "Civilian Casualties from 'Limited' Nuclear Attacks on the Soviet Union," *International Security* 12, no. 3 (Winter 1987/88): 168–89.

[7] Discussions of the possibility that such an attack could prevent U.S. retaliation by "decapitating" its command structure include Bruce G. Blair, *Strategic Command and Control: Redefining the Nuclear Threat* (Washington, D.C.: Brookings Institution, 1985), especially p. 208; John D. Steinbruner, "Nuclear Decapitation," *Foreign Policy* no. 45 (Winter 1981–82): 19; idem, "National Security and the Concept of Strategic Stability," *Journal of Conflict Resolution* 22,

although studies show that Soviet civil defense could reduce deaths, the CIA estimated that under the most favorable conditions Soviet casualties from the direct effects of U.S. retaliation could be reduced to the low tens of millions; the Arms Control and Disarmament Agency estimated Soviet fatalities from these effects at 25–35 million, and also noted that the United States could kill 75–85 million Soviets if it attacked the evacuated population.[8] In addition, civil defense would do little to protect the infrastructure that the Soviet Union would rely on to recover from a nuclear war; and massive disruption of Soviet society and possible environmental effects could threaten those who initially survived the U.S. attack.[9]

Finally, Soviet leaders appear to be fully aware of the devastating consequences of an all-out nuclear war. The political level of Soviet military doctrine has long held that a nuclear war would have catastrophic and unacceptable consequences and cannot be considered a rational means to political ends, and now also holds that neither superpower can win a nuclear war.[10] Thus, whatever ability the Soviet Union might have to reduce the damage of an all-out nuclear war appears to be far too small to embolden Soviet leaders and increase their willingness to challenge U.S. interests.

In short, the Soviet ability to protect its society appears to be quite limited and Soviet leaders recognize this. The United States has a robust capability to destroy Soviet society and there are strong reasons for believing that the

---

no. 3 (September 1978): 426; Desmond Ball, *Can Nuclear War Be Controlled?* Adelphi Paper No. 169 (London: IISS, 1981), p. 14; and Ashton B. Carter, "Assessing Command System Vulnerability," in Ashton B. Carter, John D. Steinbruner and Charles A. Zraket, eds., *Managing Nuclear Operations* (Washington, D.C.: Brookings Institution, 1987). Carter concludes that "insofar as the assured ability to retaliate with devastating force, irrespective of traditional and more stringent military damage criteria, constitutes nuclear deterrence, to this extent command system vulnerability is not a threat to deterrence" (p. 607); Blair and Steinbruner are more pessimistic. Doubts about the U.S. ability to retaliate are best dealt with by improving U.S. C^3 (command, control, and communication), not by increasing the size of U.S. forces.

[8] Director of Central Intelligence, *Soviet Civil Defense* (Washington, D.C.: CIA, 1978), p. 12; U.S. Arms Control and Disarmament Agency, *An Analysis of Civil Defense in Nuclear War* (Washington, D.C.: ACDA, 1978). See also Office of Technology Assessment, *The Effects of Nuclear War* (Washington, D.C.: GPO, May 1979), pp. 49–59, 139–45. On problems with Soviet civil defense see Fred M. Kaplan, "The Soviet Civil Defense Myth," *Bulletin of the Atomic Scientists* (March 1978): 14–20, (April 1978): 41–47. See also John M. Weinstein, "The Strategic Implications of Civil Defense," in Robert Kennedy and John M. Weinstein, eds., *The Defense of the West: Strategic and European Security Issues Reappraised* (Boulder, Colo.: Westview Press, 1984), pp. 77–116. For a range of views see Senate Committee on Banking, Housing and Urban Affairs, *Hearings on Civil Defense*, 95th Cong., 2d sess., 8 January 1979.

[9] For sources on these effects see note 44.

[10] Raymond L. Garthoff, "New Thinking in Soviet Military Doctrine," *Washington Quarterly* (Summer 1988): 133; Stephen M. Meyer, "The Sources and Prospects of Gorbachev's New Political Thinking on Security," *International Security* 13, no. 2 (Fall 1988): 135–36. See also David Holloway, *The Soviet Union and the Arms Race* (New Haven: Yale University Press, 1983), pp. 52–55.

United States will be able to maintain this capability for the foreseeable future.[11]

Some analysts believe that Soviet leaders are insensitive to damage to their society. According to this view, they do not see even very high levels of societal damage resulting in high costs, and therefore, will not be deterred by the prospect of such damage. Richard Pipes, for example, argues that:

> The novelty of nuclear weapons consists not in their destructiveness—that is, after all, a matter of degree, and a country like the Soviet Union which, as Soviet generals proudly boast, suffered in World War II the loss of over 20 million casualties, as well as the destruction of 1,710 towns, over 70,000 villages, and some 32,000 industrial establishments to win the war and emerge as a global power, is not to be intimidated by the prospect of destruction.[12]

Pipes goes on to claim that as a result of this experience in previous wars, the Soviet Union defines "unacceptable damage" at a far higher level than does the United States.[13] In short, Soviet leaders do not consider the loss of population to be as costly as do U.S. leaders and, therefore, are willing to accept extremely heavy damage to their society to achieve their objectives. This means that the Soviet Union is both harder to deter and better able to use nuclear weapons for coercion.

There are, however, serious problems with this line of argument. First, Soviet losses during World War II were not sustained voluntarily; rather, Stalin tried to avoid war with Hitler. Consequently, we can infer neither that Soviet leaders are insensitive to societal losses nor that they would accept high levels of damage in order to expand. Second, proponents have not provided evidence to support their claim that incurring heavy large losses in past wars makes states more willing to accept high levels of damage in future wars. Third, identifying 20 million deaths as an acceptable threshold is itself misleading since Soviet leaders have little chance of reducing the damage of an all-out nuclear war to this level. As discussed above, Soviet leaders recognize that a nuclear war would probably result in much greater damage to their society.[14]

In addition, a more general counterargument simply responds that Soviet

---

[11] For a detailed discussion of the robustness of U.S. assured destruction capabilities see Chapter Ten; for a structural analysis see Chapter Five.

[12] Richard Pipes, "Why the Soviet Union Thinks It Can Fight and Win a Nuclear War," *Commentary* 64, no. 1 (July 1977): 29.

[13] Ibid., 34.

[14] On these points see Holloway, *The Soviet Union and the Arms Race*, p. 52–53; Michael E. Howard, "On Fighting a Nuclear War," *International Security* 5, no. 4 (Spring 1981): 6; Bernard Brodie, "The Development of Nuclear Strategy," *International Security* 2, no. 4 (Spring 1978): 73; McGeorge Bundy, "Maintaining Stable Deterrence," *International Security* 3, no. 3 (Winter 1978/1979): 12–13.

leaders are not insensitive to damage on the scale of nuclear war. Along these lines, McGeorge Bundy argues that even a small nuclear attack would bring costs that exceed the benefits of expansion.[15] The following section suggests that Soviet behavior is consistent with this view.

WHAT ASSETS DO THE SOVIETS VALUE MOST?

Some analysts believe that Soviet leaders place the highest value on maintaining political control and military forces, and therefore conclude that the United States should threaten limited nuclear attacks against these targets. Others fear that U.S. threats against Soviet society may be ineffective. Thus, according to these analysts, threatening sufficiently high costs to deter Soviet leaders requires the United States to be able to destroy the Soviet leadership and its conventional and nuclear forces.[16]

In describing the targeting requirements of the "countervailing strategy," which was the nuclear strategy developed during the Carter administration, former secretary of defense Harold Brown provides an important example of the first type of argument: "The United States would have the option for more selective, lesser retaliatory attacks that would exact a prohibitively high price from the things the Soviet leadership prizes most—political and military control, nuclear and conventional military force, and the economic base needed to sustain a war."[17]

Colin Gray and Keith Payne take this view of Soviet leaders a step further, asserting that Soviet leaders would be most impressed by a strategy designed to lead to the demise of the Soviet state, and that "If the United States developed the targeting plans and procured the weapons necessary to hold the Soviet political, bureaucratic, and military leadership at risk, that would serve as

[15] See McGeorge Bundy's often quoted statement in "To Cap the Volcano," *Foreign Affairs* 48, no. 1 (October 1969): 10.

[16] We should not confuse this argument for targeting command and control with arguments for maintaining the ability to decapitate the Soviet retaliatory capability. Although the targeting requirements are similar, the rationales are quite different: the latter is designed to reduce the Soviet ability to inflict costs on the United States; the former is designed to increase the U.S. ability to inflict costs on the Soviet Union.

[17] Secretary of Defense Brown, *Annual Report, FY 1982* (Washington, D.C.: GPO, 1981), p. 40. For similar views on the Soviet value structure see Walter Slocombe, "The Countervailing Strategy," *International Security* 5, no. 4 (Spring 1981): 22–23; *Report of the President's Commission on Strategic Forces* (Washington, D.C.: President's Commission on Strategic Forces, April 1983) [hereafter referred to as *Scowcroft Commission Report*], p. 6; and Secretary of Defense Caspar W. Weinberger, *Annual Report, FY 1987* (Washington, D.C.: GPO, 1986), p. 75.

Brown's statement is somewhat difficult to reconcile with his statement in *Annual Report, FY 1981* (Washington, D.C.: GPO, 1980), p. 65, that "what has come to be known as assured destruction is the bedrock of nuclear deterrence." See also ibid., p. 66, and Brown, *Annual Report, FY 1982*, p. 42. For further discussion of this point see my "Why Do Strategists Disagree about the Requirements of Strategic Nuclear Deterrence?"

the functional equivalent in Soviet perspective of the assured destruction effect of the late 1960s.''[18]

These analysts are not arguing simply that the Soviet leadership is insensitive to societal losses and that as a result the United States needs a countervalue retaliatory capability greater than usually required for assured destruction. Rather they are redefining Soviet ''value targets'' to include the political and military control structure; the more extreme view proposed by Gray and Payne even appears to exclude Soviet cities and their nonmilitary economic capabilities.[19]

Let us first consider the argument that the high value of leadership and military capabilities makes them important targets for limited nuclear options. This argument is logically flawed. The effectiveness of limited nuclear options would stem from their ability to inflict costs, by destroying some valuable targets, combined with their high credibility relative to all-out attacks, which results from their preserving other targets of value as hostages. In other words, limited options inflict relatively low costs (although high in absolute terms), while maintaining the potential to inflict still greater costs. However, the United States could inflict costs, ranging from relatively low to quite high, by attacking only ''traditional'' value targets—for example, economic and industrial facilities. Thus, even if Soviet leaders do value forces and control capabilities highly, targeting them does not provide the United States with special capabilities for inflicting costs. To disagree, proponents must hold the truly extreme view that Soviet leaders place high value only on their forces and control capabilities. Furthermore, if Soviet leaders value these targets especially highly, then attacking them would be at least as risky as attacking cities; in this case, therefore, threats to attack these targets should not be more credible than threats against other value targets.[20]

---

[18] Colin S. Gray and Keith Payne, ''Victory Is Possible,'' *Foreign Policy* no. 39 (Summer 1980): 25. In the same article, p. 21, they hold that ''the most frightening threat to the Soviet Union would be the destruction or serious impairment of its political system. Thus, the United States should be able to destroy key leadership cadres, their means of communication, and some of the instruments of domestic control.''

For similar statements of his views see Colin S. Gray, ''Targeting Problems for Central War,'' *Naval War College Review* 33 (January–February 1980): 11–17, and idem, ''Nuclear Strategy: The Case for a Theory of Victory,'' *International Security* (Summer 1979): 61–69. See also Scott Sagen, *Moving Targets* (Princeton: Princeton University Press, 1989), pp. 58–97; Samuel P. Huntington, ''The Renewal of Strategy,'' in Huntington, ed., *The Strategic Imperative* (Cambridge, Mass.: Ballinger, 1982), p. 12; and Albert Wohlstetter, ''Bishops, Statesmen, and Other Strategists on the Bombing of Innocents,'' *Commentary* 75 (June 1983): 19, 27.

Another approach for threatening political control calls for breaking up the Soviet empire by targeting Great Russians while avoiding attacks on other ethnic groups. Criticizing this strategy is George H. Quester, ''Ethnic Targeting: A Bad Idea Whose Time Has Come,'' *Journal of Strategic Studies* 5, no. 1 (June 1982): 228–35.

[19] For qualifications, however, see Colin S. Gray, ''War-Fighting for Deterrence,'' *Journal of Strategic Studies* 7 (March 1984): 22–23.

[20] In addition, the United States would not want to attack Soviet command and control in a

As to the argument for threatening these control and force targets in an all-out war, it seems empirically flawed. In this case, the U.S. ability to destroy Soviet control capabilities and military forces can enhance the U.S. deterrent only if Soviet leaders believe that U.S. destruction of these targets would significantly increase the costs of an all-out war. But how could this be possible? A U.S. attack could virtually annihilate the Soviet Union, eliminating the value of political and military control targets: What possible use could military forces and political control have if one's country were destroyed? Thus, it is difficult to see how an attack that added these targets to the full array of population and industrial targets could significantly increase the costs of an all-out attack.[21]

How Do Soviet Leaders View the Benefits of Expansion?

The greater the benefits Soviet leaders see in expansion, the greater the expected costs the United States must threaten to deter the Soviet Union. Thus, analysts' views of Soviet objectives influence their assessments of U.S. deterrent requirements.

We find a wide spectrum of views of Soviet objectives in the strategic nuclear debate. At one end are analysts who believe the Soviet Union is highly aggressive with unyielding global hegemonic aims; at the other end, analysts believe that the Soviet Union has little interest in challenging the political status quo, and that it has essentially no interest in conquering Western Europe.[22] Between the extremes lie analysts who believe the Soviets are interested in expanding but are unwilling to pay high costs to do so, and those who are unsure about Soviet objectives.

Analysts who believe Soviet leaders are highly expansionist demand that the United States be able to threaten higher costs and/or that its threats be more credible than analysts at the other end of the spectrum. Analysts who are unsure about Soviet objectives are inclined to hedge against possible worst-case Soviet leaders. Therefore, they tend to conclude that the United States requires capabilities sufficient to deter a highly aggressive Soviet Union.

Although views of Soviet objectives are important, in the end it is comparisons of Soviet costs and benefits that determine U.S. requirements for deterring Soviet attack. These comparisons play a central role in determining how credible U.S. threats must be. Analysts who believe that Soviet leaders see

---

limited war because these capabilities are required to terminate the war before it becomes an unlimited all-out war.

[21] For a similar observation see Robert J. Art, "Between Assured Destruction and Nuclear Victory: The Case for the 'Mad-Plus' Posture," *Ethics* 95, no. 3 (April 1985): 509. Chapter Seven examines this argument in more detail.

[22] This debate is reviewed in Douglas Seay, "What Are Soviet Objectives in its Foreign, Military and Arms Control Policy," in Eden and Miller, *Nuclear Arguments*. See Chapter Three for other analyses of Soviet objectives and for examples from the strategic nuclear debate.

the costs and benefits as comparable require the United States to pose threats which Soviet leaders believe the United States will almost certainly carry out. Otherwise, Soviet leaders will not conclude that the expected costs of acting exceed the expected benefits, and as a result will not be deterred. Thus, these analysts conclude that the United States requires highly credible threats. In contrast, if the costs of war in Soviet eyes dwarf the benefits, then U.S. threats need not be highly credible. In this case, even analysts who believe the Soviet Union is highly aggressive could conclude that deterrence is relatively easy, since even a small chance of provoking a nuclear war should be sufficient to deter highly expansionist Soviet leaders. Divergent prescriptions for U.S. forces and strategy follow: highly credible threats demand more extensive U.S. capabilities, which leads some analysts to prescribe reacquisition of U.S. nuclear superiority.

Colin Gray, for example, finding the benefits of expansion comparable to the costs of nuclear war, worries that Soviet leaders are willing to pursue actions that greatly increase the probability of nuclear war. He argues, for example, that:

> it is possible that the posing (even credibly posing) of major economic recovery problems to the Soviet Union might be insufficiently deterring a prospect if Soviet arms could acquire Western Europe in a largely undamaged condition to serve as a recovery base; if the stakes in a war were deemed by Moscow to be high enough; and if the Soviet Union were able, in the course of the war, to drive the United States back to an agrarian economy.[23]

Given this view of Soviet benefits and costs, extended deterrence requires that the United States threaten the highest possible costs with very high credibility.

In sharp contrast, other analysts argue that even a Soviet Union that was strongly motivated to expand would be deterred by the possibility of the overwhelming costs of a nuclear war. For example, Robert Jervis finds it obvious that the costs of having one's country destroyed are so large that even extremely expansionist countries will act with restraint: "No decision maker in the world's history would embark on a course of expansion while his cities were held hostage. . . . even Hitler probably was not an example, since he knew that if he could militarily defeat the Allies he could protect his own country."[24] Thus, according to Jervis, "the argument that the American threat

---

[23] Colin S. Gray, "Nuclear Strategy: A Case for a Theory of Victory," *International Security* 4, no. 1 (Summer 1979): 66–67. Gray has, however, left himself a loophole since he does not specify the conditions that would make the "stakes . . . high enough." For a less extreme example see Paul H. Nitze, "Strategy in the Decade of the 1980s," *Foreign Affairs* 59, no. 1 (Fall 1980): 90, and idem, "SALT II and American Strategic Considerations," *Comparative Strategy* 2, no. 1 (1980): 10.

[24] Robert Jervis, "Why Nuclear Superiority Doesn't Matter," *Political Science Quarterly* 94, no. 4 (Winter 1979–80): 622.

to use nuclear weapons is not very credible glosses over the point that only a little credibility may be required."[25]

Lying between these extremes are analysts who are unsure about Soviet objectives, and therefore want to hedge against risky Soviet behavior. For example, while discussing the danger of vulnerable U.S. ICBMs, Harold Brown argued that "it is difficult to imagine any circumstances or expectations that would prompt Soviet leaders to undertake such a self-destructive attack . . . [however] the 'rubbish heap of history' is filled with authorities who said something reckless could not or would not be done."[26]

Considering previous Soviet behavior helps resolve disputes about Soviet comparisons of the benefits of expansion and the costs of war.[27] Examinations of Soviet foreign policy suggest that the Soviet Union is unwilling to use force to challenge U.S. vital interests, except possibly to defend its own vital interests.[28] This evidence casts doubt on the idea that the Soviet Union is bent on expansion and would significantly increase the probability of nuclear war to achieve this objective. Recent dramatic shifts in Soviet foreign policy only serve to reinforce this conclusion.

Consequently, given the U.S. ability to inflict overwhelming retaliatory costs, there appears to be little need for capabilities that would provide the

[25] Robert Jervis, *The Illogic of American Nuclear Strategy* (Ithaca: Cornell University Press, 1984), p. 156.

[26] Secretary of Defense Harold Brown, *Annual Report, FY 1980* (Washington, D.C.: GPO, 1979), p. 80. The desire to hedge against extremely risky behavior is also evident in Victor Utgoff, "In Defense of Counterforce," *International Security* 6, no. 4 (Spring 1982): 50.

[27] Resolving disputes about Soviet objectives is more difficult but also less important for determining U.S. military requirements. Views of Soviet objectives do, however, play a central role in the debate over the international political consequences of American military policy, which is analyzed in Chapter Three.

[28] For example, Dennis Ross, "Risk Aversion in Soviet Decisionmaking," in Jiri Valenta and William Potter, eds., *Soviet Decisionmaking for National Security* (London: Allen & Unwin, 1984), p. 247, finds that "the conclusions we draw about Soviet risktaking should not be particularly alarmist. In this regard it might be said that the character of the Soviet system and the sociology of the Soviet leaders will continue to render a general caution that is unlikely to change in the near future, and that permits the use of decisive and perhaps risky action far more readily for *defending* as opposed to *extending* Soviet gains." See also Hannes Adomeit, *Soviet Crisis Prevention and Management: Why and When Do the Soviet Leaders Take Risks?* Occasional Paper OPS-008 (Santa Monica: Rand/UCLA Center for the Study of Soviet International Behavior, October 1986), pp. 31–32: "Both the patterns and the rationale of Soviet crisis behavior thus inspire some confidence as to the future. . . . Soviet leaders have traditionally given very careful consideration to risks and cost in the conduct of their foreign policy"; idem, *Soviet Risk-Taking and Crisis Behavior: A Theoretical and Empirical Analysis* (London: Allen & Unwin, 1982); Benjamin S. Lambeth, "Uncertainties for the Soviet War Planner," *International Security* 7, no. 3 (Winter 1982/1983): 143; and William Zimmerman, "What Do Scholars Know about Soviet Foreign Policy?" in Robbin F. Laird and Erik Hoffmann, eds., *Soviet Foreign Policy in a Changing World* (Hawthorne, N.Y.: Aldine, 1986), pp. 92–93, who holds that "Soviet use of force reveals a sharp distinction between situations where there is no risk of confrontation with the United States and those with even a low risk of confrontation with the United States."

United States with highly credible nuclear threats. Nevertheless, at least in theory, a case for hedging exists since we cannot know how the Soviet Union will behave in the future. The strength of this case requires a complete policy analysis of specific hedges—one that considers the possible strategic, international political, and economic costs to the United States as well as the extent of the benefits. Following chapters provide this analysis.

Can the United States Significantly Limit Damage to Itself in an All-Out War?

Since the beginning of the nuclear age there has been a strong interest in ways to protect U.S. society from the damage it would suffer in an all-out nuclear war, and thereby to reduce the costs of such a war. A variety of programs has been put forward in the hope of limiting damage, including offensive counterforce for destroying Soviet forces before they are launched, strategic defenses for destroying Soviet forces after they are launched, and civil defense for reducing the damage from Soviet nuclear weapons that nevertheless reach the United States.

The feasibility of reducing the costs of an all-out war depends on two judgments: (1) at what level of damage would the United States have achieved significant reductions, and (2) to what level can the United States limit the damage?

AT WHAT LEVEL IS DAMAGE LIMITATION SIGNIFICANT?

For example, if a Soviet attack, without U.S. programs to reduce damage, would kill 100 million Americans, and with these programs would kill 90 million Americans, is that significant damage limitation?[29] No one questions the value of protecting U.S. cities. Rather, disagreements about the value of damage limitation center on the benefits of trying to limit damage when the

---

[29] Analysts do not agree that looking at the number of U.S. deaths and casualties is the best or only way to assess the outcome of an all-out war. Analysts have used a number of other measures to assess war outcomes. For example, how long will it take the United States to recover from the war? Given this measure, programs that significantly reduce recovery time might be said to reduce the costs of the war. Yet another way to measure war outcomes compares the United States and the Soviet Union after a war: Which country suffered more damage? Which can recover more quickly? Given these relative measures, the United States might achieve an improved war outcome by increasing its ability to inflict damage on the Soviet Union as well as by reducing the Soviet ability to attack the United States. Examples of these other measurements include Huntington, who argues in "The Renewal of Strategy," p. 39, that the "restoration of something resembling equivalent survivability in the event of nuclear exchanges at any level" should be a major U.S. goal, and Jones and Thompson, "Central War and Civil Defense," who compare the time required for the United States and the Soviet Union to recover following a variety of types of nuclear exchanges. Additional examples are discussed by Jervis, *The Illogic of American Nuclear Strategy*, p. 61.

Soviet Union retains an assured destruction capability that enables it to destroy most major U.S. cities, though not the entire U.S. population.[30]

Many analysts argue that in MAD neither superpower can reduce the costs of a nuclear war. Proponents of this view hold that if the Soviet Union can destroy the major U.S. cities, then the costs of a nuclear war cannot be reduced. This position is often described in terms of the "flat of the damage curve"—a few hundred Soviet warheads can destroy America's major cities and additional Soviet warheads would do little additional damage to American society. Thus, according to this view, there is little value in preventing the Soviet Union from attacking with more warheads; the difference would be insignificant as long as the major U.S. cities were destroyed. Analysts often state this conclusion by arguing that in MAD the United States lacks a damage-limitation capability. Put more precisely, they believe that whatever damage limitation might be possible would not significantly reduce the costs of an all-out war.[31]

In contrast, other analysts are more interested in pursuing damage limitation, even when the United States cannot protect its major cities. Specifically, they argue that the damage curve is not in fact flat, hence American forces that reduce the size of a Soviet attack can limit damage even if the Soviet attack remains large.[32] They note that tens of millions of Americans live in small and middle-sized cities that the Soviets could target if their force remained undiminished.

Although not explained in these terms, U.S. policy appears to be based on something resembling this view of damage limitation. While believing that

[30] Disagreements on this point are rarely the focus of debate, but are sometimes noted. For example, although not very specific, William R. Van Cleave and Roger W. Barnett, "Strategic Adaptability," *Orbis* 18, no. 3 (Autumn 1974): 662, argue that "there is nothing inevitable in massive population destruction or escalation. Likewise, there is a significant distinction among numbers killed, even at high levels." Carl H. Builder, "Why Not First-Strike Counterforce Capabilities?" *Strategic Review* 7, no. 2 (Spring 1979): 34, notes the existence of divergent beliefs within the national security community, arguing that "splendid counterforce"—defined as the capability to destroy the adversary's threat to one's societal survival—is unattainable and that "there are some who would dispute that conclusion, but their arguments pivot on what constitutes unacceptable damage to a society." See Herman Kahn, *On Thermonuclear War* (Princeton: Princeton University Press, 1960) for an early, rather flip discussion of distinguishing between extremely bad outcomes.

[31] We should note that some analysts making this argument may actually be using it as a kind of shorthand for the more complete argument that the benefits of reducing damage at such high levels do not warrant the costs of damage-limitation programs and, therefore, that the United States should not pursue damage limitation in MAD. Few have spelled out this position, however.

[32] In support of this claim they could cite the calculations done by the Department of Defense in the early 1960s (see Alain C. Enthoven and K. Wayne Smith, *How Much Is Enough? Shaping the Defense Program 1961-1969* [New York: Harper and Row, 1971], pp. 207–9) and more recent studies of attacks against U.S. cities (see William Daugherty, Barbara Levi, and Frank von Hippel, "The Consequences of 'Limited' Nuclear Attacks on the United States," *International Security* 10, no. 4 [Spring 1986]: 3–28).

the United States cannot protect its cities, Harold Brown has suggested that the United States could reduce the costs of an all-out war. In his annual report Brown explained that "we have always considered it important, in the event of war, to be able to attack the forces that could do damage to the United States and its allies."[33] Further, official statements held that the United States did not acquire forces in pursuit of damage limitation, but that if nuclear war occurred the United States might use its force for this purpose.[34]

TO WHAT LEVEL CAN THE UNITED STATES REDUCE THE DAMAGE?

Analysts disagree over whether the United States can escape MAD.[35] Some believe that a full-scale U.S. commitment to damage limitation would enable the United States to deny the Soviet Union its assured destruction capability. The most optimistic claims are made by Gray and Payne, who argue that "an intelligent U.S. offensive strategy, wedded to homeland defense, should reduce U.S. casualties to 20 million. . . . A combination of counterforce offensive targeting, civil defense, and ballistic missile and air defense should hold U.S. casualties down to a level compatible with national survival and recovery."[36]

[33] Brown, *Annual Report, FY 1981*, p. 66. See also Harold Brown, Senate Committee on Foreign Relations, *Hearings on Presidential Directive 59*, 96th Cong., 2d sess., 16 September 1980 (Washington, D.C.: GPO, 1981), p. 16: "usually what is meant by 'counterforce' is attacks on the other side's strategic nuclear capability so as to limit the damage to you by their strategic forces. An option regarding those forces will be one of the options that grows out of the policy in PD-59, but it is not the only countermilitary capability." See also ibid., p. 18.

[34] Senate Committee on Armed Services, *Fiscal Year 1978 Authorization for Military Procurement, Research and Development, and Active Duty, Selected Reserve and Civilian Personnel Strengths*, pt. 1, 95th Cong., 1st sess. (Washington, D.C.: GPO, 1977), p. 554.

[35] Although commonly understood to hinge on technical considerations, this question also depends on other issues. For example, the feasibility of damage limitation depends both on the extent of U.S. efforts to limit damage and the extent of Soviet reactions to offset these efforts. Disagreement about how vigorously the Soviet Union will react to U.S. damage-limitation programs could lead analysts to disagree about the effectiveness of specified U.S. programs. On these issues, see Chapter Five.

[36] Gray and Payne, "Victory Is Possible," p. 25. Huntington, "The Renewal of Strategy," pp. 39–40, advocates a combination of programs similar to Gray and Payne's, but appears less optimistic about the level to which U.S. casualties might be reduced. Also arguing that extensive damage limitation is feasible is Stephen Peter Rosen, "Foreign Policy and Nuclear Weapons: The Case for Strategic Defenses," in Huntington, ed., *The Strategic Imperative*, pp. 153–59, and Richard B. Foster, who advocates similar programs in "From Assured Destruction to Assured Survival," *Comparative Strategy* 2, no. 1 (1980): 53–74.

It also appears that the Reagan administration might have concluded that the United States could acquire a substantial damage-limitation capability. According to George C. Wilson, " 'Preparing for Long Nuclear War Is Waste of Funds,' General Jones Says," *Washington Post*, 19 June 1982, pp. 3, 21, the Fiscal Year 1984–1988 Defense Guidance, which was developed early in the Reagan administration, is reported to have argued: "Should deterrence fail and strategic nuclear war with the U.S.S.R. occur, the United States must prevail and be able to force the Soviet Union to seek earliest termination of hostilities on terms favorable to the United States. This requires:

In sharp contrast, others believe that MAD is inescapable. Jervis, for example, describes other analysts' continuing interest in protecting the U.S. population through a combination of counterforce offenses, strategic defenses, and civil defense as an attempt to escape the nuclear revolution in "the face of extensive evidence that it is simply unattainable." Spurgeon Keeny and Wolfgang Panofsky write "the thesis that we live in an inherently MAD world rests ultimately on the technical conclusion that effective protection of the population against large scale nuclear attack is not possible."[37]

Despite claims to the contrary, the available studies of U.S. damage-limitation programs show that they have virtually no chance of eliminating the Soviet assured destruction capability. A complete assessment of the U.S. ability to limit damage would combine the various types of damage-limitation systems—that is, strategic defense, offensive counterforce, and civil defense—and evaluate their effectiveness against a reactive Soviet threat. Few comprehensive studies are available in the unclassified literature. The feasibility of damage limitation was studied extensively within the U.S. government during the early 1960s. Studies done by the Systems Analysis office found that U.S. ballistic missile defenses (BMD) in combination with a U.S. first strike, when confronting Soviet efforts to offset U.S. strategic defenses, could do very little to reduce the damage of an all-out war: 120 million U.S. fatalities following a U.S. first strike without BMD; 100–110 million fatalities following a first strike with BMD.[38] Pentagon analysts found that this result "stood up under any reasonable set of assumptions."[39]

Although they do not evaluate the combined effectiveness of U.S. damage-

---

. . . Employment plans that assure U.S. strategic nuclear forces can render ineffective the total Soviet, and Soviet allied, military and political power structure through attacks on political/military leadership and associated control facilities, nuclear and conventional forces and industry critical to military power." See also Richard Halloran, "Pentagon Draws Up First Strategy for Fighting a Long Nuclear War," *New York Times*, 30 May 1982, p. 1; idem, "Weinberger Confirms New Strategy on Atom War," *New York Times*, 4 June 1982, p. 10; and Secretary of Defense Caspar Weinberger, *Annual Report, FY 1983* (Washington, D.C.: GPO, February 8, 1982), pp. I-18. On recent changes in U.S. doctrine that are consistent with these objectives see Robert C. Toth, "U.S. Shifts Nuclear Response Strategy," *Los Angeles Times*, 23 July 1989, p. 1.

Further, although not described as part of an offensive strategy, the Reagan administration's interest in ballistic missile defense for protecting the U.S. homeland, reflected in its support for SDI, suggests a belief that significant damage limitation might be possible in the future.

[37] Jervis, *The Illogic of American Nuclear Strategy*, p. 54–55; Spurgeon M. Keeny, Jr., and Wolfgang Panofsky, "MAD versus NUTS," *Foreign Affairs* 60 (Winter 1981–1982): 298.

[38] Enthoven and Smith, *How Much Is Enough?* pp. 188–90.

[39] Ibid., p. 189. Barry R. Posen and Stephen Van Evera, "Defense Policy and the Reagan Administration: Departure from Containment," *International Security* 8, no. 1 (Summer 1983): 24–27, argue that the case against the feasibility of significant damage limitation is stronger today than in the late 1960s because the Soviet force is now much larger and better protected. A possible qualification, however, is that the implications of vulnerable U.S. command and control, which are more fully recognized now than in the 1960s, were not included in these calculations.

limitation programs, recent studies support these pessimistic conclusions. Virtually all technical experts believe ballistic missile defenses capable of defeating the Soviet assured destruction capability will remain beyond the U.S. reach for the foreseeable future.[40] Calculations show that the counterforce route is hardly more promising. Given current forces, a U.S. counterforce first strike would leave the Soviet Union with a redundant assured destruction capability.[41] The one possibility for significantly reducing Soviet retaliation appears to lie in simultaneously attacking Soviet forces and their command and control facilities. If successful, such an attack would eliminate the Soviet ability to launch their surviving forces. However, the prospects for success appear to be quite low, since in a crisis Soviet leaders would be able to predelegate authority for launching their nuclear forces and prepare to launch their forces on warning; at a minimum, it is hard to see how the United States could have anything but low confidence in the prospects for success.[42] Finally, although studies disagree about the ability of civil defense to save lives by providing shelters and evacuating people from cities, the number of Americans killed by direct effects would probably remain in the many tens of millions. And civil defense has essentially no potential for protecting U.S. cities and industrial capabilities,[43] or for reducing deaths that could occur from the severe ecological, agricultural, and societal disruptions that would almost certainly follow a massive nuclear attack.[44]

[40] For studies of the feasibility of highly effective BMD, see Chapter Four.

[41] See Harold Feiveson and Frank von Hippel, "The Freeze and the Counterforce Race," *Physics Today* (January 1983): 46–47, for estimates of surviving Soviet equivalent megatonnage (EMT), which is the best measure of countervalue capability, for the forces deployed in 1982. See Salman, Sullivan, and Van Evera, "Analysis or Propaganda?" for estimates of surviving Soviet destructive potential for current forces under both day-to-day and alerted conditions, and for some possible future forces. On deaths from various attacks see Office of Technology Assessment, *The Effects of Nuclear War*, pp. 139–45, and Daugherty, Levi, and von Hippel, "The Consequences of 'Limited' Nuclear Attacks on the United States," pp. 3–45.

[42] On Soviet C[3] see Desmond Ball, *Soviet Strategic Command, Control, Communications and Intelligence (C³) System* (Canberra: Strategic and Defense Studies Centre, Australian National University, May 1985); Stephen M. Meyer, "Soviet Nuclear Operations and Command and Control," in Carter, Steinbruner, and Zraket, eds., *Nuclear Operations and Command and Control*, who discusses some of the problems the Soviet Union might have with predelegation; and Lawrence Gershwin, *Soviet Strategic Force Developments*, Joint Hearing before the Senate Subcommittee on Strategic and Theater Nuclear Forces and the Senate Subcommittee on Defense of the Committee on Appropriations, 99th Cong., 1st sess., 26 June 1985, p. 17.

[43] See note 8 and also Arthur M. Katz, *Life after Nuclear War* (Cambridge, Mass.: Ballinger, 1982), pp. 291–307; Arthur A. Broyles, Eugene P. Wigner, and Sidney D. Drell, "Civil Defense in Limited War—a Debate," *Physics Today* (April 1976): 44–57.

[44] On these effects see A. B. Pittock et al., *Environmental Consequences of Nuclear War: Scope 28, Volume I—Physical and Atmospheric Effects* (New York: John Wiley, 1986); Mark A. Harwell and Thomas C. Hutchinson, *Environmental Consequences of Nuclear War: Scope 28, Volume II—Ecological and Agricultural Effects* (New York: John Wiley & Sons, 1986); Mark A. Harwell, *Nuclear Winter* (New York: Springer-Verlag, 1984); National Research Council, *The*

Although Gray and Payne have made great claims for a full-scale U.S. commitment to damage-limitation programs—stating that U.S. casualties could be reduced to 20 million[45]—they have provided *no analysis*: we do not know the forces they hypothesize, the assumptions they make about the effects of nuclear attacks, or the scenarios they evaluate. Their claims are severely undermined by the available studies of U.S. damage-limitation capabilities.

Because the prospects for removing the Soviet assured destruction capability are so slim (and the programs so expensive), the burden of proof must lie with the advocates. They face a seemingly overwhelming challenge: the Soviet Union can afford to deploy very large numbers of nuclear weapons; cities are easily destroyed by these weapons; and there are a relatively small number of U.S. cities.[46] Until studies suggest otherwise, there is no reason to believe that the United States can escape MAD, and U.S. strategy should be developed within this constraint.

A different disagreement divides analysts who agree that the United States is stuck in MAD, but disagree about how much damage limitation is possible at such high levels of damage. In this dispute there are reasonable grounds for disagreement, partly because the outcomes of large nuclear wars are highly uncertain. Proponents of damage limitation tend to focus on more optimistic outcomes (frequently pertaining to the prompt casualties that can be calculated with some precision), while opponents focus on the pessimistic outcomes, including severe environmental effects and the total collapse of modern U.S. industrial society—which would doom those who initially survive the nuclear attack.

Whether the United States should pursue whatever damage limitation is feasible in MAD depends on one's position on the previous disagreement, that is, on the value of reducing damage at already extremely high levels of damage. Reaching conclusions also requires comparing these benefits to costs of the damage-limitation programs.

What Determines Advantages in Credibility and Capability?

RELATIVE VERSUS ABSOLUTE MEASURES

Analysts disagree about how to measure the nuclear balance; more specifically, they disagree about which features of U.S. forces and capabilities would

---

Effects on the Atmosphere of a Major Nuclear Exchange (Washington, D.C.: National Academy Press, 1985); and Starley L. Thompson and Stephen H. Schneider, "Nuclear Winter Reappraised," *Foreign Affairs* 64, no. 5 (Summer 1986): 981–1005. For an early assessment of the danger of nuclear winter see R. P. Turco et al., "Nuclear Winter: Global Consequences of Multiple Nuclear Explosions," *Science* (22 December 1983): 1283–1300.

[45] Problems with this claim are discussed in Donald W. Hanson, "Is Soviet Doctrine Superior?" *International Security* 7, no. 3 (Winter 1982/1983): 74–76.

[46] I develop this argument in greater detail in Chapter Five.

influence Soviet leaders as they considered pursuing actions that the United States wants to deter. Although this disagreement surfaces in a variety of detailed arguments, there are two basic views on this central issue. Some analysts believe that U.S. nuclear forces influence Soviet decisions primarily through their ability to inflict costs against Soviet society, and through their ability to protect U.S. society, since this affects the credibility of U.S. threats to employ nuclear weapons. In other words, these analysts believe that U.S. nuclear capability should be measured in terms of its ability to influence war outcomes. In sharp contrast, other analysts believe that Soviet leaders would also be heavily influenced by a variety of other measures, including *comparisons* of U.S. and Soviet forces that reflect neither the ability of U.S. forces to inflict damage nor their ability to limit it. For example, these analysts believe that the relative size of superpower forces could influence the Soviet willingness to attack the United States, although attacking would not reduce the U.S. ability to inflict retaliatory damage.

These fundamental differences lead to disagreements about whether, in MAD, strategic nuclear forces can provide either superpower with an advantage in capability and/or credibility. Those analysts who focus on the ability of U.S. nuclear forces to inflict and limit damage argue that strategic nuclear forces *cannot* provide these advantages in MAD.[47] When both superpowers can inflict overwhelming damage and neither can significantly reduce the costs of an all-out war, the United States and the Soviet Union have essentially equal capabilities. Because neither country possesses an advantage in capability, strategic forces cannot provide significant advantages in credibility.

These analysts reject the importance of relative measures of superpower forces precisely because they do not reflect the ability of U.S. forces to determine war outcomes. Jervis argues, for example, that "deterrence comes from having enough weapons to destroy the other's cities; this ability is an absolute, not a relative, one."[48] This is true because whether a country has enough de-

---

[47] An exception here are analysts who believe that the significant damage limitation is possible in MAD; their dissent, however, is not based on the importance of relative force size.

[48] Jervis, "Why Nuclear Superiority Doesn't Matter," p. 618. The arguments summarized in the next few paragraphs are found in ibid. and idem, *The Illogic of American Nuclear Strategy*.

Also arguing for the importance of the absolute size of retaliatory forces and/or against the importance of the relative size of forces are Brodie, "The Development of Nuclear Strategy," p. 71; Kenneth Waltz, *The Spread of Nuclear Weapons: More May Be Better*, Adelphi Paper No. 171 (London: International Institute for Strategic Studies [hereafter IISS], 1981), pp. 15, 22; Richard Ned Lebow, "Misconceptions in American Strategic Assessment," *Political Science Quarterly* 79, no. 2 (Summer 1982): 194–95; Walter Slocombe, *The Political Implications of Parity*, Adelphi Paper No. 77 (London: IISS, 1971), pp. 7–12; and Salmon, Sullivan, and Van Evera, "Analysis or Propaganda?" Steinbruner, "Beyond Rational Deterrence," argues that due to limitations on rational decisionmaking, deterrence does not depend upon detailed calculations of attack outcomes. Betts, "Elusive Equivalence," pp. 107–8, criticizes Jervis's argument, holding that the balance of resolve may be linked to the balance of forces. Jervis's position, however, is that when both superpowers have assured destruction capabilities the balance of forces does not

liverable weapons to destroy an adversary's cities depends on the number of adversary cities, not on the size of the adversary's nuclear force.

Further, according to this view, measures of relative force size would be just as misleading once a nuclear war had begun as they are during peacetime and crises. The country with the larger post-attack or post-exchange force still cannot protect its cities and cannot inflict greater costs than its adversary, and therefore has no additional leverage for imposing its will and achieving an improved political settlement of the nuclear war. Thus, relative force size following a counterforce attack or a counterforce exchange (for example, the ratio of forces surviving a counterforce exchange) is not an important measure of nuclear force capabilities.[49]

Because in MAD neither country has an advantage in military capability, it is the "balance of resolve," not the "balance of military power," that will have a greater influence on a country's ability to deter attack and achieve its objectives in a limited nuclear war.[50] Kenneth Waltz sums up this position, arguing that: "Given second-strike capabilities, it is not the balance of forces that counts but the courage to use them that counts. The balance or imbalance of strategic forces affects neither the calculation of danger nor the question of whose will is the stronger. Second-strike forces have to be seen in absolute terms."[51]

In contrast, analysts who focus on relative measures of the superpowers' strategic nuclear forces see a radically different world. They fear, for example, that the Soviet ability to improve the ratio of surviving forces increases their willingness to launch a full-scale counterforce attack against the United States, even if the U.S. assured destruction capability would remain intact. According to these analysts, shifting the ratio of surviving forces against the United States reduces the credibility of U.S. retaliation, thereby making the Soviet attack less risky. Thus, continues the argument, this capability in the hands of Soviet leaders creates far-reaching dangers. Recognizing that U.S. leaders would

---

favor either side; thus, whether the two are linked does not matter in this case. Dennis Ross, "Rethinking Soviet Strategic Policy," *Journal of Strategic Studies* 1, no. 1 (May 1978): 21–22, argues that the Soviet Union would not initiate an exchange to improve the ratio of forces because Soviet doctrine rejects this type of limited war.

[49] A possible exception is a war of attrition in which countries continue with counterforce attacks, avoiding cities until one is disarmed or nearly disarmed. In this case, the countries fight their way out of MAD and the arguments against relative force measures no longer apply. Jervis notes this exception, but argues that such a war is extremely unlikely, even compared to other quite unlikely nuclear wars, and therefore concludes that his general argument is not significantly weakened. See, for example, *The Illogic of American Nuclear Strategy*, p. 136. Analysts' views on the possibility of wars of attrition, and therefore their significance, are influenced by beliefs about the prospects for limiting a nuclear war; these are addressed in the following section.

[50] Jervis, "Why Superiority Doesn't Matter," p. 628.

[51] Waltz, *The Spread of Nuclear Weapons*, p. 18.

tend to back down in crises, Soviet leaders could adopt a more aggressive foreign policy and drive tougher bargains during crises.

Paul Nitze focused attention on these arguments during the latter half of the 1970s in what came to be known as the "Nitze scenario." He proposed that the United States acquire forces "such that the Soviet side could not hope by initiating a counterforce exchange to improve either the absolute excess in pounds of its throw-weight over ours, or the ratio of its throw-weight to ours."[52]

These analysts also believe that Soviet leaders would assess the outcome of a nuclear war in terms of relative force measures. Harold Brown, for example, argued that "an improved relative balance would appear to be a minimum condition of 'victory.' "[53] Therefore, continues the argument, because U.S. strategy is designed to deter war by denying the Soviets victory, the United States must be able to prevent an improved ratio of postwar forces.

Proponents of relative measures have failed to explain why Soviet leaders would be influenced by these comparisons of the superpowers' forces. They

[52] Paul Nitze, "Deterring Our Deterrent," pp. 195–210. A missile's throw-weight is the useful weight that it can place on a trajectory toward its target; the equivalent megatonnage (EMT) that a missile can deliver is roughly proportional to its throw-weight. For similar arguments see Nitze, "Assuring Strategic Stability in an Era of Détente," *Foreign Affairs* 54, no. 2 (January 1976): 224–25. We should note that in this article (p. 226) Nitze also mentions that absolute retaliatory capabilities are important and "will be conducive to continued effective deterrence *even if the ratios are unfavorable*" (emphasis added). This observation, which is mentioned in passing and rarely noticed, is a telling criticism of Nitze's own arguments. For a rebuttal of Nitze's analysis see Jan Lodal, "Assuring Strategic Stability: An Alternative View," *Foreign Affairs* 54, no. 3 (April 1976): 462–81. For Nitze's reply see "Strategic Stability," *Foreign Affairs* 54, no. 4 (July 1976). Other criticisms of Nitze's analysis include Gary D. Brewer and Bruce G. Blair, "War Games and National Security with a Grain of SALT," *Bulletin of the Atomic Scientists* 35, no. 6 (June 1979): 20–22; Joseph M. Grieco, *Paul Nitze and Strategic Stability: A Critical Analysis*, Occasional Paper No. 9 (Ithaca: Cornell University Peace Studies Program, 1976); and Richard Betts, *Nuclear Blackmail and Nuclear Balance* (Washington, D.C.: Brookings Institution, 1987), pp. 191–92.

[53] Brown, *Annual Report, FY 1982*, p. 58. See also ibid., p. 41: "the state of the strategic balance after an initial exchange—measured both in absolute terms and in relation to the balance prior to the exchange—could be an important factor in the decision by one side to initiate a nuclear exchange. Thus, it is important—for the sake of deterrence—to be able to deny the potential adversary a fundamental shift in the strategic balance as a result of a nuclear exchange." See also ibid., pp. 52–58. Although Brown appears to believe that some damage limitation is possible, his statements do not reflect a concern that the Soviet Union might gain a politically useful advantage by being able to inflict significantly more damage than the United States.

On the importance of relative capabilities see also Betts, "Elusive Equivalence," p. 125, and Fritz W. Ermarth, "Contrasts in American and Soviet Thought," *International Security* 3, no. 2 (Fall 1978): 152, who argues that for Soviet force planners the chief aim of combat is to achieve a more favorable balance of forces. Stephen M. Meyer and Peter Almquist, *Insights from Soviet Strategic Force Modeling*, Report to the Defense Advanced Research Projects Agency (revised April 1985), find that "Soviet analysts developed an exchange model for evaluating strategic nuclear forces based on the ratio of equivalent megatonage remaining to each side after an initial strike" and conclude that "this model . . . captures the essence of Soviet strategic thinking."

have asserted that ratios of nuclear forces matter in MAD, but have failed to supply any arguments about why and when this might be the case; they have not described how the Soviets would use advantages in force size to achieve political or military objectives. Why should relative measures matter during peacetime or crises? If the country suffering the unfavorable ratio faced the possibility of greater costs, this might in turn reduce its credibility, thereby weakening its bargaining position. In MAD, however, the ratio of forces does not reflect the countries' relative abilities to inflict damage. We have no better reason for believing that the ratio of forces would influence U.S. willingness to retaliate once a war had begun. There is no doubt that retaliating after an attack against the U.S. homeland would be extremely dangerous—but this would be because the Soviet Union retains an assured destruction capability, not because the United States suffered an unfavorable ratio of forces. Finally, the case for assessing war outcomes in terms of relative force measures is just as weak. The Soviet Union would have achieved a military victory only if its remaining strategic nuclear forces provided an enhanced capability to coerce U.S. leaders or to survive further fighting. Relative measures do not reflect these capabilities.

In short, in MAD, the logical case for using force comparison as indicators of nuclear capability or credibility is weak, proponents have done little to support their claims, and efforts to fill in the logical gaps in their arguments encounter overwhelming difficulties. The stronger arguments are clearly those that focus on the U.S. ability to inflict damage and to reduce the costs of Soviet retaliation.

PERCEPTIONS OF THE BALANCE

Proponents of the importance of relative measures of superpower forces frequently respond by arguing that Soviet advantages in these comparisons of strategic forces might have significant diplomatic implications, even if they cannot be directly related to military capabilities. In their view, comparisons of strategic forces have an importance that goes far beyond the U.S. ability to perform specific missions. America's allies and adversaries compare the superpowers' nuclear arsenals to judge the U.S. ability and determination to achieve its foreign policy objectives. In other words, comparisons of superpower forces influence key perceptions of the United States. According to this view, unfavorable comparisons will lead U.S. allies to question our ability to protect their security, and might raise Soviet doubts about American resolve, thus encouraging the Soviet Union to challenge U.S interests.

These views are reflected in the long-standing U.S. requirement that American forces maintain "essential equivalence" with Soviet forces. In the mid-1970s, for example, Secretary of Defense James Schlesinger argued that "there is an important relationship between the political behavior of many leaders of other nations and what they perceive the strategic nuclear balance to be. . . . many do react to the static measures of relative force size, numbers of warheads, equivalent megatonage, and so forth. Hence, to the degree that we wish to influence the perceptions of others, we must take appropriate steps (by their lights) in the design of the strategic forces."[54]

Again, however, the arguments for relative measures appear quite weak. The case against perceptions arguments is not that perceptions do not matter—clearly they do. But we should be skeptical of arguments that regard international leaders as being influenced by essentially meaningless measures, measures that do not accurately reflect the ability of forces to perform specific missions. The case is summed up well by Warner Schilling:

> American concern for how the strategic balance is perceived by friends, foes, and allies is not unwise. It is simply misplaced. What is questionable is the present American policy of focusing that concern on the numerical differences between Soviet and American forces as expressed in various static and dynamic indices. These numerical differences are of consequence only to the extent that they can affect the amount of destruction that would occur to targets of value in the event of a nuclear exchange. . . . But numerical differences that cannot be related to adverse war outcomes should be addressed by American declaratory policy, not redressed by American acquisition policy.[55]

Although, of course, it is not impossible that perceptions of relative force size are influential and that these perceptions cannot be altered simply by changing the way in which the United States describes its strategic requirements and capabilities, proponents of relative measures have not supported their claims about perceptions. The available research finds little support for the claim that relative force size is a key factor forming perceptions of U.S.

[54] Secretary of Defense James R. Schlesinger, *Annual Defense Department Report, FY 1975* (Washington, D.C.: GPO, 1974), p. 27. Focusing specifically on Soviet perceptions, Schlesinger reviewed the growing asymmetries in U.S. and Soviet forces, including the growing Soviet ability to attack U.S. ICBMs and bombers, and concluded: "In such circumstances we cannot exclude the possibility that future Soviet leaders might be misled into believing that such apparently favorable asymmetries could, at the very least, be exploited for diplomatic advantage. Pressure, confrontation, and crisis could easily follow from miscalculation of this nature," ibid., p. 43.

For additional examples see Brown, *Annual Report, FY 1982*, pp. 43–44, 52, where he argues that static indices may be "very important as far as perceptions of the balance are concerned." These statements appear inconsistent with a statement that follows a couple of pages later (p. 54): "We build our forces in order to accomplish certain missions and not with an eye towards how they will look stacked up against Soviet forces in a chart or table." See also *Scowcroft Commission Report*, pp. 5, 16–17; Weinberger, *Annual Report, FY 1987*, p. 38; and Jan M. Lodal, "Deterrence and Nuclear Strategy," in *U.S. Defense Policy in the 1980s, Daedalus* (Fall 1980): 163.

[55] Warner Schilling, "U.S. Strategic Concepts in the 1970s: The Search for Sufficiently Equivalent Countervailing Parity," *International Security* 6, no. 2 (Fall 1981): 67–68. See also Robert Jervis, "Cooperation under the Security Dilemma," *World Politics* 30, no. 2 (January 1978): 209–10, and Ross, "Rethinking Soviet Strategy," pp. 23–24. Richard K. Betts, "Nuclear Peace: Mythology and Futurology," *Journal of Strategic Studies* 2, no. 1 (May 1979): 87–88, disagrees, at least partially, noting the possible shortcomings of this solution.

capability.[56] Given that strategic logic is against them, we should require strong evidence before basing U.S. strategic force requirements on perceptions arguments.

Before leaving this dispute, we should recognize that advocates of U.S. efforts to escape MAD by acquiring highly effective damage-limitation capabilities have framed their arguments in terms of wartime missions, not relative measures of force. Regarding disputes over how to assess strategic nuclear forces, these analysts are essentially in agreement with analysts who stress the importance of the ability to perform missions in MAD. Their disagreements are over what capabilities the United States can eventually acquire and what capabilities it needs.

How Does the Difficulty of Limiting a Nuclear War Affect the Requirements of Deterrence?

Two questions are particularly important in determining the implications of the difficulty of limiting a strategic nuclear war. First, does the burden of escalation to the strategic nuclear level lie with the United States or the Soviet Union? Second, do Soviet leaders recognize that nuclear war will be extremely difficult to limit? Based on divergent answers to these questions, analysts use seemingly similar beliefs about the poor prospects for limiting a nuclear war to support quite different U.S. military requirements.

For clarity, we need to distinguish between a limited war and a damage-limitation capability. In a limited war, both superpowers choose to restrict the amount of damage they inflict. In contrast, a damage-limitation capability enables a country to unilaterally reduce the costs of an all-out war. In MAD neither superpower can deny its adversary the ability to destroy its cities; in other words, neither has what is commonly considered a significant damage-limitation capability. However, the superpowers could cooperate to terminate

---

[56] Donald C. Daniel, ed., *International Perceptions of the Superpower Military Balance* (New York: Praeger, 1978), p. 188. In addition, this study finds that observers seeking information on superpower capabilities relied heavily on official U.S. statements and publications (p. 187). Thus, there is reason to believe the United States can influence perceptions by how it describes its capabilities. Closely related to the perceptions issue, Barry M. Blechman and Stephen S. Kaplan, *Force Without War* (Washington, D.C.: Brookings Institution, 1978), pp. 127–29, find little support for the "hypothesis that the strategic weapons balance influences the outcome of incidents in which both the United States and the USSR are involved." Other discussions of perceptions include Freedman, *The Evolution of Nuclear Strategy*, p. 370, who notes the lack of evidence. Howard, "On Fighting a Nuclear War," p. 9, criticizes counterforce scenarios for being divorced from the political context. See also Steven Kull, *Minds at War* (New York: Basic Books, 1988), and idem, "Nuclear Nonsense," *Foreign Policy* no. 58 (Summer 1985): 28–52. Betts, "Elusive Equivalence," pp. 111–17, provides some evidence in arguing, based upon an examination of the U.S. use of nuclear threats, that nuclear superiority provided the United States with a coercive capability. He qualifies his conclusion, however, noting that the much larger number of survivable weapons on both sides today make the situations significantly different.

a nuclear war before their cities are destroyed—that is, at least in theory, a limited war is possible.[57]

We should also recognize that disagreements about whether a nuclear war can be limited do not play a central role in analysts' divergent policy conclusions. Although assertions to the contrary are common, most analysts believe the superpowers would face severe challenges in terminating a limited strategic nuclear war.[58] Among factors frequently seen as contributing to the poor prospects are the problems of using limited nuclear attacks for wartime bargaining, the pressures to launch large counterforce and counter-control attacks to reduce the costs of an all-out war, problems with controlling forces during crises, and a lack of Soviet interest in limiting a strategic nuclear war.[59]

[57] Classic works on the theory of limited nuclear war, bargaining, and the need for and use of limited nuclear options include Klaus Knorr and Thornton Read, *Limited Strategic War* (New York: Praeger, 1962); Thomas C. Schelling, *The Strategy of Conflict*; idem, *Arms and Influence*; and Morton Halperin, *Limited War in the Nuclear Age* (New York: John Wiley, 1963), especially Chapter 6. For a recent discussion see Ian Clark, *Limited Nuclear War* (Princeton: Princeton University Press, 1982). For discussion of the various interpretations of "loss of control" see Robert Powell, "The Theoretical Foundations of Strategic Nuclear Deterrence," *Political Science Quarterly* 100, no. 1 (Spring 1985): 83–92. For historical discussion of these theories see Lawrence Freedman, *The Evolution of Nuclear Strategy*, Chapters 7, 8, 14, 15, and 25. On debate over whether counterforce is required for limited nuclear options see Chapter Seven in this book.

[58] Albert Wohlstetter, "Bishops, Statesmen, and Other Strategists on the Bombing of Innocents," appears to be something of an exception, stressing that nuclear wars in which small nuclear weapons are used in highly accurate counterforce attacks would be much easier to control than other nuclear wars. See also Thomas C. Schelling, "What Went Wrong with Arms Control?" *Foreign Affairs* (Winter 1985/86): 219–33, who disagrees, arguing instead that other types of attacks are more likely to stay limited. Expressing confidence that limited use of theater nuclear weapons would probably not escalate is Edward N. Luttwak, "How to Think about Nuclear War," reprinted in his *On the Meaning of Victory* (New York: Simon and Schuster, 1986), pp. 74–75. See also Bernard Brodie, *Escalation and the Nuclear Option* (Princeton: Princeton University Press, 1966). Less optimistic, but stressing the possibility of control, are Karl Kaiser et al., "Nuclear Weapons and the Preservation of Peace," *Foreign Affairs* 60, no. 5 (Summer 1982): 1161.

[59] On the problems created by vulnerable command and control systems see note 7 above and Paul Bracken, *The Command and Control of Nuclear Forces* (New Haven: Yale University Press, 1983). A useful synthesis of the literature on the difficulty of successful limitation is Richard Ned Lebow, *Nuclear Crisis Management: A Dangerous Illusion* (Ithaca: Cornell University Press, 1987). On factors that have made conventional wars difficult to terminate see Fred Charles Ikle, *Every War Must End* (New York: Columbia University Press, 1971); Richard Smoke, *War: Controlling Escalation* (Cambridge: Harvard University Press, 1977); and Stephen Van Evera, "Causes of War," (Ph.D. diss., University of California at Berkeley, 1984), Chapter 12. On possible escalatory pressures of current conventional military operations, see Barry R. Posen, "Inadvertent Nuclear War: Escalation and NATO's Northern Flank," *International Security* 7, no. 2 (Fall 1982): 28–54. On Soviet doctrine see Jack L. Snyder, *The Soviet Strategic Culture: Implications for Limited Nuclear Options*, R-2154-AF (Santa Monica: Rand, 1977); Benjamin S. Lambeth, "Selective Nuclear Options in Soviet Strategy," in Johan J. Holst and Uwe Nerlich, eds., *Beyond Nuclear Deterrence* (New York: Crane, Russak & Company, 1977); and Stephen M. Meyer, *Soviet Theater Nuclear Forces, Part I*, Adelphi Paper No. 187 (London, IISS, 1983–84), pp. 23–24.

THE BURDEN OF ESCALATION

If the United States needs to threaten to initiate the use of strategic nuclear weapons, specifically to enhance extended deterrence—that is, to help deter conventional or theater nuclear attacks against its allies—then the high probability of uncontrolled escalation following the initial use of strategic nuclear weapons works against the United States by making its threats less credible. In theory at least, limited nuclear threats are more credible because the United States would suffer lower costs in a limited nuclear war than in an all-out war. However, if limited nuclear attacks will probably escalate to all-out war, then the expected costs of launching a limited atttack are hardly smaller than the expected costs of launching an all-out attack. As a result, American limited nuclear options (LNOs) can do little to enhance the credibility of its threats to escalate to the nuclear level. This particularly worries analysts who believe that the United States must make highly credible threats to deter the Soviet Union. Gray and Payne, for example, conclude that the United States cannot base its strategy on limited nuclear options because "deterrence may fail to be restored during war for several reasons . . . LNOs would be viable only if the United States had a plausible theory of how it could control and dominate later escalation."[60] Thus, the problems of limiting a war reinforce their conclusion that extending deterrence requires the United States to reduce the vulnerability of its homeland.[61]

If, on the other hand, the United States is attempting to deter Soviet nuclear attacks against the U.S. homeland, then Soviet expectations that launching a limited strategic nuclear attack would lead to all-out war make the U.S. task easier. Consider, for example, the requirements for deterring Soviet counterforce attacks designed to improve the ratio of surviving forces. Even if Soviet leaders do see large benefits in shifting the balance, they will recognize that the high probability of all-out war makes these benefits unattainable. Therefore, the United States could deter these attacks even if it was unable to deny the Soviets an advantage in the size of surviving forces. Although generally valid, this argument is emphasized most frequently by analysts who already believe that Soviet leaders would have little incentive to launch a counterforce attack.

SOVIET RECOGNITION OF THE DIFFICULTY OF LIMITATION

The preceding arguments—which conclude that deterring the first use of strategic nuclear weapons is made easier by the difficulty of limiting a nuclear war—assume that Soviet leaders recognize the difficulty of controlling a nu-

[60] Gray and Payne, "Victory Is Possible," p. 18. See also Gray, "Targeting Problems for Central War."

[61] Gray does favor efforts to make nuclear war controllable, however. This is primarily to reduce the costs if war occurs, not to enhance deterrence. See "Defense, Warfighting and Deterrence," *Naval War College Review* 35, no. 4 (July–August 1982): 38–39, 41.

clear war. Some analysts, however, reject this assumption and therefore do not agree that the difficulty of controlling a nuclear war reduces U.S. requirements for deterring Soviet escalation to the use of strategic nuclear weapons. According to these analysts, the United States must be worried about deterring limited Soviet attacks, even if the war is in fact very likely to become all-out. For example, Harold Brown believes that although there is a high probability that limited nuclear attacks are likely to escalate to full-scale war, "we cannot count on others seeing the prospects of a nuclear exchange in the same light we do."[62] He therefore concludes that the United States should possess nuclear forces capable of deterring Soviet leaders who might ignore the difficulties of war termination following a Soviet limited nuclear attack. Consider, for example, limited counterforce attacks that the Soviets would launch to gain the benefits of shifting the ratio of forces. Even though escalation to all-out war would probably eliminate these benefits, according to this argument the United States should nevertheless maintain nuclear forces capable of denying the Soviet Union the ability to shift the ratio of surviving forces.

Others have greater confidence that Soviet leaders will not ignore the high probability of continued escalation. Jervis, for example, argues that "decision makers, having experienced the multiple ways in which predictions prove incorrect and situations get out of control, do not commit the fallacy of believing that escalation could be carefully manipulated and thus would not place great faith in the precise options of limited nuclear warfare."[63] Thus, whatever benefits the Soviets might see a limited attack providing, they almost certainly recognize that its risks are too high.

In closing, we should note that analysts tend to use arguments about the difficulty of limiting a war to reinforce the implications of more basic beliefs about the U.S. military requirements of deterrence. Thus, some ambiguity remains about the true source of disagreement. For example, for analysts who believe that relative force size matters, the Soviets have incentives to launch large counterforce attacks and there are therefore greater risks in assuming that Soviet leaders fully recognize the dangers of escalation. In contrast, for those who believe that relative force size matters little, the Soviets lack incentives for launching these attacks and there are therefore smaller risks in making these assumptions. Consequently, the difficulty of limiting a nuclear war tends to increase the divide between analysts who already disagree.

What Is Required for Crisis Stability?

It is generally considered desirable that strategic nuclear forces not create pressures for either superpower to escalate a crisis or conventional war to an all-

---

[62] Brown, *Annual Report, FY 1981*, p. 67.
[63] Jervis, "Why Nuclear Superiority Doesn't Matter," p. 621.

out strategic nuclear war.[64] The common concern is that once nuclear war appears likely, both countries will fear the other's attack and therefore launch a preemptive attack to limit the damage. Situations that do not suffer this pressure are said to have a high degree of ''crisis stability.'' This characteristic of the nuclear balance has received tremendous attention largely because these preemptive attacks are generally believed to be the most likely route to a deliberate all-out nuclear war.

Analysts' disagreements about crisis stability are best understood in terms of disagreements over the definition of crisis stability, the effect of first-strike incentives on the probability of war, and the conditions that create first-strike incentives in MAD. These disagreements lead to divergent conclusions about the requirements for avoiding preemptive war.

According to the most generally accepted definition, crisis stability is a measure of the countries' incentives not to preempt in a crisis, that is, not to attack first in order to beat the attack of the enemy. Crisis stability is high when the incentives to strike first are low. Changes in the nuclear forces that decrease the incentives for preemption enhance crisis stability. This concept was invented by Thomas Schelling and others in the late 1950s and early 1960s.[65]

Much of the concern over crisis stability stems from the belief that ''crisis instability'' could push a serious superpower confrontation, which might otherwise be resolved, into a large nuclear war. Indeed, there are situations in which both countries would expect to be less well-off after a nuclear war than before, thus preferring not to escalate, but each would decide that its best option was to attack first, thus starting a large nuclear war. Two conditions are commonly believed to be necessary for such a preemptive attack to occur. First, decisionmakers in at least one country believe that both countries have first-strike advantages, that is, there is some advantage to attacking first rather than letting one's adversary do so.[66] Second, due to a crisis or ongoing war, these decisionmakers fear that the adversary might launch a first strike to reap the relative benefits of going first. If the adversary's first strike appears sufficiently likely, then because there is a relative advantage in going first, one's best option would be to launch a preemptive first strike.

[64] Chapter Seven describes and analyzes the opposing points of view.

[65] Schelling, *Strategy of Conflict*, pp. 207–54, and *Arms and Influence*, pp. 221–48. See also Snyder, *Deterrence and Defense*, pp. 97–114, and Daniel Ellsberg, ''The Crude Analysis of Strategic Choice,'' originally published as P-2183 (Santa Monica: Rand, December 15, 1960), reprinted in John Mueller, ed., *Approaches to Measurement in International Relations* (New York: Meredith Corporation, 1969).

[66] There are important variations on this basic argument. For example, if only one country has a first-strike advantage, but it believes incorrectly that its adversary also has one, then this country would face essentially the same pressures for preemption as if its adversary actually had a first-strike advantage.

Although most analysts appear to accept the foregoing definition, there are important exceptions and qualifications. Some analysts use a broader definition in which crisis stability reflects the probability that a crisis will escalate by accidental or unauthorized attack or by a loss of control, in addition to the probability of escalation by preemptive attack. Others use a still broader definition, arguing that crisis stability is high when the United States can deter all types of Soviet escalation. Gray, for example, argues that ''crisis stability, if possible would flow from a Soviet belief that any escalation of the military conflict would produce negative military and ultimately political returns.''[67] I prefer the standard, narrower definition because it focuses on first-strike advantages.

In addition, some analysts have raised questions about how measures of crisis stability are used to analyze U.S. security. While accepting the standard definition of crisis stability, they argue that U.S. security depends on the probability of preemptive war, not on crisis stability considered in isolation. The probability of preemptive war depends on both the probability of crises and the probability that a crisis will escalate via preemptive attack. Crisis stability measures only the second factor.[68]

This criticism correctly observes that the United States should consider how to minimize the probability of preemptive war, not just how to minimize preemptive incentives. Reductions in the probability of preemptive war could be achieved by reducing the probability of crises and by reducing incentives to preempt in crisis. If reducing one of these increases the other, then analysts should address this tradeoff.[69]

Most analysts believe that crisis instability increases the probability of a large nuclear war. Broad acceptance of this argument is reflected in the common use of crisis stability as a measure of whether specific force deployments and arms control agreements would increase U.S. security. Some analysts,

[67] Colin Gray, ''Strategic Stability Reconsidered,'' *Daedalus* 109, no. 4 (Fall 1980): 150. In this article, Gray also appears to propose an even broader definition that includes both deterring crises and deterring escalation of crises.

[68] See, for example, Utgoff, ''In Defense of Counterforce,'' pp. 55–56. His point is slightly different, however, because he does not confine his remarks to the probability of escalation of crises that result from preemptive incentives.

[69] Although few discussions address this tradeoff, analysts have examined a closely related tension in discussions of the ''stability-instability'' paradox: lowering the probability that a conventional war will escalate to a nuclear war—along preemptive and other paths—reduces the danger of starting a conventional war; thus, this low likelihood of escalation—referred to here as ''stability''—makes conventional war less dangerous, and possibly, as a result, more likely. See T. C. Schelling, ''Comment,'' in Knorr and Read, eds., *Limited Strategic War*, pp. 250–53; Glenn H. Snyder, ''The Balance of Power and the Balance of Terror,'' in Paul Seabury, ed., *The Balance of Power* (San Francisco: Chandler, 1965), pp. 184–201; and Jervis's discussion of the ''stability-instability'' paradox in *The Illogic of American Nuclear Strategy*.

however, doubt that preemptive incentives make crises more dangerous. For example, Steven Rosen argues that "it is difficult to find even one war caused by instability" and that "war will not become more likely because of the character of the two opposing nuclear forces."[70]

Nevertheless, the case for worrying about crisis instability appears to be well-founded. Historical studies support the theoretical arguments that preemptive incentives can precipitate wars, with World War I being the most carefully studied case.[71] Those who question this have not convincingly refuted the historical evidence against their position.[72] Moreover, nuclear weapons probably increase the importance of maintaining crisis stability. Given the costs of all-out war, it is hard to imagine either superpower launching a full-scale attack, except possibly to preempt the adversary's attack.

Some analysts believe that first-strike incentives are created by the ability to reduce the costs of an all-out war; if neither country has a damage-limitation capability, then first-strike incentives do not exist and crisis stability is high. For analysts who also believe that significant damage limitation is impossible in MAD, this position leads to the conclusion that crisis stability is very high in MAD.[73] The superpowers' inability to protect their societies means that counterforce does not significantly reduce crisis stability, since it cannot provide either country with a significant damage-limitation capability.[74] These

[70] Rosen, "Foreign Policy and Nuclear Weapons," pp. 142, 146. Rosen uses stability to reflect the extent of preventive incentives that result from arms race pressures and political tensions, as well as the extent of preemptive incentives. The first of the quoted statements is less contentious than the second, since most analysts believe that crisis instability can increase the probability of war once crises occur, but not that it causes war by itself. See also Gray, "Strategic Stability Reconsidered," p. 150.

For a different critique based on a formal game theory model see Robert Powell, "Crisis Stability in the Nuclear Age," *American Political Science Review* 83, no. 1 (March 1989): 61–76.

[71] For a detailed study of the role of preemptive incentives see Stephen Van Evera, "The Cult of the Offensive and the Origins of the First World War," *International Security* 9, no. 1 (Summer 1984): 71–79, and idem, "Causes of War," pp. 21–42. See also Schelling, *Arms and Influence*, pp. 221–27, and Herman Kahn, *On Thermonuclear War* (Princeton: Princeton University Press, 1961), pp. 357–75.

[72] See, however, Patrick Glynn, "The Sarajevo Fallacy: The Historical and Intellectual Origins of Arms Control Theology," *National Interest* (Fall 1987): 3–32.

[73] Steinbruner, "National Security and the Concept of Strategic Stability," accepts this measure of first-strike incentives, but argues that standard analyses of crisis stability are too narrow because they overlook the vulnerability of the superpowers' command and control systems. See also Blair, *Strategic Command and Control*, pp. 284–85.

[74] See, for example, Jervis, *The Illogic of American Nuclear Strategy*, p. 129. He points out, however, that in MAD there might be first-strike incentives if attacking first provides an advantage in bargaining. This type of first-strike incentive is not usually considered to contribute to crisis instability. See also Posen and Van Evera, "Defense Policy and the Reagan Administration," pp. 26–27, who argue that significant damage limitation is infeasible and that counterforce would

analysts believe that forces for limiting damage would be dangerous if they seriously threatened the superpowers' assured destruction capabilities, but find this outcome quite unlikely and therefore see little threat to crisis stability.[75]

In contrast, other analysts believe that first-strike advantages are also created by a country's ability to improve the relative size of its force by launching a counterforce strike. This incentive will be especially strong if one's adversary cannot remove this advantage with a counterforce retaliatory attack. This view of first-strike incentives is suggested by Brown when he argues: "Crisis stability means insuring that even in a prolonged and intense confrontation the Soviet Union would have no incentive to initiate an exchange, and also that we would feel ourselves under no pressure to do so."[76] When taken in the context of Brown's discussion of nuclear exchanges, much of which pertains to counterforce exchanges measured in post-exchange ratios, this statement suggests that first-strike incentives are measured in terms of shifting force ratios.

As a result, these analysts believe that crisis stability requires "counterforce equivalence"—that is, the United States must be able to deny the Soviets an advantage in a counterforce exchange—as well as an assured destruction capability.[77] According to this argument, survivable U.S. counterforce can increase crisis stability by enabling the United States to redress the post-attack balance of forces.[78]

This disagreement over what creates a first-strike incentive stems directly from the dispute over the significance of relative force size in MAD. As argued previously, measures of relative force size are misleading since they re-

increase the risk of war if damage limitation were feasible, but do not argue that counterforce increases the risk of war.

[75] However, many who hold this basic view appear to be inconsistent, arguing both that damage limitation is infeasible and that counterforce decreases crisis stability. On this point see Chapter Seven.

[76] Brown, *Annual Report, FY 1981*, p. 69.

[77] For a clear discussion see James A. Thompson, *Strategic Defense and Deterrence*, P-6985 (Santa Monica: Rand, May 1984), pp. 8–9. He calls the ability to shift the balance of forces in a first strike a "counterforce instability" and notes that, although this type of instability is worrisome, a large U.S. retaliatory capability would most likely deter a Soviet first strike. While this argument is rarely made explicitly, concern about Soviet counterforce attacks that improve the ratio or differential of Soviet to U.S. forces is often associated with crisis instability. For example, although Nitze in his influential articles does not describe in detail the Soviet motivation for launching counterforce attacks, they are often discussed as preemptive attacks. For a more explicit statement see Paul Nitze, "SALT II and American Strategic Considerations," pp. 11, 13.

[78] Whether counterforce weapons would actually increase this type of crisis stability depends on a variety of factors, including their survivability (vulnerable counterforce could have the opposite effect) and the survivability of the weapons the Soviets planned not to use in their first strike. For other interesting arguments about why counterforce might not reduce crisis stability see Michael M. May, "Some Advantages of a Counterforce Deterrence," *Orbis* 14, no. 1 (Summer 1970): 279–80.

flect neither the ability to inflict damage nor the ability to limit it. Thus, arguments holding that crisis stability requires counterforce equivalence are weak. The recognition by both countries that they lack significant damage-limitation capabilities should be sufficient to create a very high degree of crisis stability.

Finally, analysts who equate crisis stability with the U.S. ability to deter all types of Soviet escalation believe that crisis stability requires U.S. superiority: the U.S. advantage in the ability to inflict damage is necessary to deter crises and to reduce the probability that the Soviet Union will deliberately escalate crises. Gray, for example, argues that "the United States is most unlikely to be able to enforce stability if damage to the U.S. homeland cannot be limited severely."[79] Believing that first-strike incentives are an unimportant cause of war, these analysts conclude that extensive damage-limitation forces do not increase the probability that crises will escalate preemptively.[80]

IDENTIFYING AND EVALUATING SCHOOLS AND STRATEGIES

Having explored the key disputes, it is useful to identify three schools of thought that emerge in the debate over the military requirements of deterrence.[81] These schools are defined by analysts' positions on the disputed issues. The table below summarizes these positions.[82] Identifying schools increases our ability to examine the logical connections between analysts' positions on the disputes and the strategy and specific policies they recom-

[79] Gray, "Strategic Stability Reconsidered," p. 150. Huntington seems to reach a similar conclusion in "The Renewal of Strategy," pp. 3, 42.

[80] See Chapter Five for analysis of crisis stability in a world of U.S. superiority.

[81] For other divisions of the strategic nuclear debate see Michael Krepon, *Strategic Stalemate: Nuclear Weapons and Arms Control in American Politics* (New York: St. Martin's, 1984); Colin S. Gray, *Nuclear Strategy and Strategic Planning*, Philadelphia Policy Papers (Philadelphia: Foreign Policy Research Institute, 1984); Leon Sloss, "The Strategist's Perspective," in Ashton B. Carter and David N. Schwartz, *Ballistic Missile Defense* (Washington, D.C.: Brookings Institution, 1984), pp. 37–46; the Public Agenda Foundation in collaboration with the Center for Policy Development at Brown University (New York: Public Agenda Foundation, 1984), pp. 72–81; and Morton H. Halperin, *Nuclear Fallacy: Dispelling the Myth of Nuclear Strategy* (Cambridge, Mass.: Ballinger, 1987). For analysis of schools in the strategic debate of the early 1960s see Robert A. Levine, *The Arms Debate* (Cambridge: Harvard University Press, 1963).

[82] Some readers of early drafts of this chapter argued that the military denial school and the damage-limitation school do not differ enough to delineate two distinct schools. They did not doubt primarily the logical differences between the schools, but rather questioned their significance in the strategic nuclear debate. Readers who tend to dismiss the damage-limitation school hold that only a few analysts really hold these views. In contrast, others believe that the military denial school simply packages the damage-limitation school's beliefs for public consumption: its arguments are designed to justify many of the forces advocated more directly by the damage-limitation school without alienating a public that is unwilling to strive for superiority and to engage in an intense arms race. I have kept the schools separate because their positions are logically distinct and because I believe both are important in the debate.

mend. It also, however, requires some simplification since many analysts have not taken positions on each dispute and some do not fit neatly into these schools. This is not a serious shortcoming since the schools are best viewed as ideal types for understanding the contours of the debate.

Analysts' positions on the disputes, however, do not fully determine their conclusions about military strategy or about the forces and arms control agreements best suited to supporting their preferred strategy. Regarding strategy, the basic divide (regardless of school) is over first use—should the United States use strategic nuclear threats to help deter Soviet conventional attacks or only to deter Soviet nuclear attacks against the U.S. homeland? Regarding force posture and arms control, analysts' conclusions depend on a range of additional factors, including the political implications of various military options and their economic costs. In effect, therefore, the schools (and beliefs on which they are built) establish boundaries within which analysts' conclusions about strategy and forces are likely to fall.

After describing the schools, I examine the strategies that are compatible with each school. The remainder of this section then draws together my analysis of the disputes to reach an overall assessment of the competing schools.

Schools

The *damage-limitation school*, prominently represented by analysts such as Colin Gray and Keith Payne, argues that the United States can protect its vital interests only by escaping MAD and acquiring nuclear superiority. Because Soviet leaders are determined to expand, the United States needs highly credible threats to deter Soviet challenges to vital U.S. interests. U.S. strategic forces, however, cannot pose such threats while the U.S. homeland is highly vulnerable. U.S. threats to escalate are rendered incredible by the Soviet assured destruction capability, leaving the United States unable to extend deterrence to its allies. The only solution, then, is for the United States to have "escalation dominance,"[83] that is, the ability to defeat the Soviet Union at all levels of conflict, or at least in an all-out nuclear war.[84] Thus, the United States needs a highly effective damage-limitation capability while maintaining its

[83] This definition is close to Herman Kahn's in *On Escalation: Metaphors and Scenarios* (New York: Praeger, 1965), pp. 289–91. Escalation dominance is sometimes used to describe the requirements of the countervailing strategy. See, for example, Jervis, *The Illogic of American Nuclear Strategy*, p. 59. I will use the term "escalation equivalence" to describe the requirements of the countervailing strategy.

[84] An alternative solution, especially if damage limitation is infeasible, is to reduce U.S. commitments to allies. For example, Earl C. Ravenal, "Counterforce and the Alliance: The Ultimate Connection," *International Security* 6, no. 4 (Spring 1982): 26–43, agrees that extended deterrence requires this capability, but the economic and strategic costs of damage limitation, and its likely infeasibility, lead him to conclude that the United States should withdraw its extended deterrence commitments.

Summary of Schools of Thought in the Debate over the Military Requirements of Nuclear Deterrence

	How do Soviet leaders view the costs of nuclear war?	How do Soviet leaders view the benefits of expansion?	Can the U.S. limit damage to itself in an all-out war?	What determines advantages in credibility & capability between nuclear superpowers?	How does the difficulty of limiting a nuclear war affect the requirements of deterrence?	What is required for crisis stability?
Punitive retaliation	Extremely high, since society is vulnerable	Dwarfed by the potential costs of nuclear war	Not enough to matter	Commitment and resolve	Decreases requirements	Assured destruction capabilities
Military denial	Extremely high if, in addition to society, leadership & forces are also vulnerable	Uncertain, so the U.S. needs to hedge against worst-case Soviet leaders	Slightly, worth pursuing to save American lives	Relative force size	Unchanged, since the U.S. needs to hedge against worst-case Soviet leaders	Assured destruction capabilities, plus counterforce equivalence
Damage limitation	May not be very high, since • insensitive to societal damage • effective damage limitation • highest value on leadership & forces	Very large, possibly even comparable to costs of nuclear war	Enough to matter, worth pursuing to enhance deterrence	Relative ability to inflict damage	Increases requirements	U.S. damage-limitation capability plus superiority

ability to inflict extremely high costs on the Soviet Union. According to these analysts, nuclear superiority will reduce the probability of crises and the probability that crises will escalate.

These analysts believe that the United States can acquire the necessary damage-limitation capabilities by investing heavily in offensive counterforce, strategic defenses—including ballistic missile defenses and air defenses—and civil defense. Inflicting extremely high costs requires offensive counterforce to destroy the targets that Soviet leaders value most highly—political and military control and military forces.

This school shows little interest in limited nuclear options, largely because it sees damage limitation requiring a massive counterforce attack launched at the outset of the nuclear war. In theory, however, if damage limitation were achieved entirely by highly effective strategic defenses, then the United States might deter Soviet conventional attacks by threatening costs via limited nuclear attacks.

In sharp contrast, the *punitive retaliation school*, which includes Robert Jervis, McGeorge Bundy, and Bernard Brodie, concludes that the U.S. ability to destroy Soviet society deters Soviet attacks against the U.S. homeland and contributes extensively to extended deterrence, even in MAD. Because Soviet leaders see the costs of a large nuclear attack against their society dwarfing any benefits they place on expansion, they are deterred from pursuing actions that they think have even a small probability of provoking such a nuclear attack. These analysts therefore conclude that U.S. strategic nuclear forces can contribute significantly to extended deterrence, since they believe that Soviet leaders recognize that a large superpower war would significantly increase the probability of nuclear war. Brodie, for example, argues that "we have ample reason to feel now that nuclear weapons do act critically to deter wars between the major powers, and not nuclear wars alone but any wars. . . . It is the curious paradox of our time that one of the foremost factors making deterrence really work and work well is the lurking fear that in some massive confrontation crisis it might fail. Under these circumstances one does not tempt fate."[85]

[85] Bernard Brodie, *War and Politics* (New York: Macmillan, 1973), pp. 430–31. See also Jervis, "Why Superiority Doesn't Matter," pp. 618–19: "because statesmen know that imprudent action could lead to all-out war, the resulting deterrence covers a lot more than attacks on one's homeland. To take any major offensive action is to run an intolerably high risk of escalation."

Robert S. McNamara, who seems to hold the positions that define the punitive retaliation school, appears to disagree in "The Military Role of Nuclear Weapons: Perceptions and Misperceptions," *Foreign Affairs* (Fall 1983): 68, 73, 79, arguing that the only purpose of strategic nuclear weapons is to deter the other side's first use of its strategic forces. Jervis, *The Illogic of American Nuclear Strategy*, pp. 148–50, observes that this is because McNamara believes the "stability-instability" paradox is extreme, that is, the probability of escalation from the conventional level is judged so low that it does not contribute significantly to deterrence of conventional war. However, because he was focusing on how the United States *should* plan to use nuclear

Further, members of the punitive retaliation school find little if any value in counterforce. They believe that the United States cannot acquire a significant damage-limitation capability and therefore see no benefit in being able to destroy a fraction of Soviet forces in MAD. In addition, the United States does not require counterforce options to deter Soviet counterforce attacks. The U.S. assured destruction capability essentially eliminates the benefits of a Soviet counterforce attack by ensuring that the Soviet Union cannot significantly reduce the U.S. ability to inflict retaliatory costs. Moreover, with significant damage limitation infeasible, relative force size—both before and after counterforce attacks and exchanges—matters little. In sharp contrast to such limited benefits, a Soviet counterforce attack carries enormous risks. Even if they spared U.S. cities, Soviet leaders could not assume that the United States would not attack their society. U.S. retaliation might be deliberate or might result from the difficulty of controlling a large nuclear war.

Finally, although they find counterforce unnecessary, these analysts do not see it posing great dangers. Since neither country can significantly limit damage by launching a preemptive attack, crisis stability is high in MAD.[86]

Although they do not stress the need for limited nuclear options, most of these analysts believe that U.S. limited nuclear options might enhance deterrence of Soviet conventional attack and possibly limited nuclear attacks against the U.S. homeland. In MAD, the utility of nuclear weapons lies in their potential for influencing the Soviet Union by threatening to inflict pain. Threats of limited nuclear attack are more credible than all-out threats because they preserve Soviet incentives for restraint. At least in theory, limited nuclear options provide the capability to engage in a "competition in risk taking," to bargain with one's adversary.[87] But since limited options work by threatening costs, the need for limited options does not require the United States to deploy forces designed to destroy counterforce targets.

However, analysts in the punitive retaliation school believe that limited nuclear options, whether targeted against counterforce or countervalue targets, contribute relatively little to deterrence. The U.S. assured destruction capability provides what Bundy has termed "existential deterrence"—deterrence resulting from the possibility of extremely high costs and not from the details of the U.S. options and threats.[88] According to Jervis, "Although the United

---

weapons, McNamara may have overstated his argument and may actually believe that the superpowers' strategic arsenals do reduce the probability of large superpower conventional war.

[86] As noted above, many analysts that otherwise fit in this school appear inconsistent on this point.

[87] On this concept see Schelling, *Arms and Influence*, pp. 92–125.

[88] Bundy, "The Bishops and the Bomb," p. 4. For a related argument about why shifting to a no-first-use policy would not weaken deterrence see McGeorge Bundy et al., "Nuclear Weapons and the Atlantic Alliance," *Foreign Affairs* 60, no. 4 (Spring 1982): 753–68, especially pp. 757, 766.

States should be able to conduct limited nuclear demonstrations, it should not stress this part of its policy.''[89] Thus, arguments that emphasize the role of limited nuclear options are misleading.

Strongly disagreeing, the *military denial school* believes that in MAD an adequate U.S. deterrent requires a full spectrum of limited options, including large counterforce options. These options play a central role in deterring conventional attacks against U.S. allies and limited attacks against the U.S. homeland. This school represents views closely associated with official U.S. nuclear doctrine since at least the early 1970s and presented most fully by former secretary of defense Harold Brown.

Like the damage-limitation school, the military denial school stresses that the Soviet assured destruction capability, by reducing the credibility of U.S. threats to use nuclear weapons against Soviet cities and industry, greatly weakens the U.S. ability to extend deterrence. Unlike the damage-limitation school, however, these analysts believe that the United States cannot take its cities out of a hostage situation. Thus, the low credibility of U.S. threats must be solved by other means. To this end, the military denial school emphasizes the need for a spectrum of limited nuclear options.

This school concludes that counterforce limited options are required to enhance extended deterrence for two reasons: (1) counterforce threats are more credible than countervalue threats, since they threaten lower costs and preserve Soviet incentives for restraint,[90] and (2) counterforce options enable the United States to influence Soviet decisions during peacetime, crisis, and war, because Soviet leaders are influenced by detailed comparison of the size and qualitative features of superpower strategic nuclear forces.

Based on similar arguments about relative force size, the military denial school argues that the United States needs counterforce options to deter counterforce attacks against the U.S. homeland. Concern about Soviet efforts to gain an advantage in relative force size is reinforced by the school's concern that Soviet leaders might fail to appreciate the difficulty of limiting a large counterforce war. Thus, these analysts envision a wide range of scenarios in which Soviet leaders initiate the use of strategic nuclear weapons, including cases in which they launch counterforce attacks to increase their prospects for prevailing in Europe.

As formulated by Brown, the United States needs options that can deny the Soviet Union an advantage at whatever level of conflict it chooses.[91] I term

---

[89] Jervis, ''Why Superiority Doesn't Matter,'' p. 632. See also idem, *The Illogic of American Nuclear Strategy*, p. 168.

[90] This argument, however, does conflict with the school's argument that military forces are valued most highly by Soviet leaders.

[91] If the denial capability required for escalation equivalence were not restricted to responses at the level of conflict chosen by the adversary, then escalation equivalence would be virtually mean-

this requirement "escalation equivalence." As discussed below, however, satisfying this requirement would not meet the school's own requirement for extending deterrence with threats of strategic first use.

This school's positions support additional arguments for counterforce. For example, counterforce would enhance the U.S. deterrent by threatening higher retaliatory costs through the ability to destroy Soviet leadership and military targets. Finally, extensive counterforce capabilities might not reduce crisis stability, since the Soviet Union will retain a substantial retaliatory capability, and might even increase it by providing counterforce equivalence.

Strategies

While encompassing the key disputes in the strategic nuclear debate, these schools do not delineate the full range of basic nuclear strategies. For the most part, the schools focus on the threats and capabilities the U.S. requires for deterring given Soviet actions. The schools disagree on the conditions under which the United States *could* adequately deter these actions. Conclusions about strategy, however, require additional judgments about which Soviet actions the United States *should* use nuclear weapons to deter and about the risks and feasibility of alternative strategies.[92]

The most important divide is over whether the United States should maintain its policy of threatening first use of strategic weapons to enhance extended deterrence. Disagreements about the threats the U.S. requires to deter given Soviet actions lead to disagreements between the punitive retaliation and military denial schools about how to implement first-use and no-first-use strategies.

In broad terms, three strategies are associated with the punitive retaliation school. The first continues the U.S. policy of explicitly threatening the first use of strategic nuclear weapons to contribute to deterrence of Soviet conventional attacks. Toward this end, the United States would threaten limited nuclear attacks designed to inflict pain on the Soviet Union and to increase Soviet assessments of the costs of continued fighting. Similar threats would also be used to deter Soviet limited nuclear attacks against the U.S. homeland. These limited nuclear options are seen entirely in terms of wartime bargaining and need not threaten Soviet forces. This diverges from current U.S. policy, which sees an effective first-use policy requiring large counter-military attacks. The second strategy rejects the first use of strategic nuclear forces to deter Soviet conventional attacks, but would provide the United States with limited, essentially countervalue, options to enhance deterrence of limited Soviet attacks

---

ingless: as long as the United States has an assured destruction capability, an all-out U.S. response could always deny the Soviet Union an advantage.

[92] Gray, *Nuclear Strategy and Strategic Planning*, presents a useful and somewhat different description of the spectrum of strategies.

against the U.S. homeland. The third strategy differs from the second by re-jecting all limited options, leaving the United States with only an all-out retal-iatory option against Soviet society.

Although assertions to the contrary are common, few analysts in this school have argued that the United States should have only an all-out retaliatory ca-pability, that is, no limited nuclear options. The key argument against limited nuclear options in general is that by acquiring them the United States might convince Soviet leaders that limited nuclear war is possible, thereby making it more likely.[93] However, virtually all opposition to nuclear options has fo-cused against large counterforce options. Thus, proponents of counterforce who criticize this third variant of the punitive retaliation school are attacking something of a strawman.

Within the punitive retaliation school, disagreements about first use are not rooted in disagreements about the types of threats that influence Soviet lead-ers. Instead, they reflect divergent comparisons of the benefits and risks of a first-use strategy. Specifically, analysts disagree about how the benefits, re-ducing the probability of conventional war, compare with the costs—increas-ing the probability of nuclear war if conventional war occurs. Exploring these disagreements requires delving into the details of the debate over no-first-use and is beyond the scope of this chapter.[94]

The views presented by the military denial school are also compatible with first-use and pure second-use strategies for strategic nuclear weapons. Unlike the punitive retaliation school, however, its members are usually associated with first-use strategies. In a first-use policy the United States would deploy forces for shifting the ratio of forces with a counterforce first strike and for maintaining an advantage following Soviet retaliation in a counterforce ex-change.[95] In a second-use policy the United States would deploy forces suffi-cient to deny the Soviets the ability to acquire these ratio advantages by strik-ing first.

Given its common association with a first-use strategy, it is noteworthy that

---

[93] Analysts who have raised questions about the benefits of limited options include Jervis, "Why Nuclear Superiority Doesn't Matter," pp. 629–30; Brodie, "The Development of Nuclear Strategy," pp. 80–82; and Herbert Scoville, Jr., "Flexible Madness," *Foreign Policy* no. 14 (Spring 1974): 175–76.

[94] Among the key works in the extensive debate over shifting to a policy of no-first-use are McGeorge Bundy et al., "Nuclear Weapons and the Atlantic Alliance," pp. 753–68; Karl Kaiser et al., "Nuclear Weapons and the Preservation of Peace," pp. 1157–71; Morton H. Halperin, *Nuclear Fallacy: Dispelling the Myth of Nuclear Strategy*; John Steinbruner and Leon Sigal, eds., *Alliance Security: NATO and the No-First-Use Question* (Washington, D.C.: Brookings Institu-tion, 1983); and John J. Mearsheimer, "Nuclear Weapons and Deterrence in Europe," *Interna-tional Security* 9, no. 3 (Winter 1984–85): 19–46.

[95] Carl H. Builder, "Why Not First Strike Counterforce Capabilities," *Strategic Review* 7, no. 2 (Spring 1979): 32–39, makes essentially this argument. For related observations see Betts, *Nu-clear Blackmail and Nuclear Balance*, pp. 193–95.

the U.S. countervailing strategy does not meet the military denial school's requirements for first use. Although Harold Brown argues that it is entirely consistent with U.S. commitments to NATO,[96] measured by its own criteria the countervailing strategy prescribes forces sufficient only for second use. The logic underlying escalation equivalence suggests that a country can credibly threaten to escalate only if it would have an advantage at the new level of conflict. Thus, according to the criteria used by the military denial school, a strategic first-use policy requires that the United States be able to favorably shift the ratio of forces following a counterforce exchange that it initiates. In other words, extended deterrence requires the United States to deny the Soviet Union escalation equivalence, not simply for the United States to possess it.

Unlike the other schools, the damage-limitation school is associated with only one basic strategy. Its requirements are driven by the need to enhance extended deterrence by providing the United States with highly credible threats of first use. These analysts do not address the requirements of a pure second-use strategy.

Evaluating the Schools

Which of the schools of thought is most convincing? Which can best guide U.S. nuclear strategy? The answers depend on the strength of the positions taken in each of the six areas of dispute and on the strength of the logic that weaves them together.

Although internally consistent, the damage-limitation school suffers from some extremely weak positions on the disputed issues. Consequently, its overall argument exaggerates the requirements of deterrence and then prescribes infeasible policies to meet them. Little evidence supports the claims that Soviet leaders doubt that a nuclear war would result in overwhelming costs or that the Soviet Union is willing to significantly increase the probability of nuclear war to expand. Thus, these analysts have exaggerated the credibility the U.S. requires to deter Soviet attacks.[97]

Even if we accept that protecting current U.S. interests requires strategic nuclear superiority, the damage-limitation school fails because its prescription simply cannot be achieved.[98] It depends critically on the United States creating a highly favorable asymmetry in the superpowers' abilities to inflict costs on

---

[96] Brown, *Annual Report, FY 1982*, p. 40.

[97] This requirement is also exaggerated since it tends to assume that NATO must depend heavily on threats of escalation because its conventional forces have no hope of stopping a Warsaw Pact invasion. For citations to analyses of the conventional balance see note 12 in Chapter Five.

[98] The analysis presented here leaves open the question of whether nuclear superiority, if feasible, would be preferable to MAD. Because the damage-limitation school's overall argument is internally consistent, the case for superiority might be significantly stronger under such different conditions. Chapter Five analyzes this comparison.

one another. Yet there is overwhelming evidence that such a reduction in the vulnerability of the U.S. population, cities, and industry is impossible in the foreseeable future. Only an attack against the Soviet command and control system, in combination with a counterforce attack, holds even the slightest chance of so substantially reducing the costs of Soviet retaliation. However, this possibility of a successful counter-control attack does not satisfy the requirements of the damage-limitation school. Because a decapitation attack would have at most a very small chance of dramatically reducing Soviet retaliation, the possibility of such an attack does not significantly increase the credibility of U.S. threats. Both U.S. and Soviet decisionmakers would continue to believe that U.S. society remained highly vulnerable to Soviet retaliation in virtually all important scenarios.[99]

The choice then is between arguments about the requirements for deterring the Soviet Union in MAD. The preceding analysis suggests that the punitive retaliation school holds stronger positions on the disputed issues than does the military denial school.

The crux of the military denial school's argument is undermined because relative measures of forces are not highly significant. Ratio arguments lack a logical basis—in MAD relative measures cannot be directly related to the capability to affect war outcomes. Moreover, the importance of relative measures has not been rescued by perceptions arguments—there is essentially no evidence that relative measures affect Soviet decisions about using nuclear weapons or influence Soviet and allied perceptions of overall U.S. strength and determination. These weaknesses shatter arguments holding that counterforce can provide the United States with advantages in credibility and capability, and that Soviet counterforce threatens important U.S. capabilities.

Weaknesses in other of the school's positions further damage its arguments for counterforce. With Soviet society already extremely vulnerable, the school's claim that targeting Soviet forces and control capabilities enables the United States to threaten significantly worse war outcomes is implausible. In addition, because these analysts believe that the United States might be able to reduce the costs of an all-out war, counterforce is likely to reduce crisis stability somewhat.

Furthermore, there are additional problems with a first-use strategy based on the military denial school's requirements. Even if we accept that relative

---

[99] A second, although less important point also works against the damage-limitation school: because the command and control facilities of both superpowers suffer some vulnerabilities, the possibility of successful damage limitation based on disabling command and control capabilities might not consistently favor either superpower and would therefore not create the asymmetry that the damage-limitation school requires. While the mutual vulnerability of the superpowers' command and control systems might favor the country that attacked first, the conservative planners of the damage-limitation school could not be confident that the United States would get in the first blow if war occurs.

force size matters, U.S. counterforce options that could provide the United States with a clear advantage in relative force size seem insufficient to support a first-use strategy. Given the importance this school places on unpredictable Soviet behavior and the difficulty of limiting a nuclear war, counterforce attacks large enough to shift the relative size of surviving forces would likely carry risks of Soviet escalation that exceeded their military benefits. If so, then the only militarily significant capability that could satisfy the school's requirements would be a highly effective damage-limitation capability. These analysts, however, believe that such a capability remains beyond U.S. reach.

Faced with this problem, analysts in the military denial school could suggest that the U.S. threaten smaller counterforce attacks designed to encourage Soviet restraint. However, these smaller attacks would do little to shift relative force size. They are best understood in terms of bargaining and risk generation, and not in terms of military advantages.[100] Thus, this solution borrows heavily from the arguments emphasized by the punitive retaliation school. Once the military denial school resorts to bargaining uses, the difference between these schools is seriously blurred. At this point, both strategies depend on limited options for bargaining while disagreeing about the importance of counterforce.

Proponents of the military denial school might respond along two lines. First, although the punitive retaliation school holds strong positions on the disputed issues, it is overly confident about future Soviet behavior. Instead of being confident, the United States should hedge against unlikely but possible Soviet behavior. How can we be sure that a future Soviet leader will not run great risks to expand? And what about a leader that measures international power in terms of ratios of strategic forces, or believes that both conventional and nuclear wars are easy to limit? Further, since nuclear war is possible, should not the United States pursue damage-limitation capabilities to reduce its costs? In short, in this approach the military denial school argues that it provides good guidance because U.S. strategy should be designed to succeed under the most difficult conditions. Second, analysts in the military denial school could argue that the punitive retaliation school does an even less satisfactory job of meeting U.S. commitments to NATO. The claim is that the punitive retaliation school fails to recognize that counterforce options are required to enhance the credibility of U.S. threats to escalate to the strategic level.

Resolving these challenges to the punitive retaliation school requires moving beyond these basic disputes. Complete analysis of U.S. strategy and forces must consider a full range of more specific arguments about military require-

---

[100] The countervailing strategy does make passing references to bargaining. For example, Slocombe, "The Countervailing Strategy," pp. 22–23, argues that the need for "sharply restricted" options that demonstrate resolve is distinct from the need for "less than all-out strikes that exact high costs" by destroying highly valued targets, including nuclear forces.

ments and costs, many of which build on these disputes. This chapter provides the foundation for the more detailed analysis presented in later chapters on the benefits and costs of hedging against worst cases. In addition, reaching conclusions about which forces can best support U.S. strategy requires considering the political effects of U.S. military policy, which are explored in the following chapter.

CHAPTER THREE

Disputes about the International Political Consequences of Competing and Cooperating with the Soviet Union

U.S. STRATEGIC nuclear policy should not be based entirely on the military requirements of nuclear deterrence, but also on the policy's broader international political consequences. U.S. nuclear policy could influence Soviet images of the United States, Soviet domestic debates over foreign and military policy, and the extent of conflict of interest between the superpowers.

These broader political consequences can significantly influence U.S. security. Let us look at an example where increasing U.S. military capabilities might decrease our security. If a competitive U.S. nuclear policy communicates a hostile image of the United States and as a result increases Soviet doubts about their ability to maintain their security, Soviet leaders may in turn be more inclined to pursue provocative and risky actions simply to protect their interests in the status quo. In this case, enhancing American capabilities could be self-defeating because it also makes the Soviets harder to deter. There are also cases in which more cooperative American policies could bring negative political consequences. If, for example, an arms control agreement maintains U.S. military capabilities but nevertheless raises doubts about U.S. resolve, then Soviet leaders might be tempted to more aggressively challenge vital U.S. interests.

Considered from this perspective, the debate over the military requirements of nuclear deterrence analyzed in Chapter Two is built on an essentially static view of the Soviet Union and superpower relations. For example, it fails to take account of the broader political consequences by assuming that Soviet images of the United States are basically fixed. It focuses on an inherent Soviet desire to alter the status quo—seen as uninfluenced by U.S. policy—while paying little attention to the role of Western policies in creating Soviet insecurity that could generate pressures for hostile Soviet policies.[1]

Nevertheless, although this debate over military requirements receives the bulk of attention, disagreements about the political consequences of American nuclear policy play a central role in dividing analysts on such basic questions

---

[1] The obvious exception is the debate's concern over Soviet incentives for preemptive attack; note, however, that even this apparent exception holds the Soviet view of the United States constant: Soviet concern stems not from their view of increasingly malign U.S. intentions but from their recognition of the U.S. desire to reduce losses relative to the status quo.

as: Is the strategic nuclear arms race dangerous? Are cooperative or more threatening, competitive policies better suited to managing the U.S. relationship with the Soviet Union?

This chapter explores three broad disputes about the political consequences of U.S. strategic nuclear policy. The first dispute is over the Soviet propensity to underestimate U.S. resolve. Some analysts worry that American self-restraint and willingness to negotiate arms control agreements encourage Soviet underestimates of U.S. resolve. But others respond that the Soviets are unlikely to misperceive U.S. resolve as long as the United States maintains the military capabilities required to deter the Soviets. Underlying this dispute are disagreements about Soviet intentions: analysts who believe the Soviet Union is highly expansionist see the largest dangers in pursuing more cooperative policies.

The second dispute is over the Soviet propensity to exaggerate U.S. hostility. On one side, analysts hold that American nuclear forces that threaten Soviet deterrent capabilities project a malign image of the United States, which increases both Soviet insecurity and superpower tensions. To avoid these dangers, they tend to favor both arms control and unilateral American restraint in the most threatening weapons systems. In response, others argue that the Soviets know the United States has only defensive motives and therefore do not misinterpret American efforts to deter Soviet attacks. Accordingly, American restraint is unnecessary and nuclear policies that are more competitive and threatening do not create political dangers.

We can view these two disputes over nuclear cooperation and competition in terms of more general models of superpower behavior. Concern that U.S. restraint and bilateral cooperation will mislead highly aggressive Soviet leaders to underestimate U.S. resolve lies at the heart of the "deterrence model." According to the deterrence model, there is little risk in pursuing competitive policies since the Soviet Union understands that the U.S. is a status quo power. By contrast, concern that the Soviet Union will misperceive U.S. benign intentions is central to the "spiral model," which prescribes cooperative policies. According to the spiral model, although making concessions may carry risks, they are limited since the Soviet Union is not highly aggressive.[2]

The third dispute, unlike the first two, which view the Soviet Union essentially as a unitary actor, focuses on the Soviet domestic debate. Some analysts argue that competitive American policies increase U.S. security by reducing the influence of Soviet hard-liners, while others maintain that these policies will in fact increase the influence of hard-liners on Soviet policy.

---

[2] The classic statement of these models is Robert Jervis, *Perception and Misperception in International Relations* (Princeton: Princeton University Press, 1976), pp. 58–113; see also idem, "Rational Deterrence: Theory and Evidence," *World Politics* 39, no. 2 (January 1989): 190–93. Glenn H. Snyder and Paul Diesing raise similar distinctions in their discussion of "hardliners and softliners" in *Conflict among Nations* (Princeton: Princeton University Press, 1977), pp. 297–310.

Conclusions about these three political disputes have clear implications for key questions of U.S. strategic nuclear policy. For example, if the arguments for competition are correct, then American counterforce and strategic defense can increase U.S. security, even when Soviet responses can render these systems militarily ineffective. In this case, deploying these systems signals U.S. resolve by demonstrating a continuing willingness to invest in forces that hold some chance of enhancing American deterrent capabilities. If, on the other hand, arguments for cooperation are correct, then Soviet leaders will see American counterforce and strategic defense reflecting malign U.S. intentions, since from their perspective they appear to be necessary only if the United States still hopes to undermine Soviet deterrent capabilities. Thus, deploying even militarily ineffective counterforce and strategic defenses could decrease Soviet security and increase superpower tensions.

Similar arguments apply to whether the United States should pursue arms control agreements. If proponents of competition are correct, then the United States should be reluctant to engage in arms control. Because it risks a variety of negative political consequences, arms control must greatly enhance U.S. deterrent capabilities if it is going to increase U.S. security. On the other hand, according to proponents of cooperation, the United States should pursue arms control agreements even when they do little to enhance U.S. deterrent capabilities, since agreements that moderate superpower military competition can help avoid unnecessary superpower tensions.

The divergence between these policy conclusions and those based solely on the military requirements of deterrence makes clear the potential significance of these political consequences of nuclear policy. Viewed in terms of American military requirements of deterrence, it matters little whether the United States maintains its deterrence capabilities by engaging in an intense arms race or agreeing to a restrictive arms control regime. However, beliefs about the political consequences of cooperative and competitive policies suggest otherwise. These arguments take on special importance since even an intense superpower arms race promises to leave the superpowers in MAD.

Beyond its importance for analyzing policy, exploring the political consequences of nuclear policy can improve our understanding of the American debate over strategic nuclear policy. Although the vast majority of this debate is carried out in terms of the military requirements of deterrence, examining analysts' arguments suggests that beliefs about these political consequences may drive their conclusions more often than is readily apparent.

SOVIET AGGRESSIVE INTENTIONS AND UNDERESTIMATES OF U.S. RESOLVE

Beliefs about Soviet intentions play a central role in analysts' assessments of the requirements for discouraging Soviet underestimates of U.S. resolve. Analysts who believe the Soviet Union is highly aggressive worry that Soviet leaders, in the hope of finding support for their expansionist ambitions, are constantly looking for indications of flagging U.S. resolve.[3] They believe that as part of this search Soviet leaders design policies to probe U.S. commitments. U.S. restraint is more dangerous in these cases, since Soviet leaders are especially likely to conclude that it reflects inadequate American determination to protect its interests. Further, these analysts see additional risks in failing to respond to Soviet probes, since the Soviets are likely to conclude that if the United States lacks determination in one policy area it will also lack determination to protect its interests in quite different policy areas—U.S. credibility is therefore tightly connected across disparate issues. Finally, preventing these underestimates of American resolve deserves the highest priority, since greater U.S. credibility is required to deter a more expansionist Soviet Union.

To avoid these dangers, analysts who believe the Soviet Union is highly expansionist tend to favor competitive foreign and military policies and to see large risks in cooperative ones. In the context of U.S. strategic nuclear policy, these views translate most immediately into concern over U.S. unilateral restraint in deploying forces, especially when this means failing to match Soviet deployments, and over U.S. participation in arms control. Further, some analysts believe the United States can communicate its determination to protect its interests by pursuing military advantages and superiority, and therefore favor strategies based on counterforce and strategic defenses. From this perspective, then, the United States can increase its security by engaging in an arms race, even when it cannot ultimately achieve significant military objectives.

According to these analysts, unilateral U.S. restraint can be doubly dangerous: beyond leaving the United States with inadequate nuclear capabilities, it projects an image of overall U.S. weakness. For example, in 1969 Senator Henry Jackson argued that a U.S. decision against deploying an anti-ballistic missile system would lead the Russians to conclude that "we are made of mush over here."[4] Similarly, given this type of concern, even militarily insignificant additions to Soviet forces can have large negative political consequences, since they risk signaling advantages in Soviet resolve.[5]

---

[3] I use the terms "aggressive" and "expansionist" to reflect the amount a state would be willing to pay to change the status quo if its interests in it were not threatened. Given this use, a state that is interested in expanding only to protect its interest in the status quo is not an expansionist state. Although often discussed as dichotomous between status quo and aggressor states, the extent of aggressive intentions is continuous and can span a wide spectrum. In theory at least, at one extreme are truly status quo states—those willing to pay costs or run risks only to protect their territory, wealth, political influence, and/or other interests in the status quo. At the other extreme are states that are willing to pay the highest costs to expand even when entirely secure. On different uses of the term "intentions" see Jervis, *Perception and Misperception*, pp. 48–54.

[4] Daniel Yergin, " 'Scoop' Jackson Goes for Broke," *Atlantic Monthly* (June 1974), p. 83.

[5] Concern that disadvantages in the relative size of U.S. nuclear forces can generate dangerous

Analysts who believe the Soviets are highly aggressive see especially large risks in arms control.[6] In the first place, all agreements are suspect since the Soviets are interested in acquiring military advantages, not increasing mutual security, and are therefore unlikely to accept proposals that are in the U.S. interest. More directly relevant to the issues at hand, any U.S. concessions and all inequalities in an agreement are dangerous because the Soviets see them reflecting the U.S. desire to avoid military competition, even when this requires falling short of U.S. military requirements. Thus, engaging in arms control can encourage the Soviets to pursue more competitive military policies (with the expectation that this will yield still more valuable U.S. concessions) and become more adventurous. For example, in opposing the second Strategic Arms Limitation Talks (SALT II) agreement, some analysts argued:

> SALT II must not only pass the immediate test in regard to the balance of strategic power and mutual security, it must also pass the test of international perception. If the Soviets and their allies and sympathizers worldwide perceive the agreement as an indication of the further deterioration of U.S. and Western resolve and determination to survive, then the Communist camp will be encouraged to expand and intensify all forms of "class struggle." If the Soviets alone perceive of the agreement as our acceptance of their strategic superiority, then we can assume that the Soviets will become militarily more adventurous and daring as they seek to extend their political control.[7]

Further, Soviet compliance with arms control agreements raises intense concern since these analysts believe that allowing the Soviets to take advantage of American cooperation sends the most misleading and damaging signals. The risks are large even when Soviet violations are militarily insignificant, since failing to react to Soviet noncompliance risks undermining U.S. credibility on issues that are not closely related to the nuclear capabilities in question. Along these lines, Colin Gray argues:

Soviet misperceptions is a specific example of this more general argument and forms a link between the debates on military requirements and political consequences.

[6] Opponents of strategic nuclear arms control sometimes suggest that pursuing agreements with the Soviet Union is analogous to British appeasement during the 1930s. For example, Strobe Talbott, *Endgame* (New York: Harper & Row, 1979), p. 5, recalls that "Senator Henry Jackson of Washington, the most prominent critic of SALT II, delivered to an audience of conservative Democrats his most extreme attack to date on the President and the agreement. By going to Vienna to sign SALT II with Leonid Brezhnev, said Jackson, Carter would be following in the footsteps of Neville Chamberlain's ignominious journey to Munich in 1938." Richard Perle also compared compromising with the Soviets to appeasement. See Strobe Talbott, *Deadly Gambits* (New York: Knopf, 1984), p. 84.

[7] American Security Council, *An Analysis of SALT II* (Boston, Va.: Coalition for Peace through Strength, 1979), reprinted in Roger P. Labrie, ed., *SALT Hand Book* (Washington, D.C.: American Enterprise Institute, 1979), pp. 679–80. On their view of the Soviet Union, see ibid., pp. 683–84.

the greatest danger raised by failing to respond forthrightly to Soviet arms control cheating results from the loss of U.S. credibility. . . . Possible Soviet decisions to foment crises, to stage military demonstrations during crises, and even perhaps to fight are not very likely to be influenced by the marginal differences that arms control treaties may make to the military balance. But they are certain to be influenced by calculations of Western, and particularly American, steadiness of purpose.[8]

Thus, although not necessarily opposed to all agreements, these analysts are skeptical about the ability of arms control to increase U.S. security. Given the political risks of restraint, they conclude that agreements must provide large improvements in U.S. deterrent capabilities.

Although rarely explicit in the debate, some analysts go beyond these basic arguments, holding that a nuclear strategy that commits the United States to acquiring military advantages is essential for communicating its determination to protect its interests. According to this argument, setting American security requirements quite high and then buying forces to meet these requirements is essential for convincing the Soviets that America will not tolerate their challenges. This approach is most effective if the United States actually acquires military advantages, since this not only communicates resolve but also increases U.S. capabilities. Nevertheless, it can succeed even when the United States fails to achieve its military objectives, by demonstrating how strongly the United States is committed to maintaining its security.

Based on this argument, pursuing damage-limitation capabilities and nuclear superiority can increase U.S. security, even though massive investments in counterforce and strategic defenses hold virtually no prospect of protecting U.S. society from a nuclear attack. The credibility of U.S. extended deterrent threats would be enhanced, since the United States demonstrates its commitment to Europe by trying to achieve desirable and possibly necessary capabilities.[9] Given the broad consensus that highly effective damage-limitation capabilities are infeasible, this argument provides a more plausible case for pursuing damage-limitation capabilities than more common arguments presented by members of the damage-limitation school, which are based on U.S. military requirements of deterrence.

---

[8] Colin S. Gray, "Moscow Is Cheating," *Foreign Policy* (Fall 1984): 145.

[9] A similar-sounding but different argument holds that buying counterforce will mislead the Soviets into believing that the United States believes counterforce is usable. This argument is analyzed in Chapter Seven. For a view that seems to combine these strands see Barry M. Blechman, "Do Negotiated Arms Limitations Have a Future?" *Foreign Affairs* 59, no. 1 (Fall 1980): 111–12, who observes that some analysts believe that "by placing itself formally in a posture of seeking nuclear superiority the United States would be demonstrating a willingness to manipulate the risk of nuclear war for political objectives, thus lending credibility to the nuclear threats implicit in its foreign policy. In short, only in an environment of wide-open U.S.-Soviet competition can the United States' *necessary reliance* on nuclear weapons to underpin its foreign policy be supported successfully" (emphasis in original).

A closely related argument holds that a highly competitive nuclear strategy can help the United States protect areas where its interests are not so well-established. For example, Stephen Rosen argues that the United States should shift to a damage-limitation strategy because:

> the Soviet Union may miscalculate and challenge the United States in an area where it expects no American response. The United States, however, may well feel compelled to respond.
>
> This is the danger that makes a new nuclear strategy necessary. A doctrine making it abundantly visible that the United States is taking seriously the problems of limiting the damage resulting from a nuclear war would demonstrate to the Soviet Union that the United States would in fact take all steps necessary to stop Soviet advances. The present doctrinal confusion does not communicate any resolve to prevent war.[10]

In sharp contrast to the preceding arguments, analysts who believe the Soviet Union is less aggressive believe that misperceptions of U.S. credibility are both easier to avoid and less dangerous if they occur. The Soviets are less likely to misinterpret U.S. restraint and cooperation since they are not intent upon challenging U.S. vital interests. U.S. credibility is not tightly connected across disparate issues because most Soviet actions are not primarily probes designed to test U.S. resolve; instead, at worst, U.S. credibility is connected across issues in which U.S. interests are comparable.[11] These analysts find that both the political benefits of competitive policies and the risks of cooperation are smaller than if the Soviet Union were highly aggressive.

Regarding U.S. strategic nuclear policy more specifically, while recognizing the need to deter the Soviet Union, these analysts believe that the risks of forgoing competitive policies and pursuing arms control are small since the Soviets are far less likely to misinterpret U.S. cooperation than proponents of nuclear competition suggest. Further, the political benefits of competition are very small because: (1) U.S. commitments to protect vital American interests are sufficiently clear; (2) if necessary the United States has a variety of more direct and appropriate means for clarifying these interests; and (3) competitive nuclear policies do not enhance U.S. credibility in areas of less than vital interest.

---

[10] Stephen Peter Rosen, "Foreign Policy and Nuclear Weapons: The Case for Strategic Defenses," in Samuel P. Huntington, ed., *The Strategic Imperative: New Policies for American Security* (Cambridge, Mass.: Ballinger, 1982), p. 149.

[11] On the relationship between interests and commitments see Robert Jervis, "Deterrence Theory Revisited," *World Politics* 31, no. 2 (January 1979): 314–22, and Alexander L. George and Richard Smoke, *Deterrence in American Foreign Policy* (New York: Columbia University Press, 1974), pp. 558–61. For related arguments see Patrick M. Morgan, "Saving Face for the Sake of Deterrence," in Robert Jervis, Richard Ned Lebow, and Janice Gross Stein, *Psychology and Deterrence* (Baltimore: Johns Hopkins University Press, 1985), pp. 125–52.

How Expansionist Is the Soviet Union?

In assessing these arguments it is useful to look both at Soviet intentions and at how Soviet aggressive behavior has varied with changes in the superpowers' nuclear capabilities and the U.S. willingness to negotiate arms control agreements.

At least until the late 1980s, the spectrum of American views on Soviet intentions has been wide, running from a Soviet Union with unyielding global hegemonic aims, to a less aggressive country willing to use force only when the risks are low, to a country essentially uninterested in changing the status quo.[12] Although central to the debate over U.S. security and foreign policy, surprisingly little scholarly work has focused on resolving this dispute.[13] In part, this may reflect the difficulty of relying on Soviet foreign policy to indicate Soviet intentions: a deterred aggressor may act much like a status quo power. Thus, the fact that the Soviets have not launched a war against the United States or its key allies can be explained as the product of either effective U.S. defense policies or a low level of Soviet interest in expansion. The range of expert opinion on Soviet foreign policy behavior is therefore narrower—accepting for the most part that the Soviet Union has been cautious and avoided very risky actions—than the spectrum of views on Soviet aims.[14]

Nevertheless, although difficult to determine definitively, Soviet foreign policy behavior raises serious doubts about claims that the Soviet Union is so extremely aggressive that the United States must engage in nuclear competition either to establish or preserve its reputation. To begin with, the Soviet Union has avoided direct military confrontations with the United States and its key allies, reserving the large-scale use of military force for intervention in Eastern Europe and invasion of Afghanistan—areas in which the United States clearly did not have vital interests or major commitments. While not inconsistent with explanations based on the effectiveness of Western deterrent strate-

[12] Reviews and discussions of these positions include William Welch, *American Images of Soviet Foreign Policy* (New Haven: Yale University Press, 1970), who analyzes views expressed in academic studies; Douglas Seay, "What Are the Soviets' Objectives in Their Foreign, Military, and Arms Control Policies?" in Lynn Eden and Steven E. Miller, eds., *Nuclear Arguments* (Ithaca: Cornell University Press, 1989); Richard K. Herrmann, *Perceptions and Behavior in Soviet Foreign Policy* (Pittsburgh: University of Pittsburgh Press, 1985), pp. 12–18; Robert E. Osgood, *Containment, Soviet Behavior, and Grand Strategy* (Berkeley, Calif.: Institute of International Studies, 1981), pp. 1–18; Stanley Hoffman, "Grasping the Bear," in his *Janus and Minerva: Essays in the Theory and Practice of International Relations* (Boulder, Colo.: Westview, 1987); and George F. Kennan, "Two Views of the Soviet Problem," in his *The Nuclear Delusion: Soviet American Relations in the Atomic Age* (New York: Pantheon, 1982).

[13] An exception is Herrmann, *Perceptions and Behavior in Soviet Foreign Policy*, who finds little support for expansionist theories but also notes the problems of assessing motivations by examining behavior.

[14] On Soviet foreign policy behavior see note 28 in Chapter Two.

gies, this record provides no support for claims that the Soviets are highly aggressive. More problematic, if the Soviets were so highly aggressive, we could reasonably expect them to have launched more and riskier probes of Western resolve. Even in the face of highly effective deterrent capabilities, a Soviet Union bent on expansion in Eurasia would be willing to run substantial risks in the hope of finding that NATO would crumble under pressure. In fact, however, over the last twenty-five years the Soviets have launched few serious probes of American resolve to protect Western Europe or its other vital interests.[15] There has not been a severe superpower crisis since the Cuban Missile Crisis.[16] Finally, recent Soviet decisions to release their grip on Eastern Europe make it clear that the Soviet Union is not now bent on global expansion.

Considering how Soviet threatening behavior has varied with changes in the superpowers' nuclear capabilities raises further doubts about the arguments for nuclear competition. On their face, arguments for nuclear competition suggest that major improvements in Soviet nuclear capabilities would greatly increase Soviet willingness to launch direct challenges to American vital interests. This proposition follows logically from the proponents' beliefs that marginal improvements in Soviet forces and American restraint in matching them can significantly reduce Soviet estimates of U.S. resolve and encourage dangerous Soviet adventurism. However, contrary to this hypothesis, the shift from Soviet inferiority to superpower nuclear parity did not result in an increase in serious Soviet challenges to U.S. vital interests. In fact, the Soviet initiatives that created the greatest risk of military conflict with the United States in Europe preceded Soviet acquisition of assured retaliatory capabilities and strategic parity, as did the Cuban Missile Crisis.[17] Similarly, there is no support for concerns that U.S. willingness to pursue strategic arms control will embolden Soviet leaders to challenge America's core interests in Western Europe and Japan. Negotiations to limit strategic nuclear forces, which began in the late 1960s, were not followed by increased Soviet threats to these areas. Instead,

[15] For discussion of the factors that determine U.S. vital interests see note 11 in Chapter One.

[16] Further, a strong case can be made that those Soviet initiatives that have created the greatest risk of military conflict with the United States are reasonably understood as heavily defensive, motivated largely by their desire to protect interests in the status quo, and therefore should not be interpreted entirely as a reflection of a Soviet desire to expand. Consistent with this interpretation, serious Soviet probes of American resolve to protect Western Europe preceded the stabilization of the postwar order. See Hannes Adomeit, *Soviet Crisis Prevention and Management: Why and When do the Soviet Leaders Take Risks* (Santa Monica: Rand, 1986), p. 28, for discussion of the Berlin crises of 1948 and 1961 and the Cuban Missile Crisis.

[17] This is not to claim that Soviet tests of the United States stopped entirely. For example, Soviet efforts to establish a ballistic missile submarine base in Cuba in 1970—which challenged the U.S. commitment to the agreement that resolved the Cuban Missile Crisis—are reasonably interpreted as a test of the additional leeway provided by their then recent acquisition of nuclear parity. See Raymond L. Garthoff, "Handling the Cienfuegos Crisis," *International Security* 8, no. 1 (Summer 1983): 46–66.

as part of the overall improvement in superpower relations, the superpowers officially recognized the post-World War II boundaries in Europe.[18]

Although not conclusive, since this overview does not control for a variety of factors beyond changing nuclear capabilities, the paucity of serious Soviet challenges and their decrease instead of increase with the coming of parity, raises severe doubts about these arguments for nuclear competition. It suggests instead that the United States did not need to strive for military advantages or to deny the Soviets militarily insignificant ones to avoid raising Soviet doubts about America's commitment to protecting its vital interests. In light of recent changes in the Soviet Union the case for nuclear competition is even weaker today.

Proponents of nuclear competition may respond that, even if this is true, competing with the Soviets can help the United States protect its interests in other areas, for example the Third World, by communicating U.S. resolve; and protecting these areas may in turn be important for maintaining U.S. credibility for protecting more central interests. In supporting this argument, proponents make the observation, which is at least partially accepted by a wide spectrum of experts, that Soviet achievement of nuclear parity contributed to an increase in their military intervention.[19] Proponents of competition then go a step further, suggesting that the policies of the 1970s—which included SALT negotiations and U.S. acceptance of nuclear parity—were therefore misguided.

However, a variety of points undermine this case for nuclear competition. First, although there is some disagreement, studies of Soviet policy toward the Third World find that nuclear parity was probably far less important than a variety of other factors influencing Soviet decisions about military intervention—including improved conventional means for projecting force and the occurrence of favorable political conditions for Soviet intervention.[20] Second, even if the nuclear balance was a key factor, nuclear competition would be of limited value since the Soviets could maintain their assured destruction capabilities as well as numerical parity. Since competition would not significantly enhance U.S. nuclear capabilities, this argument for nuclear competition

[18] On these negotiations see the relevant chapters in Alexander L. George, Philip J. Farley, and Alexander Dallin, *U.S.-Soviet Security Cooperation: Achievements, Failures, Lessons* (Oxford: Oxford University Press, 1988).

[19] See, for example, Bruce Porter, *The USSR in Third World Conflicts: Soviet Arms and Diplomacy in Local Wars 1945–1980* (Cambridge: Cambridge University Press, 1986), p. 59. For additional examples and analysis of these arguments see Andrew Bennett, "Soviet Governmental Learning and the Rise and Fall of Soviet Military Intervention 1975–1987," (Ph.D. diss., Kennedy School of Government, Harvard University, 1988 draft), pp. 7–10.

[20] Raymond L. Garthoff, *Détente and Confrontation: Soviet-American Relations from Nixon to Reagan* (Washington, D.C.: Brookings Institution, 1985), p. 688; Harry Gelman, *The Brezhnev Politburo and the Decline of Détente* (Ithaca: Cornell University Press, 1984), especially pp. 165–66; and Bennett, "Soviet Governmental Learning," Chapter Two.

hinges entirely on its role in communicating U.S. resolve to protect at most secondary interests.

Third, even if nuclear competition was essential for communicating U.S. resolve, its value would be limited since U.S. security interests in the Third World are small to start with.[21] Fourth, nuclear competition promises to be an extremely blunt means of communicating this resolve, since the threat to employ nuclear weapons has little if any role to play in protecting less than vital interests, especially in MAD. A persuasive case has been made that Soviet leaders do not view their intervention in the Third World as a test of American resolve to protect more vital U.S. interests.[22] In other words, U.S. credibility is not tightly connected across these issues. Further, assuming the United States has interests that require protection, it has a variety of more appropriate means for clarifying its commitments, including providing military and economic aid, maintaining the conventional capabilities required to intervene, and guaranteeing direct military support if the Soviets attack.

In short, we have little reason to believe that the Soviet Union is so aggressive that the United States needs to deploy forces beyond those required to satisfy its military requirements in an attempt to increase Soviet assessments of its resolve. Similarly, the risks of more cooperative policies are small, as long as U.S. restraint and arms control agreements do not compromise necessary American military capabilities. This is not to claim, however, that the United States need not worry about deterring the Soviet Union. Because Soviet intentions remain uncertain and could become more aggressive in the future, the United States has strong reasons for maintaining forces that satisfy its military requirements of deterrence.

SOVIET INSECURITY AND EXAGGERATIONS OF THE AMERICAN THREAT

If the United States were concerned only with Soviet aggressive intentions, then there would be little risk in pursuing competitive policies to hedge against the possibility that the Soviet Union is extremely expansionist or that it might become so in the future. However, Soviet challenges to the status quo could stem from a second source—the Soviet Union might be motivated by the desire to maintain its security in the status quo. The United States must therefore be concerned about threatening Soviet security as well as maintaining effective deterrent capabilities. U.S. policies that make the Soviet Union less se-

---

[21] For debate on this issue see sources cited in note 11 in Chapter One.

[22] Michael C. Desch, "The Keys that Lock Up the World: Identifying American Interests in the Periphery," *International Security* 14, no. 1: 94–96, summarizes the general evidence. Theodore G. Hopf, "Deterrence Theory and Soviet Foreign Policy: Soviet Lessons from Their Victories and Defeats in the Third World" (Ph.D. diss., Columbia University, 1989), finds that American losses, including the loss of influence in Iran—an area of strategic interest—did not undermine Soviet assessments of U.S. credibility in other areas.

cure raise a tradeoff—the United States must weigh the deterrent benefits of increases in capability or credibility against the risks of decreasing Soviet security. For example, if, as some analysts believe, the United States requires a large counterforce arsenal to make its deterrent threats credible, then the United States might face such a tradeoff—Soviet leaders might see these American counterforce systems as reducing their security by threatening necessary retaliatory capabilities.

When capabilities that the United States requires for deterrence raise this kind of tradeoff, the United States faces a "security dilemma," since it cannot increase its security without reducing Soviet security. The possibility of such a dilemma is in no way restricted to forces the United States might buy to hedge against uncertainties about Soviet intentions. If the security dilemma is severe, forces that the United States regards as essential for deterrence would threaten Soviet security.

International relations theorists have argued that Soviet insecurity could increase the probability of war in a variety of ways. Soviet fears could reduce their willingness to compromise in political disputes, since their more malign view of the United States could lead them to conclude that making concessions would only encourage additional U.S. demands. In addition, the Soviets might adopt more confrontational tactics, since increased insecurity increases the benefits of winning disputes.[23] Further, heightened Soviet insecurity could increase the value they place on maintaining and acquiring territory that is useful for protecting the Soviet homeland from Western attack, thereby increasing the extent of the conflict between East and West.[24] Consequently, increasing Soviet insecurity could result in more frequent and more severe superpower crises and an increase in the probability of conventional superpower war. These changes would be especially dangerous if the nuclear balance lacks crisis stability.[25]

These propositions about the dangers of Soviet insecurity are not themselves a key source of disagreement in the debate over U.S. nuclear policy.[26]

---

[23] Stephen W. Van Evera, "Causes of War," (Ph.D. diss., University of California at Berkeley, 1984), pp. 95–98, argues that offense dominance increases insecurity, which increases the frequency and danger of fait accompli tactics.

[24] On this general point see Robert Jervis, "Cooperation under the Security Dilemma," *World Politics* 30, no. 2 (January 1978): 168–69.

[25] In addition, when a country's military capabilities are declining, an increasingly malign view of its adversary increases the country's incentives for preventive war by increasing its assessment of the probability of war in the future. This poses little danger when the superpowers are clearly in MAD, but would be important if one or both superpowers escaped from MAD.

[26] Although not prominent in the strategic nuclear debate, there is a "learning" argument that holds that under certain conditions it is desirable to decrease Soviet security. If the Soviets recognize U.S. threats to their security as reactions provoked by their own competitive behavior, then conditional American threats to Soviet security can lead to moderation in Soviet policy. On this argument for offense see Stephen Van Evera, "Offense, Defense and Strategy: When Is

Instead, analysts disagree more strongly about whether U.S. military capabilities are an important source of Soviet insecurity. On one side of the debate, analysts believe that the Soviets judge the United States by the image it projects—if the United States appears threatening, then the Soviets assume it has malign intentions and act to protect their security. Other analysts disagree, holding that the Soviets know that the United States is a status quo power with benign intentions and is therefore not a threat to Soviet security.

The former group explains Soviet insecurity in terms of the pressures created by the international system and the existence of an actual or "perceptual" security dilemma.[27] The anarchic nature of the international system drives national leaders to base their policies on conservative assumptions about one's adversary.[28] Thus, if American military policy suggests that the United States *might* have aggressive intentions, Soviet leaders will feel compelled to act as though it *does* have these intentions. Unfortunately, states facing a security dilemma often lack acceptable options for reducing how threatening they appear. Making matters worse, once decisionmakers develop a hostile image of an adversary, they tend to focus on the threatening components of the adversary's policy while overlooking defensive and cooperative behavior.[29] As a result, the Soviets are likely to see the United States as still more threatening than required by the ambiguities in the international environment. These concerns lie at the core of the spiral model.[30]

In addition, the United States may appear especially malign if it threatens Soviet security when it does not face a security dilemma. U.S. threats to Soviet deterrent capabilities that are optional, that is, go beyond American deterrent requirements, are especially likely to convince Soviet leaders that the United States harbors malign intentions.[31]

According to the security dilemma/spiral model arguments, Soviet leaders will not find all types of U.S. strategic nuclear weapons to be equally threatening. In MAD, U.S. forces that jeopardize the forces Soviet leaders believe

---

Offense Best?'' (Paper presented at the annual meeting of the American Political Science Association, Chicago, September 1987). He concludes, however, that this argument does not support American counterforce since the Soviets are unlikely to recognize their role in provoking it.

[27] On perceptual security dilemmas see Jack Snyder, "Perceptions of the Security Dilemma in 1914," in Jervis, Lebow, and Stein, *Psychology and Deterrence*, pp. 161–62.

[28] On the implications of anarchy see Kenneth N. Waltz, *Man, the State and War: A Theoretical Analysis* (New York: Columbia University Press, 1954), pp. 157–238; idem, *Theory of International Politics* (New York: Random House, 1979); and Robert Art, "The Role of Military Power in International Relations," in B. Thomas Trout and James E. Harf, ed., *National Security Affairs: Theoretical Perspectives and Contemporary Issues* (New Brunswick, N.J.: Transaction Books, 1982), pp. 13–20.

[29] On this tendency see Jervis, *Perception and Misperception*, pp. 117–202.

[30] Ibid., pp. 62–76.

[31] This distinction assumes that Soviet leaders are sensitive to the U.S. security dilemma. If this is not the case—which is a concern of the spiral model—then the political consequences of optional threats and those demanded by a security dilemma will be more similar.

are necessary for deterrence do the most to communicate malign U.S. intentions. Consequently, we expect that the U.S. strategic nuclear forces that appear most threatening to the Soviets are offensive counterforce and area-wide strategic defenses. For example, as discussed below, it appears that Soviet leaders did see the American development of the MX missile during the 1970s—which would have increased the U.S. ability to destroy Soviet missile silos—as reflecting malign intentions. By contrast, although U.S. counter-value capabilities can destroy Soviet society, they are less likely to raise Soviet doubts about U.S. intentions, since in MAD they hold no prospect of enhancing the U.S. ability to defeat or coerce the Soviet Union.

Put another way, when countries depend on deterrence to maintain their security, forces that threaten the adversary's deterrent forces are offensive, while forces that enhance one's deterrent forces are defensive. Thus, in MAD, U.S. counterforce and area-wide strategic defenses, because they threaten Soviet retaliatory capabilities, are offensive. By the same logic, U.S. counter-value capabilities are defensive.[32] Given this terminology, it is U.S. offensive weapons that communicate malign U.S. intentions, and the United States faces a security dilemma when deterring the Soviets requires offense.[33]

According to these spiral model arguments, the superpower arms competition generates dangers that go beyond its direct military effects. A U.S. military buildup increases Soviet fears of the United States both by actually increasing U.S. military capabilities and by communicating the desire for military advantages. Even if the Soviet Union offsets any military advantages that the U.S. buildup might have provided, the United States will have communicated its interest in acquiring these advantages. It is then a small step for Soviet leaders to infer that the United States hopes to use its forces to jeopardize Soviet interests. In addition, Soviet responses to the U.S. buildup will contribute to American fears. Not recognizing the Soviet security dilemma and not seeing Soviet deployments as a reaction to U.S. deployments, the

[32] In addition, strategic antisubmarine capabilities are a kind of offense. Admittedly, this terminology is potentially confusing since we commonly refer to forces that can attack as offenses— ICBMs, SLBMs, bombers, and cruise missiles—and refer to systems that can destroy the adversary's forces once they are launched as defenses—BMD and air defenses. However, since we are concerned with the incentives and opportunities that forces generate, and how they appear to one's adversary, we need to focus on the missions they can perform and the strategies these capabilities make possible. The definitions presented in the text follow directly from asking what strategies a given type of weapon supports. On these distinctions see Jervis, "Cooperation under the Security Dilemma," pp. 198, 206–10. See also Dietrich Fischer, *Preventing War in the Nuclear Age* (Totowa, N.J.: Rowman & Allanheld, 1984). On some of the potential problems with defining offense and defense and with determining which dominates see Jack S. Levy, "The Offensive/Defensive Balance of Military Technology: A Theoretical and Historical Analysis," *International Studies Quarterly*, 28, no. 2 (June 1984): 222–35.

[33] On the full range of dangers created by offense see Van Evera, "Causes of War," and idem, "Offense, Defense and Strategy," pp. 4–6. As I discuss in the concluding section, analysts disagree about whether the United States faces a security dilemma because they disagree about its military requirements of deterrence.

United States will adopt a more threatening view of Soviet intentions. Thus, the superpower arms race creates a world in which each superpower sees the other as more threatening and, therefore, each feels less secure.

Focusing on distinctions between offense and defense refines these arguments about the arms race. U.S. offense—counterforce and strategic defense—is especially likely to generate Soviet fears since these U.S. forces threaten forces that Soviet leaders believe are necessary for deterrence. In contrast, increasing defense—that is, countervalue retaliatory capabilities—is much less threatening since this only increases the redundancy of American retaliatory capabilities. Adding offense requires a Soviet reaction; adding defense does not. Adding offense communicates a desire for military advantages; adding defense does not.[34] Soviet offense has a similar effect on U.S. images of the Soviet Union. In short, it is the buildup of offense, not the buildup of forces in general, that is most likely to lead to exaggerated superpower tensions.

Important arguments in the strategic nuclear debate are based on the belief that counterforce and strategic defense will generate these negative political consequences. For example, Herbert York argues that improvements in counterforce capabilities, although unlikely to provide significant damage-limitation capabilities, are nevertheless dangerous:

> It is highly unlikely that MIRV could affect the ultimate outcome of a nuclear war between U.S. and the the U.S.S.R. It seems clear that each has ample power to destroy the society of the other, with or without multiple-warhead missiles and whether or not a surprise attack destroys the opposing force. By generating fears of the others intentions, however, MIRV's could affect the likelihood that a nuclear war will occur.[35]

George Rathjens and Jack Ruina use a similar argument to oppose deployment of strategic defense to protect the U.S. population. They find that strategic defenses would be too ineffective to create preemptive dangers during crises,

[34] For qualifications see Chapter Ten, pp. 332–37.

[35] Herbert F. York, "Multiple-Warhead Missiles," *Scientific American* (November 1973), reprinted in Bruce M. Russett and Bruce G. Blair, *Progress in Arms Control?* (San Francisco: Freeman, 1979), p. 122. In a similar vein, Richard H. Ullman, "Denuclearizing International Politics," *Ethics* 95, no. 3 (April 1985): 588, argues that nuclear doctrines that are heavily oriented toward counterforce attacks have a significant negative effect on superpower relations: "So long as nuclear weapons exist, that distrust is unlikely altogether to vanish. But the knowledge that neither possesses nuclear forces configured or deployed so as to facilitate an attack on the other might well have a transforming effect on other aspects of their bilateral relationship. In particular, it might diffuse the processes that cause nearly any incident or dispute to ratchet up the overall level of tension between Washington and Moscow." Also noting the political dangers of offense are McGeorge Bundy, "The Bishops and the Bomb," *New York Review of Books* (16 June 1983), p. 6; Herbert Scoville, Jr., *MX: Prescription for Disaster* (Cambridge: MIT Press, 1981), pp. 139–40; and Marshall D. Shulman, "U.S.-Soviet Relations and the Control of Nuclear Weapons," in Barry M. Blechman, ed., *Rethinking the U.S. Strategic Posture* (Cambridge, Mass.: Ballinger, 1982), p. 78.

but that superpower deployment of ineffective ballistic missiles defenses would nevertheless lead to an "increase in U.S.-Soviet tensions and intensification of the arms race."[36]

These political arguments seem important for understanding why some members of the punitive retaliation school find U.S. counterforce and the strategic nuclear arms race to be dangerous. This conclusion is not supported by their assessment of the military requirements of deterrence, since they believe that an arms race will not take the superpowers out of MAD and that in MAD the U.S. ability to deter the Soviet Union is quite insensitive to the details of the superpowers' forces. For example, McGeorge Bundy argues both that "the new weapons systems which are being deployed by each of the two great powers will provide neither with protection or advantage" and yet that the arms race is "totally unprecedented in size and danger."[37] Beliefs about the political effects of nuclear policy fill in a missing piece of the puzzle. Based on the belief that military competition generates fears and hostility that increase the probability of war, these analysts conclude that an arms race, and especially the offense that drives it, would be dangerous even when the superpowers remain securely in MAD.

Analysts who are concerned about Soviet insecurity see arms control as a way of reducing the threat the United States poses to Soviet capabilities.[38] According to security dilemma arguments, arms control agreements designed to make the superpowers appear less threatening would give priority to constraining counterforce and strategic defense, not countervalue weapons.[39] However, many proponents of arms control do not make this distinction, arguing instead that all types of negotiated limitations are useful in slowing the arms race and reducing the exaggerated tensions that it generates.

In sharp disagreement with these views, other analysts believe that Soviet leaders know the United States is a status quo power, and therefore reject claims that U.S. military policy generates Soviet fears of the United States. They believe that U.S. intentions are sufficiently clear to enable the Soviets to overcome the pressures created by the international system. Given this view of the Soviets, the United States need not worry about pursuing potentially

[36] George Rathjens and Jack Ruina, "BMD and Strategic Instability," *Daedalus* 114, no. 3 (Summer 1985): 241.

[37] McGeorge Bundy, "To Cap the Volcano," *Foreign Affairs* 48, no. 1 (October 1969): 1, 9–10. Similar apparent inconsistencies exist in common arguments offered specifically against counterforce. For examples see Chapter Seven, p. 244.

[38] See, for example, Lloyd N. Cutler and Roger C. Molander, "Is There Life after SALT?" *International Security* 6, no. 2 (Fall 1981): 9. Of course, the United States could shift to forces that appear less threatening entirely through unilateral measures. Thus, arms control is necessary either to make these reductions safer by simultaneously reducing Soviet counterforce/offensive capabilities or to help achieve a U.S. domestic political consensus in favor of a less threatening U.S. policy.

[39] For elaboration and qualification see Chapter Ten.

threatening military policies. The Soviets understand that whatever threat the United States poses to Soviet security is entirely conditional—the United States will not use force against them as long as they respect the status quo. In effect, these analysts reject the possibility that the United States faces a security dilemma and that optional U.S. offense could mislead the Soviets about U.S. intentions, since they see all types of U.S. forces as purely defensive.[40]

Views along these lines were influential in the Reagan administration. For example, in explaining why U.S. SDI did not pose a threat to the Soviet Union, Secretary of Defense Weinberger explained that: "The other reason [the Soviets] have no need to worry [about SDI] is that they know perfectly well that we will never launch a first strike on the Soviet Union. And all of their attacks, and all of their military preparations—I should say, and all of their acquisitions in the military field in the last few years have been offensive in character."[41] Strobe Talbott describes Weinberger's beliefs: "It was as though the Soviets should be expected to base policy or conduct of diplomacy on the assumption of their own essentially criminal nature, recognizing the United States as a restraining influence."[42] Based on similar assumptions, Richard Perle argued that the Soviets would not pay large sums to defeat the American SDI because "the Soviets will always know that the United States would never launch a first strike."[43]

Soviet Views of U.S. Intentions and Nuclear Forces

Examinations of Soviet beliefs find little support for either the general claim that the Soviet Union sees the United States as an unthreatening status quo power, or the more specific claim that the Soviets believe that U.S. offense—counterforce and strategic defense—does not pose a potential threat to their security. Instead, the available evidence suggests that U.S. nuclear policy can increase Soviet insecurity.

Soviet leaders tend to believe that the United States is interested in expansion and is a threat to Soviet interests, not that the United States is a status quo power.[44] Although there is diversity in Soviet images of the United States,

---

[40] One important implication of this position is that essentially all Soviet forces reflect hostile intent—since the Soviets know the United States has no interest in starting a war, Soviet deployments must reflect offensive and not defensive aims.

[41] NBC's "Meet the Press," March 27, 1983, quoted in Arms Control Association, *Star Wars Quotes*, July 1986, p. 51.

[42] Strobe Talbott, *The Master of the Game* (New York: Knopf, 1988), p. 200.

[43] Ibid., p. 235. For an early statement by Perle that implicitly assumes that U.S. military programs do not generate dangerous Soviet fears see Yergin, " 'Scoop' Jackson Goes for Broke,'' p. 81.

[44] For an overall assessment of Soviet views see Herrmann, *Perceptions and Behavior in Soviet Foreign Policy*. On the diversity of Soviet images of the United States and their implications for Soviet policy, see Franklyn Griffiths, "The Sources of American Conduct: Soviet Perspectives

even moderates believe the United States is hostile and needs to be deterred. Moderates recognize that the Soviet Union is partially responsible for super- power tensions, but do not believe that it is primarily responsible. They di- verge from more traditional Soviets by stressing that the United States is re- alistic enough to restrain its ambitions when faced with sufficient Soviet military capabilities, and that less threatening Soviet policies may encourage less dangerous U.S. policies by enhancing the influence of U.S. moderates. Consistent with this view of U.S. intentions, Soviet analysts tend to believe the United States is responsible for the arms race. Moderates believe only that the United States is not entirely at fault.[45]

Focusing more specifically on U.S. nuclear forces that threaten Soviet de- terrent forces, studies of Soviet official statements and internal debates find that the Soviets have seen both U.S. counterforce and strategic defenses as potential threats to their security and have interpreted U.S. interest in these forces as reflections of U.S. malign intentions. Reviewing the Soviet debate during the negotiation of the SALT I arms control agreement, Samuel Payne found that "both 'arms controllers' and 'militarists' point out the dangers and aggressive intent of American development of MIRVs and ABMs. . . . [the 'arms controllers'] have never asserted that there is no danger from the United States, or that the American government does not have aggressive intentions, but only that the danger could be averted by negotiations."[46]

---

and Their Policy Implications," *International Security* 9, no. 2 (Fall 1984): 11–46. On the views of analysts at the Institute of the United States and Canada see Morton Schwartz, *Soviet Percep- tions of the United States* (Los Angeles: University of California Press, 1978). On Soviet views through the mid-1960s see William Zimmerman, *Soviet Perspectives on International Relations, 1956–1967* (Princeton: Princeton University Press, 1969), pp. 211–41; since the mid-1960s see Allen Lynch, *The Soviet Study of International Relations* (Cambridge: Cambridge University Press, 1987). On Soviet views in the context of U.S. nuclear policy see Samuel B. Payne, "The Soviet Debate in Strategic Arms Limitation: 1968–1972," *Soviet Studies* 27, no. 1 (January 1975): 27–45; Bruce Parrot, *Politics and Technology in the Soviet Union* (Cambridge: MIT Press, 1983), pp. 181–202, 231–65; William D. Jackson, "Soviet Images of the U.S. as a Nuclear Adversary, 1969–1979," *World Politics* 33, no. 4 (July 1981): 614–38; and William B. Hus- bands, "Soviet Perceptions of U.S. 'Positions of Strength' Diplomacy in the 1970s," *World Politics* 31, no. 4 (July 1979): 495–517. On views of Gorbachev and his advisers and opponents see Jack Snyder, "The Gorbachev Revolution: A Waning of Soviet Expansionism?" *International Security* 12, no. 3 (Winter 1987/88): 117–26; Stephen M. Meyer, "The Sources and Prospects of Gorbachev's New Political Thinking on Security," *International Security* 13, no. 2 (Fall 1988): 124–63; and Bruce Parrott, "Soviet National Security under Gorbachev," *Problems of Commu- nism* (November–December 1988): 1–36.

[45] On Soviet views of the arms race, see Pat Litherland, *Gorbachev and Arms Control: Civilian Experts and Soviet Policy*, Peace Research Report Number 12 (Bradford, England: University of Bradford, School of Peace Studies, 1986), pp. 53–71.

[46] Payne, "The Soviet Debate on Strategic Arms Limitation," pp. 40–41. Payne does note, however, that the Soviet attacks on ABM "were probably directed mostly at the United States." For a somewhat different emphasis see Lawrence T. Caldwell, *Soviet Attitudes to SALT*, Adelphi Paper No. 75 (London: IISS, 1971), p. 10.

In the years following SALT I, continuing U.S. interest in counterforce raised Soviet doubts about U.S. intentions. According to Raymond Garthoff, in 1974 the Soviets believed that changes in U.S. nuclear doctrine, which became known as the Schlesinger Doctrine, and the accompanying U.S. decision to pursue enhanced counterforce, "portended the possibility of dangerous American initiatives." The Soviets recognized that U.S. pursuit of counterforce was not new and that these changes in American doctrine were evolutionary. Nevertheless, they believed that the emphasis the United States was placing on counterforce options and limited nuclear warfare worked against the objectives of arms control and détente.[47]

Continued U.S. enhancement of its counterforce systems in the second half of the 1970s led some Soviets to suspect that U.S. objectives included "strategic superiority for political intimidation, if not for even more ominous purposes." Contributing to this conclusion were the U.S. decisions to upgrade its Minuteman III ICBMs with improved warheads and guidance systems and to deploy the still more lethal MX intercontinental missile, the NATO decision to deploy the Pershing II medium range ballistic missile (which the Soviets viewed as contributing to U.S. first-strike capabilities), and the U.S. failure to ratify the SALT II Treaty.[48] Garthoff concludes that these U.S. nuclear policies played an important role in convincing the Soviets that U.S. interest in détente had greatly declined, if not ceased altogether.[49]

The Reagan administration's pursuit of highly effective strategic defenses, under the Strategic Defense Initiative, and challenges to the existing arms control regime tended to reinforce these Soviet concerns about U.S. threats to their security. The Soviets saw SDI complementing U.S. counterforce in American efforts to regain superiority and deny the Soviets the international political benefits of parity. Although many Soviet statements opposing SDI were designed to influence the Western debate, Bruce Parrott concludes that "it is evident that Soviet observers genuinely perceive the initiative as a threat to Soviet security—one with enormous offensive potential."[50]

---

[47] Garthoff, *Détente and Confrontation*, pp. 417–18.

[48] Ibid. pp. 796–800. See also David Holloway, *The Soviet Union and the Arms Race* (New Haven: Yale University Press, 1983), pp. 48, 50.

[49] Garthoff, *Détente and Confrontation*, pp. 1068, 1085–86.

[50] Bruce Parrott, *The Soviet Union and Ballistic Missile Defense* (Boulder, Colo.: Westview, 1987), p. 72; see also ibid., pp. 11–21; Sidney D. Drell, Philip J. Farley, and David Holloway, "Preserving the ABM Treaty: A Critique of the Reagan Strategic Defense Initiative," *International Security* 9, no. 2 (Fall 1984): 61–63; and Lawrence T. Caldwell and Robert Legvold, "Reagan through Soviet Eyes," *Foreign Policy* no. 52 (Fall 1983): 5, who state that "Americans, Soviet analysts think, are bent on restoring a practical form of superiority, one that would allow the United States to prosecute a war successfully or one that might deceive it into thinking it could." They go on to note (p. 6) that "this image is not the administration's self-image, nor, more important, does it fit a common U.S. conviction that the Soviets understand U.S. policy essentially as it is meant to be understood."

In short, contrary to claims that the Soviets are confident that the United States is a status quo power, the Soviets have tended to see malign U.S. intentions behind American counterforce and SDI, which they believe the United States is pursuing to regain its capability to challenge Soviet interests. Starting in the mid-1970s and continuing well into the 1980s, these views of U.S. intentions contributed to superpower tensions.

This conclusion, however, does not seem to jibe with Soviet policy in the second half of the 1980s: if American counterforce and strategic defense negatively shift Soviet views of U.S. intentions, which in turn generates more threatening Soviet behavior, what explains the more cooperative policies the Soviets have pursued under Gorbachev? This question is examined at the end of the following section.

U.S. MILITARY POLICY AS A MEANS FOR INFLUENCING THE SOVIET SECURITY DEBATE

The arguments discussed in the preceding sections view the Soviet Union as essentially a unitary actor and examine ways in which U.S. nuclear policy might influence Soviet perceptions of the United States. A second way in which U.S. military policy might interact with Soviet policy is by shifting the balance of influence between Soviet leaders who disagree among themselves about Soviet foreign policy in general, and military policy in particular. U.S. policies that increase the influence of Soviet "moderates" make the Soviet Union less dangerous, while policies that increase the influence of "hard-liners" make it more so. In very broad terms, moderates see the United States as less aggressive, believe U.S. hostility is partly conditional on Soviet behavior, see a role for cooperative diplomacy and arms control in encouraging American moderation and helping to resolve superpower disputes, and see smaller benefits and larger risks in Soviet efforts to expand. By contrast, hard-liners, primarily because they see the United States as more aggressive and unconditionally hostile, tend to place greater reliance on military solutions to Soviet security problems and see larger benefits in expansion, partly because it reduces the overall influence of the United States and its allies.[51]

Beyond these direct dangers, increasing the influence of Soviet hard-liners increases the likelihood and extent of Soviet misperceptions of U.S. intentions. Soviet hard-liners, already believing that they face a highly aggressive United States, are more likely to read the worst into the ambiguities in U.S. military and foreign policies.[52] In addition, they tend to find American forces

---

[51] For a fine-grained analysis of competing Soviet views on how to manage Soviet relations with the United States see Griffiths, "The Sources of American Conduct," pp. 3–50.

[52] This is because the more certain decisionmakers are of their image of the adversary, the more likely they are to see new information as consistent with and supporting that belief. See Jervis, *Perception and Misperception*, p. 195.

more threatening than do moderates, which further compounds their inclination to incorrectly infer hostile intentions from American forces. At the same time, however, they are less sensitive to their own security dilemma, believing that maintaining their security requires more offensive military capabilities.[53]

U.S. policies designed to influence Soviet domestic political debates would try to discredit hard-liners' arguments and support moderates. The broad choice is between competitive policies, such as relying heavily on counterforce to threaten Soviet nuclear forces, and cooperative ones, which avoid threatening these forces. Which type of American policies is more likely to achieve these results depends on a variety of factors, including whether hardliners or moderates are controlling Soviet policy, the nature of the arguments that competing Soviets use to support their policy prescriptions, the quality of Soviet understanding of U.S. policy—which will influence the plausible range of contending interpretations of American actions—and the relative skill of competing factions in pressing their interpretations.[54]

Highly competitive American policies will tend to undercut Soviet hardliners when they are in power, if they are held responsible for provoking these American policies.[55] Under these conditions, Soviet moderates can gain influence by arguing that the United States would have followed less threatening policies if the Soviets had been more cooperative.[56] On the other hand, competitive or threatening American policies could strengthen the position of Soviet hard-liners when they are in power, if they can argue persuasively that American policies are not a reaction to competitive Soviet policies, but instead reflect malign U.S. intentions. In this case hard-liners benefit because their policies are built on the belief that U.S. hostility is both great and unconditional.

[53] To see this compare the views of moderates—for example, Gorbachev and proponents of the new political thinking—with opponents of reform. See, for example, Meyer, "The Sources and Prospects of Gorbachev's New Political Thinking," and Raymond L. Garthoff, "New Thinking in Soviet Military Doctrine," *Washington Quarterly* (Summer 1988). For the potentially dramatic implications of the new thinking see Alexei Arbatov, "How Much Defense Is Sufficient?" *International Affairs* (April 1989): 31–44.

[54] On these basic points, with examples from a range of great-power cases, including the U.S.-Soviet case, see Jack Snyder, "International Leverage and Soviet Domestic Change," *World Politics* 42, no. 1 (October 1989): 1–30.

[55] According to Strobe Talbott, *The Russians and Reagan* (New York: Vintage Books, 1984), pp. 74–75, this type of argument motivated some members of the Reagan administration.

[56] Along these lines, Edward N. Luttwak, "Is There an Arms Race?" *Washington Quarterly* 2, no. 1 (Winter 1979), argued that the United States should reject SALT II so that "the moderates in Soviet policy circles will accuse the 'hardliners' of having spoiled a good thing by pushing too hard in the growth of armaments and in their foreign policy adventures (the Horn of Africa, etc.), as well as in domestic affairs. If an agreement is reached and if it is then ratified, the moderates will lose ground and the hardliners will have been confirmed in their belief that the West will in the end swallow all their domestic brutalities, all their foreign policy adventures, and also their massive military buildup, rather than competing with the Soviet Union in adequate degree."

By contrast, cooperative U.S. policies, if correctly understood to reflect the U.S. interest in mutual security, are likely to support Soviet moderates when they are in power, since their policies would be based on the expectation that the United States would reciprocate cooperation. If instead, however, Soviet hard-liners argue successfully that U.S. cooperation reflects a lack of U.S. resolve or was produced by an earlier Soviet military buildup, then U.S. co-operation could actually undermine moderates.[57] It is also possible that coop-erating in response to a Soviet buildup could support Soviet moderates, if it helps them argue successfully that the United States is willing to accept parity and other conditions that are consistent with Soviet security requirements, while hard-liners argue that the United States will always pursue superiority and therefore will forgo unilateral restraint and reject arms control agree-ments.[58]

Clearly then, the domestic political effects of U.S. policies will depend on which interpretation of U.S. motivations prevails in the Soviet debate. This will depend partly on the particulars of the Soviet debate: the power and bu-reaucratic skill of competing factions, the quality of Soviet understanding of U.S. policy and motivations, and the interaction of domestic issues with ar-guments for and against competitive policies.[59]

Although this complexity promises to make predictions difficult, two types of considerations can provide some guidance in assessing the effect of U.S. nuclear policies on the Soviet domestic debate. The first concerns the ambi-guity of U.S. policy: less threatening, more defensive U.S. policies are open to a narrower range of interpretations about U.S. motivations, and are there-fore more likely than offensive U.S. policies to support Soviet moderates and defeat Soviet hard-liners. If defense can be distinguished from offense, then defensive U.S. policies, because they do not provide the United States with military advantages, do not support the hard-line image of a malign United States; hard-liners will have trouble arguing that the United States is pursuing

[57] This creates a kind of no-win situation in which both cooperative and competitive U.S. pol-icies tend to support Soviets who favor competition. Snyder, ''International Leverage and Soviet Domestic Change,'' explains that the United States faces this type of situation when Soviet poli-cies are based on correlation of forces arguments.

[58] In U.S. domestic politics, Gorbachev's conciliatory policies seem to have worked according to this dynamic, increasing the influence of American moderates who favor more cooperative policies, while making it more difficult for American hawks to argue for competition and against arms control. By contrast, if the Soviets had continued with their competitive policies the Amer-ican hard-liners could have argued more persuasively for regaining military superiority and for-going arms control.

[59] In fact, experts disagree about the ability of the United States to influence Soviet debates. See, for example, Charles Gati, ''The Stalinist Legacy in Soviet Foreign Policy,'' and the re-sponse by William Zimmerman, ''The Soviet Union and the West,'' both in Stephen F. Cohen et al., *The Soviet Union since Stalin* (Bloomington: Indiana University Press, 1980), and Snyder, ''International Leverage and Soviet Domestic Change,'' p. 1.

military superiority. At the same time, relatively unambiguous defensive responses support the moderate image of a United States that is willing to respect Soviet security requirements. Defensive responses further help defeat hard-liners' policies by denying the Soviets military advantages, which reduces the possibility that hard-liners can successfully argue that the United States lacks resolve.[60] By contrast, offensive U.S. policies can be interpreted to support the hard-liners' image of U.S. hostility, even when the U.S. policy is designed and promoted as a reaction to threatening Soviet policies. So, for example, responding to Soviet counterforce by increasing the number or survivability of U.S. countervalue weapons (defensive response) is more likely to support moderates than if the United States responds with counterforce of its own (offensive response). Similarly, defeating Soviet BMD with countervalue weapons is more likely to succeed in supporting moderates than if the United States responds with BMD of its own.

However, while defensive responses are more likely to succeed, when U.S. offensive responses do work against Soviet hard-liners they will be more effective than defensive ones. Hard-liners held responsible for provoking U.S. offense will have reduced Soviet security; in comparison, if they provoke U.S. defense they will have wasted Soviet resources but not reduced Soviet security.

Thus, to determine whether the United States should pursue an offensive or defensive response, we need to consider the factors that influence how ambiguous American policies are interpreted in the Soviet debate. When the United States pursues policies in reaction to Soviet policies, what determines whether the Soviets recognize that they provoked these policies? More specifically, when the United States pursues offensive policies in response to threatening Soviet policies, what determines whether Soviet hard-liners can enhance their position by arguing that the United States planned a provocative buildup anyway, or whether moderates gain by arguing that the United States would have forgone offense if the Soviets had shown restraint?

A key factor is how the Soviets view their own policies. If both hard-liners and moderates believe that the Soviet Union has not pursued threatening policies, then U.S. policy will not be interpreted as a reaction and hard-liners will gain. On the other hand, if moderates are already arguing influentially that Soviet policy has threatened U.S. security, or at least that Americans believe this, then the reactive nature of U.S. policy is more likely to support the moderates.

Another factor that would influence Soviet interpretations is the clarity of U.S. policy. For example, does the timing of U.S. policy suggest that it is a

---

[60] Thus, defensive (countervalue) responses to Soviet counterforce might avoid what Snyder, in "International Leverage and Soviet Domestic Change," terms the "double wammy" that flows from correlation-of-forces arguments.

reaction to Soviet policies, or does it suggest a continuation of previous U.S. policies? Similarly, can moderates argue convincingly that U.S. competitive policies are appropriate in offsetting Soviet threats, or are hard-liners more likely to succeed in arguing that the U.S. response exceeds the one required to match Soviet deployments?

Insights from the Soviet Debate

Examinations of the Soviet debate on nuclear policy find that in fact it does divide between hard-liners, who are more skeptical about arms control and tend to favor pursuing security through competitive unilateral policies, and moderates, who see larger benefits in arms control and, at least recently, in Soviet unilateral restraint.[61] Although the center of the debate has changed over time, disagreements about Western intentions have remained at its core.

Studies of the Soviet debate since the late 1960s suggest that offensive U.S. policies have tended to support Soviet hard-liners. Discussing the period preceding SALT talks, William Jackson argues that "because of the existing apprehension about U.S. policy, American MIRV and ABM programs probably added credence in many quarters to the view that the U.S. sought a war-winning capability."[62] With the beginning of SALT talks in 1969, Soviet moderates presented a less threatening view of the United States by arguing that there were factions in the United States that favored limiting the arms race. Soviets who opposed arms control paid less attention to these divisions in the U.S. debate and focused instead on the continuing U.S. military buildup. In their view, MIRVs (Multiple Independently Targetable Reentry Vehicles) and ABMs (Anti-Ballistic Missiles) reflected hostile U.S. intentions, since these systems testified to unaltered U.S. interest in nuclear superiority and first-strike capabilities.[63] Their opposition to arms control was based primarily on doubts about whether such a hostile United States would actually accept arms limitations, not on arguments that questioned whether agreements were desirable.[64]

U.S. improvements in its counterforce weapons following SALT I tended to undermine the arguments of Soviet moderates, and the image of the United States that they used in their arguments shifted toward a somewhat more threatening, less flexible adversary. For example, G. A. Arbatov's claim following SALT I that "the bankruptcy of the flexible-response strategy of waging limited war had now been recognized," was proved incorrect by subsequent changes in U.S. force posture and refinements of its declaratory

---

[61] See note 44. Although these authors describe similar divides in the debate, the terminology varies: hard-liners are variously termed traditionalists, conservatives, militarists, and orthodox, while moderates are referred to as nontraditionalists, arms controllers, modernists, and reformers.

[62] Jackson, "Soviet Images of the U.S. as Nuclear Adversary 1969–1979," p. 618.

[63] Ibid., 619–24, and Payne, "The Soviet Debate on Strategic Arms Limitation," pp. 36–42.

[64] Payne, "The Soviet Debate on Strategic Arms Limitation," p. 42.

doctrine.[65] Such beliefs certainly fit poorly with the increasing emphasis that the Schlesinger Doctrine and then the countervailing strategy—which was developed by the Carter administration—placed on counterforce, and with improvements in American counterforce weapons that the United States pursued from the mid-1970s and into the 1980s. Apparently, the growth of U.S. counterforce capabilities put Soviet moderates on the defensive. While continuing to note the existence of American factions opposed to continuing the arms race, they argued that within SALT the United States continued pursuing counterforce "as a method of exploiting the situation of equality of strategic capabilities" and that its "new conception for the utilization of strategic forces is [thus] a series of variations on key themes of the postwar U.S. strategy: how to secure the utilization of nuclear forces without U.S. suicide."[66] Moderates worried that this shift in American doctrine supported Soviets who favored more competitive nuclear policies.[67] As the 1970s came to an end, divergence in Soviet images of the United States narrowed, placing increasing emphasis on the dominant role of reactionary forces in the U.S. debate and on U.S. pursuit of effective counterforce capabilities.[68]

The Reagan administration's pursuit of SDI put further pressure on Soviet proponents of cooperation with the United States.[69] Contrary to claims that the Reagan administration's more competitive and offensive policies defeated Soviet hard-liners, Bruce Parrott finds that the main challenge to Brezhnev's national security policy came from conservative Soviet elites: "Questioning the centrist balance between military and diplomatic security instruments struck by Brezhnev, these hard-liners asserted that détente had been permanently eclipsed by a growing American aggressiveness, and that this situation required a large increase in the Soviet defense budget."[70]

In contrast, more cooperative U.S. policies appear to have enhanced the

[65] Jackson, "Soviet Images of the U.S. as Nuclear Adversary 1969–1979," pp. 624–36, quoting Arbatov from June 1972.

[66] Ibid., p. 632, quoting Trofimenko from March 1976. See also Thomas W. Wolfe, The SALT Experience (Cambridge, Mass.: Ballinger, 1979), pp. 162–70, 202–9. While stressing the difficulty of judging how American policy influences Soviet policy, Wolfe finds "some slight hint that Brezhnev might have been more receptive to concluding a deal on MIRV had it not been for the Schlesinger strategic initiative. . . . This supposition rests on the inference that Brezhnev's own stand on MIRV was somewhat softer than that of the Soviet marshals, but that he found it expedient to bow to their position in order to avoid the appearance of having yielded to American pressure emanating from Schlesinger's Pentagon."

[67] Garthoff, Détente and Confrontation, pp. 768–70, argues that "one way in which these American military doctrines were seen to be dangerous to détente and the arms race was by provoking or giving ammunition to those in the Soviet Union most distrustful of political and military détente with the United States and most inclined to see a need for strengthening Soviet military power" (emphasis in original).

[68] Jackson, "Soviet Images of the U.S. as Nuclear Adversary 1969–1979," pp. 635–36.

[69] Parrott, The Soviet Union and Ballistic Missile Defense, pp. 9–21.

[70] Parrott, "Soviet National Security under Gorbachev," p. 2.

position of Soviet moderates. At least initially, the SALT I agreement provided support for moderate images of the United States and undermined opponents' arguments that the United States was too hostile and inflexible to accept limits on its military buildup.[71] Soviets who were interested in reforming Soviet nuclear doctrine—shifting it to a less competitive and they believed less dangerous form—supported their arguments with references to the improved superpower relationship and the SALT I agreement.[72] The signing of SALT II also supported Soviet moderates, but had a less positive effect because growth in U.S. counterforce, the long delay since the signing of SALT I, and concern about the U.S. ratification of SALT II served to raise doubts about U.S. intentions.[73]

Unfortunately, U.S. policy does not provide a good case for examining Soviet reactions to an essentially defensive U.S. nuclear strategy—one that eschews counterforce as well as strategic defense. Although the SALT negotiations of the 1970s provide some information on Soviet reactions to cooperative U.S. policies, overall U.S. policy during these years retained an important offensive cast as the United States continued to enhance its counterforce systems. Since the key measure of U.S. policy is the extent to which it is offensive, not whether it includes negotiated arms control agreements, these years are best viewed as a complex mix of cooperative and competitive policies. As discussed above, the competitive component of these policies appears to have limited the support that Soviet moderates could draw from the arms control agreements. Nevertheless, the evidence we do have suggests that a defensive policy would support Soviet moderates; virtually none of it suggests that this restraint in deploying counterforce or strategic defense would backfire, enhancing the position of Soviet hard-liners.[74]

Because many other factors influenced Soviet decisions about force deployments, military doctrine, and arms control policy, how much these shifts in the Soviet debate influenced policy outcomes is hard to determine. The less moderate image of the United States was insufficient to undermine the Soviet leadership's commitment to détente and arms control, but may have limited the extent of Soviet cooperation.[75]

---

[71] Jackson, "Soviet Images of the U.S. as Nuclear Adversary 1969–1979," pp. 624–26.

[72] Thomas N. Bjorkman and Thomas J. Zamostny, "Soviet Politics and Strategy toward the West: Three Cases," *World Politics* 36, no. 2 (January 1984): 199–204.

[73] Ibid., pp. 204–6; Jackson, "Soviet Images of the U.S. as Nuclear Adversary 1969-1979," pp. 635–36.

[74] Some qualifications are necessary, however. U.S. offensive potential may play a dual role: U.S. restraint in exercising its potential supports moderates; at the same time, by making clear that the Soviets would fare poorly in a competition between offenses, it undercuts Soviet proponents of competition. Thus, a more subtle mix of incentives may sometimes be possible. For example, Parrott, *The Soviet Union and Ballistic Missile Defense*, p. 31, argues that Soviet doubts about their ability to compete in technology innovation (which would favor BMD) contributed to Soviet willingness to begin strategic arms negotiations in the late 1960s.

[75] For example, Parrott, "Soviet National Security under Gorbachev," p. 3, argues that the

The two factors discussed at the end of the last section—Soviet views of their own policies and the clarity of U.S. policy—help to explain why U.S. offense has tended to weaken the position of Soviet moderates. First, the Soviets did not believe their nuclear policies were provocative, and therefore did not interpret U.S. counterforce as a response to their counterforce. Instead, through much of the 1970s the Soviets had doubts about whether they had fully achieved and/or could maintain parity;[76] by the late 1970s they believed that their buildup had resulted in an overall balance in which each superpower had some advantages, not that they had achieved strategic superiority.[77] In addition, the Soviets believed both that their counterforce threat to U.S. ICBMs provided little advantage and that U.S. counterforce posed a relatively large threat to their strategic force. Consequently, although the United States tended to justify new counterforce systems in terms of its need to match Soviet counterforce, the Soviets did not see themselves possessing an overall advantage or a lead in counterforce. Instead, the Soviets saw the United States making false claims to justify its own nuclear buildup.[78]

Second, the prospects that the Soviets would conclude that U.S. counterforce was a response to competitive Soviet policies was further reduced because U.S. decisions to pursue counterforce were not clearly matched to Soviet decisions to deploy counterforce. Instead, although not without some domestic opposition, the United States has continued to enhance its counterforce systems rather steadily.[79] Thus, U.S. policies did not provide Soviet moderates with solid grounds for arguing that the United States would have forgone counterforce if the Soviets had been more restrained. Somewhat ironically, the Reagan administration's pursuit of SDI, because it was a major departure, probably had greater potential for communicating American objections to Soviet policy. However, since the Soviet Union had shown no interest in scrapping the ABM Treaty, this potential could be realized only if Soviet proponents of cooperation could persuasively explain SDI as a reaction to overall Soviet foreign and military policy. Because this is a much more ambiguous link, the prospects for success were low.[80]

Soviet decision to stop arms control negotiations in 1983 resulted from the policy struggle that developed in reaction to the Carter-Reagan nuclear buildup.

[76] Garthoff, *Détente and Confrontation*, pp. 432, 554.

[77] Ibid., pp. 771–72, 797.

[78] Ibid., pp. 797–800.

[79] For basic information on U.S. missile programs see Thomas B. Cochran, William M. Arkin, and Milton M. Hoenig, *U.S. Nuclear Forces and Capabilities* (Cambridge, Mass.: Ballinger, 1984), pp. 100–146.

[80] Allen Lynch, *Gorbachev's International Outlook: Intellectual Origins and Political Consequences*, Occasional Paper Series 9, Institute for East-West Security Studies (Boulder, Colo.: Westview, 1989), pp. 39–42, however, argues that SDI led to a reevaluation of Soviet military requirements in which the condition of mutual assured destruction was found to be desirable. This shift then provides the foundation for moderates to oppose Soviet offensive policies.

The Gorbachev Revolution and the "New Thinking" in Soviet Foreign Policy

I have argued in the above sections that competitive U.S. policies tend both to communicate a malign image of the United States and to support Soviet hard-liners while discrediting moderates. Some, however, fault these arguments for failing to explain Soviet policy in the latter half of the 1980s. According to this view, the more competitive, threatening American nuclear policies that were initiated by the Carter administration and accelerated by the Reagan administration discredited Brezhnev's policies and yielded more cooperative Soviet policies under Gorbachev.[81] Specifically, proponents of competitive policies point to the U.S. strategic modernization programs—which included the MX and Trident II missiles, and under Reagan the SDI and the B-2 bomber—as important in changing Soviet policy.

This brings us into the middle of an emerging debate over the sources of Gorbachev's foreign policy. Reaching firm conclusions about the influence of competitive American nuclear policies is difficult because the case is overdetermined. A variety of domestic and international factors appears to have motivated changes in Soviet foreign policy. This case may be especially difficult to sort out because the Soviet Union faces a variety of powerful pressures for change. Taken in combination, however, these factors raise serious doubts about the importance of competitive American nuclear policies.

In the first place, Western foreign policy probably did little to support Gorbachev's rise to power. When chosen to be General Secretary, Gorbachev was not an expert in foreign affairs[82] and had not presented views on national security policy that diverged significantly from Brezhnev's.[83] Thus, to the extent that individual general secretaries play a central role in redirecting Soviet foreign policy, American foreign policy deserves little credit for recent moderation in Soviet policy.[84]

Given Gorbachev's rise to power, the issue is how American nuclear poli-

---

[81] This argument comes in two broad forms. The first is a learning argument that, challenging the basic spiral model argument, holds that creating Soviet insecurity is desirable when the Soviets recognize their role in generating offensive U.S. policies. The second type of argument focuses on the domestic political effects that this section addresses.

[82] Timothy J. Colton, *The Dilemma of Reform in the Soviet Union* (New York: Council on Foreign Relations, 1986), pp. 178–79, 187–88.

[83] Parrott, "Soviet National Security under Gorbachev," p. 2; on the evolution of Gorbachev's thinking see Timothy J. Colton, "Gorbachev and the Politics of System Renewal," in Seweryn Bialer and Michael Mandelbaum, *Gorbachev's Russia and American Foreign Policy* (Boulder, Colo.: Westview, 1987), pp. 151–86.

[84] Some analysts, however, question whether Gorbachev is the key to revolutionary changes in Soviet foreign policy. Robert Legvold, "Soviet Foreign Policy," *Foreign Affairs* 68, no. 1 (1988/89): 96, for example, stresses that the roots of change preceded Gorbachev by more than a decade, reflecting Soviet adaptation to changes in the international environment. Disagreeing is Meyer, "The Sources and Prospects of Gorbachev's New Political Thinking," pp. 126–29.

cies influenced the development and/or rise of the "new thinking" that provides the foundation for Gorbachev's radical changes in Soviet foreign and military policy. Although there have certainly been important changes in the Soviet understanding of the international environment,[85] it seems doubtful that competitive American nuclear policies deserve much credit for bringing about these changes. Evolutionary changes in Soviet understanding of the implications of the nuclear revolution are central to the new thinking. However, less competitive American policies—that would have insured that Soviet counterforce did not undermine U.S. retaliatory capabilities—would have been sufficient to confirm the basic tenets of the new thinking on nuclear weapons. The discrediting of other elements of Brezhnev's foreign policy, especially its limited success in the Third World,[86] made clear to the Soviets that they would be giving up little by shifting their foreign policy. But again, competitive American nuclear policies were not central to these Soviet failures, and therefore deserve little credit for the development of the new thinking.[87]

Whether competitive American nuclear policies contributed to the rise in influence of the new thinking is a trickier question. The Reagan administration's policies may have helped to discredit Brezhnev's policy of pursuing offensive military capabilities and Third World expansion while simultaneously pursuing détente with the United States,[88] and thereby created an opportunity for the new thinking.[89] In logical terms, however, competitive American policies need not have discredited the foundation of the Brezhnev policy—based on correlation of forces arguments, the Soviets could have concluded they were not strong enough militarily to achieve a stable détente and decided therefore to pursue still more extensive military capabilities.[90]

[85] For a discussion of key factors see Lynch, *Gorbachev's International Outlook*, especially pp. 39–40.

[86] Francis Fukuyama, *Moscow's Post-Brezhnev Assessment of the Third World* (Santa Monica: Rand, 1986).

[87] On Soviet assessments of the difficulty of advancing their ideology in the Third World see Elizabeth Kridl Valkenier, "Revolutionary Change in the Third World," *World Politics* 38, no. 3 (April 1986): 415–34. See also George W. Breslauer, "Ideology and Learning in Soviet Third World Policy," *World Politics* 39, no. 3 (April 1987): 429–48.

However, American linking of Soviet policy in the Third World to American willingness to continue with détente and nuclear arms control may have influenced Soviet new thinking. See Bialer, *The Soviet Paradox*, p. 332.

[88] See, for example, Severyn Bialer, *The Soviet Paradox: External Expansion, Internal Decline* (New York: Knopf, 1986), p. 317, who argues that Reagan's policies "brought home to Soviet leaders the unintended consequences of their own military development and expansionist policies." See also David Holloway, "Gorbachev's New Thinking," *Foreign Affairs* 68, no. 1 (America and the World, 1988/89): 66–81.

[89] On how U.S. policy might create domestic "policy windows" see Matthew Evangelista, "Sources of Moderation in Soviet Security Policy," in Philip E. Tetlock, Jo L. Husbands, Robert Jervis, Paul Stern, and Charles Tilly, eds., *Behavior, Society, and Nuclear War, Vol. 2* (New York: Oxford University Press, forthcoming).

[90] For a variety of reactions along these lines see Stephen Shenfield, *The Nuclear Predicament: Explorations in Soviet Ideology* (London: Routledge & Kegan Paul), pp. 30–39; for example (p.

Further, competitive American nuclear policies do not unambiguously support the "new thinking" that provides the foundation for Gorbachev's radical changes in Soviet foreign and military policy. In fact, in many ways competitive American nuclear policies tend to undercut the new thinking. For example, new thinkers emphasize that arms control, unilateral restraint, and concessions can moderate the American threat.[91] The Reagan administration's enthusiasm for SDI—which posed a clear future threat to the ABM Treaty—and its lack of interest in strategic arms control (at least during most of the first term) seem to challenge this claim, not support it. Similarly, arguments that Soviet force posture should be based on "reasonable sufficiency"—which opens the possibility of strategically adequate forces that do not match U.S. forces in size or sophistication—find little reinforcement in U.S. counterforce programs that the United States would find unnecessary if it accepted this criterion. Other strands of the new thinking cut in both directions. For example, concern over "mutual security" can be seen as laying the groundwork for arguing that Soviet counterforce provoked American counterforce.[92] In response, however, opponents of the new thinking argue that highly competitive American policies demonstrate that the United States does not accept this basic premise, which therefore does not provide a sound basis for Soviet policy.[93]

By comparison, the weakness of the Soviet economy provides much clearer support for the new thinking. This is significant because Gorbachev appears to be motivated heavily, if not primarily, by the need to reform the Soviet economy.[94] The basic components of the new thinking provide a framework

---

34), he quotes V. V. Zagladin's 1987 argument that "what is needed to strengthen peace is 'an increase in the economic, political and military might of world socialism.' "

[91] Snyder, "The Gorbachev Revolution," pp. 118–20; Meyer, "The Sources and Prospects of Gorbachev's New Political Thinking," p. 157.

[92] However, this argument—which sees U.S. counterforce as a reaction to Soviet counterforce—is not spelled out in the new thinking. The new thinkers have, however, criticized other Soviet policies for provoking undesirable American reactions, for example, the invasion of Afghanistan and the deployment of SS-20 missiles.

[93] Meyer, "The Sources and Prospects of Gorbachev's New Political Thinking," p. 143.

[94] For example, Meyer, "The Sources and Prospects of Gorbachev's New Political Thinking on Security," p. 128, argues that economic restructuring required Gorbachev "to gain control over and restructure the Soviet defense agenda"; also on the instrumental role of the new thinking see Lynch, Gorbachev's International Outlook, pp. 3–4. For a related argument about the role of economic imperatives see Snyder, "The Gorbachev Revolution," pp. 93–131. Disagreeing, at least in emphasis, is Raymond L. Garthoff, "New Thinking in Soviet Military Doctrine," Washington Quarterly (Summer 1988): 148: "The impetus for the new thinking on military doctrine in the Soviet Union stems basically from the new conception of security. Economic considerations are important but contributory." Also on sources of change see Seweryn Bialer, "Gorbachev's Program of Change: Sources, Significance, Prospects," in Bialer and Mandelbaum, Gorbachev's Russia and American Foreign Policy, pp. 231–50; and Alexander Dallin and Gail W. Lapidus, "Reagan and the Russians: American Policy toward the Soviet Union," in Kenneth A. Oye et al., Eagle Resurgent? The Reagan Era in American Foreign Policy (Boston: Little, Brown, 1987), pp. 241–46. Jack Snyder, "Limiting Offensive Conventional Forces: Soviet Proposals and

for reducing Soviet military spending while at the same time increasing Soviet security. In addition, the increasing weakness of the Soviet economy probably enhanced the position of reformers in a second way: many of the Soviets who developed what is now termed the new thinking have also tended to doubt the Soviet ability to compete economically and technologically with the West.[95] While in the mid-1960s this issue was more debatable, the increasing economic troubles of the Soviet system have discredited Soviets who were optimistic about these forms of competition.

Competitive American nuclear policies launched during the late 1970s and the 1980s are not primarily responsible for the weakness of the Soviet economy. Although Soviet military spending may have weakened their economy, the Carter/Reagan policies did not make a special contribution to this drain. The growth in Soviet military spending slowed starting about 1976 and did not respond significantly to the American buildup.[96] Thus, these American policies did not create the economic conditions that appear to be driving Gorbachev's policies and the Soviets would have had strong incentives to limit their defense spending without them.

It is true, however, that the prospect of a continuing American buildup probably supported the new thinking by threatening a costly arms race that would divert resources from domestic priorities. The new thinking is consistent with a variety of approaches for avoiding this danger, including not responding to U.S. deployments, responding efficiently with less costly asymmetric deployments, and pursuing ambitious arms control initiatives designed to reduce the American threat.[97]

Overall, then, within the boundaries of available information it is difficult to determine whether the conditions that would have prevailed without competitive American policies—economic weakness, the basic implications of the nuclear revolution, reduced Soviet optimism about the prospects for achieving advances in the Third World, and the "policy window" created by the leadership transition—would have been sufficient to so greatly increase the reformers' influence. Their ability to point to the failures of Brezhnev's policies may have been necessary to strengthen their overall position. However, given the logical indeterminacy of the implications of competitive American policies, it seems at least as likely that economic imperatives overwhelmed the

---

Western Options," *International Security* 12, no. 4 (Spring 1988): 57, identifies economic savings as a key factor behind Soviet interest in reducing conventional forces.

[95] Parrott, *Politics and Technology in the Soviet Union* (Cambridge: MIT Press, 1983).

[96] Richard F. Kaufman, "Causes of the Slowdown in Soviet Defense," *Soviet Economy* 1, no. 1 (1985): 9–31, and Franklyn D. Holzman, "Politics and Guesswork: CIA and DIA Estimates of Soviet Military Spending," *International Security* 14, no. 2 (Fall 1989): 108. It is true, however, that certain Soviet programs, for example, mobile ICBMs, might be unnecessary if the United States had not increased the number and lethality of its counterforce weapons.

[97] See note 77 in Chapter Seven.

logical appeal of arguments calling for the Soviet Union to compete more vigorously, thereby creating an opening for the new thinking to emerge in full force. An intermediate explanation suggests a refinement of the general arguments presented earlier in this section. The more competitive U.S. nuclear policies were probably not a sufficiently clear reaction to Soviet policies to support Soviet moderates under normal conditions. However, combined with Soviet economic weakness, they may have enhanced the reformers' position by requiring hard-liners to propose policies that were clearly unworkable.

In sum, as a rule, U.S. nuclear policies designed to influence the Soviet security debate should avoid capabilities that threaten Soviet deterrent forces while deploying forces that satisfy America's requirements of deterrence. This type of defensive policy is most likely to discredit Soviets who favor competition and military superiority, while simultaneously supporting the moderates' claim that the United States is not hostile under all conditions, and that it responds well to less threatening, more cooperative Soviet policies. American cooperation is especially likely to succeed in dealing with Gorbachev, since claims that the United States will reciprocate Soviet concessions and restraint are especially clear and prominent in the new thinking.[98]

The feasibility of these defensive American policies depends on the severity of America's security dilemma. If the security dilemma is severe, then responding to competitive Soviet policies requires increasing U.S. threats to Soviet deterrent forces, thereby increasing the prospect that Soviet hard-liners will gain influence. By contrast, when the security dilemma is mild, the United States can maintain its necessary capabilities without significantly increasing the U.S. threat to Soviet deterrent forces.

Exceptions to this rule may be appropriate when the Soviets recognize that they have pursued unnecessarily threatening policies, and when U.S. reactions can be tailored to insure that there is a reasonably high probability that the Soviets will recognize their role in provoking U.S. offensive policies. However, these conditions are both unlikely and will probably be hard for the United States to identify if they do occur. In addition, Gorbachev's shift toward more moderate policies suggests the possibility that competitive American policies are more likely to succeed when the Soviet Union faces severe economic constraints.

ANALYTIC AND POLICY IMPLICATIONS

The debate over nuclear policy often divides between analysts who focus on Soviet aggressiveness and favor competitive policies and those who focus on Soviet insecurity and favor more cooperative ones. However, the challenge

[98] Snyder, "The Gorbachev Revolution," p. 130; Meyer, "The Sources and Prospects of Gorbachev's New Political Thinking," p. 157.

facing the United States is more complicated than this polarization suggests, since the Soviet Union could be both aggressive and insecure. In this case, the United States confronts a mix of Soviet motivations and should strive for policies that simultaneously discourage Soviet underestimates of U.S. resolve while not fueling exaggerations of American hostility.[99] The dual objectives of U.S. policy stem from the mix of Soviet motives, not uncertainties about Soviet intentions.

In other words, one-dimensional characterizations of Soviet motives misconstrue the demands facing U.S. strategy. The standard formulation of spiral and deterrence models blurs this point. The choice between spiral and deterrence models is often said to hinge on Soviet intentions—if an aggressor state then pursue a competitive policy, if a status quo state then pursue a cooperative policy.[100] However, Soviet insecurity, which depends on how U.S. policy influences Soviet images of the United States, also plays a key role in defining these models. Thus, if the Soviets simultaneously have aggressive and defensive motives, then neither model does an adequate job of describing how the Soviets will react. For example, an aggressive Soviet Union might react partly according to spiral model predictions if it is also insecure.

A parallel argument applies to U.S. policies designed to influence Soviet domestic debates. Ideally, the United States would like to simultaneously undermine the position of Soviet hard-liners and enhance the standing of moderates.

The preceding analysis suggests that the United States does not face one of the simpler, extreme cases—neither a Soviet Union that is entirely secure nor one without the desire to expand. Instead, the Soviets are not confident that the United States is a status quo power, and therefore tend to see offensive U.S. policies based on counterforce and strategic defense as posing a threat to their security. Likewise, Soviet intentions are sufficiently unclear that the United States cannot be confident that policies that weaken American deterrent capabilities will not raise Soviet doubts about U.S. resolve.[101] In addition, U.S. nuclear policy appears to have some influence on the Soviet security debate.

The feasibility of a U.S. nuclear strategy that deals simultaneously with the demands of this situation depends on three factors: the severity of the security dilemma; the extent to which nuclear competition is required to signal U.S. resolve; and the effectiveness of competitive and cooperative nuclear policies

[99] For a similar point see Richard Ned Lebow, "The Deterrence Deadlock: Is There a Way Out?" in Jervis et al., *Psychology and Deterrence*, pp. 193–94.

[100] On the role of Soviet intentions in choosing between spiral and deterrence models, see Jervis, *Perception and Misperception*, pp. 100–107.

[101] In addition, of course, these policies would be risky because they would leave the United States with inadequate military capabilities.

in enhancing the position of Soviet moderates and discrediting Soviet hard-liners.

Previous sections addressed the last two factors. I found little support for the view that the Soviets are so bent on expansion that American pursuit of more cooperative, less threatening nuclear policies risks misleading the Soviets about U.S. resolve. I also argued the United States will have trouble using offensive policies to weaken the position of Soviet hard-liners, since the Soviets have tended to underestimate how threatening they look to the United States and are therefore unlikely to see U.S. offense as a response to threatening Soviet policies.[102] The success of such policies is further reduced since U.S. nuclear policy has consistently relied heavily on counterforce, thereby reducing the probability that the Soviet hard-liners would be saddled with responsibility for the next round of enhancements in U.S. offense.

Thus, the preceding analysis suggests that a nuclear strategy that provides the United States with highly effective deterrent capabilities while not threatening Soviet deterrent capabilities is likely to be most effective in generating desirable political consequences. Such a defensive nuclear strategy holds the greatest promise of avoiding Soviet underestimates of U.S. resolve while also not fueling Soviet exaggerations of U.S. hostility. In addition, effective U.S. deterrent capabilities weaken the position of Soviet hard-liners by defeating their attempts to gain military advantages, while enhancing the position of Soviet moderates by supporting their arguments that the United States is not extremely or unconditionally hostile. The feasibility of such a nuclear policy depends on the severity of the security dilemma facing the United States.

Severity of the Security Dilemma and Feasibility of Defensive Strategies

As discussed above, if the security dilemma is mild, then the United States can maintain the capabilities required to satisfy its military requirements of deterrence without significantly threatening Soviet deterrent capabilities. However, if the security dilemma is more severe, the United States faces a tradeoff between enhancing U.S. deterrent capabilities and threatening Soviet deterrent capabilities, which reduces Soviet security.

The severity of the security dilemma depends upon two factors: the degree to which offense dominates defense; and the degree to which offense and defense are ambiguous. When offense dominates, a country can defend itself best with forces that make possible a successful attack against its adversary. When offense and defense are indistinguishable, a country that deploys forces

---

[102] Ironically, however, since Gorbachev and the new thinkers appear to be more sensitive to the image that Soviet forces project, competitive U.S. policies might under certain conditions be more effective against them than when the United States confronts more traditional Soviet hard-liners. Nevertheless, a variety of other considerations suggest that conditional cooperation rather than competition is more likely to support Gorbachev.

designed to protect its territory looks much like one that is planning to take territory. Thus, when offense and defense are not clearly differentiated, a country cannot determine its adversary's intentions based on the forces it deploys.[103] The security dilemma is most severe when offense dominates defense, and the two are indistinguishable; it is least severe when defense dominates, and offense and defense are distinguishable.[104]

As discussed above, when countries depend upon deterrence to maintain their security, forces that enhance deterrence are the equivalent of defense. Like capabilities for defeating an invasion of one's territory, nuclear deterrent forces make it less attractive for the adversary to start a war. In contrast, forces that threaten the adversary's deterrent forces or increase a country's ability to compel its adversary are a form of offense. And forces that both support a country's deterrent strategy and threaten its adversary's deterrent capability are ambiguous.

Since the security dilemma depends on the U.S. military requirements of deterrence, analysts from different schools in that debate disagree about the magnitude of the U.S. security dilemma.[105] The punitive retaliation school believes that nuclear weapons essentially eliminate the security dilemma. Since the United States does not require counterforce to deter the Soviet Union, it can deploy necessary deterrent capabilities without threatening Soviet deterrent capabilities.[106] Thus, for these analysts, offense and defense are relatively unambiguous. Further, believing that neither superpower can gain a significant damage-limitation capability in an arms race, the punitive retaliation school concludes that retaliatory capabilities dominate damage-limitation

[103] A complete lack of ambiguity is probably insufficient to eliminate the security dilemma when offense greatly dominates defense. Although countries have the option of forgoing offense, they may be unable to afford to if their adversary invests heavily in offense. The lack of ambiguity might, however, help countries avoid this danger by reducing the difficulty of reaching arms control agreements that ban offense. Nevertheless, offense dominance will make reaching arms control agreements difficult because when offense dominates, agreements are more sensitive to cheating. Consequently, even when offense and defense are distinguishable, offense dominance is likely to generate an intense arms race. On this point see Van Evera, "Causes of War," p. 113; see also Chapters Four and Six.

[104] Jervis, "Cooperation under the Security Dilemma," pp. 186–214.

[105] Recall also that analysts who are not worried about Soviet insecurity tend to discount the importance of the U.S. security dilemma. To the extent that these analysts also believe the Soviets are highly aggressive, and therefore subscribe to the arguments of the damage-limitation or military denial schools, we have a debate in which the analysts whose force requirements generate the possibility of a security dilemma are the same ones who believe that the United States need not worry about Soviet insecurity, and therefore about a security dilemma.

[106] The fact that the United States has developed and deployed highly lethal ballistic missiles that can destroy Soviet missile silos and other hardened nuclear targets with high probability does not eliminate this option. The United States could still choose to retire these systems and deploy only slow and/or inaccurate systems that would be far less effective against Soviet retaliatory capabilities. The feasibility of this policy does depend, however, on the Soviet ability to determine that the U.S. deployed only these systems.

capabilities—we live in a defense-dominated world.[107] The advantage of defense over offense is overwhelming, since maintaining a redundant assured destruction capability is much easier than acquiring a significant damage-limitation capability.

This combination of offense-defense distinguishability and defense dominance essentially eliminates the U.S. security dilemma. Thus, according to the punitive retaliation school, the United States can maintain highly effective deterrent capabilities without generating the negative political consequences of more competitive, offensive policies. Because their military requirements do not establish a security dilemma, these analysts do not face a tradeoff between satisfying U.S. military requirements of deterrence and avoiding the negative political consequences that U.S. nuclear strategy might generate. Adding these political consequences to their analysis would not change their preferred nuclear strategy.

Nevertheless, the possibility of these political consequences has important policy implications for these analysts. If they based U.S. nuclear policy entirely on considerations of military capability, they might be essentially indifferent to superpower offense (counterforce and strategic defense). Assuming that defense dominance was generally recognized, they would see counterforce and strategic defense as wasteful but not very dangerous.[108] However, considering these political consequences identifies stronger reasons for U.S. unilateral restraint and for arms control agreements that severely constrain these systems.

Given the opportunity to forgo offense and project a relatively unthreatening image, U.S. pursuit of offense is especially likely to appear provocative. In certain ways, buying offense when there is no security dilemma is worse than buying offense when it is more severe. When the United States faces a security dilemma there is at least some possibility that the Soviets will recognize the dilemma and moderate their conclusions about U.S. offense. However, when there is no security dilemma, even Soviet leaders who would be sensitive to a U.S. security dilemma have little choice but to impute aggressive

---

[107] These observations are somewhat overstated because limited countervalue options could have coercive uses and therefore support an offensive strategy. See Jervis, "Cooperation under the Security Dilemma," pp. 209–10. The potential offensive uses of these limited nuclear options is constrained by two factors, however. First, in MAD, LNOs cannot provide an offensive military advantage since the Soviets can maintain a similar capability. Second, in MAD countervalue options will tend to favor the country defending the status quo because the status quo power will tend to have greater resolve, which is the key to prevailing in bargaining in MAD. For elaboration see Chapter Seven. See, however, Robert Powell, "Crisis Bargaining, Escalation, and MAD," *American Political Sciences Review* 81, no. 3 (September 1987): 717–35.

[108] Chapter Seven addresses the possibility that superpower leaders will underestimate the extent of defense dominance and argues that this is a key additional reason for opposing counterforce.

intentions to U.S. offense.[109] In this case, U.S. counterforce and strategic defense are clearly "optional" offenses—forces that go beyond those required for deterrence—and are therefore more likely to communicate malign intentions than if they were necessary for deterrence.

Fortunately, defense dominance limits the fear that this optional U.S. offense might generate. Communicating malign American intentions creates relatively little Soviet insecurity since the United States will be unable to undermine Soviet deterrent capabilities. Because nuclear weapons create a world in which defense dominates offense, an intense superpower arms race creates relatively little insecurity.[110] Nevertheless, since the United States can satisfy its requirements of deterrence without counterforce and area-wide strategic defense, members of the punitive retaliation school can argue that these negative political effects weigh heavily against these systems.

In contrast, given the military requirements established by the military denial school, the United States does face a security dilemma. These analysts believe the United States needs counterforce both to extend deterrence to its allies and to deter attacks against the U.S. homeland. In other words, these analysts believe that the United States needs counterforce for defensive purposes. However, since U.S. counterforce poses some threat to the forces that the Soviets rely on for retaliation, these U.S. counterforce requirements blur the distinction between defense and offense.

In addition, the military denial school believes the world is less defense-dominant than does the punitive retaliation school. For example, these analysts believe that U.S. counterforce capable of favorably shifting the ratio of forces enhances U.S. deterrent and war-termination capabilities. These counterforce capabilities are far easier to acquire than damage-limitation capabilities. Thus, this view of the requirements of deterrence identifies desirable offensive capabilities that, unlike significant damage-limitation capabilities, the United States can acquire.

In light of this security dilemma, members of the military denial school must consider whether the deterrent benefits of a large counterforce arsenal more than outweigh the negative political consequences of projecting a more threatening American image. Chapter Two argues that the best case for the military denial arguments is as a hedge against possibilities that are quite unlikely but not clearly impossible—for example, an extremely aggressive So-

---

[109] There are, however, other explanations for why the United States buys offense, including military organizational preferences and other domestic political factors. On militaries' inclinations toward offense see Barry Posen, *The Sources of Military Doctrine: France, Britain and Germany between the World Wars* (Ithaca: Cornell University Press, 1984), and Jack Snyder, *The Ideology of the Offensive: Military Decision Making and the Disasters of 1914* (Ithaca: Cornell University Press, 1984).

[110] In addition, defense dominance is likely to reduce the intensity of the arms race, thereby further reducing the insecurity created by American offense.

viet leader or one who sees large benefits in being able to shift the ratio of surviving nuclear forces. Given the possibility of political costs, it is no longer sufficient for these analysts to base their conclusions on the possibility that hedging will provide some deterrent benefits.

However, considering the political consequences of nuclear policy also provides members of the military denial school with an additional argument for American counterforce. Policies that fail to satisfy the U.S. military requirements of deterrence could encourage the Soviets to underestimate U.S. resolve. I argued that discouraging these underestimates does not require the United States to pursue competitive policies that provide forces in excess of American military requirements. At the same time, however, given uncertainties about Soviet intentions, it is prudent for the United States to meet these military requirements. Given their conclusion that the United States requires a large counterforce arsenal, members of the military denial school can therefore argue that forgoing counterforce risks Soviet underestimates of American resolve.

At a minimum, these analysts should place a premium on "defensive hedges," that is, measures that enhance U.S. deterrent capabilities without threatening Soviet deterrent capabilities. For example, instead of deploying counterforce to insure the U.S. ability to maintain the ratio of surviving forces, the United States could increase the survivability of its own forces. When possible, this general approach provides deterrent benefits while avoiding political costs.

Finally, the damage-limitation school establishes requirements that result in a severe security dilemma. These analysts provide two types of arguments that render U.S. offense and defense indistinguishable. By requiring a highly effective damage-limitation capability for deterrence, this school calls for capabilities that would undermine the Soviet Union's most basic deterrent capabilities. In addition, this school argues that U.S. security need not rely entirely on deterrence, but instead that counterforce and strategic defense can reduce the costs of all-out war if deterrence fails—that is, U.S. offense can serve as a traditional defense against Soviet attack.

Further, members of the damage-limitation school believe that these capabilities are not only necessary but feasible. In other words, they believe that a determined U.S. effort can create a world in which U.S. damage-limitation capabilities can dominate Soviet retaliatory capabilities—in which offense dominates defense.

Analysts in this school tend to believe that the United States does not face a security dilemma since the Soviet Union is confident that U.S. motivations are entirely defensive. Nevertheless, it seems quite likely that regaining nuclear superiority would greatly increase Soviet insecurity, which could make the Soviet Union harder to deter. Whether U.S. superiority is preferable to MAD therefore depends partly on whether the deterrent benefits of superiority are sufficient to offset this increased danger. I examine this alternative nuclear world in Chapter Five.

In closing, the implications of the political consequences of U.S. military policy are influenced by analysts' views of the military requirements of deterrence. Since my analysis in Chapter Two shows that the punitive retaliation school holds the strongest positions in that debate, I conclude here that competitive, offensive policies—those that pose some threat to Soviet deterrent capabilities—are both unnecessary for avoiding Soviet underestimates of U.S. resolve and dangerous because they communicate that the United States has malign intentions.[111] Although they hold little prospect of undermining Soviet deterrent capabilities, American counterforce and strategic defenses are dangerous since Soviet leaders are inclined to interpret them as efforts to gain military advantages, which they in turn take to reflect malign U.S. intentions. The Soviet Union's ability to maintain its necessary retaliatory capabilities— which creates a kind of defense dominance—may reduce the direct danger of competitive U.S. nuclear policies, but since these American forces are unnecessary both for avoiding Soviet misperceptions of U.S. resolve and for satisfying U.S. military deterrent requirements, the United States can safely forgo them in an effort to avoid misleading the Soviets about its intentions.

[111] My conclusion on American military deterrent requirements also depends on further analysis presented in Part III.

PART II

Alternative Nuclear Worlds

CHAPTER FOUR

Why Even Good Defenses May Be Bad

AT PRESENT, the United States cannot physically prevent the Soviet Union from virtually destroying it. Instead of defending its homeland against nuclear attacks, the United States achieves its security by deterring these Soviet attacks. The United States maintains a redundant assured destruction capability, insuring its ability to inflict extremely high levels of damage on the Soviet Union even following a full-scale attack against U.S. forces.[1] Since the Soviet Union now maintains a similar capability, the superpowers live in MAD.

This chapter analyzes the desirability of a world in which both superpowers have perfect or "near-perfect" strategic defenses—that is, systems that are capable of denying one's adversary an assured destruction capability.[2] To fa-

[1] Recall that an assured destruction capability is generally understood to require the ability to inflict a given level of retaliatory damage, which is roughly comparable to the destruction of a country's major cities. Analysts often use the levels of damage established by Robert McNamara—25 percent of the population and 50 percent of industrial capability—as a benchmark. These levels reflected the Pentagon's assessment of where the damage versus equivalent megatonage curve flattened out. A related, but conceptually distinct interpretation of assured destruction focuses on the relationship between the level of damage and the costs a decisionmaker associates with that level of damage. In this interpretation, a country has an assured destruction capability when increasing its ability to retaliate does not significantly increase its ability to inflict costs on its adversary. In other words, assured destruction occurs at the level of damage where the cost versus damage curve flattens off. In this chapter, I use assured destruction to have this second meaning. The distinction is especially important for analyzing crisis stability.

[2] Although "near-perfect" might be understood to describe less effective defenses, this more stringent definition is useful because it identifies the range of defenses that, while imperfect, are sufficiently effective to remove the superpowers from MAD. I have borrowed the term from Ashton B. Carter, *Directed Energy Missile Defense in Space* (Washington, D.C.: GPO, 1984), pp. 66–67.

How well a defense must perform to be considered near-perfect depends on three factors. First is the level to which a Soviet attack against U.S. cities must be reduced before its costs are judged significantly reduced. There is substantial disagreement: some analysts argue that defenses are of little value until potential damage is reduced far below the levels established by McNamara; others believe any reduction in the potential damage to the United States, even if above these levels, is worth pursuing. Carter, in *Directed Energy Missile Defense in Space*, for the sake of discussion uses 100 megatons as the level of penetration at which "a defense would be judged near-perfect." The arguments in this chapter do not depend upon a specific assessment of the level of retaliatory damage required for assured destruction. Although analysts disagree on the level, the arguments apply in all cases. Second, for a given U.S. defense, the Soviet ability to inflict damage depends on the size and penetrability of its force. The third factor is the type of Soviet attack against which the defense is measured. For example, a defense that could provide some protection of U.S. cities following a U.S. counterforce attack might be unable to do so if the Soviet Union launched a first

cilitate an examination of the issues that goes beyond questions of technical feasibility, I hypothesize a world in which the superpowers have deployed such highly effective defenses. My analysis does not depend heavily on the types of strategic defense technology deployed. What is most important is how effective the superpowers' defenses are against each other's offenses.

The possibility of nuclear war, and the enormous destruction that would result, generates interest in strategic defenses that would protect the United States. Even if the probability of superpower war is very low, the possibility of a nuclear war is said to make MAD too risky. Barring fundamental changes in U.S.-Soviet relations, deterrence will have to work for decades and centuries. Further, a nuclear accident could precipitate an all-out war. Knowing that a nuclear war could start along a variety of paths creates fears that the superpowers will eventually fight a nuclear war.[3]

Motivated by the dangers of U.S. vulnerability, President Reagan called for a shift from MAD to a world of highly effective defenses. Offering a future vision of "truly lasting stability" based upon the "ability to counter the awesome Soviet missile threat with measures that are defensive,"[4] he launched the Strategic Defense Initiative (SDI) and set in motion a fundamental reevaluation of U.S. nuclear policy.

The vast majority of opposition to defending the United States is based upon the judgment that perfect or near-perfect defense against a massive Soviet ballistic missile attack is infeasible.[5] Supporting this position are authoritative studies that show there is virtually no hope that the ballistic missile defense (BMD)[6] concepts now under research will provide near-perfect defense in the foreseeable future.[7] Moreover, near-perfect defense of the United States

---

strike against U.S. cities. Interestingly, most assessments of the feasibility of highly effective defenses consider the threat posed by the entire Soviet force, that is, they examine the ability of defenses to blunt a first strike.

[3] In addition to this most obvious reason for deploying strategic defense, proponents present a variety of other rationales: to reduce the fear created by the possibility of nuclear war; to make U.S. security less dependent on Soviet decisions; to reduce superpower tensions and add stability to superpower relations; and to provide the foundation for a more moral national security policy.

[4] *New York Times*, 24 March 1983, p. 20.

[5] I am using the term "defense" to refer only to area defense, that is, systems designed to protect cities and other value targets. Ballistic missile defense that would protect the United States by reducing the Soviet Union's ability to inflict damage is an area defense. By contrast, a point defense is designed principally to protect nuclear forces. This distinction is important because these two types of defense have fundamentally different strategic implications: a country's area defense, if sufficiently effective, could reduce the size of the adversary's deterrent threat; a country's point defenses, by increasing the survivability of its forces, could increase the size of the country's deterrent threat.

[6] A ballistic missile defense is a system capable of destroying Soviet missiles (or warheads) in flight. The terms "ballistic missile defense" and "anti-ballistic missile" (ABM) are usually used interchangeably.

[7] Carter, *Directed Energy Missile Defense in Space*, p. 81, concludes that the prospect of de-

would also require defenses against Soviet bombers and cruise missiles, which are also currently well beyond U.S. reach.

Whether perfect or near-perfect defenses are actually desirable has been left largely unexamined; few analysts have questioned the desirability of highly effective defenses.[8] The implicit assumption is that if effective ballistic missile defense could be developed and deployed, then the United States should pursue the BMD route and the associated change in nuclear strategy. Even analysts who strongly oppose SDI on technical grounds tend to believe that highly effective defenses, if feasible, would be desirable. So, for example, the Union of Concerned Scientists observed that: "If it were possible to put in place over-night a fully effective, invulnerable defense against nuclear weapons, there could hardly be serious objections to doing so."[9]

---

veloping near-perfect defense "is so remote that it should not serve as the basis of public expectation or national policy about ballistic missile defense (BMD). This judgment appears to be the consensus among informed members of the defense technical community." See also Office of Technology Assessment, *Ballistic Missile Defense Technologies* (Washington, D.C.: GPO, 1985), and idem, *SDI: Technology, Survivability and Software* (Washington, D.C.: GPO, 1988). Studies done outside the government concur with this assessment: Sidney D. Drell, Philip J. Farley, and David Holloway, *The Reagan Strategic Defense Initiative: A Theoretical, Political and Arms Control Assessment* (Stanford, Calif.: Center for International Security and Arms Control Studies, Stanford University, 1984); Union of Concerned Scientists, *The Fallacy of Star Wars* (New York: Vintage Books, 1983); and American Physical Society Study Group, *Science and Technology of Directed-Energy Weapons* (Woodbury, N.Y.: American Physical Society, 1987). See also Sidney D. Drell and Wolfgang Panofsky, "The Case against Strategic Defense: Technical and Strategic Realities," *Issues in Science and Technology* (Fall 1984): 45–65; James R. Schlesinger, "Reckless Rhetoric and Harsh Realities in the Star Wars Debate," *International Security* 10, no. 1 (Summer 1985): 3–12; Harold Brown, "Is SDI Technically Feasible," *Foreign Affairs* 64, no. 3 (1985): 435–54; and Kurt Gottfried, "The Physicists Size Up SDI," *Arms Control Today* 17, no. 6 (July/August 1987): 28–32.

Studies ordered by President Reagan following his announcement of the Strategic Defense Initiative were less pessimistic. The study of BMD technologies directed by James C. Fletcher concluded that "the technological challenges of a strategic defense initiative are great but not insurmountable. . . . The scientific community may indeed give the United States 'the means of rendering' the ballistic missile threat 'impotent and obsolete.' " *The Strategic Defense Initiative: Defensive Technologies Study* (Washington, D.C.: Department of Defense, March 1984), p. 23. A study of the policy implications of BMD directed by Fred S. Hoffman, *Ballistic Missile Defenses and U.S. National Security: Summary Report*, (Washington, D.C.: October 1983), prepared for the Future Security Strategy Study, is quite cautious, stating that "nearly leakproof defenses may take a very long time, or may prove to be unattainable in a practical sense against a Soviet effort to counter the defense" (p. 2). On these studies see Donald L. Hafner, "Assessing the President's Vision: The Fletcher, Miller and Hoffman Panels," *Daedalus* 114, no. 2 (Spring 1985): 91–107.

[8] Exceptions include Thomas C. Schelling, "What Went Wrong with Arms Control," *Foreign Affairs* 64, no. 2 (Winter 1985/86): 231–33, and Robert J. Art, "Between Assured Destruction and Nuclear Victory: The Case for the 'MAD-Plus' Posture," *Ethics* 95, no. 3 (April 1985): 515–16.

[9] Union of Concerned Scientists, *The Fallacy of Star Wars*, p. 153. For a similar comment, see Office of Technology Assessment, *Ballistic Missile Defense Technologies*, p. 113.

Nevertheless, whether such highly effective defenses are desirable is the central question. If near-perfect defenses would create a world far safer than MAD, then even a slight chance of eventually deploying them might be sufficient to warrant pursuing extensive research and possibly taking some risks in current policy. In contrast, if MAD is preferable to a world of perfect defenses, then even if perfect defenses are feasible, the United States should pursue policies to preserve MAD.[10]

Broadly speaking, there are two important cases in which the United States deploys such highly effective defenses. In the first case, the United States is defended but the Soviet Union is not; defenses provide the United States with a form of nuclear superiority. Chapter Five examines the desirability of U.S. superiority. The second case, in which both superpowers are defended, is the subject of this chapter.

Assuming highly effective defenses might be developed, this case is important because there is little reason for assuming the United States could maintain a technological advantage enabling only it to have near-perfect defense. Furthermore, symmetric deployment is an especially interesting case to consider because of the intuitive appeal of reducing U.S. vulnerability without threatening Soviet security. Proponents of SDI see this as a strong selling point, arguing that MAD is morally unacceptable because in this world the United States threatens enormous destruction. They also argue that defenses will reduce superpower tensions. Clearly, these claims do not apply to a world in which only the United States has effective defenses.[11]

A world in which defense wins the competition against offense, thereby eliminating the superpowers' assured destruction capabilities, is often described as one of "defense dominance." This terminology is unfortunate since, judged in terms of the strategic implications of weapons capabilities, MAD is a world of defense dominance.[12] I will refer to a world in which both

[10] This chapter does not address the question of less-than-near-perfect defenses. These systems raise fundamentally different issues since the superpowers remain in MAD. Less-than-near-perfect defenses may have some value, but they cannot reduce the costs of an all-out war. However, since some argue that deploying less effective BMD is justified partly because it is a first step toward highly effective defenses, beliefs about the desirability of near-perfect defenses are important in the debate over less-than-near-perfect defenses. Chapter Nine analyzes whether the United States should deploy these less effective defenses.

[11] For examples see Reagan, *New York Times*, 24 March 1983; Lt. Gen. James Abrahamson, "Analysis: Star Wars," *British Broadcasting Corporation* radio documentary, 10 October 1984, quoted in The Arms Control Association, *Star Wars Quotes* (July 1986): 4; and Secretary of Defense Caspar W. Weinberger, *Annual Report, FY 1988* (Washington, D.C.: GPO, 1987), p. 52, who argues that "President Reagan's SDI vision seeks to move *all* mankind away from our unsettling state of total vulnerability" (emphasis added).

[12] When countries maintain their security through deterrence by punishment, the ability to retaliate supports a defensive strategy, while the ability to deny retaliatory capabilities, that is, to limit damage, could support an offensive strategy. In MAD, retaliatory capabilities dominate

superpowers deploy highly effective defenses as BAD (Both Are Defended).[13] In other words, this chapter asks: Could BAD be preferable to MAD?

PERFECT DEFENSES

It is important to begin with an examination of the strategic implications of perfect defenses, however distant they may seem, because that is the goal toward which many advocates of strategic defense, including former President Reagan, wish to move. Despite the widespread presumption that perfect defenses are desirable if feasible, there are two major shortcomings of a world of perfect defenses that draw into question whether it would be safer than our current nuclear situation.[14]

First, there could be no guarantee that perfect defenses would remain perfect. The technical challenge of developing and deploying a defense that would make the U.S. invulnerable to nuclear attack is enormous. Such a defense is commonly referred to as ''perfect.'' The difficulty of maintaining a perfect defense indefinitely is likely to be far greater than developing it in the first place. Consequently, so-called perfect defenses should not be envisioned as a permanent technological solution to the dangers posed by nuclear weap-

---

damage-limitation capabilities, so MAD is defense-dominant. Further, in MAD, strategic defenses—BMD and air defenses—could be offensive, since these systems threaten the adversary's retaliatory capabilities. On these points see Robert Jervis, ''Cooperation under the Security Dilemma,'' *World Politics* 30, no. 2 (January 1978): 198, 206–10; see also Chapter Three.

[13] I have borrowed the term BAD from Robert J. Art, ''The Role of Military Power in International Relations,'' in B. Thomas Trout and James E. Harf, eds., *National Security Affairs: Theoretical Perspectives and Contemporary Issues* (New Brunswick, N.J.: Transaction Books, 1982), p. 23. This chapter analyzes cases in which the superpowers reduce their vulnerability to retaliatory attack through a combination of offensive counterforce systems and strategic defenses, as well as cases in which they rely entirely on strategic defenses. However, there are some important differences between these types of cases. Unlike cases of pure strategic defenses, in some situations launching a counterforce first strike could provide a country with strategic superiority; in others, striking first would enable a country to reduce the damage of an all-out war, although not to ''acceptable'' levels. Although I have included all of these different cases in this analysis of BAD, they could be considered different nuclear worlds. See Stephen W. Van Evera, ''Causes of War'' (Ph.D. diss., University of California at Berkeley, 1984), Chapter 13.

[14] The following discussion assumes that both countries know the effectiveness of both their own defense and the adversary's defense. This is admittedly unrealistic since there would always be uncertainties about the effectiveness of the defenses, and the implications of these uncertainties could be significant. I assume that the effectiveness of the defenses would be known to focus my examination of perfect defenses on the most basic issues. Some of the complications that would probably result from uncertainties about effectiveness are discussed later in this chapter.

There are cases in which uncertainty might create a safer world. For example, if defenses are in fact perfect, but decisionmakers do not know this, then they might act more cautiously—avoiding conventional confrontation—due to the believed possibility of nuclear war. However, if war occurs, nuclear attacks would not be damaging. In addition, uncertainty might reduce some dangers stemming from a lack of robustness, but would exacerbate other dangers.

ons. The far more likely course of events is that a world of perfect defenses would decay into a world of imperfect defenses, returning the superpowers to MAD. As a later section of this chapter explores in detail, a variety of structural features tend to make BAD less robust than MAD and, therefore, harder to maintain.[15]

The likelihood of decay will create a number of related dangers. A world in which strategic defenses made both superpowers invulnerable to nuclear attack would be extremely sensitive to even small improvements in the ability of one country's offense to penetrate the adversary's defense. For example, the ability to penetrate the adversary's defense with ten warheads would provide the potential for enormous destruction, especially compared to no destruction. The country that first acquired even a small capability to penetrate the adversary's defense would have attained an important coercive advantage: nuclear attack could be threatened with impunity since effective retaliation would be impossible given the adversary's inability to penetrate one's own defense.[16] Recognizing that the adversary is likely to acquire a similar capability—that is, that one's defense will not remain impenetrable—could create pressure to reap the benefits of the strategic advantage quickly. This time pressure would be especially strong if one's advantage could be used to prevent the adversary from acquiring the capability to penetrate one's defense. In other words, BAD would suffer the dangers of opening and closing "strategic windows."[17]

By contrast, when both superpowers possess redundant assured destruction capabilities, which is the case today in MAD, the addition of tens, hundreds, or even thousands of warheads would not significantly change either country's capabilities. As a result, the probability of gaining a strategic advantage is extremely low, especially when both superpowers are aware of and react to

[15] Many advocates of pursuing highly effective defense argue that even if the prospects for effective defense do not look extremely promising today, history suggests that major technological changes should be expected. For example, Keith B. Payne and Colin S. Gray, "Nuclear Policy and the Defense Transition," *Foreign Affairs* 62, no. 4 (Spring 1984): 826, observe that: "All of recorded history has shown swings in the pendulum of technical advantage between offense and defense. For the strategic defense to achieve a very marked superiority would be an extraordinary trend in light of the last 30 years, but not of the last hundred or thousand years. Military history is replete with examples of defensive technology and tactics dominating the offense." However, this argument applies more strongly to BAD than MAD, since BAD would be less robust, and therefore points to major problems that would exist in BAD.

[16] Some might question the utility of such an advantage, noting the limited value of the U.S. nuclear monopoly following World War II. See Mortin H. Halperin, *Nuclear Fallacy: Dispelling the Myth of Nuclear Strategy* (Cambridge, Mass.: Ballinger, 1987), pp. 23–47, and McGeorge Bundy, "The Unimpressive Record of Atomic Diplomacy," in Gwyn Prins, ed., *The Nuclear Crisis Reader* (New York: Vintage Books, 1984), pp. 42–54.

[17] On "windows" see Stephen W. Van Evera, "Causes of War" (Ph.D. diss., University of California at Berkeley, 1984), 60–76; see also Chapter Five.

changes in the other's nuclear force. Consequently, MAD virtually eliminates the danger of windows.[18]

In a world of impenetrable defenses, the dangers that result from this sensitivity to small offensive improvements would be increased by the strong incentives the superpowers would have to defeat each other's defense. Because there could be no guarantee that one's defenses would not be degraded, even a country that did not desire nuclear superiority would feel compelled to acquire additional strategic capabilities. Such a country would want to improve its defense to offset anticipated improvements in the adversary's offense. In addition, there would probably be a strong instinct to improve one's offense as a hedge against being unable to offset the adversary's enhanced offense with improvements in one's defense. Consequently, even if both countries would prefer to remain in a world of perfect defense, an interactive competition that threatened to reduce the effectiveness of the defenses would be likely to ensue. The possibility of strategic inferiority would create overwhelming pressures for nuclear competition.

This intense military competition would almost certainly damage superpower relations. Unfortunately, U.S. leaders would be unable to know with confidence that Soviet strategic programs were intended only to preserve an equal capability, and would conclude that the Soviet Union was interested in challenging vital American interests. As discussed in Chapter Three, we have strong reasons for expecting that Soviet leaders would reach similar negative conclusions about U.S. intentions. Thus, BAD would be plagued by all of the political dangers predicted by the spiral model. Consequently, war would be more likely for two related reasons: countries would have great difficulty maintaining military capabilities necessary to preserve their security, and their relationship would be strained by misperceptions generated by intense military competition.

We can appreciate the extent of these dangers by considering the severity of the security dilemma. First, in BAD the forces that support offensive and defensive strategies are impossible to distinguish. As discussed above, even countries that prefer BAD must prepare for a return to MAD simply to avoid inferiority. But the capability of penetrating the adversary's strategic defenses and regaining an assured destruction capability is exactly what is required to gain superiority. Similarly, while improving one's strategic defenses is necessary to preserve BAD, these improvements also support a quest for superiority, since they would provide an advantage if combined with the ability to

---

[18] This observation is built on the belief that a country's ability to deter and coerce its adversary depends on countervalue capabilities, not measures of relative force size or numbers of counterforce weapons. In other words, the punitive retaliation school believes that MAD eliminates windows, but the military denial school disagrees, as its arguments during the 1970s stressed.

penetrate the adversary's defenses.[19] Second, because national security would be sensitive to small changes in capability, both countries would fear an imminent shift from BAD, in which strategic defenses support a defensive strategy, to a world of nuclear inferiority, in which the adversary's strategic defenses are a central component of an offensive strategy. The countries would therefore be inclined to perceive each other as though they were already in a world of offense dominance. Combined with offense-defense ambiguity, this creates a severe security dilemma. Thus, whereas MAD essentially eliminates the security dilemma, BAD would bring it back in full force. It is the intensity of the security dilemma that promises to create a world plagued by the dangers predicted by the spiral model.

The second problem with a world of mutual perfect defenses is that superpower conventional war would probably be more likely than in MAD. Today's nuclear forces greatly increase the potential costs of any direct U.S.-Soviet military confrontation. Thus, nuclear weapons increase the risk of starting conventional wars and therefore contribute to deterring them. Impenetrable defenses would eliminate this contribution. Virtually all analysts believe that the superpowers' current strategic arsenals help deter conventional war, though they disagree about which features are most critical for that function.[20] Reduced capabilities for deterring conventional war could be especially dangerous when combined with the hostile superpower relationship that BAD would generate.

Perfect defenses might be in the United States' security interest despite the increased probability of conventional war. Still, because conventional war would be more likely, there is an important tradeoff to consider. As World Wars I and II demonstrated, global conventional wars can be extremely destructive. The net effect of increasing the probability of major conventional

---

[19] This example reminds us that whether a given weapons system supports an offensive or defensive strategy depends heavily on the military conditions. In MAD, adding countervalue capabilities is clearly defensive since this increases the redundancy of retaliatory capabilities. In contrast, in BAD, trying to increase countervalue capabilities is highly ambiguous and would appear quite threatening.

[20] Members of the punitive retaliation school are quite clear on this contribution. At the other end of the spectrum, members of the damage-limitation school argue that the United States cannot adequately meet its extended deterrence commitments in MAD. This is not the same as arguing that strategic forces contribute nothing to extended deterrence, however. For example, see Colin S. Gray and Keith Payne, "Victory Is Possible," *Foreign Policy* no. 39 (Summer 1980): 16, in which they admit that U.S. strategic nuclear forces do contribute to deterrence of Soviet conventional attack in Europe. For an opposing view on the effect of BAD on conventional war that is not inconsistent with his argument cited above, see Keith Payne, "Strategic Defense and Stability," *Orbis* 28, no. 2 (Summer 1984): 222–25.

Strong proponents of no-first-use appear to believe that, independent of stated doctrine, the possibility of nuclear war would contribute somewhat to deterring conventional war; see, for example, McGeorge Bundy, "The Bishops and the Bomb," *New York Review of Books*, 16 June 1983, p. 6.

war, while eliminating the possibility of more destructive, but extremely unlikely, nuclear war might not be positive. The evaluation of this tradeoff would involve many factors, including estimates of the probability of nuclear and conventional wars with and without perfect defenses, estimates of the size and costs of these wars, and the availability of options for reducing the probability and costs of conventional war. Here I can only call attention to this tradeoff, not resolve it.

In sum, what are commonly called perfect defenses would have two shortcomings. First, because the defenses would not be truly perfect but only temporarily impenetrable, BAD could decay, creating intense military competition, increased superpower hostility, and incentives for nuclear war that exceed those in MAD. Second, even if the temporary nature of impenetrable defenses is ignored, the net effect of both superpowers deploying impenetrable defenses remains unclear because major conventional wars could become more likely.

Imperfect Defense and the Probability of War

Understanding security in a world of perfect defense is relatively easy because as long as the defenses remain impenetrable there is no possibility of a strategic nuclear war.[21] The problem is more complicated in a world in which near-perfect defenses have been deployed. Since the United States would be vulnerable to Soviet strategic nuclear attacks, we need to evaluate the U.S. ability to reduce the probability of these attacks.

The following analysis considers cases in which both superpowers have near-perfect defenses, that is, each has denied the other an assured destruction capability. Implicit in this formulation is a relationship between one country's offense and the adversary's defense. When defenses are imperfect there will always be, at least in theory, an offense sufficiently large to provide an assured destruction capability. Therefore, for one country's imperfect defense to deny the adversary an assured destruction capability, either the size of the adversary's offense must be limited or the defense must be able to expand and improve to offset increases in the size of the offense. This analysis does not examine the feasibility of achieving these conditions. It assumes the establishment of a world in which neither the United States nor the Soviet Union has assured destruction capabilities.

The probability that the United States will avoid war with the Soviet Union depends upon the following three features of the nuclear situation:

---

[21] This assertion depends on the assumption made above that both countries know that the defenses are perfect. If defenses were not known to be perfect, although in fact they were, then nuclear attacks might be carried out (but would not result in damage) and nuclear threats might be used coercively.

1. The U.S. ability to deter "premeditated" Soviet nuclear attack. Deterring this type of attack requires that the Soviet Union believe that the net effect of starting a nuclear war would be negative, that is, that the Soviet Union would be worse off after the war than before it. Surprise attacks, including the infamous "bolt from the blue," fall within this category. So do limited nuclear attacks employed as a means of coercive bargaining and certain counterforce attacks employed for damage limitation.

2. The crisis stability of the nuclear forces. In a crisis, one or both superpowers might fear a nuclear attack by the other. If striking first is believed to be preferable to being attacked first, and if a country believes the probability that the adversary will strike first is sufficiently high, then launching a first strike would be preferable to taking a chance on being attacked first. This type of first strike is commonly termed a "preemptive attack." Unlike the case of premeditated attack, the country launching a preemptive attack would expect to be less well-off after the war than before it. The crisis stability of the nuclear forces is a measure of how severe a crisis must be (or how high one's estimate that the adversary will strike first must be) before striking first becomes one's best option.[22]

3. The robustness of U.S. forces. The adequacy of U.S. forces depends not only on their ability to reduce the probability of preemptive and premeditated attacks, but also on how sensitive this ability is to potential changes in Soviet forces. The more easily the Soviet Union could build forces that would either make a premeditated attack attractive or significantly increase the incentives for preemptive attack, the greater the probability of a nuclear war. The robustness of the U.S. nuclear force is a measure of the difficulty the Soviet Union would encounter in trying to undermine necessary U.S. military capabilities.

These three measures are frequently used to assess the adequacy of U.S. nuclear forces. What distinguishes the following analysis from standard analyses is the assumption that both superpowers lack assured destruction capabilities. Past analyses have asked the question: What capabilities are required to minimize the probability of war? Essentially all answers include the need for an assured destruction capability. Here we need to explore how eliminating

---

[22] The probability of preemptive nuclear war depends on the probability of crises as well as the crisis stability of the nuclear situation. For example, a change in forces that increases crisis stability but also increases the probability or severity of crises could increase the probability of preemptive nuclear war. The following comparison of the probability of nuclear war in BAD and MAD does not consider the relative probability of crises. Because BAD is likely to increase tensions between the superpowers, not including the probability of crises in this analysis probably favors BAD. Therefore, this simplification tends to reinforce the best case that this analysis makes for BAD.

assured destruction capabilities by mutual deployment of strategic defenses would affect the probability of nuclear war.

Premeditated Attacks: Is Assured Destruction Necessary for Deterrence?

If Soviet defenses eliminated the U.S. assured destruction capability, the United States would lack what is now generally accepted to be the most basic requirement for deterring Soviet nuclear attacks. A natural conclusion is that the U.S. deterrent would be inadequate.[23] But closer examination of cases in which both superpowers deploy defenses shows that the United States could maintain the capability to deter premeditated Soviet attacks without possessing an assured destruction capability.

The United States now bases its force requirements on the belief that the Soviet Union is capable of annihilating the United States. Specifically, the standard argument for possessing an assured destruction capability holds that deterring Soviet annihilation of the United States requires that the United States credibly threaten to annihilate the Soviet Union in retaliation.[24] But deterring this attack would become unnecessary if, by deploying defenses, the United States eliminated the Soviet Union's annihilation capability. Furthermore, we have difficulty imagining other Soviet actions that the United States would want to deter that require threatening annihilation. Thus, the United States could still have an adequate deterrent when the superpowers eliminated each other's annihilation capabilities by deploying defenses. Of course, the United States would still need a nuclear retaliatory capability to deter Soviet attacks that could not annihilate the United States but would still inflict high costs.

What capability would the United States need to deter attacks against its homeland when defenses had denied the Soviet Union an annihilation capability? Deterrence requires that, even after a Soviet attack, the United States have the ability to inflict costs greater than the benefits the Soviet Union would

---

[23] The belief that deterrence requires assured destruction is clearest in arguments holding that BMD would fuel an intense arms race. The inevitability of the arms race is based partly on the assertion that each superpower, to maintain an effective deterrent, would have to possess an enormous retaliatory capability. See, for example, Abram Chayes and Jerome Wiesner, eds., *ABM: An Evaluation of the Decision to Deploy Anti-Ballistic Missile Systems* (New York: Harper and Row, 1969), pp. 49–54.

[24] The following discussion assumes that the Soviet value structure closely resembles that of the United States. Some analysts believe that U.S. and Soviet leaders have different value structures and, as a result, that the United States needs to threaten more than the annihilation of Soviet society. For example, members of the damage-limitation school believe that the United States must be able to destroy the Soviet Union's political and military leadership and its military forces in an all-out war. Although rarely noted, analysts who accept this view of Soviet values should see major problems with defenses since protecting hardened leadership and military targets is much easier than protecting cities and economic capabilities.

achieve by attacking. Thus, to determine the U.S. retaliatory requirement we must estimate the value the Soviet leaders would place on attacking the United States.

This requires considering why the Soviet Union might attack the United States. In the most general terms, the Soviet Union could use its nuclear force to damage or weaken the United States and to coerce it. In the following discussion I briefly examine the capabilities the United States requires to deter these actions.

For all of the concern about Soviet attacks against U.S. cities, it is unclear why the Soviet Union would ever launch an all-out countervalue attack. Still, since such an attack is not impossible, the United States should plan to deter it. This requires estimating the value the Soviet Union might place on attacking U.S. cities. One possibility is that the Soviet Union would attack U.S. cities to weaken the United States, thereby reducing the U.S. ability to oppose its pursuit of expansionist foreign policy objectives.[25]

To deter this type of attack, the United States would need forces capable of weakening the Soviet Union as much as the Soviet countervalue attack could weaken the United States. The United States could satisfy this requirement with a countervalue capability roughly equivalent to the Soviet countervalue capability. In fact, this is a very conservative requirement. U.S. retaliation would go well beyond simply denying the Soviet Union the increase in relative world power that it desired. In addition, by retaliating the United States would inflict direct costs by destroying targets the Soviets value.

Because the Soviet Union could first attack U.S. forces, and then attack U.S. cities, U.S. forces should provide a countervalue capability essentially equal to the Soviets' both before and after a Soviet counterforce attack. I will call this an "equal countervalue capability." Based upon similar considerations, Freeman Dyson has argued for this requirement and terms the concept "live-and-let-live."[26]

[25] This rationale may underlie analysts' current concern about countervalue attacks: presumably they fear that the Soviet Union might annihilate the United States to become the dominant world power. If U.S. defenses had eliminated the Soviet ability to annihilate the United States, the analogy would be a Soviet countervalue attack designed to weaken the United States.

[26] Freeman Dyson, *Weapons and Hope* (New York: Harper and Row, 1984), pp. 272–74. A similar argument is made by Donald Brennan in "The Case for Population Defense," in Johan J. Holst and William Schneider, Jr., eds., *Why ABM? Policy Issues in the Missile Defense Controversy* (New York: Pergamon Press, 1969), pp. 100–106. An earlier version of this argument appeared in Donald Brennan and Johan Holst, *Ballistic Missile Defense: Two Views*, Adelphi Paper No. 43 (London: IISS, 1967), pp. 9–11.

Including in this analysis uncertainty and imperfect information about the level of vulnerability to countervalue attack weakens this argument. Redundant assured destruction capabilities are extremely large by any reasonable evaluation. Leaders are unlikely to underestimate the destructive potential of today's arsenals, and assessments of outcomes are therefore not sensitive to relatively small differences in force size. In contrast, in BAD, with each country's ability to inflict damage greatly reduced, relative force capabilities would be harder to evaluate and uncertainties, mis-

A second way in which the Soviet Union might use its nuclear capability is to coerce the United States. While we can question whether the Soviet Union would see benefits in actually attacking U.S. cities, the potential benefits of coercing the United States are more obvious. Specifically, if the Soviet Union could inflict enormous damage on the United States and the United States lacked the ability to deter these attacks, then the Soviet Union might be able to compel the United States to compromise its security and vital interests.[27]

As in other cases, deterring these attacks would require that the United States threaten the Soviet Union with expected costs exceeding the benefits the Soviets might achieve. The United States, however, could defeat Soviet attempts to coerce it simply by refusing to perform the action the Soviet Union demanded: any U.S. attack combined with refusal of the Soviet demand would result in a net Soviet loss. Thus, if faced with a coercive threat, the United States could refuse the Soviet demand and inform Soviet leaders that it would reciprocate attacks against U.S. value targets.

The United States could adopt this strategy only if confident in its ability to deter the Soviet Union. Maintaining this confidence would require that U.S. leaders believe that the Soviet Union finds U.S. retaliatory threats credible. A large disparity in U.S. and Soviet countervalue capabilities could undermine this confidence. For example, knowing that the United States would suffer much greater costs in an all-out war than would the Soviet Union, U.S. leaders would recognize that the risk of all-out war was not equally shared by the superpowers. As a result, U.S. leaders might worry that the Soviet Union would be more willing to launch a limited nuclear attack that increased the probability of all-out war to coerce the United States into concessions. Although it is difficult to know precisely what capabilities the United States

---

evaluations, and misperceptions would be more likely to result in a perceived advantage that could result in a failure of deterrence. However, as noted in the text, this equal countervalue requirement is conservative, which might help offset the danger of these errors.

[27] A third type of Soviet attack would be designed to eliminate the U.S. ability to deter the Soviet Union from pursuing its foreign policy objectives. For example, consider a hypothetical case in which the United States deters Soviet attack on Western Europe entirely with threats of strategic nuclear retaliation. If a Soviet counterforce attack could sufficiently reduce the potential cost of U.S. retaliation, then the Soviet Union could judge that attacking the United States, incurring U.S. retaliation, and invading and acquiring Western Europe could result in a net benefit. This type of Soviet nuclear attack on the U.S. homeland, unlike the two discussed in the text, does not depend upon the Soviet Union's ability to inflict countervalue damage on the United States. In contrast, it is a purely military attack, motivated by the desire to reduce the damage the United States could inflict on the Soviet Union. The United States could eliminate the Soviet incentive for launching this type of attack by making its forces invulnerable. However, even with invulnerable forces, and with the equal countervalue requirement satisfied, there might be cases in which the U.S. countervalue threat would be insufficiently large to deter Soviet attack on Europe. This would be true for the same reason that perfect defenses could increase the probability of conventional war: U.S. escalation to the nuclear level would no longer be sufficiently costly to deter Soviet attack.

would require to maintain confidence in its deterrent, we can reasonably require that the United States not allow the Soviet Union an advantage in countervalue capabilities: an advantage should not exist in the deployed forces, nor should the Soviet Union be able to gain a countervalue advantage in surviving forces by launching a counterforce attack. Thus, U.S. forces that satisfy the equal countervalue requirement should be sufficient to deny the Soviet Union a capability that enables it to coerce the United States.[28]

In sum, a reasonable requirement for deterring premeditated Soviet attacks is for the United States to possess an equal countervalue capability. The implications of this requirement differ significantly from an assured destruction requirement. The equal countervalue requirement explicitly couples U.S. and Soviet capabilities to inflict countervalue damage. It could be satisfied by both the United States and the Soviet Union at all levels of vulnerability to attack. According to the equal countervalue requirement, if the United States can reduce the Soviet Union's ability to inflict countervalue damage, then the United States can afford to have Soviet defenses reduce its retaliatory capability. Moreover, improvements in Soviet defenses that reduce the damage the United States could inflict on the Soviet Union could be compensated for by improvements in U.S. defenses. In contrast, the assured destruction requirement demands that the United States have a retaliatory force capable of inflicting a specific level of countervalue damage independent of the size of the Soviet ability to inflict damage. It demands that improvements in Soviet defenses be offset either by an increase in the size of the U.S. countervalue force or by an increase in the ability of American retaliatory forces to penetrate Soviet defenses.

Crisis Stability: What Would Be the Effect of Defenses?

There is a common belief that defenses capable of eliminating an adversary's assured destruction capability would decrease crisis stability: a country that can protect itself (that is, a country that can deny its adversary a second-strike annihilation capability) is more likely to strike preemptively in a crisis.[29] Under what conditions is this proposition correct?

[28] This does not mean, however, that the Soviet Union would necessarily be unable to coerce the United States. As in MAD, if the Soviet Union were able to convince U.S. leaders that it would carry out a threat to attack U.S. cities, then Soviet coercion might be successful. U.S. possession of an equal countervalue capability, by making possible a highly credible retaliatory threat comparable to the Soviet threat, would make it difficult for the Soviet Union to make its coercive threat convincing. Thus, if the Soviets were able to coerce the United States, the key to their success would be greater resolve and willingness to take risks, not an advantage in nuclear forces.

[29] See, for example, William C. Foster, "Strategic Weapons: Prospects for Arms Control," *Foreign Affairs* 47, no. 3 (April 1969): 414–15, and Robert L. Rothstein, "ABM, Proliferation and International Stability," *Foreign Affairs* 46, no. 3 (April 1969): 498–99.

Crisis stability depends upon the decisionmaker's incentives to strike preemptively in a crisis. The decision to preempt would depend upon how the costs of being attacked first compare to the costs of being attacked second.[30] If the adversary has an assured destruction capability, then there would be little if any incentive for preempting: a preemptive attack could not deny the adversary an assured destruction capability, so a decisionmaker who anticipates a countervalue attack would see little difference between the costs of being attacked first or second.[31] In MAD, the vulnerability of the adversary's forces does not create first-strike incentives because the portion of the force that would survive a counterforce attack would be able to annihilate the adversary. Since a leader's decision to preempt would be fueled by anticipation of the adversary's preemption, possession of an assured destruction capability by either country should be sufficient to create a high level of crisis stability.

If one's defense eliminates the adversary's assured destruction capability and the adversary's retaliatory capability is partially vulnerable, then striking first would reduce the damage from an all-out countervalue attack. As a result, if one's decisionmakers anticipate that the adversary is going to launch such an attack, then there would be an incentive to preempt. Since without defenses there would be virtually no incentive to preempt (because the adversary maintains an assured destruction capability), deploying defenses that eliminate assured destruction capabilities would decrease crisis stability.

However, we reach a different conclusion if the adversary's retaliatory capability is invulnerable to a first strike. In this case, there is nothing to be gained by striking first because the adversary's retaliatory strike would be no less costly than if it had attacked first—the costs to one's own country of suffering an all-out countervalue first or second strike would be essentially equal. Thus, if the adversary's forces are invulnerable there would be no incentive to

[30] Extensive discussions of crisis stability include Thomas C. Schelling, *Strategy of Conflict* (Cambridge: Harvard University Press, 1960), pp. 207–54; idem, *Arms and Influence* (New Haven: Yale University Press, 1966), pp. 221–48; and Glenn H. Snyder, *Deterrence and Defense* (Princeton: Princeton University Press, 1961), pp. 97–114. For additional sources see Chapter Two.

[31] The assumption that decisionmakers would anticipate a countervalue strike is implicit in many discussions of crisis stability. It underlies the logic that says if a counterforce attack could reduce the adversary's countervalue potential, then there will be an incentive to strike first. A crisis, however, should provoke fears of a counterforce attack. If we assume the adversary's first strike would be counterforce, then the nuclear situation is far more crisis stable than if we assume the attack would be countervalue. For a good discussion of this argument see Snyder, *Deterrence and Defense*, pp. 104–9. Assuming that both countries anticipate counterforce first strikes, the incentives to preempt would be small or nonexistent, with or without defenses.

We should note that the above arguments do not hold for decisionmakers who anticipate counterforce exchanges and believe, with members of the military denial school, that the ratio of surviving forces would be politically significant during a nuclear war. In this case, even if significant damage limitation is infeasible, preemptive incentives could exist if the superpowers can shift the ratio of surviving forces.

preempt. This would be true when neither superpower had deployed defense, even if the countries were unable to annihilate each other. Deploying survivable defenses would reduce one's societal vulnerability, but would not create an incentive to preempt.

We should not overestimate the practical significance of this case. To start with, an invulnerable retaliatory capability requires not only that the forces be invulnerable, but also that attacks against the command and control system would not reduce the size of the possible retaliatory attack. These conditions might not be achievable. Submarines in port are vulnerable to attack and much of the command system is now highly vulnerable. Consequently, while in theory survivable defenses that eliminated assured destruction capabilities need not decrease crisis stability, in practice they probably would.

To minimize possible decreases in crisis stability, the United States could pursue programs to reduce the vulnerability of its retaliatory forces. Area defenses, although not designed specifically for this mission, could increase the survivability of U.S. forces. In addition, there are many ways to further increase force survivability, including deploying point defenses.[32] If effective area defense were feasible, then American defenses could also make U.S. forces and command and control highly survivable. Thus, the United States should be able to deploy effective defenses while reducing crisis stability only slightly.

The fundamental insight we can draw from this discussion is that survivable defenses do not by themselves create incentives for preemption. In this case, the source of preemptive incentives is the vulnerability of retaliatory forces. Therefore, the effect of strategic defenses on crisis stability should not be evaluated without considering this vulnerability. By reducing retaliatory capabilities, defenses could increase the significance of remaining offensive vulnerabilities.

The preceding discussion favors BAD by overlooking the preemptive incentives that could be created by vulnerable strategic defenses. This danger must be considered, however, since space-based defenses—which would almost certainly play a key role in a highly effective strategic defense—are likely to be vulnerable.[33] The preemptive incentives created by vulnerable defenses depend upon two factors: the vulnerability of the threat to the defenses and the vulnerability of nuclear capabilities. Consider first the case in which the threat to defenses is itself vulnerable (for example, spaced-based BMDs that are effective against each other as well as against ballistic missiles). The country that attacks first destroys not only the adversary's defense but also its antidefense capability. Thus, striking first restores the attacker's assured destruction

[32] Useful analysis of a variety of options for increasing ICBM survivability are found in Office of Technology Assessment, *MX Missile Basing* (Washington, D.C.: GPO, 1981).

[33] On survivability of space-based BMD see Office of Technology Assessment, *SDI: Technology, Survivability and Software*.

capability and eliminates the adversary's ability to do the same; the country that strikes first, therefore, acquires strategic superiority. As a result, both superpowers would see large advantages in striking first against the adversary's defense. There might not be large preemptive incentives for further escalation, however. The inferior country, now vulnerable to annihilating attacks, has essentially no incentive to attack, thereby eliminating both countries' incentives for further preemptive escalation.[34] Nevertheless, the pressures to preempt against defenses remain large because doing so brings nuclear superiority.

In contrast, a world of vulnerable defenses and survivable antidefense forces is much more stable. This case could arise if space-based defenses were invulnerable to attack from other space-based defenses, but were vulnerable to survivable land-based antisatellite weapons. Striking first against the adversary's BMD would not protect one's own BMD. The adversary could destroy one's BMD in a second strike.

In this case—vulnerable defense and survivable antidefense weapons—the magnitude of first-strike incentives depends upon the survivability of the countries' nuclear capabilities. If following the destruction of the adversary's BMD the attacker can destroy the adversary's nuclear capability, then first-strike incentives would be large. Even though its defense would remain vulnerable, combining attacks against strategic defenses and then nuclear forces might enable the country that attacked first to gain a decisive advantage in countervalue capability. On the other hand, if retaliatory capabilities are highly survivable even after defenses have been destroyed, then first-strike incentives would be quite small. Both countries could destroy the other's defense and neither would be able to then destroy the adversary's countervalue forces. In many ways, this world is simply a disguised form of MAD.[35]

In sum, contrary to what many advocates of BMD maintain, effective defenses would be likely to decrease crisis stability. If defenses are survivable, it would probably be possible to keep this negative effect quite small. Vulnerable defenses, however, could generate a variety of first-strike incentives, thereby greatly reducing crisis stability.

Robustness: The Fundamental Inadequacy of BAD

We do not live in a static world. Thus, we cannot evaluate U.S. security as though both superpowers' forces could be held constant. Instead, we must also examine the effect of possible changes in Soviet forces on U.S. security and the probability of these changes. More specifically, we must evaluate not only

---

[34] Chapter Five examines crisis stability in a world of U.S. superiority in more detail.

[35] Other variations are possible: for example, whether ASATs that would be vulnerable only following destruction of BMD would create first-strike incentives would depend on whether they could be launched before the attacker's counterforce attack arrived.

the U.S. ability to deter premeditated Soviet attack and to maintain crisis stability, but also the probability of changes in Soviet forces that would undermine these capabilities.

The robustness of U.S. forces is a measure of the difficulty the Soviet Union would encounter in trying to reduce U.S. security.[36] All else being equal, the more easily U.S. security could be jeopardized by changes in Soviet forces, the less desirable the situation. A world that would be highly desirable if the two countries' forces could be held fixed, but that lacks robustness, might not be preferable to one that is less desirable when the forces are fixed, but that is more robust.

I have already discussed the lack of robustness of a world in which both superpowers have deployed perfect defenses. This section extends that analysis to mutual deployment of near-perfect defenses. The conclusion remains the same: BAD would be much less robust than MAD and would therefore suffer the military and political dangers created by strategic windows.

The following discussion compares the difficulty the Soviet Union would have undermining the U.S. ability to deter premeditated Soviet attacks in BAD and MAD. It assumes that the requirement for deterrence of premeditated attack (that is, the equal countervalue requirement) is initially satisfied. The U.S. ability to deter premeditated attacks could be undermined by improvements in Soviet defenses that reduced the U.S. ability to retaliate, and by improvements in Soviet offenses that increased the vulnerability of the U.S. homeland.

The robustness of U.S. nuclear forces to these changes in Soviet forces depends upon two related factors. The first is the magnitude of the change in potential countervalue damage required for the Soviet Union to be less deterred from launching a premeditated attack. For example, how large an increase in Soviet countervalue capability is required to provide a significant advantage? The second factor is the technical difficulty the Soviet Union

[36] "Arms race stability" is the standard measure of this characteristic of a country's forces. I use the term "robustness" to avoid the confusion that often surrounds this term. Arms race stability brings to mind at least two issues that are related to robustness but are conceptually distinct. First, arms race stability is often considered an indicator of the likelihood and/or intensity of arms races that will occur in a specific nuclear situation. Arms races, however, can occur for a variety of reasons that are only peripherally related to the effect that the adversary's buildup of nuclear forces might have on one's security. Consequently, arms races can occur in highly robust nuclear situations, as has happened in our current world of highly redundant and diversified assured destruction capabilities.

Second, using the term "arms race stability" can connote a belief that arms races cause wars. However, one can assert that the probability of war depends on the robustness of the nuclear situation without believing that, in general, arms races cause wars. Assuming a force buildup takes place either competitively or unilaterally, a war is more likely when countries' necessary capabilities are more sensitive to changes in the adversary's forces. Further, such a buildup is more likely when robustness is low. Of course, beyond these military dangers, analysts who hold a spiral model view of the world will see political dangers in this intensified competition.

would have in achieving this increase. For example, assuming that acquiring a useful advantage requires the Soviet Union to increase its countervalue capability by fifty warheads, how difficult would this be to accomplish? The combination of these two factors determines the overall difficulty of acquiring a strategic advantage. Both factors tend to make BAD less robust than MAD.

My discussion of perfect defenses focused on the first factor, the magnitude of the change, and argued that even small countervalue changes could be strategically significant. Situations in which imperfect defenses had been deployed would suffer from the same sensitivity, although less severely. Imagine three cases: (1) both superpowers have impenetrable defenses; (2) each can penetrate the other's defense with ten warheads; and (3) today's world, in which both superpowers have assured destruction capabilities. Now imagine an improvement in Soviet forces enabling fifty additional warheads to penetrate. The addition to Soviet capabilities would be most significant in the case of impenetrable defenses. Fifty penetrating warheads would provide the Soviet Union with a large advantage in the ability to inflict damage. Its still impenetrable defense would enable the Soviet Union to attack the United States without fearing retaliation and to threaten attack with high credibility. If the superpowers started with ten penetrating warheads, the addition of fifty penetrating warheads to the Soviet capability would be less dangerous for the United States, although still worrisome. The change would significantly increase the Soviet countervalue capability, quite possibly providing an advantage in coercive capability. However, the U.S. ability to retaliate would reduce the coercive value of the Soviet advantage. By contrast, in MAD the addition of fifty warheads to the Soviet arsenal is insignificant—thousands of new warheads would not significantly increase the Soviet ability to damage the United States.

In general, the less vulnerable the United States is to Soviet attack, the more sensitive its security is to improvements in Soviet capabilities.[37] This conclusion can be restated specifically in terms of defenses: the smaller the number of warheads that could penetrate the countries' defenses, the more sensitive U.S. security would be to improvements in the Soviet ability to penetrate its defenses. As a result, BAD tends to be less robust than MAD.

The technical difficulty of gaining a strategic advantage depends upon size of the requisite change. Since the size of requisite change is much larger in MAD than in a world of near-perfect defenses, the Soviet Union would likely have a much harder time gaining an advantage today than in BAD.

Other considerations reinforce this conclusion. Whereas staying in BAD requires the United States to maintain highly survivable defenses that are

---

[37] This is not to argue that the United States would necessarily be less secure when it is less vulnerable, for if war occurs, it would be less costly. I examine this tradeoff in more detail in the following section.

nearly perfect, maintaining its assured destruction capability requires only that a small fraction of the U.S. countervalue force be able to reach the Soviet Union. In BAD, the Soviet Union can require the United States to deploy increasingly effective defenses simply by enlarging its countervalue force or by adding countermeasures to defeat U.S. strategic defenses. Increasing the effectiveness of defenses tends to increase their cost at the margin,[38] making it more difficult for the United States to offset changes in Soviet offenses. Thus, even if near-perfect defenses are deployed, the prospects for maintaining low vulnerability promise to be small. In contrast, the U.S. assured destruction capability is relatively easy to maintain. In MAD, it is not necessary that a large percentage of the U.S. offense penetrate Soviet defenses. Instead, the offense needs only to get 100 or possibly a few hundred weapons through Soviet defenses. Consequently, the Soviet Union is likely to face a much greater technical challenge in trying to defeat the U.S. assured destruction capability than in trying to defeat near-perfect U.S. defenses.[39]

Further, the countries' ability to diversify their countervalue forces makes MAD easier to maintain while making BAD harder to maintain. In MAD, diversifying one's offense increases the challenge facing the adversary's defense. For example, to deny the United States the ability to inflict high levels of damage, Soviet defenses must be highly effective against both ballistic missiles and strategic bombers. In contrast, just the opposite is true in BAD: since the ability to penetrate with a single type of delivery system can eliminate low vulnerability, the adversary's ability to diversify its offense works against BAD. For example, if near-perfect BMD were technologically feasible but defenses against bombers and cruise missile were impossible, the superpowers would remain in MAD. Thus, to preserve its low vulnerability in BAD, the United States must be able to continue to defeat improvements in *all* types of Soviet delivery vehicles.

To increase the robustness of its defenses in BAD, the United States could diversify its defenses against each of the Soviet offenses. The advantage in this diversification race would remain with the offense, however. The number of improvements in offense required to defeat the adversary's defense is determined by the type of offense facing the least diversified defense. Thus, in BAD the success of diversifying defenses depends heavily on one's ability to diversify defenses against each of the adversary's offenses. For example, assume that the United States wanted to force the Soviet Union to make three technological breakthroughs before it could overwhelm the U.S. defense. If the Soviet Union had two offenses with different penetration modes, then the U.S. objective would require six defenses, three against each penetration

---

[38] On this point see Carter, *Directed Energy Missile Defense in Space*, pp. 45–46.

[39] Chapter Five provides a more complete discussion of the factors that favor retaliatory capabilities over damage-limitation capabilities.

mode.[40] By comparison, in MAD, three offenses with different penetration modes are sufficient to force the Soviet Union to make three technological breakthroughs in defense. Thus, for what could be termed "structural" reasons, BAD would be harder to make as resistant to change as MAD.[41]

In short, BAD would lack robustness for two reasons: relatively small changes in vulnerability could threaten one's security, and these changes could be achieved relatively easily both because they are small and because a variety of factors combine to make preventing changes in BAD harder than in MAD.

A lack of robustness would not be so dangerous if the United States and the Soviet Union lacked incentives to try to alter the nuclear balance. A political environment that encouraged cooperation would reduce the need to make BAD resistant to change. But, as with the case of perfect defense, in a world of near-perfect defenses the superpowers would feel tremendous pressure to try to defeat the adversary's defenses. Even in the unlikely event that BAD was highly robust, neither superpower could have high confidence in this robustness: a country could not be sure that offenses that could undermine its defenses could not be developed. Neither superpower could overlook this uncertainty because the change required to gain a strategic advantage would still be small and the adversary's incentive to pursue a strategic advantage would be obvious. As a result, while proponents of strategic defense promise a more stable and less frightening world, in fact, in BAD the United States would be unable to satisfy its security requirements with high confidence and superpower competition would be much more intense than in MAD.

Given the pressures generated by this strategic environment, the superpowers would have great difficulty reaching arms control agreements that would increase the robustness of BAD. When security is sensitive to small variations in forces, cooperation will seem especially risky.[42] The prospects for arms control in BAD appear especially poor when we consider the superpowers' experience with strategic arms control in MAD. Although they have achieved some useful agreements, neither country's security was sensitive to a complete and rapid failure of these agreements. Both countries retained highly robust—redundant and diversified—retaliatory capabilities. Nevertheless, negotiations have progressed slowly, agreements achieved during the 1970s and 1980s

[40] For simplicity, this example assumes that each type of defense is effective against only one of the adversary's offensive penetration modes. Relaxing this assumption does not weaken the overall argument.

[41] Closely related, when its defenses are not diversified, a country's low vulnerability is susceptible to catastrophic failure, because one offensive breakthrough by the adversary could render one's country vulnerable to large attacks.

[42] Recall that offense dominance tends to make cooperation more difficult; offense-defense differentiability would tend to have an offsetting effect, but with offensive breakthroughs believed to be imminent, cooperation would remain exceedingly difficult.

were modest, and ambitious proposals have failed.[43] Because the military demands would be so severe, there are strong reasons for being pessimistic about the prospects for arms control in BAD. The spiral effects of intense competition would only make matters worse.

Having raised the possibility of arms control, I should distinguish between two cases in which strategic defenses play some role in reducing the superpowers' vulnerability to attack. In the first, addressed in this chapter, the superpowers do not need to cooperate to reduce their vulnerability since each country's strategic defense can win the race against the other's countervalue forces. This relationship between the countries' capabilities is most important in a world in which the superpowers engage in military competition. If they were not competing, then the ability of strategic defense to defeat countervalue forces would not be tested and might be unimportant. In the second case, strategic defenses are far less effective. If, however, there is agreement to limit offenses, then defenses might play a role in helping the superpowers reduce their vulnerability. Here the key to reduced vulnerability is cooperation, not defense; this case shares more with disarmament than with BAD.

This distinction is important since, contrary to proponents' claims, deploying defenses in the foreseeable future is unlikely to encourage such extensive cooperation. The far more likely result is that defenses will make it much more difficult to reduce offenses.[44] Each country's defense reduces the ability of the adversary's countervalue forces to perform their missions, thus increasing the marginal value of warheads. On the other hand, once the superpowers are already committed to reducing their societal vulnerability through arms control, defenses might help reduce the risks of cooperating.[45] But these necessary conditions for ambitious arms control do not exist today and defenses will not create them.

Overall, then, the probability of nuclear war would be greater in BAD than in MAD. In static conditions, the United States might be able to deter premeditated nuclear attacks and maintain crisis stability as well in BAD as in MAD. In many cases, however, defenses would decrease crisis stability relative to MAD, with special dangers and complications created by vulnerable defenses. Probably more important, the world would not be static and the superpowers would compete intensely for strategic advantage, or at least to prevent one another from gaining one. Because BAD would be far less robust than MAD, this military competition would be more likely to create conditions and opportunities for a nuclear war.

---

[43] For qualifications and extensions of these observations see Chapter Ten.

[44] Chapter Nine explores this issue in detail. See also Albert Carnesale, "Special Supplement: The Strategic Defense Initiative," in George E. Hudson and Joseph Kruzel, eds., *American Defense Annual: 1985–1986* (Lexington, Mass.: Lexington Books, 1985), p. 220.

[45] Chapter Six examines the role of defenses in "reinforcing disarmament" and argues that defenses could create more problems than they solve.

COULD DEFENSES CREATE A PREFERABLE NUCLEAR WORLD?

A comparison of alternative worlds requires a measure that combines two U.S. security objectives: minimizing the probability of war and minimizing the costs if war occurs. These objectives should be evaluated simultaneously.[46] Examining either dimension alone is insufficient to understand the net effect of a shift from MAD to BAD. For example, a policy that would reduce the damage of a nuclear attack, but would also increase its probability, might not improve U.S. security. The correct measure of security is the expected cost of war, defined as the probability of war multiplied by the cost if it occurs.

It is crucial to keep these two aspects of U.S. security in mind when analyzing defenses. Much of the debate over BMD tends to ignore the need for simultaneous evaluation. Proponents emphasize the reductions in damage that defenses might provide. Opponents argue that deploying BMD would increase the probability of nuclear war by undermining deterrence and decreasing crisis stability. Neither argument is sufficient for drawing a conclusion about area defenses: each looks at only one aspect of U.S. security. Previous sections examined the probability of war. Here we compare its costs in BAD and MAD and consider the tradeoffs that are required to reach a conclusion about which world is preferable.

If U.S. security depended only on the probability of nuclear war, then, since the probability of war would be higher in BAD, mutual deployment of highly effective defenses would decrease U.S. security. However, because defenses would decrease the damage of certain wars, they would have some positive effects as well as negative ones.

To examine these issues in greater detail, consider the possible paths to nuclear war. Begin by assuming that the superpowers' forces are held constant, the superpowers have deployed near-perfect defenses, and the equal countervalue requirement is satisfied. The Soviet Union might launch a premeditated attack even when the requirements of deterrence are satisfied; this is true today, when both superpowers have assured destruction capabilities, and it would be true in BAD. The damage in an all-out countervalue war would be lower in BAD. Since the probability of premeditated nuclear war might not be greater in this world of near-perfect defenses, the expected cost along this path to nuclear war could be lower than in MAD.

In BAD the damage from a preemptive war could be lower than in MAD.[47] The probability of preemptive war, and therefore the expected cost of a preemptive attack, would depend on the level of crisis stability. If BAD were less

---

[46] On this point see Snyder, *Deterrence and Defense*, p. 4–5.

[47] By definition the costs of countervalue retaliation following preemptive attack would be lower in BAD than in MAD. There are, however, cases in which the collateral damage from a preemptive attack would be higher in BAD than MAD. How the total costs in these wars compare depends upon how the superpowers fight following the preemptive attack.

stable in crises than MAD, then the probability of preemptive attack would be higher. In this case, BAD would have a higher probability of preemptive attack and lower costs if the preemptive attack occurred. Therefore, it is unclear whether the expected cost from preemptive war would be greater in BAD or MAD. If, on the other hand, BAD were as stable in a crisis as MAD (which is possible if the retaliatory capabilities and defenses are invulnerable), then the expected cost along the preemptive path would probably be lower than in MAD.

Now suppose the superpowers' forces are not held constant. In this case, both the United States and the Soviet Union might deploy forces that increase their adversary's vulnerability or decrease their own. Unlike the preceding case, the damage in BAD might not be lower than in MAD. Although the adversaries begin in a world of near-perfect defenses, the damage of war is not constrained by the status quo forces. The superpower competition might restore one or both countries' assured destruction capabilities. If the Soviet Union could build out of BAD (i.e., regain its assured destruction capability), then the United States might suffer costs as high as in MAD. Therefore, the expected cost of nuclear wars resulting along this path could be greater in BAD than in MAD since BAD's lack of robustness increases the probability of war.

Defenses might also reduce the costs of an accidental Soviet attack or an attack launched by another state with nuclear weapons. Assuming that defenses do not somehow increase the probability of these attacks, they would reduce the expected cost along these paths.

All in all, although defenses could reduce the damage done by certain types of wars, this positive effect would tend to be offset by the increased probability of wars resulting from the lack of robustness of BAD and possibly from a reduction in crisis stability. Consequently, the net result of both superpowers deploying near-perfect defenses might be to decrease U.S. security. This outcome seems especially likely because BAD would generate intense military competition that would lead to hostile political relations.

This conclusion runs counter to the commonly held belief that BAD, and so-called defense dominance, would be clearly preferable to MAD. Even after making the best case for defenses (that is, ignoring questions of technical and economic feasibility, the effect on the probability of superpower conventional wars, and a number of other issues discussed briefly at the end of this chapter), MAD is probably preferable to a world in which the superpowers' defenses drastically reduced their vulnerability to nuclear attack.[48]

[48] This analysis also leads to another controversial conclusion: the transition from MAD to BAD might be less dangerous than the endpoint. For a detailed discussion see Charles L. Glaser, "Managing the Transition," in Samuel F. Wells and Robert S. Litwak, eds., *Strategic Defenses and Soviet-American Relations* (Cambridge, Mass.: Ballinger, 1987). Also analyzing the transition are Glenn A. Kent and Randall J. DeValk, *Strategic Defense and the Transition to Assured Survival*, R-3369-AF (Santa Monica: Rand, October 1986), and Dean Wilkening, Kenneth Wat-

The policy implications of this conclusion are obvious, and profound. Whether the United States could be more secure in a world of highly effective defenses should no longer be viewed primarily as a technological issue. The United States should examine more completely the strategic and political issues associated with defense against nuclear attack before deciding to pursue such a fundamental change in nuclear strategy.

ADDITIONAL PROBLEMS WITH STRATEGIC DEFENSE

Several additional factors further weaken the case for pursuing highly effective defense.

Uncertainty

The effectiveness of U.S. defenses would be uncertain and small uncertainties would be highly significant. In addition to the uncertainties inherent in the operations of complex systems, the effectiveness of defenses would be uncertain due to the severe limits on testing. The defense could not be tested against a full-scale attack or against Soviet offenses. And while estimates could be made of effectiveness against deployed Soviet offenses, there would always be reasonable questions about Soviet penetration aids that could be quickly added to their offensive force.

Small uncertainties would be significant because, with the large counter-value forces that are currently deployed, a small difference in the percentage of penetrating weapons would translate into a large difference in destructive potential. The uncertainties involved with a defense that was in fact perfect would probably be large enough to leave the United States unsure about whether it was vulnerable to an annihilating attack by the Soviet Union. While the strategic implications of uncertainty are ambiguous—in some cases it might enhance deterrence—uncertainty about necessary capabilities would frighten political leaders and exacerbate superpower tensions.

Uncertainty would affect U.S. policy in a number of ways. First, the United States would never feel adequately defended (nor would the Soviet Union). Even without uncertainties, there would always be arguments that the United States needed additional defense to improve its protection against Soviet attacks and as a hedge against Soviet offensive breakthroughs. These arguments would be more telling than those made about the inadequacy of today's strategic nuclear forces since the capability to defeat attacks against the United States would start to become redundant only once American defenses were perfect. The existence of uncertainties would probably result in unrelenting requests for additional defenses, yet fulfilling these requests would yield little

man, Michael Kennedy, and Richard Darilek, ''Strategic Defenses and First-Strike Stability,'' *Survival* 29, no. 2 (March/April 1987).

satisfaction and add little to the public's sense of security. Because uncertainties would persist, even fantastic advances in strategic defense would do little to reduce domestic fear of nuclear war.

Second, uncertainty would fuel fears that the Soviet Union had a superior defensive capability. Prudent military analysis could require assessing uncertainties in favor of Soviet defense and against U.S. defense. As a result, even if the United States and Soviet Union had comparable capabilities for protecting their homelands, the United States could not be confident that it was maintaining capabilities adequate to deter the Soviet Union. This conclusion would contribute to the demands for improving defenses.

This uncertainty might not increase the probability of war: if both countries employed these conservative assumptions, uncertainty might reduce the danger of low robustness. On the other hand, if political leaders believed that these uncertainties created strategic inferiority, they might feel pressure to run greater risks to protect their basic interests. This could increase the probability of war.

Allies

Any comprehensive analysis of BAD must consider the reaction of U.S. allies and the implications for their security.[49] One issue of great importance to them has already been raised, that is, the effect of defenses on the probability of conventional war. If strategic defense were believed to increase the probability of conventional war, then we should expect tremendous resistance from our European allies. Many expect a conventional war in Europe to be so costly that it is barely less unacceptable than a nuclear war. A second concern focuses on the vulnerability of allies to nuclear attack. A policy that drastically reduces U.S. vulnerability while leaving our European and other allies highly vulnerable cannot look good from their perspective. A third concern would be the effect of defenses on the independent deterrent capabilities of the French, British, and Chinese. A highly effective but imperfect Soviet defense would leave the United States with a modest retaliatory capability, but would probably eliminate the value of these independent deterrents.

Suitcase Bombs and Future Nonnuclear Technologies

The ability to defend effectively against ballistic missiles, cruise missiles, and bombers could greatly increase the importance of clandestinely delivered nuclear weapons. Nuclear bombs could be placed on Soviet ships and commer-

[49] For a discussion of the likely alliance reactions to extensive U.S. homeland defense see Ivo H. Daalder and Lynn Page Whittaker, "SDI's Implications for Europe: Strategy, Politics, and Technology," in Stephen J. Flanagan and Fen Osler Hampson, eds., *Securing Europe's Future* (London: Croom Helm, 1986), and David S. Yost, "Ballistic Missile Defense and the Atlantic Alliance," *International Security* 7, no. 2 (Fall 1982): 154–58.

cial airplanes, or could be carried into the United States by Soviet agents. These alternative types of delivery are possible today, but are not of great importance due to the large Soviet ballistic missile and air-breathing threats.

These alternative forms of delivery would not necessarily render defense useless: the Soviet ability to clandestinely deliver weapons in a crisis might be severely limited; hiding weapons before a crisis would be risky unless early detection was known to be impossible; and the damage from clandestine attacks might be less extensive than is currently possible without defenses. Still, the observation that defense against the delivery systems that are most important today would not eliminate vulnerability to nuclear attack raises basic issues about strategic defense. What threats must the United States be able to defend against? How would a "partial defense," that is, a defense against standard delivery systems, affect the political and military uses of nuclear weapons? How would the United States deter clandestine attacks—would credible retaliatory threats be available?

In addition, we need to consider future nonnuclear means of mass destruction. These might be biological or chemical weapons that are far more destructive than varieties now developed. Moreover, entirely new types of destructive capabilities might be invented. Would future strategic defenses that work against nuclear capabilities also be highly effective against these as yet unknown threats? If not, then the United States might be just as vulnerable as it is today.

Multipolarity

In the future the United States might face many adversaries possessing large nuclear arsenals capable of surviving attack. Would the United States be more secure in a multipolar world of countries with perfect or near-perfect defenses or in a multipolar world of countries with assured destruction capabilities?

To begin with, we need to reconsider our definitions of perfect and near-perfect defenses. A defense that is perfect against one country's offense might provide essentially no protection when attacked by two or more large nuclear powers. For example, by combining forces two U.S. adversaries might be able to overwhelm America's defenses, leaving all of its cities vulnerable to attack. Is this a perfect defense or no defense at all? While recognizing this ambiguity, I will term this a perfect defense. Similarly, an imperfect defense that is capable of eliminating one adversary's assured destruction capability will be considered near-perfect.

Highly effective defenses run into problems in a multipolar world that would not exist in a bipolar world. First, the requirements for deterring a premeditated attack cannot be satisfied by all countries. In BAD, both countries can have equal countervalue capabilities, and a position of parity is sufficient to allow the United States to maintain the capabilities required for deterrence. In a multipolar world this would no longer be possible. If each country has an equal countervalue capability against each of its adversaries, then it lacks such a capability against an alliance of adversaries.[50]

In contrast, this problem could be avoided in a multipolar world of countries with assured destruction capabilities. Each country could maintain an assured destruction capability against all of its adversaries. More than an assured destruction capability would be unnecessary since the redundancy of adversaries' forces does not pose an increased threat.

The possibility of each superpower maintaining forces sufficient to deter all of its adversaries, even against the most threatening alliance, makes strategic nuclear multipolarity quite different from prenuclear multipolarity. Kenneth Waltz argues that the danger in multipolar worlds stems from uncertainty:

> With three or more powers flexibility of alliances keeps relations of friendship and enmity fluid and makes everyone's estimate of the present and future relation of forces uncertain. So long as the system is one of fairly small numbers, the actions of any of them may threaten the security of others. . . . [In contrast, in bipolarity] states are less likely to misjudge the strength and reliability of opposing coalitions. Rather than making states properly cautious and forwarding the chances of peace, uncertainty and miscalculation cause wars.[51]

This danger of multipolarity might not arise in a world of many states with highly redundant assured destruction capabilities, but would exist in a multipolar world of near-perfect defenses.

This last point leads us directly to the second danger of a multipolar world with near-perfect defenses: the robustness of U.S. forces would be even more tenuous in this world than in a bipolar world. There would be more countries that could defeat U.S. defenses, making low vulnerability more difficult to maintain than in a bipolar world. Further, U.S. security would depend heavily upon alliances. If it could not maintain its share of allies, the United States would fall into strategic inferiority. Unless alliances are quite inflexible, which is unlikely in a world of true multipolarity, the United States will have little confidence in the future adequacy of its forces.

Once again, a multipolar world of assured destruction capabilities would not encounter these problems—U.S. forces could be quite robust. A highly redundant force could be made relatively insensitive to changes in adversaries' forces and the United States would not need to depend upon superpower allies. In addition, this world would be less competitive and provide greater opportunities for arms control than would a world of highly effective defenses.

Any final conclusions about these multipolar worlds must consider that war occurring in the defensive world might be less costly than in the assured de-

---

[50] Dyson, *Weapons and Hope*, p. 284, makes a similar observation.

[51] Kenneth N. Waltz, *Theory of International Politics* (New York: Random House, 1979), pp. 163–76, quote from p. 168. See also Waltz, "The Stability of a Bipolar World," *Daedalus* 93, no. 3 (Summer 1964): 881–909.

struction world. Still, the difficulties of maintaining adequate capabilities, and the intense competition this is sure to generate, counts heavily against the multipolar world of highly effective defenses.

CONCLUSION

Strategic defense and the prospect of being invulnerable to nuclear attack have undeniable appeal. But there is no excuse for being romantic or unrealistic about the nature of a world in which the superpowers have built tens of thousands of nuclear weapons and sophisticated delivery systems. Strategic defense cannot return us to a prenuclear world. BAD has not been studied as carefully or extensively as MAD. There are, however, reasons to believe that BAD would be more complex and more difficult to manage than MAD.

The best of worlds in which both superpowers have perfect or near-perfect defenses would not be so good and would probably not be preferable to today's world of redundant assured destruction capabilities: in all but the case of perfect defense, the United States would still depend upon deterrence by retaliation for its security; BAD's lack of robustness would make it sensitive to small changes in forces and would create strong incentives for both countries to pursue threatening improvements in countervalue forces, which would then increase the probability of nuclear war; the probability of large conventional wars between the superpowers and their allies would probably increase; and the threat posed by clandestinely delivered nuclear weapons would be much more significant than today.

Any serious policy for deploying defenses must address the dangers that would result from the difficulty of maintaining the low vulnerability of U.S. society. Even if defenses greatly reduced U.S. vulnerability, it is hard to imagine how this capability could be made highly robust. The lack of robustness will be particularly dangerous because BAD will be a highly competitive world in which the superpowers find cooperation extremely difficult.

This brings to the forefront the issue of U.S.-Soviet relations in a world of highly effective defenses. Statements by former President Reagan and other proponents of BMD have suggested that effective strategic defenses would eliminate the need for nuclear weapons that could be employed against the adversary's society.[52] This outcome is extremely unlikely. A more realistic assessment is that deploying defenses would lead to an intense competition between the superpowers' strategic nuclear forces and to tense, strained superpower relations. Arms control agreements to limit or reduce countervalue nuclear forces would be difficult, if not impossible, to negotiate. Careful thought should be given to whether in BAD a cooperative relationship between the superpowers would be possible, and to whether the pressures for confron-

---

[52] *New York Times*, 30 March 1983, p. 14.

tation could be kept low. If, as I believe, these would be impossible, then the prospects for improving U.S. security by shifting to a world of effective defenses must be judged to be especially gloomy.

No evidence indicates that the U.S. interest in highly effective defense is based upon a complete analysis of a world of near-perfect defense. Unfortunately, a world in which both superpowers deployed effective defense is far less attractive than its proponents suggest. Even on the most optimistic assumptions, BAD would probably be less secure than MAD; and with more realistic assumptions, we find that deploying BMD would definitely reduce U.S. security.

Until a convincing argument is presented for this fundamental change in U.S. nuclear weapons policy, the United States should severely restrain its enthusiasm and funding for strategic defense, attempt to repair the damage that is likely to have occurred in Soviet understanding of U.S. nuclear weapons policy, and pursue with renewed determination a prudent policy of offensive weapons acquisition and arms control.

CHAPTER FIVE

Why U.S. Superiority Is Probably Inferior to MAD

WOULD A WORLD in which the United States had strategic nuclear superiority—the ability to protect at least some of its cities while maintaining its assured destruction capability against Soviet society—be preferable to the current world of Mutual Assured Destruction?

The desirability of U.S. strategic superiority is a question that is rarely addressed explicitly. Superiority is most often debated in terms of the feasibility or infeasibility of attaining it. In fact, virtually the entire case against pursuing strategic superiority has been based on its technical infeasibility. As discussed in earlier chapters, available assessments are quite pessimistic about U.S. prospects for regaining superiority—they find that even intense competition between U.S. damage-limitation capabilities and Soviet retaliatory capabilities would almost certainly leave the United States stuck in MAD.

Despite the exceedingly poor prospects for achieving superiority, the concept of strategic superiority continues to exert a powerful influence on the nuclear debate. In large part this is because the conventional wisdom holds that U.S. superiority would alleviate MAD's two most serious shortcomings and therefore is preferable to MAD. First, it would restore the credibility of U.S. extended deterrent threats that was lost when the Soviets deployed an assured destruction capability in the mid to late 1960s.[1] Second, superiority would reduce the cost to the United States in an all-out nuclear war.[2]

---

[1] On the problems created by MAD see, for example, Henry A. Kissinger, "NATO: The Next Thirty Years," *Survival* 21, no. 6 (November/December 1979): 264–68. Questioning how good this supposed period of advantage looked to U.S. leaders is Richard K. Betts, "A Nuclear Golden Age? The Balance before Parity," *International Security* 11, no. 3 (Winter 1986–87): 3–32. Questioning the value of nuclear threats during this period are McGeorge Bundy, "The Unimpressive Record of Atomic Diplomacy," in Gywn Prins, *The Nuclear Crisis Reader* (New York: Vintage Books, 1984), and Morton Halperin, *Nuclear Fallacy: Dispelling the Myth of Nuclear Superiority* (Cambridge, Mass.: Ballinger, 1987), pp. 23–47. On the constraints U.S. leaders felt during this period see John Lewis Gaddis, "The Origins of Self-Deterrence: The United States and the Non-Use of Nuclear Weapons, 1945–1958," in his *The Long Peace* (Oxford: Oxford University Press, 1987). Reviewing U.S. policy during this period is Harland B. Moulton, *From Superiority to Parity: The United States and the Strategic Arms Race, 1961–1971* (Westport, Conn.: Greenwood Press, 1973).

[2] In addition, proponents argue that superiority would further reduce the probability of nuclear war by enabling the United States to compel the Soviets to terminate a conventional war on acceptable terms. On war termination see Linton F. Brooks, "Conflict Termination through Maritime Leverage," in Stephen J. Cimbala and Keith A. Dunn, eds., *Conflict Termination and Military Strategy* (Boulder, Colo.: Westview, 1987), but note however, that his argument is based on the implications of superiority in force ratios, not in the ability to limit damage.

Taking these arguments a step further, members of the damage-limitation school argue that the United States cannot adequately protect its interests in MAD. They believe that U.S. strategic nuclear forces now contribute little or nothing to deterring Soviet attacks against Western Europe and other areas of vital interest. According to these analysts, this creates a severe shortfall, since NATO's conventional forces are incapable of defending Western Europe. Proponents of superiority therefore conclude that it is not only desirable, but necessary. Colin Gray argues that "if there is no theory of political victory in the U.S. SIOP, then there can be little justification for nuclear planning at all. . . . If it is true, or at least probable, that a central war could be won or lost, then it has to follow that the concept of strategic superiority should be revived in popularity in the West.[3]

For many, the promise of superiority has held continued political attractiveness. The 1980 Republican Party Platform called for the United States "to achieve overall military and technical superiority over the Soviet Union" and claimed that "our strategy must encompass the levels of force required to deter each level of foreseeable attack and to prevail in conflict in the event deterrence fails."[4]

Moreover, the belief in the desirability of U.S. strategic superiority continues to influence U.S. nuclear policy in fairly explicit terms. For example, the Fiscal Year 1984–1988 Defense Guidance, which was developed early in the Reagan administration, is said to have called for the United States to have the ability to prevail in strategic nuclear war and to "force the Soviet Union to seek earliest termination of hostilities on terms favorable to the United States." According to the Defense Guidance this requires "plans that assure U.S. strategic nuclear forces can render ineffective the total Soviet, and Soviet allied, military and political power structure through attacks on political/military leadership and associated control facilities, nuclear and conventional forces and industry critical to military power."[5]

In addition, there may be greater support for pursuing superiority than is readily apparent in the nuclear debate. There is now substantial interest in

[3] Colin S. Gray, "Nuclear Strategy: The Case for a Theory of Victory," *International Security* 4, no. 1 (Summer 1979): 69, 82, 84–86. SIOP stands for the Single Integrated Operational Plan; it is the U.S. strategic nuclear warplan. For other recent proponents of this position see Chapter Two. For earlier arguments for such an asymmetric capability see Herman Kahn, *On Thermonuclear War* (Princeton: Princeton University Press, 1961).

[4] 1980 Republican Platform Text, p. 20, reprinted in *Congressional Quarterly*, 19 July 1980, p. 2049.

[5] George C. Wilson, " 'Preparing for Long Nuclear War Is Waste of Funds,' General Jones Says," *Washington Post*, 19 June 1982, p. 21. See also Richard Halloran, "Pentagon Draws Up First Strategy for Fighting a Long Nuclear War," *New York Times*, 30 May 1982, p. 1; idem, "Weinberger Confirms New Strategy on Atom War," *New York Times*, 4 June 1982, p. 10; and Secretary of Defense Caspar W. Weinberger, *Annual Report, FY 1983* (Washington, D.C.: GPO, February 8, 1982), p. I–18.

developing highly effective area-wide ballistic missile defenses, with the stated long-term goal of achieving a world in which both superpowers can protect themselves against full-scale nuclear attacks (BAD). However, many proponents of these strategic defenses probably prefer superiority to BAD. We might expect this since superiority would solve the key problems suffered by BAD: it enhances the U.S. ability to deter conventional war, while mutual defenses are said to make the world "safe for conventional war"; and, although both of these alternatives to MAD are sensitive to improvements in Soviet forces, superiority will appear less dangerous, since it promises to decay back into MAD, not into serious U.S. inferiority. Thus, although we tend to envision these alternatives to MAD as separate strategic options, U.S. decisions to move toward BAD would probably be converted into decisions to pursue superiority.

Although calls for U.S. superiority have been prominent since at least the late 1970s, the desirability of regaining superiority remains essentially unchallenged. Members of both the punitive retaliation and military denial schools believe that the United States can adequately protect its security in MAD, which provides grounds for questioning how much safer a world of superiority would be. Nevertheless, little in their arguments suggests that superiority would not be preferable.[6]

I am convinced that skeptics of superiority, by ignoring fundamental questions about its desirability, concede too easily half the argument against superiority. Arguing that superiority is infeasible fails to respond to key arguments for superiority. Some analysts conclude that even a slim prospect of gaining superiority is sufficient to warrant pursuing it, since living in MAD for the indefinite future poses unacceptable risks that superiority would eliminate. If, however, superiority is not preferable to MAD, then its feasibility is really of secondary importance. In addition, arguments in favor of strategic superiority, whether or not they are translated directly into proposals for developing and deploying forces, shift the center of debate and lend support to less ambitious but highly competitive policies.

This chapter analyzes the desirability of U.S. strategic superiority. The first section looks at possible types of superiority. The remaining sections of the chapter examine the effect of U.S. superiority on the probability of war. I assess the U.S. ability to deter premeditated attacks, maintain crisis stability, and maintain robust capabilities as the Soviets attempt to regain their assured destruction capability.

I find that there are four fundamental flaws in the case for the desirability of U.S. superiority: First, the benefits of nuclear superiority are dramatically

---

[6] The possible exception is their concern that U.S. damage-limitation capabilities would reduce crisis stability. However, as discussed later in this chapter, their arguments concerning this are flawed.

overrated. The U.S. already has a highly effective deterrent to major Soviet aggression. Consistent with the positions presented by the punitive retaliation school, I argue that the combination of extensive conventional capabilities, theater nuclear forces and a flexible assured destruction capability are sufficient to deter the Soviet Union from attacking U.S. vital interests. Thus, at most, U.S. superiority could only slightly reduce the probability of superpower war. Second, U.S. superiority could reduce crisis stability. If U.S. damage-limitation capabilities are vulnerable, then the Soviet Union would have a "back-to-MAD" capability that could generate preemptive incentives. Third, U.S. superiority would lack robustness. As a result, it would generate an intense arms race and strategic windows, which create incentives for preventive war. Finally, U.S. superiority, and the intensified military competition which it would generate, would increase Soviet insecurity and worsen superpower relations. This could make the Soviet Union more difficult to deter. As a result, even with enhanced U.S. nuclear capabilities, superiority could increase the probability of war. These dangers must be weighed against the possibility of reducing the costs of an all-out war. I conclude that in virtually all cases MAD is preferable to a world in which the United States had strategic superiority.

TYPES OF SUPERIORITY

In broad terms, the U.S. has superiority when it can deny the Soviet Union an assured destruction capability while maintaining its own assured destruction capability. In other words, U.S. superiority is distinguished from MAD by the U.S. ability to protect at least some of its cities.[7]

This definition rejects claims about superiority that are based on perceptions of superpower forces in MAD, including especially ratio arguments. Instead, as defined here, superiority is measured in terms of the superpowers' ability to inflict damage. Neither superpower can have superiority in MAD: when both superpowers have assured destruction capabilities, advantages in force size or number of counterforce weapons do not translate into significant advantages in the ability to inflict damage.

U.S. superiority could come in a variety of significantly different forms. Basic types of superiority are usefully distinguished along two dimensions (see the table below). The first dimension is the *effectiveness of the U.S. damage-limitation capability*.[8] At one extreme, the United States could have es-

---

[7] Broader definitions of superiority, covering cases in which the United States lacks an assured destruction capability but nevertheless maintains a significant strategic advantage over the Soviet Union, are possible. Recall, for example, the analysis of asymmetries in countervalue capability that might result from an arms race in BAD. For the purposes of this chapter, however, the more restricted definition is adequate.

[8] A more extensive typology might usefully cover additional dimensions, including the extent of U.S. decisionmakers' confidence in their damage-limitation capabilities, the vulnerability of

sentially perfect damage-limitation capabilities, which would leave at most a few U.S. cities vulnerable. At the other extreme, most U.S. cities would remain vulnerable but the Soviet Union would still lack an assured destruction capability. The category of imperfect U.S. damage-limitation capabilities is therefore quite wide, ranging from a small number of vulnerable cities to near total vulnerability of U.S. cities.

The second dimension is the *dependence of U.S. damage-limitation capabilities on striking first* against Soviet forces. Can the United States protect its cities only by first destroying some of the Soviet nuclear force before it is launched? Or, can it instead protect U.S. cities even if the Soviet Union launches a first strike against them?

Three degrees of dependence are important. U.S. damage limitation could be independent of striking first. Damage limitation in this case is achieved entirely by strategic defenses, including both ballistic missile and air defenses.[9] In contrast, the U.S. damage-limitation capability could be entirely dependent on striking first—U.S. cities are totally vulnerable to a Soviet first strike, but not to Soviet retaliation. This type of damage-limitation capability might rely entirely on offensive counterforce, that is, U.S. forces that can destroy Soviet forces before they are launched. On the other hand, this type of damage-limitation capability might combine strategic defenses with offensive counterforce; if it does, however, the strategic defenses are inadequate by

Types of Superiority

	Effectiveness of U.S. Damage-Limitation Capability	
	Perfect	Imperfect
Damage limitation entirely dependent on U.S. striking first	All U.S. cities vulnerable to Soviet first strike; invulnerable to Soviet retaliation	All U.S. cities vulnerable to Soviet first strike; some vulnerable to Soviet retaliation
Damage limitation partially dependent on U.S. striking first	Some U.S. cities vulnerable to Soviet first strike—U.S. has near-perfect defenses; invulnerable to Soviet retaliation	Some U.S. cities vulnerable to Soviet first strike; U.S. has near-perfect defenses; fewer cities vulnerable to retaliation
Damage limitation independent of whether U.S. strikes first	U.S. cities invulnerable to Soviet first strike—U.S. has perfect defense	Some U.S. cities vulnerable to Soviet first strike; same number vulnerable to second strike—U.S. lacks offensive counterforce

U.S. damage-limitation capabilities to Soviet attack, and a wider range of scenarios under which damage limitation might occur—including protracted conventional war and multiple counterforce exchanges.

[9] As discussed in Chapter Three, area-wide strategic defense should be considered a type of offense since, like offensive counterforce, it threatens the adversary's deterrent capability.

themselves to protect U.S. cities against a Soviet countervalue first strike. In between these possibilities is the case in which U.S. damage limitation depends partially on striking first—strategic defenses can protect some cities from a Soviet first strike, and striking first can further reduce American vulnerability.

U.S. superiority would most likely combine offensive counterforce and strategic defense, since in combination each faces a less difficult task. Proponents of superiority advocate U.S. deployment of both types of systems. Following sections employ the distinctions laid out here when the type of superiority influences its desirability.

WOULD U.S. SUPERIORITY REDUCE THE PROBABILITY OF WAR?

Using the framework developed in the previous chapter, this section analyzes claims that U.S. strategic superiority would reduce the probability of war. It assesses the U.S. ability to deter premeditated Soviet attacks, minimize crisis instability (and, more generally, the probability of preemptive war), and avoid the dangers of low robustness.

I undertake this analysis in two stages. First, these criteria are examined while assuming that U.S. superiority does not have broad political consequences. For example, this discussion assumes that U.S. superiority influences neither Soviet views of U.S. intentions nor the superpowers' overall relationship. Thus, U.S. superiority does not change the value either superpower places on altering or maintaining the political status quo. In this world of U.S. superiority, superpower leaders are assumed to contemplate the same actions that they would in MAD, and to place the same value on achieving them.

The second stage completes this analysis by including the possible political consequences of U.S. nuclear superiority. In fact, most analysts believe that highly competitive American military policies would have consequences for superpower relations, but disagree about whether the consequences would be positive or negative. I argue that although there is some uncertainty, the spiral model is likely to be correct in predicting that highly competitive U.S. policies would generate negative political consequences. Thus, by excluding these political effects, the analysis that assumes that superpower politics remain essentially constant makes something of a best case for U.S. superiority.

Deterring Premeditated Attacks

U.S. superiority could enhance extended deterrence only slightly, since current U.S. capabilities are sufficient to deter Soviet conventional and nuclear attacks. At most, therefore, its benefits appear to be relatively small.

First, superiority is overrated because even in MAD U.S. strategic nuclear capabilities contribute significantly to deterrence of Soviet invasion of Western Europe. The possibility of U.S. escalation to the strategic nuclear level—although reduced by the vulnerability of the U.S. homeland—makes Soviet aggression enormously risky, since the costs of nuclear war would be so large. Soviet leaders recognize that a large conventional war could escalate in numerous unpredictable ways, both planned and inadvertent, to full-scale strategic nuclear war. Among other things, they are unlikely to ignore either that the United States has a variety of limited strategic nuclear options in addition to its assured destruction capability, or that fighting a large conventional war could generate pressures for escalation.[10] Thus, Soviet decisionmakers who believed that war could be avoided would almost certainly see the risks of initiating a large conventional war exceeding all possible benefits.

In other words, proponents of superiority greatly exaggerate the extent of the stability-instability paradox. MAD does not make the world safe for conventional war; U.S. flexible assured destruction capabilities deter more than attacks against the U.S. homeland. The damage-limitation school disagrees, but, as we saw in Chapter Two, the punitive retaliation school makes the stronger arguments.[11]

Second, even before recent reductions in Soviet conventional military capabilities, NATO's conventional and theater nuclear forces contributed extensively to deterrence of Soviet conventional attack against Western Europe. Contrary to conventional wisdom, analyses of NATO forces showed that the Soviets should doubt their ability to win a conventional war in Europe, especially a quick one.[12] The likelihood that NATO can deny the Soviets a quick

[10] Beyond the "fog of war" in general, leaders might, for example, worry about the interaction of command and control systems once on increasingly high alert, the limited endurance of nuclear forces on alert, and the inadvertent pressures generated by conventional operations. On the first, see Paul Bracken, *The Command and Control of Nuclear Forces* (New Haven: Yale University Press, 1983); on the last, see Barry R. Posen, "Inadvertent Nuclear War? Escalation and NATO's Northern Flank," *International Security* 7, no. 2 (Fall 1982): 28–54.

[11] We should recall also that the military denial school believes that U.S. extended deterrence requirements can be satisfied in MAD, although they require much more extensive capabilities than does the punitive retaliation school.

[12] Arguing that NATO's prospects are reasonably good are John J. Mearsheimer, "Why the Soviets Can't Win Quickly in Central Europe," *International Security* 7, no. 1 (Summer 1982): 3–39, and "Numbers, Strategy and the European Balance," *International Security* 12, no. 4 (Spring 1988): 174–85; Barry R. Posen, "Measuring the European Conventional Balance: Coping with Complexity in Threat Assessment," *International Security* 9, no. 3 (Winter 1984/85): 47–88; idem, "Is NATO Decisively Outnumbered?" *International Security* 12, no. 4 (Spring 1988): 186–202; Joshua M. Epstein, *The 1988 Defense Budget* (Washington, D.C.: Brookings Institution, 1987); and idem, "Dynamic Analysis and the Conventional Balance in Europe," *International Security* 12, no. 4 (Spring 1988): 154–65. For an opposing view see Elliot A. Cohen, "Toward Better Net Assessment: Rethinking the European Conventional Balance," *International Security* 13, no. 1 (Summer 1988): 50–89; see *International Security* 13, no. 4 (Spring 1989): 128–79 for responses by Mearsheimer, Posen, and Cohen. Raising a variety of important methodological points is Steven D. Biddle, "The European Conventional Balance: A Reinterpretation

victory in a European conventional war goes a long way toward deterring these attacks.[13] In addition, large numbers of theater nuclear weapons, deployed in support of NATO's doctrine of flexible response, make the possibility of nuclear war, and escalation to strategic nuclear war, still harder for Soviet leaders to overlook.

Proponents might challenge this conclusion, holding that the above arguments do not cover highly aggressive Soviet leaders. Thus, since we cannot be confident of current Soviet intentions and, more important, since a future Soviet leader might be bent on expansion, superiority provides the United States with valuable insurance. However, leaders who are willing to initiate a major war against an adversary capable of destroying their country are extremely rare. As Jervis notes, even Hitler would probably have been unwilling to run such large risks.[14] Thus, although superiority would be more valuable if the United States ever faced such a dangerous Soviet leader, its expected benefits are quite small because this case is so improbable. Furthermore, as discussed below, such risk-accepting Soviet leaders are most likely when Soviet security is severely threatened. Therefore, U.S. superiority might play a central role in creating the circumstances in which it might provide more than marginal benefits.

Third, and less general, superiority would fall short of providing even these limited benefits unless the United States acquires an essentially perfect, high-confidence damage-limitation capability that does not require striking first.[15] Superiority based on imperfect damage-limitation capabilities would enhance U.S. credibility less, since many U.S. cities and tens of millions of Americans could remain vulnerable to Soviet retaliation. The United States would not be vulnerable to virtual annihilation, but would remain vulnerable to unacceptable costs. When confronting large Soviet forces, small uncertainties about damage-limitation systems would raise doubts about whether the United States could actually protect any of its cities. If damage limitation depends on a massive U.S. first strike, the Soviets might overcome it by launching their forces on warning.[16] Soviet leaders, recognizing the potential costs and vast uncer-

---

of the Debate,'' *Survival* 30, no. 2 (March/April 1988): 99–121. Reviewing this debate is Charles A. Kupchan, "Setting Conventional Force Requirements: Roughly Right or Precisely Wrong," *World Politics* 41, no. 4 (July 1989): 536–78.

[13] On the requirements of conventional deterrence see John J. Mearsheimer, *Conventional Deterrence* (Ithaca: Cornell University Press, 1983).

[14] Robert Jervis, "Why Nuclear Superiority Doesn't Matter," *Political Science Quarterly* 94, no. 4 (Winter 1979–80): 622.

[15] Questioning whether the Soviet assured destruction capability and parity further reduced the credibility of U.S. threats is Warner R. Schilling, "U.S. Strategic Nuclear Concepts in the 1970s: The Search for Sufficiently Equivalent Countervailing Parity," *International Security* 6, no. 2 (Fall 1981): 63. See also Harold Brown, *Annual Report, FY 1981* (Washington, D.C.: GPO, 1980), p. 68.

[16] Further, in this case U.S. leaders would be less willing to employ LNOs coercively since a

tainties facing the United States, might question the U.S. willingness to escalate a conventional war, thereby robbing superiority of some of its increased credibility. This would be most serious when superiority might otherwise provide relatively large benefits—that is, if the United States ever faces a very risk-accepting Soviet leader.

Although all types of superiority are now beyond the U.S. reach, it is significant that the United States is least likely to acquire the types that would contribute most to deterrence: developing perfect damage-limitation capabilities promises to be especially difficult; not relying on striking first requires U.S. strategic defenses that are more effective; and eliminating uncertainties in such complex and untested systems would probably be impossible.

In sum, while the argument that superiority would enhance the credibility of U.S. extended deterrence threats is logically sound, the contribution to deterrence is much smaller than its proponents suggest. Given that the United States already has capabilities adequate for deterring the Soviet Union, superiority would not reduce the probability of premeditated attacks significantly.

Crisis Stability

A world of U.S. superiority would be plagued by crisis instability—a situation in which both countries prefer to strike first rather than be attacked first—if two conditions exist. First, the U.S. ability to limit damage is vulnerable to Soviet attack. In this case, the Soviets would have a "back-to-MAD" capability:[17] a Soviet counterforce attack could not reduce the U.S. ability to destroy Soviet cities, but could instead restore the Soviet ability to destroy American cities. For example, if the United States has strategic defenses that can protect its cities and the Soviet Union can destroy the defenses, the Soviets have a back-to-MAD capability. Second, the Soviet back-to-MAD capability is vulnerable to U.S. attack.

In combination, these conditions create first-strike incentives for both countries. Striking first enables the Soviets to fight their way back to MAD, thereby eliminating U.S. superiority. On the other hand, striking first against Soviet back-to-MAD capabilities enables the United States to secure its superiority. Thus, both countries would prefer to strike first than be attacked first. For the Soviets, striking first is the difference between returning to MAD and being locked into inferiority. For the United States, it is the difference between retaining superiority and returning to the high societal vulnerability of MAD. In a crisis, the combination of these first-strike incentives would create pressures for each side to launch a preemptive attack on the other before it was too late.

---

full-scale Soviet response would then overwhelm U.S. strategic defenses. Thus, the United States would have difficulty increasing the credibility of its nuclear threats by raising the prospect of a limited nuclear war that resulted in lower costs than all-out war.

[17] This term was coined by Stephen Van Evera.

An example helps to illustrate the pressures created by this type of situation. Consider a case in which the United States has deployed highly effective space-based strategic defenses that can protect American cities against a massive Soviet attack. The Soviet Union in turn has deployed antisatellite weapons that can destroy these American space-based systems. And finally, the United States has deployed weapons that can destroy the Soviet antisatellite weapons.[18] If the Soviet Union attacks first with its antisatellite weapons, it destroys the U.S. strategic defense and, with it, U.S. superiority. If the United States attacks first against Soviet antisatellite weapons, then the Soviets no longer have the capability to destroy American strategic defenses. They are left without options for escaping inferiority.

Before exploring these first-strike incentives in greater detail, it is useful to make two comparisons to MAD. First, a world of American superiority in which the Soviets have vulnerable back-to-MAD capabilities suffers greater crisis instability than MAD does. In MAD crisis instability is essentially eliminated, since neither superpower can significantly reduce the costs of an all-out war by attacking first. Thus, this type of nuclear superiority would lack one of MAD's important advantages.

Second, it is important to recognize that there are other types of U.S. superiority that, like MAD, would not suffer crisis instability. If the Soviet Union lacks a back-to-MAD capability, then U.S. damage-limitation capabilities would not reduce crisis stability. Without either damage limitation or back-to-MAD capabilities, the Soviet Union would lack first-strike incentives. In turn, the United States would not face pressures to launch a preemptive attack in a crisis.[19] Thus, the potential dangers created by U.S. damage-limitation capabilities could be quite different in a world of U.S. superiority than on the edges of MAD.[20] In the latter case, which has been the focus of most

[18] The Soviet antisatellite systems and the American threat to these systems could be either space-based or ground-based.

In another, somewhat more complicated example, vulnerable Soviet back-to-MAD capabilities are comprised of vulnerable Soviet ICBMs that could return them to MAD by destroying American offensive counterforce weapons that the United States relies on for damage limitation. If the United States attacks first, then the Soviets are left without a back-to-MAD capability, as well as diminished retaliatory capabilities. If the Soviets attack first against U.S. ICBMs, then they have restored their assured destruction capability if after destroying the American ICBMs they still hold enough forces in reserve for assured destruction. Of course, in this case U.S. damage-limitation capabilities depend on the Soviet Union not launching their forces on warning of American attack.

[19] Similar points are made by Keith B. Payne, ''Strategic Defense and Stability,'' *Orbis* 28, no. 2 (Summer 1984): 220. Many proponents of U.S. damage limitation, apparently having overlooked this argument, present less convincing reasons for not worrying about policies that create first-strike incentives—for example, that states do not act according to the predictions of theories of crisis instability.

[20] Opponents of superiority have tended to overlook this qualification. Instead, to the extent that their criticism has gone beyond infeasibility and addressed desirability, opponents have

concern about crisis instability, if both countries can reduce the costs of war by striking first, then there would be preemptive incentives in a crisis.[21]

When possessing back-to-MAD capabilities, Soviet first-strike incentives could reflect a variety of concerns. Returning to MAD would reduce the U.S. ability to coerce the Soviet Union during a crisis or conventional war. It would therefore help the Soviet Union protect its political interests. The Soviets might also strike first to reduce the probability of a U.S. attack against Soviet society. Although a Soviet first strike would not reduce the vulnerability of its homeland, Soviet leaders might expect U.S. attacks against their homeland to be more likely when the United States could protect its own homeland than when the vulnerability of American society had been restored by a Soviet back-to-MAD attack. Finally, if the U.S. damage-limitation capability would employ nuclear weapons against the Soviet homeland, then the Soviets might have additional first-strike incentives. Striking first would prevent the collateral damage from the U.S. attack, since the United States would no longer be able to launch it.

The United States could also have a variety of incentives for destroying the Soviet back-to-MAD capability. The United States might strike to enhance its power: as long as the Soviet Union could fight back to MAD, the United States would not enjoy the full political benefits of its advantage, and would be constrained from pressing too hard for Soviet concessions during a crisis or ongoing war. The United States might also attack Soviet back-to-MAD capabilities simply to reduce the costs of an all-out war. Finally, the United States might strike first to avoid the collateral damage from the Soviet back-to-MAD strike.

Based on these considerations, we would expect that both countries' first-strike incentives would increase with the effectiveness of U.S. damage-limitation capabilities. For the United States, first-strike incentives would increase because maintaining superiority promises greater reductions in the costs of an all-out war, and greater political benefits from locking-in Soviet inferiority. For the Soviets, the benefits of a back-to-MAD attack would increase since it enables them to avoid the greater coercive pressure and the higher probability of attacks against their homeland that would accompany more effective U.S. damage-limitation capabilities.

A Soviet decision to preempt would also depend on the probability that it would lead to U.S. escalation. For example, Soviet leaders might be more likely to preempt when the collateral damage from their attack would be lower, since the United States might be less likely to retaliate. Thus, an attack against

tended to argue incorrectly that U.S. damage-limitation capabilities would create preemptive incentives.

[21] For qualifications see Chapter Four.

U.S. space-based strategic defenses would be less risky, and therefore more attractive, than a nuclear attack against U.S. land-based counterforce.

How likely is it that U.S. superiority would be accompanied by vulnerable Soviet back-to-MAD capabilities, and therefore by crisis instability? This is impossible to judge with any confidence, since the prospects for technological breakthroughs that would provide the United States with a significant damage-limitation capability are by their nature unpredictable. Nevertheless, it is worth noting that it now appears that if highly effective strategic defenses are deployed, they are likely to include space-based components; furthermore, the prospects for making space-based defenses survivable are especially slim, and certain of the key threats to these strategic defenses would be space-based and vulnerable.[22] Thus, if American technologies currently under investigation ever advance far enough to provide the United States with highly effective strategic defenses, the chances are that the Soviet Union could deploy a back-to-MAD capability that would itself be vulnerable.

Finally, it is useful to note that even survivable Soviet back-to-MAD capabilities could create first-strike incentives. This could occur if the U.S. damage limitation depends on striking first and the Soviet back-to-MAD capability consists of the ability to destroy these American first-strike forces. This might occur, for example, if survivable Soviet space-based lasers could destroy the forces the United States would employ to destroy Soviet retaliatory capabilities, but could do little damage to U.S. cities. The United States would need to launch its damage-limitation attack before the Soviet lasers destroyed its first-strike forces, while the Soviets would want to attack first against the American offensive counterforce capability. Other survivable back-to-MAD capabilities do not create this type of first-strike incentive. If the U.S. superiority relies on a combination of offensive counterforce and strategic defenses, and if the Soviets can fight back to MAD by destroying U.S. strategic defenses, then they do not need to attack first. They could instead absorb the U.S. offensive counterforce attack, then return to MAD by destroying U.S. strategic defenses.[23] Further, if U.S. damage-limitation capabilities rely entirely on strategic defenses and not on striking first, then this question of Soviet first-strike incentives does not arise.[24]

[22] See Office of Technology Assessment, *SDI: Technology, Survivability and Software* (Washington, D.C.: GPO, May 1988).

[23] In fact, if Soviet back-to-MAD capabilities are survivable and do not depend on destroying U.S. offensive counterforce, then this case is actually a disguised form of MAD since both superpowers would know that the Soviets could fight back to MAD. Presumably, this would reduce or eliminate the deterrent and coercive advantages of the U.S. damage-limitation capability.

[24] Beyond the preemptive incentives discussed in this section, U.S. leaders might face a kind of "tactical window" that created pressure to launch a damage-limitation attack early in a superpower war. This could occur if Soviet attacks along other (non-preemptive) paths appeared sufficiently likely. Possible paths include a bargaining war in which the Soviets slowly attack U.S. cities, irrational Soviet escalation driven by crisis pressures, and a failure of Soviet command and

In sum, there are a variety of ways in which U.S. superiority could generate preemptive incentives. Although it is hard to predict exactly what a world of U.S. superiority would look like, such a world may well suffer dangerous crisis instability.

Robustness: The Danger of Strategic Windows

This section argues that U.S. superiority would be far less robust than MAD—that is, much harder to maintain in an arms race with the Soviet Union—and would therefore suffer dangers that do not exist in MAD. The probability of war depends not only on the military capabilities deployed at a given moment, but also on expectations about future capabilities. Because superiority would lack robustness, the United States would expect to lose its superiority; its declining military capabilities would create a "strategic window" that could create pressures for war.

WHY U.S. SUPERIORITY WOULD LACK ROBUSTNESS

Achieving superiority would require technological breakthroughs that are currently well beyond the reach of the United States. However, even if the United States made these advances, a variety of structural and political factors would continue to favor Soviet retaliatory capabilities over U.S. damage-limitation capabilities in a long-term competition. Thus, U.S. superiority would almost certainly lack robustness.

The structure of the damage-limitation mission. Four structural features favor the Soviet assured destruction capability over U.S. damage-limitation capabilities. First, the number of major U.S. cities—which determines the number of targets the Soviets must destroy—is essentially fixed. The *percentage* of the Soviet force that the United States must be able to destroy is therefore determined by the *absolute* size of the Soviet force: the larger the Soviet force, the higher the percentage of that force the United States must be able to destroy to protect its cities. Thus, as the Soviet Union increases the size of its force, the United States must disproportionately increase the size and/or effectiveness of its damage-limitation capabilities. As a result, the marginal cost of

---

control that allows unauthorized counter-city attacks. These pressures would not arise, however, if U.S. superiority were built entirely on strategic defenses.

U.S. damage-limitation capabilities might also create other types of pressures for Soviet escalation. This could occur, for example, if U.S. superiority depended on strategic antisubmarine warfare (ASW) capabilities that were vulnerable to Soviet attack. Since U.S. ASW would probably be slow, the Soviets would not need to escalate before the United States launched its ASW campaign. In a somewhat different context, analysts argue that these pressures are especially worrisome since Soviet escalation would take the war across the nuclear threshold. See Barry R. Posen, "Inadvertent Nuclear War: Escalation and NATO's Northern Flank," *International Security* 7, no. 2 (Fall 1982): 28–54.

U.S. damage-limitation capabilities increases with the size of the Soviet force.[25]

For example, if the Soviets double the size of their ballistic missile force, the United States cannot maintain its damage-limitation capability by doubling the size of its BMD system. That would simply hold constant the percentage of Soviet weapons that leak through the system. With the Soviet force now twice its original size, the number of penetrating Soviet warheads would double. Hence the United States must also increase the effectiveness of its BMD to cut the leakage rate in half.[26]

In addition, nuclear weapons make it relatively cheap to destroy cities: cities cannot be significantly protected against the destructive effects of nuclear weapons; and nuclear weapons are relatively cheap to make and deliver. Given the comparatively small number of major U.S. cities, the Soviet Union can easily afford a force many times the size required to destroy them (and has built such a force). Admittedly, maintaining a highly survivable force promises to be far more expensive than simply maintaining a very large one. But an assured destruction capability does not require highly survivable forces; a large, moderately survivable force provides a redundant capability against cities.

Taken together, the fixed number of U.S. cities and the Soviet ability to deploy a large force means that the U.S. damage-limitation system must work extraordinarily well to protect U.S. cities. Closely related, by building a large force the Soviet Union increases the marginal cost of the U.S. damage-limitation capability, and its total cost becomes extremely high.[27]

As discussed in Chapter Four, the Soviet Union's ability to diversify its retaliatory capabilities makes successful U.S. damage-limitation even more difficult. Damage limitation requires that the United States defeat *all* types of Soviet retaliatory forces. Thus, by diversifying their retaliatory capabilities in MAD the Soviets insure that a single U.S. technological breakthrough cannot make damage limitation easy and that the United States cannot improve the other components of its damage-limitation system before they react. By contrast, if the United States achieves superiority, the Soviet Union can restore its assured destruction capability with a single delivery system that can survive and reach the U.S. homeland.

Finally, the United States will be unable to effectively test its damage-limitation system against Soviet attack. Because damage limitation is much more

[25] This argument requires some modification if we entertain less ambitious damage-limitation objectives, for example, saving Americans that do not live in cities. On this issue, see Chapter Seven.

[26] This relationship is reflected in the increasing marginal cost of area-wide strategic defense. See Ashton B. Carter, *Directed Energy Missile Defense in Space—Background Paper* (Washington, D.C.: Office of Technology Assessment, April 1984), p. 45.

[27] This conclusion is not, however, independent of technological considerations since advances in damage-limitation technologies would reduce the cost.

complex than retaliation, this favors retaliation and reduces U.S. prospects for perfecting and then maintaining its damage-limitation systems.[28]

The implications of these structural factors are most severe for an essentially perfect damage-limitation capability, since it must allow only an extremely small percentage of Soviet forces to reach the United States.

Soviet reactions. Defeating American damage-limitation programs would be a top Soviet strategic priority. The Soviet Union relies on strategic nuclear weapons to protect its vital interests. Deterrence is the key objective of Soviet nuclear policy, and assured retaliation plays an important role in this strategy. Soviet doctrine holds that if deterrence fails the Soviet Union should be able to launch crippling attacks against the U.S. homeland. The priority targets in this assured retaliation attack would be economic-industrial and population targets.[29]

Consequently, the Soviet Union would probably react vigorously to defeat U.S. damage-limitation programs and be willing to pay disproportionate sums both to maintain and regain its retaliatory capabilities, possibly many times what the United States invests in damage-limitation capabilities. Thus, even a highly favorable cost-exchange ratio of U.S. damage-limitation capabilities to Soviet retaliatory capabilities might not enable the U.S. to maintain a damage-limitation capability.

Soviet deployments reflect this priority—the Soviet Union has made extensive efforts to maintain a second-strike capability. In response to the increasing vulnerability of their ICBMs, which continue to make up a large fraction of the Soviet force, the Soviets have hardened their ICBM silos and are deploying mobile ICBMs. In addition, they have invested in quieting their SSBNs (nuclear powered ballistic missile submarines), which makes them harder to find, and deployed longer-range SLBMs (Submarine-Launched Ballistic Missiles), which enable the Soviets to keep their SSBNs in a protected bastion. They are also deploying a new long-range bomber and air-launched cruise missiles, which add diversity to Soviet retaliatory capabilities.[30]

[28] On the problems created by the complexity of the software tasks demanded by SDI see Herbert Lin, "The Development of Software for Ballistic Missile Defense," *Scientific American* (December 1985), and Greg Nelson and David Redell, "Could We Trust the SDI Software," in Union of Concerned Scientists, *Empty Promise: The Growing Case against Star Wars* (Boston: Beacon Press, 1986). On uncertainties in ballistic missile attacks against hardened silos see note 2 in Chapter Eight.

[29] Stephen M. Meyer, "Soviet Strategic Programmes and the US SDI," *Survival* (November/December 1985): 277–83, argues that "Soviet military specialists use higher minimal damage requirements for assured retaliation than do their American counterparts: 70% of American industry and 50% of her population must be destroyed" (p. 279). For a divergent view see William T. Lee, "Soviet Nuclear Targeting Strategy," in Desmond Ball and Jeffery Richelson, eds., *Strategic Nuclear Targeting* (Ithaca: Cornell University Press, 1986), pp. 84–108.

[30] On these programs see Robert P. Berman and John C. Baker, *Soviet Strategic Forces: Requirements and Responses* (Washington, D.C.: Brookings Institution, 1982), pp. 62–69, and U.S.

At the most general level, Soviet determination to maintain their retaliatory capabilities is suggested by balance of power theory. Kenneth Waltz observes that "maintaining the status quo is the minimum goal of any great power" and that "the first concern of states is not to maximize their power but to maintain their positions in the system."[31] Thus, even if the United States gains superiority, we should expect that the Soviet Union will rely upon "internal" balancing to restore its assured destruction capability and superpower status.

Skeptics may counter that earlier Soviet behavior does not appear to support these arguments, noting that the Soviet Union accepted inferiority in the early postwar years, failing to acquire a large retaliatory capability in which it could have high confidence until well into the 1960s. A few observations seriously weaken this counterargument, however. First, during the early postwar years Soviet policy may have been going through a transition, shifting from traditional policies that focused on fighting a war in Europe to policies that gave greater prominence to deterring U.S. nuclear attacks.[32] Second, since the Soviet Union believed that much of the U.S. attack would be launched from bases in Europe, its medium-range forces might have provided the best available option for blunting a U.S. attack.[33] Neither of these considerations would moderate Soviet policy in the future. Third, having enjoyed the benefits of strategic equality, the Soviet Union would probably be less willing to accept a return to strategic inferiority than it was to accept a "second-best strategic posture" when starting from severe inferiority.[34]

U.S. willingness to sustain the competition. Because the Soviet Union will almost certainly commit itself to defeating U.S. damage-limitation systems, acquiring and maintaining superiority would require the United States to engage in an unending competition against Soviet retaliatory capabilities. Such a sustained U.S. effort seems unlikely for a variety of reasons.

First, damage-limitation capabilities promise to be enormously expensive. As discussed above, strategic defenses would probably play a major role in a U.S. quest for superiority. A first-generation ballistic missile defense designed

---

Department of Defense, *Soviet Military Power: Prospects for Change, 1989* (Washington, D.C.: GPO, 1989), pp. 42–48.

[31] Kenneth N. Waltz, *Theory of International Politics* (New York: Random House, 1979), pp. 191, 126.

[32] Thomas W. Wolfe, *Soviet Military Power in Europe, 1945–1970* (Baltimore: Johns Hopkins University Press, 1970), p. 41, argues that while the Soviets did experience technical and operational problems with intercontinental delivery capabilities, their decision to focus nuclear forces on Europe was heavily influenced by "a military tradition in which intercontinental strategic bombing had not hitherto won a firm hold, as well as by the general focus of Soviet attention upon the European politico-military arena." See also ibid., p. 180.

[33] Ibid., p. 180.

[34] On Soviet views on parity see David Holloway, *The Soviet Union and the Arms Race* (New Haven: Yale University Press, 1983), pp. 43–55. On Khrushchev's decision not to pursue parity see Wolfe, *Soviet Military Power in Europe*, pp. 133–36.

to protect the United States would cost in excess of half a trillion dollars.[35] This investment, however, would only be the tip of the iceberg. A first-generation system would not be sufficiently effective to protect U.S. cities. In addition, the United States would have to deploy effective air defense against Soviet bombers and cruise missiles. Moreover, unless these strategic defenses were essentially perfect, the United States would also have to continue expanding and modernizing its offensive counterforce systems. Finally, the Soviet Union would certainly respond, thereby requiring the United States to make still larger investments.

Second, many Americans will dispute the benefits of U.S. superiority, thereby reducing the prospects for a sustained consensus on such large investments. Many analysts believe that the United States can protect its vital security interests in MAD. Thus, consistent with arguments presented earlier in this chapter, they would find that the benefits of superiority are less than is suggested by the conventional wisdom. In addition, many analysts and much of the American public favor cooperation and arms control over competitive approaches to dealing with the Soviet Union.[36] Thus, even if superiority would provide the United States with important military advantages, these Americans might conclude that U.S. security had decreased. They will be especially concerned if U.S. superiority depends heavily on offensive counterforce. While a damage-limitation capability based solely on strategic defense can be presented as entirely benign—recall former President Reagan's description of SDI—one which depends on the United States launching a massive counterforce attack will unavoidably appear extremely provocative.

Third, the benefits of the ongoing and intense competition will be difficult to demonstrate. Whether any damage limitation is in fact possible would be known only following a large strategic nuclear war. Until then, the uncertainties in an untested system, which must perform almost perfectly, would leave plaguing doubts about the benefits of enormous investments.

In sum, although a major accomplishment, winning the first round in this competition would be a poor indicator of U.S. prospects for maintaining superiority in following rounds. The Soviets would probably develop new systems and approaches for defeating U.S. damage-limitation forces. In each round, the United States would have to achieve a new and still more over-

---

[35] Barry M. Blechman and Victor A. Utgoff, "The Macroeconomics of Strategic Defenses," *International Security* 11, no. 3 (Winter 1986–87): 33–70. They argue, however, that we need to put this figure in perspective: deploying these systems would require the United States to devote approximately one additional percent of its GNP to the defense budget. Examination of U.S. defense spending since 1945 raises doubts about the feasibility of continued growth during peacetime. See Samuel P. Huntington, "The Defense Policy of the Reagan Administration, 1981–82," in Fred I. Greenstein, ed., *The Reagan Presidency: An Early Assessment* (Baltimore: Johns Hopkins University Press, 1983), pp. 82–116.

[36] On the moderating influence of divergent American views on which policies can provide the greatest security see Miroslav Nincic, "The United States, the Soviet Union, and Politics of Opposites," *World Politics* 40, no. 4 (July 1988): 452–75.

whelming technological advantage. Moreover, the Soviet Union will probably be more determined to regain its retaliatory capabilities than the United States would be to continue denying them.[37] The Soviet Union would therefore probably regain its assured destruction capability, returning the superpowers to MAD. The transitory nature of U.S. superiority would raise the prospect of strategic windows. Hence the question becomes: Would a limited period of U.S. superiority increase U.S. security?

APPLYING WINDOW LOGIC

The lack of robustness of U.S. superiority would create a strategic window: the United States would expect that its military advantage would last for a limited period and would be followed by a return to MAD, or possibly a decline into inferiority; in other words, the United States would face a closing window of military advantage.

The key danger created by a strategic window is pressure for preventive war.[38] A country that fears war in the future might prefer fighting sooner to

[37] This analysis of robustness also suggests that proponents of superiority have exaggerated the promise of technological breakthroughs for eventually achieving superiority, since these same structural and political factors make superiority quite difficult to achieve in the first place.

Yet another factor making superiority difficult to achieve is the dependence of U.S. damage-limitation capabilities on the timing of a U.S. attack. Damage limitation will be most difficult in the scenarios that are most important. The United States would have the best chance of limiting damage in a surprise attack, since Soviet forces would not be on alert. This, however, is the least important case since it is hard to imagine the United States launching a first strike in the absence of a crisis. (As discussed below, this is true even for preventive war.) By comparison, once the superpowers are involved in a serious crisis or conventional war, any U.S. damage-limitation capabilities would be greatly reduced. The possible exception are scenarios in which the United States attacks Soviet strategic nuclear forces with conventional forces during a superpower conventional war. For example, the United States currently plans an attrition campaign against Soviet SSBNs before a superpower war escalates to the nuclear level. In these cases, U.S. damage-limitation capabilities could increase as the conventional war continues.

[38] Windows can exert a second kind of danger by pressuring the superior country to pursue expansion before the window closes. (On the danger created by time pressures see Stephen W. Van Evera, "Causes of War," pp. 33–39, 67–71.) A window exerts this pressure on an expansionist power, but not on a status quo power. An aggressor sees a "window of opportunity." The real source of danger here is the aggressor's military advantage, not the window. The window, however, might increase the probability of war by encouraging the aggressor to employ its military advantage quickly. If the aggressor's objectives might be achieved through patient diplomacy backed by a coercive military advantage, then the window increases the probability of war by reducing the time available for finding diplomatic solutions. We might term these "rushed premeditated wars." If, on the other hand, the aggressor's demands are so extreme as to foreclose any compromise, then the window does not increase the probability of war but only encourages the aggressor to initiate it sooner. Further, in this case windows might actually decrease the probability or number of wars. Without a window the aggressor might maintain its advantage indefinitely and continue fighting until it achieves hegemony. Windows, then, can be viewed as limiting the period during which an aggressor can be successful. Unsatisfied aggressors will therefore be tempted to fight to keep windows open.

In contrast, a status quo power with superiority does not want to use its military advantage to

risking trying to avoid war later—fighting sooner prevents some of the costs of fighting later without a military advantage. Both status quo and expansionist powers could be influenced by preventive motives. Studies of the causes of war show that preventive incentives have influenced leaders' decisions. In the most extensively examined case, analysts find that preventive incentives contributed to Germany's decision for war in 1914.[39]

The magnitude of U.S. incentives for launching a preventive nuclear war would depend on three factors.[40] The first is the probability that the United States would lose its superiority. This is the probability that the United States actually faces a window. The more likely the United States is to lose superiority, the greater its incentives for launching a preventive war, since fighting sooner would be more likely to be better than fighting later. Thus, judged along this dimension, U.S. superiority would be plagued by preventive incentives. U.S. leaders would expect to lose superiority, since it would probably suffer a severe lack of robustness.

The second factor is the difference between the cost of war while the United States has superiority and the cost of war following superiority. This difference determines the magnitude of the window. Anticipating a return to MAD, U.S. leaders would compare the costs of war while the United States still has its damage-limitation capability to the costs once the Soviet Union has re-

---

achieve political gains, and therefore the window does not create this type of pressure. Instead, the status quo power sees a "window of enhanced security" during which its deterrent capabilities are more effective. Judged in terms of this type of pressure, U.S. superiority would not create dangers as long as the United States remains a status quo power dedicated to containment and not expansion.

[39] Stephen Van Evera, "The Cult of the Offensive and the Origins of the First World War," *International Security* 9, no. 1 (Summer 1984): 79–85; Jack L. Snyder, "Perceptions of the Security Dilemma in 1914," in Robert Jervis et al., *Psychology and Deterrence* (Baltimore: Johns Hopkins University Press, 1985), pp. 168–78. Both find that Germany overestimated its preventive incentives—because they inflated the advantages of offense, German leaders exaggerated both the size of the window and the future threat to German security. For an opposing view on the influence of windows see Richard Ned Lebow, "Windows of Opportunity: Do States Jump through Them?" *International Security* 9, no. 1 (Summer 1984): 147–86. For useful background on Germany's view of its military and political situation see also Holger H. Herwig, "Imperial Germany," in Ernest R. May, ed., *Knowing One's Enemies* (Princeton: Princeton University Press, 1986), pp. 62–97.

Other cases involving preventive incentives are discussed in Van Evera, "Causes of War," pp. 60–76; Richard K. Betts, "Surprise Attack and Preemption," in Graham T. Allison et al., *Hawks, Doves & Owls* (New York: W. W. Norton, 1985), pp. 56–57, 61–63; and Alfred Vagts, *Defense and Diplomacy: The Soldier and the Conduct of Foreign Relations* (New York: King's Crown Press, 1956), pp. 263–350.

[40] These factors are presented in more general form in Van Evera, "Causes of War," p. 72. See also Snyder, "Perceptions of the Security Dilemma in 1914," pp. 160–61; Betts, "Surprise Attack and Preemption"; and Robert Gilpin, *War & Change in World Politics* (Cambridge: Cambridge University Press, 1981), pp. 186–210. Reviewing the literature on preventive war is Jack S. Levy, "Declining Power and the Preventive Motivation for War," *World Politics* 40, no. 1 (October 1987): 82–107.

gained an assured destruction capability. The more effective the U.S. damage-limitation capability is, the larger the difference in these costs will be and, therefore, the greater the incentive to launch a preventive war.[41] Thus, a perfect damage-limitation capability would create larger preventive incentives than a near-perfect one that leaves a large fraction of U.S. cities vulnerable.

The third factor is the U.S. estimate of the probability of war with the Soviet Union once the window closes. Thus, U.S. estimates of the probability of war influence the significance of the window. If U.S. leaders were confident that war could be avoided, then even a large window would create only small preventive incentives. U.S. incentives for launching a preventive war grow larger with higher estimates of the probability of superpower war.[42]

U.S. estimates of the probability of war would be influenced by expectations about the adequacy of future U.S. military capabilities. Starting from U.S. superiority, the most likely outcome of superpower competition is a return to MAD.[43] Expecting this outcome, analysts would disagree about the U.S. ability to deter the Soviet Union. Members of the damage-limitation school, believing that the Soviet Union is highly aggressive and that superiority is necessary for extended deterrence, would anticipate a higher probability of war and therefore would see larger preventive incentives. In contrast, members of the punitive retaliation school would see U.S. capabilities as still adequate, and therefore see smaller preventive incentives. Although far less likely, U.S. leaders might fear that U.S. superiority would pass into U.S. inferiority instead of MAD. For example, if confronting extensive Soviet strategic defenses, U.S. leaders might fear that improvements in these systems could jeopardize the U.S. assured destruction capability at the same time that additions to already large Soviet missile forces restore their assured retaliatory capability. To the extent that U.S. leaders anticipate this outcome, they would project a higher probability of superpower war, since they foresee clearly inadequate military capabilities.[44]

In short, U.S. superiority would create preventive incentives that vary in-

[41] In general, when offense has larger advantages over defense, military advantages will be larger and windows will create greater pressures; in this case, the extent of offense advantage is reflected in the effectiveness of the U.S. damage-limitation capability.

[42] We should note a fourth factor that might influence incentives for preventive attack. Decisionmakers may place greater value on events that they expect may take place in the near future than in the more distant future. If so, they will be inclined to postpone incurring costs. A complete comparison of war now and war later would therefore "discount" future costs. This inclination might be especially strong if the future costs would become the responsibility of a future leader.

[43] This outcome is most likely because the structural factors favor retaliation over damage limitation.

[44] Thus, although both U.S. superiority and BAD would be plagued by a lack of robustness, the dangers are more worrisome in BAD. Superiority is likely to decay back to MAD, so the United States confronts a window of advantage. In contrast, BAD is more likely to decay into U.S. inferiority, so the United States would anticipate windows of disadvantage.

versely with the robustness and directly with the effectiveness of the U.S. damage-limitation capability. In addition, preventive incentives would be larger if U.S. leaders believe that the Soviet Union cannot be adequately deterred in MAD, and even larger if they fear that the United States might fall into strategic inferiority.

There is support for these arguments in the history of U.S.-Soviet competition. Following World War II, the United States faced a strategic window. The United States initially enjoyed a nuclear monopoly and the Soviet Union failed to acquire an assured destruction capability until well into the 1960s;[45] and U.S. leaders recognized that their superiority would eventually be lost. Nuclear war would have been much less costly if the United States had crippled Soviet nuclear capabilities before the Soviet Union acquired a large survivable arsenal. In addition, many analysts feared that the Soviet Union was highly expansionist, which created the expectation that avoiding a large superpower war might be impossible. Thus, the conditions that generate preventive incentives were all in place.

U.S. preventive incentives were recognized both inside and outside the U.S. government, and did influence U.S. policy debates.[46] Marc Trachtenberg

[45] There are, however, a number of questions about how large the U.S. advantage was and about how U.S. leaders understood their advantage at the time. See Betts, "A Nuclear Golden Age"; Lebow, "Windows of Opportunity," pp. 170–71; and George H. Quester, *Nuclear Diplomacy: The First Twenty Years* (New York: Dunellen, 1970), pp. 1–9.

In addition, we should note that the United States, at least during the period of monopoly, did not pursue the buildup of nuclear capabilities that preparation for a future preventive war would have dictated. See Wolfe, *Soviet Power and Europe: 1945–1970*, p. 33.

[46] The most thorough discussion is Marc Trachtenberg, "A 'Wasting Asset': American Strategy and the Shifting Nuclear Balance, 1949–1954," *International Security* 13, no. 3 (Winter 1988/89): 5–49. See also David Alan Rosenberg, "The Origins of Overkill: Nuclear Weapons and American Strategy, 1945–1960," *International Security* 7, no. 4 (Spring 1983): 33–34, 47; Tami Davis Biddle, "Handling the Soviet Threat: 'Project Control' and the Debate on American Strategy in the Early Cold War Years," *Journal of Strategic Studies* 12, no. 3: 271–302; Lebow, "Windows of Opportunity," pp. 168–70; Glenn H. Snyder, "The New Look of 1953," in Warner R. Schilling et al., *Strategy, Politics and Defense Budgets* (New York: Columbia University Press, 1962), pp. 407–9; and Vagts, *Defense and Diplomacy*, pp. 329–35.

Preventive war was one of four options considered, and rejected, in NSC 68. See "United States Objectives and Programs for National Security, NSC 68, April 14, 1950," reprinted in Thomas H. Etzold and John Lewis Gaddis, eds., *Containment: Documents on American Policy and Strategy, 1945–1950* (New York: Columbia University Press, 1978), pp. 431–32.

Bernard Brodie addressed preventive war in some detail in *Strategy in the Missile Age* (Santa Monica: Rand, 1959), pp. 227–41: "Preventive war seems today no longer a live issue, though it was that only a few years ago among a small but important minority of American citizens. The pressure in favor of it diminished as the Soviets developed a nuclear capability, and especially as Americans became acclimated to living with those nuclear bombs that had provoked the idea in the first place" (pp. 227–28). Interestingly, Brodie's reflections over a decade later present a somewhat different impression: "In the days of American nuclear monopoly there was some small, politically unimportant following for the advocacy of 'preventive war,' " *War and Politics* (New York: Macmillan, 1973), p. 322.

concludes that "support for a highly aggressive strategy was much more wide-spread than has ever been recognized. But these explicit calls for a showdown with the Soviets 'before it was too late' were just the tip of the iceberg, a surface manifestation of a much more pervasive, but also more amorphous, set of concerns about what the loss of America's nuclear advantage might lead to."[47] According to David Rosenberg, "although seldom explicitly discussed in writing, preventive war was implicit in some of the major policy deliberations of the time." For example:

> Formal recognition that the survival of the U.S. might be in doubt generated renewed pressures for the consideration of preventive war. In May 1954, Eisenhower was briefed on a paper by the JCS's Advance Study Group which proposed that the U.S. consider "deliberately precipitating war with the USSR in the near future," before Soviet thermonuclear capability became a "real menace."[48]

According to Bernard Brodie, a preventive war policy was "for several years certainly the prevailing philosophy at the Air War College."[49]

Proponents of superiority, however, point to this postwar window to argue that the decay of regained American superiority would not be dangerous. Since the conditions for preventive war were satisfied and yet the superpowers avoided nuclear war, they conclude that concern about preventive incentives should not inhibit the United States from trying to regain superiority.

However, this argument is flawed. Even though a preventive war did not occur, the postwar window might nevertheless have increased its probability.[50] For example, if the probability of preventive war increased, but remained low, then we would still expect war not to have occurred. Thus, the proponents' counterargument does not provide strong evidence against the danger of strategic windows. By comparison, the fact that American leaders recognized and were influenced by this window provides much stronger support for the argument that windows can be dangerous.

In fact, the influence of U.S. preventive incentives was never seriously tested.[51] Preventive incentives would be most important during a superpower conventional war, and far less influential during peacetime and relatively mild

---

[47] Trachtenberg, "A 'Wasting Asset,' " p. 7.

[48] Rosenberg, "Origins of Overkill," pp. 33, 34.

[49] Quoted in Trachtenberg, "A 'Wasting Asset,' " p. 10.

[50] Lebow, "Windows of Opportunity" (although not a proponent), seems to overlook this possibility, focusing instead on the nonmilitary factors that led U.S. leaders to ignore preventive pressures; he does not address how these pressures might have contributed to decisions for nuclear war.

[51] Preventive incentives are not special in requiring us to consider the conditions under which they influence outcomes. Rather, the influence of many types of escalatory incentives is conditional. Familiar arguments about preemptive incentives provide a useful reminder. According to these arguments, preemptive incentives will not lead to preemption unless there is a crisis. Thus, cases in which a preemptive war did not occur may tell us little about whether preemptive incentives existed or how they would have influenced escalation of a crisis.

crises.[52] First, the influence of preventive incentives might grow sharply if conventional war broke out in Europe. Even limited Soviet aggression could convince U.S. leaders that the probability of a nuclear war in the future was much higher than previously estimated, thereby increasing U.S. incentives for launching a preventive attack. Second, once a conventional war began, U.S. leaders would probably consider a variety of arguments for launching a nuclear attack, including narrower military purposes—winning the conventional war and preempting Soviet nuclear attack—as well as preventive war. Thus, preventive incentives would not bear the full burden of the U.S. decision to escalate; rather, in combination with other arguments they could contribute to a decision to launch a nuclear war. Finally, Soviet aggression might reduce barriers to a preventive U.S. attack by enabling the United States to blame the Soviets for starting the war.[53]

In addition, we need to be careful in using the postwar window as a general analogy for evaluating U.S. superiority, since it is possible that future windows could be more dangerous. For example, U.S. preventive incentives during the 1950s were moderated by the belief that U.S. superiority would most likely be followed by nuclear parity, not inferiority.[54] If future superiority were accompanied by the fear that the arms race would drive the United States into inferiority,[55] then its preventive incentives would be larger.[56]

[52] One consideration does, however, favor preventive attack during peacetime—a surprise attack would be more effective and would therefore promise a greater reduction in the costs of war.

[53] For example, the moral costs are discussed by Brodie, *Strategy in the Missile Age*, pp. 235–37; Lebow, "Windows of Opportunity," pp. 171–75; and moral arguments were important in the short discussion rejecting preventive war in NSC 68.

Reflecting the importance of these barriers, Brodie described nuclear war launched according to the principal of massive retaliation as "preventive war, save that we have waited for an excuse, a provocation." *Strategy in the Missile Age*, pp. 255–57.

[54] A number of studies during this period warned of future vulnerabilities in U.S. retaliatory capabilities but also proposed solutions—inferiority was seen as avoidable if the United States responded to growing Soviet capabilities. See Rosenberg, "The Origins of Overkill," pp. 38–40, 46–49.

[55] It is also possible that U.S. superiority would decay into parity at reduced vulnerability. In this case the Soviet Union acquires a damage-limitation capability but does not eliminate the U.S. damage-limitation capability. In other words, superiority could decay into a world in which both countries can protect themselves with strategic defenses or into a world in which both countries have damage-limitation capabilities that depend on an offensive counterforce first strike. If the U.S. leaders expect one of these outcomes and that it will last, then they might not see increasing costs of war in the future; this would tend to reduce the pressure for preventive war. However, since these worlds are likely to lack robustness and can suffer severe crisis instability, U.S. leaders might expect the probability of war in the future to increase, thereby increasing incentives for preventive attack.

[56] As laid out above, U.S. preventive incentives would also vary with the effectiveness of the U.S. damage-limitation capability. During the 1950s, U.S. leaders believed the Soviet Union could inflict enormous costs, first on Western Europe and shortly thereafter on the United States. (See Betts, "A Golden Nuclear Age," on U.S. views of its vulnerability during this period.) As a result, by the mid-1950s preventive war was discouraged by high costs. If the United States acquires a high-confidence, essentially perfect damage-limitation capability, U.S. leaders would

Broader Political and Military Effects of U.S. Superiority

The preceding analysis presents a partially static view by assuming that U.S. acquisition of strategic superiority changes only the superpowers' military capabilities. However, U.S. superiority could have a variety of broader political consequences. Most obvious of these, the intense military competition required to gain and then maintain U.S. superiority would influence U.S.-Soviet relations. As discussed in Chapter Three, alternative views of the Soviet Union support divergent predictions. On the one hand, some analysts believe that competitive American policies communicate resolve, thereby enhancing the U.S. ability to deter the Soviet Union. On the other hand, others worry that these competitive policies increase Soviet insecurity, which in turn generates the dangers identified by the spiral model, leaving the Soviet Union harder to deter. Judgments about this basic dispute play an important role in reaching an overall assessment of the desirability of U.S. superiority. Another possible political consequence, although rarely noted, is that superiority would encourage the United States to pursue a more ambitious foreign policy.

In addition, U.S. superiority could have broader military consequences. It could pressure the Soviets into provocative or risky military deployments designed to restore their assured destruction capability, which could then generate superpower crises. If so, the number of paths to superpower conflict would increase in comparison to MAD, since the Soviets would find these policies necessary in a world of U.S. superiority, but not in MAD.

This section first argues that U.S. superiority is likely to generate the negative political consequences predicted by the spiral model. It next briefly explores the political and military consequences of superiority noted above, and then considers their implications for the probability of war.

WHY SPIRAL EFFECTS ARE LIKELY

Some analysts argue that Soviet leaders understand that the United States is a status quo power deploying military capabilities solely to defend its vital interests. Were the Soviet Union to hold such a benign view of American intentions, we would not need to consider the negative political consequences of superiority that are predicted by the spiral model.

However, as discussed in Chapter Three, Soviet leaders have in fact tended

---

be less deterred. Of course, the more likely case of near-perfect superiority would not eliminate this barrier.

In addition, at least if U.S. decisions are influenced by moral considerations, U.S. willingness to launch a preventive attack might depend on the damage to the Soviet Union. The lower the costs associated with destroying Soviet capabilities for returning to MAD, the more likely the United States would be to launch a preventive attack. If these costs were lower than in the 1950s, then a preventive U.S. attack would be more likely. This might occur if the United States could destroy Soviet capabilities with highly accurate conventional or small nuclear weapons.

to believe that the United States is a hostile power that will, if given the opportunity, take advantage of the Soviet Union. They are therefore likely to view American policies that challenge their military capabilities as threats to their security and to impute hostile American intentions. U.S. military capabilities are most likely to bring Soviet leaders to these conclusions when they threaten military capabilities that the Soviets rely on to protect their vital interests. Consequently, U.S. acquisition and maintenance of nuclear superiority is especially likely both to create Soviet insecurity and to convince the Soviets that the United States is more hostile than previously assumed.

Soviet military doctrine leaves no doubt that U.S. superiority would undermine the most basic Soviet requirements. Soviet doctrine now states that strategic parity is compatible with both superpowers' security requirements, but leaves no doubt that the Soviet Union needs an assured retaliatory capability.[57] Given these beliefs, Soviet leaders would see U.S. nuclear superiority leaving the Soviet Union short of the capabilities required to protect its vital interests while providing the United States with capabilities exceeding its security requirements. Soviet leaders are therefore likely to see superiority reflecting a U.S. desire to challenge the political status quo. U.S. superiority would tend to confirm Soviet fears about the U.S. desire to expand, while discrediting opposing views that see the United States as less threatening.

Achieving and maintaining U.S. superiority is likely to generate larger spiral effects than competing militarily in MAD. In MAD, the clear dominance of retaliatory capabilities (that is, defense dominance) moderates the negative political effects of an arms race. Even as military competition continues, the superpowers' large retaliatory capabilities severely limit the threat that either country can pose to the other's vital interests.

For U.S. superiority to have positive political consequences Soviet leaders would have to believe that the U.S. decision to pursue superiority was a natural reaction to highly expansionist Soviet policies.[58] In this case, Soviet leaders, well aware that they threatened U.S. security, might understand that superiority provided the United States with necessary protection, not excess capabilities. Although possible in theory, Soviet leaders are in fact most unlikely to adopt this perspective. In the first place, Soviet leaders are likely to link U.S. decisions for superiority to Soviet foreign policy behavior only if that behavior has been extremely aggressive, far beyond what we have experienced during the Cold War. Otherwise, Soviet leaders would doubt that the United States saw them severely threatening its vital interests and thus would find U.S. policies excessive. Furthermore, even if U.S. pursuit and acquisi-

[57] See citations in notes 29 and 34; and note 94 in Chapter Three.

[58] A related argument holds that U.S. superiority might contribute to the "mellowing" of Soviet intentions. On this possibility, and why it is unlikely in the Soviet case, see Stephen Van Evera, "Offense, Defense, and Strategy: When Is Offense Best?" (Paper delivered at the annual meeting of the American Political Science Association, Chicago, September 1987).

tion of superiority did correlate with such aggressive Soviet behavior, Soviet leaders might miss the connection. Since they have been inclined to see the United States as aggressive, Soviet leaders might overlook their role in provoking U.S. superiority. This would be especially likely if Soviet expansionist policies were partly motivated by insecurity, since U.S. superiority would then make the Soviets feel even more insecure.

CHANGES IN POLITICAL CALCULATIONS

Feeling more threatened, Soviet leaders might be less willing to compromise in political disputes, and might even pursue a variety of more aggressive policies simply to protect the status quo.

Having become convinced that the United States is more hostile, Soviets leaders might conclude that their credibility for defending their interests is tightly connected across all issues (in other words, the Soviets might adopt a deterrence model view of the United States). In this case, U.S. superiority could convince Soviet leaders that reductions in their global influence were more costly than in MAD. Soviet leaders might, for example, come to see even small losses as significantly increasing the prospects for a complete decline in Soviet influence. With the potential costs of incremental losses having increased, they would be less willing to make compromises and more willing to run large risks to protect the political status quo.[59]

This decreased Soviet willingness to compromise would be most likely to raise the probability of crises in "grey areas"—places in which both superpowers believed they had important interests, but that lay outside of their spheres of influence. For example, the Soviets might feel greater pressure to support faltering allies in the Middle East. For its part, the United States would probably find Soviet involvement and military intervention as unacceptable as in MAD, and therefore would be at least as likely to respond.[60] For similar reasons, the Soviets would have stronger incentives for responding to U.S. intervention in grey areas.

In addition, increased insecurity might pressure the Soviets to pursue riskier policies where their interests are greater—most importantly, in Europe. Studies of Soviet foreign policy behavior suggest that superiority might create the conditions under which Soviet leaders would be willing to run such large risks. Although generally risk-avoiding, Soviet leaders are more likely to run large risks to protect the status quo than to expand.[61] Soviet incentives for risky

---

[59] In addition to the possibilities discussed below, conflict might increase because intense military competition and scarce security for the Soviets might encourage greater secrecy, fait accompli diplomacy, and militarism. On the sources and danger of these reactions see Van Evera, "Causes of War."

[60] If, however, U.S. interests in these grey areas were based on concerns for U.S. security, then the United States might feel less need to intervene, assuming that superiority made it feel more secure.

[61] See note 28 in Chapter Two.

behavior and the probability of miscalculation seem greater in a world of U.S. superiority, since under MAD the Soviet Union can protect its vital interests without resorting to provocative policies.

The recent events in Eastern Europe offer an interesting case for comparison. We should remember that the dramatic reduction of Soviet control of Eastern Europe occurred during a period in which the Soviets could be confident of their assured retaliatory capabilities and while Soviet nuclear doctrine was increasingly stressing the adequacy of those capabilities. Thus, even while struggling with severe economic problems, the Soviets could count on nuclear weapons to protect their truly vital interests. Further, Soviet leaders see these capabilities as playing a central role in their ability to maintain superpower status.[62]

But what of a world in which the United States had nuclear superiority? U.S. superiority, by reducing their security and robbing them of their international position, might pressure the Soviets to pursue a quite different foreign policy. Eastern Europe might once again seem necessary to the Soviets as a buffer zone against conventional attack. They might even be more willing to attack a NATO country that lent support to a major uprising in Eastern Europe.

U.S. superiority could also influence U.S. political calculations. First, the United States might conclude that a more determined foreign policy was necessary to protect American interests.[63] The United States would probably interpret the Soviet Union's more aggressive foreign policy, which is defensive from the Soviet perspective, as increasingly offensive. Convinced that the Soviets were becoming more dangerous, U.S. leaders might then conclude that there was a growing need to oppose the Soviets in all areas, especially in grey areas. This conclusion could be reinforced by the intense arms competition generated by U.S. superiority. Although the Soviets would see their efforts to regain an assured retaliatory capability as defensive, U.S. leaders—believing that protecting U.S. security required nuclear superiority—might conclude that Soviet military efforts reflected still more aggressive intentions. Second, although rarely considered, we should not entirely overlook the possibility that the United States would adopt a more expansionist foreign policy. Superiority would eliminate a key barrier to a more aggressive U.S. policy since, if extremely effective, U.S. damage-limitation capabilities would reduce the costs of war with the Soviet Union. Counting against this possibility is the well-established U.S. commitment to protecting the status quo, as reflected in its policy of containment.[64] Nevertheless, U.S. interest in rolling back Soviet

---

[62] Meyer, "The Sources and Prospects of Gorbachev's New Political Thinking on Security," p. 160.

[63] For example, based on highly aggressive views of the Soviet Union, NSC 68 called for the United States to adopt a more ambitious foreign policy, including "dynamic steps to reduce the power and influence of the Kremlin inside the Soviet Union and other areas under its control." Reprinted in Etzold and Gaddis, eds., *Containment*, p. 435.

[64] John Lewis Gaddis, *Strategies of Containment* (New York: Oxford University Press, 1982).

control was certainly greater when the United States had superiority than it is today.[65]

Soviet efforts to regain their assured destruction capability could provoke U.S. reactions that lead directly to military conflict. U.S. leaders would reasonably expect Soviet efforts to build back to MAD by expanding their arsenal, increasing its survivability, and improving its ability to penetrate U.S. strategic defenses. They might, however, find other types of Soviet reactions more provocative, concluding that the Soviets were changing the rules of competition. In reaction, the United States might demand a reversal of Soviet policy or might even destroy new Soviet systems.

For example, consider a U.S. damage-limitation capability that depended on destroying Soviet missiles just after they were launched. The Soviets might defeat such a system by placing nuclear weapons in earth orbit during peacetime. The United States might find this solution provocative—because it changed the "rules" of competition—and also dangerous if nuclear weapons in orbit increased the probability of accidental nuclear attack. Even if the Soviets recognize likely U.S. objections, they might be willing to run substantial risks if unable to restore their assured destruction capability via a more "normal" buildup. A crisis could follow if the United States decided to prevent the Soviet Union from implementing this solution. In another possibility, the U.S. damage-limitation capability might depend on satellites—possibly for locating Soviet forces, for improving the accuracy of U.S. missiles, and/or for basing strategic defenses. Soviet deployment of a space-based antisatellite capability might then restore their retaliatory capability. Soviet leaders might see such a deployment as crucial, and the United States would have strong incentives for preventing it. The United States might decide that its security required the destruction of Soviet antisatellite weapons, even if it risked initiating a superpower war. These examples are suggestive of ways in which Soviet efforts to overcome U.S. superiority could create crises or lead directly to military conflict.

The Cuban Missile Crisis is an example of such a confrontation.[66] Soviet

---

[65] For an overview of arguments presented in the late 1940s and into the 1950s see Bennett Korvig, *The Myth of Liberation: East-Central Europe in U.S. Diplomacy and Politics since 1941* (Baltimore: Johns Hopkins University Press, 1973), pp. 99–125. According to Snyder, "The 'New Look' of 1953," pp. 406–9, the Eisenhower administration considered the option of "liberation" during a reexamination of U.S. strategy, but completely rejected it. For an influential statement of the arguments see James Burnham, *Containment or Liberation: An Inquiry into the Aims of the United States Foreign Policy* (New York: John Day, 1952).

Recent discussions of policies open to the United States show that U.S. options are severely constrained by Soviet retaliatory capabilities. See, for example, Aaron Wildavsky, ed., *Beyond Containment: Alternative American Policies toward the Soviet Union* (San Francisco: ICS Press, 1983).

[66] The other Soviet motivation was extended deterrence of U.S. conventional attack against

leaders saw the deployment of missiles in Cuba as a quick fix to their strategic inferiority. If the Soviet Union had an assured destruction capability the incentives for deploying missiles in Cuba would have been much smaller and the crisis would have been less likely to have occurred. On the U.S. side, some believed that, because the missiles would increase Soviet military capabilities, either the Soviets had to remove them or the United States had to destroy them.

In addition, if unable to quickly regain their assured destruction capability, the Soviet Union might pursue offsetting conventional military advantages that might in turn increase superpower tensions. Soviet leaders might conclude that advantages in conventional forces would reduce the coercive potential of U.S. nuclear superiority. This is plausible since this is how they viewed their conventional strength in Europe during the period of U.S. nuclear monopoly.[67] The United States, however, would probably not recognize this conventional buildup as a reaction to its strategic superiority, but see it instead confirming Soviet hostility.[68] If so, the United States might conclude that it needed to win the conventional arms race, even while retaining nuclear superiority. Alternatively, a crisis could result directly if the United States decided to use nuclear threats—backed by its damage-limitation capability—to pressure the Soviets to end their buildup.

THE PROBABILITY OF WAR REASSESSED

If, as argued above, U.S. superiority is likely to increase Soviet interest in pursuing a variety of risky foreign and military policies, then U.S. superiority might actually generate crises, not deter them. In addition, once involved in a confrontation, Soviet leaders might be willing to run larger risks since superiority increases the costs of backing down and losing political influence.

Cuba. For discussion of Soviet motivations see Bruce J. Allyn, James G. Blight, and David A. Welch, "Essense of Revision: Moscow, Havana, and the Cuban Missile Crisis," *International Security* 14, no. 3 (Winter 1989/90): 136–72; Raymond L. Garthoff, *Reflections on the Cuban Missile Crisis* (Washington, D.C.: Brookings Institution, 1989); Richard K. Betts, *Nuclear Blackmail and Nuclear Balance* (Washington, D.C.: Brookings Institution, 1987), pp. 110–14; Graham T. Allison, *The Essence of Decision: Explaining the Cuban Missile Crisis* (Boston: Little, Brown, 1971), pp. 240–41; Richard Ned Lebow, "The Cuban Missile Crisis: Reading the Lessons Correctly," *Political Science Quarterly* 98, no. 3 (Fall 1983): 451–54; and Holloway, *The Soviet Union and the Arms Race*, p. 85.

[67] Holloway, *The Soviet Union and the Arms Race*, p. 27; and Wolfe, *Soviet Power in Europe*, pp. 33–34: "Stalin's main recourse in the military field lay in making the threat of Soviet land power against Europe the counterpoise to U.S. nuclear power." But for reassessment of this period see Matthew A. Evangelista, "Stalin's Postwar Army Reappraised," *International Security* 7, no. 3 (Winter 1982/1983): pp. 110–38.

[68] Apparently, Stalin's policy had this effect. Wolfe, *Soviet Power in Europe*, p. 35, notes that this policy created "apprehension in the West as to the intentions behind the Soviet military posture" and "Western uncertainty about Soviet intentions [stemmed] in part from what was perceived as a Soviet posture of readiness to use massive conventional forces against Western Europe." This seems to be a clear example of spiral model predictions: the Soviet Union faced a severe security dilemma; the United States interpreted Soviet policy as quite threatening.

Thus, the preceding analysis of the probability of war made something of a best case for U.S. superiority by overlooking these broader political and military consequences. The remainder of this section briefly reassesses the U.S. ability to deter premeditated Soviet attacks, maintain crisis stability, and avoid the dangers of low robustness.

Under these conditions, there is not a clear general answer to whether superiority would increase or decrease the probability of premeditated Soviet attacks. While superiority might enhance the U.S. deterrent by increasing the credibility of U.S. nuclear threats, as discussed above, the Soviet Union would be harder to deter since the benefits of aggressive and risky policies would now be greater.

Whether U.S. superiority increased the probability of premeditated war might depend on the quality of the U.S. damage-limitation capability. Essentially perfect, high-confidence damage-limitation capabilities would provide the largest increase in U.S. credibility, and thus have the best prospect for offsetting the negative spiral effects. By contrast, imperfect capabilities that could barely defeat the Soviet assured destruction capability, and left doubts about this, would increase U.S. credibility far less. In this case, the United States might then end up with the worst of both worlds—intense competition and increased Soviet risk-taking with little increase in the credibility of its threats.[69]

The probability of premeditated attacks could also depend on the quality of Soviet perceptions—studies of the causes of war warn that countries that believe they face severe threats to their vital interests may underestimate the adversary's resolve, ignore warnings that continued aggressive behavior will lead to war, and focus on optimistic scenarios in which overwhelming military capabilities do not result in catastrophic outcomes.[70] Thus, U.S. superiority might not provide the expected enhancement of American credibility, in which case the probability of war is more likely to increase.

As concluded earlier, U.S. superiority could under a range of conditions reduce crisis stability. Whatever crisis instabilities U.S. superiority creates would be especially dangerous if superiority also generates crises for any of the political or military reasons described above. In this case, U.S. superiority would increase the probability of preemptive war in two ways: the frequency and severity of superpower crises would increase; and these crises would be more likely to escalate via preemptive attacks due to the decrease in crisis stability.

---

[69] On the other hand, less effective U.S. damage-limitation capabilities would pose a smaller threat to the Soviet Union and might therefore put less pressure on them to pursue risky policies. However, even in this case, U.S. pursuit of overwhelming superiority would communicate malign intentions.

[70] See, for example, Richard Ned Lebow, *Between Peace and War* (Baltimore: Johns Hopkins University Press, 1981).

Finally, the tensions and exaggerated images of hostility that would probably accompany U.S. superiority would make its low robustness still more dangerous. Recall that U.S. incentives to launch a preventive war—which involves the decision to fight sooner instead of risking being attacked later—grow with estimates of the probability of war with the Soviet Union. The intense military competition that could accompany U.S. superiority is likely to convince the United States of still more malign Soviet intentions and therefore that war will be harder to avoid than previously believed. These changes in American judgments of Soviet intentions will further increase U.S. incentives for preventive war under conditions of U.S. superiority.

The influence of preventive incentives would be further increased if the overall effect of U.S. superiority was to increase the probability of conventional war. Conventional war would confirm Soviet hostility, thereby increasing American estimates of the probability of all-out war in the future and in turn increasing the incentives for preventive war. This observation is important because, as discussed above, U.S. superiority might increase the probability of conventional war in a variety of ways.

CONCLUSION

Contrary to widely held views and the specific claims of the damage-limitation school, the foregoing analysis suggests that U.S. superiority could increase the probability of both conventional and nuclear war. Even in the best case, U.S. superiority would reduce the probability of war only slightly, since the United States poses highly effective deterrent capabilities in MAD. The best case, however, is defined by quite restrictive conditions: U.S. damage-limitation capabilities are essentially perfect, highly robust, and leave the Soviet Union without a back-to-MAD capability; and Soviet leaders do not respond politically according to the spiral model.

In less attractive cases, superiority could increase the probability of war. Less effective damage-limitation capabilities would contribute far less to the credibility of U.S. extended deterrence threats, since much of U.S. society would remain vulnerable. If political spirals leave the Soviet Union harder to deter, the net effect could be an increased probability of war. Further, crisis stability would be reduced if the Soviets possess back-to-MAD capabilities that are vulnerable or depend on destroying the first-strike component of U.S. damage-limitation capabilities. The implications of reduced crisis stability will be greater if combined with spiral effects that increase the probability of crises. In addition, the likely low robustness of U.S. superiority would create strategic windows that create incentives for preventive war. These incentives would be largest if U.S. damage-limitation capabilities were essentially perfect. Thus, even if these highly effective damage-limitation capabilities reduce the probability of conventional war, the probability of nuclear war could increase, since the United States would have greater preventive incentives for escalating. Finally, the dangers of the less attractive cases are particularly significant since they are far more likely than the best case.

Consequently, in all but the best case, U.S. superiority would be preferable to MAD only if the increased probability of war were more than offset by reductions in its costs. This tradeoff is especially complicated because the probability of war might increase as the U.S. damage-limitation capability becomes more effective. Preemptive and preventive incentives could be higher when the United States is better able to reduce the costs of an all-out war. In addition, the Soviet Union might feel more threatened, and run larger risks, if the United States achieves decisive superiority than if it acquires a modest damage-limitation capability.

In assessing this tradeoff, two considerations suggest that MAD would be preferable to U.S. superiority, except in its best case. First, unless U.S. damage-limitation capabilities are essentially perfect, the costs of all-out war would remain incredibly high. Second, unless U.S. damage-limitation capabilities are highly robust, the U.S. ability to reduce the costs of war would be short-lived, but the probability of war might remain increased after the superpowers return to MAD. For example, the spiral effects of increased competition would continue, especially if the United States tried once again to regain superiority and the Soviet Union persisted in trying to defeat its efforts. There could also be military dangers. For example, the United States is more likely to misevaluate its capabilities while on the edge of MAD, believing incorrectly that striking first could still reduce damage somewhat and thereby creating perceived preemptive incentives.[71] The United States could then face the worst of both worlds: the probability of war would increase but the United States would no longer be able to reduce the costs of an all-out war.

There is, however, little doubt that U.S. superiority would be preferable to BAD, that is, a world in which both superpowers have highly effective strategic defenses. Although the preceding analysis shows that they suffer some similar shortcomings, U.S. superiority "solves" two of BAD's key problems. First, BAD might make the world safer for conventional war, while superiority increases the credibility of U.S. extended deterrent threats. Second, BAD could easily decay into U.S. inferiority, while U.S. superiority is most likely to decay back to MAD.

Recognizing that U.S. superiority is preferable to BAD provides another perspective on why the latter would be so competitive. Even if both superpowers were committed to the political status quo, they would wage an intense arms race to gain superiority's benefits, as well as to avoid inferiority's disadvantages. Thus, this evaluation of superiority provides a further warning

---

[71] Preemptive incentives in this case would also require the belief that the Soviets had some reason to strike first.

against starting down the strategic defense route under the illusion that BAD would be less scary and competitive than MAD. If at all successful, efforts initially directed toward BAD would almost certainly turn into a bitter competition for superiority.

The clear dangers and limited and questionable benefits of superiority suggest that in virtually all cases MAD is preferable to U.S. superiority. Consequently, the United States should steer clear of this highly competitive world and plan to base its security on the multiple advantages of MAD. Even analysts who disagree with this net assessment will hopefully recognize that superiority's advantages relative to MAD are greatly overrated. Since investing heavily in long shots only makes sense when they can provide overwhelming benefits, this undercuts their case for pursuing superiority.

CHAPTER SIX

Why Disarmament Is Probably More Dangerous than MAD

CALLS FOR disarmament play an important role in the nuclear debate, providing a long-term vision in which superpower cooperation eradicates their vulnerability to nuclear annihilation. In 1986 Mikhail Gorbachev presented a plan for complete nuclear disarmament by the year 2000.[1] Presidents Reagan and Carter expressed support for similar goals.[2] At the Reykjavik summit, Reagan and Gorbachev discussed the possibility in some detail.[3] This interest in nuclear disarmament is neither new nor confined to the rhetoric of national leaders.[4]

Although usually dismissed as utopian, disarmament nevertheless influences the policy debate by offering a distant alternative judged preferable to MAD. Although there appears to be a consensus that arms control should be

---

[1] On Gorbachev's arms control proposals see Matthew Evangelista, "The New Soviet Approach to Security," *World Policy Journal* (Fall 1986): 561–99.

[2] Ronald Reagan, Inaugural Address, 20 January 1985, reprinted in *Weekly Compilation of Presidential Documents* (Washington, D.C.: GPO, 1985), p. 69; Jimmy Carter, Inaugural Address, 20 January 1977, reprinted in *Weekly Compilation of Presidential Documents* (Washington, D.C.: GPO, 1977), p. 89.

[3] On the Reykjavik meeting see Michael Mandelbaum and Strobe Talbott, "Reykjavik and Beyond," *Foreign Affairs* 65, no. 2 (Winter 1986/87): 215–35. And the preambles to the ABM Treaty and the SALT II Treaty both state the superpowers' interest in general and complete disarmament: *Arms Control and Disarmament Agreements* (Washington, D.C.: Arms Control and Disarmament Agency, 1980), pp. 139, 207.

[4] For example, Philip Noel-Baker, *The Arms Race: A Programme for World Disarmament* (New York: Oceana Publications, 1958); J. David Singer, "Part III: Disarmament: Modifying the Environment," in his *Deterrence, Arms Control, and Disarmament* (Columbus: Ohio State University Press, 1962; Lanham, Md.: University Press of America, 1984); Richard J. Barnett and Richard A. Falk, eds., *Security in Disarmament* (Princeton: Princeton University Press, 1965); John H. Barton, "The Proscription of Nuclear Weapons: A Third Regime," in David C. Gompert et al., *Nuclear Weapons and World Politics* (New York: McGraw-Hill, 1977); Jonathan Schell, *The Abolition* (New York: Avon Books, 1984); and U.S. Catholic Conference, *The Challenge of Peace: God's Promise and Our Response* (Washington, D.C., 1983). See also Thomas C. Schelling, who while noncommittal on the desirability of disarmament, provides a framework for analyzing its military requirements: *The Stability of Total Disarmament*, Institute for Defense Analysis, Study Memorandum Number 1 (Washington, D.C., October 6, 1961); and idem, *Arms and Influence* (New Haven: Yale University Press, 1966), pp. 248–59. On early superpower arms control efforts focused on disarmament see Bernard G. Bechhoefer, *Postwar Negotiations for Arms Control* (Washington, D.C.: Brookings Institution, 1961). For discussion of prenuclear disarmament see Salvador de Madariaga, *Disarmament* (New York: Coward-McCann, 1929).

directed at reducing the size of the superpowers' arsenals, few proponents explain why smaller forces are preferable. The answer is not obvious, since the Soviet Union would retain its assured destruction capability. The appeal of disarmament probably explains much of this interest in reductions.[5] The INF (Intermediate-range Nuclear Forces) Treaty—which eliminated long-range theater missiles from Europe—reduced doubts about the feasibility of reductions and reinvigorated calls for reducing superpower strategic arsenals.

This influence is warranted only if disarmed worlds are preferable to MAD worlds. There is little analysis supporting this view, however. Instead, as with the other alternatives to MAD, mutual disarmament is simply assumed preferable because U.S. society is so vulnerable in MAD.

This chapter compares disarmed and MAD worlds by addressing three basic issues. The first section asks: What are the military requirements of a disarmed world? Military requirements would not disappear with disarmament, since rearmament would be possible. U.S. security would depend on being able to deny the Soviet Union a decisive military advantage in a nuclear rearmament race. Without this capability disarmament would not increase U.S. security. Further, without confidence in this capability, U.S. leaders would refuse to disarm. Thus, answering this question helps us understand the extent to which military requirements are a barrier to disarmament. In addition, this section considers two commonly discussed approaches for reducing the military risks of, and therefore the barriers to, a disarmed world: near-disarmament, which is proposed to reduce U.S. societal vulnerability while hedging against the danger of Soviet rearmament; and disarmament reinforced with strategic defenses, which are proposed to defeat Soviet rearmament.

The second section addresses the political requirements of disarmament. For example, could the military requirements of disarmament be achieved under current international and domestic political conditions? Military requirements cannot be defined separate from political conditions. Rather, beliefs about Soviet intentions influence how effectively the United States must be able to respond to Soviet rearmament. Doubts about the Soviet commitment to disarmament and the political status quo support more stringent U.S. military requirements.

The primary purpose of this assessment is not to determine whether disarmament is feasible, but instead to determine the political conditions that would

---

[5] On the consensus that arms control should reduce force size see Michael Krepon, *Strategic Stalemate: Nuclear Weapons and Arms Control in American Politics* (New York: St. Martin's, 1984), p. 132. Noting the lack of strong arguments in favor of reducing force size is Thomas C. Schelling, "What Went Wrong with Arms Control?" *Foreign Affairs* 64, no. 2 (Winter 1985/86): p. 226; see also Chapter Ten.

Further, not only proposals calling for reductions are linked to the future prospects of disarmament. See, for example, Randall Forsberg, "A Bilateral Nuclear-Weapon Freeze," *Scientific American* (November 1982): 61.

have to accompany superpower nuclear disarmament. I argue that although carefully designed military plans for rearmament could reduce the risk of disarmament, the superpowers would not agree to disarm until after their political relationship had fundamentally improved. Unlike the feasibility of competitive alternatives to MAD, which were evaluated in Chapters Four and Five, the desirability and feasibility of disarmament are tightly intertwined. Consequently, the most important comparison of disarmament to MAD assumes that superpower relations have improved in both worlds. There would be an important exception to this claim if the superpowers could improve their relationship by disarming, but I argue that they could not.[6]

To control for the importance of the superpowers' political relationship, the third section compares four worlds that are defined along two dimensions: the military dimension, where the possibilities are MAD and disarmament; and the political dimension, where the possibilities are superpower relations that resemble today's and superpower relations that have radically improved. Most discussions of disarmament focus on the least likely combination—disarmament with today's superpower relationship—and do little more than assume that disarmament under these conditions would increase U.S. security.

I conclude that without fundamental improvements in superpower relations the United States is likely to be at least as secure in MAD as in a nuclear disarmed world. In the latter, the probability of conventional war is likely to be greater and, unless disarmament is implemented very well, the probability of escalation to nuclear war would also probably be higher than in MAD. Moreover, the United States would be safer in MAD with fundamentally improved superpower relations than in a disarmed world with today's political relations.

Consequently, long-term efforts for increasing U.S. security should not focus on military plans for overcoming today's technical barriers to disarmament. Instead, the United States should explicitly commit itself to living in MAD while pursuing policies directed toward improving superpower relations.

In terms of military policy, this means the United States should adopt a strategy that appears as defensive (unthreatening) as its military requirements allow. At the strategic nuclear level, achieving this balance is relatively easy since retaliatory capabilities dominate damage-limitation capabilities; the United States should emphasize the former while forgoing the latter, including area-wide strategic defenses. Consideration of moving toward nuclear disarmament should wait until there have been truly radical improvements in superpower relations—sufficient to essentially eliminate not only current conflicts of interest, but also possible future ones. In the unlikely event that such

---

[6] As discussed below, it is even possible that disarmament could damage superpower relations, which would then put still greater stress on disarmament plans.

fundamental changes occur, however, the world would be so safe that disarming would not increase either country's security very much, and there would still be good reasons not to disarm.

THE MILITARY REQUIREMENTS OF NUCLEAR DISARMED AND NEAR-DISARMED WORLDS

Nuclear Disarmed Worlds

Neither superpower will agree to disarm if its adversary might gain a decisive military advantage by cheating, that is, by rearming or hiding nuclear weapons. This would be true even if superpower relations had improved fundamentally, since both countries would have to worry about the possibility of a less harmonious future. Moreover, disarming under the mistaken belief that these military dangers had been eliminated might reduce U.S. security: Soviet rearmament might leave the United States militarily inferior and unable to protect its vital interests. We should also note that even disarmament that meets these criteria might nevertheless reduce U.S. security if the probability of conventional war increases because nuclear deterrence is weakened. This key issue is explored in later sections.

FORCE-PLANNING CRITERIA

In broad terms, the military and deterrent requirements of a disarmed world resemble today's. Not only must the Soviet Union lack a significant military advantage, but it must be unable to acquire one by launching an arms race. In addition, the possibility of nuclear rearmament must not create pressures for preemptive or preventive rearmament; and, if a rearmament race begins, it should not create incentives for preemptive or preventive war. In other words, U.S. capabilities must be highly robust in the face of Soviet rearmament.

This robustness is required for three closely related reasons. Robustness helps deter rearmament: the ability to deny a significant military advantage greatly reduces Soviet incentives for rearming in the first place. In addition, robustness provides a kind of defense: if the Soviets do break out of the disarmament agreement, the ensuing arms race will create fewer dangers for the United States. Finally, because of these military considerations, robustness increases the feasibility of disarmament. Unlike the highly competitive alternatives to MAD—in which technology is the key to reducing societal vulnerability—the feasibility of disarmament is more closely related to its desirability. If both superpowers preferred a disarmed world to MAD, then disarmament would be feasible. However, if breakout threatened either's vital interests, then disarmament is less desirable, hence less feasible.

The robustness of disarmament will depend on four factors: the equality of rearmament rates, the magnitude of rearmament rates, the time to detect the adversary's rearmament, and the vulnerability of rearmament capabilities. First, if rearmament rates are unequal, then the country that can rearm more quickly might gain a strategically significant advantage, even if both countries begin rearming simultaneously. Thus, a Soviet advantage in rearmament rate might encourage it to break out of disarmament, even if it cannot gain a large head start. Along these lines, Thomas Schelling has argued:

> The essential requirement is for some stable situation of "rearmament parity." If disarmament is to be durable, it must be so designed that the disadvantages of being behind in case an arms race should resume are not too great and so that, in the face of ambiguous evidence of clandestine rearmament or overt evidence of imminent rearmament, nations can react without haste. The straightforward elimination of so-called "military production facilities" might, by sheer coincidence, provide the stability; but stability is more likely if there is a deliberately designed system of "stable equal readiness for rearmament."[7]

Second, even with equal rearmament rates, the absolute speed with which countries can rearm influences the value of a head start in rearmament. The slower the rate of rearmament, the smaller the advantage the Soviets can acquire before the United States also begins to rearm. In addition, by making a head start in rearmament less significant, slower rearmament rates might allow the superpowers to react less quickly to ambiguous indicators that the agreement is breaking down, thereby providing more time for resolving political disputes and for collecting information before making a decision to rearm. Thus, slower rates reduce pressures for preemptive rearmament. Furthermore, slower rearmament capabilities might reduce the dangers if a rearmament race occurred. Schelling argues that:

> It is not certain that maximizing the time required to rearm is a way to deter it. Lengthening the race course does not necessarily lessen the incentive to be first under the wire. It may, however, reduce the advantage of a small headstart; it may allow time to renegotiate before the race has too much momentum; and it may reduce the confidence of a fast starter that he could win if he called for a race.[8]

Third, the more quickly a Soviet breakout attempt can be detected, the smaller the lead that will be gained before the United States can react. Better monitoring capabilities might reduce the importance of achieving slow rearmament rates, and vice versa.

Finally, vulnerable rearmament capabilities can create pressures and incentives to rearm, and to initiate war once rearmament has begun. For example, if a small lead in breaking out of disarmament would enable the Soviet Union

[7] Thomas C. Schelling, *Arms and Influence*, pp. 248–59, quote from p. 257; idem, *The Stability of Total Disarmament*. For a recent application of this logic see Schell, *The Abolition*.

[8] Schelling, *Arms and Influence*, pp. 257–58.

to prevent U.S. rearmament, then breakout could confer large benefits. The Soviet Union could use its first weapons to destroy U.S. rearmament capabilities, and could then build as large a force as it desired, while denying the United States the ability to rearm. The Soviets might launch this breakout to pursue renewed expansionist objectives. But they might also act out of defensive concerns. If they feared that the United States would rearm in the future, then the Soviets might rearm and attack U.S. rearmament capabilities to guarantee the future invulnerability of Soviet society. In contrast, if U.S. rearmament capabilities were survivable, the Soviet Union might acquire a momentary lead but could not prevent the United States from acquiring a substantial retaliatory capability in the future. Although this "window of opportunity" might provide the Soviets with valuable coercive potential, their advantage would be far less decisive than if they could prevent the United States from rearming.[9]

In addition to insuring robustness against arms races, the superpowers would have to overcome the threat posed by the possibility of hidden weapons. Given the large arsenals the superpowers have deployed, it seems virtually impossible that either superpower could be sure that its adversary had not hidden tens or hundreds of weapons.[10] A country would certainly not destroy all of its nuclear weapons if it believed that its adversary had the ability to maintain a clandestine stockpile.

Some analysts believe that this problem could be solved if the superpowers have essentially equal capabilities to hide weapons.[11] According to this argument, each country would be deterred from using its hidden weapons by the possibility that the other had a comparable hidden supply with which to retaliate. Furthermore, recognizing the deterrent value of their *potential* for maintaining hidden arsenals, both countries would be willing to disarm. Some analysts have argued that the United States would suffer under such a scheme since its open society promises to make maintaining a clandestine stockpile more difficult.[12]

---

[9] There may be a tension between establishing survivable rearmament capabilities and slow rearmament rates. For example, one way to increase survivability is to allow large numbers of rearmament facilities, only a fraction of which are necessary to rebuild a nuclear force. Destroying this rearmament capability then requires one's adversary to rebuild a larger number of deliverable weapons. This approach, however, might provide the superpowers with faster rearmament rates since it allows more facilities.

[10] For example, Barton, "The Proscription of Nuclear Weapons," p. 157, estimates that the superpowers could hide a fraction of a percent of their current arsenals, which might provide in the low hundreds of weapons. Even when the number of weapons was much smaller than today, the possibility of a significant number of hidden weapons was considered unavoidable. Concern about the problems posed by hidden nuclear weapons dates back to 1946; see Noel-Baker, *The Arms Race*, pp. 288–94.

[11] Schell, *The Abolition*, p. 179.

[12] James N. Miller, Jr., "Zero and Minimal Nuclear Weapons," in Joseph S. Nye, Jr., Graham

SATISFYING THE FORCE-PLANNING REQUIREMENTS

Satisfying these requirements for robustness promises to be exceedingly difficult because U.S. security would be extremely sensitive to small differences in Soviet capability. Starting from a disarmed world, building a small number of nuclear weapons could provide the Soviet Union with a significant advantage in countervalue capability that could be used to coerce a still disarmed United States. Similarly, a relatively small number of nuclear weapons might constitute a decisive counterforce capability, enabling the Soviets to cripple the U.S. rearmament capability. Small numbers of hidden weapons raise similar dangers. By contrast, MAD is extremely robust.

Consequently, both superpowers would establish severe criteria for judging whether plans for disarmament guarantee sufficient robustness and equality in the ability to hide weapons. For starters, both superpowers would require virtually unlimited on-site inspection of all areas in which nuclear weapons had been deployed and all facilities that once produced or stored nuclear weapons and their delivery vehicles. Both countries would probably want to station large, essentially permanent, teams of inspectors in the other's country, and to send them throughout the country unannounced.

Further, commercial nuclear energy plants would be viewed as part of a country's rearmament potential. Adequately monitoring large nuclear energy programs would in itself pose an important challenge.[13] Beyond monitoring clandestine breakout, however, the superpowers would also insist that nuclear energy capabilities could not provide an advantage in an overt rearmament race. Therefore, the superpowers might have to coordinate their nuclear energy programs.

In addition, the superpowers would want to regulate conventional military capabilities that might provide advantages in nuclear rearmament.[14] In particular, nuclear rearmament capabilities would have to be invulnerable, or at least equally vulnerable, to the adversary's conventional forces. Consequently, all long-range delivery vehicles, bombers and missiles, would probably have to be limited. Limits would also have to cover shorter-range systems located nearer the adversary's homeland. For example, Soviet leaders might see a threat in conventional missiles and bombers located in Western Europe. Further, all systems that could easily be moved within range of the adversary's

---

T. Allison, and Albert Carnesale, eds., *Fateful Visions*, (Cambridge, Mass.: Ballinger, 1988), p. 18.

[13] For assessments of the challenges that nuclear power poses for limiting nuclear proliferation see *Nuclear Power and Choices: Report of the Nuclear Energy Policy Study Group*, sponsored by the Ford Foundation, administered by the MITRE Corporation (Cambridge, Mass.: Ballinger, 1977), and Amory B. Lovins, L. Hunter Lovins, and Leonard Ross, "Nuclear Power and Nuclear Bombs," *Foreign Affairs* 58, no. 5 (Summer 1980): 1137–77.

[14] Also, as discussed below, the superpowers would probably not agree to nuclear disarmament without conventional arms control agreements that provide high confidence that they can defend their vital interests against conventional attack.

homeland would have to be limited, including bombers on aircraft carriers, cruise missiles on naval vessels, and even medium-range bombers and missiles deployed in the United States, since they could be redeployed to Europe.

Further complicating matters, long-range delivery vehicles could pose another kind of threat—the means for delivering nuclear weapons. Trying to ban delivery systems would extend constraints beyond conventional military capabilities to include civilian aircraft. However, since delivering nuclear weapons might require a small number of planes, these restraints are beyond the limits of superpower cooperation. The ability to deliver nuclear weapons would remain a source of superpower concern.

In short, an acceptable disarmament agreement would require unprecedented superpower cooperation across a wide range of issues. The United States would demand high confidence in all of these arrangements since its security would remain sensitive to small disadvantages in rearmament.

Near-Disarmed Worlds

One way to reduce the risks of disarmament is for both superpowers to maintain very small nuclear forces. Small forces would increase robustness by guaranteeing the United States at least some ability to retaliate if the Soviets break out of the disarmament agreement. The prospects for achieving near-disarmament might therefore be greater than for total disarmament.[15]

In near-disarmament the superpowers would lack assured destruction capabilities. From their forces of over 10,000 strategic weapons, the superpowers might retain from a few tens to at the very most a few hundred nuclear weapons.[16] Forces in a near-disarmed world would be smaller than in a "minimum deterrent" force, which provides an assured destruction capability but not redundant retaliatory capabilities or counterforce weapons. Unlike a minimum deterrent force, near-disarmament promises to reduce the potential costs of an all-out war.[17] Of course, this benefit of near-disarmament is much smaller if

[15] Some analysts also see significant benefits in maintaining some nuclear weapons for deterring conventional attacks. A further reason for considering near-disarmament is that it would constitute the transition from MAD to disarmament and is therefore important to understand before moving to disarmament.

[16] This description includes useful simplifications about the extent of force reductions required to reduce the costs of an all-out war. First, it assumes that forces are highly survivable, and therefore that there is a close relationship between force size and retaliatory capability. The other possibility—in which the superpowers agree to forgo assured destruction capabilities by retaining large but vulnerable forces—is far less interesting for a variety of reasons, including the dangers of crisis instability. Second, the correct measure of destructive potential is equivalent megatonage, not the number of weapons. Thus, if we define near-disarmament to begin where the superpowers no longer have assured destruction capabilities, this boundary actually corresponds to a given number of survivable equivalent megatons, not a given number of weapons.

[17] Proponents favor minimum deterrent forces because they would forgo dangerous counterforce weapons and the strategies that require them, and avoid unnecessary economic costs. See,

the superpowers remain near the edges of MAD—retaining hundreds of weapons—than if they press near true disarmament.

Contrary to the common belief that an assured destruction capability is necessary, the following discussion suggests that the United States could adequately deter Soviet nuclear attacks in near-disarmament. In addition, the allowed nuclear weapons might continue to play some role in deterring conventional attacks. Rearmament, however, would continue to pose a serious threat, although a diminished one. Thus, near-disarmament would have advantages over total disarmament, but reducing the danger of rearmament would still encounter daunting barriers.

FORCE-PLANNING CRITERIA

In contrast to disarmament, in near-disarmament U.S. security would depend on the danger posed by allowed Soviet nuclear forces. Specifically, the United States would have to deter premeditated Soviet nuclear attacks and maintain crisis stability, in addition to maintaining high robustness.[18]

A reasonable requirement for deterring premeditated Soviet nuclear attacks against the U.S. homeland is for the United States to be able to inflict costs essentially equal to those the Soviet Union could inflict. From one perspective, this is a conservative requirement: the United States might be able to deter the Soviet Union without an ability to inflict roughly equal costs, since deterrence requires only that the Soviets expect to be worse off after starting a war than before it, not that they expect to be worse off than the United States. However, from another perspective the requirement is quite reasonable: if the Soviets can inflict greater costs than the United States, then the risk of a crisis or conventional war escalating to all-out nuclear war would not be shared equally by the two countries; as a result, the credibility of U.S. threats might be reduced and the Soviet ability to coerce the United States might be increased.

Because the Soviet Union could first attack U.S. forces and then its cities, the United States should possess this "equal countervalue capability" both before and after a Soviet counterforce attack. If the United States relies on its nuclear weapons solely for deterring Soviet nuclear attack, then its deterrent requirements could be satisfied at any level of countervalue capability. In contrast, if the United States plans to deter Soviet conventional attacks as well, then it must retain retaliatory capabilities above some minimum level, but

for example, Harold A. Feiveson, "Finite Deterrence," in Henry Shue, *Nuclear Deterrence and Moral Restraint* (Cambridge: Cambridge University Press, 1989), pp. 271–93.

[18] The following arguments parallel my arguments about deterrent requirements in a world of near-perfect defenses; their logical underpinnings are laid out in more detail in Chapter Four. The similarity arises because deterrence depends foremost on the ability to threaten costs and not on the means by which these costs are threatened. Thus, when considering whether basic U.S. military requirements of deterrence are satisfied, it matters little whether symmetric reductions in the superpowers' societal vulnerability stem from mutual deployment of highly effective strategic defenses or from mutual reductions of countervalue forces.

quite likely well below the level usually required for assured destruction.[19] Requiring a U.S. equal countervalue capability should not create special troubles in negotiating near-disarmament, since Soviet possession of a similar capability would be compatible with an agreement based on parity in superpower capabilities.

In theory, the superpowers could also negotiate a near-disarmed world that maintained crisis stability. If both countries had invulnerable forces and command and control there would be no incentive to preempt since a counterforce attack could not reduce the adversary's ability to inflict retaliatory damage. Unlike today, however, partially vulnerable forces would create preemptive incentives.[20] Thus, in near-disarmament, eliminating the vulnerability of superpower forces would be much more important than in a world of redundant assured destruction capabilities.

Whether the superpowers could actually make their forces and command and control nearly invulnerable is partially a technical issue. If, however, the superpowers were seriously interested in moving to very small nuclear forces, they could almost certainly cooperate to reduce dramatically the vulnerability of each other's forces.

Three examples illustrate the possible role of cooperation. The superpowers could agree to eliminate ballistic missiles entirely, leaving only air-breathing capabilities.[21] Because air-breathing threats are relatively slow, a country with good warning capabilities could thwart the adversary's counterforce attack by launching its bombers before the adversary's weapons arrived. In addition, by allowing the stationing of observers at their air bases the superpowers could increase their confidence that they would receive early warning of bomber attack.[22] The superpowers could also employ deception and/or mobility to make their forces highly survivable. For example, using deceptive basing, the

[19] It is true, however, that extended deterrence might be enhanced by a U.S. ability to inflict costs that greatly exceeded Soviet benefits in a conventional war, since in this case even threats of relatively low credibility might threaten high expected costs.

[20] Given today's forces, partial vulnerability does not create large first-strike advantages because the forces are so large that the survivable fraction can inflict costs essentially as large as the entire force.

[21] The possibility of getting rid of all ballistic missiles was raised at the Reykjavik summit. This plan, however, did not call for radical cuts in air-breathing forces and therefore was not viewed as a plan for near-disarmament. On these discussions see Mandelbaum and Talbott, "Reykjavik and Beyond," pp. 226–28. For a spectrum of views on the merits of getting rid of ballistic missiles while staying in MAD see the Policy Focus section in *International Security* 12, no. 1 (Summer 1987): 175–96.

[22] A possible analogy is the recent proposal for placing sensors in the adversary's ICBM fields. See Victor A. Utgoff, "On-site Automated Monitoring: An Application for Reducing the Probability of Accidental Nuclear War," in Barry M. Blechman, ed., *Preventing Nuclear War* (Bloomington: Indiana University Press, 1985), pp. 126–43, and Michael M. May and John R. Harvey, "Nuclear Operations and Arms Control," in Ashton B. Carter, John D. Steinbruner, and Charles A. Zraket, *Managing Nuclear Operations* (Washington, D.C.: Brookings Institution, 1987), pp. 717–18.

superpowers could achieve whatever level of survivability they desired by increasing the number of shelters while fixing the number of allowed weapons. Of course, the countries would have to implement cooperative measures to insure that shelters were not being used to hide illegal weapons.[23]

The principal advantage of near-disarmament is that, all else being equal, U.S. capabilities would be more robust in near-disarmament than in total nuclear disarmament. Assuming they remained survivable, allowed U.S. forces would reduce the dangers of Soviet cheating by providing the United States with at least some retaliatory capability. Soviet advantages in rearmament would be less effective in coercing the United States; and, following breakout, the United States would be better able to deter Soviet nuclear attack than if starting from total nuclear disarmament. Robustness would increase with the size of the superpowers' forces, since an advantage in rearmament matters less when the forces already deployed are relatively large and survivable.

However, although more robust than disarmament, near-disarmament would tend to be less robust than MAD, especially redundant and diversified MAD. Falling behind in a rearmament race might leave the United States vulnerable to coercion, since U.S. society would be more vulnerable than Soviet society. This danger would be larger for near-disarmed worlds that approached complete disarmament, both because the U.S. retaliatory threats would be smaller and because the Soviet Union could gain a larger advantage in the ability to inflict costs. In addition, Soviet advantages would be still more dangerous if rearmament threatened U.S. forces or rearmament capabilities, since the Soviet Union might then be able to eliminate U.S. retaliatory capabilities. U.S. leaders would also have to worry about Soviet breakout in strategic defenses, since they might work well against the relatively small forces allowed in near-disarmament.

Achieving robustness comparable to MAD's would require the superpowers to design near-disarmament according to the same criteria as total disarmament. Specifically, they would reduce and coordinate rearmament rates, reduce the warning time of breakout, and make allowed forces and rearmament facilities survivable. Unless they had high confidence in these measures, U.S. leaders would believe that moving to near-disarmament carried serious risks.

FEASIBILITY RELATIVE TO DISARMAMENT

Although probably less severe than for total disarmament, the technical barriers to near-disarmament would remain daunting. Although allowing small forces would create additional deterrent requirements, these are not the key problem; meeting U.S. requirements for deterring premeditated attacks and

---

[23] The United States considered this type of basing for the MX missile. See Office of Technology Assessment, *MX Basing Study* (Washington, D.C.: GPO, 1981). An MPS type basing mode might encounter less political opposition in a near-disarmed world: because it would have to defeat a relatively small attack, the system would require less land and be far less costly.

maintaining crisis stability would be relatively straightforward. By contrast, achieving adequate U.S. robustness to Soviet rearmament would still be exceedingly difficult. Because allowed weapons provide a hedge against Soviet cheating, the United States might accept greater uncertainty about its "equal readiness for rearmament" and a less comprehensive inspection regime. Nevertheless, if the United States had only ten or a few tens of nuclear weapons, its security would remain far more sensitive to Soviet rearmament than to any Soviet buildup that is possible today in MAD. Thus, the United States would demand extensive protection against breakout, with the resulting agreement approaching the complexity required for total disarmament.

The superpowers could reduce these barriers somewhat by staying close to MAD. At a point, however, this defeats the entire purpose of such drastic reductions. Forces that approach the minimum required for assured destruction cannot promise to reduce the costs of all-out war very much. Occupying a narrow slice on the spectrum between disarmament and today's forces, near-disarmament provides little room to hedge against rearmament.

Finally, the feasibility of near-disarmament might suffer from a relative lack of political appeal. Compared to total disarmament, near-disarmament would leave the United States vulnerable to extensive nuclear damage. On balance, therefore, reduced technical barriers might fail to make near-disarmament easier to achieve than total disarmament.

Strategic Defenses to Reinforce Disarmament

Some analysts argue that strategic defense can increase the prospects for disarmament by reducing technical barriers. These defenses would be unnecessary for reducing the countries' vulnerability to allowed weapons, since simply agreeing to get rid of all weapons would be a more direct and less expensive route to societal invulnerability. Defenses might, however, play a valuable role in reducing the risks of rearmament and hidden weapons.

The following discussion examines the potential for strategic defenses to reinforce disarmament and near-disarmament. Unfortunately, although strategic defenses could provide some benefits, they could also create severe problems of their own.

Point defenses and area defense would play different roles in reinforcing disarmament. Point defenses—systems designed to protect a small area and incapable of protecting cities—might increase the survivability of the countries' rearmament capabilities.[24] In near-disarmament, they could also increase the survivability of each side's allowed forces. Since defending these capabilities increases the size of the force required to destroy them, it reduces

---

[24] This feature of Schell, *The Abolition*, has received special attention. Schelling, *The Stability of Total Disarmament*, p. 17, also notes the potential value of this approach.

the significance of the adversary's hidden weapons and increases the time available to react to breakout. As a result, each country could afford to be less concerned about its adversary's ability to launch a rearmament race.

Point defenses are an alternative to other means of increasing survivability, which for rearmament capabilities include hardening and proliferation, and for forces include hardening, mobility, and deception. Each approach could increase robustness, and there is no general reason to prefer one over the others.

Area defense, on the other hand, might increase robustness by reducing the adversary's ability to gain an advantage in countervalue potential.[25] First, U.S. area defense could help reduce the effective rate at which the Soviet Union could rearm, since only a fraction of redeployed Soviet forces would then be able to reach the United States. This could reduce the significance of a Soviet head start in a rearmament race, which might in turn reduce the demands the United States placed on warning capabilities.

Second, area defenses could reduce the effective difference in superpower rearmament rates. Ideally, disarmament would provide countries with the ability to rearm at equal rates. However, given the complexity of rearmament capabilities, achieving confidence in equal rearmament rates might be impossible. Defenses might reduce this danger. Given different rearmament rates, strategic defenses could increase the time required for the leader to acquire a large advantage in countervalue capability. Third, area defenses could reduce the danger posed by hidden weapons. By reducing the effective size of hidden stockpiles, area defenses could reduce their coercive potential.

The preceding observations make clear that strategic defenses are best viewed as an alternative and complement to other means of creating robustness. Determining whether defenses would be the preferred option requires examining the problems they could create. Unfortunately, these problems could be considerable, especially for area defenses.

Superior area defenses could provide an advantage in rearmament, because one country's area defense reduces its adversary's effective rearmament capability.[26] Thus, an unconstrained competition in defenses could provide military advantages and convince one or both superpowers that a race to rebuild nuclear weapons and delivery vehicles was imminent.

Consequently, if disarmament is to be reinforced by defenses the superpowers would have to coordinate defenses with the same confidence with which they coordinate the entire spectrum of capabilities for building and delivering nuclear weapons. Since there is no reason to believe that defenses will be

---

[25] The following discussion assumes that area defenses would be effective against all relevant delivery systems. If not, their effects would be greatly diminished.

[26] Similarly, superior defenses might confer an advantage in hidden weapons: for example, if two countries are equally capable of hiding weapons, the country with superior defenses might have an advantage in countervalue potential. If, however, both countries' defenses could easily defeat all possible hidden arsenals, this advantage would be insignificant.

easier to balance, they appear to have no clear advantage in enhancing robustness against the adversary's breakout.

The need to limit defenses is even more obvious in near-disarmament.[27] In this case, unequal defense capabilities not only provide an advantage in effective rearmament capability but also leave one superpower less vulnerable than the other.

Further, rearmament parity would require equality in the ability to deploy additional defenses and in the ability to improve deployed defenses. An advantage in the ability to deploy area defenses is essentially equivalent to an advantage in offensive (countervalue) rearmament: new defenses reduce the effective rate of the adversary's rearmament; thus, an advantage in the defense race confers an advantage in the offense race. As a result, whether or not the superpowers agree to deploy some strategic defenses, disarmament would require the coordination of "defensive breakout" capabilities. Banning defenses, and the capabilities for building them, might reduce both superpowers' fears about a race in strategic defenses.

In addition, defenses could create further problems if their capability is uncertain. Uncertainty in defenses translates into uncertainty in relative rearmament rates, and in near-disarmament, into uncertainty about the vulnerability of one's society. Each country's analysts, looking through their conservative planning lenses, would judge their own defenses pessimistically and the adversary's optimistically. Assuming they have established parity in the ability to rebuild offenses, this interpretation of defenses would leave both countries convinced they suffer a disadvantage in effective rearmament rates.

Finally, defenses would create further complexities if they were vulnerable to deployed or rebuilt offenses. At a minimum, this vulnerability increases the ways that one's adversary might attempt to gain a decisive advantage, thereby making it more difficult to achieve high confidence in rearmament parity.

In sum, while strategic defenses might make some contribution to the robustness of disarmament, they could also create a host of problems and complexities. At a minimum, the superpowers would need to constrain defenses as well as offenses: advantages in defense would destroy the delicate balance of rearmament capabilities. Although their net effect necessarily depends on many particulars, defenses appear likely to increase the difficulty of coordinating superpower capabilities in disarmament.

In closing, we should distinguish these arguments from arguments that hold that defenses will create a commitment to disarmament. The former see defenses as a technical fix that increases the prospects for disarmament between countries *already* dedicated to this objective. From this perspective, defenses

---

[27] Determining how to mix offenses and defenses in near-disarmament promises to be extremely tricky. A given level of vulnerability could be achieved with larger offenses and more effective defenses, or with smaller offenses and less effective defenses. Robustness then depends on the difficulty of changing vulnerability by a given amount.

are much like other means for increasing robustness, including improving monitoring capabilities and coordinating, slowing, and hardening rearmament capabilities. In contrast, the latter view sees defenses as the key to disarmament. Its proponents hold that U.S. defenses could persuade the Soviet Union to agree to bilateral disarmament, even when neither country would otherwise be interested in disarming. This is the extreme form of the common argument that strategic defenses increase the prospects for arms control. Because this argument is severely flawed, I have focused on the role of defenses as a means of reducing the technical barriers to disarmament.[28]

THE POLITICAL REQUIREMENTS OF DISARMAMENT

Superpower judgments about whether a disarmament plan provides adequate assurance against breakout and cheating would depend on their political relationship. American beliefs about Soviet leaders' intentions and their commitment to disarmament would affect U.S. assessments of the probability that the Soviets would attempt to take advantage of flaws in the design and implementation of disarmament, and in turn whether disarmament would increase U.S. security. Thus, if the United States believes the Soviets harbor malign intentions and expansionist objectives, then the United States would hold plans for disarmament to a much higher standard than if it was confident that the Soviets were committed to maintaining the political status quo for the foreseeable future.

Therefore, in evaluating whether disarmament is desirable, we should control for the political conditions that would accompany it. For example, if, as I argue below, disarmament would be possible only after superpower relations have fundamentally improved, then the most important comparison of disar-

---

[28] For detailed analysis of the flawed claim that deploying BMD increases the prospects for reducing offenses see Chapter Nine. A possible exception to the arguments presented there might exist if strategic defenses had a cost-exchange ratio that strongly favored them in a competition to maintain assured destruction capabilities. See Albert Carnesale, "Special Supplement: The Strategic Defense Initiative," in George E. Hudson and Joseph Kruzel, eds., *American Defense Annual: 1985–1986* (Lexington, Mass.: Lexington Books, 1985), p. 200.

A closely related argument does not argue explicitly that defenses can increase countries' willingness to disarm, but notes that the United States can reduce the vulnerability of its homeland by deploying moderately effective defenses (ones that cannot deny the Soviet Union its assured destruction capability in a competitive world) if the superpowers agree to constrain their offenses. See, for example, D. G. Brennan, "Post-Deployment Policy Issues in BMD," in *Ballistic Missile Defense: Two Views*, Adelphi Paper No. 43 (London: IISS, 1967), pp. 8–9. Although correct, this statement is simply an observation about exchange calculations. The parallel observation about very deep reductions is: today's nuclear force can inflict greater costs than one that is dramatically reduced. Neither statement tells us anything about the prospects for achieving these arrangements.

mament to MAD is the one that assumes that superpower relations have improved in both worlds.[29]

As a result, although the preceding section is useful, reminding us that disarmament would depend on deterring rearmament and identifying the complexities that a disarmament agreement must cope with, it can also be misleading. By focusing on the military requirements of disarmament, these arguments can incorrectly imply that the key to escaping from nuclear vulnerability lies in designing carefully balanced rearmament capabilities. Although clearly necessary, this is almost certainly insufficient.

This section argues that disarmament would require fundamental changes in superpower relations, and that achieving these improvements will require overcoming an array of the most imposing barriers. The anarchic nature of the international system breeds skepticism and demands caution when vital interests are at stake.[30] As a result, the superpowers would probably not find even the most extensive plans for robust disarmament to be adequate until after their political disputes were entirely resolved and the possibility of future conflicts appeared vanishingly small. It is also possible that the constraints imposed by anarchy could make disarmament appear undesirable even under the most promising political conditions. The key point for our analysis, however, is not that disarmament might be infeasible, but instead that disarmament, if ever feasible, would occur only once superpower relations had fundamentally improved. In addition, disarmament would have to overcome a variety of imposing domestic political barriers. Near-disarmament would probably require less radical but still dramatic changes.

This need for political change is suggested by the lack of historical precedents. Great power adversaries have never cooperated on the scale required for disarmament. Instead, the most extensive security cooperation has been restricted to a moderation of competition inherent in the balance of power system, reflected in the countries' willingness not to exploit each others' short-term vulnerabilities.[31] Furthermore, national leaders have shown a strong

[29] However, a partial exception exists if the transition to disarmament would itself be a key factor in generating the necessary improvement in superpower relations. But, as discussed in the closing section of this chapter, moving to disarmament is quite unlikely to have this effect and could well have the opposite one, that is, it could strain superpower relations.

[30] Many analysts reach similar conclusions, with some seeing a world government or a world police force as an alternative. For a variety of views see in Barnet and Falk, *Security in Disarmament*: Richard J. Barnet, "Inspection: Shadow and Substance," pp. 30–36; Richard A. Falk, "Inspection, Trust, and Security," pp. 37–49; idem, "The Limitations of Inspection for Drastic Disarmament," 226–39; and Arthur I. Waskow, "Conflicting National Interests in Alternative Disarmed Worlds," pp. 373–83. See also Barton, "The Concept of Proscribing Nuclear Weapons," pp. 159–91, and Singer, *Deterrence, Arms Control and Disarmament*, pp. 180–91, 232–37.

[31] Robert Jervis, "From Balance to Concert: A Study of International Security Cooperation," *World Politics* 38, no. 1 (October 1985): 58–59.

preference for unilateral measures in protecting their vital interests.[32] This behavior, however, cannot be explained by a shortage of plans for extensive cooperation—rather, the past is better characterized by the consistent rejection of the plans that have been developed.[33] At a minimum, this raises doubts about whether technical arrangements can so dramatically redirect the superpowers' security policy.

International Barriers

Because the international order is anarchic—that is, states cannot count on a world government or international organization to resolve disputes and protect them from attack by others—cooperating on issues related to national security tends to be difficult. In the extreme case of disarmament, the tendencies created by anarchy are strongly reinforced because the superpowers will see threats to their vital interests and because these threats would arise from small deviations from the allowed military capabilities. In combination, these factors promise to drive the military requirements for disarmament beyond the superpowers' reach. Closely related, anarchy creates a barrier to disarmament by preserving a role for military force until both superpowers are satisfied with the political status quo and are highly confident that their adversary is satisfied as well.

International anarchy is the most fundamental barrier to disarmament, making countries reluctant to engage in extensive cooperation on security issues. Anarchy pressures states to be conservative, inclining them toward worst-case analysis focused on the adversary's capabilities. The alternative—moderating assessments of potential threats based on one's view of the adversary's relatively benign intentions—is too risky since intentions are easily misjudged and the adversary's objectives can always shift against one's interests. Robert Art describes the conservative lens through which states see the world: "Anarchy breeds skepticism about the motives of others and constrains statesmen to focus on what others can do, not on what they say they intend to do. . . . Anarchy literally constrains statesmen to be short sighted. . . . the avoidance of defeat is mightily prized."[34]

However, it is not anarchy alone that promises to make disarmament so

[32] Robert Jervis, "Security Regimes," *International Organization* 36, no. 2 (Spring 1982): 359–60.

[33] See, for example, Noel-Bake, *The Arms Race.*

[34] Robert J. Art, "The Role of Military Power in International Relations," in B. Thomas Trout and James E. Harf, eds., *National Security Affairs: Theoretical Perspectives and Contemporary Issues* (New Brunswick, N.J.: Transaction Books, 1982), pp. 15–16. See also Kenneth N. Waltz, *Theory of International Politics* (New York: Random House, 1979), pp. 171–72, who argues that bipolarity makes the superpowers even more conservative. Joseph M. Grieco reviews this literature in "Anarchy and the Limits of Cooperation: A Realist Critique of the Newest Liberal Institutionalism," *International Organization* 42, no. 3 (Summer 1988): 485–507.

difficult to achieve. Anarchy does not dictate intense competition and under certain conditions some security cooperation is quite possible. Even in a self-help system countries may be able to pursue security and protect their position in the system through cooperative means.[35] In particular, they can attempt to maintain necessary capabilities by agreeing to reciprocal restraint in military forces.

Rather, the difficulty of achieving acceptable plans for disarmament stems from the conservative inclinations generated by anarchy in combination with two additional factors.[36] First, decisionmakers will see the failure of disarmament posing a severe threat to their most vital interests, including maintaining their position in the international system and even possibly their sovereignty. Thus, they will be extremely reluctant to chance a breakdown in disarmament, since in this case the costs of falling into military inferiority would be overwhelmingly unacceptable. Consequently, plans for disarmament will be subjected to the most severely conservative scrutiny. With their most vital interests at stake, leaders will be extremely reluctant to base their national security policy on judgments about their adversary's future intentions. This would be true even when history provides examples of apparently similar situations in which military inferiority did not result in massive costs. For example, arguing that the United States did not use its nuclear monopoly to extract crippling concessions from the Soviet Union would probably be of little use in persuading decisionmakers to run the risks of disarmament. By comparison, countries

[35] Waltz, *Theory of International Politics*, p. 118, seems to underemphasize the potential role of cooperation, arguing that states can pursue security through internal balancing (increasing their capabilities) and external balancing (gaining and strengthening allies). At least in theory, states could pursue "cooperative balancing," as described by arms control theorists. Disarmament is a special case of this general approach. In addition, states could pursue policies designed to moderate their adversaries' aggressive intentions, thereby making them less dangerous although not necessarily less capable. The latter approach, however, is not easily handled by structural explanations of international politics.

For recent work on cooperation under anarchy see Robert Axelrod, *The Evolution of Cooperation* (New York: Basic Books, 1984); Kenneth A. Oye, ed., *Cooperation under Anarchy* (Princeton: Princeton University Press, 1986); and Robert O. Keohane, *After Hegemony: Cooperation and Discord in the World Political Economy* (Princeton: Princeton University Press, 1984). Grieco, "Anarchy and the Limits of Cooperation," challenges these arguments for failing to include states' concerns about relative gains. However, the severity of the relative gains constraint depends on considerations of offense and defense and their impact on the security dilemma, and therefore may not be a general feature of anarchy.

Applied to disarmament, however, this literature suggests that the prospects for disarmament are extremely poor. Among other problems, the possibility that defection could lead to catastrophic failure forces states to have an extremely short shadow of the future. For relevant points on security cooperation see Charles Lipson, "International Cooperation in Economic and Security Affairs," *World Politics* 37, no. 1 (October 1984): 12–18.

[36] Samuel P. Huntington, "Arms Races: Prerequisites and Results," *Public Policy* 8 (1958): 81, touches on these points.

are less conservative when judging security cooperation that involves less important interests.

Second, security in a disarmed world is sensitive to small changes in military capability. For example, tens of weapons provide a large advantage in the capability to inflict damage, and therefore a potentially large advantage in the ability to coerce. Because small changes in military capability could be decisive, decisionmakers would have to worry about even the most unlikely and ineffective routes to rearmament.

This sensitivity to small asymmetries in capability combined with the very conservative framework that countries must use to assess threats to vital interests greatly reduces the prospects for disarmament. The possibility that the Soviets harbor aggressive intentions will force U.S. decisionmakers to assume that the Soviet Union is planning to break out of the disarmament agreement, is willing to run high risks to break out—including forgoing the benefits of disarmament—and is likely to employ fully any military advantage it acquires. These fears would probably drive the standards for adequate rearmament parity beyond the reach of all conceivable plans for disarmament.

In contrast, in MAD there are greater possibilities for superpower arms control involving strategic nuclear weapons. Although today's analysis is conservative and vital interests are involved in negotiations over strategic nuclear force postures, MAD is much less sensitive to even large differences in forces. As a result, the prospects for superpower arms control are incomparably greater than for disarmament. Nevertheless, as I discuss below, the superpowers have made only modest progress in strategic arms control.

Extremely conservative decisionmaking also creates problems for overcoming the threat posed by hidden weapons. Recall that the key argument holds that neither country would benefit from its hidden weapons: the possibility that one's adversary has a hidden retaliatory capability deters the use of hidden weapons and, since both countries recognize this, the possibility of hidden weapons is acceptable. However, while countries in a disarmed world might be deterred by this possibility, decisionmakers considering disarmament are likely to find inadequate assurance in these arguments. Assessments of whether the adversary believes one's country has hidden weapons would be too uncertain to form the basis for one's security. For example, U.S. leaders, fearing that Soviet leaders might believe the United States had complied with the disarmament agreement, could easily foresee catastrophic results. In other words, the United States will not base its security on the hope that the Soviets believe we are cheating on an agreement that we are going to the greatest lengths to convince them we are complying with![37]

[37] In addition, imagine the problems of achieving domestic support for this agreement. Proponents could argue that the United States is going to comply with the treaty, in which case Soviet hidden weapons will provide an unacceptable advantage. Or, they can argue publicly that the

In addition, anarchy will tend to make disarmament still more difficult to achieve because its influence reaches beyond states' concern for their security: anarchy preserves a role for military force in the competition between major powers for international influence. Countries with conflicting international interests will continue to see force as the final arbiter of political disputes. Consequently, the United States and the Soviet Union will be unwilling to disarm until both are confident that the changes they desire in the political status quo can be accomplished peacefully. Much more demanding, each superpower must also be confident that the changes the other might desire can be achieved peacefully, without significantly compromising its own interest.[38] Consequently, the superpowers will find disarmament unacceptable until serious conflict in their relationship is virtually eliminated. Although insufficient, since future threats are possible, this is probably a necessary condition for disarmament.

Recent changes in Soviet policy appear to have reduced U.S. concern about Soviet determination to alter the status quo, but they also highlight the limits imposed by anarchy. Gorbachev's commitment to reducing and restructuring Soviet military forces, and his willingness to accept dramatic changes in Eastern Europe, have convinced many in the West that Soviet intentions are far less hostile than during the Cold War and that the Soviets might welcome a political status quo that is mutually acceptable. And these changes may create valuable opportunities for much more extensive superpower cooperation, both in reducing political conflicts and negotiating arms control agreements. Nevertheless, with rare exception, even strong proponents of policies designed to increase the chances that Gorbachev's domestic and international initiatives will succeed call for long-term American policies that provide protection against reversals in Soviet policy.

We should still ask whether the superpowers might agree to *nuclear* disar-

---

United States is going to cheat, which promises to make the agreement unacceptable to the Soviet Union.

[38] On this relationship between disarmament and the existence of political disputes see, for example, Merze Tate, *The United States and Armaments* (Cambridge: Harvard University Press, 1948), pp. 3–23, who argues that ''the greatest obstacle to effective disarmament always has been the impossibility of securing the acceptance of the *status quo*. . . . In the final analysis, effective disarmament can only be realized with the elimination of the dangers of war. Therefore, the supreme task of statesmanship is to find a substitute for war; to solve the problem of how provision for peaceful change within the international order can be made'' (pp. 22–23); Hans J. Morgenthau, *Politics among Nations*, 4th ed. (New York: Alfred A. Knopf, 1966), pp. 391–95: ''So long as nations advance contradictory claims in the contest for power, they are forced by the very logic of the power contest to advance contradictory claims for armaments. Therefore, a mutually satisfactory settlement of the power contest is a precondition for disarmament'' (p. 394); and Huntington, ''Arms Races,'' p. 81.

Recognition of this reality has generated work on peaceful change. See, for example, Richard A. Falk, ''Provision for Peaceful Change in a Disarming World,'' in Barnet and Falk, eds., *Security in Disarmament*.

mament without feeling confident that important political differences were resolved. One could argue that since neither superpower believes their political disputes are sufficiently important to warrant resort to nuclear weapons, both should be willing to accept the abolition of nuclear weapons while rejecting the abolition of conventional weapons.[39] Arguments for no-first-use of nuclear weapons would seem to be based on a similar conclusion about the relative costs and benefits of relying on nuclear weapons.[40] Given the interest in no-first-use, one could argue that it is not politically unrealistic to imagine the superpowers eventually forgoing strategies that depend on first use of nuclear weapons. Then, continues this argument, since nuclear weapons would be used only to deter the adversary's use of nuclear forces, and not to pursue political objectives, nuclear disarmament should be possible.

While identifying the need to moderate the boldest claims about the implications of political disputes, this counterargument is overstated. As long as the superpowers were concerned that they might fight a large conventional war over important interests, resort to nuclear rearmament would be a concern. Unlike today, U.S. leaders would fear that Soviet leaders might acquire a clear strategic nuclear advantage that might enable them to compel the United States to terminate a war on unfavorable terms.

In fact, superpower concern over the adequacy of their conventional forces could create another barrier to nuclear disarmament. Neither superpower would rely on the threat of nuclear rearmament to make up for a shortfall in its conventional forces. Thus, both would require high confidence in their conventional deterrents. Among other reasons, this confidence will be elusive because net assessments of conventional capabilities are extremely complex, uncertain, and controversial, far more so than nuclear net assessments.[41] In addition, confidence in future conventional capabilities would require a comprehensive conventional arms control agreement. Although serious discussions are now underway, their objectives are more modest than those that

---

[39] This argument seems consistent with John Mueller, "The Essential Irrelevance of Nuclear Weapons: Stability in the Postwar World," *International Security* 13, no. 2 (Fall 1988): 55–79. See also comments by Robert Jervis, "The Political Effects of Nuclear Weapons: A Comment," *International Security* 23, no. 2 (Fall 1988): 80–90.

[40] For citations to the debate over no-first-use see note 94 in Chapter Two. Note, however, that some proponents of no-first-use do point out that nuclear arsenals would have value for deterring conventional war even under a no-first-use policy. See, for example, McGeorge Bundy, "The Bishops and the Bomb." The basic observation is not weakened by this caveat.

Further, we should not confuse a willingness to forgo threats of first use with a belief that the superpower relationship necessarily permits NATO to have less than a highly effective military deterrent. Rather, many proponents of no-first-use require highly effective conventional forces and believe that such a change in doctrine should be accompanied by additions to NATO's already extensive conventional capabilities. See, for example, McGeorge Bundy et al., "Nuclear Weapons and the Atlantic Alliance," *Foreign Affairs* 60, no. 4 (Spring 1982): 759.

[41] On these issues see note 12 in Chapter Five.

would be required to support nuclear disarmament.[42] Further, because nuclear weapons contribute to deterrence of conventional war, reaching these agreements should be much easier today than in a nuclear disarmed world.[43]

In sum, although the logic that identifies rearmament parity as a necessary condition for superpower disarmament remains sound, international anarchy, combined with the lurking possibility of catastrophic failure in rearmament capabilities, virtually guarantees that the superpowers will establish extremely demanding standards for rearmament parity. The conservative lens that anarchy requires raises doubts about whether the superpowers could ever develop and implement plans for disarmament that met these standards. It seems virtually certain that fundamentally improved superpower relations, capable of moderating these standards somewhat, would be required before the superpowers agreed to disarm.

Domestic Political Barriers

In addition to these international barriers, at least three domestic political barriers would stand in the way of disarmament: elites who tend to exaggerate the adversary's hostility; militaries that are inclined to establish overly conservative force requirements; and domestic groups that would resist disarmament because their interests would be impinged upon by the disarmament agreement. Consequently, a disarmed world would be free of the dangers that can be created by myopic elites and overly influential militaries,[44] and would be created by superpowers whose societies were willing to make enormous sacrifices to avoid international conflict. Since disarmament would not create these conditions, comparisons of MAD and disarmament should assume that the MAD world benefits from similar domestic political conditions.

First, in both superpowers, severe doubts among political elites about the other superpower's intentions are likely to cripple efforts toward disarmament.[45] Americans who continue to fear that the Soviet Union is an expan-

---

[42] On the ongoing Conventional Forces in Europe (CFE) negotiations see Chalmers Hardenbergh, ed., *The Arms Control Reporter* (Brookline, Mass.: Institute for Defense and Disarmament Studies, 1990). On the previous failure of conventional arms control talks see Jonathon Dean, *Watershed in Europe: Dismantling the East-West Confrontation* (Lexington, Mass.: Lexington Books, 1987).

[43] Anarchy creates yet another barrier by requiring a state that is considering disarmament to consider future threats from states that are not included in the agreement, including current allies. Regarding nuclear disarmament, both superpowers are even less likely to disarm if other states could pose a nuclear threat in the future. Thus, superpower disarmament would be contingent on other nuclear powers agreeing to join the disarmament agreement and on nonnuclear powers accepting prohibitions on acquiring nuclear weapons. The superpowers would require essentially the same high confidence in these agreements that they would require in their bilateral agreement.

[44] On the possible dangers see Stephen W. Van Evera, "Causes of War" (Ph.D. diss., University of California at Berkeley, 1984).

[45] On the spectrum of views see Chapter Three.

sionist power will demand a level of rearmament parity that is even higher than that demanded by anarchy. Further, they will question whether engaging in extensive cooperation is the safest way to manage the superpower relationship. As described by the deterrence model, cooperating with an aggressor increases the probability of future challenges to one's interests; extensive cooperation might encourage Soviet leaders to underestimate U.S. resolve. These analysts will strongly oppose disarmament on general political grounds, long before the details of a disarmament plan become a serious barrier. Thus, until there is an overwhelming consensus among U.S. elites that the Soviet Union is essentially a status quo power, even near-disarmament will be blocked by fundamental disagreements about how to deal with superpower conflict.[46] It is true that Gorbachev's recent initiatives appear to have moderated the views of U.S. hard-liners, or at least have reduced their influence. Nevertheless, convincing skeptics will be far more difficult if superpower cooperation becomes extensive and carries much larger risks.

The superpowers' militaries will present a second domestic barrier to disarmament. We expect that superpower militaries would establish extremely conservative force-planning requirements, thereby making the requirements of rearmament parity impossible to satisfy. In part, this is because the military is responsible for focusing on the threats posed by the adversary's military capabilities. The result is often an exaggeration of the adversary's hostility and neglect of nonmilitary means of attaining security.[47] In addition, the military would have strong organizational reasons for opposing nuclear disarmament, since even near-disarmament would require the virtual elimination of large portions of the superpowers' military services.[48] From the military's perspective, protecting their organizational interests would be entirely consistent

---

[46] Such a consensus would be especially important since the U.S. public, although hopeful that U.S.-Soviet relations will continue to improve, remains wary of Soviet intentions. As a result, elites who oppose such extensive cooperation will be able to generate extensive opposition to "overly" cooperative policies. On recent views of the American public see Daniel Yankelovich and Richard Smoke, "America's 'New Thinking,' " *Foreign Affairs* 67, no. 1 (Fall 1988): 1–17; for comparison to the early 1980s see Public Agenda Foundation, *Voter Opinion on Nuclear Arms Policy: A Briefing Book for the 1984 Election* (New York: Public Agenda Foundation, 1984). See also Bruce Russett, "Democracy, Public Opinion and Nuclear Weapons," in Philip E. Tetlock et al., *Behavior, Society and Nuclear War* (New York: Oxford University Press, 1989), pp. 174–208, and Miroslav Nincic, "The United States, the Soviet Union, and the Politics of Opposites," *World Politics* 40, no. 4 (July 1988): 452–75.

[47] Jack Snyder, *The Ideology of the Offensive* (Ithaca: Cornell University Press, 1984), p. 28.

[48] One possible counterargument is that a buildup of conventional forces might offset, in organizational terms, the loss of nuclear forces. However, this ignores distribution effects between and within the military services. Probably more important, nuclear disarmament is likely to be accompanied by severe limits on conventional forces, not substantial additions.

On military organizational interest see Barry Posen, *The Sources of Military Doctrine* (Ithaca: Cornell University Press, 1984), and Morton H. Halperin, *Bureaucratic Politics & Foreign Policy* (Washington, D.C.: Brookings Institution, 1974).

with protecting the national interest, since both motivations reinforce the call for the most demanding military standards for disarmament.

The superpowers will almost certainly not proceed with plans for disarmament if their militaries find them dangerous.[49] The militaries will play a central role because they possess special expertise in military issues. For example, the U.S. military would be asked to assess the Soviet ability to hide weapons and break out from the agreement, and the U.S. ability to respond.

Superpower experience in nuclear arms control provides a useful benchmark. At least in the United States, military support for agreements is considered essential for their ratification. As a result, the military has significantly influenced the formulation of U.S. arms control policy and has been able to protect its priority programs.[50]

Of course, if superpower relations were so dramatically transformed that potential military threats could be heavily discounted, then the influence of the military might be reduced. In part, military influence reflects the international and domestic context in which political decisions are being made.[51] This possibility, however, only serves to reinforce the conclusion that political changes are a prerequisite for acceptable plans for disarmament.

A third domestic barrier to disarmament would probably result from the need to coordinate and restrain many activities not usually thought to have military implications. Each superpower is likely to see the other's civilian economy having implications for rearmament and therefore posing a threat that must be constrained. Most obviously, the superpowers would have to agree to severe control of their nuclear power plants and their fuel cycles. In addition, a variety of nonnuclear production capabilities would pose a greater concern. For example, facilities that produce civilian aircraft and missiles for space programs might provide a base for building strategic delivery vehicles; and research in electronics and material science might provide a capability for defeating the adversary's defenses. Moreover, because disarmament would make other means of mass destruction more important, limiting and monitoring research in areas related to biological and chemical weapons would take on much greater importance. Further, because the clandestine delivery of nuclear weapons to one's territory would be much more threatening in a disarmed world, the superpowers would feel pressure to secure their borders more effectively than is necessary today. Without imagining all the details, it is clear that a disarmed world would demand constraints that reached far beyond standard military capabilities.

<hr />

[49] On the extensive influence of militaries see Stephen Van Evera, "Causes of War" (Ph.D. diss., University of California at Berkeley, 1984), pp. 202–50.

[50] On this point see Steven E. Miller, "Politics over Promise: Domestic Impediments to Arms Control," *International Security* 8, no. 4 (Spring 1984): 79–82.

[51] This observation also suggests caution in generalizing to the Soviet Union based on U.S. experience, since the Soviet military operates in a different institutional and political setting.

Disagreements about the Political Requirements

FEAR OF NUCLEAR WAR DWARFS POLITICAL BARRIERS

One response is that the preceding arguments, although logically sound, might nevertheless be poor predictors of superpower behavior. Faced with the horror of nuclear annihilation, might not the superpowers become determined to eliminate or ignore these barriers? If so, then disarmament would not have to be preceded by fundamental international and domestic political changes. However, our experience to date in MAD provides essentially no support for this hope.

Consider the limited accomplishments of superpower arms control in MAD. The comparison is useful because in today's world, characterized by redundant assured destruction capabilities, the superpowers should find cooperating much easier than in a disarmed or near-disarmed world.[52] The risks of cooperating in MAD are really quite small. None of the proposals the superpowers have seriously considered would have reduced or constrained key U.S. capabilities: U.S. retaliatory capabilities would have been well insured; and the United States has essentially no prospect of gaining a significant damage-limitation capability with or without arms control. In addition, because the permitted capabilities would have been insensitive to even relatively large changes in Soviet forces, feasible Soviet cheating would have been strategically insignificant. Nevertheless, the superpowers have found reaching limitations on strategic nuclear forces quite difficult.

The limited accomplishments of arms control during the 1970s and 1980s are not explained by a lack of innovative and ambitious arms control proposals. Instead, the international and especially the domestic factors explored above have been the major constraints on superpower arms control. For example, deep divisions within the United States about what type of arms control, if any, would serve U.S. interests have severely limited the range of feasible agreements. Analysts on the American political right argue that even in MAD there are large risks to modest agreements. In an effort to gain their support, U.S. negotiators have set standards for adequate verification that are far more demanding than necessary to identify strategically significant cheating in a timely manner. In addition, in large part to satisfy its political right, the United States has had to avoid asymmetries in permitted forces. Yet in MAD, these asymmetries could create at most marginal Soviet military advantages, and then only if one accepts critics' implausible scenarios. Nevertheless, the carefully negotiated SALT II Treaty was harshly judged along these

---

[52] We expect that cooperation would be relatively easy when there is little or no security dilemma. Thus, cooperation should be easy in MAD and much more difficult in disarmament.

dimensions.[53] Projecting similar constraints onto disarmament—where small differences in capability could produce large differences in security—makes it clear that no disarmament plan would be acceptable without unprecedented change in U.S. domestic politics.

In addition, as noted above, the military has been able to protect its most valued weapons systems, even when the strategic rationale for additional or improved systems has been weak. If anything, the military will be able to make much stronger arguments against disarmament.

In short, in our current MAD world, which provides the opportunity for relatively easy cooperation, the superpowers have maintained their security primarily through unilateral means. Until the superpowers demonstrate a much greater capacity to cooperate in MAD, we have no grounds for believing that disarmament can be made possible by even the most carefully designed plans for establishing rearmament parity. The prerequisite is political change.

MOVING TO DISARMAMENT ELIMINATES POLITICAL BARRIERS

Another response to the preceding arguments holds that nuclear weapons are a source of superpower tensions and, therefore, moving toward disarmament can eliminate these tensions and enable the superpowers to disarm. In other words, reducing the size of nuclear arsenals in MAD and then beginning to disarm (that is, moving out of MAD) will eliminate the political barriers to disarmament. Consequently, disarmament is both more desirable and more feasible than I suggest. This counterargument, however, both overlooks a more promising approach for reducing superpower tensions and exaggerates the potential contribution of disarming.

To reduce the tensions and misperceptions created by their strategic nuclear forces, the superpowers should give priority to avoiding nuclear forces that threaten the military capabilities that their adversary requires for deterrence. This is the most basic approach because it attempts to eliminate the insecurity that is generated by the combination of anarchy and the security dilemma, which in turn gives rise to the dangers identified by the spiral model. In general, to accomplish this objective the superpowers should adopt defensive strategies while avoiding offensive ones. Nuclear weapons provide a special opportunity to pursue this approach since they essentially eliminate the security dilemma. Recall that the nuclear revolution strongly favors defensive (countervalue and retaliatory) strategies over offensive (counterforce and preemptive) strategies, and makes the forces required by these strategies distinguishable. Both superpowers can satisfy their military deterrent requirements without threatening the other's necessary deterrent capability.

---

[53] On Carter administration efforts to satisfy its critics see Strobe Talbott, *Endgame: The Inside Story of SALT II* (New York: Harper & Row, 1979). For a classic criticism of the treaty see Edward N. Luttwak, "Ten Questions about SALT II," *Commentary* (August 1979).

Consequently, in attempting to reduce whatever tensions their nuclear forces create the superpowers should first take full advantage of the nuclear revolution by shifting away from offensive counterforce doctrines and rejecting the possibility of future competitive worlds that rely on strategic defenses. In other words, instead of pursuing reductions to get out of MAD, the superpowers should first forgo offense in MAD.[54] Furthermore, considering feasibility also suggests that this approach deserves priority: it faces less severe barriers than disarming and, closely related, it is essentially risk-free since defensive strategies have a clear advantage over offensive ones.[55]

By comparison, it is far less clear that reducing countervalue capabilities below the levels required for assured destruction would further reduce the tensions generated by nuclear capabilities, and it might increase them. On the one hand, the ability to destroy each other's societies might contribute to the superpowers' perceptions of each other as threatening. In this case, agreeing to reduce the vulnerability of their societies might help reduce tensions.[56] However, these tensions would already be quite small if both superpowers believe that their adversary has little interest in expansion and are confident that their own military deterrent requirements are satisfied. Defensive nuclear strategies based on highly robust countervalue capabilities can help bring about these conditions by providing highly effective deterrent capabilities while avoiding the negative political consequences predicted by security dilemma and spiral model arguments.

On the other hand, moving toward disarmament is likely to reduce the robustness of the superpowers' deterrent capabilities and could therefore become a source of superpower tension if one or both countries see an increased possibility of military threats to their security. Of course, the extent to which robustness would be reduced would depend on how far the superpowers move below the capabilities required for assured destruction. In fact, even while still in MAD, reducing the diversity and redundancy of assured destruction capabilities could result in somewhat reduced robustness. Robustness will be

---

[54] In a sense, pursuing rearmament parity is an attempt to recreate a type of defense dominance by creating a situation in which getting a head start in a rearmament race provides little advantage. In other words, adding additional capabilities to existing forces matters little, which is the situation when defense has the advantage over offense. However, because security in a disarmed world is sensitive to small changes in capabilities, creating this type of defense dominance promises to be quite difficult.

[55] Furthermore, in narrower military terms, a shift away from counterforce is probably a prerequisite for agreeing to reduce force size enough to escape MAD. Reducing force size would be easier—since a larger fraction of the force would survive—and would provide near-disarmament with necessary crisis stability.

[56] In other words, these reductions help to eliminate the "survival dilemma." Nuclear weapons are a revolution for the defense and thus eliminate the security dilemma; but, unlike defense dominance based on denial capabilities, deterrence based on retaliation creates a survival dilemma. On the survival dilemma see Van Evera, "Causes of War," Chapter Four.

harder to maintain as the superpowers move below assured destruction into near-disarmament, and still more difficult as they approach total disarmament. It is true, however, that well-designed rearmament capabilities might help to minimize the reduction of robustness.

Whether moving toward disarmament would reduce superpower tensions depends on comparing these competing effects. If U.S. attitudes during the 1970s and 1980s are any guide to the future, then we should expect that the superpowers will worry a great deal about even unlikely future threats to their nuclear deterrent capabilities. If so, then trading robustness for reductions in societal vulnerability is likely to generate more concern than it eliminates. It is also possible that past behavior is not a good guide to the future. As other sources of conflict are reduced, the superpowers might become less concerned about threats to their military capabilities, which would in turn make reductions in robustness less worrisome. However, in this case, the political benefits of reducing societal vulnerability would also be smaller, since war would be less likely.

SECURITY IN DISARMED AND MAD WORLDS

Having explored the military and political requirements of disarmament, we are prepared to compare U.S. security in disarmament and in MAD. Imagine four worlds: in two the superpowers disarm and in the other two they maintain assured destruction capabilities; in one of the disarmed worlds and in one of the MAD worlds superpower relations remain essentially as they are today; in the other worlds superpower relations have fundamentally improved. These possibilities are presented in the chart below.

Consider each of the four worlds. The first, a world with superpower politics unchanged where each side has an assured destruction capability is, of course, the present world. The second, a world with superpower politics unchanged but in which the superpowers have nevertheless disarmed, is, as argued in the preceding section, exceedingly unlikely to ever occur. For the sake of analysis, however, assume that the superpowers agree to disarm, even though most of today's political conflicts remain unresolved and doubts about the adversary's intentions persist. Maybe the superpowers were shocked into disarmament by a small nuclear war, possibly one initiated by a country that

		Force Structure	
		MAD	Disarmed
Superpower Politics	Unchanged	I	II
	Fundamentally Improved	III	IV

had recently acquired a small nuclear arsenal.[57] Or perhaps disarmament resulted from the coincidence of overly optimistic leaders in both countries, an extended lull in overt conflict, and an exceptionally broad-based political consensus on the urgency of getting rid of nuclear weapons. The following discussion does not depend heavily on the details of how disarmament occurred when seemingly necessary conditions were unsatisfied.

In the third of the worlds considered here, a world with fundamentally improved relations yet still in MAD, the superpowers are able to overcome the international and domestic barriers described above. Disarmament might be possible, but the superpowers choose to keep their large nuclear arsenals. Since these arsenals are politically unnecessary and domestic pressures for expanding and modernizing military capabilities no longer exist, we can assume that, unlike our current MAD world, the superpowers focus on maintaining retaliatory capabilities and forgo threats to one another's forces. These nuclear forces might be maintained under the guidance of formal arms control agreements or through reciprocated unilateral restraint. The fourth world considered here is one in which superpower relations have fundamentally improved and the superpowers have disarmed.

This section argues that U.S. security would be greater in the two worlds with fundamentally improved relations than in the worlds that politically resemble today's. This is true even though U.S. society is more vulnerable in MAD with improved relations than in disarmament with unchanged relations. Further, the United States would probably be safer in today's world—MAD with current superpower relations—than in the nuclear disarmed world with current superpower relations. Finally, if superpower relations improve dramatically, the United States would have little reason to move from MAD to disarmament and, somewhat ironically, doing so could even reduce U.S. security.

Comparison of worlds with current superpower relations to those with fundamentally improved relations sounds tautological: superpower war is less likely when the countries have much less to fight over, when the countries find each other unthreatening, and when domestic pressures to create enemies have been eliminated. This apparent circularity, however, reflects an essential feature of these worlds: by assuming that the necessary conditions for disarmament have been achieved, we have posited the most obvious conditions for continuing peace between the superpowers. In other words, to make disarmament possible we had to first eliminate the problem disarmament was designed to solve. As we will see below, this realization greatly reduces the relative desirability of disarming when it might be possible.

---

[57] Jervis, "Security Regimes," p. 378, observes that a security regime might require such a shock. See also Herman Kahn, *Thinking about the Unthinkable* (New York: Horizon Press, 1962), pp. 148–49.

Comparing Worlds II and III

Some analysts might challenge the importance that the above argument places on superpower relations, arguing instead that it is safer to disarm with superpower relations unchanged than to remain in MAD with improved relations.[58] According to this argument, a world of large nuclear arsenals is more dangerous than a disarmed world because the risks of living with societies vulnerable to nuclear devastation are simply too great.

This argument has important shortcomings. In a world in which superpower relations have been fundamentally improved, the danger posed by nuclear arsenals is primarily limited to nuclear accidents. Yet in such a world the danger of accidents is greatly reduced. First, even with today's forces, the probability of accidents in peacetime is extremely low; although the probability increases in severe crises,[59] we expect that these crises will not occur once superpower relations are fundamentally improved. Second, with the superpowers having restructured their nuclear arsenals into purely countervalue forces, the pressures to go on high alert during a crisis and to react quickly to warning of attack would be eliminated, thereby greatly reducing the probability that a crisis would lead to an accidental attack. Third, the probability that an accident would turn into a large war would be much lower in the world of improved relations than it is today. Given the change in relations, an accident would not be confused with deliberate attack. Further, with superpower forces restructured, the attacked country would lack incentives for retaliating quickly and could take the time necessary to eliminate confusion about the adversary's intentions.

Still unconvinced, some proponents of disarmament will argue that even after a fundamental improvement in relations, the superpowers might become involved in a deliberate war and, therefore, that their nuclear arsenals would continue to present unacceptable risks. This argument, however, suffers two shortcomings. If the superpowers are still thinking this way, then we would not consider their relationship to have fundamentally improved and they would probably remain unwilling to disarm. Second, this counterargument overlooks a key point: any war can become a nuclear war, even in a disarmed world. Disarmament cannot make a nuclear war impossible; it increases the amount of time before nuclear weapons can be used. Therefore, since nuclear war can occur in either of these worlds we need to ask: In which world is it more likely? If nuclear war occurs, in which world would it be more costly?

Because the superpowers have more to fight over, the probability that superpower conflict would lead to crises or conventional war is greater in the

---

[58] This belief seems to underlie arguments for disarmament that focus on technical solutions rather than political problems. See, for example, Schell, *The Abolition*.

[59] See Paul Bracken, "Accidental Nuclear War," in Graham T. Allison et al., *Hawks, Doves, & Owls* (New York: W. W. Norton, 1985).

world with unchanged relations. These conflicts are likely to eventually lead to nuclear rearmament. If this takes place during a conventional war, then rearmament might lead directly to nuclear war. If not, then rearmament might lead back to MAD, that is, back to today's world. Under less fortunate circumstances, rearmament itself may generate pressures for preemptive and/or preventive war. Faced with its first serious test, the superpowers' supposed slow and equal capabilities to rearm might demonstrate unforeseen flaws that create windows of opportunity or preemptive incentives. In contrast, while nuclear war is possible without delay in MAD with improved relations, according to our assumptions the superpowers would lack reasons for going to war for the foreseeable future. Thus, deliberate nuclear war seems less likely starting from this world than from a disarmed world in which relations remain unimproved. Furthermore, as discussed shortly, nuclear wars occurring in MAD might not result in greater damage than those occurring from disarmament, since MAD can create conditions favorable for terminating a limited nuclear war.

Comparing Worlds II and I

Would a disarmed world be preferable to today's world if superpower relations remained fundamentally unchanged? In certain ways, this question may be more interesting than the previous one, since we lack clear ideas about how to bring about and maintain worlds in which superpower relations have been fundamentally transformed. Keep in mind, however, that this is also an artificial comparison. As argued above, there are strong reasons to believe that the superpowers would not disarm before their relationship improves fundamentally. That said, we ask: If the superpowers could somehow develop technical arrangements that overcome today's technical and political barriers, would not disarmament be preferable to remaining in MAD? To answer this question we need to compare the probability of superpower conventional war in these worlds, the probability that these wars would escalate to nuclear wars, and the costs of wars if they occur.

The probability of conventional war would be higher in this nuclear disarmed world than it is today. Most analysts believe that the possibility of nuclear war adds to deterrence of large conventional war.[60] If so, then as long as

[60] The logic here parallels the argument that perfect defenses would increase the probability of conventional war. As noted in that discussion, analysts disagree about how much and what types of wars U.S. nuclear weapons help to deter in MAD. For general disagreement see Mueller, "The Essential Irrelevance of Nuclear Weapons."

The following arguments do not, however, cover the possibility of what some people think of as "crazy" leaders who are insensitive to the nuclear deterrent threats facing them. In such a rare case, disarmament would not increase the probability of war and, as discussed below, might provide opportunities for avoiding nuclear war once conventional war has begun.

the incentives and pressures for war are not diminished, removing the possibility of escalation to the nuclear level weakens the U.S. ability to deter Soviet aggression, increasing the probability of conventional war. In addition, in a world without nuclear weapons, both superpowers might exercise less restraint in their global competition, thereby increasing the number and intensity of crises that might escalate to conventional war, even though the initiator did not anticipate armed conflict.

Although these arguments are essentially correct, three qualifications are in order. First, since nuclear arsenals could be rebuilt, both superpowers would know that nuclear escalation is possible, just not as quickly as in the nuclear armed world. Thus, the possibility of escalation to the nuclear level might still hold some deterrent value. There is the danger, however, that if disarmament were designed well enough to convince superpower leaders that their security was adequately protected, nuclear rearmament might then be too slow. As a result, states might try to fight and win conventional wars before rearmament was possible. This would reduce the deterrent value of the possibility of reacquiring nuclear weapons. It is also hard for proponents of disarmament to have it both ways: either nuclear rearmament is so well controlled that it has little deterrent value or it is not so well controlled and conventional wars are more likely to escalate to the nuclear level.

Second, recognizing that intense competition would create pressure for rearmament, the superpowers might moderate their behavior. If the benefits of disarmament (most immediately, reduced vulnerability to nuclear attack) greatly exceed the potential benefits of competition, then disarmament might generate its own incentives for cooperation.[61] Yet this argument overlooks an obvious point: states that are so worried by the possibility of nuclear attack should act even more cautiously in an armed world than in a disarmed world.

Third, one could argue that the probability of conventional war would be low because the superpowers would agree to nuclear disarmament only if they reached agreements on conventional forces that insured their ability to deter each other. Given this condition, the enhanced deterrent capability of a country's conventional forces might offset the loss of its nuclear deterrent. Again, the counterargument fails to hold superpower politics constant: superpowers that could reach such effective conventional agreements in a nuclear disarmed world should be able to reach the same conventional agreements in a nuclear armed world. In fact, because nuclear weapons make the conventional balance less important, conventional agreements should be easier to reach in the nuclear armed world. If so, then the armed world could provide the best of both deterrents: highly effective conventional deterrence reinforced by the clear

---

[61] In a similar vein, Morton Halperin, *Limited War in the Nuclear Age* (New York: John Wiley, 1963), notes that more modest arms control agreements might help deter limited war if the superpowers believed that war would end the agreements.

possibility of escalation to nuclear use. In short, given the assumption that superpower relations resemble today's, the probability of conventional war is likely to be higher in the disarmed world than in MAD.

The probability that a conventional war would escalate to the nuclear level in a nuclear disarmed world depends on two factors: the probability that the superpowers rearm and the probability that a rearmed country chooses to launch a nuclear attack. It seems virtually certain that a large conventional superpower war would lead to rearmament. By confirming one's worst fears about the adversary's intentions, a large conventional war would make continuing with nuclear disarmament far too risky. Technical arrangements for insuring rearmament parity that were adequate during peacetime would be found inadequate once a large conventional war was underway. Making matters worse, certain arrangements, for example on-site inspection, would probably stop functioning.

Whether the rearming countries would be more or less likely to escalate than countries that had remained in MAD depends on the quality of rearmament capabilities. As noted above, one possibility is that rearmament capabilities turn out to be poorly matched, creating preemptive and/or preventive incentives, or providing one country with a nuclear capability useful for compelling its adversary to terminate the war on favorable terms. In these cases, the probability of conventional war leading to nuclear use would be higher than in MAD. On the other hand, rearmament might turn out to be so well designed that the transition back to MAD was not plagued by instabilities and military advantages. In this case a return to MAD is more likely, and the probability of escalation to nuclear war seems comparable to the case in which the superpowers had maintained their assured destruction capabilities. Nuclear war might occur before the superpowers entirely rebuild their capabilities to annihilate each other, or following reacquisition of assured destruction capabilities. A third possibility is that rearmament rates were so low that the conventional war is terminated before the superpowers reacquired deliverable nuclear weapons. In this case, escalation of the conventional war is impossible and the superpowers are likely to build back to MAD following the war, unless preventive incentives make nuclear attack especially attractive. In short, whether escalation from conventional to nuclear war is more likely starting from disarmament or from MAD appears to depend on the details of the disarmament plans.

Although it is hard to know which of these rearmament scenarios is more likely, we should recall that this is a world in which superpower relations have not fundamentally improved. In such a world it would be difficult for the superpowers to have confidence that their plans for slow and equal rearmament capabilities would in fact eliminate military pressures and opportunities in a rearmament race. The United States would not know how effective its rearmament capabilities were, since they would be complex and untested; neither would the Soviets. Given doubts about each other's intentions and the relative effectiveness of their rearmament capabilities, both superpowers would probably make efforts to maintain some secrecy about those rearmament capabilities. Thus, without fundamentally improved relations we expect that the superpowers would go to great lengths to hedge against the adversary's rapid rearmament, thereby making mismatched capabilities more likely.

As noted above, in terms of reducing costs, the advantage of disarmament is clearest when rearmament would take place so slowly that neither superpower reacquires nuclear weapons before the conventional war is terminated. If instead nuclear weapons become available during the conventional war, but slowly enough that neither country regains its ability to annihilate the other before the war is terminated, then nuclear war would be possible but less costly than an all-out war in MAD. If rearmament takes place more quickly, then (assuming that rearmament capabilities are survivable) the potential costs of a nuclear war would be the same as in MAD. In effect, if rearmament capabilities are sufficiently slow, then disarmament can reduce the costs of an all-out war by providing the superpowers with additional time for terminating the conventional war, and possibly a limited nuclear war, before they can once again annihilate each other.

Whether disarmament is necessary to provide time for terminating a limited war depends heavily on the nature of the MAD world we compare it to. MAD provides the superpowers with the capability of immediately annihilating each other; however, it eliminates the incentives to act quickly and creates incentives to maintain the adversary's cities and other value targets as hostages. Consequently, a nuclear war in MAD need not proceed quickly. In fact, it "should" proceed slowly.[62] If wars in MAD would be fought according to this logic, the time provided by rearmament might be of little or no value. Of course, by emphasizing counterforce and marginal damage-limitation capabilities in their current nuclear doctrines, the superpowers have failed to take advantage of this opportunity to fight slowly, and consequently they are more likely to fight a nuclear war quickly in a few massive attacks. But this says much about current thinking in MAD and little about the opportunities that alternative policies might provide for limiting a nuclear war. If the superpowers could agree to disarm, then they could almost certainly agree to these more modest changes in nuclear strategy.

In sum, assuming that superpower relations remain essentially unchanged, the case for disarmament is mixed, leaving serious doubts about whether the United States would be more secure in this disarmed world than in MAD. In this world disarmament would probably bring a range of dangers. Conventional wars promise to be more likely than in MAD, which is not to be taken lightly since large conventional wars could be extremely costly. Further, even

---

[62] See Schelling, *Arms and Influence*, pp. 166–220.

well-designed disarmament might not reduce the probability of escalation from conventional to nuclear war, and if rearmament capabilities turn out to be poorly balanced the probability of nuclear escalation would be higher than in MAD. This possibility is especially worrisome, since implementing adequate disarmament plans promises to be extremely difficult when superpower relations have not fundamentally improved. In addition, disarmament might not reduce the costs of nuclear war, both because disarmament would be designed to enable the superpowers to rebuild their nuclear arsenals and because nuclear wars in MAD need not be all-out. Finally, if conventional war occurs but does not escalate, or if nuclear war occurs but does not make recovery impossible, the countries will rebuild their assured destruction capabilities and once again face the dangers of living in MAD.

On the other hand, disarmament in this world might provide advantages. Starting from disarmament the costs of all-out nuclear war could not immediately be as high as in MAD. Thus, disarmament might provide the opportunity to terminate a conventional war before nuclear weapons could be used, or at least before they were available in the numbers required to destroy the superpowers' societies.

Moving to near-disarmament, instead of disarmament, might provide the opportunity to moderate this tradeoff between the probability and costs of war. The probability of conventional war might not increase relative to MAD, since even a small nuclear arsenal could inflict costs that would probably overwhelm the benefits of Soviet expansion.[63] In addition, all else being equal, near-disarmament would be more robust than total disarmament; as a result, rearmament might be less dangerous than if starting from total nuclear disarmament. Against these advantages must be weighed near-disarmament's key shortcoming—nuclear weapons would be available for immediate use, so near-disarmament would not provide a period of time during which a conventional war might be terminated before nuclear escalation is possible. It is true, however, that the costs of a nuclear war could not immediately be as large as in MAD.

Comparing Worlds III and IV

The final comparison is between worlds in which superpower relations have fundamentally improved. As argued above, these worlds are safer than the worlds with current relations. The question here is: Given improved relations, should the superpowers disarm? The answer according to many discussions of disarmament is yes. Starting from an interest in disarmament, these analyses recognize the political barriers and conclude that in pursuit of disarmament the superpowers will first have to resolve their political differences. However,

---

[63] In a world of equal but reduced societal vulnerability, there might be doubts about the credibility of U.S. threats to escalate. Compared to MAD, threats with low credibility might be less effective since the costs of all-out war would be lower; on the other hand, U.S. threats might be more credible, since the United States would be less vulnerable.

analysts appear to have confused the problem with its solution. Once the superpowers resolve their disputes and develop confidence that these problems will remain resolved, there would be essentially no need to disarm. Given the crystal-clear lack of political disputes, the adversary's weapons would not be a source of concern.[64] Fundamental changes in superpower relations greatly reduce the importance of disarming.

Moreover, there would still be good reasons *not* to disarm. If relations ever improve so dramatically, the superpowers' principal objective should be to preserve this harmony. Disarmament might not serve this purpose. A disarmed country is likely to be more worried about possible changes in an adversary's intentions than a country that can protect itself (either through deterrence or defense). When one's security is sensitive to small changes in the adversary's capabilities, leaders will have to scrutinize the adversary's intentions extremely carefully. There will be little leeway for the fluctuations in relations that even the most peaceful relationships are likely to experience. In other words, unless disarmament is quite robust to rearmament it could strain superpower relations and therefore be self-defeating.[65]

The alternative would be for the superpowers to maintain forces that appear as unthreatening as possible while at the same time providing a deterrent capability that was relatively insensitive to changes in the adversary's forces. Such a force would emphasize countervalue retaliatory capabilities while rejecting counterforce capabilities, that is, it would emphasize defense over offense (where retaliatory capabilities are understood to be defensive, strategic area defenses are understood to be offensive, etc.). A force with redundant assured destruction capabilities would be most insensitive to changes in the adversary's force. The superpowers might consider reducing their vulnerability somewhat, however, trading robustness for reductions in societal vulnerability. Such a "sub-minimum deterrent" might take advantage of dramatically improved superpower relations without jeopardizing its underpinnings.

CONCLUSIONS

In many respects, calls for disarmament appear to confuse the problem with its solution. Until superpower relations improve dramatically, there is virtually no prospect that the superpowers will give up their nuclear weapons. Plans

[64] Richard K. Betts, "Nuclear Peace: Mythology and Futurology," *Journal of Strategic Studies* 2, no. 1 (May 1979): 87, commenting on Barton's chapter in *Nuclear Weapons and World Order*, makes essentially the same observation: "The question also arises of whether disarmament is to be the route to peace, or peace the route to disarmament. In a world sufficiently rid of tensions and disputes to make allegiance to a supra-national authority plausible, how much reason would there be to worry about nuclear weapons anyway?" See also Schelling, *Arms and Influence*, footnote on p. 256. These arguments do assume that the probability of nuclear accidents does not represent a serious danger. This seems reasonable, especially since the probability of accidents in peacetime appears to be extremely low.

[65] For a similar observation see Schelling, *Arms and Influence*, pp. 258–59.

for extending nuclear deterrence into the disarmed world recognize that the superpowers would disarm only if assured that rearmament could not threaten their vital interests. However, until the United States is convinced that the Soviet Union has no desire to challenge its interests, it will never be convinced that the proposed "equal readiness to rearm" provides sufficient assurance to make disarmament preferable to MAD. The same, of course, holds for the Soviet Union. In short, the infeasibility of virtually all plans for disarmament stems largely from a mismatch between means and ends—these plans try to find a technical fix to a fundamentally political problem. Furthermore, although exceedingly unlikely, if the superpowers ever disarm before their relationship is fundamentally transformed, they might be reducing their security. In this world, the probability of conventional war would be higher than it is today in MAD, and the probability of nuclear war might also be higher. Finally, if the superpowers were able to transform their relationship, disarmament would be unnecessary since in such a world the probability of war would be extremely low. Unfortunately, we lack a clear picture of how to overcome the international and domestic barriers to such dramatically improved superpower relations.

Because it lacks clear advantages relative to MAD, the United States should not maintain nuclear disarmament as a long-term goal. Instead, the United States should explicitly commit itself to living in MAD as safely as possible.

Allowing the supposed desirability of disarmament to influence current policy has important opportunity costs, directing our energy away from policies that are more likely to be productive. For example, arms control gives priority to reducing force size in part because reductions are loosely connected to disarmament. However, since disarmament should not be a U.S. goal, reductions should not be pursued as first steps toward disarmament. Their desirability will have to be established by other arguments (but we find in Chapter Ten that arguments for giving priority to arms reductions tend to be quite weak).

Instead, the United States should be more sensitive to how its military policy might influence its relationship with the Soviet Union. Examining disarmament reminds us that ignoring the importance of superpower politics leads to poor analysis of military policy. We can usefully apply this lesson to living in MAD. While we do not know how to transform international relations, we have a better idea of how to reduce the tensions generated by superpower military policies. The United States should maintain its deterrent capability while posing as little threat as possible to necessary Soviet capabilities. In other words, the United States should try to minimize the possible "spiral effects" of its military policy by buying retaliatory capabilities (defense) and forgoing forces designed for damage-limitation (offense). This military policy will not eliminate superpower tensions. Among possible nuclear policies, however, this policy offers the greatest prospects for improving superpower relations while insuring that the United States has adequate capabilities for deterring the Soviet Union. At a minimum, superpower relations will not be unnecessarily damaged by military competition and the superpowers will be able to devote more energy to constructive diplomacy.

The remainder of the book considers in detail the strategic nuclear policies the United States should adopt to maximize its security in MAD.

PART III

Decisions in MAD

CHAPTER SEVEN

Does the United States Need Counterforce in MAD?

THE DEEPEST divide over U.S. nuclear strategy and force requirements in MAD is about counterforce—systems capable of destroying Soviet nuclear forces. While accepting that the United States needs forces for an assured destruction capability, debate focuses on whether counterforce can enhance the U.S. ability to deter Soviet attacks and reduce the costs if war occurs.

American counterforce forces include highly accurate ballistic missiles, such as the Minuteman IIIA ICBM, the MX ICBM, and the D-5 (Trident II) SLBM, which are distinguished from other counterforce systems by their "promptness."[1] Their high accuracy enables them to destroy targets that the Soviet Union has hardened against nuclear attack, specifically ICBM silos and command bunkers.[2] American strategic bombers and cruise missiles can also destroy hardened targets, but are generally considered to pose a much smaller threat to Soviet forces because they lack the promptness of ballistic missiles. As a result, these systems are often not even considered counterforce systems, and most of the debate over both the benefits and risks of counterforce has

[1] SLBMs are sometimes not considered prompt because of the time required to communicate with strategic submarines; see Congressional Budget Office, *Modernizing U.S. Strategic Offensive Forces: Costs, Effects and Alternatives* (Washington, D.C.: GPO, November 1987), pp. 19, 24. Some analysts note that cruise missiles, although not prompt, pose a larger threat than is generally assumed. Because they are difficult to detect, the available warning time may be much smaller than the actual flight time. See Bruce G. Blair, *Strategic Command and Control: Redefining the Nuclear Threat* (Washington, D.C.: Brookings Institution, 1985), p. 301, and Theodore A. Postol, "Banning Nuclear SLCMs: It Would Be Nice if We Could," *International Security* 13, no. 3 (Winter 1988/89): 193–202.

[2] For a classification of warheads according to their capability to destroy targets of different hardness see Congressional Budget Office, *Trident II Missiles: Capability, Costs and Alternatives* (Washington, D.C.: GPO, July 1986). Also on counterforce see Congressional Budget Office, *Modernizing U.S. Strategic Offensive Forces: Costs, Effects and Alternatives*; Congressional Budget Office, *Modernizing U.S. Strategic Offensive Forces: The Administration's Program and Alternatives* (Washington, D.C.: GPO, May 1983); and Congressional Budget Office, *Counterforce Issues for the U.S. Strategic Nuclear Forces* (Washington, D.C.: GPO, January 1978).

In addition, although usually not classified as counterforce, less accurate nuclear weapons could be used to destroy Soviet nuclear forces that have not been hardened, including submarines in port and bombers on the ground, and to destroy conventional military forces. Furthermore, weapons not accurate enough to efficiently destroy hardened silos could be useful against mobile ICBMs. The counterforce potential of a missile force employed in a barrage attack against mobile missiles is proportional to its throw-weight and not especially sensitive to the accuracy of the missiles; see Office of Technology Assessment, *MX Missile Basing* (Washington, D.C.: GPO, September 1981), pp. 257–65.

focused on prompt counterforce. However, this leg of the strategic triad could be used in counterforce attacks,[3] and arguments for the B-2 (Stealth) bomber hold that it might provide special counterforce capabilities since a penetrating bomber is necessary to attack mobile Soviet missiles, a capability that neither ballistic missiles nor cruise missiles can provide.[4]

Furthermore, we should not restrict our definition of counterforce to these accurate offensive systems. A key counterforce mission—reducing U.S. costs in an all-out war—would probably require both offensive and defensive strategic forces.[5] The United States would first use its offensive force to attack Soviet forces before they are launched. Ballistic missiles would be used to attack Soviet ICBMs, SLBMs in port, bomber bases, and command and control facilities. Antisubmarine forces would be used against Soviet strategic submarines.[6] Then the United States would employ strategic defenses to destroy remaining Soviet forces in flight, after they are launched against American cities. Air defenses and area ballistic missile defenses help to limit damage and should therefore be considered a type of counterforce weapon, along with their offensive cousins.[7] Thus, although its focus is on prompt offensive

[3] On counterforce missions for penetrating bombers see Jasper Welch, ''Assessing the Value of Stealth Aircraft and Cruise Missiles,'' *International Security* 14, no. 2 (Fall 1989): 54–56. On the role of cruise missiles in attacks against ICBMs see Richard K. Betts, ''Complexities, Uncertainties and Dilemmas,'' in Betts, ed., *Cruise Missiles: Technology, Strategy and Politics* (Washington, D.C.: Brookings Institution, 1981), pp. 518–26.

Systems that are not prompt might play a role in damage limitation even if the Soviets get warning of an American attack. Strategic bombers and air-launched cruise missiles take many hours, instead of approximately half an hour, to reach their targets. These weapons are not usually seen as contributing to a damage-limitation capability because the Soviet Union would have plenty of warning time before the air-breathing systems reached their targets and could therefore launch its weapons before they were destroyed. If, however, a U.S. attack against Soviet C^3 makes immediate retaliation impossible, then these slower systems might arrive before the Soviets can retaliate. In this case, these air-breathing systems might be used to ''mop up'' surviving Soviet systems following an attack on Soviet strategic nuclear forces and command and control. On U.S. concern about a mop-up role for Soviet bombers see Strobe Talbott, *Endgame: The Inside Story of SALT II* (New York: Harper & Row, 1979), p. 33.

[4] There are, however, severe doubts about whether penetrating bombers will be able to perform this mission. See Michael E. Brown, ''The U.S. Manned Bomber and Strategic Deterrence in the 1990s,'' *International Security* 14, no. 2 (Fall 1989): 13–14, and Michael Brower, *The Stealth Bomber and Targeting Mobile Nuclear Forces* (Cambridge, Mass.: Union of Concerned Scientists, 1988). On penetrating versus stand-off bombers see Congressional Budget Office, *The B-1 Bomber and Options for Enhancement* (Washington, D.C.: GPO, 1988), pp. 46–59.

[5] Civil defense might be considered a third stage of a damage-limitation attack, reducing the effects of weapons that reach U.S. territory.

[6] Strategic antisubmarine warfare (ASW) is therefore a type of counterforce. ASW operations are likely to unfold slowly, in which case they could not contribute to a quick damage-limitation campaign. An attrition campaign, however, might be fought during the conventional phase of a superpower war. At least in theory, this could provide the time necessary for destroying much of the Soviet submarine force.

[7] I will sometimes use the term ''offensive counterforce'' to distinguish forces that can attack Soviet forces before they are launched from the full range of systems that might contribute to

counterforce, this chapter also analyzes whether the United States should acquire these other counterforce systems in pursuit of damage limitation.

This chapter considers three basic questions. First, can counterforce reduce the costs that American society would suffer in an all-out war in MAD? Some counterforce advocates argue that American counterforce, while unable to eliminate the Soviet assured destruction capability, can still save a significant number of American lives. They sometimes suggest that counterforce can reduce American losses by reducing the size of the Soviet attack, even if the absolute size of that attack remains very large. Others argue that American counterforce can save American cities because most of the Soviet force is targeted against U.S. forces, not its cities. Achieving these damage-limitation goals would require an extensive American counterforce arsenal, ideally one capable of threatening the entire Soviet force with a high probability of destruction. My analysis concludes that these slim hopes for damage limitation are too small, uncertain, and risky to lend support to such extensive counterforce.

Second, can counterforce enhance deterrence or provide other political benefits? Reflecting its central role in the debate over American nuclear strategy, proponents have generated a large number of arguments. No single argument seems to be consistently crucial to the overall case for counterforce, and the relative importance of arguments shifts over time. Most proponents offer a combination of arguments, but many find that a single argument (although not the same one) is sufficient to conclude in favor of counterforce. I divide these arguments into three categories, corresponding to the broad purposes for which the United States might deploy counterforce.

The first set covers arguments about the role of counterforce in deterring a conventional or nuclear Warsaw Pact attack against American allies—that is, in enhancing extended deterrence. A key argument here is that counterforce provides the United States with limited nuclear options that are necessary to make credible U.S. threats to escalate to the use of strategic nuclear weapons. The second category covers arguments about the contribution of second-strike counterforce to deterring limited Soviet nuclear attacks against the United States. An influential argument holds that second-strike counterforce can deny the Soviet Union the ability to coerce the United States by providing the capability to redress the ratio of nuclear forces following a Soviet counterforce attack. Another argument holds that counterforce can enhance deterrence by threatening the targets the Soviets value most, thereby increasing the threat-

---

damage limitation. The more encompassing definition is used in Barry R. Posen and Stephen Van Evera, "Defense Policy and the Reagan Administration: Departure from Containment," *International Security* 8, no. 1 (Summer 1983): 24–25.

All of the forces that I have classified here as counterforce could play a role in an offensive strategy, that is, one that threatens Soviet retaliatory capabilities. Thus, when we consider their strategic purpose, in MAD all of these types of counterforce, including strategic defense, are offense, while forces dedicated to retaliation are defense.

ened costs of an all-out war. The final category covers arguments that hold that counterforce can provide broader political benefits useful in managing U.S.-Soviet relations. For example, proponents argue that engaging the Soviet Union in an arms race can help communicate U.S. resolve to protect its interests.

Although the number of arguments for counterforce is large, they are based on a smaller number of more basic positions. The disputes addressed in Chapters Two and Three surface in a variety of guises as arguments about the ability and inability of counterforce to enhance deterrence. Many arguments for counterforce rest on positions developed by the military denial school—including prominently the belief that relative force size matters in MAD—and suffer the shortcomings identified in Chapter Two. Others ignore the potential political dangers of competitive military policies, commonly associated with the spiral model, that were evaluated in Chapter Three. In addition, some of these arguments fail to identify alternatives to counterforce and therefore exaggerate the benefits of counterforce relative to other policies. Overall, the arguments for counterforce identify at most small benefits.

The third question I ask is: What strategic, political, and economic costs are raised by pursuing counterforce systems in MAD? I argue that for several reasons large counterforce forces, especially prompt ones, bring relatively large costs. Most important, continued acquisition of counterforce reflects and encourages misunderstanding of MAD, which could increase the probability of large-scale nuclear war. In reality, U.S. first-strike incentives in MAD are not large enough to warrant a preemptive damage-limitation attack. Nevertheless, decisionmakers who believe that counterforce provides hope of limiting damage may, as a result, be spurred to strike first in a severe superpower crisis. Concern about this possibility is warranted since American leaders have not excluded the possibility of limiting the damage the United States would suffer in an all-out war. Thus, although there are virtually no situations in which preemption would be the best U.S. option, large counterforce arsenals are dangerous because American leaders might fail to fully appreciate this. These dangers will be compounded if Soviet leaders also retain some interest in damage limitation.

In addition, pursuit of a larger and more advanced counterforce arsenal could create a variety of other dangers. It could increase the probability of crises by fueling an arms race that causes the superpowers to exaggerate each others' hostility. During crises and war, counterforce could strain the superpowers' abilities to control their forces, raising the risk of unwanted escalation.

On balance, these costs appear to outweigh the meager benefits identified by the arguments for counterforce. Given its costs, maintaining and expanding a large counterforce arsenal reduces U.S. security. Important implications for U.S. strategy follow. A flexible assured destruction capability—a countervalue force that provides U.S. leaders with the ability to launch a range of limited nuclear attacks—can provide the United States with essentially all the deterrent capability that strategic nuclear forces can offer in MAD.

COUNTERFORCE TO REDUCE THE COSTS OF ALL-OUT WAR

MAD is commonly understood to be a condition of mutual vulnerability in which neither superpower can significantly reduce the damage the other can inflict. According to this view, which is central to arguments presented by the punitive retaliation school, although American counterforce can destroy some of the Soviet nuclear force, this is of little value since the surviving Soviet forces could inflict essentially the same amount of damage as the full Soviet force. Thus, the United States should not deploy counterforce for damage limitation. However, some analysts suggest that, even in MAD, counterforce can reduce the harm that American society would suffer in an all-out war because: (1) the damage curve is not flat; (2) most Soviet weapons are not targeted on U.S. cities; and (3) some relatively "good" outcomes are possible.

The Damage Curve Is Not Flat

As discussed in Chapter Two, analysts disagree about the level at which damage limitation becomes significant; this leads to disagreements about counterforce. Counterforce opponents often use "flat of the damage curve" arguments to demonstrate that counterforce provides little benefit. Since a few hundred Soviet warheads can destroy America's major cities, anything short of an extremely effective counterforce system is not useful. Less capable counterforce can destroy only those Soviet warheads that would do relatively little additional damage to U.S. society.

In response, some counterforce proponents answer that the damage curve is not in fact flat, hence American forces that reduce the size of a Soviet attack can limit damage even if the absolute size of the Soviet attack remains very large. While counterforce might not save the citizens of large cities, it might save Americans that live in small cities and rural areas. In a sense, these analysts see counterforce as an insurance policy that is inadequate but still worth having since all-out nuclear war might occur.[8]

Efforts to save American lives have undeniable appeal. Nevertheless, although this argument has some validity since the damage curve may not be flat, it exaggerates the benefits that counterforce can provide. First, the Soviets

---

[8] In addition, some analysts argue that the United States has a moral responsibility to try to save these lives. This argument is offered more frequently in support of strategic defenses than offensive counterforce. Ethical discussions, however, tend to focus on questions of deterrence and targeting dilemmas. For a spectrum of views see Henry Shue, ed., *Nuclear Deterrence and Moral Restraint* (Cambridge: Cambridge University Press, 1989), and Russell Hardin, John J. Mearsheimer, Gerald Dworkin, and Robert E. Goodin, eds., *Nuclear Deterrence: Ethics and Strategy* (Chicago: University of Chicago Press, 1985).

are likely to react to American counterforce programs by increasing the size of their survivable forces, thereby restoring the damage their force can do to its previous level. If so, arguments for the feasibility of damage limitation by counterforce may rest on "fallacy of the last move" thinking, that is, arguments that fail to account for Soviet responses to U.S. arms programs. Furthermore, if the Soviet Union overcompensates for U.S. offensive counterforce or BMD, which is likely, then a Soviet attack might actually result in greater damage.

Second, even putting aside likely Soviet reactions, this argument overstates the ability of counterforce to save lives by focusing on prompt fatalities. American counterforce operations might reduce prompt fatalities—deaths occurring immediately due to blast and fire—but many of those saved would probably perish from longer-term consequences of nuclear war, including famine, plague, ecological damage, and the collapse of American society. We cannot precisely forecast the effects on a modern industrial society when its major population and economic centers are destroyed, its transportation capabilities are crippled, and its standard sources of energy are unavailable.[9] However, it seems probable that many survivors would not survive for long. If so, counterforce deployed to increase the number of these survivors serves little purpose; it merely defers their death.

Third, while counterforce might preserve the right of some Americans to live, it cannot preserve their right to enjoy the rights they possess today. All human life is precious, but quality of life is not uniform. Postwar lives would be lived in a radioactive stone age; American economic, political, and cultural institutions would no longer exist. Saving lives in an all-out nuclear war would be an accomplishment, but a smaller accomplishment than saving the same lives in peacetime. Thus, this argument for counterforce exaggerates the potential value of American counterforce by failing to place the saving of these lives in the context of the inconceivable catastrophe of all-out nuclear war.

Most Soviet Weapons Are Not Targeted on U.S. Cities

Some proponents argue that U.S. counterforce requirements are inflated by analysts who assume that all Soviet weapons are targeted at U.S. cities. This assumption underlies the common argument that as long as the Soviet Union can deliver approximately 100 or 200 weapons the United States cannot protect its major cities. However, they point out that Soviet forces, like U.S. forces, are not targeted primarily on cities.[10] Proponents then argue that an

---

[9] On these effects see notes 43 and 44 in Chapter Two.

[10] For an estimate of Soviet targeting plans see Desmond Ball, "Soviet Strategic Planning and the Control of Nuclear War," *Soviet Union/Union Sovietique* 10, parts 2–3 (1983): 204–11, and William T. Lee, "Soviet Nuclear Targeting Strategy," in Desmond Ball and Jeffrey Richelson, *Strategic Nuclear Targeting* (Ithaca: Cornell University Press, 1986).

American counterforce attack could protect some major cities, even if the Soviets are left with enough surviving weapons to destroy all of them, since Soviet commanders might not retarget their forces to replace Soviet warheads that were targeted at American cities but were destroyed by American attack.[11] In this view, the American attack might prevent Soviet retargeting by damaging the Soviet command apparatus, or Soviet leaders might choose not to retarget their forces because they place higher priority on destroying withheld American forces than on destroying cities. Either way, some American cities would survive Soviet all-out retaliation.

Again, although there is some validity to this argument since the Soviet Union does not target only U.S. cities, it exaggerates the potential of American counterforce to limit damage. The Soviet Union can insure its ability to destroy U.S. cities and industrial capabilities without dedicating most of its force to these targets. Instead, a relatively small, highly survivable reserve force dedicated to U.S. value targets can perform this mission.[12] Soviet mobile ICBMs and their new generation of quieter SSBNs will probably be sufficiently survivable to play this role.[13] With this type of Soviet targeting, a U.S. attack that destroyed the majority of the Soviet force would leave a disproportionate share of surviving weapons that were targeted against U.S. value targets. Further, Soviet doctrine suggests that a retaliatory strike should be able to inflict massive damage against U.S. "military-economic facilities, political-administrative centers, and economic-industrial infrastructure."[14] Thus, although we cannot be certain, there are strong reasons for believing that the Soviets plan their targeting to insure this retaliatory capability. If so, American

[11] Applying this argument to strategic defenses is Fred S. Hoffman, "The SDI in U.S. Nuclear Strategy," *International Security* 10, no. 1 (Summer 1985): 16.

[12] If, however, the U.S. damage-limitation capability included strategic defenses, then the size of the survivable Soviet reserve force would still need to substantially exceed the number of U.S. value targets the Soviet Union was committed to destroying.

[13] On the difficulty of destroying Soviet mobiles see note 4 and Desmond Ball and Robert C. Toth, "Revising the SIOP: Taking War-Fighting to Dangerous Extremes," *International Security* 14, no. 4 (Spring 1990): 77–81, 88–90. On the quieting of Soviet submarines see *Report of the Advisory Panel on Submarine and Antisubmarine Warfare*, House Armed Services Subcommittees on Research and Development, and Seapower and Strategic and Critical Materials, March 21, 1989; on the poor prospects for a successful campaign against Soviet SSBNs see Tom Stefanick, *Strategic Antisubmarine Warfare and Naval Strategy* (Lexington, Mass.: Lexington Books, 1987).

[14] Stephen M. Meyer, "Soviet Perspectives on the Paths to Nuclear War," in Graham T. Allison et al., *Hawks, Doves & Owls* (New York: W. W. Norton, 1985), p. 174; see also idem, "Soviet Nuclear Operations," in Ashton B. Carter et al., eds., *Managing Nuclear Operations* (Washington, D.C.: Brookings Institution, 1987), pp. 496, 529–31, on possible Soviet target priorities in a retaliatory attack. Lee, "Soviet Nuclear Targeting Strategy," stresses the Soviet interest in targeting only selected population groups and in avoiding unnecessary collateral damage; nevertheless, the Soviets would inflict extremely high levels of damage in attacking the economic targets that he places on their strategic target list.

counterforce would provide almost as little ability to protect U.S. cities as if the entire Soviet force were targeted against them.

Some Relatively "Good" Outcomes Are Possible

Some proponents of counterforce argue that, although the United States might suffer the gravest damage in an all-out nuclear war, significantly better outcomes are also possible. According to these analysts, opponents of damage limitation ignore these possibilities by making pessimistic assumptions about the effectiveness of U.S. counterforce attacks. Proponents believe this is misguided because nuclear war might occur and if it does the United States should be prepared to do the best it can. Unless it makes a major commitment to damage limitation, the United States will have no option but to accept the worst.

In support of this argument, proponents point out that standard calculations of war outcomes assume that U.S. attacks against Soviet command and control fail to prevent Soviet retaliation, that Soviet retaliation is against cities, and that U.S. strategic antisubmarine warfare is ineffective. They also note that pessimists frequently argue that Soviet leaders can launch their vulnerable forces on warning of U.S. attack, thereby rendering U.S. offensive counterforce useless. While accepting that all of these outcomes are possible, proponents argue that they are not certain. Since the superpowers have never fought a nuclear war, there is always the possibility that U.S. counterforce might perform surprisingly well. In addition, the Soviet Union might not launch on warning since the United States would have enormous countervalue capabilities in reserve.[15] In short, according to this view, Soviet destruction of American society in an all-out war is not absolutely assured and the United States should not overlook opportunities to survive a nuclear war. This is not an argument for regaining U.S. superiority, which these analysts agree is infeasible, but instead for maintaining some chance of significantly reducing the costs of all-out nuclear war once it becomes unavoidable. The strongest case for this argument posits a scenario in which U.S. leaders are absolutely certain that the Soviets are about to attack the United States. In such a case the United States has nothing to lose,[16] and preemption might reduce the costs of the imminent Soviet attack.

[15] Amoretta M. Hoeber and Francis P. Hoeber, "The Case against the Case against Counterforce," *Strategic Review* 3, no. 4 (Fall 1975): 55–56, and Victor Utgoff, "In Defense of Counterforce," *International Security* 6, no. 4 (Spring 1982): 52. If, however, this argument is correct, then the U.S. ability to destroy Soviet forces does little to protect the U.S. homeland since the Soviets are already deterred.

[16] This claim is actually more conditional than it sounds. It assumes that the Soviets were not planning to shift from counterforce targets in their first strike to countervalue targets in their second strike; and closely related, that they were not planning to withhold a countervalue reserve force, which they would then use in response to such a large U.S. attack.

However, this line of argument suffers two serious weaknesses. First, it seems quite unlikely that U.S. leaders could be certain that the Soviet Union was going to launch an all-out attack. Although hard to predict, it seems more likely either that U.S. leaders would face great uncertainty about whether the Soviets were planning a massive attack or that they would mistakenly conclude that such a Soviet attack was unavoidable. The complexity, magnitude, and novelty of military operations in the midst of a severe crisis or during a large-scale superpower conventional war are more likely to create confusion than certainty. Further, the stress and time pressures of crisis decisionmaking on the verge of nuclear war would probably create an environment incompatible with the careful analysis required for certainty. Thus, the United States is unlikely to find itself in a situation in which there is actually nothing to lose by preempting. Instead, U.S. leaders would probably have to risk launching a massive counterforce first strike against the Soviet Union at a moment when nuclear war might still be avoided.

Second, this argument implicitly assumes that the probability of Soviet attack is independent of U.S. preparations for damage limitation. However, it seems likely that a Soviet decision to launch a massive attack would largely be the result of preemptive pressures created by U.S. damage-limitation capabilities; the Soviets would have few if any other motivations for launching a massive attack.

Consequently, the benefits of preemption must be weighed against its risks. As already discussed, available analyses strongly suggest that the prospects for significantly protecting the United States are quite slim. Although proponents of pursuing damage limitation have identified some important qualifications to claims that damage limitation is literally impossible in MAD, the probability of American success remains low and the reduction in costs to U.S. society are likely to be small. Thus, it appears that even in a severe crisis the risks of preemption would outweigh the expected benefits.

In sum, although marginal damage limitation may not be impossible, the United States should plan its strategy and forces as though it were.

COUNTERFORCE TO ENHANCE EXTENDED DETERRENCE IN MAD

Many analysts believe that the Soviet assured destruction capability makes U.S. threats to initiate strategic nuclear war incredible, thereby undermining the U.S. ability to extend deterrence to its allies. The straightforward solution to the credibility problem—deploying highly effective offensive counterforce in combination with strategic defenses to protect the U.S. homeland and regain strategic superiority—is infeasible. (Moreover, as indicated in Chapter Five, in almost all cases it is undesirable.) Proponents argue that offensive counterforce can nevertheless increase the credibility of American first use of strategic nuclear weapons by: (1) providing limited nuclear options; (2) improving the ratio of forces; (3) *de*creasing crisis stability; and (4) misleading the Soviets about American willingness to use nuclear weapons. In addition, based on closely related arguments, some proponents believe that the United States needs counterforce to enhance the U.S. ability to terminate a war.

The number and type of weapons prescribed by these arguments in favor of counterforce cover a wide spectrum. For example, certain limited nuclear options can be provided by one or a few counterforce weapons. However, most of the arguments examined in this and following sections prescribe a large American counterforce arsenal consisting of thousands of counterforce weapons. Arguments for extending deterrence tend to place less importance on survivable counterforce than do arguments for deterring attacks against the U.S. homeland, which require survivable counterforce for striking back. Most require the promptness of ballistic missiles—the ability to reach Soviet targets quickly, possibly before the Soviets can launch their forces; a few arguments require only the slower counterforce capabilities that could be provided by strategic bombers and cruise missiles.

Providing Limited Nuclear Options

Proponents argue that counterforce provides the United States with limited nuclear options (LNOs) that enhance extended deterrence. As discussed in Chapter Two, although analysts disagree about their importance, most believe that limited nuclear options can strengthen the U.S. ability to deter Soviet conventional and nuclear attacks against U.S. allies. The critical question here is: Do these limited options require counterforce?

COUNTERFORCE OPTIONS VERSUS COUNTERVALUE OPTIONS

In theory at least, limited nuclear options enhance the U.S. ability to deter limited Soviet attacks—conventional and nuclear—by enabling the United States to make threats that are more credible than the threat of all-out retaliation.[17] U.S. threats to employ LNOs are more credible because they preserve Soviet incentives for restraint in retaliation.[18] Limited attacks achieve this by leaving unattacked targets that the Soviets value, which continue to be U.S. hostages. Soviet leaders, recognizing that the United States expects less costly Soviet retaliation, will find U.S. threats more credible.[19] Thus, in MAD,

[17] On the key works see note 57 in Chapter Two.

[18] Limited options might also increase the credibility of U.S. threats by providing possible responses to limited Soviet attacks that would appear less disproportionate than all-out American retaliation.

[19] Limited nuclear options strengthen deterrence if one believes that the increase in the adversary's assessment of the probability that the threat will be carried out more than offsets the reduction in the costs that are threatened (where "costs" include the expected cost of the entire war, not just the cost of the option).

American limited options create the possibility of a nuclear war that is less costly for the United States than an all-out war by preserving Soviet incentives for not launching an all-out attack. This approach to limiting the costs of a nuclear war (and thereby enhancing the credibility of threats for launching it) is fundamentally different from one that relies on counterforce to significantly degrade Soviet retaliatory capabilities, and which is essentially infeasible in MAD.

The United States can have a broad array of limited nuclear options even if it targets only Soviet cities. Although all Soviet cities are vulnerable, American attacks against cities need not be all-out, unlimited attacks.[20] Without minimizing the horror of attacks against people, we should acknowledge that there is a vast difference between an attack against a small town, or even a major city, and a full-scale attack against Soviet population centers. The need for limited options does not, therefore, lead immediately to a requirement for counterforce.

Confusion on this point has been fueled by analysts who mischaracterize MAD. These proponents of counterforce suggest that the U.S. choice is between MAD and counterforce—between all-out retaliation against Soviet cities and limited counterforce options. Then, since the United States needs limited options it must reject MAD and acquire counterforce. For example, Albert Wohlstetter argues:

> Perhaps the most disturbing aspect of the dogma of Mutual Assured Destruction is that while it appears to be a description of a supposed fact, a state of affairs—the impossibility of discriminate attacks, the impossibility of maintaining control—it is really a policy which resists any *Western* improvements in precision and discrimination and any *Western* attempts to keep destruction within less than suicidal bounds.[21]

Even if LNOs strengthen deterrence of conventional attacks they might nevertheless increase the probability of nuclear war, since the probability of nuclear use if the Soviets launch a conventional war could increase. This might occur because the Soviets were more willing to escalate, since U.S. LNOs convince them that the Americans believe a nuclear war could remain limited, and because the U.S. is more willing to escalate because it has options that open some prospect of less than all-out war.

[20] Thomas C. Schelling, *Arms and Influence* (New Haven: Yale University Press, 1966), pp. 162–66. Also discussing limited attacks against cities are Leo Szilard, "Disarmament and the Problem of Peace," *Bulletin of the Atomic Scientists* 11, no. 8 (October 1955): 298–99, and Morton A. Kaplan, *The Strategy of Limited Retaliation*, Policy Memorandum No. 19 (Princeton: Center for International Studies, Princeton University, 1959).

[21] Albert Wohlstetter, "Between An Unfree World and None," *Foreign Affairs* 63, no. 5 (Summer 1985): 988–89. For similar positions see idem, "Bishops, Statesmen, and Other Strategists on the Bombing of Innocents," *Commentary* 75 (June 1983): 23; Hoffman, "The SDI in U.S. Nuclear Strategy," p. 14; Carl H. Builder, *A Conceptual Framework for a National Strategy on Nuclear Arms*, R-2598-AF (Santa Monica, Calif.: Rand, 1980); and Fred Charles Ikle, "Can Nuclear Deterrence Last Out the Century," *Foreign Affairs* 51, no. 2 (January 1973): 267–85.

This description is misleading because MAD *is* a state of affairs—a condition of mutual societal vulnerability to retaliation—not a policy or strategy. Within this condition of MAD the United States can deploy a wide range of forces—including an extensive counterforce arsenal. Closely related, a wide range of targeting options—including counterforce options—and employment policies are possible in MAD. Whether counterforce increases U.S. security is an entirely different question, however.

Most discussions of limited nuclear options, while less misleading than Wohlstetter's, blur the distinction between the need for counterforce and the need for options. They assume that forces are the most important, if not the only, targets for limited options.[22] For example, former Secretary of Defense Brown argued:

> Under many circumstances large-scale countervalue attacks may not be appropriate—nor will their prospect be sufficiently credible—to deter the full range of actions we seek to prevent. . . . [therefore] we must be able to deter Soviet attacks of less than all-out scale by making it clear to the Kremlin that, after such an attack, we

Not only strong proponents of counterforce have suggested that MAD means the United States lacks options. See, for example, Leon Wieseltier, "When Deterrence Fails," *Foreign Affairs* 63, no. 4 (Spring 1985): 832.

[22] Former Secretary of Defense Schlesinger came close to avoiding this confusion, stressing that increasing the flexibility of U.S. plans would not require *additional* counterforce weapons, and raising the possibility of limited nuclear attacks not directed at forces—specifically noting the targeting of oil refineries. See his testimony in Senate Committee on Foreign Relations, *Hearings on U.S. and Soviet Strategic Doctrine*, 93rd Cong., 2d sess. (1974); and Senate Committee on Foreign Relations, *Briefings on Counterforce Attacks*, 93rd Cong., 2d sess. (1974). However, additional counterforce was not required largely because the United States already possessed forces capable of threatening much of the Soviet force. In addition, Schlesinger did blur the relationship between LNOs and counterforce as he laid the foundation for acquiring more and/or more lethal counterforce weapons. While new forces were not required, he notes that "accuracy contributes somewhat to the effectiveness of the new targeting doctrine" (*Briefings on Counterforce Attacks*, p. 39). Moreover, he argues that limited nuclear attacks may be best deterred by retaliation in kind, thereby linking the rationale for LNOs with Soviet counterforce capabilities (ibid., p. 9). Leon Sloss and Marc Dean Millot, "U.S. Nuclear Strategy in Evolution," *Strategic Review* 12, no. 2 (Winter 1984): 26, suggest a closer link between the development of limited options and U.S. counterforce capability, noting that "the development of highly accurate, individually-targeted multiple warheads made limited options appear more feasible. This was an important factor that influenced the Nixon Administration's consideration of limited options."

Also noting that limited options might not require additional counterforce weapons but giving little attention to countervalue attacks are Lynn Etheridge Davis, *Limited Nuclear Options: Deterrence and the New American Doctrine*, Adelphi Paper No. 121 (London: IISS, 1975/76), and William R. Van Cleave and Roger W. Barnett, "Strategic Adaptability," *Orbis* 18, no. 3 (Autumn 1974): 223–45.

Critics of this change in doctrine included Ted Greenwood and Michael Nacht, "The New Nuclear Debate: Sense or Nonsense," *Foreign Affairs* 52, no. 4 (July 1974); Herbert Scoville, "Flexible Madness," *Foreign Policy* no. 14 (Spring 1974); Barry E. Carter, "Nuclear Strategy and Nuclear Weapons," *Scientific American* 230, no. 5 (1974): 20–31; and G. W. Rathjens, "Flexible Response Options," *Orbis* 18, no. 3 (Fall 1974).

would not be forced to the stark choice of either making no effective *military* response or totally destroying the Soviet Union. We could instead attack, in a selective and measured way, a range of military, industrial, and political control targets, while retaining an assured destruction capacity in reserve.[23]

But why could not the United States rectify the inadequacy of "large-scale countervalue attacks" by possessing a full spectrum of counter*value* options? Options at the low end of this spectrum need not include the targeting of cities. The United States could, for example, attack oil refineries, relatively isolated industrial targets, and railroads. The high accuracy of counterforce weapons is not required to destroy these targets. What then would counterforce options add to this full spectrum?

Similar questions are raised by arguments that focus on the U.S. need for highly lethal ICBMs—those with warheads that combine yield and accuracy sufficient to destroy hard targets with high probability—to threaten limited nuclear attacks.[24] For example, although the Scowcroft Commission does not spell out the logic of limited options in detail, ICBMs are said to be valuable in "helping to deter Soviet threats of massive conventional or limited nuclear attacks by the ability to respond promptly and controllably against hardened military targets."[25] But why would these forces be especially effective in deterring such Soviet attacks?

In fact, counterforce can contribute little, if anything, to the deterrent value of limited nuclear options. In MAD, limited nuclear options should be designed to do two things. The first is to increase the credibility of U.S. threats, primarily by preserving Soviet incentives for restraint in retaliation. As we have already seen, increased credibility does not require counterforce—a countervalue arsenal enables the United States to threaten a wide spectrum of attacks that would preserve Soviet incentives for restraint. The second is to provide the United States with the ability to inflict costs on the Soviet Union. Analysts who stress that limited options require counterforce overlook this. The role of inflicting limited costs results partly by default—in MAD it is impossible for counterforce attacks to improve U.S. military capabilities.[26] In addition, we should not lose sight of the basic fact that threatening costs lies at the core of deterrence.[27] Limited options enhance deterrence by threatening

[23] Secretary of Defense Harold Brown, *Annual Report, FY 1981* (Washington, D.C.: GPO, January 1980), pp. 65–66, emphasis added.

[24] On lethality see Kenneth W. Thompson, ed., *Kosta Tsipis on the Arms Race* (New York: University Press of America, 1987), pp. 50–90.

[25] *Scowcroft Commission Report*, April 1983, p. 12.

[26] Analysts who believe that the ratio of forces matters in MAD reject this position. I address ratio arguments as a separate argument.

[27] Deterrence by denial is the exception to this statement, but is not relevant here. There is, however, a denial argument for counterforce that envisions using nuclear weapons against Soviet conventional forces to help defeat (and thereby deter) Soviet conventional attacks. In this role,

costs with greater credibility than threatening the still higher costs of an all-out war. Obviously, counterforce is unnecessary for inflicting costs.

In other words, counterforce is unnecessary because the capabilities it provides for deterring limited Soviet attacks and engaging in bargaining during a limited war are already provided by a spectrum of countervalue options. For example, it is true that counterforce options might be useful for bargaining— employing a limited counterforce option would increase the probability of Soviet nuclear attacks against the United States and would therefore communicate U.S. resolve. But counterforce attacks achieve this in essentially the same way as countervalue attacks—that is, by crossing the strategic nuclear threshold and by inflicting costs on the Soviet Union. The costs of the counterforce attack result from what is usually considered the collateral damage—that is, the damage to Soviet society inflicted while trying to destroy Soviet forces. While bargaining in MAD, however, inflicting this damage is actually the purpose of the counterforce attack.[28] Thus, counterforce options contribute very little since a comparable level of damage could easily be inflicted by limited countervalue attacks.

COUNTERFORCE LIMITED OPTIONS AND ESCALATION THRESHOLDS

To press this conclusion further, we need to consider more specific arguments for counterforce options. Proponents of counterforce respond that the deterrent and bargaining value of limited options is not determined solely by

---

the high accuracy of counterforce weapons would have an important advantage—it would make possible lower collateral damage, which might make escalation to countervalue attacks less likely. On this role for nuclear weapons see Henry S. Rowen and Albert Wohlstetter, "Varying Response with Circumstance," in Johan J. Holst and Uwe Nerlich, eds., *Beyond Nuclear Deterrence* (New York: Crane, Russak, 1977), pp. 225–38.

In contrast to arguments that require counterforce to threaten Soviet nuclear forces, this argument is consistent with the logic of MAD and the nuclear revolution. Unlike Soviet nuclear forces, the Soviet conventional forces threatened by this counterforce would not be redundant. This said, there are powerful arguments for not viewing these attacks primarily in terms of their military effect on battlefield capabilities, but instead in terms of bargaining. See, for example, Schelling, *Arms and Influence*, pp. 105–16; and for similar observations, Malcomb W. Hoag, "On Stability in Arms Races," *World Politics* 13, no. 4 (July 1961): 518. U.S. doctrine calls for targeting Soviet conventional forces (see, for example, Secretary of Defense Brown, *Annual Report, FY 1982* [Washington, D.C.: GPO, 1981], p. 41) but says little about when and why the United States would employ strategic nuclear weapons against them.

Other analysts have argued primarily on moral grounds for targeting Soviet conventional forces. See, for example, Joseph S. Nye, Jr., *Nuclear Ethics* (New York: Free Press, 1986), pp. 97–115.

[28] Arguments holding that counterforce, specifically improvements in the accuracy of delivery systems, is necessary to reduce the collateral damage of a counterforce attack overlook this point. Again, the denial of conventional victory, discussed in the preceding note, is the exception. For related issues regarding the benefits of conventional attacks against strategic forces see Carl H. Builder, *The Prospects and Implications of Non-Nuclear Means of Strategic Conflict*, Adelphi Paper No. 200 (London: IISS, 1987).

the costs they would inflict. Soviet decisions about escalation would depend on other factors as well. For example, proponents argue that U.S. counterforce threats are more credible because a counterforce attack would respect an important threshold between force and value targets. According to this argument, a U.S. counterforce attack would be less escalatory than an attack against Soviet value targets that inflicted comparable costs on Soviet society. If the Soviets respect this threshold, then their retaliation might be less costly and would not lead to all-out war. Continuing, this argument holds that the United States would therefore be more willing to launch a counterforce attack and, since the Soviet leaders recognize this, U.S. counterforce threats are more credible than even small countervalue threats.

However, other considerations probably more than offset the benefits identified by this threshold argument. Tacit bargaining requires that one's adversary understand the message that employing force is designed to communicate. A relatively small number of weapons delivered against lesser value targets, or even cities, would make more apparent the bargaining purpose of the U.S. attack, and the likely nature of future U.S. attacks—more cities would be destroyed—thereby making the U.S. strategy relatively easy to understand.[29] In addition, these attacks might be more effective in demonstrating U.S. restraint. During the attack the Soviets might recognize that the United States had launched only a small number of weapons; and following the attack the limited nature of the U.S. attack would be immediately clear.

By comparison, a large counterforce attack appears less well suited for communicating either the purpose of the U.S. attack or its restraint. A large counterforce attack might mislead Soviet decisionmakers to believe that the United States was pursuing a damage-limitation strategy, not a bargaining strategy. As a result, Soviet leaders would be more likely to respond as if the United States had forgone all restraint. Avoiding Soviet command and control would help to avoid this confusion, but could be insufficient since a large counterforce attack would still be extremely disruptive. In addition, a large attack against Soviet forces, which would include thousands of warheads, could easily be mistaken for an unrestrained attack. The costs of such a large attack, in

---

[29] In general support of this position, Thomas C. Schelling, "What Went Wrong with Arms Control?" *Foreign Affairs* 64, no. 2 (Winter 1985/86): 230, argues that "the choice is presented as one between a counterforce campaign that is subject to control and a purely retaliatory campaign that is a total spasmodic response. I find it more plausible that the actual choice is between the two opposite alternatives. A controlled retaliatory capability seems to me supremely important, as these things go, and probably achievable, at least if somewhat reciprocated on the other side. But it is unlikely that 'controlled' counterforce warfare on the scale typically envisioned could be sustained all the way to a termination that left populations and their economic assets substantially intact; indeed *uncontrolled* counterforce is probably what you would get." See also Kenneth N. Waltz, *The Spread of Nuclear Weapons: More May Be Better*, Adelphi Paper No. 171 (London: IISS, 1981), p. 24.

addition to being high, would be hard to determine quickly, which could lead Soviet leaders to underestimate U.S. restraint.

A rejoinder is that small U.S. counterforce attacks would communicate restraint at least as effectively as small countervalue attacks. Although correct, this argument does not generate a requirement for highly effective (lethal) counterforce weapons. The United States would not need to attack Soviet forces most "efficiently," that is, with a highly favorable weapons exchange ratio, because the purpose of a limited attack is primarily to demonstrate U.S. willingness to use nuclear weapons—and to inflict the associated costs and accept the associated risks—not to destroy Soviet forces.[30] Consequently, the United States would always have the capability to threaten this type of limited attack, even if it did not deploy any highly lethal forces. Whether small-scale attacks against Soviet nuclear forces would be more successful than equally costly countervalue attacks would necessarily depend on how Soviet leaders interpret them. As noted above, a possible shortcoming is that limited counterforce attacks might communicate a military purpose, thereby confusing the Soviets about the U.S. bargaining strategy. And if the Soviets are not confused but instead recognize that small U.S. attacks against their nuclear forces lack a military purpose, then they are interpreting them as relatively low-cost countervalue attacks anyway.[31]

Improving the Ratio of Forces

Some proponents of counterforce argue that the United States can enhance extended deterrence by maintaining the ability to launch a first strike that would improve the ratio of nuclear forces. Carl Builder, for example, argues:

> First-strike counterforce capabilities could provide the advantageous counter-initiative needed to deter the Soviets at the conventional level of conflict. As defined here,

[30] This point is also made by Robert Sherman, "The Fallacies of Counterforce," *Strategic Review* 3, no. 2 (Spring 1975): 52. Further, even if favorable exchange ratios were required, the United States would not need enhanced counterforce. While many discussions suggest otherwise, current U.S. ICBMs have a high probability of destroying even very hard Soviet silos: Minuteman III with Mark 12A warheads has a single shot probability of kill of 57 percent against a 5,000 psi silo (Congressional Budget Office, *Trident II Missiles*, p. 10). Assuming SS-18s are in such hard silos, this means that the United States can on average destroy approximately five SS-18 warheads with each of these Minuteman III warheads.

[31] A second rejoinder points out that Soviet doctrine appears to reject the possibility of limited strategic nuclear war, and therefore, since limited American attacks will lead to all-out war, they are no more credible than threats of all-out war. As discussed below, limited options could nevertheless increase the credibility of U.S. threats if Soviet leaders believe the United States will employ them. However, even accepting this rejoinder, it undermines the case for counterforce options at least as severely as the case for countervalue options.

Yet another rejoinder points out that even if we accept this logic against counterforce options, superpower leaders do not think this way, which restores the case for counterforce. I address this argument below.

CF1 capabilities represent a potential military advantage that could provide the United States with a credible threat to shift the strategic balance if the Soviets unleash their preponderance of conventional forces.[32]

To provide the greatest advantage, highly lethal counterforce weapons are required for this first-strike option.[33] In addition, the United States would require prompt counterforce if the Soviets would launch their forces before slower systems arrive, but not before American ballistic missiles could reach their targets.

Unlike the preceding arguments, here counterforce attacks are not themselves part of a bargaining strategy. They are not undertaken to communicate resolve. Instead, the threat of counterforce attacks promises to place the United States in a stronger military position, enhancing its ability to bargain. This argument is built on the belief—advanced by the military denial school—that superpower leaders are influenced by the ratio of their strategic nuclear forces, even in MAD.

However, the ratios argument for counterforce options is flawed because there is no reason why relative force size should influence a country's bargaining position in MAD. As discussed in Chapter Two, ratios of nuclear forces do not measure countries' relative ability to inflict costs and therefore to deter and coerce. Further, there is little evidence that leaders whose countries could be annihilated place significant weight on these ratios.

[32] Carl H. Builder, "Why Not First-Strike Counterforce Capabilities?" *Strategic Review* 7, no. 2 (Spring 1979): 37. CF1 is defined as "the capability to strike first and thereby foreclose to an opponent the possibility of advantageous force relationships in any subsequent counterforce exchange" (p. 35). It is not a damage-limitation capability. A similar belief about force ratios underlies Admiral James D. Watkins' claim that attacking Soviet SSBNs can provide advantages by shifting the strategic balance. See his "The Maritime Strategy," supplement to U.S. Naval Institute *Proceedings* 112/1 (January 1986): 13–14.

Two additional arguments for how counterforce first strikes can provide military advantages are worth noting. First, some analysts argue that destroying Soviet counterforce would leave the Soviets without acceptable retaliatory options. For example, Builder, "Why Not First-Strike Counterforce Capabilities?" p. 37, argues that following a U.S. first strike "the Soviets would have to contemplate the possibility that exploiting their advantage at the level of conventional theater conflict might prompt a counterforce campaign where they would face the prospective choice of escalating to countervalue attacks or desisting." This is a threshold argument and suffers the weaknesses discussed above.

Second, proponents argue that counterforce could enhance deterrence by providing the United States with an advantage in long-term survivable reserve forces. See Utgoff, "In Defense of Counterforce," pp. 44–60. This argument is logically sound, since it focuses on asymmetries in the ability to inflict damage. It is extremely doubtful, however, that such an advantage would be politically useful since leaders would have to be influenced by the outcome of an attrition war carried out over months.

[33] As noted in Chapter Two, the countervailing strategy does not offer this argument for first-strike counterforce. It is, nevertheless, the logical extension of the views I have associated with the military denial school.

Decreasing Crisis Stability

Some analysts worry that MAD makes the world safe for conventional war. Two features of MAD create this danger. First, the United States has great difficulty in making credible limited nuclear threats because its homeland is vulnerable to Soviet retaliation. Second, MAD creates a high degree of crisis stability that severely reduces or eliminates the probability that crises will escalate via preemptive attack. As a result, some fear that Soviet leaders might be confident that even a large superpower conventional war would not escalate to nuclear war. These analysts then conclude that a high degree of crisis stability at the strategic nuclear level, although usually considered desirable, might actually increase the probability of conventional war and is therefore undesirable.[34] To manage this stability-instability paradox they recommend that the United States deploy counterforce to reduce crisis stability.[35]

According to these analysts, decreased crisis stability would enhance extended deterrence in two ways. As already mentioned, Soviet leaders would see greater risks in launching a conventional war since now conventional war might precipitate an all-out nuclear war via a preemptive strategic attack. In addition, creating preemptive incentives would add a dimension to the bargaining uses of U.S. limited nuclear options. The United States could employ limited nuclear options to manipulate the risk of escalation to all-out war via preemptive attack. Employing a limited option increases the intensity of the war and makes all-out war appear more likely. Thus, following a limited nuclear attack, both superpowers would be more likely to launch a preemptive attack. Therefore, once there is some crisis instability, threats to employ limited nuclear options can serve as "threats that leave something to chance." Consequently, in a world of preemptive incentives a U.S. limited nuclear attack communicates resolve by demonstrating U.S. willingness to increase the probability of all-out preemptive war as well as to increase the probability of limited Soviet retaliation.[36]

---

[34] Similar arguments hold that eliminating the possibility of accidental and unauthorized nuclear escalation makes the world safer for conventional war. Thus, counterforce could reduce the probability of conventional war by increasing these dangers. The arguments pro and con closely parallel the arguments over decreasing crisis stability. How counterforce might create these dangers is discussed in the last section of this chapter.

[35] This assumes the Soviets would also have some first-strike incentive. For discussion of this argument at the theater nuclear level see Leon V. Segal, *Nuclear Forces in Europe* (Washington, D.C.: Brookings Institution, 1984), pp. 46–49.

[36] On this distinction see Robert Powell, "The Theoretical Foundations of Strategic Nuclear Deterrence," *Political Science Quarterly* 100, no. 1 (Spring 1985): 75–83. On "threats that leave something to chance" see Schelling, *The Strategy of Conflict*, pp. 187–203.

There is, however, some question about whether reducing crisis stability would make limited nuclear threats more effective. Employing limited options would now be riskier for the United States, which might reduce Soviet estimates of U.S. credibility. If so, the net result is unclear

The first question is whether U.S. counterforce can create crisis instability in MAD. Some analysts believe that MAD essentially eliminates preemptive incentives by leaving both superpowers without the ability to protect their cities and social structure. As discussed above, however, others disagree, pointing out that even when the Soviet Union can retaliate massively, a U.S. counterforce attack could save lives. Thus, these analysts conclude that by building a large and highly lethal counterforce arsenal the United States can create a first-strike advantage. According to this view, Soviet counterforce can also create first-strike incentives. Therefore, if superpower leaders hold this view of damage limitation, counterforce can reduce crisis stability.

The second question is whether this crisis instability is desirable. The benefits of reducing crisis stability—a reduction in the frequency of Soviet challenges that could lead to crises or war—must be weighed against the increased risks: if the superpowers nevertheless become engaged in a severe crisis or conventional war, crisis instability increases the probability of all-out nuclear war.

To assess the net effect of decreasing crisis stability we can consider two paths to superpower conventional war. In the first, the premeditated path, Soviet leaders consider the full range of U.S. threats and capabilities before making a decision on launching a major attack against Western Europe. As spelled out in detail by the punitive retaliation school, even without increased crisis instability the risks are enormous. A Soviet leader could not be confident that launching a major conventional attack against Western Europe would not lead to nuclear war. Given its costs, even a small probability of escalation would deter even a highly expansionist Soviet leader.[37] Therefore, decreasing crisis stability in MAD would add little to deterrence of deliberate conventional attacks against vital U.S. interests. On the other hand, since the probability of crises occurring along this path is quite low, the risks of decreasing crisis stability might also be small, even though the costs of a nuclear war would be so large. Thus, although the benefits are small, they might be comparable to the risks.

Along the second path, the superpowers become involved in a major confrontation in Europe or elsewhere following unforeseen escalation from another dispute—for example, following fighting that originated in Eastern Europe and did not initially include NATO countries, or following a direct superpower confrontation over less vital interests outside of Europe. In this case, crisis instability probably helps very little in deterring the initial Soviet move because the Soviets never foresaw becoming involved in a conventional superpower war. Then, even if the increased crisis instability made both su-

---

since the United States is left with less credible threats that carry higher expected costs when the increased probability of escalation is factored in.

[37] Of course, Soviet leaders face much more than the U.S. strategic nuclear deterrent—NATO's conventional and theater nuclear capabilities pose powerful deterrent threats themselves.

perpowers more cautious, a variety of actions taken for defensive purposes—
for example, mobilizing conventional forces for protecting Europe and increasing reconnaissance for making sure that a large attack was not being
planned—might intensify the crisis further. Thus, in this inadvertent scenario,
increased crisis instability would do less to reduce the probability of severe
crises while still increasing the probability that they would escalate to all-out
war. In this case, the risks of decreasing crisis stability appear to more clearly
exceed the benefits.

Even without crisis instability, the risks involved in attacking Western Europe or other areas of vital American interests are so large that Soviet leaders
are extremely unlikely to launch a deliberate attack. Thus, although both types
of scenario appear quite improbable, the inadvertent scenario appears to be at
least as important as the premeditated one. This tends to undercut the case for
decreasing crisis stability.

Misleading the Soviets about American Willingness to Use Nuclear Weapons

Some proponents of counterforce prescribe counterforce as a way of falsely
convincing the Soviets that U.S. leaders believe it provides usable nuclear
options. If the United States invests heavily in counterforce weapons, for example, it might look as though the United States is pursuing a significant damage-limitation capability and planning to prevail in an all-out war. Therefore,
the argument continues, although U.S. leaders in fact recognize these objectives are infeasible, the counterforce policy fools the Soviets, convincing them
that U.S. escalation from conventional war is more likely and thereby enhancing deterrence.

Another version of this argument focuses on limited counterforce nuclear
options. Emphasizing the role of counterforce options in U.S. doctrine, and
buying the forces those options require, misleads Soviet leaders into believing
that U.S. leaders expect that large but limited counterforce wars are possible.
As a result, though U.S. leaders would not order limited counterforce attacks,
the credibility of U.S. threats to escalate to such attacks increases.[38] In addition, proponents point out that this approach is especially important because
Soviet leaders have not adjusted to the nuclear revolution. Thus, even if the
logic against counterforce options is sound, counterforce limited options remain more credible than countervalue limited options because the Soviets continue to view nuclear weapons in conventional terms.[39]

---

[38] Examples of these types of arguments are included in Steven Kull, *Minds at War: Nuclear
Reality and the Inner Conflicts of Defense Policymakers* (New York: Basic Books, 1988), pp.
156–74, 178–80.

[39] On conventionalization see Jervis, *The Illogic of American Nuclear Strategy*, pp. 57–58, and
Hans Morgenthau, "The Fallacy of Thinking Conventionally about Nuclear Weapons," in David

Logically, since the effectiveness of the U.S. deterrent depends on Soviet beliefs, not U.S. beliefs, policies that mislead Soviet leaders could enhance deterrence. In addition, there are reasons to believe the bluff might work. Studies of Soviet writings suggest that U.S. counterforce policies have influenced Soviet assessments of how the United States would use nuclear weapons to achieve political and possibly military objectives.[40] Furthermore, the structure of Soviet forces has certainly influenced U.S. views of how the Soviets plan to fight a war.

Nevertheless, the benefits of misleading the Soviets as to U.S. beliefs about counterforce are small and the risks are relatively high. As discussed previously, Soviet leaders are likely to be deterred already by the catastrophic potential of U.S. countervalue capabilities, even if these capabilities appear unusable. Further, even if we accept the need to search for small additional increments of deterrence, bluffing about counterforce options may not be more effective than bluffing about the U.S. willingness to use countervalue options. At least there is a clear logical rationale for limited countervalue options. This is more than can be said for counterforce attacks that shift the ratio of forces but cannot limit damage. Once analysts stop intertwining the requirements for counterforce and limited options, understanding of MAD will probably increase, which will tend to increase the credibility of limited countervalue threats.

Moreover, bluffing about counterforce attacks could bring costs of its own. A large American counterforce arsenal is more likely to convince Soviet leaders that U.S. leaders believe some damage-limitation is possible than that they are willing to fight a limited counterforce war. The former is likely to be the most convincing bluff, since it is the only one based on the ability to affect the outcome of an all-out war. As a result, a large American counterforce arsenal might convince the Soviets that the United States would be willing to strike first, if necessary, in a severe crisis. However, as argued above, the deterrent benefits of reducing crisis stability are outweighed by the risks.

In addition, U.S. counterforce policies based on bluff will be dangerous if they also fool U.S. decisionmakers. In practice, decisionmakers may be unable to maintain a clear line between their own beliefs and the ones they intend to project to Soviet leaders.[41] They might underestimate the escalatory implications of limited counterforce attacks and/or exaggerate the U.S. ability to limit damage. If so, the United States might use nuclear weapons when a clearer view concludes against it.

In short, misleading the Soviets might contribute a little to deterrence, but

---

Carelton and Carlo Schaerf, eds., *Arms Control and Technology Innovation* (New York: John Wiley & Sons, 1976), pp. 255–64.

[40] See Chapter Three for discussion of these points and citations.

[41] On this possibility see Kull, *Minds at War*, pp. 169–74.

the contribution would probably be more than offset by the dangers of bluffing.

Enhancing the U.S. Ability to Terminate a War

Proponents argue that beyond deterring war, limited nuclear options enhance the U.S. ability to control escalation and to terminate both conventional and nuclear wars. Because limited options are usually seen to require counterforce, it is only a short step to the argument that the United States needs counterforce to enhance its ability to terminate a nuclear war.[42]

At least in theory, this general argument for limited nuclear options is sound. In MAD, limited nuclear threats might increase the U.S. ability to terminate a war by deterring further Soviet escalation and possibly by compelling the Soviet Union to accept certain U.S. conditions. As with prewar deterrence, limited nuclear options might be necessary because all-out threats are incredible. In other words, war termination can be viewed as a bargaining process in which limited options are bargaining tools.[43] In intra-war bargaining, the United States would carry out limited attacks to communicate its resolve. Attacking the Soviet Union increases the probability of Soviet attacks against the United States; thus, limited nuclear attacks communicate U.S. resolve by demonstrating the U.S. willingness to run great risks to reach an acceptable outcome.

However, as with arguments about prewar deterrence, the step from the need for limited nuclear options to the need for limited counterforce options is quite weak. To see the flaw we need to recognize only that limited nuclear options would play essentially the same role in helping to terminate a war as in deterring it. Thus, the arguments that counterforce limited options will not

---

[42] This argument applies to both first use and second use of counterforce; I have included it in this category on extended deterrent uses because its basic logic resembles the preceding arguments for limited options.

For examples of the basic argument see Secretary of Defense James R. Schlesinger, *Annual Report, FY 1975*, p. 40; Brown, *Annual Report, FY 1982*, p. 40; and Secretary of Defense Caspar W. Weinberger, *Annual Report, FY 1985*, p. 29. Even some analysts who see little other value in counterforce accept this viewpoint. Leon Wieseltier, "When Deterrence Fails," *Foreign Affairs* 63, no. 4 (Spring 1985): 840–42, for example, argues that "a strike against cities, or generally against a population, will almost certainly preclude the possibility of preventing any future strikes.

"This is the good news, and all the good news, about counterforce. The theory of war termination suggests something important about (horrible dictu) the character of a first strike, which is that it must be seriously limited. A massive first strike will make war termination impossible. . . . But in the initial stage of nuclear war, at least, counterforce is not yet warfighting."

[43] The bargaining involved in war termination is not entirely special to MAD. Schelling, *Arms and Influence*, pp. 126–31, observes that war can end in two ways: complete exhaustion of forces—an all-out war in the strongest sense, in which bargaining plays no role in termination—and "conditional restraint," in which each country's decision to stop fighting depends partly on expectations about the other's restraint. Bargaining is a key component in this latter type of war.

significantly enhance U.S. war termination capabilities are essentially identical to those in the previous case and I do not repeat them here. The basic point is that the United States would engage in intra-war tacit bargaining by threatening and possibly inflicting costs, and counterforce is neither required for inflicting costs nor likely to be especially beneficial in this role. In addition, as I argue in detail below, an extensive U.S. counterforce arsenal could encourage escalation and actually make termination more difficult.

COUNTERFORCE TO DETER SOVIET NUCLEAR ATTACKS AGAINST THE U.S. HOMELAND

In addition to the preceding arguments—which focus on increasing the credibility of U.S. threats to use nuclear weapons first—analysts also argue that counterforce is necessary to deter Soviet nuclear attacks against the U.S. homeland. Proponents argue that second-strike counterforce—that is, counterforce that can be used to retaliate following a Soviet strategic nuclear attack—is necessary to: (1) retaliate in kind; (2) restore the ratio of forces; (3) defeat the Soviet damage-limitation campaign; and (4) hold at risk what Soviet leaders value most.

Arguments for the first two capabilities closely resemble arguments addressed in the previous section, except that they focus on second use of strategic weapons instead of first use. Since they are built on similar basic assumptions and thus suffer similar weaknesses, I will deal with them rather briefly. Further, as elaborated below, many arguments for second-strike counterforce suffer an additional weakness: even if we accept the proponents' basic argument, increasing the survivability of U.S. forces can substitute for deploying counterforce and has important advantages.

Retaliating in Kind

Proponents of counterforce worry that the lack of counterforce retaliatory options would leave the United States with only incredible threats against Soviet society.[44] They argue that deterring limited Soviet counterforce attacks against the U.S. homeland requires a capability for U.S. counterforce retaliation—as highlighted by the "Nitze scenario," in which a Soviet attack against U.S.

---

[44] See, for example, Schlesinger, *Briefing on Counterforce Attacks*, p. 9. Nitze's prominent articles do not spell out this argument in detail, but his description of U.S. options after a Soviet counterforce attack suggests that the United States would be left primarily with countervalue options and that the lack of other options is the key problem. See, for example, Paul H. Nitze, "Deterring Our Deterrent," *Foreign Policy* no. 25 (Winter 1976–77): 204–6. For critiques of Nitze's analysis see citations in note 52 in Chapter Two. Also noting this danger in ICBM vulnerability are Hoeber and Hoeber, "The Case against the Case against Counterforce," pp. 55–56.

ICBMs is said to leave the United States with two unacceptable options, either suicide or surrender. Further, some analysts want U.S. retaliation to resemble the Soviet attack as closely as possible. Accordingly, retaliation in kind should be narrowly defined. For example, if the Soviets use ICBMs to attack American ICBMs, then the United States should be able to retaliate with ICBMs against Soviet ICBMs. This type of retaliation is said to be even more highly credible since the United States would clearly match—but not exceed—the Soviet attack, thereby further reducing the probability of continued escalation.[45]

The argument that the United States requires counterforce for retaliation in kind misses the basic point that in MAD the limited use of nuclear weapons should be understood in the context of tacit bargaining. As argued above, in such a tacit bargaining situation the United States needs to be able to threaten costs, not destroy forces. Thus, while the United States might want the capability to inflict retaliatory costs comparable to those that the Soviet attack would inflict, this does not require counterforce. A relatively small countervalue retaliatory attack could probably match the societal costs inflicted by the Soviet counterforce attack. Thus, calls for counterforce retaliation are essentially built on the belief that an important threshold is crossed in moving from counterforce to countervalue attacks. But as argued in detail above when considering the role of counterforce in threats of limited first use, retaliating in kind following a large Soviet counterforce attack might not be the best U.S. option. A smaller attack against Soviet value targets might send a clearer message of restraint and of the nature of future U.S. attacks. Furthermore, the United States does not need counterforce systems to avoid crossing the countervalue threshold. Less lethal weapons used against Soviet forces can serve the same purpose. In addition, regarding the narrower requirement of retaliation in kind, there is little benefit in retaliating with the same type of weapon that the Soviets used in the initial attack. The United States would demonstrate restraint through the targets it attacks and the costs it inflicts, not the type of weapons it employs.

Restoring the Ratio of Forces

DENIES THE SOVIETS COERCIVE ADVANTAGES

Some proponents of second-strike counterforce worry that the Soviets might launch a limited counterforce attack to favorably shift the ratio of surviving forces and thereby enhance their ability to coerce the United States. They conclude that to deter these Soviet attacks the United States should be able to deny the Soviets that ability to favorably shift the ratio of surviving forces. U.S. second-strike counterforce helps deter these Soviet counterforce attacks by

---

[45] On the general argument for retaliation in kind as a means of communicating restraint in a tacit bargaining situation see Schelling, *Arms and Influence*, pp. 141–51.

enabling the United States to restore the ratio by retaliating efficiently against Soviet forces. Secretary of Defense Brown, for example, argues that "our countervailing strategy seeks to deny the Soviets victory, and an improved relative balance would appear to be a minimum condition for 'victory.' . . . [analysis] reveals the special contributions in the late 1980s that the MX in survivable basing mode would make to the post-exchange ratios."[46] Similarly, the Soviet ability to shift the ratio of forces is one of the key dangers identified in the Nitze scenario.

Like the argument calling for counterforce to enable the United States to favorably shift force ratios when striking first, this argument is flawed because ratios do not matter in MAD. A Soviet attack that cannot limit damage should be understood as part of a bargaining strategy; but improving the ratio of forces would not enhance the Soviet bargaining position. Thus, as the punitive retaliation school argues, Soviet leaders have no incentive to launch such an attack in the first place.

Yet even if one accepts the importance of relative force size, the United States would not require counterforce if it could make its forces highly survivable. In this case, a Soviet counterforce attack could not improve the relative size of its force—the attack would consume at least as many Soviet weapons as it destroys.[47] Thus, this argument is even weaker than its troubled brother— whereas attempts to enhance extended deterrence by threatening to strike first to improve the ratio of forces definitely require U.S. counterforce, denying the Soviets the ability to shift the ratio of forces does not.

For example, if the MX missile had been deployed in the basing mode proposed by the Carter administration—which provided twenty-three shelters for each missile—the Soviet Union could not have improved the relative size of its force in a full-scale attack against U.S. ICBMs. To destroy an MX—which has ten warheads—would have required at least twenty-three warheads.[48] Therefore, in this basing mode, the countersilo capability of MX could not be justified by the U.S. need for a retaliatory capability to redress shifts in relative force size. Similarly, Soviet attacks against mobile ICBMs would result in unfavorable warhead exchange ratios.

[46] Brown, *Annual Report, FY 1982*, p. 58. See also Walter Slocombe, "Preplanned Options," in Carter et al., *Managing Nuclear Operations*, p. 127.

[47] Deploying only single warhead ICBMs, even if not highly survivable, would also confront the Soviets with an unfavorable warhead exchange ratio against American ICBMs. We should note, however, that when the attacking country has an initial advantage in force size, an attack that consumed as many warheads as it destroyed would improve the ratio of surviving forces in favor of the attacker.

[48] On MX based in MPS see Office of Technology Assessment, *MX Missile Basing*, pp. 33–107. The Soviet Union might have improved its relative force size in a partial attack against U.S. ICBMs, one directed against only Minuteman IIIs; I am unaware of concern over this possibility. An attack against MX/MPS and the Minuteman force could not have favorably shifted surviving force size. A complete analysis would consider attacks against *all* U.S. forces with/without MX in a variety of basing modes under a variety of alert conditions.

Consequently, proponents of counterforce retaliatory options designed to deny Soviet advantages in relative force size need to explain why counterforce retaliation is their preferred option (and for most of them, the *only* option). At a minimum, this requires demonstrating that for a given investment less survivable counterforce weapons can better maintain the relative size of U.S. forces than more survivable but less lethal weapons.[49]

The alternative of increased survivability has clear advantages. First, this approach works against even optimistic Soviet leaders since it does not depend on a U.S. decision to retaliate. Thus, analysts who worry that the United States would not retaliate following a large Soviet counterforce attack should see clear advantages.[50] Second, as discussed in Chapter Three, increased survivability avoids the political dangers of military competition identified by the spiral model. By contrast, enhancing counterforce solves the same problem with forces that appear more threatening to the Soviets. Therefore, analysts who believe that prudence requires the United States to hedge against the possibility of a Soviet counterforce attack launched to shift relative force size, but who see little other need for counterforce, ought to give special weight to solutions based on increased survivability.

In sum, the argument for second-strike counterforce to shift the ratio of forces shares the fundamental flaw of the entire family of ratio arguments. This argument for second-strike counterforce is further weakened because it fails to consider alternative, noncounterforce means.

INCREASES CRISIS STABILITY

Contrary to the common claim that counterforce reduces crisis stability (and to the previous argument for reducing crisis stability), some proponents argue that U.S. counterforce can increase it. If relative force size matters, the Soviet Union has a first-strike advantage when a counterforce attack would improve the ratio of forces following a counterforce exchange. According to this argument, if both superpowers have such a capability, the Soviet Union might launch a preemptive attack during a crisis because it fears that the United States might launch a "ratio-shifting" counterforce attack. Additional U.S. counterforce weapons might reduce this pressure: if sufficiently survivable, improved U.S. counterforce retaliation could restore the ratio of surviving forces, thereby reducing Soviet first-strike incentives.

Like the preceding argument, although internally consistent, this argument

---

[49] There are, of course, a number of ways to improve force survivability, and thereby to improve post-attack ratios. Increasing ICBM survivability has received the bulk of attention. Other alternatives include moving toward a strategic dyad instead of a triad and increasing the alert rate of bombers and the fraction of SSBNs at sea.

[50] In addition, since the Soviet Union would probably be able to launch its weapons before U.S. missiles arrived, a retaliatory counterforce attack might be ineffective. While there might be insufficient time to successfully implement launch-on-warning (LOW) against a bolt from the blue, LOW in reaction to the adversary's *retaliatory* attack would be much easier.

fails because improving relative force size is of little value in MAD. Preemptive incentives are small and crisis stability is high when both superpowers have assured destruction capabilities. Further, whatever crisis instability might exist would reflect first-strike advantages in reducing costs at very high levels of damage, not the ability to favorably shift ratios.

Furthermore, even if ratios matter, deploying survivable counterforce is not the best solution. Increasing the survivability of deployed U.S. forces while decreasing their ability to destroy Soviet forces would be preferable. This has the dual advantages of reducing the U.S. ability to destroy Soviet forces in a first strike—thereby reducing Soviet fear of a U.S. preemptive attack initiated to shift ratios or to limit damage—and of reducing the Soviet ability to destroy U.S. forces, thereby reducing any benefits they might see in a first strike.

Defeating the Soviet Damage-Limitation Campaign

Some proponents argue that counterforce can enhance the U.S. ability to deter the Soviet Union from launching a damage-limitation attack during a severe crisis.[51] In contrast to the most common damage-limitation scenario, which imagines a single massive Soviet attack against American retaliatory capabilities, they argue that the Soviets plan to limit damage by launching repeated attacks. The Soviets would use ICBMs in follow-on attacks against American forces that survive their initial attack and would launch repeated attacks against command and control in the hope of further disrupting U.S. retaliation.[52] Proponents then argue that American second-strike counterforce could help defeat a Soviet damage-limitation attack by destroying the forces the Soviets would employ in these follow-on attacks. Recognizing that the United States can interrupt their damage-limitation campaign, the Soviets would be convinced not to launch it.

According to this argument, the United States should be concerned about Soviet efforts to limit damage for a variety of reinforcing reasons: although American retaliatory capabilities are likely to remain massive, a Soviet counterforce and counter-control attack might nevertheless reduce the American ability to inflict retaliatory damage; the Soviet military remains interested in

---

[51] The most thorough and compelling statement of this overall argument is Scott Sagan, "Second-Strike Counterforce," in his *Moving Targets: Nuclear Strategy and National Security* (Princeton: Princeton University Press, 1989); my summary draws heavily on his chapter. See also Testimony of General Larry D. Welch, Senate Armed Services Committee, *Department of Defense Authorization for Appropriations for Fiscal Year 1987*, pt. 4, 99th Cong., 2d sess., 20 March 1986, pp. 1563–64, 1571, who holds that "high confidence deterrence demands that the Soviet war planner be convinced that we possess the forces necessary to promptly disrupt a Soviet attack and preclude successful follow-on attacks."

[52] On the latter point see Lawrence K. Gershwin, *Soviet Strategic Force Developments*, Joint Hearing before the Senate Subcommittee on Strategic and Theater Nuclear Forces of the Committee on Armed Services and the Senate Subcommittee on Defense of the Committee on Appropriations, 99th Cong., 1st sess., 26 June 1985, p. 18.

damage limitation; the Soviet military may judge its prospects for success according to narrow military criteria that exaggerate the prospects for success; and the Soviet military would probably be influential in Soviet decisions to launch a preemptive attack during a severe crisis. Thus, the United States should plan to deter not only Soviet political leaders, but also the Soviet military. This in turn requires that the United States be able to deny Soviet military war aims, of which limiting damage is probably the most important.

The central point of this argument—that the United States should plan to deter *actual* Soviet decisionmakers, including military leaders as well as civilians—is well taken.[53] Thus, to the extent that Soviet decisionmakers might conclude in a severe crisis that striking first might significantly limit damage— however they measure it—the United States should consider policies that would make it an even more unattractive option than massive American retaliatory capabilities already do. If Soviet decisionmakers fully appreciated the implications of the nuclear revolution, then such measures would be unnecessary. However, Soviet military doctrine maintains an interest in damage limitation even when the absolute level of damage would remain extremely high.[54] Although such uncertain and marginal damage-limitation capabilities are militarily irrelevant during peacetime, there is some danger in overlooking their potential influence on decisionmakers during a severe crisis or, more importantly, a large superpower conventional war. Under these conditions, decisionmakers may run grave risks, make poor decisions, and be overly influenced by available military options.[55] Thus, taking the basic arguments presented by the punitive retaliation school to their logical extreme—assuming that leaders act as though damage limitation is entirely infeasible—probably underestimates the potential danger of Soviet counterforce in these situations.[56]

However, even accepting the value of hedging against the possibility of such risky and misguided Soviet behavior, counterforce is not the best hedge. Instead, if the danger of such a preemptive damage-limitation attack is judged sufficiently large to warrant corrective action, the United States should give top priority to increasing the survivability of its forces and get rid of highly

[53] I argue along these lines in the following section that American counterforce may be dangerous because American decisionmakers—both civilian and military—have not fully accepted that the United States should not pursue damage limitation.

[54] On the long-standing Soviet interest in limiting damage if war occurs see David Holloway, *The Soviet Union and the Arms Race* (New Haven: Yale University Press, 1983), pp. 48–58.

[55] On some of the psychological factors that could contribute to poor decisions see Robert Jervis, *The Meaning of the Nuclear Revolution: Statecraft and the Prospects of Armageddon* (Ithaca: Cornell University Press, 1989), pp. 148–73.

[56] I find this qualification of the basic punitive retaliation school arguments far more persuasive than those that focus on perceptions of force ratios and other relative measures, both because it focuses on capabilities for influencing outcomes during wartime and because the Soviet military appears to maintain an interest in limiting damage.

vulnerable ones.[57] This would eliminate targets for the Soviets to attack, thereby reducing the difference they might see between striking first and being attacked first.[58] Since pressures for preemptive damage-limitation attacks would arise only in a severe crisis, forces that were highly survivable at high levels of alert might be adequate.

Three points favor giving priority to reducing the vulnerability of American retaliatory capabilities over maintaining counterforce to defeat a Soviet damage-limitation campaign. First, as noted above, this is the "defensive" hedge—it reduces U.S. force vulnerability, thereby reducing Soviet incentives to preempt, while not threatening Soviet forces, which could increase Soviet incentives to preempt. Given the near certain U.S. ability to retaliate massively, preemption could become a relatively attractive option only if Soviet leaders conclude that large-scale nuclear war is very likely or inevitable—that is, that the United States is going to launch a massive attack. Although it is impossible to predict with any certainty how the Soviets might reach such a conclusion, it seems likely that fear of an American damage-limitation attack would be the most important factor. Thus, American policy for reducing further the likelihood of Soviet preemption should attempt to reduce the pressures that could encourage the Soviets to preempt in addition to reducing its possible benefits; this counts against an extensive counterforce arsenal.[59]

Second, at least given current forces, the United States can do far more to reduce Soviet preemptive incentives by reducing the vulnerability of its forces than by maintaining the ability to protect its forces against follow-on attacks. Vulnerable U.S. ICBMs currently provide the Soviets the opportunity to destroy approximately 80 percent of that force in a first strike, amounting to about 2,000 warheads; denying the Soviets the ability to launch follow-on attacks against the ICBMs that survive a first strike could protect at most the remaining 20 percent, or about 500 warheads.[60] Follow-on attacks are likely

---

[57] Scott D. Sagan, "1914 Revisited: Allies, Offense, and Instability," *International Security* 11, no. 2 (Fall 1986): 174, notes the importance of survivable forces to a second-strike counterforce strategy, but does not find that they could be sufficient.

[58] Proponents could respond, however, that counterforce is nevertheless a second-best solution, since the United States is unwilling to make its forces sufficiently survivable, as demonstrated (for example) by the difficulties of finding an acceptable survivable ICBM basing mode.

[59] Sagan, *Moving Targets*, pp. 89–94, argues that the United States can, by depending heavily on slow counterforce, develop a second-strike counterforce capability that would look less like a first-strike capability to the Soviet Union. If possible, this is clearly preferable to one that might appear far more capable of damage-limitation. However, in terms of defeating Soviet damage limitation efforts this approach has no advantages over the alternative of increasing the survivability of American forces. Further, we need to consider whether this counterforce arsenal, which would still include some prompt counterforce, might still create fears about American preemption when viewed through a Soviet worst-case lens. Adopting a worst-case perspective is appropriate since this entire case for second-strike counterforce is built on the possibility that the Soviets will take extremely risky actions once they fear nuclear attack.

[60] On the vulnerability of ICBMs see note 2 in Chapter Eight.

to be even less significant against the other legs of the triad, since their vulnerable portions are soft targets that the Soviets should be able to destroy with high confidence in their initial attack. Furthermore, increasing the survivability of American forces would reduce the number of warheads vulnerable to Soviet follow-on attacks, thereby reducing the marginal value of these attacks for limiting damage.

Third, American second-strike counterforce forces would be unable to defeat Soviet follow-on attacks if the Soviets deploy survivable counterforce, possibly for example in mobile ICBMs. In this case, the Soviets would employ their vulnerable counterforce in the first wave, saving the survivable forces for follow-on attacks.

In short, although the United States will be unable to make its strategic nuclear force entirely survivable, reducing its vulnerability would greatly reduce whatever danger results from Soviet efforts to limit damage at the margin. Further, significantly increasing the survivability of American forces would leave little if any role for counterforce in disrupting Soviet follow-on damage-limitation attacks.[61]

Holding at Risk What Soviet Leaders Value Most

Some proponents argue that the United States needs counterforce to threaten what Soviet leaders value most highly—specifically, political and military control, military forces, and their own lives.[62] Given this view of Soviet leaders, the ability to destroy these targets increases the costs the United States can threaten and therefore enhances its ability both to extend deterrence and to deter Soviet attacks against the U.S. homeland.[63] Some analysts go so far as to argue that the United States can threaten the high costs usually associated with an assured destruction capability—which provides the ability to destroy the adversary's society—only if it maintains second-strike counterforce to destroy these targets.[64]

As evidence, these analysts observe that the Soviet Union has invested heavily in many hundreds of relocation shelters for national and regional leaders, including deep underground shelters for the top national leadership.[65] They infer that these shelters were built because Soviet leaders want to insure

[61] There are also questions about whether second-strike counterforce could greatly impede Soviet follow-on attacks. Some of these issues are addressed in Chapter Eight, pp. 262–68.

[62] On the importance of these arguments in current U.S. plans to expand its counterforce arsenal see Congressional Budget Office, *Modernizing U.S. Strategic Offensive Forces*, pp. 14–15.

[63] I have included this argument in the section on deterring attacks against the American homeland because, as argued below, the strongest case for targeting the Soviet leadership focuses on reducing Soviet incentives for preemption.

[64] For citations to these arguments see Chapter Two, pp. 25–26.

[65] On the existence of these shelters see Gershwin, *Soviet Strategic Force Developments*, and Department of Defense, *Soviet Military Power 1988* (Washington, D.C.: GPO, 1988), pp. 59–62.

their ability to direct the recovery of the Soviet state as well as protect their own lives. Thus, American counterforce dedicated to counter-leadership targeting can enhance deterrence by promising to deny these Soviet war aims.

Proponents add that counterarguments that focus on rational calculations of total costs and benefits miss the point, since in a severe crisis Soviet leaders, especially military leaders, might focus on achieving their specific military objectives. During such a crisis, for example, these leaders might judge their personal survival in isolation from the broader consideration of the absolute level of damage in an all-out war, and would, in effect, exaggerate the importance of that survival.

Chapter Two presented the basic problems with this overall argument. First, an attack against Soviet society would inflict such high costs that even a highly aggressive Soviet leader would be unwilling to significantly increase its probability in pursuit of expansionist objectives. Thus, even if threatening these targets would increase the prospective costs of war, doing so is unnecessary. Second, even if Soviet leaders place especially high value on military forces and control capabilities during peacetime, destroying their society would eliminate the value of these capabilities. There would not be much left to protect or control. Thus, destroying these targets in an all-out war would not significantly increase Soviet costs. In short, the U.S. ability to destroy Soviet society should be more than sufficient to deter premeditated Soviet attacks.[66] And if not, it is hard to imagine why threatening to destroy these additional targets would make an important difference.

But if this is true, why have the Soviets built these shelters? We should note first that the Soviets may have built the very hard shelters primarily to reduce the U.S. ability to decapitate their retaliatory capabilities.[67] In this case, these shelters are best understood as part of the Soviet effort to deter U.S. attacks by guaranteeing the Soviet ability to retaliate, not as preparation for their survival and the Soviet Union's postwar recovery.

Yet even if we accept that the overall Soviet shelter program is motivated partly by the leadership's desire to survive a nuclear war,[68] we need to ask in what situations would leadership survival be a war aim that would influence

[66] This judgment is now explicit in Soviet doctrine. See, for example, Stephen M. Meyer, "The Sources and Prospects of Gorbachev's New Political Thinking on Security," *International Security* 13, no. 2 (Fall 1988): 134–38. In addition, experts believe that the Soviet ability to limit damage at the margin would not influence Soviet willingness to launch premeditated attacks. See, for example, Director of Central Intelligence, *Soviet Civil Defense* (Washington, D.C.: CIA, July 1978), p. 12, which concludes "We do not believe that the Soviets' present civil defenses would embolden them deliberately to expose the USSR to a higher risk of nuclear war."

[67] This possibility is consistent with Meyer, "Soviet Nuclear Operations," in Carter et al., eds., *Managing Nuclear Operations*, pp. 485–87, 501–3.

[68] This position is reasonable because some of these shelters would be used to house nonmilitary personnel. See Donald Latham, Senate Committee on Armed Services, *Department of Defense Authorization for Appropriations for Fiscal Year 1983*, pt. 7, 97th Cong., 2d sess., pp. 4673, 4675.

Soviet decisions? As argued above, there is no reason to believe that the ability of Soviet leaders to survive a nuclear war would influence their peacetime decisions about challenging American interests in ways that increase the probability of nuclear war with the United States or its allies. Clearly, the best way to guarantee their ability to survive a nuclear war is to avoid one altogether.

Whatever danger exists must lie in the possibility that some ability to reduce nuclear damage, including protecting its leadership, might increase Soviet interest in launching a preemptive attack in the midst of a severe crisis. Even in this more demanding case, however, we have reasons to doubt that the U.S. ability to destroy Soviet military forces and control targets would make a significant difference. As with Soviet decisions in peacetime, if the United States can defeat the overall Soviet damage-limitation program Soviet leaders would probably see little special value in their own survival, since there would be so little left to control. Thus, Soviet first-strike incentives would remain very small and Soviet leadership survival is unlikely to contribute significantly to them.

Nevertheless, what if Soviet leaders do see some benefit in their own survival, even in the face of catastrophe? Analysts may disagree about whether prudence requires the United States to hedge against this possible danger. Those who worry that in a severe crisis Soviet leaders may consider their own survival in isolation—and thereby exaggerate its benefits—will tend to favor hedging.

But the United States can hedge against these possible dangers without maintaining counterforce to threaten Soviet leaders. In fact, it is counterforce—specifically, vulnerable American forces capable of destroying the Soviet leadership shelters—that creates these Soviet preemptive incentives. If the United States does not deploy these forces, then Soviet leaders, including military leaders, should recognize that these shelters would survive whether or not they preempt. Thus, the United States can eliminate these Soviet incentives to preempt by *not* deploying counterforce capable of destroying Soviet leadership bunkers. The United States can afford to concede this war aim to the Soviets since doing so would not compromise the American ability to deter premeditated Soviet attacks; it would, however, eliminate whatever marginal first-strike incentives American targeting of Soviet leaders might generate.

COUNTERFORCE TO PROVIDE BROADER POLITICAL BENEFITS

Avoiding Perceptions of Counterforce Inferiority

Proponents of counterforce argue that specific perceptions of U.S. counterforce inferiority could have broad negative political consequences. Perceptions of counterforce inferiority could occur if the Soviet Union has better counterforce weapons—for example, missiles that are larger or warheads that have greater yield and/or accuracy—and if the Soviet Union has more counterforce weapons than the United States. Along these lines, the Carter administration argued:

There are political as well as military reasons to develop and deploy U.S. hard-target-kill capabilities. . . . An asymmetry in this measure of relative U.S. and Soviet capabilities could lead to perceptions of Soviet advantage that could have adverse political and military implications, including (1) greater Soviet and less U.S. freedom of action in the employment of conventional forces; (2) greater Soviet latitude in the implicit utilization of nuclear strength for political coercion. . . .[69]

And, Amoretta and Francis Hoeber, arguing in support of U.S. counterforce deployments, hold that the "image of power conveyed by Soviet superiority in ICBM numbers and throw weight does count and the Soviets know it."[70]

The counterforce inferiority argument is a type of perceptions argument, because comparisons of the superpowers' counterforce weapons, and of their ICBMs in particular, do not reflect the U.S. ability to perform necessary military missions.[71] Judged in terms of the military requirements of U.S. strategy, these arguments are flawed because U.S. counterforce requirements are determined by the targets the United States needs to be able to destroy, not by the number or quality of Soviet counterforce missiles and warheads.[72]

---

[69] Senate Committee on Foreign Relations and House Committee on Foreign Affairs, *Fiscal Year 1981 Arms Control Impact Statements* (Washington, D.C.: GPO, 1980), pp. 56–57.

[70] Hoeber and Hoeber, "The Case against the Case against Counterforce," p. 55. Also arguing the danger of imbalance in counterforce capabilities is General Bennie Davis, commander in chief of SAC, before the Senate Committee on Armed Services, *Department of Defense Authorization for Appropriations for Fiscal Year 1986*, pt. 7, 99th Cong., 1st sess., 1985, p. 3710: "MX is an urgent military requirement that is absolutely essential to reduce the current disparity in U.S. and Soviet forces. It will counter the Soviet's superiority in prompt counter-military capability . . . This Soviet advantage, more than any other factor in the current strategic situation, undermines stability and threatens peace. If not redressed, it may lead the Soviets to believe their political objectives can be successfully attained through the use of coercion or force." See also *Scowcroft Commission Report*, pp. 14, 16, and Blair Stewart, "MX and the Counterforce Problem: A Case for Silo Deployment," *Strategic Review* 9, no. 3 (Summer 1981): 16–26.

Although I have argued that these comparisons are not meaningful, we should also note that taken on their own terms they are somewhat misleading. For example, focusing entirely on Soviet counterforce suggests incorrectly that the United States has little capability to destroy Soviet silos. However, according to Congressional Budget Office, *Trident II Missiles*, p. 16, in 1985 the United States would be able to destroy 40 percent of 2,000 targets hardened to 5,000 psi, and about 60 percent of them if hardened to 2,000 psi. Plans for deploying MX and D-5 would increase the latter figure to about 90 percent (p. 30). According to Warner R. Schilling, "U.S. Strategic Nuclear Concepts in the 1970s," *International Security* 6, no. 2, (Fall 1981): 71–72, in 1982, without MX and D–5, the United States with 1,650 Minuteman III warheads could have expected to destroy 4,300 Soviet ICBM warheads, which comprise 39 percent of their total force; by comparison, the Soviet Union with 2,100 SS-18 warheads could destroy 1,960 U.S. ICBM warheads, equal to 18 percent of the American force.

[71] See Salman, Sullivan, and Van Evera, "Analysis or Propaganda?" who term these arguments "number games" (pp. 178–82) and "subcategory games" (p. 193).

[72] Robert Jervis, *The Illogic of American Nuclear Strategy* (Ithaca: Cornell University Press,

In line with persuasive arguments presented by the punitive retaliation school, the counterforce perceptions argument suffers the general weakness of arguments that hold that superpower leaders are influenced by comparisons of nuclear forces that do not reflect their ability to affect war outcomes: as discussed in Chapter Two, we have virtually no evidence supporting these claims. In addition, comparisons of specific types of forces are even less likely to influence Soviet and allied perceptions of U.S. capability and resolve since they overlook the remainder of the superpowers' forces.

Engaging the Soviet Union in an Arms Race

Some proponents of counterforce favor pursuing a damage-limitation capability, even if infeasible, because they believe the United States can increase its security by competing with the Soviet Union. Additional U.S. countervalue systems cannot generate this competition since increasing the redundancy of the U.S. ability to destroy Soviet society puts little pressure on the Soviet Union to react. In contrast, additional weapons that threaten Soviet retaliatory forces could jeopardize the Soviet capability for deterring the United States. Even if U.S. offensive counterforce and strategic defenses are ineffective when deployed, Soviet leaders will respond to insure that the cumulative effect of U.S. efforts is insignificant. Proponents argue that pressing this arms race can provide three types of benefits.

DEMONSTRATION OF U.S. RESOLVE

Some counterforce proponents argue that by striving to enhance its military capabilities the United States demonstrates resolve to protect its interests. Thus, pursuing a damage-limitation capability and engaging the Soviet Union in an arms race contributes to deterrence by increasing the credibility of U.S. nuclear threats rather than by actually improving the U.S. ability to perform military missions. Proponents also raise the flip side of this argument—forgoing this military competition and pursuing instead either unilateral restraint or negotiated arms control is dangerous because Soviet leaders will see these more cooperative policies as reflecting a lack of U.S. determination to protect its interests.[73]

This line of argument, however, is based entirely on the deterrence-model view of the Soviet Union—which assumes the Soviets are bent on expansion—and fails to adequately incorporate guidance from the spiral model by ignoring the possibility that competitive policies will increase Soviet insecurity. As argued in Chapter Three, the United States should strive for a nuclear

---

1984), especially pp. 111–18, presents a number of arguments against counterforce matching. See also Sherman, "The Fallacies of Counterforce," pp. 53–54.

[73] Chapter Three provides examples and elaboration of these arguments and the counterarguments that follow.

policy that simultaneously addresses the dangers identified by both models. Strategic nuclear weapons provide an opportunity to achieve this balance relatively easily because defense (retaliatory capabilities) dominates offense (damage-limitation capabilities). Consequently, this argument for pursuing an arms competition suffers two more specific shortcomings.

First, because Soviet leaders are unlikely to be convinced that the United States is entirely benign, fueling a counterforce arms race will raise Soviet doubts about U.S. intentions. The more likely effect of a U.S. buildup of counterforce would therefore be to convince Soviet leaders that the United States threatens their security, not that it is determined to protect its own.

U.S. counterforce policies are especially likely to be self-defeating when Soviet leaders favor cooperative policies. In this case, competitive U.S. policies tend to discredit Soviet moderates and to support elites who favor competition. Specifically, U.S. counterforce policies seem more likely to eventually undermine Gorbachev's calls for moderation than to generate support for additional concessions.

In contrast, the conditions under which U.S. counterforce might encourage conciliatory Soviet policies are far less likely. According to this approach, the United States deploys counterforce in reaction to competitive Soviet policies; recognizing that their policies provoked these threatening U.S. programs, the Soviets learn they are self-defeating and Soviet hard-liners who sponsored them are discredited. However, the Soviets are unlikely to recognize the reactive and conditional nature of U.S. counterforce policies. Although often restrained, the United States has continued to deploy and upgrade its offensive counterforce systems since the early 1960s. Thus, the Soviets are most likely to understand U.S. counterforce as they have in the past—as U.S. attempts to acquire military advantages, not as the United States punishing the Soviet Union for its competitive policies. Further complicating this approach, U.S. counterforce programs are not easily turned on and off in response to Soviet policy. Rather, they take years to develop, gain domestic constituencies, and become far more expensive if developed and deployed in a stop and go fashion.

Second, this argument for fueling an arms race exaggerates the risks of a more cooperative U.S. policy. More cooperative policies are unlikely to raise Soviet doubts about U.S. resolve since the United States would not be depriving itself of necessary military capabilities by deciding to forgo competition in counterforce. In other words, there is not a tradeoff between maintaining an adequate military capability and pursuing a relatively nonprovocative policy. The difficulty of balancing the competitive and cooperative dimensions of security policy—which is potentially a key point dividing spiral and deterrence model theorists—is greatly reduced because nuclear weapons virtually eliminate the security dilemma and its associated dangers.

Admittedly, these same factors tend to reduce the danger of a counterforce arms race. U.S. counterforce will appear less threatening because it has little hope of providing a highly effective damage-limitation capability.

Nevertheless, the Soviets have tended to see even ineffective U.S. offense reflecting U.S. interest in military superiority and whatever political benefits it might provide. Thus, the negative political effects of American counterforce policies are not entirely eliminated by defense dominance.

FURTHER WEAKENING OF THE SOVIET ECONOMY

Some analysts advocate an arms race to weaken the Soviet economy. One version of this argument holds that because the U.S. economy can better afford the diversion of resources to the military, an intensified arms race would place the United States in a relatively stronger position. Another version maintains that a weakened economy keeps Soviet leaders focused on domestic problems, and that such an inward-looking adversary is less likely to challenge U.S. interests.[74] Consistent with these arguments the Reagan administration adopted a policy of economic warfare that "involved shaping U.S. military policies and programs so as to maximize the economic burden they placed on the Soviet Union. . . . it set as a guideline for decisions on U.S. programs not just their military usefulness to the United States but also the economic burdens they could impose on the Soviet Union."[75]

In support of this strategy, proponents argue that the cooperative international policies pursued by Gorbachev are driven primarily by the weakness of the Soviet economy. In addition, as discussed in Chapter Three, the prospect of a continuing expensive arms race with the United States may have enhanced the domestic standing of Soviets who favor more cooperative policies. Furthermore, Gorbachev has stressed the importance of curbing military spending, thereby suggesting its importance for solving domestic problems.

Nevertheless, there are serious questions about both the feasibility and desirability of further weakening the Soviet economy (or preventing its improvement). U.S. counterforce would probably be at most of secondary importance, possibly aggravating the problems of Soviet economic growth but neither cre-

[74] Reviewing arguments on Soviet decline is Kurt M. Campbell, "Prospects and Consequences of Soviet Decline," in Graham Allison, Albert Carnesale, and Joseph Nye, eds., *Fateful Visions* (Cambridge, Mass.: Ballinger, 1988), pp. 153–57. Arguing that U.S. policy should be directed at Soviet economic vulnerabilities is Richard Pipes, *Survival Is Not Enough* (New York: Simon and Schuster, 1984). Some analysts argue that severe Soviet decline could lead to highly risky Soviet behavior: see, for example, Hannes Adomeit, *Soviet Crisis Prevention and Management: Why and When Do the Soviet Leaders Take Risks?* Occasional Paper (Santa Monica: Rand, October 1986), pp. 27–33.

[75] Samuel P. Huntington, "The Defense Policy of the Reagan Administration, 1981–1982," in Fred I. Greenstein, ed., *The Reagan Presidency: An Early Assessment* (Baltimore: Johns Hopkins University Press, 1983), p. 94. See also Leslie H. Gelb, "What We Really Know about Russia," *New York Times Magazine*, 28 October 1984, p. 25, and information on the leaked FY 1984–1988 Defense Guidance reported in the *New York Times*, 30 May 1982.

ating them nor greatly impeding their solution.[76] In addition, the Soviets might reduce the potential costs of responding to U.S. counterforce by finding relatively inexpensive countermeasures for defeating U.S. counterforce, particularly SDI, instead of matching it. "New thinking" on Soviet nuclear doctrine has emphasized the importance of such asymmetric responses.[77]

Still, why not invest in counterforce to achieve these marginal reductions in the prospects for Soviet economic recovery? To begin with, as discussed above, American counterforce might lead to more competitive Soviet policies. This broad argument is supported by analyses of the current Soviet security debate. The Soviet reformers who favor shifting investment from the military to the civilian sector also favor shifting to less confrontational policies and increasing Soviet reliance on diplomatic instruments to resolve superpower disputes. Thus, U.S. policies that help defeat these reformers would increase the prospects that the United States will face a more confrontational Soviet Union.[78]

In addition, U.S counterforce deployments that require costly Soviet reactions will also be expensive for the United States. Thus, even assuming that superpower military spending slows economic growth, the United States might not emerge in a relatively stronger position. Further, even if economic growth is not slowed, both countries would be worse off in absolute terms since the arms race has opportunity costs, shifting nondefense spending and/ or personal consumption to defense spending.

GENERATING A QUALITATIVE ARMS RACE

Samuel Huntington argues that qualitative arms races reduce the probability of war and that the United States should therefore pursue new counterforce systems: "vigorous competition in the development and deployment of new weapons, which has been central to the Soviet-American arms race, does not

[76] On sources of Soviet economic weakness see Ed A. Hewett, *Reforming the Soviet Economy* (Washington, D.C.: Brookings Institution, 1988).

The relationship between defense spending and economic growth is not firmly established. See Aaron L. Friedberg, "The Political Economy of American Strategy," *World Politics* 41, no. 3 (April 1989): 392–405. These points are not necessarily inconsistent with Gorbachev's emphasis on reducing defense spending—these reductions would make possible increases in personal consumption and investment in future consumption even if the rate of Soviet economic growth did not increase. On the effect of reduced defense spending on consumption see Mark M. Hopkins and Michael Kennedy, *The Tradeoff between Consumption and Military Expenditures for the Soviet Union during the 1980s*, R–2927-NA (Santa Monica: Rand, November 1982).

[77] Matthew Evangelista, "Economic Reform and Military Technology in Soviet Security Policy," *Harriman Institute Forum* 2, no. 1 (January 1989): p. 7; idem, "The Domestic Politics of the Soviet Star Wars Debate" (unpublished paper, 1987); and Raymond L. Garthoff, "New Thinking in Soviet Military Doctrine," *Washington Quarterly* (Summer 1988): 142–43.

[78] Evangelista, "Economic Reform and Military Technology in Soviet Security Policy," and Jack Snyder, "International Leverage on Soviet Domestic Change," *World Politics* 42, no. 1 (October 1989): 1–30.

increase the probability of war but instead does just the reverse. History shows rather conclusively that such qualitative arms races function as a substitute for war rather than a stimulus to war."[79]

This argument suffers at least three important weaknesses. In the first place, there are doubts about whether the historical record supports this conclusion. Paul Kennedy argues that the distinction is misleading and that both types of arms races have had similar effects.[80]

Moreover, the logic underlying Huntington's conclusion fails when applied to the particular case of the superpower nuclear arms race. Among his key points are that a qualitative race, if vigorously pursued by both countries, "acts to stabilize the relationship between the two competitors," while a country that pursues a quantitative buildup sends a "fairly clear sign that it was intending to go to war in the immediate future."[81] However, although both types of arms races are likely to leave the superpowers in MAD, a quantitative race holds little hope of providing significant military advantages. In contrast, qualitative advances—for example, in ASW (antisubmarine warfare) and strategic defense—would be necessary before either superpower could acquire a significant damage-limitation capability. Thus, there is no reason to believe that a quantitative strategic nuclear race is more likely to suggest preparation for launching nuclear war; if anything, just the opposite is true.

Finally, comparing qualitative and quantitative races is insufficient; we must also compare these two possibilities to avoiding an arms race altogether. Clearly, not pursuing Huntington's qualitative race is an important option for "stabilizing" the military balance.

COSTS OF COUNTERFORCE

The preceding analysis has already identified one key danger—contrary to the proponents' argument that arms racing will communicate U.S. resolve, extensive U.S. investments in counterforce are more likely to generate the misperceptions and tensions predicted by the spiral model. The rest of this chapter explores additional costs, of which decreasing crisis stability is probably the most important.

Before beginning, I should add that the extent of these costs varies with the ability of American counterforce to destroy Soviet forces and command and

---

[79] Samuel P. Huntington, "The Renewal of Strategy," in Samuel P. Huntington, ed., *The Strategic Imperative* (Cambridge, Mass.: Ballinger, 1982), p. 41. This conclusion is based upon Huntington, "Arms Races: Prerequisites and Results," *Public Policy*, Yearbook of the Graduate School of Public Administration, Harvard University, vol. 8 (1958), pp. 41–86.

[80] Paul Kennedy, *Strategy and Diplomacy, 1870–1945* (Aylesbury, England: Fontana, 1984), p. 176, although Kennedy is reacting to the claim that qualitative races are dangerous.

[81] Huntington, "The Renewal of Strategy," p. 41, and idem, "Arms Races," p. 72. He acknowledges that arms races may "foster suspicion and insecurity," but believes that qualitative and quantitative races generate very different domestic pressures for war ("Arms Races," pp. 83, 75–76).

control in a first strike. All else being equal, they increase with the size, lethality, reliability, and promptness of American forces. For example, a large force of only air-launched cruise missiles would create smaller preemptive incentives than an equally large and lethal force of ballistic missiles, since slow counterforce poses a smaller first-strike threat. In theory at least, the United States could deploy a counterforce arsenal that posed such a limited threat to Soviet retaliatory capabilities that these dangers would not arise. However, the current American arsenal, and its planned modernization, are beyond this threshold. Thus, the following discussion addresses the dangers of counterforce on this scale, which I sometimes refer to as "extensive" counterforce.[82]

Exaggeration of First-Strike Incentives

Although the United States should never launch a preemptive attack, extensive American counterforce could nevertheless reduce crisis stability because U.S. leaders may not fully appreciate this.

I am not making the standard argument against American counterforce, which holds that it reduces crisis stability by providing the United States with damage-limitation capabilities, thereby creating "real" first-strike incentives that would make preemption its best option in a severe crisis. According to this argument, if both the United States and the Soviet Union can reduce the costs of a nuclear war by striking first, then in a severe crisis both could feel pressure to attack quickly—that is, before the other attacks. However, MAD essentially eliminates the superpowers' abilities to reduce the costs of an all-out war, and thereby virtually eliminates first-strike incentives.[83] Even if we accept the possibility, discussed early in this chapter, that some damage limitation may be possible in MAD, the risks of a preemptive attack—which requires the United States to launch a massive first strike and thereby guarantee an all-out war—exceed the probably marginal benefits of striking first. Thus, preemption would never be the United States' best option.

However, if American leaders do not accept this conclusion, and instead believe that counterforce could provide sufficient protection for American so-

---

[82] Because the preceding analysis finds that the United States requires little if any counterforce, I do not explore how to design counterforce deployments that could perform specific counterforce missions while minimizing the danger of crisis instability. On this issue see Sagan, *Moving Targets*, pp. 89–95.

[83] Some opponents of counterforce argue both that damage limitation is impossible in MAD and that continued U.S. deployment of counterforce creates crisis instability. As presented, these arguments are internally inconsistent since counterforce that is too ineffective to limit damage would not create first-strike incentives. See, for example, Louis Rene Beres, "Tilting toward Thantos: America's 'Countervailing' Strategy," *World Politics* 34, no. 1 (October 1981): 27–31; Randall Forsberg, "A Bilateral Nuclear-Weapons Freeze," *Scientific American* (November 1982): 2; and Herbert Scoville, Jr., *MX: Prescription for Disaster* (Cambridge: MIT Press, 1981), pp. 137–48.

ciety to warrant launching a preemptive attack, then counterforce would reduce crisis stability, even if significant damage limitation is in fact unattainable.[84] Counterforce would create the same types of pressure predicted by the
basic logic of crisis instability.[85] The danger in this case would stem from
exaggerations of the benefits of striking first, not from the actual benefits
themselves.

Based on this latter argument, I conclude that we have grounds for concern.
As already discussed, some influential U.S. civilian leaders continue to hold
some hope of limiting damage if all-out war occurs. While U.S. declaratory
policy has not emphasized damage limitation since the early 1960s, the possibility of pursuing damage limitation by striking first has not been ruled out.
This section explores the U.S. military's views.

Although infrequently stated as an objective, a variety of considerations
suggest that the U.S. military has a continuing interest in limiting damage if
war occurs. To begin with, some public statements by top U.S. military leaders indicate that they believe at least some damage limitation is feasible and
that this belief underlies their commitment to continued improvements in U.S.
counterforce systems. For example, in 1987 General Russell Dougherty, a
former commander in chief of the Strategic Air Command (SAC), while arguing for continued ICBM modernization, wrote: "The purpose of promptness is to remove warfighting resources from Soviet control, thereby disrupting and blunting the ongoing Soviet attack and *limiting damage to the U.S.
and our allies.*"[86] In a similar vein, in 1982 General Bennie Davis, then commander in chief of SAC, argued:

> In a comprehensive strategy of deterrence, our strategic forces are the controlling
> rods—if escalation can be controlled. If it can't be controlled, and ultimate degrees
> of nuclear weaponry are employed, the size and strength of our weapons and the
> comprehensive planning of target selection and weapon laydown will determine the
> extent to which it is possible for our society to emerge from such a conflict with
> advantage and [be] able to control its destiny.[87]

---

[84] This assumes that U.S. leaders also believe that the Soviets might launch a damage-limitation
attack. Further, as discussed above, the Soviets are likely to see extensive American counterforce
deployments reflecting an interest in damage limitation; therefore, this would probably be a key
contributor to any Soviet decision to launch a preemptive attack.

[85] This is the basic lesson of recent studies of World War I. See Stephen Van Evera, "The Cult
of the Offensive and the Origins of the First World War," *International Security* 9, no. 1 (Summer
1984): 71–79.

[86] Russell E. Dougherty, "The Value of ICBM Modernization," *International Security* 12, no.
2 (Fall 1987): 169, emphasis added.

[87] Quoted in Bruce G. Blair, *Strategic Command and Control* (Washington, D.C.: Brookings
Institution, 1985), p. 29. Having noted the widespread belief that full-scale nuclear war is likely
once the nuclear threshold is crossed, Blair concludes that "this fatalism is sufficiently deep and
wide that strategy for fighting a war is probably valued more for its contribution to damage limitation than to nuclear diplomacy" (ibid., p. 29).

For an earlier example see General Earle Wheeler, Chairman of the Joint Chiefs of Staff, who

These views are hardly surprising since the United States has a long history of planning for damage limitation. U.S. warplans are reported to have included options for preemptive attack through the 1970s and current warplans emphasize counterforce and counter-leadership targeting that would be necessary for limiting damage.[88]

Furthermore, the U.S. military has not simply developed the full range of options available in deployed forces. Rather, priority has often been given to acquiring damage-limitation capabilities—sometimes at the expense of increasing U.S. retaliatory capabilities—and to insuring that arms control agreements would not reduce the U.S. ability to destroy Soviet forces. For example, the Air Force welcomed MIRV only after becoming convinced of its advantages against hard targets.[89] In contrast, during the early 1960s the Air Force was unenthusiastic because questions remained about MIRV's hard-target capability. At that time some proponents saw MIRV enhancing U.S. retaliatory capabilities, since it would provide more survivable warheads and increase the U.S. ability to penetrate future Soviet defenses. Thus, Air Force pursuit of MIRV was driven by the priority it placed on improving U.S. counterforce.

The military's continued interest in damage limitation is also evident in their positions on U.S. arms control policy. For example, Strobe Talbott explains that while the Joint Chiefs of Staff endorsed the low warhead ceiling in the Reagan administration's START (Strategic Arms Reduction Talks) proposal, this was acceptable only if there was an even lower launcher ceiling:

> Among the most important targets they would have to cover in the SIOP were Soviet ICBM silos and ballistic-missile-firing submarines. If START was going to leave the U.S. with fewer warheads, then there would have to be fewer Soviet launchers for the U.S. to "take-out" in a war. Therefore, the outcome of START should be a high ratio of American warheads to Soviet launchers.[90]

---

in 1968 said "Yes, you attack the urban industrial base, that is the population base and industry, but we also have always held to the view that we must attack those forces of the Soviet Union which are able to inflict destruction on ourselves and our allies," quoted in Ted Greenwood, *Making the MIRV: A Study of Defense Decision Making* (Cambridge, Mass.: Ballinger, 1975), p. 59.

[88] On U.S. nuclear warplans up to 1960 see David Alan Rosenberg, "The Origins of Overkill: Nuclear Weapons and American Strategy, 1945–1960," *International Security* 7, no. 4 (Spring 1983): 3–71. On the existence of preemptive options in the 1960s and 1970s see Desmond Ball, "U.S. Strategic Nuclear Forces: How Would They Be Used?" *International Security* 7, no. 3 (Winter 1982/1983): 33–38. See also Secretary of Defense Harold Brown, *Nuclear War Strategy*, Hearing before the Senate Committee on Foreign Relations, 96th Cong., 2d Sess., 16 September 1980, p. 18. On current warplans see Ball and Toth, "Revising the SIOP," pp. 65–92. For additional sources on U.S. nuclear targeting see note 6 in Chapter One.

[89] Greenwood, *Making the MIRV*, especially pp. 37–43, 57–73.

[90] Strobe Talbott, *Deadly Gambits: The Reagan Administration and the Stalemate in Arms Control* (New York: Alfred A. Knopf, 1984), p. 257. It is important to note, however, that Talbott also explains that the Chiefs' position was designed to meet the Reagan administration's Defense Guidance.

The Pentagon's interest in banning mobile missiles provides a third example of its interest in damage limitation. A Reagan administration arms control official explained that the proposed ban "was largely the Pentagon's doing" and that "although a variety of factors were involved, there was substantial pressure from the Joint Chiefs [of Staff] to eliminate what they see as a major irritant—namely, untargetable Soviet missiles."[91] At the time of this proposed ban, the United States was also considering the small mobile missile as the leading candidate for restoring the survivability of the ICBM leg of its triad. Finally, reflecting continuing concern with survivable Soviet forces, hunting for Soviet mobile ICBMs is one of the primary missions being proposed for the B-2 Stealth bomber.

This continuing interest in damage limitation is worrisome since military leaders' assessments of U.S. prospects for damage limitation are likely to influence U.S. decisions about escalation. As a superpower war grows, military leaders would play a key role in evaluating U.S. options and briefing top political decisionmakers. Escalation is more likely if the U.S. military believes significant damage limitation is possible. In contrast, military leaders could probably veto arguments for preemption if they conclude against the feasibility of damage limitation.[92]

The military will be less likely to play this restraining role, and more likely to see benefits in large counterforce attacks, if the United States continues to invest in counterforce. Doing so preserves the illusion that preemption could be the best U.S. option. Furthermore, military leaders have a better chance of successfully making the case for damage limitation if they can point to a U.S. force designed to attack the entire Soviet force. In this vein, Morton Halperin argues that "if military commanders get what they want—forces necessary for this kind of war-fighting capability—and if they are permitted to draw up contingency plans for using these forces, they are likely to take the contingency planning for nuclear war more seriously than if they are restricted to forces designed and justified for retaliation against cities."[93]

Thus, the clearest and potentially most effective way to influence future

[91] R. Jeffrey Smith, "Proposal to Ban Mobile Missiles Favors Targeting over Arms Control," *Science* (22 August 1986): 831. See also the recent statement by Larry Welch, the Air Force chief of staff: "survivability has been overplayed. . . . The real issue is capability," quoted in Robert C. Toth, "Proposed Arms Pact Launches Strategic Debate," *Los Angeles Times*, 25 July 1989, p. 10.

[92] Richard K. Betts, *Soldiers, Statesmen and Cold War Crises* (Cambridge, Mass.: Harvard University Press, 1977), p. 96, finds that military advice has its greatest influence when the military finds U.S. capabilities inadequate to the task at hand. In these cases the military was essentially able to veto intervention. Morton Halperin, "Clever Briefers, Crazy Leaders, and Myopic Analysts," *Washington Monthly* (September 1974): 43, argues that the president would not launch a major nuclear attack if the military did not support it.

[93] Halperin, "Clever Briefers, Crazy Leaders, and Myopic Analysts," p. 44.

military advice away from considerations of damage limitation is not to provide the extensive counterforce forces necessary for attempting damage limitation. In contrast, continuing to buy counterforce weapons, even if justified by arguments other than pursuit of damage limitation, works against this objective; it provides some of the necessary forces and it may suggest tacit civilian support for a damage-limitation strategy. Therefore, buying counterforce as a hedge against unforeseeable Soviet calculations, as recommended by the military denial school, has larger costs than is generally recognized.

In sum, U.S. policies that emphasize counterforce are dangerous because influential civilian and military decisionmakers retain an interest in limiting damage and believe that preemption could be the best U.S. option in a severe crisis. Continuing to acquire counterforce both reflects and reinforces this misunderstanding about MAD. In addition, U.S. counterforce policies will be even more dangerous if Soviet leaders believe that their counterforce can provide some damage limitation worth pursuing; U.S. counterforce might then provoke Soviet preemption.

Fortunately, even given this misunderstanding, crisis stability will remain higher than if the superpowers gained highly effective damage-limitation capabilities. In that case, everyone would see a first strike offering large benefits and in a severe crisis preemption might actually be the best U.S. option.

It would be imprudent, however, to be confident that misunderstandings about counterforce will not lead to a catastrophic decision in the future. Of course, if ever raised in a severe crisis, all arguments for damage limitation might be rejected by U.S. decisionmakers. But this is not certain, and exaggerating the benefits of striking first in MAD makes decisions for preempting more likely. Because nuclear war would be so costly, all scenarios in which a crisis escalates to full-scale war seem quite unlikely. Relative to the other possibilities, however, the scenario in which misconceived first-strike incentives lead to preemptive war deserves serious attention.

Other Costs

In addition to damaging superpower relations and misleading decisionmakers about whether and how to use nuclear weapons, an American counterforce policy could result in a number of additional specific costs and dangers.

ACCIDENTAL AND INADVERTENT WAR

U.S. counterforce could increase the danger of accidental or inadvertent war that is created by vulnerable command, control, and communications (C³).[94] An extensive U.S. counterforce arsenal could pressure the Soviet

---

[94] With increased awareness of the implications of the vulnerability of command and control, analysts have argued that in a crisis both superpowers would probably feel pressure to shift to

Union to shift to high alert sooner, that is, at a lower level of crisis or war. This is because a U.S. attack against Soviet forces complements an attack against its C^3, increasing U.S. prospects for damage limitation. Believing that U.S. prospects for damage limitation are better, Soviet leaders would fear that U.S. leaders might preempt at a lower level of crisis. Thus, extensive U.S. counterforce pressures the Soviet Union to shift to higher alert sooner, thereby increasing the amount of time during which an accident—for example, incorrect information about a nuclear attack—might trigger the launch of a large Soviet nuclear attack, and during which predelegation might lead to unauthorized Soviet attack.[95]

Furthermore, to the extent that it makes the United States appear to have a damage-limitation strategy, an extensive counterforce arsenal might increase Soviet willingness to launch on warning in response to ambiguous indicators of U.S. attack. Thus, U.S. counterforce not only encourages a Soviet launch-on-warning policy but also makes it more dangerous.[96] Similarly, counterforce could make predelegation of authority more dangerous. If forces were not highly vulnerable, then although the vulnerability of C^3 would still pressure the superpowers to predelegate launch authority, military commanders would not have to launch their forces quickly. Thus, counterforce further increases the probability of undesired escalation.

---

higher levels of alert, including adoption of a LOW posture, even if the adversary lacked an extensive counterforce arsenal. My argument here is that counterforce could exacerbate the dangers of high alert, but would not create them. On these dangers created by vulnerable C^3 see Paul Bracken, *The Command and Control of Nuclear Forces* (New Haven: Yale University Press, 1983), and idem, "Accidental Nuclear War," in Allison, Carnesale, and Nye, eds., *Hawks, Doves and Owls*, pp. 25–53.

The danger in forcing the Soviet Union to a launch-on-warning posture was a key argument against counterforce in the early 1970s. See, for example, Scoville, "Flexible Madness?" pp. 170–71, and Carter, "Nuclear Strategy and Nuclear Weapons," *Scientific American* (May 1974): 27. This argument was presented more recently in Harold Feiveson and Frank von Hippel, "The Freeze and the Counterforce Race," *Physics Today* (January 1983): 36–49.

[95] Utgoff, "In Defense of Counterforce," p. 56, argues, however, that these dangers are small since the probability of mistaken information during the few days or weeks of a crisis is quite small. On the potential for confusion and misunderstandings while on high alert see Scott D. Sagan, "Nuclear Alerts and Crisis Management," *International Security* 9, no. 4 (Spring 1985): 99–139. On the relationship between the danger of accidental war and the pressure to strike first see Schelling, *Arms and Influence*, pp. 227–32.

[96] Counterforce systems that can reach C^3 targets especially quickly (for example, Pershing II missiles based in Europe—which are now banned by the INF Treaty—and highly accurate SLBMs launched from close range) would further increase this danger by essentially eliminating any possibility of waiting to determine the accuracy of the earliest warning information, thereby increasing the possibility of escalation based upon faulty information. Bracken, *The Command and Control of Nuclear Forces*, pp. 244–45, identifies other dangers of short-flight-time systems: they encourage greater predelegation of authority and stimulate informal arrangements by military commanders that increase the ambiguity in the command system.

In addition, a counterforce strategy could create pressures for the United States to adopt a launch-on-warning policy, bringing with it the dangers of quick decisions. Although a Soviet attack against U.S. C^3 would almost certainly leave the United States with massive countervalue capabilities, it would greatly reduce U.S. retaliatory capabilities against Soviet military targets.[97] Thus, pursuing the military objectives for which a counterforce strategy is built creates pressure for the United States to attack before its forces and C^3 are destroyed. By contrast, planning for countervalue retaliation would not create these time pressures.

Finally, counterforce could contribute to the political difficulty of resolving crises at low levels of conflict. For example, a Soviet decision to increase its alert level could also increase the intensity of the crisis, since the United States might see the Soviet alert as provocative, not defensive. The United States might then further increase its alert level, thereby increasing Soviet fears.[98]

ESCALATORY PRESSURES FROM STRATEGIC ASW

Strategic antisubmarine warfare (ASW) is likely to be a necessary component of any U.S. policy that hopes to limit the damage from an all-out war. In combination with other American counterforce forces, strategic ASW could create special problems for terminating a superpower war at the conventional level.

First, it could create pressures for Soviet escalation especially early in a conventional war. Strategic ASW is likely to be a relatively slow attrition process. Destroying most of the Soviet SSBN force, if possible at all, would probably require weeks or months.[99] Therefore, if the United States hopes to keep open the possibility of damage limitation, it will have strong incentives to initiate a strategic ASW campaign well before the conflict is clearly likely to escalate to the strategic nuclear level, and possibly even before conventional fighting has begun in Europe.[100] Similar time pressures would exist if, instead of damage limitation, the ASW campaign is intended to provide the United States with coercive advantages by shifting the ratio of forces.

Although the U.S. Navy holds that an ASW campaign would contribute to termination of a conventional war on favorable terms, the Soviet Union might instead react by escalating to nuclear use. American ASW would be most threatening when combined with U.S. forces that pose a major threat to Soviet

---

[97] Ashton B. Carter, "Assessing Command System Vulnerability," in Carter, Steinbruner, and Zraket, eds., *Managing Nuclear Operations*, pp. 557, 607–9.

[98] In addition, Meyer, "Soviet Perspectives on Paths to Nuclear War," p. 196, notes that a U.S. shift to high alert status during a crisis might lead to Soviet preemption.

[99] On the difficulty of destroying Soviet SSBNs see note 13.

[100] Watkins, "The Maritime Strategy," p. 9, stresses the importance of initiating a strategic ASW campaign early, but does not identify this rationale.

land-based forces. Under these conditions, if the Soviets conclude that the U.S. strategic ASW campaign has a reasonable chance of destroying most of their SSBNs, they might see increased incentives for tactical use of nuclear weapons. Relatively few nuclear weapons might severely degrade the U.S. ASW campaign.[101] Soviet leaders might conclude that the risks of this escalation were justified to protect the sea-based leg of their strategic forces. Although seemingly less likely, if the Soviets see ASW as the first phase of an American damage-limitation campaign, they might use strategic nuclear weapons to pressure the United States to halt the campaign, to deny the United States the ability to destroy the Soviet land-based force, or to try to limit damage if the probability of all-out war appears sufficiently high.[102]

Second, the United States might launch an ASW campaign under the mistaken belief that U.S. conventional operations against Soviet strategic nuclear weapons do not significantly increase the risk of nuclear war. The United States might see strategic ASW as part of the conventional phase of the war, both because the United States would be employing conventional weapons and because the Navy plans to attack Soviet SSBNs as part of its strategy for protecting American sea lines of communication, which is its key mission during a conventional war. The Soviets, however, might focus on the destruction of their strategic nuclear force and not on the type of weapons the United States used to destroy their strategic missile submarines. From their perspective, American ASW could look like the initial phase of a nuclear war.

BARRIERS TO ARMS CONTROL

U.S. pursuit of offensive counterforce in particular and forces for damage limitation in general will reduce the superpowers' ability to reach arms control agreements.[103] Most important, as argued in detail in Chapter Ten, superpower arms control policy can provide its greatest benefits by limiting forces that threaten the adversary's deterrent capabilities—this is clearly incompatible with a continuing U.S. commitment to modernizing its offensive counterforce. In addition, U.S. counterforce could be a barrier to reducing force size, since the Soviet Union needs a larger force to perform retaliatory missions when more of its force is vulnerable. Although U.S. offensive force modernization does not appear to have had this effect in the ongoing START negotiations, U.S. interest in future deployment of ballistic missile defenses has cre-

---

[101] See Barry R. Posen, "Inadvertent Nuclear War?" Escalation and NATO's Northern Flank," *International Security* 7, no. 2 (Fall 1982): 42–43, and John J. Mearsheimer, "A Strategic Misstep: The Maritime Strategy and Deterrence in Europe," *International Security* 11, no. 2 (Fall 1986): 52, note 129.

[102] For more on these possibilities see Mearsheimer, "A Strategic Misstep."

[103] Chapters Nine and Ten examine this relationship in more detail.

ated this type of barrier.[104] In addition, U.S. counterforce may have increased barriers to agreement by forcing the Soviet Union to shift to mobile ICBM basing modes, which makes verification of agreements more difficult.[105]

ECONOMIC COSTS

A counterforce strategy increases the economic cost of U.S. strategic forces. The need to target a large fraction, if not all, of the Soviet force increases the required size of the U.S. force, especially if Soviet forces expand unconstrained by arms control. In addition, counterforce weapons are more expensive than weapons that are not designed to be so lethal. Further, pursuit of counterforce capabilities can require more frequent replacement and upgrading of systems. For example, Trident II missiles will add tens of billions of dollars to the cost of the Trident program, partly because Trident I missiles will be replaced early and partly because the Trident II missiles are more expensive.[106] Bombers—like the B-2—that are designed to penetrate Soviet air defenses and destroy Soviet mobile ICBMs are another example of expensive counterforce systems. The proposed B-2 force would be many tens of billions of dollars more expensive than a comparable force of air-launched cruise missile carriers.[107]

Moreover, maximizing counterforce capabilities could come at the expense of other desirable features, most importantly survivability. For example, making a mobile missile, for example Midgetman, highly lethal requires either making it larger—which could reduce its mobility and therefore its survivability—or reducing its range and ability to carry penetration aids. Offsetting these potential reductions in survivability requires larger investments in these systems.[108]

Finally, to the extent that U.S. counterforce blocks agreements limiting So-

[104] See, for example, Strobe Talbott, "Why START Stopped," *Foreign Affairs* 67, no. 1 (1988): 53–54. The Soviet Union did, however, eventually agree to proceed with a START agreement even if the United States did not agree to abide by the traditional interpretation of the ABM Treaty. See James P. Rubin, "Baker, Shevardnadze Generate Arms Control Progress," *Arms Control Today* 19, no. 8 (October 1989): 26.

[105] Soviet counterforce has had similar effects, including stimulating interest in deploying BMD to protect U.S. ICBMs, thereby threatening the ABM Treaty.

[106] On the cost of Trident II see Government Accounting Office, *Trident II System: Status and Reporting* (Washington, D.C.: GAO, May 15, 1984), and Congressional Budget Office, *Trident II Missile*.

[107] See Michael E. Brown, "The U.S. Manned Bomber and Strategic Deterrence in the 1990s," *International Security* 14, no. 2 (Fall 1989): 5–46.

[108] This point is made by Matthew Bunn and Joseph Romm, "Is a Counterforce Capability Desirable?" (unpublished paper, 1986). Counterforce SLBMs provide another example: the range of the D-5 is reduced to achieve its high lethality, thereby possibly reducing the area Soviet ASW would have to search. (However, given the high survivability of U.S. SSBNs, this is not a very costly tradeoff.)

viet counterforce, it also adds to the costs of increasing the survivability of U.S. retaliatory capabilities.

CONCLUSION

This chapter has shown that U.S. counterforce policies can provide only scant benefits. The United States should not pursue counterforce to reduce the costs of all-out war—it cannot provide a damage-limitation capability that is sufficiently effective to offset the risks of preemption. Counterforce can also contribute little to reducing the probability of war. Contrary to common claims, counterforce is not required for extending deterrence or for deterring attacks against the U.S. homeland. Although proponents argue that counterforce is necessary for limited nuclear options, a flexible assured destruction capability—that is, a countervalue force that provides U.S. leaders with a range of countervalue options—provides essentially all of the deterrence possible from strategic forces in MAD. Although the United States probably needs the ability to attack more than major Soviet cities, threatening less valuable economic and industrial targets is sufficient. Thus, counterforce is not required for limited nuclear options and would do little if anything to enhance them. These conclusions about U.S. strategy hold for a first-use policy designed to extend deterrence as well as for a purely retaliatory policy designed to deter attacks against the U.S. homeland.

By comparison, the costs of extensive counterforce are relatively large. Counterforce policies can create a variety of pressures for escalation during superpower crises and conventional war. Probably most important, an extensive American counterforce arsenal reduces crisis stability: although the United States should not preempt to limit damage, U.S. decisionmakers might fail to recognize this; if this misunderstanding of MAD prevails, counterforce generates the dangers commonly associated with larger first-strike advantages. In addition, extensive U.S. counterforce makes any Soviet misunderstanding of the effectiveness of their damage-limitation capabilities more dangerous, by creating pressure for Soviet preemption. Furthermore, counterforce policies exacerbate superpower tensions, increase the probability of accidental war, create barriers to valuable arms control agreements, and increase the economic costs of U.S. forces.

Given these costs, the United States can increase its security by forgoing additions and improvements to the full range of counterforce systems. Probably the most worrisome are highly lethal ballistic missiles—such as the MX and D-5—that can reach their targets promptly. Also dangerous are other counterforce weapons that increase the threat posed by prompt American counterforce, such as forces for strategic ASW and area-wide strategic defenses (including SDI). In addition, although less dangerous, there appears to be little reason for providing relatively slow nuclear systems, for example bombers and cruise missiles, with the ability to destroy hardened and mobile Soviet nuclear forces. Thus, although the United States should maintain effective air-breathing capabilities, the case for penetrating bombers designed to search for Soviet forces that survive the first wave of a U.S. attack—such as the B-2 bomber—appears quite weak; and the high accuracy of nuclear cruise missiles is of little value. Furthermore, the United States should not give priority to retaining its prompt threats to Soviet forces—the Minuteman III and MX missiles—and should probably reduce these forces unilaterally. Finally, as long as the United States maintains a large number of counterforce weapons it is important for American decisionmakers to recognize that these forces do not give the United States a meaningful damage-limitation capability.

The arguments presented in this chapter also suggest that U.S. security would be increased by Soviet rejection of counterforce policies. Consequently, the United States would be most secure if both superpowers decided to forgo counterforce. The most obvious route to this end is through arms control. The ABM Treaty is especially important for this reason.

In deciding whether the United States should abandon offensive counterforce unilaterally or pursue arms control instead, we need to consider which route is more likely to succeed. The key shortcoming of arms control is that if the United States needs to continue to develop and deploy counterforce systems as "bargaining chips," pursuit of arms control might undermine efforts to stop U.S. deployment of counterforce.[109] The danger then is that pursuing the best outcome could increase the probability of missing the next best outcome.

On the other hand, we should not underestimate the difficulty of achieving unilateral restraint. Traditional military thinking, current U.S. doctrine, and strong military organizational interests continue to favor counterforce. In addition, many analysts believe that the United States needs counterforce weapons comparable to the Soviet Union's. Therefore, as the strategic debate of the 1970s and 1980s demonstrates, Soviet acquisition of counterforce makes establishing and sustaining U.S. restraint more difficult. Arms control, then, in addition to providing the benefits of Soviet restraint, might increase the prospects for U.S. restraint on counterforce. For example, the ABM Treaty has probably had this effect since the United States would probably not have allowed extensive Soviet deployments to go unmatched, even when additions to U.S. retaliatory forces could have defeated the Soviet BMD. Chapter Ten compares these alternatives in detail and concludes that the United States should focus on restraining counterforce unilaterally while pursuing arms control with somewhat reduced bargaining leverage.

In closing, U.S. strategic doctrine, which relies on counterforce to perform a variety of missions, is now poorly matched to its security objectives. A strat-

---

[109] On a range of related issues see Chapter Ten.

egy built around a flexible assured destruction capability, and that essentially rejects counterforce, would sacrifice little if any deterrence of the Soviet Union while avoiding significant risks. Instead, in a world in which large counterforce attacks make no sense, the United States continues to acquire forces and reinforce traditions that increase the probability that crises will escalate to all-out war. Given the range of dangers, constraining counterforce deserves the highest priority.

CHAPTER EIGHT

Does the United States Need ICBMs?

SINCE AT LEAST the late 1960s the United States has feared that its ICBMs in fixed silos would become highly vulnerable to a massive Soviet attack.[1] Growth in the size and improvements in the accuracy of Soviet ICBMs during the 1970s meant that, in theory at least, U.S. ICBMs would be highly vulnerable in the near future. By the late 1970s, many held that 90 percent of U.S. ICBMs would soon be vulnerable to Soviet attack.[2] The notorious "window of vulnerability" was based largely on these claims.

Solving the ICBM vulnerability problem has been a priority for over a decade. After much searching, the Carter administration proposed an extensive deceptive basing mode that might have enabled a large percentage

---

[1] On the history of the ICBM vulnerability problem see Lawrence Freedman, *U.S. Intelligence and the Soviet Threat*, 2d ed. (Princeton: Princeton University Press, 1986); Lauren H. Holland and Robert A. Hoover, *The MX Decision: A New Direction in U.S. Weapons Procurement Policy?* (Boulder, Colo.: Westview, 1985); and Antonia Handler Chayes, "Managing the Politics of Mobility," *International Security* 12, no. 2 (Fall 1987): 154–62.

[2] By the late 1980s authoritative estimates still found U.S. ICBMs less than 90 percent vulnerable. See Congressional Budget Office, *Trident II Missiles: Capability, Costs, and Alternatives* (Washington, D.C.: GPO, July 1986), p. 15, which estimates 84 percent; Department of Defense, *Soviet Military Power: An Assessment of the Threat, 1988* (Washington, D.C.: GPO, 1988), p. 46, which estimates between 65 and 80 percent; and Joshua M. Epstein, *The 1988 Defense Budget* (Washington, D.C.: Brookings Institution, 1988), pp. 22–23, who estimates 74 percent vulnerability.

On calculating silo vulnerability see Lynn Ethridge Davis and Warner R. Schilling, "All You Ever Wanted to Know about MIRV and ICBM Calculations but Were Not Cleared to Ask," *Journal of Conflict Resolution* 17, no. 2 (June 1973): 207–42. On the importance of including uncertainties about key variables see John D. Steinbruner and Thomas M. Garwin, "Strategic Vulnerability: The Balance between Prudence and Paranoia," *International Security* 1, no. 1 (Summer 1976): 138–81; Matthew Bunn and Kosta Tsipis, "The Uncertainties of Preemptive Nuclear Attack," *Scientific American* (November 1983): 38–47; and Bruce W. Bennett, *How to Assess the Survivability of U.S. ICBMs*, R-2577-FF, and *Appendixes*, R-2578-FF (Santa Monica: Rand, June 1980). Steinbruner and Garwin find that relatively small variations in factors included in and left out of the standard calculations would result in both lower vulnerability and greater uncertainty about the degree of vulnerability. These effects would, however, be offset somewhat by highly accurate medium-yield MIRVs (pp. 167–68), which the Soviets have deployed since then.

On the debate over bias in ICBM accuracies see Andrew Cockburn and Alexander Cockburn, "The Myth of Missile Accuracy," *New York Review of Books* (November 20, 1980): 40–44; J. Edward Anderson, "Strategic Missiles Debated: Missile Vulnerability—What We Can't Know," *Strategic Review* (Summer 1981); and General Robert T. Marsh, "Strategic Missiles Debated: Missile Accuracy—We Do Know!" *Strategic Review* (Spring 1982): 35–37.

of MX missiles to survive.[3] The Reagan administration rejected this solution but had troubles of its own in finding a satisfactory alternative. In large part to save the MX missile, the dangers of vulnerable ICBMs were downgraded by the Scowcroft Commission, which recommended deploying MXs in vulnerable silos.[4] The commission also recommended that the ICBM vulnerability problem eventually be solved by deploying single warhead missiles, possibly in a mobile basing mode. By 1988 this solution was suffering a variety of challenges and a new solution—rail-mobile MXs—had gained favor.[5]

Although frequently taken for granted, the benefits of increased ICBM survivability deserve scrutiny. This is especially important because U.S. policy on other strategic nuclear issues is influenced by the desire to solve this vulnerability problem. Attempts to decrease ICBM vulnerability have gone beyond searching for a basing mode. Analysts have often looked to arms control to contribute to a solution. Many arms control proposals generated in the 1980s focused on this goal,[6] and the deceptive basing mode proposed by the Carter administration required SALT II limits to insure the survivability of MX. Other analysts have looked to ballistic missile defense as a possible solution. Because near-perfect area defense is now generally recognized to be infeasible, defending ICBMs has become one of the key arguments for deploying BMD. Whether the desire to increase ICBM survivability should exert this broad influence on U.S. strategic nuclear policy depends on the benefits of increasing survivability.

This chapter analyzes a number of related questions about U.S. ICBMs.

[3] For description and analysis of this basing mode see Congressional Budget Office, *The MX Missile and Multiple Protective Structure Basing* (Washington, D.C.: GPO, 1979). For analysis of a variety of options for increasing ICBM survivability, including MPS, see Office of Technology Assessment, *MX Missile Basing* (Washington, D.C.: GPO, 1981).

[4] *Report of the President's Commission on Strategic Forces* (Washington, D.C.: President's Commission on Strategic Forces, April 1983); hereafter referred to as *Scowcroft Commission Report*.

[5] Analyses of mobile basing modes include Jonathon Medalia, *Small Single-Warhead Intercontinental Ballistic Missiles: Hardware, Issues, and Policy Choices*, Report No. 83–106 F (Washington, D.C.: Congressional Research Service, May 1983); Congressional Budget Office, *Modernizing U.S. Strategic Offensive Forces: Costs, Effects and Alternatives* (Washington, D.C.: GPO, November 1987), pp. 69–73; General Accounting Office, *ICBM Modernization: Status, Survivable Basing Issues, and Need to Reestablish a National Consensus* (Washington, D.C.: GAO, 1986); Defense Science Board, *Final Report: Task Force on ICBM Modernization* (1986); Les Aspin, *Midgetman: Sliding Shut the Window of Vulnerability* (Washington, D.C.: House Armed Services Committee, February 10, 1986); House Armed Services Committee, *MX Rail Garrison and Small ICBM: A Program Review* (Washington, D.C.: HASC, 1988); and Barry E. Fridling and John R. Harvey, "On the Wrong Track? An Assessment of MX Rail Garrison Basing," *International Security* 13, no. 3 (Winter 1988/89): 113–41.

[6] See Chapter Ten for citations.

First, does the United States require highly survivable ICBMs? Proponents of survivable ICBMs have offered two basic lines of argument: (1) survivable ICBMs are a necessary hedge against technological advances that threaten the other legs of the strategic triad; and (2) ICBMs possess necessary capabilities that do not exist in other legs of the triad.

Second, should the United States keep its vulnerable ICBMs? If the United States decides against deploying new, highly survivable ICBMs, then its choice is between moving to a dyad—a force of strategic submarines and bombers but not ICBMs—and maintaining a triad that includes vulnerable ICBMs.[7] If, on the other hand, the United States deploys a survivable ICBM, it will still have to decide whether to retain its vulnerable Minuteman missiles. Vulnerable ICBMs might provide some benefits. For example, even highly vulnerable ICBMs would almost certainly provide the United States with a large number of surviving warheads; and ICBMs increase the overall survivability of U.S. strategic forces by complicating an attack against U.S. bombers. To assess whether the United States should keep its vulnerable ICBMs we must therefore consider the dangers they bring. Two lines of argument are especially prominent: (1) vulnerable ICBMs reduce crisis stability; and (2) vulnerable ICBMs provide the Soviet Union with political and/or military advantages that leave the United States open to coercion.

Third, assuming the United States decides to "solve" the ICBM vulnerability problem, what would constitute a satisfactory solution? Because it is defined by a variety of arguments, there are actually many vulnerability problems, not a single one. Many of the proposed solutions, consisting of a specific ICBM and basing mode, solve certain problems but not others.

I conclude that the benefits of increased ICBM survivability are relatively small. While survivable ICBMs are preferable to vulnerable ones, for the foreseeable future the United States can maintain more than adequate capabilities without them. Thus, the United States can now safely forgo deploying survivable ICBMs. As a hedge against future threats to the other legs of the strategic triad, the United States should develop a survivable basing mode, but then deploy it only if serious Soviet threats actually begin to materialize. Finally, the dangers posed by large numbers of vulnerable ICBMs appear to be at least as large as their benefits. Consequently, the United States should consider getting rid of its vulnerable ICBMs, or at least greatly reducing the size of this force.

---

[7] Another possibility would be moving to a dyad consisting of highly survivable ICBMs and SLBMs. This choice would depend on: the relative cost of survivable and penetrating ICBM warheads and bomber weapons; judgments about relative military advantages of bombers and ICBMs; and the overall diversity of the different dyads. Considerations relevant to this decision are discussed in following sections of this chapter. On the advantages and costs of bombers see Michael E. Brown, "The U.S. Manned Bomber and Strategic Deterrence in the 1990s," *International Security* 14, no. 2 (Fall 1989): 5–46.

WHY DEPLOY SURVIVABLE ICBMs?

Insurance against Technological Advances

This line of argument holds that the United States needs a highly survivable ICBM force to increase the robustness of its strategic nuclear forces. American retaliatory capabilities are more resistant to Soviet technological advances when the diversity of their survivable basing modes and/or penetration modes is greater. Because survivable ICBMs increase diversity, a highly survivable triad is more resistant to technological advances than a highly survivable dyad.[8]

According to this argument, the United States should base its force requirements on the expectation that the Soviet Union will continue modernizing its forces; thus, prudence requires the United States to maintain the survivability of each leg of its strategic forces. This approach guarantees that the Soviet Union must achieve numerous technological breakthroughs to render the entire American strategic force vulnerable to a Soviet attack. Furthermore, the diversity of the triad forces the Soviets to spread their research and development efforts, and force deployments, across the wide spectrum of U.S. retaliatory capabilities. Conversely, once the Soviets have rendered the ICBMs "satisfactorily" vulnerable, they could increase their efforts in antisubmarine warfare, ballistic missile defense, and air defense. Not only would more resources be available for improving these capabilities, but the Soviets would see greater strategic value in increasing them.

The general logic of this argument is correct—increasing the diversity of highly survivable forces provides insurance against unforeseeable technological breakthroughs. Because a strategic force that provides high confidence in the U.S. assured destruction capability is a basic requirement for deterring premeditated attacks and maintaining crisis stability, the United States should give priority to maintaining such a capability for the foreseeable future.

Nevertheless, before deciding that the United States needs survivable ICBMs, we must consider the probability that advances in Soviet forces will actually undermine U.S. retaliatory capabilities. The smaller this probability, the less the United States should be willing to pay—economically and politi-

---

[8] See, for example, Thomas J. Downey, "How to Avoid Monad—and Disaster," *Foreign Policy* no. 24 (Fall 1976): 186, who argues that "if we could have absolute confidence in the submarine-based system, we could scrap our ICBMs and bombers today and save a great deal of money. But you can never have confidence in anything made by man and opposed by man; the more hedges we have against an unexpected Soviet breakthrough, the more secure we are. This is why we have spent such a great deal to build a triadic deterrent"; Colin S. Gray, "The Strategic Forces Triad: End of the Road?" *Foreign Affairs* 56, no. 4 (July 1978): 783–84; Brown, *Annual Report, FY 1982*, pp. 58–59; *Scowcroft Commission Report*, pp. 7, 15; and Weinberger, *Annual Report to Congress, FY 1984*, p. 54. See also Office of Technology Assessment, *MX Missile Basing*, pp. 303–05, on how various basing modes affect the overall diversity of U.S. forces.

cally—for a highly survivable ICBM force. In addition, we need to consider how quickly the Soviets could translate these breakthroughs into effective counterforce systems. The United States might insure its future capabilities by developing systems for responding quickly, but then not deploying them until real Soviet threats materialize.

Other American nuclear forces promise to provide massive retaliatory capabilities for the foreseeable future, and therefore reduce the value of maintaining a highly survivable ICBM force. Probably most important, threats to the survivability of U.S. SLBMs remain highly theoretical. Unlike the case of ICBMs, in which the nature of the emerging threat to survivability was obvious (that is, Soviet ICBMs with multiple warheads and increased accuracy), the nature of an effective antisubmarine threat is unknown. Whereas ICBM vulnerability was anticipated for more than a decade, no serious threat to the sea-based leg of the triad is expected to emerge in the foreseeable future.[9] Furthermore, while it is not incredible that an ASW threat will develop, it is extremely unlikely that the threat would develop so quickly that the United States could not respond. Antisubmarine warfare is a multifaceted mission that requires many different components working together in an integrated manner. A breakthrough in any single area does not lead automatically to a breakthrough in overall capability. Rather, major advances would probably have to be made in many components before the Soviet antisubmarine warfare threat improved dramatically. If such a threat begins to develop, then there would probably be time for the United States to restructure its land-based forces while trying to counter the Soviet ASW capability.

In addition, current modernization programs further reduce the likelihood of a future threat to the sea-based leg of American strategic nuclear forces. The Trident submarine is quieter than its predecessor and its longer-range missiles increase its patrol area, thereby making it still harder to locate.[10] And, although not always classified as strategic weapons, the introduction of sea-launched cruise missiles (SLCMs) into the U.S. nuclear force in the 1980s increased the diversity of threat facing the Soviet Union. The pre-launch survivability of SLCMs is comparable to that of SLBMs, and defending against these sea-based components will require both air defenses and ballistic missile defenses. Furthermore, increasing the number of submarines carrying nuclear weapons makes the Soviet strategic ASW mission more difficult.

Further, although more vulnerable than American submarines, U.S. bomb-

---

[9] For more detailed assessment of the destructive potential of future U.S. retaliatory capabilities see Chapter Ten.

[10] There are, however, serious questions about whether the Trident force should have been designed to have a relatively small number of SSBNs, with each carrying a relatively large number of SLBMs. Expressing concern along these lines is The Discussion Group on Strategic Policy, Harold Brown, Cochairman, *Deterring through the Turn of the Century* (Washington, D.C.: Foreign Policy Institute and CSIS, January 1989), pp. 5–6.

ers and air-launched cruise missiles (ALCMs) will probably continue to provide a massive retaliatory capability. At peacetime alert levels, at least 25 percent of U.S. bombers are expected to survive a Soviet attack; on generated alert, a much larger fraction would survive. ALCMs help to increase (or at least maintain) the penetrability of the air-breathing leg. Cruise missiles are expected to be able to penetrate Soviet air defenses into the next century due to their small radar cross-sections, the large number that will be deployed, and their flexible and low-altitude flight paths. This leg of the triad now provides a massive retaliatory capability. It is true, however, that the retaliatory capability of the current American bomber force may decrease by the late 1990s as the United States retires its B-52s.[11]

In short, while survivable ICBMs would provide some added insurance against future threats to U.S. retaliatory capabilities, the value of this insurance appears to be relatively low. Although there is great value in maintaining high confidence in U.S. assured destruction capabilities, this does not now require survivable ICBMs. Further, because threats to American SSBNs are unlikely to become severe quickly, developing a survivable basing mode that could be deployed rapidly would provide almost as much insurance as deploying survivable ICBMs now.[12]

Unique and Necessary Capabilities

In contrast to the above argument, this one focuses on a special characteristic of ICBMs: the United States is said to need ICBMs because they possess a variety of features—secure communications, high accuracy, and the speed of ballistic missiles—that enable them to perform missions that require *reliably*

---

[11] On the size of current bomber leg retaliatory capabilities see Joshua M. Epstein, *The 1988 Defense Budget* (Washington, D.C.: Brookings Institution, 1987), p. 22, and Salman, Sullivan, and Van Evera, "Analysis or Propaganda?" p. 216; on alternative bomber force structures into the 1990s see Congressional Budget Office, *Modernizing U.S. Strategic Offensive Forces*; on future capabilities, assuming the B-52s are retired, see Michael E. Brown, "The U.S. Manned Bomber and Strategic Deterrence in the 1990s," pp. 26, 38, 40. Brown also notes that advances in Soviet SLBM forces could further reduce the bombers' pre-launch survivability (ibid., pp. 17–26).

[12] Another argument for survivable ICBMs is based on a perceptions argument. For example, Secretary of Defense Harold Brown, *Annual Report, FY 1980* (Washington, D.C.: GPO, 1979), pp. 118, stated sympathy for the following argument: "Given the past importance of our ICBM force and the traditional emphasis of the Soviets (and of many military observers throughout the world) on ICBMs, it can be argued that a decision not to modernize the ICBM force would be perceived by the Soviets, and perhaps others, as demonstrating U.S. willingness to accept inferiority, or at least as evidence that we were not competitive in a major (indeed, what the Soviets have chosen as *the* major) area of strategic power." See also Harold Brown, *Thinking about National Security* (Boulder Colo.: Westview, 1983), p. 67. However, the punitive retaliation school offers a persuasive counterargument, holding that in general these perceptions arguments are dominated by arguments about the ability of U.S. forces to perform necessary missions.

prompt counterforce attacks in either a controlled and limited strike or in a massive response.[13] The other legs of the triad cannot provide this capability. Thus, the United States requires survivable ICBMs.

Promptness results from the short flight time of ballistic missiles. ICBMs take only half an hour to reach targets in the Soviet Union; the air-breathing leg of the triad (that is, heavy bombers and cruise missiles) takes approximately eight hours. Reliability results from secure communications that provide the ability to give commands at the desired moment and of the necessary complexity. The air-breathing components of the strategic force may be reliable and flexible, but because of their long flight times are not prompt. Although the Trident II missile will provide the missile submarines with silo-killing capability, doubts will remain about their ability to launch attacks quickly after a U.S. decision to do so.[14] Further, SLBMs are generally considered ill-suited for limited attacks.[15] Thus, only ICBMs can provide reliably prompt counterforce capabilities.

Reliable promptness therefore makes possible attacks on targets that are considered time-urgent. Time-urgency distinguishes between targets that must be destroyed in the first half-hour and in the first eight hours after the initial Soviet attack.[16] The targets that are often considered time-urgent include Soviet ICBMs in reserve and reloads,[17] political and military leadership and other C[3] capabilities, submarine bases, airfields, and certain conventional forces.

In fact, there are questions about whether ICBMs could be launched reliably following a full Soviet attack against U.S. forces and command and control. The secure lines of communication would be destroyed. Airborne command

[13] See, for example, Brown, *Annual Report, FY 1980*, p. 118. See also Weinberger, *Annual Report to Congress, FY 1984*, p. 220, who argues that "a more survivable and powerful ICBM is essential to redress the significant asymmetry in prompt counterforce capability"; *Scowcroft Commission Report*, pp. 8, 12; and Leon Sloss, Senate Committee on Armed Services, *Department of Defense Authorization for Appropriations for Fiscal Year 1986*, pt. 7, 99th Cong., 1st sess., p. 3763.

[14] For example, Brown, *Annual Report, FY 1980*, p. 118, expresses "considerable doubt that SLBM command, communications and control (C[3]), responsiveness and accuracy can ever be made as reliable as a CONUS-based ICBM force." See also Ashton B. Carter, "Assessing Command System Vulnerability," in Ashton B. Carter, John D. Steinbruner, and Charles A. Zraket, *Managing Nuclear Operations* (Washington, D.C.: Brookings Institution, 1987), p. 577. Closely related see also Sidney D. Drell and Thomas H. Johnson, "Managing Strategic Weapons," *Foreign Affairs* 66, no. 5 (Summer 1988): 1028. On the responsiveness of the submarine force see Office of Technology Assessment, *MX Missile Basing*, pp. 209–10.

[15] For important qualifications see Carter, "Assessing Command System Vulnerability," pp. 577–78.

[16] The time delay would actually be somewhat longer since the United States would require some time to decide to retaliate and because its forces take some time to launch.

[17] For analysis of which Soviet ICBMs need to be attacked promptly see Scott D. Sagan, *Moving Targets: Nuclear Strategy and National Security* (Princeton: Princeton University Press, 1989), pp. 90–91.

posts would be used to communicate with both the ICBMs and the SLBMs.[18] In addition, SLBMs might have some advantages in counterforce retaliation since forces at sea would be undamaged and would therefore not require retargeting. Thus, in responding to a full-scale attack, ICBMs have clear advantages in reliably prompt retaliation only if they are launched on warning of a Soviet attack, that is, before Soviet weapons reach their targets, in which case their survivability is not an issue.

However, assuming that ICBMs are the only strategic system that can perform reliably prompt counterforce missions, we must identify situations that would require this capability. How would the ability to perform these missions enhance the U.S. ability to deter Soviet attacks or to achieve improved war outcomes?

The answer clearly depends upon basic beliefs about the requirements of deterrence. The punitive retaliation school concludes that, in general, counterforce is of little value. Chapter Seven looked at the full range of arguments for counterforce in detail and found them wanting. Since reliably prompt counterforce is a subset, it is clearly unnecessary according to these more general arguments. As we have seen, however, other analysts see a greater U.S. need for counterforce. Members of the military denial school believe that American counterforce retaliatory options enhance deterrence and increase the prospects for controlling escalation once the Soviets have launched a nuclear attack.

If we assume for the sake of analysis that these general arguments for counterforce should guide U.S. force planning, we still need to evaluate whether they generate a requirement for survivable ICBMs. If not, the case for survivable ICBMs is extremely weak, given that these are highly favorable starting assumptions.

Flexibility—the ability to choose between a variety of limited nuclear attacks—is likely to be most important in low- and medium-level nuclear conflicts (those in which the Soviets have not launched a massive attack against U.S. forces and C³). However, the United States does not need highly survivable ICBMs to insure that it has a wide range of reliably prompt counterforce options in these scenarios since a large number of its ICBMs would remain unattacked.

Thus, the question becomes: How would a reliably prompt second-strike counterforce option help the United States deter a *full-scale* Soviet attack against its ICBMs and possibly other targets, or achieve an improved outcome following such an attack? Answers depend on two considerations: first, the existence of time-urgent targets following such an attack; and second, the importance of being able to destroy them if they exist.

---

[18] On post-attack communications see Bruce G. Blair, *Strategic Command and Control* (Washington, D.C.: Brookings Institution, 1985), especially pp. 182–211.

PROMPTNESS FOR ATTACKING SOVIET ICBMS

The ability to retaliate against Soviet ICBMs in a time-urgent manner receives the most attention. This focus could be anticipated, for the most obvious effect of the Soviet attack would be to create an asymmetry in ICBM capabilities. Among the rationales for possessing a time-urgent response capability against Soviet ICBMs are limiting damage to the United States, redressing the balance of surviving forces in a counterforce exchange, and defeating the Soviet damage-limitation campaign.

Prompt American retaliation could not significantly enhance U.S. prospects for limiting damage to its homeland since the Soviet Union could launch its ICBMs on warning of U.S. attack. Whether the United States attacks with ICBMs or with bombers and cruise missiles, the Soviet Union could launch its reserve ICBMs on warning. Launch on warning is usually considered in the context of responding to a first strike. In this case it is technically demanding because extremely high confidence in early warning information is required—a false alarm would be disastrous—and because there would be so little time for making the critical decision.[19] In contrast, for the initiator of an exchange faced with launching the third strike, launch on warning poses a far less demanding problem. After attacking the United States, the Soviets would have good reason to believe information suggesting that a retaliatory missile attack had been launched and, because this reaction would be anticipated, there would be more than enough time to launch the reserve missiles before the American warheads arrived.[20] Whether the Soviets would launch on warning against American countervalue targets is another question; but the answer is unlikely to depend on whether American second-strike counterforce is prompt or slow.

In an alternative scenario—one frequently used to argue that the United States needs a prompt counterforce capability—the Soviets launch a first strike in the hope of achieving a coercive advantage by improving the ratio of surviving forces. Prompt second-strike counterforce capabilities are said to enhance deterrence of this attack by providing the ability to redress the balance of surviving forces. However, slow American counterforce could redress the balance if the Soviets do not launch their remaining forces before American retaliatory weapons arrive. And, as noted above, promptness could not pre-

[19] For a range of views on launch-on-warning and launch-under-attack see Richard L. Garwin, "Launch under Attack to Redress Minuteman Vulnerability," *International Security* 4, no. 3 (Winter 1979/80): 117–39; Office of Technology Assessment, *MX Missile Basing*, pp. 146–64; John Steinbruner, "Launch under Attack," *Scientific American* (January 1984): 37–47; and Blair, *Strategic Command and Control*, pp. 234–38.

[20] In addition, promptness is not required to destroy reloads because U.S. bombers could reach the Soviet Union before the Soviets could reload their silos. For sources on this point see William J. Durch, *The ABM Treaty and Western Security* (Cambridge, Mass.: Ballinger, 1988), pp. 134–35, note 35.

vent the Soviets from launching on warning. Thus, the proponents' argument hinges on the belief that the U.S. president should have the option to redress the imbalance of surviving forces as quickly as possible.[21]

Even assuming that an imbalance in the ratio of nuclear forces could provide coercive advantages, it is quite difficult to see how the time difference between prompt and slow retaliation could make a significant difference. Because proponents never spell out how coercion occurs, we have few details against which to assess Soviet options. Nevertheless, it seems extremely unlikely that the outcome of such a bargaining situation could hinge on such a small difference in bargaining time. Thus, promptness is of essentially no value in reducing whatever danger these scenarios pose.

A third rationale for possessing the ability to retaliate promptly against Soviet ICBMs involves enhancing deterrence by maintaining the ability to defeat the damage-limitation campaign that Soviet leaders might launch during a severe crisis. As discussed in Chapter Seven, some analysts argue that the United States requires counterforce to defeat a multiwave Soviet damage-limitation campaign. The most important targets in follow-on attacks would be U.S. ICBMs and command and control. I responded that the United States could better reduce whatever danger the possibility of these Soviet attacks creates by deploying highly survivable forces and getting rid of highly vulnerable ones. However, assuming the United States decides to pursue the second-strike counterforce solution, we still need to examine whether the U.S. ability to defeat the Soviet damage-limitation campaign depends on prompt retaliation.

For promptness to be important there would have to be follow-on attacks that the Soviet Union could not launch within the first half hour to an hour after launching its initial attack but could launch within about eight hours.[22] Further, preventing such attacks would have to result in a significantly different outcome.

---

[21] The standard coercive scenario assumes a single counterforce exchange. It is possible to generate additional arguments for prompt American retaliation by imagining scenarios in which the Soviets plan to gain advantages in the ratio of surviving forces by engaging in two or more counterforce exchanges. In these scenarios prompt American retaliation could matter if it was necessary to prevent the Soviets from preparing their follow-on counterforce waves. Issues relevant to these scenarios are considered in the following discussion on disrupting Soviet damage-limitation attacks.

[22] I raise the possibility of an hour instead of half an hour because, assuming that the United States does not retaliate until Soviet ICBMs reach its territory, the Soviet Union has the half hour its ICBMs take to reach the United States plus the half hour it takes U.S. ICBMs to reach the Soviet Union. The United States might be able to reduce this interval somewhat by launching on warning. In addition, even if the United States does not launch on warning, the period from the launch of the Soviet first wave to the impact of U.S. retaliation on Soviet targets could be somewhat less than an hour if the Soviets had simultaneously launched SLBMs from near the U.S. coasts. However, the following arguments about timing do not change significantly, even if the United States launches on warning of Soviet attack.

If the Soviets plan to launch a second wave against all U.S. ICBMs, there is no obvious reason why more than half an hour would be required between Soviet attacks. Avoiding fratricide would not require waiting more than half an hour.[23]

The basic alternative to attacking all U.S. ICBMs again is for the Soviet Union to launch the second wave against only those U.S. ICBMs that survived the first wave. This requires that the Soviets wait until their weapons have reached the United States in order to assess the results of the first wave and retarget for the second wave. The time required for this process might leave remaining Soviet ICBMs vulnerable to prompt U.S. retaliation, but not slower retaliation. Whether this is the case would depend on how long it takes the Soviets to retarget and how quickly the United States launches a retaliatory attack.[24] The United States could reduce the time available to the Soviets by launching on warning instead of riding out a Soviet attack (this would not require survivable ICBMs, however!). Launching on warning would provide the additional advantage of avoiding damage to U.S. forces and command and control, which could be far more important for disrupting the Soviet damage-limitation campaign than for inflicting retaliatory damage.

However, these operational details are not now crucial since the Soviet Union currently lacks the post-attack assessment capabilities required to determine which American targets were destroyed by its counterforce attack.[25] Consequently, this type of attack does not justify prompt American retaliatory capabilities now, but might if the Soviets acquire this assessment capability in the future.

Another possible role for prompt retaliation is against Soviet ICBMs that failed to launch. Lacking attack assessment capabilities, the Soviets might plan to launch the second wave against U.S. ICBMs that were targeted by Soviet ICBMs that failed to launch in the first wave.[26] If assessing launch failures and creating a new attack option takes the Soviet Union over half an hour, then there might be some additional time-urgent targets. It is hard to imagine, however, that Soviet judgments about the benefits of initiating their damage-limitation campaign could hinge on the U.S. ability to destroy this correction to the first massive wave.

Finally, prompt retaliation could do little to protect critical American command and control capabilities, and therefore cannot help defeat a Soviet dam-

---

[23] Bennett, *How to Assess the Survivability of U.S. ICBMs: Appendixes*, pp. 39–41, estimates that the "second window" following the detonations would begin after about 20–30 minutes.

[24] There could also be constraints on the U.S. ability to retaliate promptly. If the United States plans to target only missiles that might be used in follow-on waves and not empty Soviet silos, then U.S. retaliation would be delayed by whatever time is required for attack assessment and retargeting.

[25] Paul Bracken, *The Command and Control of Nuclear Forces*, p. 108.

[26] This possibility is noted in Sagan, *Moving Targets*, p. 80.

age-limitation campaign that relies on decapitating the United States. Critical American command and control targets are sufficiently small in number that the Soviets could afford to attack all of them again in a second wave. Thus, the Soviets would not have to delay their second wave until attack assessment and retargeting were completed. Consequently, the need for prompt retaliation hinges on the importance of preventing the third wave and possibly additional follow-on attacks that could be launched before slower counterforce systems could arrive. However, even the Soviet second wave is unlikely to have significant influence on the success of a Soviet decapitation attack. The critical targets after the initial Soviet attack would be mobile American command posts, especially airborne command posts. Assuming these targets survive the first wave, they would not be vulnerable to Soviet follow-on attacks that could be launched before slower American counterforce systems reach the Soviet Union.

PROMPTNESS FOR ATTACKING OTHER TARGETS

In addition to ICBMs, other time-urgent targets might include the Soviet Union's political and military leadership, other strategic nuclear forces, and conventional forces.

Current U.S. nuclear doctrine calls for targeting the Soviet political and military leadership to threaten what the Soviets value most, thereby enhancing deterrence. Chapters Two and Seven identify a variety of serious weaknesses in this position, which is held by the military denial and damage-limitation schools. However, even taken on its own terms, this position does not suggest that the United States needs to be able to destroy Soviet leadership targets quickly. Proponents argue that targeting the Soviet leadership would enhance deterrence because the United States could threaten higher costs, not because it could deny Soviet military capabilities. The effectiveness of the U.S. deterrent would not depend on inflicting these costs promptly.

Since slow counterforce is as lethal as prompt counterforce, the time difference could influence the U.S. ability to destroy the Soviet leadership, and inflict these costs, only if the United States expected to know where the leadership would be in half an hour but not in eight hours. How could this occur? The Soviet leadership is likely to move to hardened command posts. Thus, promptness will not matter if the United States knows the location of the command posts. If the United States does not know their location, then promptness could matter if it enabled the United States to hit Soviet leaders before they got to their hidden command posts. This seems most unlikely. In almost all scenarios the leaders would have time to disperse to these command posts well before launching a massive attack. The possible exceptions are extremely unlikely surprise attacks in which early dispersal might provide the United States with warning. Thus, promptness would almost never determine the U.S. ability to destroy Soviet leaders in a retaliatory attack.

The other basic argument for attacking Soviet command and control would be to limit damage. Again, however, promptness would probably make little difference in a retaliatory attack. The argument here resembles the argument about why prompt retaliation cannot stop the Soviets from launching their ICBMs on warning—Soviet leaders would probably be able to give key orders before a prompt attack arrived. To make the case for promptness requires inventing exotic scenarios. Suppose, for example, that the Soviets avoided giving the United States strategic warning of their initial attack by not increasing the number of missile submarines on patrol. In that case, it is likely that they would rush to get their SSBNs out of port as soon as they launched their ICBMs, but the orders to do so could be issued well before the United States could detect the initial Soviet attack, perhaps days earlier. Thus, the submarines themselves might be time-urgent targets, but the communications links to them still would not. Command, control, and communications for tactical nuclear and conventional operations raises more complicated issues, many of which depend on the specifics of the scenario—for example, the stage of a war in Europe. Nevertheless, it seems likely both that important commands could be communicated before the United States could destroy the Soviet C^3 and that a small number of hours would make little difference anyway.

Submarine bases and airfields could be time-urgent second-strike targets in the unlikely event of a Soviet "bolt from the blue." Since the Soviets maintain their missile submarines and strategic bombers at a relatively low level of alert, prompt retaliation might catch a large fraction of these forces at their bases. However, even in this scenario it is doubtful that destroying Soviet submarine bases and airfields quickly would have a significant effect on the outcome of the war, since the Soviets could launch their withheld ICBMs on warning and a substantial fraction of their SSBNs at sea would probably survive. If, as is far more likely, the Soviets were to attack during a crisis, they could have increased the percentage of submarines on patrol and bombers on alert, in which case the promptness of the U.S. response would make an even smaller difference.

Besides the strategic nuclear targets considered above, there are conventional forces that are often considered time-urgent. It is argued that if the Soviets were to invade Western Europe, the United States might want to attack troop concentrations, transportation routes, and other military targets in the Soviet Union and Eastern Europe in an effort to interrupt the Soviet battle plan. Consequently, in an attempt to reduce the U.S. ability to interfere, the Soviets might attack U.S. ICBMs before the invasion. These targets, however, are not time-urgent—could the outcome of a war in Europe really depend on whether conventional military targets were attacked with strategic nuclear weapons in half an hour or in eight hours? Furthermore, even if these conventional targets were time-urgent, it is hard to imagine Soviet leaders launching a large strategic nuclear war to secure the objectives of their conventional attack.

In sum, even starting with assumptions that favor counterforce, it appears that there would now be few, if any, time-urgent targets following a massive attack against U.S. ICBMs. Scenarios that require prompt second strikes tend to be incredible and extremely unlikely, and even in these cases promptness appears to make little difference. Thus, the special characteristic of survivable ICBMs—reliably prompt second-strike counterforce—would do very little to enhance U.S. deterrent capabilities.

WHY RETAIN VULNERABLE ICBMS?

If the United States decides against increasing the survivability of its ICBMs, the question of retaining the vulnerable ones will remain. How do the benefits of a large and highly vulnerable force compare to its risks? This section first examines two arguments that identify risks of maintaining vulnerable ICBMs.[27] Although these arguments are commonly used to support increasing ICBM survivability, upon examination they turn out to be arguments only against maintaining highly vulnerable ones. The section ends with an examination of arguments for retaining vulnerable ICBMs.

Vulnerable ICBMs Reduce Crisis Stability

A common argument for increasing ICBM survivability is that vulnerable ICBMs reduce crisis stability. Analysts are often imprecise about how vulnerable ICBMs would create preemptive incentives, but two types of arguments appear to underlie this concern. First, large numbers of vulnerable U.S. weapons are seen as encouraging or tempting a Soviet leader to attack during a crisis. For example, Congressman Les Aspin argues that the high vulnerability of U.S. ICBMs is "quite unhealthy," in part because "in a crisis the vulnerability of our ICBMs would even invite the Soviet attack—make them more likely to launch a first strike. Thus it creates a situation of instability."[28]

A second argument focuses on the exchange ratio in a first strike, holding that a country that can destroy more warheads or missiles than it employs in the first strike will see first-strike advantages and therefore will be more likely

---

[27] Another possible cost of keeping vulnerable ICBMs is that they somehow convey the sense that the entire U.S. strategic nuclear force is inadequate. For example, Thomas C. Schelling, "Abolition of Ballistic Missiles," *International Security* 12, no. 1 (Summer 1987): 179–80, notes that "the entire deterrent force seemed for a while to suffer a kind of 'vulnerability by association.' " Consequently, getting rid of vulnerable ICBMs could provide benefits because it would "clean the atmosphere psychologically to have no strategic forces around that attracted so much preemptive attention."

[28] Aspin, *Midgetman: Sliding Shut the Window of Vulnerability*, pp. 1–2.

to attack preemptively in a crisis. Based on this logic, Paul Nitze, writing for the Committee on The Present Danger, argued that:

> The third casualty [in the SALT II negotiations], and the most worrisome, is "crisis stability." Over the past fifteen years it would not have profited either side to attack first. It would have required the use of more ICBMs by the attacking side than the attack could destroy. By the early 1980s that situation will have changed. By that time, the Soviet Union will be in position to destroy 90% of our ICBMs with an expenditure of a fifth to a third of its ICBMs.[29]

This same basic logic underlies many calls for shifting from MIRVed missiles to single warhead missiles. If the United States did not have MIRVed ICBMs, then the Soviet Union would have to spend at least one warhead to destroy each U.S. warhead.[30] In practice, since Soviet missiles are not perfectly accurate and reliable, attacking the U.S. ICBMs would require far more warheads than would be destroyed. Much of the interest in deploying a single warhead missile to solve the ICBM vulnerability problem is based partly on this kind of argument.

Both lines of argument suffer serious problems. As maintained by the punitive retaliation school, as long as the United States retains an unquestionable assured destruction capability, the Soviet Union should lack significant first-strike incentives. Essentially independent of how many U.S. ICBMs can be destroyed, Soviet leaders would be unable to significantly reduce the costs they expect in an all-out war and would therefore lack first-strike incentives.[31] Similarly, a favorable weapons exchange ratio should not create first-strike incentives. At its core, this argument is based upon the importance of the ratio of surviving forces. Force ratios, however, do not translate into the ability to inflict damage. Rather, the correct measure of the outcome of the Soviet attack

[29] Paul H. Nitze, *Is Salt II a Fair Deal for the United States?* (16 May 1970), reprinted in Charles Tyroler II, ed., *Alerting America: The Papers of the Committee on The Present Danger* (New York: Pergamon-Brassey, 1984), p. 160. Although it illustrates the argument's basic logic, this particular quote exaggerates the supposed problem by casting it in terms of the percentages and fractions of the country's ICBMs. Even according to the argument's own logic, we should care about the exchange ratio of ICBMs, not about the fraction of Soviet ICBMs employed or the percentage of U.S. ICBMs destroyed. Since the Soviet ICBM force is larger than America's, a smaller fraction of the Soviet force could carry as many warheads as a much higher percentage of the U.S. force. We should note that this logic differs from that in other prominent arguments by Nitze that are discussed in the next section. It is not, however, inconsistent with these arguments.

[30] For views on the benefits of deMIRVing see Downey, "How to Avoid Monad—and Disaster," p. 191; Jan M. Lodal, "Finishing START," *Foreign Policy* no. 48 (Fall 1982): 77; *Scowcroft Commission Report*, p. 14; and Drell and Johnson, "Managing Strategic Weapons," pp. 1031–32.

[31] Further, crisis instability would not result unless the Soviet Union believes the United States has first-strike incentives. Most arguments which hold that U.S. ICBM vulnerability adds to crisis instability fail to describe the nature of U.S. first-strike incentives and/or Soviet perceptions of such incentives.

is the absolute size of the surviving U.S. force. The ability to favorably shift the ratio of forces should not create first-strike incentives as long as the Soviet Union continues to lack a damage-limitation capability.

Nevertheless, these weaknesses do not completely undermine concerns about vulnerable ICBMs. The more complete argument about crisis stability is that although vulnerable forces should not create first-strike incentives, there is some chance that they might anyway. During a severe crisis, Soviet leaders might mistakenly conclude that attacking vulnerable U.S. forces could provide a better outcome than if the United States attacks first. Such a judgment could occur in a variety of ways. For example, there is the possibility that the Soviet military does not fully appreciate the reality of MAD and the ineffectiveness of its counterforce arsenal.[32] Related to this is the possibility that Soviet leaders could fall victim to conventionalized views of nuclear war in which being attacked by fewer weapons is assumed to be preferable to being attacked by more weapons.[33] To the extent that these misunderstandings of MAD prevail, large vulnerable U.S. forces could increase the probability of Soviet preemptive attack.[34] This said, we can reasonably expect that the extent of this danger is greatly reduced by the size of the U.S. retaliatory forces and Soviet recognition of the damage they could inflict.

Even accepting this possible danger, however, these arguments do not necessarily support a U.S. requirement for survivable ICBMs. To the contrary, if this danger is worth hedging against, these arguments tend to support the conclusion that the United States should not maintain large numbers of highly vulnerable ICBMs.[35]

Vulnerable ICBMs Leave the United States Open to Coercion

This argument also comes in two forms. The first holds that vulnerable U.S. ICBMs contribute to the Soviet ability to gain a strategic advantage by launching a counterforce attack or initiating a counterforce exchange that improves

---

[32] In part, this concern is supported by Soviet doctrine, which reflects a continuing interest in "doing as well as possible" should war appear inevitable. See David Holloway, *The Soviet Union and the Arms Race* (New Haven: Yale University Press, 1983), pp. 48–58.

[33] These dangers exist on the U.S. side as well, as discussed in more detail in Chapter Seven.

[34] This argument does not find the vulnerability of ICBMs to be special; rather, all vulnerabilities in U.S. retaliatory capabilities, including C^3, become a potential source of danger. Whether from this perspective ICBMs are especially worrisome depends on the scenario. For example, under day-to-day conditions submarines in port and bombers not on alert would account for a large fraction of vulnerable U.S. weapons; further, command and control would be at its most vulnerable. The relative vulnerability of ICBMs, assuming that they would not be launched on warning, would grow as the overall level of alert increased.

[35] The argument that an unfavorable weapons exchange ratio is dangerous supports only an even narrower conclusion—that the United States should not have highly vulnerable MIRVed ICBMs.

the ratio of surviving forces.[36] In his influential articles, Nitze measured these post-exchange ratios in terms of the throw-weight available to each country.[37] According to this argument, the Soviet goal in initiating the counterforce exchange would be to produce an asymmetry so great that the Soviets would gain a coercive position. The Committee on The Present Danger argued:

> Suppose that the Soviet Union possessed so numerous a force of powerful and accurate nuclear weapons that it could attack our intercontinental ballistic missiles (ICBMs) and other military installations and still have greater numbers of more powerful weapons left than we had, would it then be wise for any American President to plan to launch a retaliatory attack on Russian cities and industries, knowing they could respond in kind and much more powerfully? Or would it be wiser for him to seek a political settlement, even if it were unfavorable to our interests, before the threat of a first strike could escalate to such a holocaust.[38]

The second form of the argument that ICBM vulnerability enables the Soviet Union to coerce the United States focuses on the lack of U.S. options for counterforce retaliation, not on relative force size. In what is commonly referred to as the "Nitze scenario," a Soviet attack against U.S. ICBMs leaves the United States with two unacceptable options—surrender or suicidal counter-city retaliation—and without a second-strike counterforce option. Recognizing that it could be placed in such a compromised position, the United States could be coerced by the threat of such a Soviet attack.[39] This

[36] By focusing on measures of forces after the initial attack or exchange, this formulation assumes that the superpowers do not engage in a counterforce war of attrition.

[37] See Paul Nitze, "Deterring Our Deterrent," *Foreign Policy*, no. 25 (Winter 1976–77): 198–204, and idem, "Assuring Strategic Stability in the Era of Detente," *Foreign Affairs* 54, no. 2 (January 1976): 223–26. Nitze also measures outcomes in terms of the difference in surviving throw-weight. He maintains that throw-weight, though only a gross indicator of capability, is the appropriate measure of residual forces since after the counterforce exchange the superpowers would shift to countervalue targets. Because they are soft—unlike hardened ICBM silos—accuracy is far less important for destroying them. Actually, the correct measure of countervalue capability is equivalent megatonage. EMT, however, is roughly proportional to throw-weight; therefore, the absolute amount of throw-weight is a good proxy. On this point, see Office of Technology Assessment, *MX Missile Basing* (Washington, D.C.: GPO, 1981), p. 259.

[38] Committee on The Present Danger, "Is America Becoming Number 2?" reprinted in Tyroler, ed., *Alerting America*, p. 41. The remainder of the paragraph is also relevant: "A clearly superior Soviet *third*-strike capability, under the assumption of clear Soviet strategic nuclear superiority, would undermine the credibility of our second-strike capacity, and could lead us, either to accommodation without fighting or to the acceptance of unmanageable risks."

[39] Nitze does not spell out this argument in detail. However, his description of U.S. options after a Soviet counterforce attack suggests that the United States would be left primarily with countervalue options and that the lack of other options is the key problem. See, for example, his "Deterring Our Deterrent," pp. 204–6. Similar suggestions are included in many of the arguments finding great danger in vulnerable ICBMs. In 1978 the Congressional Budget Office, *Counterforce Issues for the U.S. Strategic Nuclear Forces* (Washington, D.C.: GPO, 1978), pp. 1–4, identified this argument as central to the debate over U.S. counterforce requirements.

argument is often combined with the argument about relative force size. For example, the above quote from the Committee on The Present Danger posits both that the Soviet Union acquires advantages in post-attack force size and that the United States' only remaining retaliatory option is to attack Soviet value targets.

These arguments are more far-reaching than the ones discussed in the previous section: whereas arguments about crisis stability apply only to situations in which a Soviet leader concludes that all-out war is quite likely, these arguments hold that vulnerable American ICBMs influence Soviet and U.S. behavior during peacetime, during crises in which nuclear war is not imminent, and during severe crises in which Soviet leaders do not fear that the United States is going to preempt. By making U.S. ICBMs highly vulnerable, the Soviet Union has acquired the ability to coerce or blackmail the United States. Recognizing its inferior position, the United States might stop defending its foreign policy and security interests.

We first need to recognize that these arguments identify dangers of vulnerable ICBMs, not a requirement for survivable ones. If the criterion for force planning is that a counterforce exchange cannot improve the relative size of Soviet forces, then simply getting rid of its vulnerable MIRVed ICBMs would help the United States meet this requirement. If the remaining survivable force was judged too small, the United States could deploy more survivable weapons on submarines and possibly bombers. Further, getting rid of vulnerable ICBMs would eliminate targets for Soviet counterforce, thereby reducing asymmetries in the U.S. ability to retaliate in kind with a prompt attack against Soviet ICBMs.[40]

These arguments do not, however, establish a very strong case for getting rid of vulnerable ICBMs. In fact, vulnerable ICBMs would not provide the Soviets with significant opportunities for coercing the United States; by comparison, the dangers of crisis instability identified above are larger. In the first place, these arguments about Soviet coercion are built on flawed assumptions. As with the above crisis stability argument, arguments based on ratios fail because measures of relative force size do not reflect the ability of the United States to perform its missions and therefore tell us little about the U.S. ability to deter Soviet attacks and avoid Soviet coercion. As argued by the punitive retaliation school, as long as the United States maintains its assured destruc-

---

[40] Moreover, even if one accepts that the United States needs survivable counterforce for retaliation in kind, this still does not establish a clear case for survivable ICBMs. In the first place, there are some soft strategic targets that could be destroyed by less accurate weapons. In addition, even at the time this scenario rose to prominence the surviving U.S. bombers and ICBMs could have destroyed hardened targets. For a variety of criticisms of the Nitze scenario see note 52 in Chapter Two. This point is even more telling today—U.S. bombers carry highly accurate cruise missiles and the Trident II missile, which will have a high probability of kill against hardened Soviet silos, will be deployed during the 1990s. On U.S. forces see Congressional Budget Office, *Modernizing U.S. Strategic Offensive Forces.*

tion capability the Soviets would be unable to inflict significantly greater costs than the United States and therefore could not gain a coercive advantage by destroying U.S. ICBMs. In MAD, whatever coercive advantages might exist will reflect the superpowers' understanding of each other's resolve and willingness to run risks.

Also based on faulty assumptions, arguments focusing on the lack of U.S. counterforce options fail because the United States does not need large counterforce retaliatory options to deter Soviet counterforce attacks or to respond to them. As argued in Chapter Seven, in MAD, American limited nuclear options are useful essentially for influencing Soviet assessments of future costs, not for reducing Soviet military capabilities. In this role, counterforce options have no special claim over other limited options, including both inefficient attacks against forces and selective attacks against cities and industry. The possible exception is retaliation in kind, which might enable clearer communication of U.S. restraint. This advantage, however, is overwhelmed by the problems created by the size of the U.S. attack and the variety of ways in which Soviet leaders could misinterpret it.

Furthermore, even if a Soviet attack against U.S. ICBMs would provide some of these purported benefits, the risk of such an attack leading to all-out war would greatly exceed these benefits. Arguments that examine post-exchange ratios and counterforce retaliation assume that the United States responds to the Soviet attack by striking at Soviet forces rather than Soviet cities. In support of this assumption, analysts argue that attacking cities would be irrational, inviting a Soviet response in kind. However, as stressed by the punitive retaliation school, Soviet leaders could not confidently assume the United States would respond with a "purely" counterforce attack[41]; they are far more likely to focus on the enormous costs of an all-out war, even a small chance of which would be sufficient to deter them. Especially in the absence of a severe crisis, a variety of factors would probably raise enormous doubts about U.S. restraint. For example, millions and probably tens of millions of Americans would die as the result of a Soviet attack on U.S. ICBMs, bombers, and ballistic missile submarines in port.[42] The level of destruction would probably be difficult to assess in the period immediately following such an attack, and might be exaggerated. And the American president would have to decide on a response under conditions of poor information, unprecedented destruction, and possibly damaged command, control, and communications.

In short, because the benefits of such an attack would be small (or nonex-

[41] Of course, even such a response would inflict high levels of collateral damage. See Barbara G. Levi, Frank N. von Hippel, and William H. Daugherty, "Civilian Casualties from 'Limited' Nuclear Attacks on the Soviet Union," *International Security* 12, no. 3 (Winter 1987/88): 168–89.

[42] On the costs of various Soviet counterforce attacks see William Daugherty, Barbara Levi, and Frank von Hippel, "Consequences of 'Limited' Nuclear Attacks on the United States," *International Security* 10, no. 4 (Spring 1986): 3–45.

istent), current U.S. forces should be a powerful deterrent to such a Soviet attack. Thus, while Soviet counterforce attacks designed to shift the ratio of surviving forces or to reduce U.S. counterforce options are possible, their likelihood is extremely low and the conclusions that follow from considering them should be weighted accordingly.

Benefits of Vulnerable ICBMs

Against these risks of maintaining vulnerable ICBMs, we need to compare their benefits. Commonly noted is that the U.S. ICBM force makes a Soviet first strike difficult, and perhaps impossible, to orchestrate. A Soviet attack designed to simultaneously destroy U.S. ICBMs and bombers would provide tactical warning that increases the ability of U.S. alert bombers to survive Soviet SLBM attacks.[43] Although often used to suggest that the United States needs survivable ICBMs, this argument really requires only vulnerable ones.

Second, a large but highly vulnerable ICBM force still provides a large retaliatory capability. An attack effective against 90 percent of the current U.S. ICBMs would leave about 100 ICBMs and 250 nuclear warheads surviving—a retaliatory force unlikely to be viewed as negligible by a Soviet decisionmaker. Although Soviet forces were not this effective in the late 1980s, they are expected to be in the future. Moreover, even if 90 percent destruction was the expected outcome of an attack on U.S. silos, many outcomes less damaging to American forces would be possible. All but the most risk-accepting or poorly informed Soviet decisionmaker would pay attention to these less favorable outcomes. Further, Soviet decisionmakers could not ignore the possibility that the United States would launch its ICBMs on warning of Soviet attack.

Although important to consider, the magnitude of these benefits is not now large. Whether or not the United States retains its vulnerable ICBM force, very large numbers of SLBM warheads would survive as would a large fraction of alert U.S. bombers, even without the increased tactical warning that could be provided by a simultaneous attack against ICBMs.

Additional benefits are more contentious. In the wake of anything less than a massive Soviet attack against the United States, U.S. ICBMs would remain available for reliably prompt counterforce missions that the other legs of the triad would be unable to perform. These additional options, however, provide

---

[43] See, for example, *Scowcroft Commission Report*, pp. 7–8, and Downey, "How to Avoid Monad—and Disaster," pp. 184–86, who raises the possibility that this synergism would be eliminated by Soviet development of counterforce SLBMs, which would make possible short warning time, simultaneous attacks against bombers and silos. Also noting this danger is Harold A. Feiveson and John Duffield, "Stopping the Sea-Based Counterforce Threat," *International Security* 9, no. 1 (Summer 1984): 193.

scant benefits: as the preceding arguments suggest, promptness is not very important in the bargaining uses of limited nuclear options.[44]

In sum, both the benefits and costs of maintaining the current vulnerable ICBM force appear to be relatively small. There is a sound but not overwhelming case for getting rid of these ICBMs.[45] The primary risk is that under severe crisis pressures Soviet leaders might evaluate their first-strike incentives incorrectly, focusing on the ability to destroy a large fraction of the U.S. force (or large numbers of its weapons) instead of the massive U.S. ability to retaliate following such an attack. U.S. retaliatory capabilities should deter such a Soviet attack. Nevertheless, these misunderstandings are not entirely implausible, especially when compared to the competing scenarios leading to a large nuclear war. This danger may be worth hedging against, but simply getting rid of vulnerable ICBMs should be essentially as effective as replacing them with more survivable ones. Further, it is clear that increasing the size of the vulnerable ICBM force—for example, by placing MX missiles in vulnerable silos—makes no sense. Doing so tends to increase the risks of maintaining the silo-based ICBMs while not increasing the benefits they provide.

WHAT CONSTITUTES A "SOLUTION"?

The preceding analysis suggests that the benefits of increasing ICBM survivability are much smaller than is generally assumed. Depending on the costs of the solutions, the problem may not be worth solving. Nevertheless, for over a decade the United States has made solving the ICBM vulnerability problem a priority among strategic nuclear programs and this commitment continues. Thus, examining the benefits offered by various possible solutions is important.

Because survivable ICBMs are said to be necessary (and vulnerable ones dangerous) for a variety of reasons, proposals that qualify as a "solution" according to certain arguments fail according to others. In assessing potential solutions we should be explicit about which problem(s) would be solved and, thus, about which benefits would be provided.

Percentages, Exchange Ratios, and Absolutes

The ICBM vulnerability problem is most often identified with a high percentage of vulnerable ICBMs (for example, over 90 percent vulnerability has often

---

[44] Analysts who believe the United States needs counterforce for first strikes, either for shifting the size of survivable forces or for limiting damage, might see additional benefits. Vulnerability matters less in these missions because it is the United States that launches the first massive strategic nuclear attack.

[45] For a variety of views on this question see *International Security* 12, no. 1 (Summer 1987): 175–96.

been used to suggest a serious danger). This vulnerability problem is at other times described in terms of favorable Soviet launcher or warhead exchange ratios (for example, the Soviet Union can destroy almost 1,000 U.S. launchers with 200 of its missiles) or in terms of the inadequate absolute size of the survivable ICBM force (for example, the United States will be left without an ICBM retaliatory option). As discussed above, each of these descriptions is closely related to a different explanation of why highly vulnerable ICBMs are dangerous. Analysts tend to use percentages in quite general descriptions that imply the United States is in a dire situation. Exchange ratios are the key to arguments focusing on shifting the relative size of surviving forces. Absolutes are central both to the "Nitze scenario" claim that the United States will lack a counterforce retaliatory option and to arguments calling for a hedge against future threats to the other legs of the triad.

Not all "solutions" help with each of these "problems." For example, deploying a moderate number of mobile missiles and getting rid of the current highly vulnerable silo-based force could enable a high percentage of ICBMs to survive and create an exchange ratio quite unfavorable to the Soviet Union, while at the same time not significantly increasing the expected number of surviving American ICBM warheads.[46] In contrast, deploying the same mobile force while keeping the current ICBM force would provide additional surviving warheads and could guarantee an unfavorable exchange ratio, but might not provide a significantly higher percentage of survivable ICBMs. This last point has frequently been overlooked in recent discussions of mobile ICBMs. For example, some "solutions" call for deploying 500 single warhead mobile missiles, promising that 50 percent would survive.[47] If, however, the United States retains its current silo-based force, and assuming for this example that this force is 90 percent vulnerable, then the overall U.S. ICBM force would still be about 85 percent vulnerable. Should this count as a solution? Will analysts who have focused so much attention on the high vulnerability of U.S. ICBMs be satisfied with a force that is more than 80% vulnerable? Finally, deploying additional ICBMs in silos or deploying more warheads per missile—for example, replacing Minuteman missiles with MX missiles—would increase the number of warheads expected to survive but would leave unchanged the percentage expected to survive and, in the latter option, would provide the Soviet Union with a more favorable warhead exchange ratio.

[46] For example, compare: (1) 20 percent survival of the current ICBM force, which would result in approximately 500 surviving warheads, and (2) 500 mobile single warhead ICBMs, which if very highly survivable could be expected to provide a roughly equal number of surviving warheads.

[47] The percentage of mobile missiles that would actually be expected to survive depends upon a variety of factors, including the size of the Soviet force, the entire target set this force is asked to cover, the size of the mobile missile deployment area, the hardness of the mobile vehicles, and the amount of warning time for plans that require dispersal on warning. For elaboration of these basic factors and evaluation of specific plans see note 5.

Clearly, evaluating proposed solutions is possible only following conclusions about the importance of the various ICBM vulnerability problems.

Because hedging against future threats to the triad is the strongest argument for increasing ICBM survivability, we should first assess the ability of proposed solutions to enhance American retaliatory capabilities. Planners should ask how large a retaliatory capability the United States needs in its ICBM leg, and then measure the proposed solutions against the threat the Soviet Union could pose during the lifetime of the proposed solution.

Further, we should be wary of other measures. For example, proposals that could deny the Soviet Union a highly favorable exchange ratio but cannot provide a large number of survivable weapons (and EMT—Equivalent Megatonage) should be rejected. These solutions do not provide an adequate hedge against threats to the other legs of the triad. By far the most likely reason for launching a massive attack against U.S. forces would be to reduce the costs of an all-out war. Faced with this decision, exchange ratios would probably be of little importance to Soviet leaders. Thus, we should be skeptical of such arguments as: "Midgetman might have trouble surviving. But in all likelihood . . . they [the Soviets] would use six warheads to destroy at most one of ours, a bad enough exchange rate to discourage attacks in the first place."[48]

Beyond increasing the absolute number of surviving weapons, solutions should avoid significantly increasing the number of vulnerable ones. In addition, simply getting rid of vulnerable ICBMs could provide benefits comparable to increasing survivable ones. As discussed above, although the number of vulnerable weapons should not influence Soviet decisions, during a severe crisis a Soviet decisionmaker might misjudge the benefits of attacking and be tempted by the ability to greatly reduce the size of the U.S. retaliatory force. Consequently, although deploying more warheads in silos would increase the number of survivable ICBM warheads, this is a poor way to solve the vulnerability problem.[49]

Finally, because single warhead missiles have received so much attention, it is important to note that the key argument for these missiles—that single warhead missiles guarantee unfavorable warhead exchange ratios—does not apply to mobile missiles. Assuming the Soviet Union cannot locate mobiles, the only way to attack them is with a barrage attack that covers the areas in which the mobiles might be deployed. The exchange ratio will be influenced by the number of U.S. warheads in the area the Soviet Union is able to attack; it will not, however, depend upon the number of warheads per missile. All

---

[48] Aspin, *Midgetman: Sliding Shut the Window of Vulnerability*, p. 20.

[49] If only the number of survivable warheads mattered, then the choice between these options, as well as others, would be determined by the cost per survivable warhead. Based upon this measure, it is possible that less survivable basing modes could be efficient. For example, the cost of a survivable MX warhead in Minuteman silos and of Midgetman appear to be comparable. On the cost of various alternatives see Jan M. Lodal, "SICBM Yes, HML No," *International Security* 12, no. 2 (Fall 1987): pp. 182–86.

else being equal, for a given total number of warheads on mobile missiles, the exchange ratio is independent of whether American missiles are MIRVed.[50] So is the number of warheads that would be expected to survive. As a result, there is little basis for insisting that a relatively small mobile missile—for example, Midgetman—have a single warhead. One rejoinder is that MIRVs are more threatening to the Soviet Union. If, however, the number of U.S. warheads is fixed, then this argument is also incorrect. The threat to Soviet forces is determined by the number and lethality of U.S. warheads. There is no obvious reason why fifty MX missiles with ten warheads each would be any more threatening than 500 equally lethal single warhead missiles.

Dependence of Survivability on Warning

Assuming that the United States decides to "solve" the ICBM vulnerability problem, should it deploy a system that relies on reacting to warning of Soviet attack to survive? Historically, one of the advantages of ICBMs was their ability, unlike bombers, to survive without warning of Soviet attack. Many of the proposed solutions lack this virtue. Some would require tactical warning of a Soviet attack (which provides 15-30 minutes of warning); others would require strategic warning (which provides more than an hour and possibly days or weeks).[51]

At first glance, the dependence of ICBMs on warning to survive may appear to be a detail. It is not, however, since this dependence influences their contribution to the diversity of survivable American strategic forces.[52] The survivability of U.S. bombers currently depends on their ability to react to tactical warning. No technical barrier stops the Soviets from being able to destroy U.S. bombers on the ground; rather, the bombers can survive because they will be gone before Soviet warheads arrive. If ICBMs were also to rely on tactical warning to survive, then both of these legs of the triad would be highly vulnerable if the United States fails to receive and react to tactical warning.[53]

[50] This argument assumes that the dispersal speed of the missiles in a dash-on-warning basing mode does not depend on missile size. If this is not true, and larger MIRVed missiles are slower, then there would be some relationship between warhead exchange ratios and MIRVing. On this issue see Aspin, *Midgetman*, pp. 25–29; also, Donald Hicks, "ICBM Modernization: Consider the Alternatives," *International Security* 12, no. 2 (Fall 1987): 177–78.

[51] This difference is currently seen as separating the rail-mobile option, which requires strategic warning, and certain Midgetman options that require less warning. On this issue see House Armed Services Committee, *MX Rail Garrison and Small ICBM*.

[52] Stressing this point is John C. Toomay, "Strategic Forces Rationale—A Lost Disciple," *International Security* 12, no. 2 (Fall 1987): 193–202.

[53] It is possible that the ICBMs might be more vulnerable since they can be attacked by Soviet ICBMs on day-to-day alert. In contrast, the key threat to bombers comes from SLBMs launched from Soviet SSBNs patrolling near the U.S. coasts, and possibly from low warning time "sneak" attacks by SLCMs. Under normal peacetime conditions, the Soviets do not have enough SSBNs on such patrols to threaten most bomber bases. The necessary increase in the number of Soviet SSBNs patrolling near U.S. coasts would probably be observed by the United States, providing

Thus, an ICBM basing mode that depends on tactical warning does less to diversify the survivability of U.S. retaliatory capabilities than one that is independent of warning.[54]

Even with this limitation, however, an ICBM force that survives by reacting to tactical warning does contribute to diversity because ballistic missiles have a different penetration mode than air-breathing forces. It could therefore be viewed as a hedge against advances in Soviet air defense that would reduce the penetrability of bombers and cruise missiles. In addition, ICBMs that can survive with tactical warning could serve as a hedge against certain types of enhanced Soviet ASW capabilities. For example, if the United States reacts to tactical warning, then these ICBMs could provide a secure reserve force, capable of surviving during and after a successful attrition campaign against U.S. SSBNs. Survivable ICBMs would be especially valuable if the Soviet Union achieves major breakthroughs in both air defense and ASW, and if the United States is unable to counter them. In this extremely unlikely case, survivable ICBMs would be the only leg of the triad capable of surviving an attack and penetrating to the Soviet homeland. Although dependence on warning would be a shortcoming, in this particular case the United States would be far better off with these ICBMs than without them.

Similar arguments apply to ICBM basing modes that require strategic warning to survive. The limitations are less significant, however, since neither SSBNs nor alert bombers depend primarily on strategic warning to survive. For example, although a surprise attack would enable the Soviets to destroy these ICBMs, it would not now enable them to destroy either SSBNs at sea or most alert bombers. If, however, the Soviets achieve breakthroughs in ASW that enable them to launch an effective ASW campaign without providing the United States advance warning of a coming missile attack, then at least two legs of the American triad might be left highly vulnerable to surprise. Avoiding this danger would require the United States to deploy ICBMs that can survive without strategic warning.

Some analysts believe there is now a stronger case for deploying ICBMs that can survive without warning, arguing that otherwise the United States is left without a hedge against a surprise attack.[55] Although some bombers would

---

advance warning of attack and enabling the United States to increase the alert rates of its bombers, including dispersing them to a larger number of bases. However, Brown, "The U.S. Manned Bomber and Strategic Deterrence in the 1990s," p. 20, questions the U.S. ability to get this type of warning in the future.

[54] This shortcoming is probably smaller than the above discussion suggests since the United States would almost certainly receive strategic warning. By deciding to disperse its mobile missiles well before the Soviets launch an attack, the United States could avoid the danger of not reacting immediately to tactical warning of a Soviet attack.

[55] Arguing the need for ICBMs that can survive without warning are Toomay, "Strategic Forces Rationale," p. 201, and Brown, "The U.S. Manned Bomber and Strategic Deterrence in the 1990s," p. 42. Far less concerned about independence of warning is Hicks, "ICBM Modernization," p. 175.

survive, assuming they receive and react to tactical warning, the only leg of the U.S. triad that is highly survivable in the face of a "bolt from the blue" would be its strategic submarines. Thus, a dramatic breakthrough in ASW would leave all legs of the American strategic triad highly vulnerable to surprise.

This argument overstates the importance of deploying ICBMs that can survive without warning for at least three reasons. First, the United States will almost certainly receive strategic warning. A superpower conventional war would provide clear political warning of the greatly increased probability of nuclear war. Thus, to achieve surprise the Soviets would have to attack before conventional fighting started. Unless the Soviets are confident that they can virtually disarm the United States such a decision is implausible, except in the extremely unlikely case in which Soviet leaders conclude both that conventional war is nearly inevitable and that its escalation to all-out nuclear war is virtually certain.[56] Second, the United States would almost certainly respond to this strategic warning if its ability to retaliate depended on doing so. Thus, although maintaining one type of strategic weapon that can survive without warning is certainly prudent, it is also more conservative than is generally assumed. Third, and probably most important, as argued above, the United States would probably be able to restore the survivability of other legs of its triad before technological advances enable the Soviets to deploy a force that poses a severe threat to American SSBNs.

In short, ICBMs that rely on warning would hedge against most but not all of the possible future threats that independently survivable ICBMs would hedge against. In weighing choices between basing modes, it is important to remember that there is not now a compelling case for deploying survivable ICBMs to insure against these dangers. Thus, if the United States decides to deploy survivable ICBMs, and if basing modes that survive independent of warning are much more expensive than others, then it would be reasonable to buy a basing mode that relies on warning. Within this context, basing modes that could be converted to become independent of warning, should Soviet breakthroughs occur, would be especially attractive.

Counterforce and Promptness

Are counterforce ICBMs a necessary component of solutions to the ICBM vulnerability problem? Once again, the answer depends on which of the numerous vulnerability problems is to be solved. Solving certain of the ICBM vulnerability problems requires survivable, reliably prompt counterforce systems, solving others requires at least counterforce, while the solution to yet others requires only a survivable countervalue capability. Obviously, if

---

[56] On the general problem of surprise attack see Richard K. Betts, *Surprise Attack* (Washington, D.C.: Brookings Institution, 1982); on points especially relevant to this discussion see pp. 234–38, 253–54.

ICBMs are valued for providing reliably prompt second-strike counterforce options, then nothing less can provide a satisfactory solution. On the other hand, eliminating the dangers advertised by the Nitze scenario calls for survivable counterforce, but not clearly for reliably prompt counterforce. Survivable cruise missiles and SLBMs should be able to solve this problem. So might survivable ICBMs that could not be fired quickly—for example, ICBMs placed in a deep underground basing mode.[57]

Redressing the decreasing diversity of the triad resulting from a vulnerable ICBM force requires neither promptness nor counterforce. Thus, inaccurate but survivable mobile missiles would solve this problem. So would ICBMs placed in a deep underground basing mode. Since this is the only problem that might be worth solving, the counterforce capability of the MX missile and the planned counterforce capability of the small mobile missile are unnecessary.

CONCLUSION

This chapter indicates that the benefits provided by survivable ICBMs are smaller than is generally assumed. The United States does not need a survivable capability for prompt large-scale counterforce attacks; and although more diversity is preferable to less, survivable ICBMs are not now a necessary component of an adequately diverse and redundant strategic force. This examination also finds that vulnerable U.S. ICBMs carry less significant liabilities than is generally assumed. Contrary to oft-repeated arguments, the Soviets cannot gain a meaningful coercive advantage by launching a counterforce attack. The greatest danger of vulnerable ICBMs lies in the possibility that they will encourage a Soviet leader to exaggerate the advantages of striking first in a severe crisis; however, this crisis instability is unlikely to be large, since the United States would retain massive retaliatory capabilities.

Thus, the United States should be unwilling to pay enormous costs—political or economic—to "solve" the vulnerability problem. Evaluating the dollar value of the benefits of programs designed to reduce the probability of nuclear war is extremely difficult and highly subjective. Nevertheless, in light of such limited benefits, the high dollar cost of many of the proposed solutions counts against them.[58] These doubts are all the more telling once we recognize that

---

[57] On this basing mode see Office of Technology Assessment, *MX Missile Basing*, pp. 269–74.

[58] Of course, these costs must be compared to the cost of the other legs of the triad. In scenarios in which the United States does not react to strategic warning, the cost of surviving and penetrating ALCMs (Air-Launched Cruise Missiles) is much greater than the cost of surviving ICBM warheads; the costs are comparable in scenarios in which the United States does react to strategic warning. See Brown, "The U.S. Manned Bomber and Strategic Deterrence in the 1990s." Since most of the bomber leg (except the B-2) and cruise missiles have already been procured this is not an argument for buying ICBMs now. However, these considerations would be more important in future decisions on strategic modernization. We would, however, want to consider the cost of ALCMs deployed on a plane that, unlike the B-1, was procured as an ALCM carrier, not as a penetrating bomber.

many of these current proposals would not actually eliminate the problems they are supposed to solve. For example, current proposals would not provide the United States with a highly survivable ICBM force—the United States might add 500 survivable warheads, while under a START agreement keeping approximately 1,500 highly vulnerable ones. Although lacking a sound strategic foundation, the high percentage vulnerability of the ICBMs has been the focus of much public concern. Thus, these solutions might over time give way to the conclusion that the ICBM vulnerability problem was left unsolved.

Consequently, the United States should probably forgo deploying a highly survivable ICBM for the foreseeable future. As a hedge against future threats to the other legs of its strategic nuclear triad, the United States should develop a survivable basing mode and have plans to deploy it relatively quickly. However, the United States need not deploy a survivable ICBM until a serious threat actually begins to materialize. A variety of observations suggest this approach is reasonable. American SSBNs are expected to remain essentially invulnerable for the foreseeable future. In the unlikely event that a threat to their survivability arises, well-developed plans for deploying a survivable ICBM would probably enable the United States to respond before its SSBNs were highly vulnerable. Further, threats to mobile missiles appear more likely to develop than threats to SSBNs, which reduces the expected value of deploying survivable ICBMs as a hedge against the future vulnerability of SSBNs.

Other possible approaches to increasing the survivability of the ICBMs include deploying ballistic missile defenses and arms control, since the effectiveness of most plans for deploying mobile missiles depends on the size of the Soviet force. The following chapters examine these approaches. In light of the limited benefits, these analyses find that the United States should not reserve top priority in arms control for increasing the survivability of its ICBMs; and, that the benefits of increasing ICBM survivability are insufficient to warrant amending or abrogating the ABM Treaty, which would increase the possibility of intense competition in ballistic missile defenses.

Finally, this analysis finds that the risks of maintaining a large vulnerable ICBM force are at least comparable to the benefits. The United States should therefore seriously consider getting rid of its vulnerable ICBMs, or at least dramatically reducing them, to minimize the prospect that in a severe crisis Soviet leaders will be tempted to launch a preemptive attack to limit damage.

CHAPTER NINE

Should the United States Deploy Limited Ballistic Missile Defenses?

ALTHOUGH DEBATE over ballistic missile defense (BMD) has focused on near-perfect systems—those necessary for escaping from MAD—the United States could deploy BMD in pursuit of a variety of more modest strategic goals. Possible goals for ballistic missile defense of more limited capability include increasing the survivability of American military forces and reducing the damage that a small nuclear attack would inflict on American cities. Unlike near-perfect defenses, less-than-near-perfect defense capable of satisfying some of these goals might be available in the relatively near future.[1]

President Reagan's March 1983 speech[2]—which raised the hope that U.S. cities could be protected in an all-out war—and the strategic defense initiative (SDI) that followed, have restored legitimacy to strategic defenses in general, even though the speech focused on near-perfect BMD. The combination of this renewed legitimacy and the dubious prospect for near-perfect defenses has lent political and budgetary support to BMD capable of achieving only more modest objectives.[3] At least within the defense community, therefore, whether the United States should deploy less-than-near-perfect BMD is likely to be debated for many years.

Limited BMD would not have the radical implications of near-perfect de-

[1] For discussion of the factors that influence whether defenses are near-perfect and for references on the infeasibility of near-perfect defenses see notes 2 and 7 in Chapter Four.

[2] *New York Times*, 24 March 1983, p. 20.

[3] During the 1960s the United States experienced a similar shift in the objectives of BMD as it became clear that the available systems could not protect U.S. cities from Soviet ballistic missile attack. There is a striking resemblance between the debate over anti-ballistic missile (ABM) systems of the late 1960s and early 1970s and the current BMD debate. Many of the arguments examined in this chapter played a role in that earlier debate. Representative arguments against ABMs are found in Abram Chayes and Jerome B. Wiesner, eds., *ABM: An Evaluation of the Decision to Deploy an Antiballistic Missile System* (New York: Harper and Row, 1969); representative arguments in favor are found in Johan J. Holst and William Schneider, Jr., eds., *Why ABM? Policy Issues in the Missile Defense Controversy* (New York: Pergamon Press, 1969). See also Morton H. Halperin, "The Decision to Deploy ABM: The Bureaucratic and Domestic Politics in the Johnson Administration," *World Politics* 25, no. 1 (October 1972): 62–95; David N. Schwartz, "Past and Present: The Historical Legacy," in Ashton B. Carter and David N. Schwartz, eds., *Ballistic Missile Defense* (Washington, D.C.: Brookings Institution, 1984); and Ernest J. Yanarella, *The Missile Defense Controversy: Strategy, Technology, and Politics* (Lexington: University Press of Kentucky, 1977).

fenses since it would leave the United States vulnerable to massive Soviet attacks. As discussed in Chapters Four and Five, near-perfect defenses would fundamentally alter U.S. nuclear strategy either by restoring American nuclear superiority or providing both superpowers with protection against all-out nuclear attacks. By contrast, less-than-near-perfect BMD would leave unchanged the basic challenges the United States faces in MAD.

Nevertheless, decisions about these less capable ballistic missile defenses will play an important role in shaping the strategic environment in MAD. The ABM Treaty now essentially prohibits both superpowers from deploying militarily significant BMD. Thus, extensive U.S. deployments would require amending or terminating the treaty, thereby allowing Soviet deployment of BMD. Decisions about deploying BMD must therefore consider whether the United States is better off when both superpowers deploy BMD, not only whether limited American BMD can perform some useful missions. In addition, limited BMD could create further complications since there may not be a clear line between BMD deployed to achieve limited goals and BMD intended eventually to protect a superpower's homeland against large attacks. American deployments of limited BMD might therefore lead the Soviets to conclude that the United States is pursuing a damage-limitation capability and nuclear superiority, and vice versa. Thus, analysis of limited BMD must consider whether it would create undesirable confusion about either superpower's objectives and nuclear strategy.

This chapter examines the following arguments for deploying BMD that is capable of performing certain limited missions, but is incapable of significantly reducing the vulnerability of U.S. cities:[4]

Increasing ICBM survivability

Protecting command and control and other military targets

Defeating small Soviet attacks, thereby raising the strategic nuclear threshold

Increasing the uncertainty confronting the attacker

Encouraging and supporting arms control, especially reduction of offensive forces

Protecting against accidental, unauthorized, nth country, and terrorist attacks

Acquiring the political and economic benefits of U.S. technical superiority

[4] From the mid- to late 1980s another important argument held that the United States should deploy BMD to counter Soviet violations of the ABM Treaty. The Soviet commitment in 1989 to dismantle the Krasnoyarsk radar, which is the clearest violation, greatly reduced the salience of this argument; see James Rubin, "Baker, Shevardnadze Generate Arms Control Progress," *Arms Control Today* 19, no. 8 (October 1989): 27. For assessment of this violation see Gloria Duffy, project director, *Compliance and the Future of Arms Control* (Cambridge, Mass.: Ballinger, 1988), pp. 105–12. Calling for deployment of BMD was Colin S. Gray, "Moscow Is Cheating," *Foreign Policy* no. 56 (Fall 1984): 141–52. Proposing other American reactions were Duffy, *Compliance and the Future of Arms Control*, p. 207; Thomas K. Longstreth, John E. Pike, and John B. Rhinelander, *The Impact of U.S. and Soviet Ballistic Missile Defense Programs on the ABM Treaty* (Washington, D.C.: National Campaign to Save the ABM Treaty, March 1985), pp. 67–74; and Michael Krepon, "Both Sides Are Hedging," *Foreign Policy* no. 56 (Fall 1984): 170–71.

Many proponents of BMD recommend an evolutionary deployment strategy based on these arguments: the United States should develop and deploy "intermediate" systems (i.e., BMD capable of performing these less demanding missions) as soon as possible. The United States would first deploy BMD capable of performing the least demanding missions, possibly beginning with the defense of ICBMs or protection against accidental attacks. Then, in the hope that BMD technologies improve faster than penetration techniques, defenses would take on more demanding missions, with the final objective remaining perfect defense. Proponents argue that an evolutionary strategy is not risky because at each stage of deployment the benefits provided by BMD exceed its costs.[5]

Furthermore, some proponents believe an evolutionary strategy increases the probability that the United States will eventually develop and deploy near-perfect ballistic missile defenses and therefore see benefits that go beyond those provided by limited BMD. From this perspective, the benefits of deploying limited BMD include termination of the ABM Treaty, increased legitimacy for a U.S. nuclear strategy that incorporates strategic defenses, and institutions and constituencies that will insure continuing large investments in BMD research and development. Specifically, members of the damage-limitation school, who have argued for regaining nuclear superiority by marrying BMD with air defense, civil defense, and offensive counterforce, tend to favor an evolutionary deployment strategy for these reasons. This viewpoint is assessed at the conclusion of the chapter, following a comparison of the costs and benefits of BMD deployment.

In sharp contrast, I conclude that deploying limited or intermediate BMD would, on balance, reduce U.S. security. The benefits of deploying these systems are found upon examination to be much less than the proponents' arguments at first suggest. And unless one desires to provoke an intensified competition with the Soviet Union, the costs of BMD deployment are more impressive: the ABM Treaty would have to be either amended or, more likely, terminated, thereby eliminating restraints on Soviet BMD;[6] each superpower, believing that the other's BMD threatens its security, would probably react by expanding and improving its offensive force in order to have confidence in its ability to overcome the adversary's defense; this competition between offense and defense would strain U.S.-Soviet relations; these changes in the political

---

[5] See, for example, Fred S. Hoffman, Study Director, *Ballistic Missile Defenses and U.S. National Security: Summary Report* (Washington, D.C.: October 1983), prepared for the Future Security Strategy Study, reprinted in Steven E. Miller and Stephen Van Evera, eds., *The Star Wars Controversy* (Princeton: Princeton University Press, 1986), pp. 273–90, and hereafter cited as *Hoffman Report*; and Keith B. Payne and Colin S. Gray, "Nuclear Policy and the Defensive Transition," *Foreign Affairs* 62, no. 4 (Spring 1984): 820–42.

[6] As discussed below, the key possible exception is a BMD system designed to provide some protection against accidental launches while complying with the ABM Treaty. However, although its costs would be smaller, the case for deployment is not compelling since the expected benefits are also small.

and strategic situation would make arms control agreements much harder to reach than today; and finally, the economic costs of U.S. strategic nuclear forces would increase immensely. Thus, deployment of less-than-near-perfect BMD and the associated evolutionary strategy should be rejected.

Increasing ICBM Survivability

BMD could probably help reduce the vulnerability of U.S. ICBMs. As discussed in the previous chapter, many analysts see a variety of serious dangers in this vulnerability, including reduced crisis stability, a Soviet capability to coerce the United States, a threat to necessary capabilities that are unavailable in the other legs of the triad—specifically, reliably prompt second-strike counterforce—and reduced robustness of U.S. retaliatory capabilities stemming from decreased diversity of survivable U.S. forces. Given that the dangers of vulnerable ICBMs have received so much attention, it is not surprising that one of the key arguments for deploying less-than-near-perfect BMD is to protect ICBMs.[7]

Upon examining the supposed dangers, however, the benefits of increasing ICBM survivability were found to be relatively small, especially since reducing the size of the vulnerable force would provide many of the same benefits.[8]

[7] On assessing active defense of ICBMs see Ashton B. Carter, "BMD Applications: Performance and Limitations," in Carter and Schwartz, eds., *Ballistic Missile Defense*; and Congressional Budget Office, *Strategic Defenses: Alternative Missions and Their Costs* (Washington, D.C.: GPO, 1989), pp. 39–59. The benefits of defending ICBMs are discussed in Payne and Gray, "Nuclear Policy and the Defensive Transition," pp. 823–25; George A. Keyworth, II, "The Case for Strategic Defense: An Option for a Disarmed World," *Issues in Science and Technology* (Fall 1984): 38–42; and Ronald Reagan, "The President's Strategic Defense Initiative" (Washington, D.C.: The White House, January 1985), p. 3.

Renewed interest in protecting ICBMs with BMD preceded SDI. Addressing this issue are "ABM Revisited: Promise or Peril," *Washington Quarterly* 4, no. 4 (Autumn 1981): 53–85; G. E. Barash et al., *Ballistic Missile Defense: A Potential Arms-Control Initiative* (Los Alamos, N.M.: Los Alamos Scientific Laboratory, 1981); Albert Carnesale, "Reviving the ABM Debate," *Arms Control Today* 11, no. 4 (April 1981): 1–2, 6–8; Colin S. Gray, "A New Debate on Ballistic Missile Defense," *Survival* 23, no. 2 (March/April 1981): 60–71; Jan M. Lodal, "Deterrence and Nuclear Strategy," *Daedalus* 109, no. 4 (Fall 1980): 166–74; Michael Nacht, "ABM ABCs," *Foreign Policy* no. 46 (Spring 1982): 155–74; and Office of Technology Assessment, *MX Missile Basing* (Washington, D.C.: GPO, 1981).

[8] In addition to the arguments discussed in Chapter Eight, some proponents of BMD argue that the United States needs survivable ICBMs to maintain crisis stability during the transition from MAD to BAD. The crisis instability would result when the Soviet Union could partially defend itself against a retaliatory attack, but not against a U.S. first strike. See, for example, Payne and Gray, "Nuclear Policy and the Defensive Transition," p. 284. However, this argument does not support the near-term deployment of BMD since the Soviet Union will be unable for the foreseeable future to defend its cities against U.S. retaliation. That decision could wait until the superpowers develop defenses capable of the more difficult task of significantly reducing the vulnerability of their homelands. If this ever occurs, they could then defend their forces before deploying

Although survivable ICBMs are preferable to vulnerable ones, vulnerable ICBMs neither leave the United States without necessary retaliatory capabilities nor create large Soviet incentives for attack. Following directly from this conclusion, BMD deployed to increase ICBM survivability would provide only relatively small benefits.

Further, even analysts who see larger dangers in vulnerable ICBMs must consider two additional issues before concluding in favor of BMD. First, those who believe there are important time-urgent second-strike targets must consider the net effect of *both* superpowers deploying BMD. Mutual deployment of BMD might not increase the U.S. prompt second-strike capability: although U.S. BMD would make its ICBMs harder to destroy in a first strike, Soviet BMD would make it harder for surviving U.S. ICBMs to destroy Soviet targets in a second strike. In addition, Soviet BMD would reduce the effectiveness of U.S. counterforce SLBMs.

Second, and probably more important, BMD must be compared to the alternatives for "solving" the ICBM vulnerability problem. Finding that BMD can provide net benefits is insufficient. The BMD solution must also be compared to other means for increasing ICBM survivability, including mobile and deceptive basing and arms control, and to reducing Soviet exaggerations of their first-strike incentives by moving to a strategic dyad.

Protecting C³ and Other Military Targets

ICBMs do not represent the only U.S. military capability vulnerable to Soviet nuclear attack. The other legs of the triad—long-range bombers and ballistic missile submarines—are partially vulnerable; the command, control, and communications (C³) systems for the strategic forces can be severely degraded by even relatively small attacks; and U.S. conventional military forces are especially vulnerable to nuclear attack. These forces could be subjected to attacks of varying intensity: at one end of the spectrum are nuclear attacks against a few conventional force targets, for example critical ports needed to support forces fighting in Europe, while at the other end of the spectrum are full-scale attacks against U.S. strategic nuclear forces, including C³.

Proponents of BMD tend to favor protecting military targets against the entire range of attacks because they believe that increasing the survivability of military targets reduces the adversary's ability to achieve its objectives, thereby strengthening deterrence.[9] In contrast, opponents of BMD do not believe there is much value in defending these targets against any type of attack: the United States already has large retaliatory capabilities and defense can add little to its ability to deter such attacks by threatening retaliation. This section

---

defenses to protect their homelands. For more detailed discussion of crisis stability in BAD see Chapter Four; on transitions see note 48 in that chapter.

[9] See, for example, *Hoffman Report*, p. 1.

examines the arguments for defending C^3. The two following sections examine arguments that apply to a wider range of military targets.

Some proponents of BMD argue especially that the United States should defend its C^3 against a large Soviet attack, maintaining that less-than-near-perfect defenses can deny the Soviet Union high confidence in its ability to destroy these targets.[10] The counterargument has two components. First, the United States need not be able to defeat a Soviet attack on its C^3 in order to deter it. A Soviet leader would believe that any full-scale attack on U.S. C^3 targets would result in full-scale retaliation: the attack would result in a large number of U.S. casualties; it would probably destroy the U.S. ability to control, and therefore limit, retaliation;[11] and the Soviets would not launch such an attack as part of a bargaining strategy since the attack would destroy the U.S. capabilities required for damage assessment, communication, and war termination. Consequently, if the Soviet Union attacked U.S. command and control it would almost certainly also attack U.S. strategic nuclear forces. The damage then would be still higher than if only C^3 were attacked, thereby reducing further any U.S. incentives for restraint. In short, the only rational reason for launching a full-scale attack against C^3 is to reduce the damage the United States could inflict in retaliation.

This goal, however, is infeasible for the Soviets. Although C^3 is considered the weak link in U.S. strategic capabilities, analysts believe that the United States would almost certainly be able to retaliate massively after a Soviet attack against its command and control.[12] Therefore, the Soviet Union cannot reasonably hope to significantly reduce the U.S. ability to inflict damage by attacking its C^3 and thus has virtually no incentive to launch such an attack. In this case, therefore, denial of the ability to attack C^3 targets adds little, if anything, to deterrence. Consequently, the benefits of protecting C^3 with BMD would be small.[13]

Again, we can understand disagreement over the benefits of defending C^3 as partially rooted in disagreements over the requirements of deterrence. For example, some members of the military denial school would extend its arguments for hedging against extremely risky Soviet actions to the defense of C^3. First, members of the military denial school might argue that the United States

[10] Ibid., pp. 9–10.

[11] Desmond Ball, *Can Nuclear War Be Controlled?* Adelphi Paper No. 169 (London: IISS, 1981); and John D. Steinbruner, "Nuclear Decapitation," *Foreign Policy* no. 45 (Winter 1981–82): 18.

[12] Ball, *Can Nuclear War Be Controlled?* p. 37; Steinbruner, "Nuclear Decapitation," pp. 18–19; and Ashton B. Carter, "Assessing Command System Vulnerability," in Ashton B. Carter, John D. Steinbruner, and Charles Zraket, eds, *Managing Nuclear Operations* (Washington, D.C.: Brookings Institution, 1987), p. 607.

[13] This may, however, underestimate the value of more survivable C^3 by focusing on decapitation and overlooking the dangers of moving to high alert, which is driven partly by C^3 vulnerability.

needs highly survivable C^3 to insure its ability to retaliate effectively against Soviet *military* targets, a capability that others find unnecessary. A Soviet ability to gain a military advantage might undermine deterrence; and attacking U.S. C^3, while not very useful for limiting damage to Soviet society, could reduce the U.S. ability to destroy military targets.[14] Second, Soviet interest in the possibility of prolonged nuclear war requires that the United States have enduring capabilities. However, as the above discussion suggests, it is most unlikely that counter-C^3 attacks would end in a limited war—these scenarios are far less plausible than the counter-ICBM exchanges that the military denial school worries Soviet leaders might envision ending in bargained outcomes. Consequently, effective counter-military retaliation and enduring forces would be of little consequence following a full-scale counter-C^3 attack. We can reasonably assume that the Soviets would launch such an attack only in pursuit of damage limitation, a capability that the United States can deny without BMD.

Nevertheless, if nuclear war appeared very likely, a Soviet leader, because of the slight hope of significantly reducing U.S. retaliation, might decide to launch a preemptive attack against U.S. C^3. Thus, the importance of the second component of the counterargument: defending American C^3 would not significantly increase its ability to survive a dedicated Soviet attack. There are on the order of 100 critical fixed C^3 targets.[15] Assuming that U.S. BMD is quite effective and could raise the ''attack price'' to twenty (i.e., the Soviet Union would have to allocate twenty warheads to each target to have confidence that it would be destroyed),[16] the Soviet Union would have to allocate 2,000 warheads to C^3 targets instead of the 100 to 200 required without BMD. However, such an attack would leave the Soviet Union with approximately 4,000 ICBM warheads for attacks against U.S. ICBMs and other military targets. Consequently, BMD could raise the price of an attack on C^3, but even very effective BMD could not deny the Soviet Union the ability to destroy

---

[14] Carter, ''Assessing Command System Vulnerability,'' pp. 607–8.

[15] Ball, *Can Nuclear War Be Controlled?* p. 35; Steinbruner, ''Nuclear Decapitation,'' p. 18. Also describing the small number of C^3 targets is John J. Hamre, Richard H. Davison, and Peter T. Tarpgaard, *Strategic Command, Control and Communications: Alternative Approaches for Modernization* (Washington, D.C.: Congressional Budget Office, 1981), p. 13.

[16] An attack price of twenty is quite optimistic for systems that might be available in the next two decades, so this argument is weighted toward the defense. Most disagreement on the attack price that might be achieved with traditional endoatmospheric systems (those that target incoming warheads after they reenter the atmosphere) involves figures between two and eight, with many analysts skeptical of estimates above five. Experts find it difficult to estimate the attack price that might be achieved by adding exoatmospheric systems (those that target incoming warheads before they reenter the atmosphere) because the performance of these systems depends heavily on the specific system architecture and its ability to defeat a wide variety of potentially devastating penetration tactics. See Carter, ''BMD Applications: Performance and Limitations,'' pp. 110–30.

these targets with a first strike.[17] Moreover, raising the total attack price would significantly discourage the Soviet Union from starting an all-out war only if the price exceeded the forces available: in an all-out war, holding forces in reserve would be of little value. If this point were ever reached, the Soviet Union could expand its offensive force to offset the U.S. BMD.

Defeating Small Soviet Attacks, Thereby Raising the Strategic Nuclear Threshold

Some proponents of BMD assert that a moderately effective BMD could reduce the probability of nuclear war by protecting the United States from a small, deliberate Soviet nuclear attack. Without BMD, nuclear war could start with the use of only one or a few nuclear weapons. Therefore, goes the argument, because a thin defense might completely intercept a small attack, it would require the attacker to launch a larger attack. But, the argument continues, the Soviet Union might be unwilling to launch a large attack because it would constitute too large an escalation. Thus, even if the United States could not prevent the Soviet Union from destroying certain targets, there is value in requiring the Soviet Union to attack with a large number of weapons. Donald Brennan argues that "it is very likely that a government that would otherwise plausibly consider escalating an intense crisis to the strategic nuclear level would have second thoughts about the matter if it was obliged to fire a large-scale salvo rather than one or a very few weapons."[18]

It is far more likely, however, that both attacker and defender would care more about the number of targets destroyed than about the number of warheads that were launched. Consequently, this argument for BMD is flawed because American BMD would not force the Soviet Union to attack more

[17] This argument, while essentially sound, requires three qualifications. First, Carter, "Assessing Command System Vulnerability," explains that there are potentially thousands of targets in a decapitation attack. While less critical, destroying these targets might increase somewhat the prospects for success. Assuming the Soviet force does not grow proportionally (which it probably could), a large BMD system might protect some of these targets, thereby reducing further the probability of successful Soviet damage limitation. Second, if U.S. BMD protected both strategic forces and C^3, then the current Soviet force might not be large enough to cover this target set. Because destroying forces complements destroying C^3 in a damage-limitation attack, such an extensive U.S. BMD system would further reduce Soviet prospects for damage limitation, unless they respond to overwhelm it. Third, the START agreement currently being negotiated would greatly reduce the number of Soviet warheads, leaving them with many fewer warheads after a counter-C^3 attack than my discussion suggests. However, as discussed shortly, the Soviet Union would probably find these arms control limits unacceptable if the United States deploys an extensive BMD system.

[18] Donald G. Brennan, "BMD Policy Issues for the 1980s," in William Schneider, Jr. et al., *U.S. Strategic-Nuclear Policy and Ballistic Missile Defense: The 1980s and Beyond* (Cambridge, Mass.: Institute for Foreign Policy Analysis, 1980), p. 27. For a similar argument see Jan M. Lodal, "Deterrence and Nuclear Strategy," *Daedalus* 109, no. 4 (Fall 1980): 167.

targets, only to use more weapons. A thin defense could increase the attack price, but could not prevent the Soviet Union from destroying a relatively small number of targets. This larger Soviet attack would not do significantly more damage than a smaller attack that did not have to cope with BMD: if U.S. BMD works as expected, only a portion of the larger Soviet attack would reach American targets, inflicting damage comparable to the smaller attack; if U.S. BMD works less well, the Soviets would simply have destroyed the same targets with more weapons, which would not result in significantly greater damage. Therefore, BMD should not significantly influence Soviet decisions unless the attack price was high enough to severely deplete the Soviet force, thereby placing the Soviet Union at meaningful military disadvantage. A moderately effective BMD protecting a relatively small number of targets could not have this effect, however.

Thus, less-than-near-perfect BMD would not deny the Soviet Union the ability to use limited nuclear attacks for military or bargaining purposes. As part of a bargaining strategy, the Soviet Union could still escalate a war with a nuclear attack against a small number of targets to demonstrate its resolve and to increase the United States' assessment of the probability that the war would escalate to yet higher levels.

More important in the context of the current debate, the Soviet Union would still be able to mount limited nuclear strikes for military purposes. For example, the Hoffman Report argues that during a large conventional war in Europe the Soviet Union might launch a limited strategic nuclear attack against U.S. force projection targets in order to deny the United States the ability to provide military support to Western Europe. The report then suggests that BMD could play a key role in deterring this type of attack: by forcing the Soviet Union to increase the size of its attack, BMD would reduce Soviet confidence in its ability to destroy these targets without running too high a risk of further escalation.[19]

However, the Soviet Union can remain highly confident of destroying the small number of U.S. force projection targets by increasing the number of weapons directed at each target. As argued above, increasing the total number of weapons, while holding the number of targets fixed, would not significantly increase the damage to the United States. Therefore, the larger attack seems

[19] The *Hoffman Report*, pp. 10–11, maintains that: "In the event of imminent or actual large-scale conflict in Europe, another high-priority Soviet task would be to prevent quick reinforcement and resupply from the United States. . . . In the absence of defenses, the Soviets . . . could also accomplish this task with higher confidence by means of quite limited nuclear attacks on such [reception] facilities in Europe and on a restricted set of force projection targets in CONUS. . . . An intermediate ballistic missile defense deployment of moderate capabilities could force the Soviets to increase their attack size radically. This would reduce or eliminate the Soviets' confidence that they could achieve their attack objectives while controlling the risks of a large-scale nuclear exchange."

to be hardly riskier than the smaller attack. Moreover, a Soviet leader willing to attack the United States with nuclear weapons is presumably prepared to run extremely large risks. BMD would not significantly increase the risk of attacking a few U.S. targets and therefore would be unlikely to change such a leader's decision.[20]

Increasing the Uncertainty Confronting the Attacker

Proponents maintain that BMD would strengthen deterrence by increasing Soviet uncertainty about the success of an attack, thereby making it less attractive. The Hoffman Report argues that "uncertainty about the offense-defense engagement itself contributes to deterrence of attack by denying confidence in the attack outcome."[21] An administration description of SDI states:

> Effective defenses against ballistic missiles have potential for enhancing deterrence. . . . they could significantly increase an aggressor's uncertainties regarding whether his weapons would penetrate the defenses and destroy our missiles and other military targets. It would be very difficult for a potential aggressor to predict his own vulnerability in the face of such uncertainties.[22]

These arguments, however, overstate both the potential of defenses to increase relevant Soviet uncertainties and the benefits if these uncertainties were increased. These errors reflect a number of problems underlying these arguments, which are incomplete and only correct under certain conditions. First, by framing their arguments in terms of uncertainty rather than in terms of missions that BMD can help perform, proponents create unnecessary confusion, which helps to hide the inadequacies of their arguments. This problem is illustrated by a few general observations about the relationship between uncertainty and deterrence. Increasing uncertainty does not in general enhance deterrence. Certainty is often preferable to uncertainty. For example, all else being equal, a Soviet leader certain that the United States possesses an assured destruction capability is more likely to be deterred than a Soviet leader that wonders whether the United States possesses this capability. Further, focusing on uncertainty tends to create confusion by overlooking more basic issues, such as: Is the expected outcome of U.S. retaliation sufficient to deter Soviet attacks? What uncertainties about U.S. capabilities already exist? Only after

---

[20] If this argument for BMD were not logically flawed, a further problem would arise. Assuming that *both* superpowers had defenses that reduced the credibility of limited attacks, the net effect could well be negative: NATO doctrine calls for credible first use threats; while problematic in MAD, if BMD eliminated the low levels of the escalation ladder, things would be even worse. Presumably, this would be especially troublesome for members of the military denial school, since they are especially concerned with the problems of credible escalation in MAD.

[21] *Hoffman Report*, p. 10.

[22] Reagan, "The President's Strategic Defense Initiative," p. 3.

answering these questions can we effectively examine additional uncertainties that BMD might create and their implications for Soviet assessments of the less likely but possible outcomes of U.S. retaliatory attacks.

In addition, the attacker's willingness to take risks influences how increased uncertainty would affect deterrence.[23] For example, a conservative Soviet decisionmaker would probably overestimate the capability of the U.S. defense and underestimate the capability of the Soviet defense. As a result, deterrence would be strengthened. However, an overconfident Soviet decisionmaker would underestimate the capability of America's defense and overestimate the Soviet defense capability; hence deterrence would be weakened. It may well be that, more often than not, decisionmakers who face potentially catastrophic outcomes will act cautiously. However, uncertainty is not unambiguously good, and we should not overlook the possibility of a decisionmaker who in a dire situation optimistically evaluates uncertainties about force capabilities.[24]

Second, looking more specifically at the proponents' argument shows that BMD would not in general increase Soviet uncertainty about U.S. capabilities. To begin with, the argument is incomplete, overlooking the effect of Soviet BMD. If both superpowers deployed defenses, the Soviet Union could face greater uncertainty about both the effectiveness of its attack and the effectiveness of U.S. retaliation. In addition, the net effect of BMD depends on the targets that are defended, its effectiveness, and the targets that each country plans to attack. In general, therefore, the net effect of defenses on Soviet uncertainty about the outcome of a nuclear exchange is indeterminate.

Further, the argument that BMD will significantly increase uncertainty applies only to large attacks against military targets. As discussed above, if the number of targets is not large, then the attacker can overcome the defense by increasing the size of the attack. Uncertainties about the effectiveness of the defense could require the attacker to further increase the size of the attack to insure high confidence of success. For BMD available in the next two decades, however, compensating for uncertainties could make the overall attack price prohibitively high only for a large target set. Moreover, the Soviet Union

[23] Because deterrence probably depends at least as much on the expected outcome of an attack as on the magnitude of uncertainties about the outcome, we should not overlook the fact that defenses could shift the most probable outcome of an attack as well as the distribution that surrounds it. Thus, there are cases in which defenses would tend to strengthen deterrence, independent of the nature of the decisionmaker. For example, if both countries deploy BMD that unambiguously protects only forces, then a decisionmaker considering a counterforce attack and anticipating countervalue retaliation would find that BMD makes attacking less attractive. In this case, as in others, the effect of uncertainty about the adversary's BMD depends on the specific decisionmaker.

[24] Crises in which ill-founded expectations of military success may have led to riskier crisis policies and, as a result, wars, are discussed in Richard Ned Lebow, *Between Peace and War: The Nature of International Crisis* (Baltimore: Johns Hopkins University Press, 1981), pp. 242–47.

could reduce the significance of the increased attack price by expanding its offensive force—which would probably cost less than the U.S. BMD. Therefore, the questions become: Is the expected outcome of U.S. retaliation sufficient to deter a large Soviet counterforce attack? What uncertainties already exist about the success of large Soviet attacks against U.S. forces? Would mutual deployment of BMD produce the desired results?

Third, answering these questions shows the basic flaw in the uncertainty argument for BMD. For reasons already discussed, large Soviet attacks against U.S. ICBMs, C^3, and other military targets are now adequately deterred. The U.S. assured destruction capability truly is assured, that is, the Soviet Union should be certain about the U.S. ability to retaliate massively. The punitive retaliation school has explained in detail why this capability is sufficient to deter large Soviet nuclear attacks. Assuming the Soviet Union does not deploy area defenses, U.S. BMD could increase the number of U.S. weapons that could survive and penetrate to the Soviet homeland, and might increase Soviet uncertainty about the size of this retaliatory attack. Nevertheless, because the U.S. ability to retaliate massively is already certain, these changes in size and uncertainty should have essentially no effect on deterrence.

Some members of the military denial school will disagree, arguing that U.S. BMD will increase Soviet uncertainty about success in a counterforce exchange, thereby increasing the U.S. ability to maintain a favorable ratio of forces. However, even if we overlook arguments holding that ratios do not influence deterrence, this argument for BMD is problematic: when *both* countries defend their forces, the net effect may not be an improvement in U.S. post-exchange ratios or an increase in Soviet uncertainty about these ratios.

Finally, even putting aside these basic problems, if we accept the proponents' assertion that uncertainty is desirable, we should recognize that there are currently enormous uncertainties about the detailed outcome of a nuclear exchange. Especially germane to this argument is the fact that large technical and operational uncertainties already exist about the effectiveness of a Soviet attack directed at hardened targets and command and control.[25] A decisionmaker who could be deterred by uncertainties about attack outcomes would probably be deterred by the uncertainties that already exist. In contrast, if these uncertainties in combination with the other reasons for not launching a counterforce attack are not adequate to deter a Soviet decisionmaker, then the additional uncertainty created by BMD is likely to have little effect.

---

[25] On attacks against ICBMs see John D. Steinbruner and Thomas M. Garwin, "Strategic Vulnerability: The Balance between Prudence and Paranoia," *International Security* 1, no. 1 (Summer 1976): 138–81, and Matthew Bunn and Kosta Tsipis, "The Uncertainties of a Preemptive Nuclear Attack," *Scientific American* (November 1983): 38–47. On command and control see Carter, "Assessing Command System Vulnerability," pp. 558–60.

*Encouraging and Supporting Arms Control, Especially Reduction of
  Offensive Forces*

Proponents of BMD maintain that defenses reduce the military utility of nuclear weapons, thereby making it easier to trade away existing offensive weapons and less attractive to build additional ones. Moreover, if the cost of building ballistic missiles to defeat BMD is greater than the cost of building BMD (i.e., the "cost-exchange ratio" favors BMD), then U.S. deployment of defenses might force the Soviet Union to give up its ballistic missiles. Presumably, President Reagan's statement that research and development of BMD "could pave the way for arms control measures to eliminate the weapons themselves" was based upon these views.[26]

Opponents, however, argue convincingly that deploying BMD will not facilitate arms control. The basic reason is obvious: if BMD reduces the Soviet Union's ability to perform necessary strategic missions, then it will simply increase the size and penetrability of its nuclear force in order to restore these capabilities. Moreover, because reducing the size of ballistic missile forces would further reduce Soviet capabilities, it will be harder for the superpowers to limit offensive forces once the U.S. deploys BMD.[27] This counterargument rests on five points.

First, U.S. BMD would not reduce the value the Soviet Union places on being able to perform certain missions with nuclear weapons; rather, BMD might increase the difficulty of performing these missions. Therefore, the utility of nuclear weapons would remain high, and the Soviet Union is likely to react to U.S. BMD by increasing the size and penetrability of its ballistic missile force to defeat the U.S. BMD.

From this perspective, the adversary's BMD actually *increases* the value of ballistic missiles, and other nuclear forces as well—forces that were previously redundant become necessary to perform valued military missions. In other words, contrary to proponents' claims, U.S. BMD increases the marginal value of Soviet warheads. In addition, each superpower is likely to conclude that it should maintain a larger hedge against improvements in the adversary's forces than if neither superpower had deployed BMD. Looking to the future through a conservative planning lens, both superpowers are likely to fear improvements in the other's BMD that leave it at a strategic disadvan-

[26] *New York Times*, 24 March 1983, p. 20. See also Reagan, "The President's Strategic Defense Initiative," p. 6; Gray, "A New Debate on Ballistic Missile Defense," pp. 68–69; Payne and Gray, "Nuclear Policy and the Defensive Transition," p. 839; Keyworth, "The Case for Strategic Defense," pp. 35–44; James C. Fletcher, "The Technologies for Ballistic Missile Defense," *Issues in Science and Technology* (Fall 1984): 28–29; and *Hoffman Report*, p. 11.

[27] See, for example, McGeorge Bundy, George F. Kennan, Robert S. McNamara, and Gerard Smith, "The President's Choice: Star Wars or Arms Control," *Foreign Affairs* 63, no. 2 (Winter 1984–85): 264–78.

tage; if extensive BMD systems are deployed, the superpowers might even become uneasy about their future ability to maintain confidence in their assured destruction capabilities. Reducing the size of ballistic missile forces would make the possibility of improvements in the adversary's defense more threatening; BMD therefore makes negotiated reductions less likely. Consistent with this argument, the Soviets have identified SDI as a key barrier to reaching agreement on reductions in strategic nuclear forces; until 1989 their willingness to proceed was contingent on a U.S. commitment to the ABM Treaty.[28]

Some analysts respond that if both superpowers deploy BMD, then the value of being able to carry out counterforce and countervalue attacks would be reduced. Both superpowers, therefore, would be willing to forgo their ability to perform these missions. For example, if U.S. BMD eliminates the Soviet ability to destroy U.S. forces, then the United States need not be able to destroy Soviet forces; in turn, Soviet defense of its own forces would not threaten a necessary U.S. mission and the United States would be willing to reduce the forces it now deploys to hold Soviet forces at risk.[29] This logic, however, fails to explain superpower behavior heretofore. Presumably, each superpower could reduce the other's counterforce and countervalue requirements by unilaterally reducing the size of its own offensive force, or by negotiating mutual reductions. Thus, if this logic were powerful we should have already witnessed large mutual reductions of the superpowers' offensive forces, going well beyond the roughly 50 percent cuts now being negotiated in START. Yet over twenty years of superpower negotiations have not produced even minor reductions in strategic nuclear offensive forces. Furthermore, although completion of a START agreement now appears likely, it will not reduce either country's countervalue retaliatory capabilities and at least the United States shows little inclination toward moving away from its counterforce doctrine. Why should we expect deployment of BMD to totally reverse the way the superpowers define their security requirements and plan their

[28] Strobe Talbott, "Why START Stopped," *Foreign Affairs* 67, no. 1 (Fall 1988): 53–56; although the Soviets loosened their position on the ABM Treaty as a condition for agreement, they reserved the right to enlarge their force if the United States deploys BMD—see Rubin, "Baker, Shevardnadze Generate Arms Control Progress," p. 26.

[29] D. G. Brennan, applying this logic, argues that BMD could lead to symmetric reductions in the homeland vulnerability of the superpowers; see "Post-Deployment Policy Issues in BMD," in D. G. Brennan and Johan J. Holst, *Ballistic Missile Defence: Two Views*, Adelphi Paper No. 43 (London: IISS, November 1967), p. 9. Arguing in a similar vein, Payne and Gray maintain that the Soviet Union's reluctance to reduce its ICBM force stems in part from its doctrinal requirement for a damage-limitation capability. Currently, ICBMs form the core of this capability, providing an offensive counterforce capability. Therefore, continues the argument, because Soviet strategic defense could substitute for Soviet ICBMs in this damage-limitation role, Soviet deployment of defenses would make the Soviet Union more willing to reduce the size of its offensive force; see "Nuclear Policy and the Defensive Transition," p. 839.

forces? Earlier chapters on mutual near-perfect defense and disarmament explain why this type of cooperation would be quite difficult once the superpowers press near, or below, the edges of MAD.

Second, even if the superpowers followed this unrealistic logic, BMD would not spur the radical reduction of Soviet forces required to protect U.S. society. The BMD proponents' argument holds that the superpowers will give up the capabilities threatened by the adversary's BMD. However, in the coming decades each superpower could deploy a moderately effective BMD at best, leaving its adversary with a redundant assured destruction capability and the ability to destroy a large fraction of its fixed military targets. There would be no more incentive than today to trade away these capabilities that threaten societies.

Third, the cost-exchange argument of proponents of BMD, while not without merit, suffers serious weaknesses. According to this argument, the superpowers should be willing to reduce their countervalue forces, or at least freeze them, if the cost of maintaining an assured destruction capability exceeds the cost of the strategic defense system required to deny this capability. However, in the unlikely event that the United States develops strategic defense technologies that are sufficiently effective to pose some threat to the Soviet assured destruction capability, the cost-exchange ratio is likely to heavily favor Soviet maintenance of its assured destruction capabilities. For one thing, the only concepts proposed for highly effective area defense require expensive boost-phase technologies that still appear susceptible to defeat by relatively inexpensive countermeasures.[30] In addition, defenses become more costly as they are asked to perform more demanding missions since they must be able to defeat the full range of offensive countermeasures, which in turn makes the cost-exchange ratio more favorable to the offense.[31] Furthermore, because each superpower would believe that its fundamental security interests were threatened by the adversary's defense, it would probably be willing to pay a disproportionate sum to defeat it; even if a favorable cost-exchange ratio existed, it would be insufficient to subdue competition between each superpower's countervalue retaliatory capability and the other's damage-limitation capability.[32]

Fourth, the inclination to offset the adversary's BMD would probably be

[30] On the existence of countermeasures see Carter, *Directed Energy Defense in Space*, pp. 45–52, 69–70.

[31] Ibid., pp. 45–46. In addition to technical countermeasures, such as decoys, there are tactical countermeasures. A city defense must engage almost all of the attacking warheads. Thus, unlike a defense of silos, it does not benefit from the leverage provided by preferential defense. In fact, just the opposite applies, since the offense can defeat the defense by concentrating its attack on cities of especially high value; see Carter, "BMD Applications," in Carter and Schwartz, *Ballistic Missile Defense*, p. 170.

[32] For example, Brennan argues that the cost-exchange ratio would probably have to exceed 5 to 1 to dominate U.S. planning; see "Post-Deployment Policy Issues," in Brennan and Holst, *Ballistic Missile Defence: Two Views*, p. 7.

reinforced by military institutions: no organization is likely to concede that its missions that are threatened by the adversary's strategic defense are not vital to the country's security. For example, it is hard to imagine the U.S. Air Force accepting the argument that Soviet BMD was so effective that the United States should no longer maintain the capability to target Soviet forces or that U.S. ICBMs had become virtually worthless and should be retired. Indeed, past Soviet defense deployments have instead motivated American offensive programs: the American MIRV was spurred in part by Soviet BMD, and the current B-1, Stealth, and air-launched cruise missile programs are responding to Soviet air defense deployments.

Finally, and possibly most important, deploying BMD will not facilitate the limitation and reduction of offensive forces if it has a destructive effect on overall superpower relations. If the Soviets understood American deployment of strategic defenses to reflect aggressive intentions, as they almost certainly would, then the superpowers are less likely to be able to achieve offensive limits or any other form of arms control.[33] Disagreement on this point reflects analysts' divergent views of the Soviet Union. Analysts who tend toward a spiral model view of superpower relations believe that competitive U.S. policies reduce the prospects for arms control by making the United States appear more hostile and therefore more dangerous to cooperate with. U.S. deployment of effective area-wide strategic defenses would suggest malign intentions because they pose a potential threat to Soviet deterrent capabilities. From this perspective, strategic defenses are a key component of an offensive American nuclear strategy that will appear more threatening to the Soviet Union than a relatively defensive strategy built on countervalue capabilities. In contrast, other analysts believe that the Soviet Union will cooperate only under pressure from the United States; by helping to convince the Soviets that the United States is determined to protect its interests, American BMD demonstrates the futility of trying to compete with the United States.[34]

In addition to arguing that BMD increases the superpowers' incentives for arms control, proponents also argue that BMD would make possible large reductions in strategic nuclear forces by reducing the difficulty of adequately verifying such an agreement. At force levels much lower than today's, the superpowers would require extremely effective verification capabilities because even small numbers of illegal nuclear weapons could be strategically

---

[33] On Soviet views of American BMD see Bruce Parrott, *The Soviet Union and Ballistic Missile Defense* (Boulder, Colo.: Westview, 1987), and Benjamin S. Lambeth, "Soviet Perspectives on the SDI," in Samuel F. Wells, Jr., and Robert S. Litwak, *Strategic Defenses and Soviet-American Relations* (Cambridge, Mass.: Ballinger, 1987).

[34] Both groups of analysts, however, could accept that U.S. BMD has tactical value as a bargaining chip in arms control negotiations. Nevertheless, they tend to disagree over the prospects for success, with the former worrying that the negative political effects could more than offset the additional bargaining leverage.

significant. BMD reduces the danger of cheating and breakout at these low levels by reducing the importance of an advantage in the number of weapons. Thus, BMD could increase U.S. confidence in its ability to detect significant violations by raising the level at which cheating becomes militarily significant. Therefore, continues this argument, BMD would allow the United States to relax its verification requirements for agreements that radically reduce the size of strategic nuclear forces.[35]

This argument, however, does not support deployment of BMD in the near future. Although often identified as the key barriers, adequate verification and protection against breakout are not the most serious impediments to successful negotiation of reductions on the scale now under consideration.[36] Moreover, for the reasons discussed above, deployment of BMD will reduce the superpowers' prospects for success in these negotiations. The dangers of Soviet cheating would, however, be far more significant if the superpowers ever negotiate agreements that draw their assured destruction capabilities into question. (However, Chapter Six shows that even in this case strategic defenses might reduce the prospects for agreement.)

Protecting against Accidental, Unauthorized, Nth Country, and Terrorist Attacks

Some BMD proponents focus on the danger posed by certain small nuclear attacks and maintain that BMD could reduce the damage if one of these attacks occurred.[37] The source of these small attacks could be an accidental or unauthorized launch of Soviet missiles, some country other than the Soviet Union (an *n*th country), or a terrorist group.

Clearly, if one of these small ballistic missile attacks occurs, the United States would be better off with a ballistic missile defense that can reduce the damage than without one. BMD would be especially valuable if these attacks could precipitate a large superpower nuclear war.[38] The importance of this

[35] See, for example, Payne and Gray, "Nuclear Policy and the Defensive Transition," p. 838. For a related argument see Fred Hoffman, "The SDI in U.S. Nuclear Strategy," *International Security* 10, no. 1 (Summer 1985): 23.

[36] On this issue see Steven Edward Miller, "The Limits of Mutual Restraint: Arms Control and the Strategic Balance" (Ph.D. diss., Fletcher School of Law and Diplomacy, 1988).

[37] See, for example, Reagan, "The President's Strategic Defense Initiative," p. 4; Fletcher, "The Technologies for Ballistic Missile Defense," pp. 26–27; Keyworth, "The Case for Strategic Defense," pp. 41–42; and Payne and Gray, "Nuclear Policy and the Defensive Transition," p. 825. Senator Sam Nunn, "Arms Control in the Last Year of the Reagan Administration," *Arms Control Today* 18, no. 2 (March 1988): 7, recommends exploration of this possibility.

[38] Richard K. Betts, "Heavenly Gains or Earthly Losses? Toward a Balance Sheet for Strategic Defense," in Harold Brown, ed., *The Strategic Defense Initiative: Shield or Snare?* (Boulder, Colo.: Westview Press, 1987), pp. 256, 261, argues that a defense of Washington, D.C., would reduce the probability that an accidental launch would lead to all-out war and that such a defense would be a good investment.

argument, however, also depends upon the likelihood of such attacks and the availability of approaches for making them less likely. As with all nuclear attack scenarios, estimating probabilities of occurrence, even relative probabilities, is highly speculative. Nevertheless, the probability of an accidental or unauthorized Soviet ballistic missile attack, at least during normal peacetime conditions, is generally believed to be quite small.[39] The probability would increase during severe crises, however. Approaches available to the United States for reducing, although not eliminating, this danger include unilateral restraint in counterforce systems that pose the greatest threat to Soviet retaliatory capabilities,[40] arms control agreements that improve superpower communications and reduce the probability of false alarms, and cooperation with the Soviets that might improve their command and control capabilities.[41]

The probability of nth country attacks depends on the number of countries that threaten the United States with nuclear weapons carried on ballistic missiles. Referring to this as the nth country problem suggests there will be many countries that might launch small ballistic missile attacks against the United States. In fact, of the countries that now have this capability—the Soviet Union, China, France, and the United Kingdom—only the Soviet Union is not a U.S. ally. During the late 1960s the possibility of a Chinese ballistic missile capability was presented as the principal reason for deploying a light area defense.[42] That capability has developed more slowly than was anticipated at the time and the Chinese have now deployed only a few ICBMs.[43] More importantly, U.S.-Chinese relations have improved significantly. Furthermore, few additional countries are likely to acquire the capability to attack the United States with nuclear weapons delivered by ballistic missiles in the near future. In addition to acquiring nuclear weapons, they face the difficult task of building long-range ballistic missiles. Although more developing countries are acquiring ballistic missiles, none is likely to produce an intercontinental missile before the end of the century.[44] The United States might reduce the future size

[39] See, for example, Paul Bracken, "Accidental Nuclear War," in Graham T. Allison, Albert Carnesale, and Joseph S. Nye, Jr., eds., *Hawks, Doves and Owls: An Agenda for Avoiding Nuclear War* (New York: W. W. Norton, 1985), pp. 25–53. On Soviet efforts to avoid accidental and unauthorized launches see Stephen M. Meyer, "Soviet Perspectives on the Paths to Nuclear War," in ibid., pp. 187–92, and "Soviet Nuclear Operations," in Carter, Steinbruner, and Zraket, *Managing Nuclear Operations*, pp. 487–93.

[40] Chapter Seven discusses how counterforce might increase this danger.

[41] On the latter possibilities see Sagan, *Moving Targets*, pp. 149–64, 173–74.

[42] A persuasive argument against deploying BMD in response to the Chinese threat was made by Allen S. Whiting, "The Chinese Nuclear Threat," in Chayes and Wiesner, *ABM*, pp. 160–70. The opposing argument was made by Frank E. Armbruster, "The Problem of China," in Holst and Schneider, *Why ABM?* pp. 221–34.

[43] International Institute for Strategic Studies, *The Military Balance 1989–1990* (London: IISS, 1989), p. 146.

[44] International Institute for Strategic Studies, "Missile Proliferation in the Third World," in

of *n*th country and terrorist threats by giving higher priority to slowing the proliferation of nuclear weapons and ballistic missiles.[45]

Possibly most important in terms of this argument, BMD could not prevent a determined adversary from attacking the United States with nuclear weapons by some other means of delivery. The country or terrorist group could deliver nuclear weapons by aircraft, ship, and a variety of clandestine means much more easily than by building intercontinental missiles. In addition, although the proliferation of nuclear weapons and advanced means of delivery does increase somewhat the threat of nuclear attack against the United States, the U.S. ability to retaliate should be sufficient to deter most countries—especially since most would presumably lack a second-strike capability and would thus stand at America's mercy after they attacked.

This discussion does not, of course, prove that accidental or *n*th country ballistic missile attack is impossible, nor that a light BMD would be of no value. It does, however, suggest that these attacks are highly unlikely and that BMD is unlikely to make a significant difference in preventing *n*th countries from delivering nuclear weapons to U.S. cities if they want to.

Acquiring the Political and Economic Benefits of U.S. Technical Superiority

Some proponents believe that even if BMD cannot meet its military objectives it can contribute more broadly to U.S. strategy. For example, Colin Gray identifies the economic benefits of competing with the Soviets in ballistic missile defense: "If, as seems unavoidable, the United States must sustain military competition with the Soviet Union for many decades to come—since the political fuel for the competition cannot be cut off—it is cost effective to compete most vigorously in those areas wherein the structural basis for an enduring lead is present, and with regard to which the Soviet Union, for excellent reasons, harbors the deepest of anxieties."[46]

In light of the preceding analysis, which suggests that the benefits of less-than-near-perfect BMD are quite small, this argument may reflect a key un-

Strategic Survey (London: IISS, 1988–1989), pp. 14–25; Aaron Karp, "Ballistic Missiles in the Third World," *International Security* 9, no. 3 (Winter 1984–85): 166–95.

[45] As a first step, in 1987 seven countries agreed to restrict the export of technologies useful for building ballistic missiles. See "Missile Proliferation in the Third World," pp. 21–23, and Janne E. Nolan, "Ballistic Missiles in the Third World—The Limits of Nonproliferation," *Arms Control Today* 19, no. 9 (November 1989): 9–14.

[46] Colin S. Gray in Carter and Schwartz, eds., *Ballistic Missile Defense*, p. 407. For a similar view see Richard N. Perle, Senate Armed Services Committee, *Department of Defense Authorization for Appropriations for Fiscal Year 1987*, pt. 4, 99th Cong., 2d sess. (1986), p. 1634, who holds: "So, it seems to us that to compete with the Soviet Union in the production and deployment of offensive missiles is tantamount to playing on their field; to play where they are strong. In contrast, the introduction of defenses that would offset the Soviet offensive deployment gives an opportunity to exploit our strength."

derlying source of disagreement on BMD policy. From this perspective, the BMD debate becomes a proxy for answers to questions like: Is intense military competition a necessary and/or desirable extension of ongoing political competition? Would U.S. security be increased by a competition that threatens the Soviet Union with the specter of technological, if not strategic, inferiority? Should the United States use military competition to drain the inferior Soviet economy, thereby weakening the Soviet Union overall?

BMD then is part of a general national security debate that, with some danger of oversimplification, can be characterized as occurring between analysts who stress the existence of common U.S. and Soviet interests and analysts who emphasize the existence of conflict and competition. In other words, once again, analysts' policy preferences reflect beliefs about the nature of the Soviet Union and, more broadly, assessments of how to balance the guidance that the spiral and deterrence models offer for U.S. policy. It is useful to make explicit the potential role of BMD in this debate.

First, even if military competition between the United States and the Soviet Union will continue for the foreseeable future, the United States has some control over its intensity. Deploying BMD will almost certainly increase the competition: American deployment of BMD would increase Soviet leaders' doubts about the adequacy of their deterrent capabilities and Soviet BMD will generate similar fears in the United States, assuming they match U.S. deployments. As a result, there will be heightened pressure to increase the size of retaliatory forces and a new, full-fledged competition in defenses would probably be set in motion.[47] Thus, analysts who believe competition increases U.S. security could favor BMD even if it could not perform important military missions. Alternatively, the United States could choose to moderate the military competition by maintaining only its retaliatory capabilities, forgoing systems that threaten Soviet retaliatory capabilities, including BMD with some potential to protect large areas. Such a policy promises to maintain necessary U.S. military capabilities (at least as required by the punitive retaliation school) while making it less likely that the Soviet Union will see U.S. programs reflecting hostile intentions. This latter option essentially eliminates the security dilemma and is therefore attractive to analysts who believe that superpower relations are plagued by the dangers that the spiral model describes.

Advocates of BMD often disagree with the above arms race prediction, pointing to the buildup of strategic nuclear forces since the signing of the ABM Treaty to support their case. Their argument, however, which compares the arms buildup we have experienced to no buildup, is misleading. The correct comparison is between the buildup we have experienced and the one we

---

[47] On Soviet responses see Stephen M. Meyer, "Soviet Strategic Programmes and the U.S. SDI," *Survival* (November/December 1985): 274–92; and note 77 in Chapter Seven.

would have experienced had there been no ABM Treaty (and had extensive BMD been deployed).

Second, a competition in BMD combined with an increased competition in the offensive forces that the BMD challenged would greatly increase the economic cost of strategic nuclear forces to both the United States and the Soviet Union. Since this competition would not significantly increase U.S. security, it could be "cost effective" only in the sense that it places more of a strain on the Soviet economy than on the U.S. economy.[48]

Third, the use of BMD to achieve military advantages is incompatible with the achievement of arms control agreements—the Soviet Union is quite unlikely to accept highly inequitable agreements that jeopardize its necessary military capabilities. Analysts cannot argue consistently that BMD is a means of achieving both objectives.

In short, there is virtually no doubt that BMD would increase the intensity of nuclear weapons competition and exacerbate superpower tensions. Thus, it is clear that disagreements about the role of competition and cooperation in improving U.S. security result in divergent conclusions about the deployment of BMD. Analysts who believe that intensified superpower competition and initiatives to weaken or intimidate the Soviet Union are in the U.S. interest will tend to favor deployment of BMD, and vice versa.

THE COSTS OF DEPLOYING BMD

The strategic, political, and economic costs of deploying BMD would depend on the missions the United States designs its BMD system to perform. The ABM Treaty now severely restricts the BMD deployments of both superpowers. BMD systems permitted by the ABM Treaty could provide some protection against a small subset of accidental, unauthorized, and nth country attacks.[49] Systems deployed to perform other missions, or to provide more effective protection against an accidental launch, would require more exten-

---

[48] This argument assumes the Soviets would follow the United States in deploying BMD. It is interesting to note, however, that if the Soviet Union responds by increasing and improving only its offensive force, it would probably cost far less to offset the U.S. BMD than it cost the United States to build it, i.e., the cost-exchange ratio is likely to heavily favor the Soviet response. In this case, which is a possibility stressed in Gorbachev's "new thinking," the U.S. deployment of BMD would move the arms competition into an area of U.S. disadvantage—its security would not be increased and its economy would be drained more than the Soviet Union's. On arguments for these asymmetric responses see the preceding note.

[49] Anthony Fainberg, "Limited Missile Defenses—What Can They Protect?" *Arms Control Today* 19, no. 3 (April 1989): 17–22, which draws heavily on Office of Technology Assessment Staff Paper, *A Treaty-Compliant Launch Protection System* (1988); Ted H. Postal, "The Implications of Accidental Launch Protection Systems for U.S. Security," *Hearing before the Panel on the Strategic Defense Initiative of the House Committee on Armed Services* 100th Cong., 2d sess. (1988). On whether proposed systems would comply with the ABM Treaty see Congressional Budget Office, *Strategic Defenses*, pp. 31–32.

sive U.S. deployment of BMD. They can be obtained only by amending or terminating the treaty, thereby allowing Soviet deployment. Switching from a world in which neither superpower has extensive BMD to one in which both do would have significant costs for the United States. Deploying BMD allowed by the ABM Treaty could avoid many of these costs.

The costs of extensive BMD deployments depend on whether the ABM Treaty is amended or terminated. The vulnerability of ICBMs has created interest in amending the treaty to allow defense only of ICBMs. Such a treaty would, in theory, continue to restrict the most important potential threat to U.S. capabilities from Soviet BMD—reduction of the U.S. ability to retaliate against Soviet value targets, including cities and economic and industrial capabilities. Therefore, the costs of amending the treaty are smaller than for terminating it because the strategic capability of Soviet BMD would continue to be constrained. In practice, however, such an amendment is likely to represent a large step toward termination of the treaty. First, U.S. attempts to amend the treaty might be unsuccessful, with one possible outcome being the total loss of constraints on BMD. For example, having committed itself to an amendment allowing deployment of ICBM defenses, the United States might, following unsuccessful renegotiation, choose to withdraw from the treaty altogether instead of allowing the Soviet Union to block its deployment of BMD. Negotiating an amendment that allows defense only of ICBMs promises to be especially difficult because the Soviet Union is likely to be more interested in protecting leadership, command and control, other military targets, and economic targets than in protecting ICBMs.[50]

Second, Soviet systems ostensibly deployed to protect ICBM silos might provide some protection for other targets as well. Even if the actual area defense capabilities of these systems were small, U.S. analysts and targeting staff would tend to give them the benefit of the doubt, creating fears about whether the amended treaty serves U.S. interests and spurring moves toward complete termination of the treaty. Finally, extensive Soviet deployment of BMD would increase concern that the Soviet Union could gain a strategic advantage through breakout. Concern about Soviet breakout potential has been an important factor in recent reassessments of U.S. strategic defense policy.[51] These concerns would only be increased by ICBM defenses that provide a base for a nationwide defense. Moreover, amendments to the treaty that allowed still more extensive deployment (e.g., defense of C^3 and ICBMs, or a thin area defense) would suffer even more severely from these problems. In short, amending the ABM Treaty is likely to hasten its termination.

Expanded Soviet deployments of BMD allowed following the amendment

---

[50] On Soviet BMD programs see Sayre Stevens, "The Soviet BMD Program," in Carter and Schwartz, *Ballistic Missile Defense*, pp. 182–220.

[51] See, for example, Perle, *Department of Defense Authorization for Appropriations for Fiscal Year 1987*, pp. 1634–35.

or termination of the ABM Treaty would reduce the ability of current U.S. reentry vehicles to penetrate to their targets. However, strategic defenses available in the foreseeable future could not deny the United States the ability to perform its key deterrent missions. Most importantly, the Soviet Union would remain unable to protect its cities and industry. The United States now has a large survivable force, only a small fraction of which must penetrate Soviet defenses to destroy a large fraction of Soviet value targets. The Soviet Union, like the United States, will be unable to deploy anything approaching the necessarily near-perfect strategic defense in the foreseeable future. Moreover, to eliminate any possible reduction in its ability to retaliate, the United States could, and almost certainly would, increase the number and penetrability of its ballistic missiles and continue to maintain bombers and cruise missiles to penetrate Soviet air defenses. If necessary it could also increase the survivability of its ICBMs with BMD or by other means.

By maintaining an unquestionable ability to retaliate massively against cities and other targets of value, the United States could insure a high degree of crisis stability: the Soviet Union would be unable to reduce significantly the costs of a U.S. attack, so striking first and incurring U.S. retaliation would be essentially as bad as being attacked first.[52]

---

[52] For a similar conclusion on crisis stability see George Rathjens and Jack Ruina, ''BMD and Strategic Stability,'' *Daedalus* 114, no. 3 (Summer 1985): 241–42. My argument here differs from that of opponents of BMD who argue that mutual deployment of BMD will undermine the United States' deterrent capabilities and reduce crisis stability. In fact, at least to first order, it appears inconsistent to argue both that retaliatory capabilities will prevail in a competition between countervalue retaliatory capabilities and damage-limitation capabilities, and that the superpowers' deployment of BMD would have these negative effects. It is possible, however, to make such an argument by including what might be considered second-order considerations. For example, one could argue that uncertainties and/or misperceptions created by BMD could increase the probability that a risk-taking decisionmaker would launch a preemptive attack in a severe crisis. However, while this argument has merit, it might not apply if the superpowers reacted to each other's defenses with retaliatory forces that offset not only the most probable performance of the defense but also worst-case estimates that far exceed the most likely estimate. In this case, which is the one BMD opponents use to predict an endless expansion of offensive forces, the uncertainties about damage-limitation capabilities created by BMD would be quite small, especially when compared to the uncertainties that already exist. This conclusion is reinforced by the fact that defending forces is less demanding than defending cities. Thus, mutual deployment of BMD might actually increase both countries' ability to retaliate against cities and industrial capabilities, tending to increase crisis stability. This is one reason why mutual deployment of BMD is less likely to result in dangerous misperceptions of damage-limitation capabilities than is mutual deployment of offensive counterforce systems.

If defenses in combination with offensive counterforce ever begin to provide a significant damage-limitation capability, then crisis stability would be reduced. Working against crisis stability is the fact that BMD would be more effective against a ragged retaliatory attack, one not optimized to defeat the defense, and against a smaller retaliatory attack than a larger first strike. Even then, however, the decrease in crisis stability might not be large since such highly effective defenses would greatly increase the survivability of retaliatory forces.

Furthermore, whether Soviet BMD could protect military targets would depend upon the value the United States places on being able to destroy them. Soviet BMD could make the total price of attacking large target sets, for example ICBMs and other military targets, quite high. However, an expanded and improved U.S. ballistic missile force would probably be able to offset the Soviet BMD. The question, then, is would the United States be willing to pay potentially vast sums to maintain its full menu of retaliatory options against Soviet strategic forces and other military targets? There is substantial disagreement about the American need for such a capability. Ironically, many advocates of deploying BMD to strengthen deterrence believe that counter-military retaliation is important for deterrence, especially extended deterrence; they are likely to see Soviet defense of military targets as more threatening than do opponents of BMD. In particular, members of the military denial and damage-limitation schools are more likely to find Soviet BMD threatening than are members of the punitive retaliation school. The former analysts, because they find post-exchange ratios strategically significant and/or because they believe the United States must hold at risk Soviet political and military control targets and military forces, will tend to find that Soviet BMD threatens necessary U.S. capabilities.

A large expansion of Soviet BMD deployments might reduce significantly the threat posed by the French, British, and Chinese nuclear forces. Most analysts believe these independent nuclear forces increase U.S. security and therefore would consider this effect of Soviet BMD to be negative. In addition, because their nuclear capabilities would be threatened by amendment or termination of the ABM Treaty, efforts by the United States to change the treaty would probably strain U.S. relations with these allies.

While the United States would be able to maintain its deterrent capabilities, the political costs of this offense-defense competition could be large. Soviet area-wide BMD will appear threatening to the United States, and vice versa. Many American analysts would see Soviet BMD reflecting aggressive intentions, reinforcing conclusions based on their understanding of the current Soviet threat to U.S. strategic nuclear forces. Analysts would probably see deployment and improvement of Soviet BMD as attempts to gain a strategic advantage, undermine U.S. deterrent capabilities, and, in the long run, disarm the United States. Soviet defenses would raise U.S. force requirements, making agreements to limit offensive forces harder to achieve than today and making U.S. security seem harder to maintain. Uncertainties about the effectiveness of Soviet defenses would continue to drive U.S. force requirements upward. The natural tendency of U.S. force planners to assume the best about Soviet defenses and the worst about their own could generate unending fears that both U.S. ballistic missile forces and BMD were inadequate. U.S. deployment of an extensive BMD system would generate similar reactions in the Soviet Union. In this environment of increased mutual fear and hostility the superpowers would be more likely to overlook their common interests and to see only hostility in each other's actions. The result could well be a reduction in their ability to avoid and manage crises.

Once again, this interpretation rests on what is essentially a spiral model view of the consequences of increased military competition. As noted above, analysts who are inclined to believe that the Soviet Union harbors aggressive intentions reach a different conclusion based upon the deterrence model. Especially if they believe that the Soviet Union recognizes that the United States is not a threat to Soviet interests, these analysts believe the United States is safer competing than cooperating.

The economic costs of deploying BMD would depend on a variety of factors, including the objectives of the U.S. BMD, the BMD technologies that would be deployed, and the size and penetrability of the Soviet offense. Any militarily significant BMD will cost tens of billions of dollars.[53] No one knows how much a highly effective multilayer BMD including boost-phase intercept (if ever developed) would cost; rough estimates range from $500 billion to $1 trillion.[54] Whatever the goal of the BMD system, the ultimate cost of deploying BMD would be far greater that the cost of the initial BMD system. The United States would have to improve its BMD to offset changes in the Soviet ballistic missile force. In addition, there would be the cost of improving and/or expanding the U.S. offensive force to offset Soviet BMD. Moreover, certain strategic defense goals (e.g., defeating small Soviet attacks) require the United States to deploy expensive air defenses against Soviet bombers and cruise missiles.[55]

[53] Congressional Budget Office, *Strategic Defenses*, pp. 39–42, estimates that BMD to defend 527 ICBMs against Soviet forces constrained by a START agreement would cost approximately $19 billion (in FY 1990 dollars). The ten-year life cycle costs of this system would be $35 billion, which is comparable to the cost of mobile ICBMs that would provide a similar number of surviving warheads. The study notes, however, that there would be greater uncertainty about the ability of the BMD system to perform its mission as projected than about the ability of mobile ICBMs to survive (pp. 45–46, 51–52). A BMD system designed to protect deceptively based missiles might cost less, largely because it takes advantage of the investment in the basing mode. The Army projected that its Low-Altitude Defense System (LoADS), designed to defend 200 MX missiles based in 4,600 multiple protective shelters (MPS), would cost $8.6 billion in 1980 dollars, not including the cost of various necessary support systems; see Office of Technology Assessment, *MX Missile Basing*, p. 125. Defense of ICBMs is discussed in detail in Carter, "BMD Applications," in Carter and Schwartz, *Ballistic Missile Defense*, pp. 122–46. Estimated costs of a treaty-compliant accidental launch protection system are $10-$16 billion; see Fainberg, "Limited Missile Defense," p. 17, and Congressional Budget Office, *Strategic Defenses*, p. 35.

[54] See, for example, R. Jeffrey Smith, "Schlesinger Attacks Star Wars Plan," *Science* (November 9, 1984): 673, and Barry M. Blechman and Victor A. Utgoff, "The Macroeconomics of Strategic Defenses," *International Security* 11, no. 3 (Winter 1986–87): 33–70.

[55] Betts, "Heavenly Gains or Earthly Losses?" argues that there are large opportunity costs in investing in BMD. The United States is likely to pay for BMD by reducing its investment in other forces, conventional forces in particular. The net result then could be a weakening of extended deterrence and an overall reduction in U.S. security.

CONCLUSION

This analysis finds that the deployment of less-than-near-perfect defenses would provide, at most, small benefits for concerns of second- or third-order importance; deterrence would not be strengthened significantly. This conclusion is based largely on the arguments presented by the punitive retaliation school: because the U.S. strategic nuclear deterrent is already highly effective, BMD could add little to deterrence. In contrast, members of the military denial school find greater need for strengthening U.S. strategic forces, and some believe BMD is the preferred means.[56] By comparison, the costs of deploying BMD would be large: U.S. offensive force requirements would increase, U.S.-Soviet competition would intensify, serious arms control efforts would probably disappear, and the economic costs of strategic nuclear forces could increase immensely. Based on the dangers identified by the spiral model, this competition could damage superpower relations and increase the probability of conflict.

The possible exception is a BMD system that could provide protection against accidental, unauthorized, and nth country attacks. If permitted by the ABM Treaty and clearly not the first step toward an extensive U.S. deployment, such a system could avoid the most important costs. Even in this case, however, the benefits might not exceed the costs.

Even granting this possible exception, this analysis undermines the argument for an evolutionary deployment of BMD that hinges on the belief that less-than-near-perfect defenses would provide net benefits at each stage of deployment. My analysis reaches the opposite conclusion: large-scale U.S. deployment of the ballistic missile defense that might be available in the foreseeable future, assuming the Soviet Union also deployed BMD, would reduce U.S. security. Thus, an evolutionary strategy might be defended only with the hope that perfect or near-perfect defenses will someday be developed.[57]

This argument, however, fails on two grounds. First, as discussed in detail in Chapters Four and Five, the United States is probably safer in MAD than it would be in these alternative worlds. Thus, even if dramatic improvements in U.S. strategic defenses were likely to occur eventually, this possibility would not justify the deployment of less-than-near-perfect defenses today. Second,

[56] Having identified Harold Brown as a key member of the military denial school, I should add that he has not supported near-term deployment of BMD. See Harold Brown, "The Strategic Defense Initiative: Defensive Systems and the Strategic Debate," *Survival* 27, no. 2 (March/April 1985): 55–64, and idem, "Too Much, Too Soon," *Arms Control Today* 17, no. 4 (May 1987): 2–3.

[57] This point is slightly overstated since the evolutionary strategy might also promise to reduce the damage of an all-out war in MAD by eventually providing strategic defenses that, although not near-perfect, could provide some protection to U.S. society. Chapter Seven, however, concludes that in MAD U.S. security would be decreased by policies that combine strategic defense and offensive counterforce to reduce damage at the margin.

even for analysts who disagree with my judgment of these alternative worlds, the extremely low probability that such effective strategic defenses will ever be developed and deployed should be sufficient to reject the evolutionary deployment strategy.

Because extensive deployment of less-than-near-perfect BMD is not in its interest, the United States should give priority to preserving the ABM Treaty. Most important is for the United States to redirect and scale back the Strategic Defense Initiative. Development and testing now planned in SDI will strain the limits of the treaty, and the BMD deployments envisioned by SDI will require its termination. In addition, the United States should reestablish its commitment to the ABM Treaty and pursue measures to strengthen it.

In effect, the United States should completely reverse the policies that the Reagan administration set in motion. Although stressing that SDI was only a research program and was therefore permitted by the ABM Treaty, the Reagan administration appeared interested in undermining the treaty: the magnitude of the planned U.S. R&D effort, the interest of at least some members of the Reagan administration in early deployment of BMD,[58] and the administration's promotion of the "new interpretation"—which allowed for development and testing that was banned by the traditional interpretation[59]—all lent support to this conclusion.

Somewhat ironically, the United States should continue research and development of BMD as permitted by the ABM Treaty in order to reduce the potential benefits to the Soviet Union of withdrawing from the treaty.[60] However, such a policy designed to deter Soviet deployment of BMD requires a careful balancing of conflicting pressures. Pursuit of BMD activities allowed by the treaty could have two negative effects. First, U.S. R&D could provide support in the Soviet Union for increased BMD R&D. This would be counterproductive if the net effect was to increase pressure in the Soviet Union to amend or withdraw from the treaty. Second, the larger the U.S. R&D effort, the stronger the domestic pressure to loosen the treaty constraints: larger budgets will increase the influence of those responsible for BMD, and successful R&D will create pressures for deployment. The momentum of R&D could threaten the objective it was initiated to achieve.

[58] On interest in and plans for early deployment see John H. Cushman, Jr., "Preliminary Tests Gain Approval in 'Star Wars,' " *New York Times*, 19 September 1987, p. 5, and John Gardner et al., *Missile Defense in the 1990s*, 2d ed. (Washington, D.C.: George C. Marshall Institute, 1987). Criticizing plans for early deployment is Matthew Bunn, "Deploying a Disaster," *Arms Control Today* (March 1987): 21–24.

[59] For review and analysis of this issue see Duffy, *Compliance and the Future of Arms Control*, pp. 120–24, and Alan B. Sherr, "Sound Legal Reasoning or Policy Expedient? The 'New Interpretation' of the ABM Treaty," *International Security* 11, no. 3 (Winter 1986–87): 71–93.

[60] On possible approaches see Congressional Budget Office, *Strategic Defenses*, pp. 19–30, and Center for International Security and Arms Control, *Strategic Missile Defense: Necessities, Prospects, and Dangers in the Near Term* (Stanford, Calif.: Stanford University, 1985).

To avoid undermining the ABM Treaty, the United States should be absolutely clear about its reasons for pursuing R&D: (1) to deter Soviet withdrawal from the treaty; and (2) to hedge against Soviet breakout from the treaty. To make these rationales for pursuing R&D convincing, both to the Soviet Union and domestic constituencies, the United States should pursue policies that clearly indicate its long-term interest in avoiding extensive BMD deployments by either superpower. To begin with, U.S. leaders should clearly reject claims that highly effective BMD may provide substantial security benefits in the future. In addition, we should recognize that there are significant advantages to pursuing R&D at less than the fastest possible rate since this will reduce any negative effects of R&D. The "best" rate requires a balance between keeping reasonable pace with the Soviet Union and controlling the pressures stimulated by R&D for amendment of the ABM Treaty. The United States should give priority to developing countermeasures to Soviet BMD since they might provide a cheap means of insuring that the Soviets have no incentive for breaking out from the treaty,[61] while at the same time not misleading them about the U.S. commitment to it.

R&D that approaches the constraints imposed by the ABM Treaty should be understood to have served its purpose: the Soviet Union would no longer be able to achieve an advantage in this area of BMD technology. The treaty should not be amended to allow R&D to continue since this would be unnecessary to achieve either of the objectives stated above. Analysts hoping to escape MAD, including some who oppose the current SDI, may find this advice difficult to swallow. These analysts should reconsider the dangers of BAD and U.S. superiority before supporting treaty amendments that will increase superpower competition with little hope of increasing U.S. capabilities.

Beyond these changes in its current policy, the United States should also explore ways to strengthen the ABM Treaty. First, the United States should pursue initiatives to clarify the limits imposed by the treaty. Most basic, it should confirm its intention to abide by the traditional/narrow interpretation of the treaty. In addition, because certain treaty constraints are open to conflicting interpretations, the United States and the Soviet Union should, in the Standing Consultative Commission,[62] try to develop a shared understanding of the treaty's boundaries. Where permitted research ends and prohibited development begins is not absolutely clear; whether certain technologies are components of an ABM system, and therefore banned, or are something less than components, and therefore allowed, can be even less clear. The United

---

[61] Congressional Budget Office, *Strategic Defenses*, pp. 20–21.

[62] The SCC was established by Article XII of the ABM Treaty. It provides a forum to consider: "questions concerning compliance"; "possible proposals for further increasing the viability of this Treaty, including proposals for amendments"; "proposals for further measures aimed at limiting strategic arms"; and other issues related to compliance with and implementation of the treaty.

States and the Soviet Union are likely to undermine the treaty if they press the limits of possible interpretations.[63] Working through these issues will require that each superpower believes the other is interested in preserving the treaty. Changes in current U.S. policy are therefore a prerequisite for strengthening the treaty.

Second, the ABM Treaty is threatened by potentially dual-capable weapons, including anti-tactical ballistic missiles, surface-to-air missiles, and antisatellite weapons, that are not banned and could reduce its effectiveness. The ABM Treaty covers only strategic ballistic missiles and therefore does not ban anti-tactical ballistic missiles (ATBMs). ATBMs could, however, contribute to the unraveling of the ABM Treaty. Drawing a precise line between ABMs and ATBMs is necessarily difficult: certain strategic weapons, for example, short-range SLBMs, have trajectories similar to long-range tactical ballistic missiles. An extensive ATBM deployment would have some capability against strategic offensive systems and would be certain to create fears that its ABM capability could be upgraded.[64] In addition, there is an important asymmetry: Soviet ATBMs can be deployed on Soviet territory. Because, by definition, the U.S. homeland is beyond the reach of tactical missiles, U.S. deployment of ATBMs on its territory would violate the ABM Treaty. This asymmetry is reinforced by the INF Treaty, which bans Soviet long-range theater nuclear missiles, thereby eliminating NATO's need for ATBMs against these nuclear threats, but does not restrict British, French, and Chinese missiles. The combination of this asymmetry with the ATBM's ability to intercept certain strategic missiles could place the United States in a situation where the Soviet Union appears to have an extensive ABM capability and the United States has none. A ban on ATBMs would close this loophole in the ABM Treaty.[65]

[63] These and other legal issues are discussed in Abram Chayes, Antonia Chayes, and Eliot Spitzer, "Space Weapons: The Legal Context," *Daedalus* 114, no. 3 (Summer 1985): 193–218, and Alan B. Sherr, *Legal Issues of the "Star Wars" Defense Program* (Boston: Lawyers Alliance for Nuclear Arms Control, 1984). On approaches for clarifying the treaty limits and securing it against weaknesses discussed below see Antonia Chayes and Paul Doty, eds., *Defending Deterrence: Managing the ABM Treaty into the 21st Century* (New York: Pergamon-Brassey, 1989), and Herb Lin, *New Weapons Technology and the ABM Treaty* (New York: Pergamon Brassey, 1988).

[64] Stephen Weiner, "Systems and Technology," in Carter and Schwartz, *Ballistic Missile Defense*, p. 73. On the technical and political issues surrounding ATBMs see Donald L. Hafner and John Roper, eds., *ATBMs and Western Security* (Cambridge, Mass.: Ballinger, 1988). The relationship between ABM and ATBM is cast in a positive light by the *Hoffman Report*, p. 3, which states that "the advanced components, though developed initially in an ATM mode, might later play a role in continental United States (CONUS) defense."

[65] Analysis of whether the net benefit of mutual deployment of ATBMs exceeds the risk that such deployment poses to the ABM Treaty is beyond the scope of this chapter. Potential benefits of NATO deployment of ATBMs are discussed in the *Hoffman Report*, pp. 3, 10–11; William E. Odom, "The Implications of Active Defense of NATO for Soviet Military Strategy," in Fred S.

There is also substantial overlap between BMD and antisatellite (ASAT) technologies.[66] The point at which an ASAT system qualifies as an ABM system (i.e., is capable of intercepting strategic ballistic missiles in flight trajectory) is unclear. Thus, the potential dual capability of ASAT weapons may provide an opportunity to circumvent the ABM Treaty. Agreement to limit or ban ASAT testing and deployment would reinforce the treaty. Although a complete assessment of ASAT arms control is beyond the scope of this chapter,[67] it is important to note that the BMD issue is of much greater moment than the ASAT issue. This assertion is not intended to minimize the significance of ASATs, but rather to highlight the central importance of strategic defenses. Area defenses could, at least in theory, threaten the adversary's capability to retaliate, which is essential for deterrence. By contrast, satellites provide extensive military support but their role is not entirely irreplaceable.[68] In this sense the BMD and ASAT issues are incommensurate: the importance of the area BMD decision overwhelms the ASAT decision. This weighs heavily in favor of limiting ASAT capabilities.

While this chapter argues against the deployment of BMD and in favor of strengthening the ABM Treaty, the foregoing analysis also suggests a general observation about BMD policy: because almost all American BMD deployment would carry costs, we must address difficult tradeoffs. Arguments in the BMD debate that suggest that deploying BMD brings only benefits are incomplete. Analyses of the benefits of defending U.S. targets tell only part of the story and will almost always favor deploying BMD. At one extreme, making the United States invulnerable to Soviet attack has undeniable appeal, but is an unrealistic objective and only distorts U.S. defense policy. U.S. security requires complete analysis of the more realistic limited BMD options. Such analysis, however, will direct the United States away from BMD and toward policies to maintain and strengthen the ABM Treaty.

Hoffman, Albert Wohlstetter, and David S. Yost, *Swords and Shields* (Lexington, Mass.: Lexington Books, 1987), pp. 159–74; Hafner and Roper, eds., *ATBMs and Western Security*; and Manfred Worner, "A Missile Defense for NATO Europe," *Strategic Review* (Winter 1986): 13–20.

[66] See Ashton B. Carter, "The Relationship between ASAT and BMD Systems," *Daedalus* 114, no. 2 (Spring 1985): 171–89.

[67] Arguing that ASAT arms control is not in the overall interest of the United States is President Reagan, *Report to the Congress on U.S. Policy on ASAT Arms Control* (Washington, D.C., 31 March 1984). Opposing opinions are found in William J. Durch, *Anti-Satellite Weapons, Arms Control Options, and the Military Use of Space* (Report prepared for the U.S. Arms Control and Disarmament Agency, July 1984); Richard L. Garwin, Kurt Gottfried, and Donald L. Hafner, "Antisatellite Weapons," *Scientific American* (June 1984): 45–55; John Pike, "Anti-Satellite Weapons and Arms Control," *Arms Control Today* 13, no. 11 (December 1983): 1, 4–7; and Paul B. Stares, *Space and National Security* (Washington, D.C.: Brookings Institution, 1987), pp. 142–86.

[68] Office of Technology Assessment, *Arms Control in Space: Workshop Proceedings* (Washington, D.C.: GPO, 1984), p. 11.

CHAPTER TEN

What Type of Arms Control in MAD?

ARMS CONTROL does not lack for proposals. Since the signing of SALT II, analysts have suggested a wide variety of competing proposals, including comprehensive freezes on the deployment of strategic nuclear weapons,[1] ceilings on the number of strategic warheads,[2] and reductions in the size of offensive forces.[3]

Missing is a clear picture of *why* the United States should pursue strategic nuclear arms control.[4] Much of the debate focuses on the details of these proposals, for example, where various ceilings will be set and what verification measures will be necessary. Less regularly explored, and more important, are the broad purposes toward which the United States should direct its arms con-

---

[1] Randall Forsberg, "A Bilateral Nuclear-Weapon Freeze," *Scientific American* (November 1982): 2–11; Harold Feiveson and Frank von Hippel, "The Freeze and the Counterforce Race," *Physics Today* (January 1983): 36–49; and Leon V. Segal, "Warming to the Freeze," *Foreign Policy* no. 48 (Fall 1982): 54–65.

[2] Jan M. Lodal, "Finishing Start," *Foreign Policy* no. 48 (Fall 1982): 66–81.

[3] On the Reagan administration START proposals and the current status of the negotiations see Chalmers Hardenbergh, ed., *Arms Control Reporter* (Brookline, Mass.: Institute for Defense and Disarmament Studies), and Walter B. Slocombe, "Force Posture Consequences of the START Treaty," *Survival* (September/October 1988). On the proposals discussed at the Reykavik mini-summit see Michael Mandelbaum and Strobe Talbott, "Reykavik and Beyond," *Foreign Affairs* 65, no. 2 (Winter 1986/87): 215–35. Other reductions proposals include: George Kennan, "A Proposal for International Disarmament," speech delivered on accepting the Albert Einstein Peace Prize, May 19, 1981, reprinted in *The Nuclear Delusion* (New York: Pantheon Books, 1983), pp. 175–82; Harold A. Feiveson, Richard H. Ullman, and Frank von Hippel, "Reducing U.S. and Soviet Nuclear Arsenals," in Len Ackland and Steven McGuire, *Assessing the Nuclear Age* (Chicago: Educational Foundation for Nuclear Science, 1986), pp. 311–24; and Richard Garwin, "A Blueprint for Radical Weapons Cuts," *Bulletin of the Atomic Scientists* 44, no. 2 (March 1988): 10–13. "Build-down" proposals, designed to simultaneously reduce force size and increase force survivability, include: Alton Frye, "Strategic Build-Down: A Context for Restraint," *Foreign Affairs* 62, no. 2 (Winter 1983/1984): 292–317, and Glenn A. Kent with Randall J. DeValk and Edward L. Warner, III, *A New Approach to Arms Control* (Santa Monica: Rand, 1984). Alvin M. Weinburg and Jack N. Barkenbus, "Stabilizing Star Wars," *Foreign Policy* no. 54 (Spring 1984), call for reducing offenses and deploying defenses. Michael Krepon, "Assessing Strategic Arms Reduction Proposals," *World Politics* 35, no. 2 (January 1983): 216–44, assesses eight proposed reductions schemes.

[4] Bernard Brodie raised essentially the same criticism more than ten years ago. See his "On the Objectives of Arms Control," *International Security* 1, no. 1 (Summer 1976): 17. Colin S. Gray, "SALT II: The Real Debate," *Policy Review* no. 10 (Fall 1979): 7–22, makes a similar observation from a different perspective. Also relevant is Thomas C. Schelling, "What Went Wrong with Arms Control?" *Foreign Affairs* 64, no. 2 (Winter 1985/86): 219–33.

trol policy. We should first ask: How can this type of cooperation with the Soviet Union increase U.S. security? Only then are we prepared to assess types of proposals. The last step would be working out the details of promising types of proposals.

Like the acquisition of forces, arms control is a means of achieving U.S. national security. Although we often speak of the objectives of arms control, arms control has no fundamental objectives of its own. Writing in the late 1950s and early 1960s, the developers of the modern theory of arms control were quite clear on this point.[5] They spelled out three basic objectives for arms control.[6] The first two, to reduce the probability of war and to reduce the damage if war occurs, are fundamental objectives of U.S. security policy; obviously they should be pursued whether the United States engages in arms control or pursues its security through entirely unilateral means. The third objective of arms control, to reduce the economic costs of military capabilities required to maintain U.S. security, is also an important factor in unilateral U.S. defense planning.[7] Thomas Schelling and Morton Halperin observed that:

---

[5] Key early works include Thomas C. Schelling and Morton H. Halperin, *Strategy and Arms Control* (New York: Twentieth Century Fund, 1961; Pergamon Press, 1985); Hedley Bull, *The Control of the Arms Race: Disarmament and Arms Control in the Missile Age* (New York: Praeger, 1961); Donald G. Brennan, ed., *Arms Control, Disarmament and National Security* (New York: George Braziller, 1961); Arthur T. Hadley, *The Nation's Safety and Arms Control* (New York: Viking Press, 1961); and J. David Singer, *Deterrence, Arms Control, and Disarmament: Toward a Synthesis in National Security Policy* (Columbus: Ohio State University Press, 1962; Lanham, Md.: University Press of America, 1984). Analyzing this literature is Steven E. Miller, "The Limits of Mutual Restraint: Arms Control and the Strategic Balance" (Ph.D. diss., Fletcher School of Law and Diplomacy, 1988).

[6] For a range of current views on these objectives see "Has Arms Control Worked?" *Bulletin of the Atomic Scientists* 45, no. 4 (May 1989): 26–45.

[7] Schelling and Halperin, *Strategy and Arms Control*, p. 2, state the third objective to include the political as well as economic costs of preparing for war. This objective is usually considered more narrowly to include only economic costs. The narrower definition has analytic advantages, since political costs might influence the probability of war.

This chapter does not address the role of arms control in reducing economic costs. Analyzing this potential use of arms control raises some complicated issues, including judgments about the forces the United States and Soviet Union would have deployed if arms control agreements had not been pursued and, related, about whether arms control can enable the United States to adopt a nuclear strategy that requires less costly forces. Relevant discussions include Roger George, "The Economics of Arms Control," *International Security* 3, no. 3 (Winter 1978/1979): 94–125; Congressional Budget Office, *SALT and the U.S. Strategic Forces Budget*, Background Paper No. 8 (Washington, D.C.: GPO, 1976); Brodie, "On the Objectives of Arms Control," p. 19, who concludes that saving money deserves priority among arms control's objectives; Albert Carnesale and Richard N. Haass, "Conclusions: Weighing the Evidence," in Carnesale and Haass, eds., *Superpower Arms Control: Setting the Record Straight* (Cambridge, Mass.: Ballinger, 1987), pp. 342–46; and Steven Alexis Cain, *The START Agreement: Strategic Options and Budgetary Savings* (Washington, D.C.: Defense Budget Project, 1988).

What is striking is not how novel the methods and purposes of arms control are, and how different from the methods and purposes of national military policy; what is striking is how much overlap there is. There is hardly an objective of arms control to be described in this study that is not equally a continuing urgent objective of national military strategy—of our unilateral military plans and policies.[8]

In general, therefore, arms control and force deployments are best thought of as alternative but complementary means of achieving the same objectives. The question we need to answer is: Given current superpower nuclear forces and expectations about future forces, how can arms control help the United States achieve these objectives?

Also generally missing in the arms control debate are assessments of the feasibility of competing proposals. By overlooking feasibility, the United States may pursue proposals that have a relatively low probability of success while forgoing attractive proposals more likely to lead to agreement. Lacking a clear picture of both the benefits and the feasibility of competing proposals, the United States has failed to establish priorities among its arms control options.

This chapter systematically analyzes the role of arms control in U.S. security policy. The first section considers the benefits that arms control might provide. The second section evaluates the potential costs of arms control; and the concluding section considers the feasibility of agreements in order to reach recommendations about the arms control policies the United States should pursue.

The chapter reaches three broad conclusions. First, arms control may have greater potential for providing political benefits than strategic benefits. Specifically, arms control may be more valuable for moderating superpower competition than for enhancing the U.S. ability to maintain the forces required for deterring the Soviet Union. Because the U.S. assured destruction capability is highly robust, even an all-out arms race is extremely unlikely to deny the United States necessary military capabilities. Thus, arms control is not necessary for this purpose. However, maintaining these capabilities by competing with the Soviet Union may generate tensions and misperceptions, as predicted by the spiral model, thereby increasing the probability of superpower conflict. Arms control might play a valuable role in reducing these dangers.

Second, the focus of U.S. arms control efforts should be constraining counterforce, including area-wide strategic defense as well as offensive counterforce. Although this is a standard conclusion of traditional arms control theories, my conclusion is not based primarily on the same arguments. Limiting Soviet counterforce provides little in added U.S. capability because the United States can easily offset Soviet counterforce via unilateral actions. Instead,

---

[8] Ibid., p. 4. We should note, however, that they consider unilateral restraint a form of arms control.

330 · Chapter 10

counterforce should be limited for two other reasons. Limiting counterforce minimizes the dangers predicted by the spiral model, since counterforce fuels the arms race even when it does not create military dangers. In addition, arms control should limit counterforce to reduce the misunderstandings of military capability that can accompany nuclear doctrines that are based heavily on counterforce targeting.

Third, most current analysis of arms control places far too much importance on reducing the size of superpower arsenals. Although there appears to be a consensus on this priority, analysts rarely explain how or why reductions would increase U.S. security. In fact, the strategic and political benefits of reductions are much smaller than is generally assumed. In part, this conclusion reflects my broader conclusion that the United States should reject disarmament as a long-term goal; hence, reductions cannot be justified as a first step toward this goal. Moreover, reductions do not significantly increase the future prospects of disarmament. Thus, even analysts favoring eventual disarmament should not give them priority. Further, pursuing reductions could be counterproductive. Emphasizing reductions misdirects attention toward the size of forces and away from the missions they are designed to perform, thereby leading to poor analysis of proposals. Pursuing reductions also has opportunity costs if reductions are harder to achieve than ceilings on force levels. Reductions deserve priority only if they reduce counterforce, in which case they are better envisioned as limits on counterforce.

ARMS CONTROL AND THE PROBABILITY OF WAR

Agreed limits on superpower forces might reduce the probability of war in two ways. First, arms control might enhance U.S. military capabilities, thereby improving America's ability to deter the Soviet Union and to maintain crisis stability. A proposal has "deterrent value" if it serves this purpose. Second, arms control might moderate the superpower competition in strategic nuclear forces, thereby reducing the political dangers predicted by the spiral model—exaggerated conflicts of interest and misperceptions—while enabling the United States to maintain necessary deterrent capabilities. The extent to which a proposal serves this purpose is measured by its "diplomatic value."[9]

Most discussions emphasize the deterrent value of arms control. This em-

[9] Arms control might also reduce the probability of war by reducing the probability of accidental and inadvertent war and by otherwise improving the superpowers' ability to manage crises. Falling into this category are agreements to improve communications, for example, by establishing the "hot line," and agreements that reduce the ambiguity in the exercising and operation of forces, which are frequently grouped under the label "confidence building measures." For examples, see Barry M. Blechman, ed., *Preventing Nuclear War: A Realistic Approach* (Bloomington: Indiana University Press, 1985); John Borawski, ed., *Avoiding War in the Nuclear Age* (Boulder, Colo.: Westview, 1986); and Scott D. Sagan, *Moving Targets: Nuclear Strategy and National Security* (Princeton: Princeton University Press, 1989), pp. 135–75.

phasis may be the product of the early development of arms control theory, much of which applied strategic nuclear deterrence theory directly to cooperative policy.[10] It may also reflect the less extensive development of theories about the international political consequences of military policies and greater disagreement over them. Nevertheless, although rarely spelled out, the belief that moderating military competition can increase U.S. security is a common theme in the arms control debate. I have separated the value of agreements into deterrent and diplomatic components largely to focus attention on those aspects of arms control that are not adequately captured by standard considerations of military capabilities.[11]

In the following analysis, I assess deterrent value essentially from positions presented by the punitive retaliation school, and from the more extensive arguments in the preceding chapters. My assessment of diplomatic value stresses the dangers identified by the spiral model. Having made these arguments, I then address disagreements based on competing foundations.

Deterrent Value of Arms Control

An arms control agreement has deterrent value if it provides the United States with necessary military capabilities that could not be maintained without the agreement. To assess deterrent value, we need first to compare the capabilities the United States would have under an arms control agreement with those it would have if the superpowers' strategic forces were unconstrained. Next, we need to ask whether these additional capabilities matter: how much more effectively would the United States be able to deter the Soviet Union? The greater this increase, the greater the agreement's deterrent value. If the U.S. ability to deter the Soviet Union is not enhanced, then the arms control agreement lacks deterrent value. Even in this case, however, an agreement might provide diplomatic value and/or economic savings, and therefore be worth pursuing. I end the section by briefly examining which of the standard types of arms control proposals would provide these benefits.

[10] Schelling and Halperin, *Strategy and Arms Control*, p. 6, for example: "we are concerned mainly with the direct relation of arms control to the military environment. Arms control can also affect, for good or for ill, our political relations with allies, neutrals and potential enemies. It can reduce tensions or hostilities; it can reduce vigilance. . . . we have not meant to depreciate the more purely political and psychological consequences. We have just not covered the whole subject. We do, however, incline to the view that the political and psychological benefits that may stem from arms control will be the more genuine, the more genuine is the direct contribution to international security." An early exception is Singer, *Deterrence, Arms Control and Disarmament*, pp. 167–91, which is a modification of his earlier "Threat-Perception and the Armament-Tension Dilemma," *Journal of Conflict Resolution* 2 (March 1958): 90–105.

[11] Although unilateral force planning should also be sensitive to possible spiral effects, these considerations are even less evident in that realm.

POTENTIAL CONTRIBUTION TO U.S. CAPABILITIES

We should measure the deterrent value of arms control in terms of its ability to enhance and/or preserve the U.S. assured destruction capability. This is because a flexible assured destruction capability satisfies the U.S. military requirements of deterrence, providing essentially all the deterrent capability that strategic nuclear weapons can provide in MAD. It deters premeditated nuclear attacks against the U.S. homeland, including counterforce attacks, by making the risks of all-out war so great that they clearly exceed all conceivable benefits. In addition, because a large superpower war increases the probability of all-out war, an assured destruction capability helps the United States to deter Soviet conventional attacks against U.S. allies. Further, although limited nuclear options might enhance deterrence of Soviet conventional and limited nuclear attacks, these options do not require extensive counterforce capabilities. Finally, an assured destruction capability makes significant damage limitation impossible, thereby essentially eliminating Soviet first-strike incentives and creating a high level of crisis stability.[12]

The United States currently has a highly redundant and diversified assured destruction capability. Even an all-out arms race is quite unlikely to threaten this capability or reduce U.S. confidence in it. At the most general level of analysis, the United States should be able to retain its assured destruction capability because a variety of structural and technical factors strongly favor retaliatory forces over damage-limitation forces. No foreseeable technical change will alter this condition.[13] In other words, strategic nuclear capabilities strongly favor retaliation (defense) over damage limitation (offense). The United States will therefore be able to prevent an unconstrained arms race from jeopardizing its assured destruction capability and would certainly do so, since maintaining this capability will remain a top security priority.

It follows immediately that the deterrent value of arms control is relatively small.[14] The United States can satisfy its military requirements of deterrence unilaterally, that is, without arms control.

In theory, however, arms control might still provide some deterrent benefits if agreements could provide the United States with a more diversified and redundant assured destruction capability than would be possible without arms control. This would increase the robustness of U.S. capabilities to changes in Soviet forces, providing additional insurance against unforeseeable technological advances. It might also be valuable in reducing the chances that Soviet leaders would mistakenly conclude that some damage limitation was feasible.

A more fine-grained look at U.S. capabilities does show that arms control

---

[12] These arguments are described in detail in Chapters Two and Seven.

[13] These arguments are explored in Chapter Five.

[14] For similar conclusions see Benjamin S. Lambeth, "Deterrence in the MIRV Era," *World Politics* 24, no. 2 (January 1972): 234, and Brodie, "On the Objectives of Arms Control," pp. 17–36.

might play a role here, but even these benefits will be relatively small. At least for the foreseeable future, the United States can maintain quite robust retaliatory capabilities without arms control. Possibly the largest deterrent benefits would be in reducing any Soviet misperceptions of their ability to limit damage that might be created by vulnerable U.S. forces. And even these benefits might be largely achieved through unilateral U.S. decisions to retire its most vulnerable forces.

To support these conclusions, I examine the competition between U.S. retaliatory forces and Soviet damage-limitation forces, identifying capabilities that can be acquired or maintained only through limiting this competition; I then evaluate the contribution of these additional capabilities to the U.S. ability to deter the Soviet Union.

Ballistic missile submarines are the most survivable leg of the strategic triad. SSBNs are highly survivable while on patrol. During peacetime, on day-to-day alert, U.S. submarines on patrol carry over 2,500 deliverable warheads and about 400 equivalent megatons (EMT), approximately twice the capability usually required for assured destruction. This capability would be larger under conditions of generated alert.[15]

No foreseeable advance in Soviet ASW capabilities poses a serious threat to U.S. SSBNs. In addition, should advances occur, experts believe that emerging threats can be countered by changes in submarine operations, jamming, and/or decoys.[16] Moreover, if these measures failed to provide sufficient confidence that enough SLBM warheads would survive a Soviet attack, the United States could deploy more SSBNs. Consequently, the United States can count on maintaining the survivability of its SSBNs without arms control.

U.S. bombers face two types of threats—Soviet missiles can destroy them before they leave their bases and Soviet air defenses threaten their ability to penetrate into the Soviet Union. However, faced with these threats, U.S. bombers attacked while on day-to-day alert are estimated to be able to deliver

---

[15] On the number of SSBN warheads see Joshua M. Epstein, *The 1988 Defense Budget* (Washington, D.C.: Brookings Institution, 1987), p. 22; on the EMT see Michael Salman, Kevin J. Sullivan, and Stephen Van Evera, "Analysis or Propaganda? Measuring American Strategic Nuclear Capability, 1969–1988," in Lynn Eden and Steven E. Miller, *Nuclear Arguments* (Ithaca: Cornell University Press, 1989). On submarine deployments and alert rates for the period 1986 to 2000 see Congressional Budget Office, *Modernizing U.S. Strategic Offensive Forces: The Administration's Program and Alternatives* (Washington, D.C.: CBO, 1983), pp. 80–82, 95.

[16] Richard L. Garwin, "Will Strategic Submarines Be Vulnerable," *International Security* 8, no. 3 (Fall 1983): 52–62; William J. Perry, "Technical Prospects," in Barry M. Blechman, ed., *Rethinking The U.S. Strategic Posture: A Report from the Aspen Consortium on Arms Control and Security Issues* (Cambridge, Mass.: Ballinger, 1982), pp. 136–39; Lawrence K. Gershwin, *Soviet Strategic Force Deployments*, Joint Hearing before the Senate Subcommittee on Strategic and Theater Nuclear Forces of the Committee on Armed Services and the Senate Subcommittee on Defense of the Committee on Appropriations, 99th Cong., 1st sess. (1985), p. 17; Donald Daniel, *Anti-Submarine Warfare and Superpower Strategic Stability* (Urbana: University of Illinois Press, 1986); and Thomas Stefanick, *Strategic Antisubmarine Warfare and Maritime Strategy* (Lexington, Mass.: Lexington Books, 1987).

approximately twice the EMT required for assured destruction; their retaliatory capability from generated alert would be much larger.[17]

The principal threat to the pre-launch survivability of the U.S. bomber force is from Soviet SLBMs, which due to their short flight time can catch some of the alert bombers at or near their bases. Nevertheless, an increase in the number of Soviet SLBM warheads will not significantly increase the future threat to the bombers. Pre-launch survivability is most sensitive to the interval between the first SLBM launch and the first bomber fly out, and is also sensitive to the flight time of Soviet SLBMs, but is relatively insensitive to increases in the number of SLBM warheads.[18] Thus, a freeze on the size of the Soviet SLBM force will have little effect on U.S. bomber survivability. The development of depressed-trajectory SLBMs would decrease bomber survivability since they have an especially short flight time.[19] A ban on the testing of these SLBMs would therefore help to prevent such a decrease.[20] Even if this increased threat develops, however, in most cases the number of surviving bombers would be decreased by no more than a third, leaving a large retaliatory capability. Further, if the United States decided this reduction in pre-launch survivability was unacceptable, it could increase the size and alert rate of its bomber force.[21]

Although the Soviet Union has invested heavily in air defense, available analyses suggest that the competition between U.S. air-breathing capabilities—bombers and cruise missiles—and Soviet air defenses will continue to favor penetration.[22] Analysis of this competition depends on the mission the

[17] See Salman, Sullivan, and Van Evera, "Analysis or Propaganda?"; also Epstein, *The 1987 Defense Budget*, p. 14.

[18] For example, Congressional Budget Office, *Modernizing U.S. Strategic Forces*, pp. 107–10, found that the difference in pre-launch survivability between SALT-constrained and unconstrained threats would be about 3 percent in the mid-1990s. For a less optimistic view of future bomber capabilities see Brown, "The U.S. Manned Bomber and Strategic Deterrence in the 1990s."

[19] Congressional Budget Office, *Modernizing U.S. Strategic Forces*, pp. 99–110.

[20] See Harold A. Feiveson and John Duffield, "Stopping the Sea-Based Counterforce Threat," *International Security* 9, no. 1 (Summer 1984): 196–98, and Alton H. Quanbeck and Archie L. Wood, *Modernizing the Strategic Bomber Force: How and Why* (Washington, D.C.: Brookings Institution, 1976), pp. 58–59. A related measure would establish SSBN stand-off zones, thereby either increasing SLBM flight times or providing warning of attack when the adversary violates the agreement; see ibid., pp. 59–60; Feiveson and Duffield, "Stopping the Sea-Based Counterforce Threat," p. 198; Garwin, "Will Submarines Be Vulnerable?" p. 67; and Alan J. Vick and James A. Thomson, "The Military Significance of Restrictions on the Operations of Strategic Forces," in Blechman, ed., *Preventing Nuclear War*, pp. 114–22.

[21] On other possibilities for offsetting an increased threat to bomber pre-launch survivability see Archie L. Wood, "Modernizing the Strategic Bomber Force without Really Trying—a Case against the B-1 Bomber," *International Security* 1, no. 2 (Fall 1976): 105–6.

[22] Congressional Budget Office, *Retaliatory Issues for U.S. Strategic Nuclear Forces* (Washington, D.C.: CBO, 1978), pp. 13–14. See also Gershwin, *Soviet Strategic Force Developments*, p. 17.

air-breathing leg must perform, since protecting a small number of cities is much harder than protecting a large number of military targets. It is virtually certain that the U.S. cruise missile force of the 1990s could by itself destroy most major Soviet cities.[23] Therefore, assuming the United States continues to react to improvements in Soviet air defenses, there are strong reasons for believing that the destructive potential of this leg of the triad can be preserved. As with the sea-based leg, arms control appears unnecessary for preserving the retaliatory capability of this leg of the triad.

U.S. ICBMs based in today's hardened silos are, at least in theory, highly vulnerable to attack. Standard calculations find a Soviet attack destroying approximately 75 percent of the U.S. ICBM force.[24] This would leave approximately 450 reliable ICBM warheads surviving, amounting to over 200 EMT. Consequently, although the ICBM force is now highly vulnerable, its survivable portion is still large enough to meet the assured destruction standard. However, continued improvements in the accuracy of Soviet ICBMs would reduce this capability. The United States is unlikely to be able to greatly delay this decrease by further hardening its silos.[25]

Almost all approaches for maintaining or increasing ICBM survivability require some type of limitation on Soviet forces. For example: a ban on flight testing might help to maintain the current level of survivability;[26] survivable mobile basing probably requires limits on Soviet throw-weight; and deceptive basing in multiple shelters requires limits on the number of Soviet warheads.[27] Thus, increasing the survivability of U.S. ICBMs would probably depend partly on arms control.[28]

[23] Gordon MacDonald, Jack Ruina, and Mark Balaschak, "Soviet Strategic Air Defenses," in Richard K. Betts, ed., *Cruise Missiles: Technology, Strategy, Politics* (Washington, D.C.: Brookings Institution, 1981), pp. 70–82.

[24] Epstein, *The 1987 Defense Budget*, pp. 22–23; Salman, Sullivan, and Van Evera, "Analysis or Propaganda?" On the calculation of silo vulnerability and the range of important uncertainties see note 2 in Chapter Eight.

[25] Epstein, *The 1987 Defense Budget*, pp. 17–18.

[26] Discussions of restricting flight testing include Sidney D. Drell and Theodore J. Ralston, "Restrictions on Weapons Tests as Confidence Building Measures," in Blechman, ed., *Preventing Nuclear War*, pp. 86–98; Martin Einhorn, Gordon L. Kane, and Miroslav Nincic, "Strategic Arms Control through Test Restraints," *International Security* 8, no. 3 (Winter 1983–84): 119–24; Farooq Hussain, *The Future of Arms Control (Part IV): The Impact of Weapons Test Restrictions*, Adelphi Paper No. 165 (London: IISS, 1981); Robert Sherman, "Deterrence through a Ballistic Missile Flight Test Ban," pp. 8–13; and Walter B. Slocombe, "A Flighty Idea," pp. 14–15, both in *Arms Control Today* 17, no. 10 (December 1987).

[27] These approaches are discussed in some detail in Office of Technology Assessment, *MX Missile Basing* (Washington, D.C.: GPO, 1981); see also Chapter Eight.

[28] There are at least two possible exceptions. First, simply deploying a much larger number of ICBMs in fixed silos might provide a large amount of surviving EMT, even if the percentage of survivors was quite small—this, however, is rarely judged a satisfactory solution. Second, deep underground basing might not depend on arms control for survivability—there are, however, technical questions about its feasibility.

The ability of ballistic missiles to penetrate to Soviet targets is now guaranteed by the ABM Treaty, which limits ballistic missile defense to militarily insignificant levels. If the treaty is terminated and the Soviet Union deploys an extensive BMD system, Soviet BMD would reduce the penetrability of U.S. ICBMs and SLBMs. However, BMD available in the foreseeable future holds little promise of protecting Soviet cities against the thousands of survivable warheads carried by U.S. SSBNs. In addition, once unconstrained by the ABM Treaty, the United States could deploy BMD to increase the survivability of its own ICBM force. Since point defense is easier than area defense, the net effect of superpower deployment of BMD would probably be an increase in the number of U.S. ICBM warheads that can survive and penetrate to Soviet cities. Further, in the unlikely event that Soviet BMD seriously threatened U.S. ballistic missile retaliatory capabilities, the United States could increase the size of its ballistic missile force and pursue a variety of countermeasures. Therefore, although the ABM Treaty provides other benefits, it is unnecessary to protect U.S. retaliatory capabilities.[29]

We also need to consider the role of arms control in reducing the Soviet threat to the *U.S. command and control system*. The vulnerability of the command system stems largely from the existence of a relatively small number of key targets—approximately 100 fixed ground-based targets that are vulnerable to Soviet attack.[30] In addition, there are possibly over 1,000 targets the Soviets might attack to increase their confidence in the success of a decapitation attack.[31] Unilateral measures are incapable of making these elements of the command system survivable. To reduce the danger created by this vulnerability the United States deploys a variety of more survivable airborne, space-based, and ground mobile elements that can perform many of the same functions as the fixed elements. In addition, U.S. procedures for operating forces during crises are designed to further reduce the danger of command system vulnerability.

Constraints on Soviet forces can probably make only a relatively small contribution to increasing the survivability of U.S. C³. Even extremely deep cuts in offensive forces would not protect the roughly 100 key fixed targets or, for that matter, the larger target set of approximately 1,000 targets.[32] Large reduc-

---

[29] Sources on BMD capabilities are provided in note 6 in Chapter Four.

[30] On the U.S. command and control system see note 7 in Chapter Two. Also describing the small number of C³ targets are John J. Hamre, Richard H. Davison, and Peter T. Tarpgaard, *Strategic Command, Control and Communications: Alternative Approaches for Modernization* (Washington, D.C.: Congressional Budget Office, 1981), p. 13.

[31] Ashton B. Carter, "Assessing Command System Vulnerability," in Ashton B. Carter, John D. Steinbruner, and Charles A. Zraket, eds., *Managing Nuclear Operations* (Washington, D.C.: Brookings Institution, 1985), pp. 560–69.

[32] On the difficulty of using arms control to increase the survivability of earth-based command centers see Michael M. May and John R. Harvey, "Nuclear Operations and Arms Control," in Carter et al., *Managing Nuclear Operations*, pp. 727–29.

tions might, however, reduce the Soviet ability to destroy this larger number of C³ targets while also attacking the full range of U.S. strategic forces. These cuts, however, would probably have to go beyond the roughly 50 percent cuts that the superpowers have been discussing in START.[33]

Possibly more promising are arms control agreements that constrain the Soviet ability to destroy key command targets on very short warning, thereby giving the United States more time to prepare for retaliation. These agreements, which would be similar to agreements designed to protect bombers, might ban depressed-trajectory SLBMs, establish ASW stand-off zones, and possibly ban forward-based cruise missiles.[34] Finally, arms control might play some role in protecting the satellites that support U.S. command and control, thereby reducing the paths by which crises might escalate to nuclear war.[35]

In sum, the United States can maintain the retaliatory capability of the air-breathing and submarine legs of its strategic triad without arms control, but maintaining or increasing the capability of the ICBM leg probably requires arms control. In addition, arms control is unlikely to play a large role in increasing the survivability of C³.

DETERRENT BENEFITS OF INCREASING SURVIVABILITY

Having explored U.S. capabilities we can now assess the potential deterrent benefits of arms control in more detail. In light of the preceding analysis it is clear why ICBM survivability has been a central concern of U.S. arms control policy. This leg of the triad is most vulnerable, and at least in theory can benefit most from arms control limits on Soviet forces. The key question for evaluating proposals designed to increase ICBM survivability is: How important are survivable ICBMs to the U.S. ability to deter the Soviet Union?

[33] This observation depends on the strategic forces the United States deploys under the reductions agreement. For example, attacking a mobile ICBM basing area could require a large fraction of the Soviet force; if the Soviets gave priority to attacking these targets, then they might be left without enough warheads for attacking C³ targets. In fact, if the dispersal area was large enough, then even without reductions the Soviets might lack the warheads required to cover U.S. strategic forces and C³.

[34] For discussion of these possibilities see May and Harvey, "Nuclear Operations and Arms Control," pp. 719–22, who point out that an effective coastal ASW capability is a unilateral means of achieving some of the benefits of a verifiable SSBN stand-off zone, and Blair, *Strategic Command and Control*, p. 301.

[35] For varying assessments of the dangers created by ASAT and discussion of unilateral and arms control measures for reducing these dangers see Paul B. Stares, "Nuclear Operations and Antisatellites," in Carter et al., *Managing Nuclear Operations*, pp. 694–703; idem, *Space and National Security* (Washington, D.C.: Brookings Institution, 1987); Kurt Gottfried and Richard Ned Lebow, "Anti-Satellite Weapons: Weighing the Risks," *Daedalus* 114, no. 2 (Spring 1985): 154–70; Ashton B. Carter, "Satellites and Anti-Satellites: The Limits of the Possible," *International Security* 10, no. 4 (Spring 1986): 67–98; and Donald M. Hafner, "Approaches to the Control of Anti-Satellite Weapons," in William J. Durch, ed., *National Interests and the Military Use of Space* (Cambridge, Mass.: Ballinger, 1984).

After examining this question in detail, Chapter Eight concluded that although survivable ICBMs are preferable to vulnerable ones, the benefits of increasing ICBM survivability, by whatever means, are relatively small. U.S. ICBM vulnerability neither increases the Soviet ability to coerce the United States nor creates sufficient incentives for Soviet attack during a crisis, since significant damage limitation is infeasible. Further, although survivable ICBMs would make U.S. strategic forces somewhat more resistant to improvements in Soviet forces, the large retaliatory capabilities of the other legs of the U.S. triad greatly reduce the value of this hedge. Based on these arguments, the deterrent value of an agreement that increases ICBM survivability is quite small.

Nevertheless, vulnerable ICBMs may be dangerous if Soviet leaders do not fully appreciate that they lack first-strike incentives. Chapter Seven argues that the superpowers' continuing commitment to large counterforce arsenals could both support and reflect the illusion that the risks of an all-out damage-limitation attack are warranted. In this case, large numbers of vulnerable U.S. weapons might help mislead a desperate Soviet leader into launching such an attack. As a result, arms control agreements that constrain Soviet counterforce in general, and threats to U.S. ICBMs in particular, might reduce pressures for escalation in severe crises; such agreements would not significantly increase U.S. retaliatory capabilities, but might reduce the probability that Soviet leaders will misevaluate them.

The deterrent value of arms control depends on whether the benefits of such an agreement could be achieved unilaterally. The United States could avoid these misunderstandings by getting rid of its ICBMs unilaterally. Strictly speaking, therefore, an agreement that increases ICBM survivability has little additional deterrent value. However, for a variety of reasons the United States may be unwilling to move to a strategic dyad. Hence, we might want to credit such an agreement with some additional deterrent value.

Although probably infeasible, we should still consider the deterrent benefits of an agreement that increases the survivability of U.S. C^3. Although the command system is highly vulnerable, Soviet prospects for greatly reducing the U.S. ability to inflict retaliatory damage appear quite slim.[36] As a result, the system's vulnerability creates little incentive for the Soviet Union to launch an all-out attack.[37]

[36] For a relatively optimistic assessment see Carter, "Assessing Command System Vulnerability," p. 607. For possible disagreements, at least in emphasis, see Blair, *Strategic Command and Control*, p. 208, and Steinbruner, "Nuclear Decapitation," p. 19.

[37] This argument is presented in more detail in Chapter Nine, where I consider the benefits of protecting C^3 with BMD. In addition, the Soviet Union would be extremely unlikely to launch a limited attack against the U.S. command and control system: first, limited attacks make sense only if the attacker believes the war can be terminated short of all-out attacks—but attacks against C^3 greatly reduce this possibility. Second, and related, attacking C^3 for limited military purposes

Nevertheless, two types of dangers remain. Vulnerable C³ is still the weakest link in the U.S. retaliatory capability. Thus, if in a severe crisis a Soviet leader is tempted/pressured to launch a preemptive attack, the vulnerability of command and control offers the best hope of limiting damage. The size of survivable U.S. forces reduces this danger, but may not eliminate it. A second danger is that vulnerable C³ could increase the probability of accidental and inadvertent war starting from a severe crisis or conventional war. By shifting to high levels of nuclear alert to reduce the danger of decapitation, the superpowers reduce their ability to maintain tight control of their forces and risk possibly dangerous interactions between their C³ systems.[38] Consequently, agreements that increased the survivability of the C³ system would have some deterrent value. Unfortunately, as discussed above, agreements that would greatly increase the survivability of the key C³ nodes are probably infeasible, although arms control might play a role in constraining the threat from Soviet attacks that would provide especially short warning.

TYPES OF ARMS CONTROL AGREEMENTS

A wide variety of arms control agreements might provide some of the deterrent benefits that the preceding analysis identifies. I briefly consider three types of agreements: a freeze, ceilings, and reductions.

A qualitative and quantitative freeze on the superpowers' forces might stop any further decrease in the already low survivability of U.S. ICBMs, thereby maintaining some of the value of this dwindling deterrent asset.[39] However, banning new types of missiles might not be sufficient to accomplish this since the Soviet Union might be able to increase the accuracy of already deployed systems. Thus, the possible deterrent benefits of a freeze would depend partly on whether a ban on flight testing would stop improvements in the accuracy of deployed systems and/or reduce leaders' confidence in their reliability and accuracy. Quantitative limits on Soviet forces would do little to help maintain the current survivability of the U.S. ICBM force. A freeze might ban the further development and deployment of ASATs.

We should also note the possible deterrent costs of a freeze. If U.S. retaliatory forces were frozen without freezing all Soviet counterforce systems (including ASW and air defenses), confidence in U.S. capabilities might even-

---

promises scant benefits and large risks. (Carter, "Assessing Command System Vulnerability," pp. 606.) Consequently, the vulnerability of C³ should not greatly reduce the U.S. ability to deter limited attacks since the Soviet Union would attack it only in an all-out war.

[38] Paul Bracken, *The Command and Control of Nuclear Forces* (New Haven: Yale University Press, 1983), and idem, "Accidental Nuclear War," in Graham T. Allison et al., *Hawks, Doves & Owls: An Agenda for Nuclear War* (New York: W. W. Norton, 1985).

[39] Further, following from the analysis presented in Steinbruner and Garwin, "Strategic Vulnerability," one could argue that holding accuracy at current levels would also maintain the uncertainty introduced by the factors often left out of standard analyses, thereby making counter-silo attacks less attractive.

tually decrease. Some freeze proposals developed in the early 1980s took this into account by allowing the continued modernization of SSBNs. Without limits on air defenses it would also be preferable to allow the continued deployment and modernization of bombers and cruise missiles. In addition, by constraining the U.S. ability to increase the survivability of its ICBMs, a freeze could entail forgoing the limited benefits of this increased survivability.[40]

A second type of proposal places ceilings on the size of superpower forces but does little to limit qualitative advances. This type of proposal is designed to increase ICBM survivability by limiting the Soviet threat while allowing the United States to deploy ICBMs in a mobile or deceptive basing mode. SALT II is an important example of this type of agreement. The Carter administration planned to combine SALT II limits with deceptive basing to make MX reasonably survivable.[41] Without these limits, the Soviet Union could have overwhelmed all feasible deceptive basing modes. Similarly, limits on Soviet throw-weight would help insure the high survivability of mobile ICBMs. Proposals that set a ceiling on the total number of warheads without limiting the number of launchers provide another example of this type of agreement. These proposals aim to increase survivability by encouraging the superpowers to move toward single warhead missiles, leaving them with at most one warhead to cover each of the adversary's targets.[42]

A third type of proposal calls for reducing the size of the superpowers' offenses. Although there is widespread support for reduction of offensive forces,[43] this is rarely clearly connected to deterrent benefits. As argued above, the air-breathing and sea-based legs of the U.S. triad are now reasonably survivable and, along with C^3, are relatively insensitive to even rather large reductions in Soviet forces, say on the order of 50 percent.

Reductions might increase the number of U.S. ICBMs that would survive a Soviet attack, although they need not. Even large reductions in Soviet ICBMs would not increase the survivability of current fixed land-based missiles; and

[40] It might, however, leave open certain routes to increased survivability, for example, allowing further hardening of silos while banning improvements in Soviet warhead lethality.

[41] On the assumptions underlying the ability of SALT plus MPS to accomplish this see Office of Technology Assessment, *MX Missile Basing*, pp. 40–44.

[42] This condition is often said to be beneficial because it guarantees a poor warhead-exchange ratio. This argument is flawed, however, since at root it is based on the importance of the ratio of surviving forces. A stronger argument is that if both countries are allowed a given number of warheads, then a force of single warhead missiles will provide more survivable weapons than a force of MIRVed missiles.

[43] Possibly most prominent among the criticisms of SALT II was the treaty's failure to substantially reduce the size of the superpowers' offensive forces. President Reagan called for "real arms control," i.e., reductions. Noting broad support for reductions are Michael Krepon, *Strategic Stalemate: Nuclear Weapons and Arms Control in American Politics* (New York: St. Martin's, 1984), p. 132, and Alan Platt, "The Politics of Arms Control and the Strategic Balance," in Blechman, ed., *Rethinking the U.S Strategic Posture*, pp. 173–74.

their survivability might continue decreasing as allowed Soviet missiles became more lethal. Reducing Soviet forces would decrease the demands placed on U.S. mobile and deceptive basing modes, thereby making them less expensive and more feasible.[44] However, the increased survivability that might be achieved by reducing the Soviet ability to attack U.S. forces would tend to be offset by required reductions in U.S. forces. Even if a reductions agreement increased the percentage of the U.S. force that would survive, U.S. retaliatory capabilities might decrease since the total deployed force would be smaller.[45]

Given the redundancy of current forces a decrease in the size of U.S. retaliatory capabilities might not be significant. In addition, even if the total size of the U.S. retaliatory force was somewhat reduced, agreements that increased the size of the survivable ICBM force would increase the diversity of U.S. retaliatory capabilities, and agreements that reduced the number of vulnerable weapons might reduce the probability that Soviet leaders would misjudge their prospects for damage limitation. Clearly, the deterrent benefits of mutual reductions in force size depend heavily on the details of the reductions agreement.

Diplomatic Value of Arms Control

The United States can continue satisfying its requirements of military deterrence with high confidence without arms control, but doing so may require engaging in an arms race. If this arms race strains superpower relations, then the probability of war could increase even if U.S. military capabilities are undiminished. The spiral model predicts that arms races can have this effect. Even a country that is confident of its ability to counter challenges to its deterrent forces may conclude that its adversary is striving for military advantage. Building on these beliefs, the spiral model predicts that arms races can increase the probability of war by generating misperceptions about the adversary's hostility, lending support to more aggressive foreign policies, making offensive military doctrines appear necessary and attractive, and by increasing the influence of both superpowers' hard-liners. As discussed in Chapter Three, military competition could generate these effects even if the Soviet Union does not entirely match the spiral model's basic assumptions: the spiral model assumes that the competing states are insecure status quo powers, but military

[44] Calls for increasing survivability by moving away from MIRVs and toward single warhead missiles are often closely associated with reductions. However, these approaches are analytically separable: we could hold the number of warheads constant but deploy them on single warhead missiles. All else being equal, this would provide a larger survivable force than would a smaller force of single warhead missiles.

[45] See, for example, Michael M. May, George F. Bing, and John D. Steinbruner, "Strategic Arsenals after START: The Implications of Deep Cuts," *International Security* 13, no. 1 (Summer 1988): 90–133.

competition could have negative political consequences if the Soviet Union is an insecure expansionist power. Arms control agreements that moderate the arms race can help to avoid these negative effects. Even if entirely lacking in deterrent value, these agreements would provide diplomatic value. This section considers the types of proposals that could provide these benefits.

LIMITS ON COUNTERFORCE

Agreements designed to provide diplomatic value should give priority to limiting counterforce. U.S. leaders are likely to see Soviet counterforce as a reflection of malign intentions because it threatens forces that the United States maintains for deterrence. This conclusion is especially likely because counterforce is a necessary component of an offensive doctrine but not of a more defensive one. Thus, according to the spiral model, offense (forces dedicated to damage limitation) is dangerous even when defense (forces dedicated to retaliation) dominates. Although Soviet counterforce is unlikely to provide a military advantage, U.S. leaders tend to see the Soviet commitment to counterforce reflecting an interest in gaining a military advantage, an advantage that would be unnecessary if the Soviet Union was willing to respect the status quo. The American strategic nuclear debate during much of the 1970s and 1980s illustrates this. The growth of Soviet counterforce systems contributed to American acceptance of an increasingly malign view of Soviet intentions and was an important factor in the decline of détente; American moderates were discredited, while hard-liners gained influence. By comparison, Soviet countervalue capabilities and Soviet achievement of rough nuclear parity created much less concern over Soviet intentions. Thus, while doing relatively little to enhance U.S. military capabilities, limits on Soviet counterforce could provide diplomatic benefits.

Naturally, much the same logic applies in reverse as well. Chapter Three found that the Soviets are inclined to see U.S. counterforce reflecting a desire to regain military superiority and political advantages at Soviet expense. However, the United States could avoid projecting this image by unilaterally restraining its deployment of counterforce. Arms control is necessary therefore only if U.S. willingness to forgo counterforce is contingent on Soviet restraint.

It is not a coincidence that proposals designed to provide diplomatic value closely resemble proposals designed to provide deterrent value. The former should limit counterforce because perceptions of the adversary's intentions are influenced by the military missions its forces can perform. The adversary's counterforce projects an image of aggressive intentions precisely because it threatens retaliatory capabilities believed necessary for deterrence.

As discussed in Chapter Seven, counterforce includes the full range of systems that could be used for damage limitation. Therefore, in addition to ballistic missiles, which have received so much attention because they can destroy hard targets promptly, counterforce includes strategic ASW and strategic defense—BMD and air defenses. According to these arguments about diplomatic value, we should be interested in limits on all of these systems.

The value of the ABM Treaty is clearest from this perspective. The ABM Treaty is not necessary to protect the U.S. ability to retaliate massively with ballistic missiles. In contrast, the political implications of a competition between ballistic missile defense and retaliatory capabilities would be more significant. A superpower that deploys an extensive nationwide strategic defense is likely to convince its adversary that it desires strategic superiority and believes there is a reasonable chance of obtaining it. This outcome is especially likely if strategic defenses are accompanied by other counterforce systems. Soviet efforts to gain military advantages are likely to be interpreted as a reflection of aggressive intentions, which supports a general shift from cooperative U.S. policies to more competitive ones. The ABM Treaty helps the superpowers avoid these dangers by moderating strategic nuclear competition.

At least in theory, there exists a broad array of other anti-counterforce proposals that could play a similar role. These include limits on strategic air defense, strategic ASW, depressed-trajectory SLBMs (since they could increase the threat to bombers and C^3), advances in ballistic missile accuracy that would pose an increased threat to silo-based ICBMs (although advances in ICBM accuracy are approaching their limit), and antisatellite weapons. In addition, we might include proposals designed to reduce the size and effectiveness of the counterforce systems that are already deployed in the category of anti-counterforce proposals. For example, all proposals for decreasing U.S. ICBM vulnerability can be seen as anti-counterforce. As described in the previous section, some of these proposals focus on actually reducing the number of highly lethal Soviet ballistic missile warheads; others propose to increase ICBM survivability by combining limits on the growth of the Soviet arsenal with U.S. deployment of ICBMs in mobile or deceptive basing modes.

How large are the diplomatic benefits of limits on counterforce? On the one hand, the diplomatic value of these limits depends on the offense-defense balance: offense is more threatening when it has the advantage. Because defense (retaliatory capability) now dominates, and will for the foreseeable future, the diplomatic benefits of limiting counterforce are smaller than if damage limitation was easier. In other words, agreements limiting counterforce are less valuable because the security dilemma is less severe. On the other hand, the diplomatic value of limiting counterforce is greater when offense and defense can be distinguished: if defense dominates and is clearly different from offense, then a country that buys offense probably communicates a strong commitment to offensive capabilities. Thus, limits on systems clearly dedicated to damage limitation—for example, thick area BMD, strategic ASW in the Soviet bastion, and highly lethal ballistic missiles—would tend to have larger diplomatic value than if the nature of their missions was more ambiguous.[46]

---

[46] Chapter Three presents these arguments in some detail.

In addition, the diplomatic value of specific limits on counterforce depends on the existing agreements that restrict counterforce. Because a damage-limitation capability would benefit from combining a variety of counterforce systems, limiting some of these systems would reduce the threat posed by the continuing deployment of other counterforce systems. In effect, limiting certain types of counterforce shifts the offense-defense balance toward defense. Consequently, the ABM Treaty reduces the diplomatic value of other anti-counterforce agreements that might follow it. For example, by guaranteeing the ability of ballistic missiles to penetrate it makes limits on air defenses less important. Nevertheless, Soviet investment in counterforce, both in ballistic missiles and air defense, continues to be a source of concern in the United States.

Finally, in terms of diplomatic value there may be a difference between agreements that halt the deployment of counterforce and those that would reduce counterforce that has already been deployed. To the extent that the U.S. image of the Soviet Union is formed by the *ongoing* competition, halting counterforce deployments would provide larger benefits than reversing them. This would be especially true when the deployed counterforce does not pose a large military threat.

LIMITS ON OTHER TYPES OF FORCES

Beyond limits on counterforce, other types of agreements might also have diplomatic value. Placing ceilings on the size of superpower arsenals and limiting modernization might help to reduce the sense of competition that often accompanies ongoing deployment of superpower strategic nuclear forces.

The rationale for placing ceilings on the size of the superpowers' forces is less obvious than the one for limiting counterforce. In theory, in MAD a larger Soviet force should be no more threatening to the United States than a smaller one, assuming that it does not pose a larger threat to U.S. capabilities. In other words, if increases in Soviet counterforce weapons are already banned, then increases in the size of the Soviet force should be of little consequence. Unlike increases in Soviet counterforce, the United States need not respond to increases in Soviet countervalue forces to maintain the diversity and redundancy of its deterrent forces. Further, a larger Soviet force does not threaten the United States with significantly higher costs in an all-out war. Why then would this type of Soviet buildup generate concern in the United States? In other words, why might ceilings have diplomatic value?[47]

---

[47] A common argument is that ceilings can increase the ability of each superpower to predict the future size of the other's forces. If, however, counterforce were limited, then there is no obvious strategic reason why the United States would need to predict the future size of Soviet forces since increases in size without increases in counterforce would not threaten U.S. capabilities. Therefore, increased predictability is valuable either for gauging future counterforce capability—which we could better view as a limit on future counterforce—or for reasons I discuss in

First, the line between counterforce and countervalue capabilities is not as sharp as these arguments suggest. For example, SLBMs that are not highly effective against hard targets can be targeted against such soft strategic targets as bomber bases and certain C³ targets. Bombers and cruise missiles can destroy hard targets, but are considered less threatening than equally lethal ballistic missiles because they take longer to reach their targets. This difference notwithstanding, these systems might contribute to a damage-limitation attack; or at least worst-case analysts might fear that they could. Relatively slow systems could be used against weapons that survive the initial counterforce attack but cannot be launched quickly, possibly because command and control has been damaged. Thus, even increases in Soviet forces that are not clearly designed for counterforce could be seen as adding somewhat to the size of its counterforce arsenal.

Ceilings on these less threatening forces would probably lack deterrent value, but could have diplomatic value. Assuming that both countries continue to expand these forces, the likely net effect of a mutual buildup would be an increase in the size of the U.S. retaliatory force. Thus, ceilings would lack deterrent value. However, since some U.S. analysts would read the growth in Soviet forces as reflecting a Soviet desire to undermine U.S. capabilities, ceilings would have diplomatic value.

Second, and probably more important, because much of the U.S. debate does not distinguish between the missions that Soviet forces might perform, virtually all increases in the size of the Soviet force can be portrayed as threatening.[48] Ceilings on force size would help reduce the fears generated by these arguments.[49]

Closely related, many analysts believe that numbers influence perceptions, even when they cannot be related to military capabilities. This claim is central to the arguments presented by the military denial school. As a result, these

the text below. Among the many analysts who see arms control benefits in increased predictability are Harold Brown and Lynn E. Davis, "Nuclear Arms Control: Where Do We Stand?" *Foreign Affairs* 62, no. 5 (Summer 1984): 1159; Charles A. Sorrels, "Limiting Strategic Forces," in Richard Burt, ed., *Arms Control and Defense Postures in the 1980s* (Boulder, Colo.: Westview, 1982), pp. 166–68; and Richard Burt, "Relevance of Arms Control in the 1980s," *Daedalus* 110, no. 1 (Winter 1981): 173. Carnesale and Haass, *Superpower Arms Control*, pp. 344–45, find that "reduction of uncertainty and enhancement of predictability may well be the principal contribution of the arms control experience."

[48] For important examples of numerical comparisons used to demonstrate that the United States is falling behind and/or is inferior to the Soviet Union see Charles Tyroler, II, ed., *Alerting America: The Papers of the Committee on The Present Danger* (Washington, D.C.: Pergamon-Brassey's, 1984). See also Department of Defense, *Soviet Military Power* (Washington, D.C.: GPO, March 1987), p. 23–24.

[49] Ceilings, however, will not be sufficient to undermine arguments that the United States is inferior, or that changes in Soviet forces are weakening the United States—analysts will always be able to find measures of superpower forces that support these conclusions. On the misuse of measures see Salman, Sullivan, and Van Evera, "Analysis or Propaganda?"

analysts might see growth in Soviet forces reflecting the pursuit of political advantage, even while recognizing that the U.S. ability to perform its military missions would not be jeopardized.

Even analysts who believe that a larger Soviet force is neither militarily nor politically more threatening than a smaller one might see ceilings playing a useful role in the U.S. debate over strategic nuclear policy. Specifically, members of the punitive retaliation school who are not worried by increasing numbers of weapons, but who recognize that other analysts will be worried, could support ceilings to reduce fears and reactions generated by arguments with which they disagree.[50] Their alternative is prevailing in the debate over the insignificance of numbers and relative force size in MAD. However, since experience suggests that this debate will not be resolved in the near future, ceilings complement efforts to win it on logical and empirical grounds.

Similar arguments suggest that agreements constraining qualitative advances in the superpowers' forces, beyond those already limited by constraints on counterforce, would have some diplomatic value. These agreements would limit the modernization of deployed retaliatory systems and the addition of new types of retaliatory systems.[51] For example, this type of agreement might ban the modernization of bombers and SSBNs. Similarly, in the 1970s and early 1980s such an agreement might have banned cruise missiles and mobile missiles. The rationale behind such proposals is that deployment of new systems, much like the growth in the size of arsenals, will be interpreted as an attempt to gain a strategic advantage, even when the system does not add to counterforce capabilities.

The U.S. strategic debate is littered with arguments that demonstrate that virtually all changes in Soviet forces can be portrayed as threatening U.S. security. For example, although mobile missiles are generally understood to reflect a commitment to a second-strike capability, the United States proposed a ban on mobile missiles in part because of ''a growing concern in the Pentagon and the National Security Council staff about what they see as a new kind of Soviet first-strike threat. By this theory, Moscow could launch its large SS-18 and SS-19 missiles and then disperse mobile SS-24 and SS-25 missiles to avert American retaliation.''[52] According to this logic, which sees survivable

[50] I should note, however, that the punitive retaliation school is divided over whether increasing numbers of weapons are dangerous, and many of its members are strong proponents of reducing superpower arsenals. The rationale for these reductions is based on arguments that go beyond the basic features I used to characterize the schools. I address these issues in the text.

[51] On the difficulty of controlling technology see Karl Lautenschlager, ''Controlling Military Technology,'' Ethics 95, no. 3 (April 1985): 692–711.

[52] Gerald M. Boyd, ''Reagan Proposes U.S.-Soviet Accord on Mobile Missiles,'' New York Times, 2 November 1985, p. 4. For an earlier and similar argument see Eugene V. Rostow, ''The Case against SALT II,'' Commentary 76, no. 2 (February 1979): 24. Also showing indiscriminate concern over Soviet modernization, the Department of Defense observed that: ''Despite the USSR's recently renewed interest in arms control, Soviet production of newer, more lethal stra-

Soviet forces threatening the U.S. deterrent, virtually all Soviet systems reflect malign intent.

However, while helping to reduce the material available for such distorting arguments, limits on the modernization of retaliatory capabilities could be counterproductive if not accompanied by a ban on the counterforce threats that oppose them. Holding retaliatory forces constant while allowing counterforce to improve could reduce the redundancy of retaliatory capabilities. For example, if air defenses are unconstrained, a ban on the modernization of U.S. air-breathing capabilities could reduce the retaliatory capability of this leg of the triad. Reducing the adequacy of the U.S. deterrent could generate greater fears, thereby bringing larger diplomatic costs than an unconstrained competition. Thus, the diplomatic benefits of this type of proposal must be weighed first against its possible deterrent costs, and then against its possible future diplomatic costs. Limits on modernization should probably be pursued only if the opposing counterforce threat is constrained. In addition, these limits must provide for the replacement of aging retaliatory systems.

AGREEMENTS REDUCING FORCE SIZE

Finally, we need to consider the diplomatic value of proposals for reducing the size of the superpowers' nuclear arsenals. Although rarely spelled out, many analysts believe that reducing the superpowers' arsenals would contribute to improved relations.

One such argument focuses on the relationship between reductions and the purposes for which the superpowers maintain nuclear arsenals. Reductions are seen as a means of eliminating counterforce weapons, thus turning the superpowers away from warfighting strategies and slowing the arms race. Arguing for a "finite deterrent" of about 2,000 warheads, Feiveson, Ullman, and von Hippel hold that "the adoption of finite deterrence would make possible a 10-fold reduction of the superpowers nuclear arsenals and the elimination of their most destabilizing weapons. Thus, it could transform the relationship between the United States and the Soviet Union, reducing the dangerous fantasies and paranoia that feed and are fed by the arms race and making it much easier to build the foundations for a more satisfactory *modus vivendi*."[53]

This argument, however, is based primarily on beliefs about counterforce and nuclear strategy, and only secondarily on reductions in force size. The superpowers could maintain the size of their forces while at the same time eliminating their counterforce weapons. It is counterforce and strategies for its

---

tegic nuclear weapons continues . . . two new ballistic missile submarines, and the flight-testing of a new strategic bomber, they are developing another generation of air-, sea-, and ground-launched nuclear capable cruise missiles" (*Soviet Military Power*, March 1987, p. 23).

[53] Harold A. Feiveson, Richard H. Ullman, and Frank von Hippel, "Reducing U.S. and Soviet Nuclear Arsenals," in Len Ackland and Steven McGuire, eds., *Assessing the Nuclear Age* (Chicago: Educational Foundation for Nuclear Science, 1986), p. 312.

use that drive the arms race, not the size of forces per se. Admittedly, if the superpowers forswear counterforce, then strategic nuclear forces as large as today's would be clearly unnecessary and, consequently, reductions might follow. The key, however, is the change in strategy, not the reductions in force size. Ullman himself makes this point while arguing for "denuclearizing international politics," which he believes would provide the opportunity for improvements in superpower relations: "reductions are not necessarily a concomitant of denuclearization. The term connotes the way in which governments plan to use (or, indeed, not to use) the nuclear forces at their disposal. Even very large and diverse nuclear forces can be reserved strictly for second strike, retaliatory roles."[54]

A second and more common argument for reductions depends directly on the positive effect of reductions themselves, not on changes in strategy. For example, Joseph Nye argues that "reductions may help maintain or restore public confidence in nuclear deterrence both at home and among U.S. allies. . . . Reductions could also reassure the American public about Soviet intentions, and reassure the Soviets about U.S. policies. . . . Potentially, a change in U.S.-Soviet relations may be the most important benefit of a series of reductions of the magnitude currently under discussion [25–30 percent]."[55]

In theory at least, reductions should not have this effect. These cuts would not reduce the costs the Soviet Union could inflict in a nuclear war. Why then should today's Soviet force of approximately ten thousand warheads be less threatening when reduced to say five thousand? Further, reductions will not in general enhance U.S. retaliatory capabilities. If they do, it is because reductions in U.S. forces would be more than offset by reductions in Soviet counterforce. Replacing Soviet counterforce weapons with countervalue weapons could provide similar increases in U.S. retaliatory capabilities. Moreover, reducing numbers of weapons substantially could actually make the adversary's weapons appear more threatening—after reductions both the forces still deployed and the forces that might be acquired could pose a greater threat to one's retaliatory capabilities.[56]

Although these arguments suggest otherwise, in practice reductions might

---

[54] Richard H. Ullman, "Denuclearizing International Politics," *Ethics* 95, no. 3 (April 1985): 584. Also on this point see Richard L. Garwin, "Reducing Dependence on Nuclear Weapons: A Second Nuclear Regime," in David C. Gompert et al., *Nuclear Weapons and World Politics* (New York: McGraw Hill, 1977), pp. 81–147, especially p. 98.

[55] Joseph S. Nye, Jr., "Farewell to Arms Control?" *Foreign Affairs* 65, no. 1 (Fall 1986): 7. But see also Nye, "Don't Count on Counting," *Bulletin of the Atomic Scientists* 45, no. 4 (May 1989): 43.

[56] For example, once there was some prospect of a START agreement, experts began expressing related concerns about the Reagan administration's reduction proposal. See Michael R. Gordon, "Experts Criticize Reagan Proposal for Weapons Cuts," *New York Times*, 13 July 1986, p. 1. This should not be a major problem, however, since awareness of this increased threat will constrain the type and extent of reductions that the superpowers would be willing to negotiate.

reduce fears and improve superpower relations.[57] Just as some analysts worry about militarily insignificant increases in the size of Soviet forces, others might be relieved by reductions, even when they do not enhance U.S. capabilities or reduce the potential costs of an all-out war. In addition, interested publics in the United States and Western Europe are likely to focus on numbers at least as much as capabilities.

Nevertheless, reductions could create more problems than they solve. Giving priority to reductions is likely to fuel the belief that future agreements will, and should, lead to deeper reductions, with the eventual goal of disarmament. Doubting the wisdom of disarmament (as argued in Chapter Six), I believe that these expectations will be counterproductive. Further, because continually deeper cuts will be increasingly difficult to accomplish (as I argue in a moment), these frustrated expectations are likely to crush the arms control endeavor, which experience shows is severely strained by even modest objectives. In contrast, ceilings in combination with constraints on counterforce are more likely to communicate the ''right'' message: a willingness to moderate competition in the hope of reducing exaggerated tensions and misperceptions of intentions. Further, because ceilings might be understood to create a plateau that would be maintained indefinitely, they could provide a partial foundation for a long-term policy designed to make MAD as safe as possible. Reductions cannot provide such a foundation because they misconstrue the dangers we face and thereby misdirect our attention away from counterforce.

In sum, agreements designed to reduce superpower competition and improve superpower relations should give priority to limiting counterforce. While less important, agreements limiting the size and modernization of superpower arsenals might provide diplomatic value by clarifying further the superpowers' desire to forgo competition in strategic nuclear forces. By contrast, focusing on reducing the size of the superpowers' arsenals may actually create more problems than it alleviates.

Disagreements Based on Competing Theories and Facts

My assessment of the deterrent and diplomatic benefits of arms control is based heavily on the arguments of the punitive retaliation school and the need to address the dangers identified by the spiral model. In this section I briefly consider disagreements stemming from different theories and facts.

The arguments presented by the damage-limitation school appear to preclude virtually all arms control agreements. Strategic superiority, which it requires for extended deterrence, is incompatible with the most basic requirement for agreement, namely rough parity. Even if the Soviets are willing to accept unequal force sizes, they certainly will not agree to radically inferior

---

[57] The INF Treaty had this effect, at least in the short run.

capabilities. Thus, members of the damage-limitation school see arms control reducing U.S. security by constraining its pursuit of necessary strategic nuclear superiority. From this perspective, arms control not only lacks deterrent value, it has deterrent costs. While most strong opponents of arms control have focused on the details of specific proposals, Colin Gray, to his credit, presents the argument that may go to the heart of the matter:

> why should it matter whether or not the agreement [SALT II] is closely balanced in its terms? The United States requires a strategic force posture that could take the strategic initiative, dominate a process of escalation, and limit damage to the American homeland. These are serious questions. Much less serious questions would pertain to the true "balance" achieved in a SALT II regime, the verifiability of that regime, and the prospects for follow-on negotiations. Lurking behind the detail of the SALT II debate are fundamental issues of strategic adequacy.[58]

Also opposing arms control are analysts who believe that U.S. policy should be guided entirely by the deterrence model, and not balanced with spiral model concerns. According to these analysts, the Soviet Union will mistake U.S. concessions for a lack of resolve and will then be more likely to challenge U.S. interests. These analysts might still conclude that arms control can increase U.S. security. But this is possible only if agreements provide deterrent benefits that are large enough to more than offset the diplomatic costs.[59]

Members of the military denial school probably believe that I have underestimated the potential deterrent value of arms control. Believing that the ratio of superpower strategic forces influences the U.S. ability to deter Soviet attacks in MAD, they would argue that my analysis underestimates the value of arms control by overlooking relative force size and focusing instead on the absolute size of U.S. forces required for specific missions. Related, because these analysts tend to see greater dangers in ICBM vulnerability, they will see greater deterrent value in agreements that contribute to a solution.

Interestingly, from this perspective we would expect the military denial school to support arms control more strongly than the punitive retaliation school. The standard image, however, is that the punitive retaliation school is more politically liberal and thus tends to see greater value in arms control. In fact, the degree of support for arms control may depend on the specific proposal. Many members of the military denial school were strong supporters of

[58] Gray, "SALT II: The Real Debate," p. 11.

[59] However, analysts who see benefits in intense competition are unlikely to see arms control as providing large deterrent benefits. Because a competitive policy requires the United States to continue deploying counterforce, these analysts are likely to believe that the United States needs an extensive counterforce capability to adequately deter the Soviet Union. On a related point see Barry M. Blechman, "Do Negotiated Arms Limitations Have a Future?" *Foreign Affairs* 59, no. 1 (Fall 1980): 110–12.

SALT II, partly because it could contribute to survivable basing for MX. In contrast, many members of the punitive retaliation school were quite disappointed with SALT II, and some chose not to support it. Being less concerned with ICBM vulnerability and more concerned with slowing the deployment of new counterforce weapons, these analysts saw less value in SALT II.[60]

Although members of the military denial school see larger benefits in agreements that decrease ICBM vulnerability, they may see deterrent costs in agreements that limit U.S. counterforce. Unlike members of the punitive retaliation school, these analysts argue that the United States needs large numbers of counterforce weapons even if damage limitation is infeasible. The United States needs counterforce—even if the Soviet Union does not deploy counterforce—for limited nuclear options and for threatening targets that Soviet leaders value highly. There may be agreements that can balance the need to increase U.S. force survivability while preserving the U.S. ability to threaten Soviet forces and control targets. However, I have found little analysis of arms control designed to balance these objectives.[61]

ARMS CONTROL AND THE COST OF WAR

In theory, arms control agreements could lower the costs of war in two ways: reducing the destructive potential of superpower arsenals by radically reducing their size; and reducing incentives for escalation, thereby increasing the probability that a war, once started, would remain limited instead of becoming all-out.[62]

Reducing the Potential Damage

Although usually implicit, the extensive interest in reducing the size of superpower forces probably stems largely from the desire to reduce the destructive potential of the superpowers' arsenals. Nonetheless, we have strong reasons to believe that pursuing reductions will fail to achieve this objective.

Reductions that have any serious chance of being achieved in the foreseeable future will not significantly reduce the costs of an all-out war. For example, although now considered quite ambitious, 50-percent cuts in the super-

---

[60] Note, however, that arguments for limiting counterforce are more powerfully supported by spiral model arguments and concerns about misunderstandings of damage-limitation capabilities than by the strategic arguments I have identified with the punitive retaliation school.

[61] Sagan, *Moving Targets*, pp. 94–96, suggests that slow counterforce may provide at least a partial solution to this dilemma.

[62] The probability of escalation might also be reduced by improving the superpowers' ability to manage intra-war negotiations and avoid accidental and unauthorized escalation. This type of agreement would resemble agreements designed to reduce these dangers before the war starts, that is, during crises. See note 9 for discussion of these possibilities.

power arsenals would leave both countries with highly redundant assured destruction capabilities.[63]

Consequently, if the goal is reducing the cost of all-out war, today's plans for reducing the size of superpower forces should be viewed as only the first step toward still more ambitious agreements. Therefore, these reductions help reduce the destructive potential of arsenals only if they increase the future probability of achieving the truly radical reductions required to protect major cities.

They are quite unlikely to have this effect, however. Reductions that leave the superpowers with high confidence in their assured destruction capabilities would have implications wholly different from those that eliminate assured destruction capabilities. Because even deep cuts would not begin to take the superpowers' cities out of hostage status, they do not alter the most important features of MAD. U.S. security would continue to depend heavily on maintaining large retaliatory capabilities. In addition, much like today, U.S. retaliatory capabilities would remain large and diversified and therefore highly robust, relatively insensitive to all but very large changes in Soviet forces. Agreeing to these reductions, therefore, would not greatly increase the degree to which U.S. security depended on cooperation with the Soviet Union. And the danger of Soviet cheating would be only slightly greater than with an agreement to maintain forces at current levels. Thus, these so-called deep reductions would not dramatically change either the risks of cooperating with the Soviet Union or the requirements for adequately verifying the arms control agreement.[64]

In sharp contrast, truly radical offensive reductions would greatly increase the degree to which U.S. security depended on cooperation with the Soviet Union. Continued Soviet compliance with the arms control agreement would be crucial, since relatively small changes in Soviet forces might jeopardize U.S. deterrent capabilities. In other words, arms control that could reduce the costs of all-out war would begin to encounter the difficulties of achieving disarmament. As argued in Chapter Six, achieving disarmament or near-disarmament is likely to require fundamental improvements in the superpowers' relationship. There is little reason, however, to believe that large reductions in strategic nuclear forces will bring about these changes. As argued above, reductions are less likely to have this effect than limits on counterforce. Until

---

[63] For example, Feiveson, Ullman, and von Hippel, "Reducing U.S. and Soviet Nuclear Arsenals," show that 80 percent cuts would leave the superpowers with assured destruction capabilities. They do note, however, that cuts of this size would reduce the costs of a war to the superpowers' allies and noncombatant nations (pp. 317–18). Of course, the extent of retaliatory capabilities would depend on which forces the countries keep.

[64] In addition, roughly 50 percent cuts would not require a fundamental change in U.S. targeting requirements. Deeper cuts would raise this issue and thus would probably confront additional barriers. See, for example, May, Bing, and Steinbruner, "Strategic Arsenals after START."

these political changes occur, the barriers to near-disarmament will remain severe.[65]

In short, the difficulty of achieving reductions is not constant, but increases as the redundancy of retaliatory capabilities is reduced, and becomes extreme as this redundancy is drawn into question and eliminated. For example, 10-percent cuts should not be considered one tenth of the way to disarmament. In fact, following 10-percent cuts we would be essentially no closer to achieving disarmament than we are today. (A good analogy is someone who wants to swim from the United States to Europe: jumping into the Atlantic would be a necessary first step, but would not increase the probability of reaching Europe.) Thus, the value of deep cuts as the first step toward far more extensive reductions is very small.

Finally, the value is even smaller since, as argued in Chapter Six, we should not even be interested in moving toward disarmament since the United States is probably as secure in MAD as in disarmed worlds. Once the political conditions necessary for disarmament are established, there would be hardly any reason to disarm.

Reducing the Probability of Escalation

The second way in which arms control might reduce the costs of war is by reducing incentives and pressures for escalation once a conventional war or limited nuclear war is underway.[66] Because these pressures would be similar to those that would exist during crises, arms control agreements pursued to reduce the probability of war would also reduce the probability of escalation.[67] Agreements that have deterrent value could be important once a war occurs. For example, agreements that reduce incentives for preemptive attack would also increase the prospects for reaching a diplomatic resolution to a limited nuclear war; lacking damage-limitation capabilities, neither superpower should feel strong pressures to escalate to all-out war.[68] Similarly, increasing the superpowers' abilities to manage their forces at high levels of alert would

[65] A possible exception is that extensive experience with cooperative means of verification might help to overcome some of the technical barriers. Nevertheless, my basic conclusion remains unchanged since more fundamental barriers would remain unaffected.

[66] Thomas C. Schelling, "From an Airport Bench," *Bulletin of the Atomic Scientists* 45, no. 4 (May 1989): 29–31, stresses this possibility and the importance of unilateral measures for accomplishing this objective.

[67] Stephen W. Van Evera, "Causes of War" (Ph.D. diss., University of California at Berkeley, 1984), Chapter 12, discusses the relationship between theories of causes of war and theories of escalation.

[68] We should note, however, that the stability-instability paradox exists during war as well as before war begins. At least in theory, reducing escalatory incentives, specifically preemptive incentives, could make limited escalation less risky and therefore more likely.

increase the prospects for terminating a limited nuclear war as well as a severe crisis.

In fact, whatever contributions arms control can make to reducing incentives and pressures to escalate might be especially valuable if nuclear weapons are ever used in a limited attack. Any use of nuclear weapons would increase decisionmakers' assessments of the probability of all-out war. Consequently, launching a counterforce attack in pursuit of some damage limitation would become relatively more attractive following a limited nuclear attack. Therefore, as with prewar deterrence, arms control might make its greatest contribution to reducing the costs of nuclear war by moving the superpowers away from counterforce doctrines.

WHAT COSTS MIGHT ACCOMPANY ARMS CONTROL?

To assess the net effect of arms control we need to assess possible deterrent and diplomatic costs that arms control might generate. This section considers three types of costs that have been prominent in the arms control debate, reflecting concern that arms control: creates a lulling effect, supports bargaining chips, and encourages exaggeration of superpower tensions. I find that these potential costs do not come close to outweighing the potential benefits of arms control.

Lulling Effect

According to proponents of the "lulling effect" argument, negotiating and/or achieving arms control agreements will lull the U.S. public or congress into reducing necessary support for defense programs.[69] Arms control creates the mistaken impression that the Soviet threat has been greatly reduced and that U.S. forces are adequate. The United States then underinvests in military programs. The overall result of arms control is therefore a reduction in U.S. military capabilities and U.S. security.

In theory, analysts might believe that the benefits of an agreement more than offset the costs of the lulling effect. However, many analysts who have focused on the lulling effect tend to oppose arms control in general and have been strong opponents of specific agreements.[70] Because it does not depend upon the details of agreements, the lulling effect argument appears to be a general criticism of arms control. For example, Paul Nitze argued that SALT

[69] Sean M. Lynn-Jones, "Lulling and Stimulating Effects of Arms Control," in Carnesale and Haass, eds., *Superpower Arms Control: Setting the Record Straight*, pp. 223–73, provides a valuable review and analysis of the lulling effect arguments.

[70] There are exceptions, however. See, for example, Joseph J. Kruzel, "Arms Control and American Defense Policy: New Alternatives and Old Realities," *Daedalus* 110, no. 1 (Winter 1981): 155–56.

II "will incapacitate our minds and will. And that is more important than the specific provisions of the treaty."[71]

A common form of the lulling argument holds that SALT I encouraged the United States to stand still while the Soviet Union raced ahead in strategic forces. For example, Eugene Rostow, after comparing U.S. and Soviet forces at the signing of SALT I and during 1979 concludes: "Lulled by the treaty— as well as by illusions about 'overkill,' and by the high hopes we had invested in détente—into thinking that the 'arms race' was being brought under control, we allowed ourselves to fall behind in most relevant categories of military power: behind in production; behind in research and development; and behind in programming."[72]

A first step in assessing the lulling argument is simply to examine U.S. strategic development and deployment programs. During the period from the signing of SALT I to the beginning of the Reagan administration, the United States increased substantially the number and capability of its MIRVed ICBMs; developed and began producing a new SLBM (Trident I) and proceeded with the development of a more lethal SLBM (Trident II); developed a new ICBM (MX); developed and began producing a new strategic bomber (B-1) and continued work on a more advanced strategic bomber; and developed a variety of cruise missiles that were ready for deployment in the early 1980s.[73] The prospect of reaching another arms control agreement certainly did not stop the United States from developing and deploying nuclear systems.

Proponents could still argue that lulling occurred, even though U.S. modernization continued. The question more specifically bearing on the lulling effect is: Did arms control reduce U.S. defense efforts in general, and investments in strategic forces in particular? Assessing this question is complicated by the wide range of other factors that could have influenced U.S. security

[71] Senate Committee on Foreign Relations, *The SALT II Treaty, Hearing before the Committee on Foreign Relations*, pt. 1, 96th Cong., 1st Sess. (Washington, D.C.: GPO, 1979), p. 511, cited in Lynn-Jones, "Lulling and Stimulating Effects of Arms Control," p. 224. Nitze's point may be less general than it sounds, since he has supported other agreements.

[72] Eugene V. Rostow, "The Case against SALT II," *Commentary* 76, no. 2 (February 1979): 25. See also Leopold Labedz, "The Illusion of SALT," *Commentary* 68, no. 3 (September 1979): 57. For a related observation on how SALT II supports dangerous misperceptions of U.S. military strength see Paul Nitze, "Is SALT II a Fair Deal for the United States?" reprinted in Tyroler, ed., *Alerting America*, p. 162.

[73] Thomas B. Cochran, William M. Arkin, and Milton M. Hoenig, *Nuclear Weapons Data Book: Volume 1, U.S. Nuclear Forces and Capabilities* (Cambridge, Mass.: Ballinger, 1984), pp. 100–193. See also Michael Nacht, *The Age of Vulnerability: Threats to Nuclear Stalemate* (Washington, D.C.: Brookings Institution, 1985), pp. 129–34. Some might object to including the B-1 in this list since it was canceled by the Carter administration. However, this was the result of narrow military considerations and executive branch politics. See Robert J. Art and Stephen E. Ockenden, "The Domestic Politics of Cruise Missile Development, 1970–1980," in Richard K. Betts, ed., *Cruise Missiles: Technology, Strategy, Politics* (Washington, D.C.: Brookings Institution, 1981), pp. 373–79.

policy during this period, including the antidefense spirit that followed U.S. involvement in Vietnam, the weakness of the U.S. economy during some of this period, competition within the defense budget from conventional forces, and the arrival of strategic nuclear parity. Nevertheless, in a careful analysis Sean Lynn-Jones finds little evidence of lulling: "Given its potentially limited or nonexistent impact on prevailing support or opposition for defense programs, it would be a mistake to argue against future arms control agreements on the grounds that they will inevitably lull the United States into reduced military expenditures."[74] In fact, some arms control agreements may have had a small stimulating effect.

Underlying disagreements about the lulling effect may be more fundamental disputes. The most basic question is whether U.S. programs were adequate to meet its security requirements. Analysts who found U.S. deployment plans inadequate may have blamed arms control when in fact the real disagreement was over the forces required for deterrence.[75] For example, in 1976 Nitze argued that to restore its deterrent capabilities the United States should deploy 550 MX missiles.[76] In contrast, the Carter administration proposed deploying 200 MXs; and many analysts believed that the MX was unnecessary, independent of the outcome of the SALT II negotiations. These lower requirements for MX did not reflect lulling but rather divergent assessments of the requirements of deterrence. Similarly, analysts who believe that the Soviet Union is highly aggressive, and therefore tend to oppose arms control based on deterrence model arguments, could argue that negotiations have lulled proponents of arms control. In fact, however, most proponents of arms control started with a less malign view of the Soviet Union.

Bargaining Chips

Some analysts believe that pursuing arms control makes the United States more likely to acquire weapons that it should forgo. They observe that new weapons systems often receive support because they are believed to be necessary to enhance the U.S. bargaining position in arms control negotiations. If negotiations then fail, the United States is left with "bargaining chips" that it would have been better off without. These critics point out that while the bargaining chip rationale has been employed to support a wide variety of U.S. strategic systems—including ABM, MIRV, Trident submarines, cruise mis-

---

[74] Lynn-Jones, "Lulling and Stimulating Effects of Arms Control," pp. 263–64. See also Nacht, *The Age of Vulnerability*, p. 134.

[75] Some analysts went a step further and incorrectly blamed SALT for creating ICBM vulnerability. See, for example, American Security Council, *An Analysis of SALT II* (Boston: Coalition for Peace through Strength, May 1979), reprinted in Roger P. Labrie, ed., *The SALT Handbook* (Washington, D.C.: American Enterprise Institute, 1979), p. 676.

[76] Paul Nitze, "Deterring Our Deterrent," *Foreign Policy*, no. 25 (Winter 1976–77): 209.

siles, MX, and ASAT—only ABM has been traded away.[77] Arms control can therefore undermine desirable unilateral restraint. Critics conclude that not only do bargaining chips increase the economic cost of the U.S. arsenal since the systems are unnecessary, but more importantly they reduce U.S. security since the systems are dangerous.

These critics, however, exaggerate this cost of arms control since the United States would most likely have failed to exercise unilateral restraint in the absence of arms control negotiations. None of the systems that critics commonly describe as failed bargaining chips were originally developed for this reason. Instead, they grew out of advances in technology and/or were developed with military missions in mind, often with strong support from the military services and/or the Department of Defense. This is true even for cruise missiles, which are often said to have been developed as bargaining chips.[78] Further, there is no reason to believe that the United States would not have deployed MIRVs in the absence of arms control, and little reason for believing that arms control was critical to the decision to deploy ALCMs.[79] On the other hand, the Reagan administration used bargaining chip arguments effectively in gaining support for the MX; these arguments may have actually tipped the balance.[80] Even in this case, however, the impact of bargaining chip arguments might be exaggerated: we should ask whether some other combination of arguments would have eventually succeeded in getting funding for a limited number of MXs. In short, critics of bargaining chips may actually be identifying the failure of their

[77] For critical assessments of bargaining chips see Jane M. O. Sharp, "Bargaining Chips," *Foreign Service Journal* 61, no. 3 (March 1984): 30–35; Robert J. Bresler and Robert C. Gray, "The Bargaining Chip and SALT," *Political Science Quarterly* 92, no. 1 (Spring 1977): 65–88; and George Rathjens, "Are Arms Control Negotiations Worthwhile?" in Paul Abrecht and Ninan Koshy, eds., *Before It's Too Late: The Challenge of Nuclear Disarmament* (Geneva: World Council of Churches, 1983), pp. 273–75.

[78] On the history of cruise missiles see Art and Ockenden, "The Domestic Politics of Cruise Missile Development, 1970–1980," pp. 359–413, especially p. 368. For a description that places greater emphasis on the bargaining chip considerations see Ron Huisken, "The History of the Modern Cruise Missile Programs," in Richard K. Betts, ed., *Cruise Missiles: Technology, Strategy, Politics* (Washington, D.C.: Brookings Institution, 1981), p. 86.

Useful histories of other weapons systems that have been suggested as possible bargaining chips include Ted Greenwood, *Making the MIRV: A Study in Defense Decision-Making* (Cambridge, Mass.: Ballinger, 1975); Ernest J. Yanarella, *The Missile Defense Controversy: Strategy, Technology, and Politics, 1955–1972* (Lexington: University Press of Kentucky, 1977); Paul B. Stares, *The Militarization of Space: U.S. Policy, 1945–84* (Ithaca: Cornell University Press, 1985); and John Edwards, *Super Weapon: The Making of the MX* (New York: W. W. Norton, 1982). See also Matthew Evangelista, *Innovation and the Arms Race: How the United States and the Soviet Union Develop New Military Technologies* (Ithaca: Cornell University Press, 1988).

[79] I should add that I do not believe the United States should have agreed to ban ALCMs and therefore do not consider this particular deployment to be a failure of arms control.

[80] Steven E. Miller, "The Viability of Nuclear Arms Control: US Domestic and Bilateral Factors," *Bulletin of Peace Proposals* 16, no. 3 (1985): 269–70.

views to prevail in the debate over U.S. force requirements, and mistakenly blaming this on arms control.

If so, then ironically arms control might be the critics' best tool for stopping the United States from deploying these bargaining chip systems. The U.S. debate can be divided into three types of preferences for deploying the weapons systems in question.[81] First, some analysts believe the United States would be more secure without the system, even if the Soviets deploy it. These analysts are the critics of bargaining chips—they prefer an arms control agreement, but favor unilateral restraint over matching Soviet deployment. Second, some analysts agree that the United States is most secure if neither country deploys the system, but, if the Soviet Union deploys it, believe the United States would be more secure with the system than without it. These analysts favor trading the system, but oppose unilateral restraint. Thus, for these analysts the weapons system is not really a bargaining chip. Third, some analysts believe the United States is more secure when both superpowers have the system than when both are without it. These analysts oppose an arms control agreement. Unilateral restraint is possible only if the first group of analysts can prevail in the domestic political debate. If, however, this is impossible, arms control might still enable the first and second groups to develop a coalition that can dominate the third group, resulting in bilateral limits. For example, support for the ABM Treaty probably reflected this type of coalition.[82] In this type of case, arms control may be the critics' only realistic option for restraint.

In contrast, the bargaining chip critics face serious risks when they possess sufficient influence to prevail in the U.S. domestic political debate. The weapons system is then a "pure bargaining chip," that is, one that would otherwise be restrained unilaterally. If critics of bargaining chips believed the United States was willing to trade the weapons system they might support it as a pure bargaining chip in the hope of achieving an arms control ban, thereby gaining limits on Soviet forces. If, however, negotiations fail, these analysts lose the opportunity to secure their second-best outcome and end up with their least desirable outcome.[83] It is this case, therefore, in which using bargaining chips

[81] My discussion assumes the superpowers are trading only weapons of the same type. In practice this is often not the case, but the basic arguments apply more generally. For an excellent in-depth discussion of these considerations see Thomas C. Schelling, "A Framework for the Evaluation of Arms-Control Proposals," *Daedalus* 104, no. 3 (Summer 1975): 187–200.

[82] On the debate over ABM see Yanarella, *The Missile Defense Controversy*; for a useful brief summary see David N. Schwartz, "Past and Present: The Historical Legacy" in Ashton B. Carter and David N. Schwartz, eds., *Ballistic Missile Defense* (Washington, D.C.: Brookings Institution, 1984).

[83] The United States could always decide to retire unwanted systems, however. Thus, this argument rests on the assumption that stopping a weapons system before deployment is easier than retiring it early.

could bring arms control costs.[84] Critics argue as though cases of pure bargaining chips have been common. In fact, however, none of the cases identified by the bargaining chip critics falls clearly into this category.

When the possibility of using bargaining chips does pose a dilemma, analysts need to assess the value of the weapons system in the specific negotiation.[85] The larger the increase in the probability of an agreement, the more sense it makes to support a weapon system as a bargaining chip.[86]

Judging this effect will often be difficult, simply because so many factors can influence the outcome of negotiations. Nevertheless, there are some general questions we should ask. How likely is success without the bargaining chip? The basic logic of needing weapons to trade (or at least the credible threat to deploy them in the future) seems unassailable, since it is the possibility of U.S. concessions that creates the Soviet incentive to negotiate. If, however, the United States can trade forces that are already deployed, then the dilemma of bargaining chips is less severe. Conversely, if the probability of success is low, can the bargaining chip significantly increase its prospects?

More specifically, we should ask what trade is actually being proposed and why the bargaining chip increases the probability of success. Claims for bargaining chips are often quite general—for example, the United States needs to bargain from strength. Confronted with this argument, we need to consider whether the United States is already "strong enough" to bargain effectively with the Soviet Union. For example, why did the Reagan administration believe the MX was necessary for bargaining when the United States was already preparing to deploy thousands of highly lethal Trident II warheads and had greatly increased the lethality of its Minuteman IIIs? What concessions was the MX supposed to achieve in the START negotiations?

Although basic, the arms control debate sees little analysis of the benefits bargaining chips are supposed to provide. Schelling observes, for example, that "no one has given an estimate of the likelihoods of successful disarmament negotiations with and without MX: if the prospect were ten percent without MX and 30 percent with it—a differential I find implausible—it could still be a bad bargain if it is not the weapon we want."[87] Similarly, since there were strong reasons for believing that the early Reagan administration was not seriously committed to achieving an agreement on strategic nuclear weapons,

[84] Analysts who oppose arms control might resort to bargaining chip tactics to attract analysts from the first and second groups. However, if analysts in the first group could not have prevailed on their own, then the costs are low, since the United States would have matched Soviet deployment anyway.

[85] Some critics have argued that bargaining chips can actually reduce the Soviet interest in agreement. See, for example, Sharp, "Bargaining Chips," p. 34.

[86] We are actually concerned with the expected benefits of the bargaining chip, which equals this probability times the benefit of the agreement.

[87] Schelling, "What Went Wrong with Arms Control?" p. 231.

and that the prospects for success were low, supporting MX as a bargaining chip was a bad bet. In other words, analysts can reduce the risk of employing bargaining chips by more carefully gauging whether supporting the weapons system will yield success in arms control.

In sum, although it is possible in theory that arms control would undermine unilateral U.S. restraint, in practice this appears to be rare. Instead, for analysts who favor unilateral restraint, arms control will often be their best option for achieving any type of restraint. In the unusual case of a pure bargaining chip, the risk of employing bargaining chip tactics can be reduced by more carefully evaluating its negotiating value.

Exaggeration of Superpower Tensions

Analysts have identified a variety of ways in which arms control could contribute to superpower tensions. If these additional tensions overwhelm the diplomatic benefits of arms control, then the superpowers might be better off forgoing arms control. The following discussion considers three ways in which arms control might create tensions. It finds that although arms control might create some tensions, these usually substitute for more serious problems that would exist without arms control.

The first argument holds that arms control reduces U.S. tolerance for differences in the superpowers' forces by focusing attention on numbers and types of weapons. As a result, the United States feels pressure to buy systems in which it would otherwise have little interest and worries more about Soviet systems that would otherwise appear less threatening. As with bargaining chip arguments, these arguments are often presented by analysts who tend to favor arms control in theory, but who have come to question its benefits in practice.[88]

While there is a grain of truth in these concerns, they exaggerate this negative effect of arms control. Arms control proposals do focus attention on specific forces or asymmetries that would otherwise be unlikely to receive much attention. A good example from SALT II is the Soviet backfire bomber. Treaty opponents complained bitterly that this bomber was not included under the treaty's limits. Outside of the SALT debate, however, analysts have been essentially unconcerned about the strategic threat posed by the Backfire. A second example is the extensive attention that proposals to eliminate long-range theater missiles in Europe focused on previously unpublicized asymmetries in shorter-range missiles in Europe.[89]

---

[88] See, for example, Jane Sharp, "Restructuring the SALT Dialogue," *International Security* 6, no. 3 (Winter 1981/1982): 152–61, who notes other costs, including the retention of obsolete forces and the creation of tensions within the NATO alliance.

[89] On the Backfire issue see Strobe Talbott, *Endgame: The Inside Story of SALT II* (New York:

However, although much of the debate over arms control proposals focuses on numerical differences and asymmetries, these comparisons play an influential role throughout the strategic nuclear debate. Arms control is not the source of these comparisons, nor is it primarily responsible for their extensive use in the nuclear debate.[90] Instead, analysts who already accept the importance of these measures and comparisons use them in the arms control debate. Equally important, analysts who oppose arms control can always find (or invent) measures that make a proposal look unattractive. Thus, in this regard, arms control is hardly special: with and without arms control, analysts favoring the acquisition of forces will have available comparisons that support their case.[91] The additional distortions created by arms control seem to be quite small.

The second argument holds that pursuing arms control lends support to U.S. weapons acquisition, which in turn generates the spiral effects arms control is supposed to reduce. Analysts worry that U.S. unilateral restraint is undermined by bargaining chip arguments and by the stimulating effect of the domestic bargaining that is usually required to gain support for arms control. From this perspective, arms control helps fuel the arms race and thereby increases superpower tensions. As discussed above, however, these side effects of arms control are quite probably smaller than the pressures that would exist in its absence.

The third argument holds that concerns about Soviet compliance with agreements are themselves an important source of superpower conflict. Some compliance problems are probably unavoidable, since arms control agreements establish provisions that are sometimes ambiguous and open to a range of interpretations.[92] Further, even if the United States accepts that the Soviets are following the letter of an agreement, its expectations about Soviet behavior under the agreement may be disappointed, leading to the damaging conclusion

---

Harper & Row, 1979); on the effect of INF negotiations see Jesse James, "Controversy at Short Range," *Arms Control Today* 17, no. 5 (June 1987): 11–15.

[90] Numerical comparisons played an important role before the United States started with SALT. For example, Alain C. Enthoven and K. Wayne Smith, *How Much Is Enough? Shaping the Defense Program, 1961–1968* (New York: Harper and Row, 1971), note that "some people believe that the way to measure the adequacy of U.S. forces is to compare them directly with those of the Soviets. If the Soviets outnumbered us by some particular criterion—for example, megatons—this is supposedly prima-facie evidence that the Soviet forces are superior to ours and that ours are inadequate. Even though such direct comparisons are meaningless, so many people insist on playing the comparisons game that the Secretary of Defense is often compelled to participate, if only in self-defense" (p. 179). Michael Nacht, "Toward an American Conception of Regional Security," *Daedalus* 110, no. 1: 8–9, however, argues that the coming of parity did increase the importance of numbers in the U.S. debate.

[91] Numerical comparisons can also, of course, be mustered against further acquisitions. See Salman, Sullivan, and Van Evera, "Analysis or Propaganda?"

[92] Richard N. Haass, "Verification and Compliance," in Carnesale and Haass, eds., *Superpower Arms Control*, p. 321.

that the Soviets are violating the spirit of the agreement. Further, the Soviets may actually violate treaties—the Krasnoyarsk radar violation of the ABM Treaty being the prime example.

We need first to consider the magnitude of tensions generated by compliance problems. Although the SALT experience has been plagued from the beginning by compliance problems, their severity has varied greatly. Until the Reagan years, the superpowers were quite successful at resolving compliance disputes and, as a result, the political costs were small. By contrast, compliance problems were at the center of the arms control debate for much of the Reagan administration.[93] The Reagan administration argued that these violations reflected malign Soviet intentions and were a serious barrier to future agreements.[94] However, critics countered convincingly that the Reagan administration had exaggerated these compliance problems and failed to take advantage of the more constructive, less public means of resolving these disputes.[95] With the possible exception of the Krasnoyarsk radar, these possible compliance problems might have been resolved with much smaller negative effect on superpower relations.[96] Thus, although compliance issues were an important source of tension during the Reagan years, costs of this magnitude were not a necessary companion of strategic arms control.

Nevertheless, compliance problems cannot be totally eliminated by reducing the ambiguity of treaties, improvements in Soviet compliance, and a more constructive U.S. approach to resolving disputes. We must therefore compare the diplomatic costs of working out compliance problems with arms control's potential diplomatic benefits in reduced competition and increased predictability. Assuming the Soviets are interested in preserving the arms control agreement, questionable Soviet activities are likely to be militarily insignificant: the United States will agree to arms control proposals only if they are adequately verifiable; given the Soviet interest in the treaty, the U.S. ability to withdraw from it will deter extensive violations; and, if necessary, the United States could react before its military capabilities are significantly reduced. Nevertheless, if compliance problems cannot be resolved within the

[93] For thorough discussions of the compliance record see Gloria Duffy, *Compliance and the Future of Arms Control* (Cambridge, Mass.: Ballinger, 1988), and James A. Schear, "Arms Control Treaty Compliance: Buildup to a Breakdown?" *International Security* 10, no. 2 (Fall 1985): 141–82.

[94] Ronald Reagan, *Soviet Noncompliance with Arms Control Agreements*, President's Report to Congress (Washington, D.C.: The White House, January 23, 1984; February 1, 1985; December 23, 1985; and March 10, 1986).

[95] See, for example, James P. Rubin and Matthew Bunn, "Analysis of the President's Report on Soviet Noncompliance with Arms Control Agreements," (Washington, D.C.: Arms Control Association, March 1987); Thomas K. Longstreth, "Report Aims to Sabotage Arms Control," *Bulletin of the Atomic Scientists* (January 1985): 29–34; and Duffy, *Compliance and the Future of Arms Control*.

[96] For additional sources on this radar issue see note 4 in Chapter Nine.

consultative mechanisms established by the treaty, they will generate diplomatic costs by raising doubts about whether the Soviets negotiated in good faith. On the other hand, without arms control, the United States would probably confront a larger Soviet buildup, which is likely to generate larger doubts about Soviet objectives. Consequently, although compliance problems will generate frictions within the context of a cooperative arrangement, these tensions are likely to be smaller than if the Soviets pursue a military buildup unconstrained by arms control.[97]

FEASIBILITY AND SPECIFIC RECOMMENDATIONS

Overall, this analysis finds that arms control could increase U.S. security. Contrary to most of the debate, however, the benefits that arms control might provide are found to be relatively modest. Primarily this is because the United States can maintain a high degree of security without arms control. In addition, the United States could acquire many of these arms control benefits unilaterally by shifting its strategic doctrine and forces away from counterforce. Further, because disarmament is probably not preferable to MAD, arms control cannot increase U.S. security by promising disarmament in the future. Nevertheless, although modest, the benefits of arms control exceed its costs. Critics' arguments often exaggerate the costs of arms control by failing to consider the analogous costs in an unconstrained regime.

In general terms, the benefits are modest because strategic nuclear weapons essentially eliminate the security dilemma. In this world, even without cooperation, both superpowers can maintain high confidence in the capabilities necessary for deterrence; and they can adopt essentially defensive (countervalue) postures without jeopardizing their military capabilities, which enables them to appear relatively unthreatening to each other. Further, the dominance of retaliatory capabilities tends to reduce the political dangers of whatever military competition does occur.[98]

Arms control may nevertheless have a valuable role to play because the superpowers have not taken full advantage of the nuclear revolution. Although retaliatory capabilities have an overwhelming advantage over damage-limitation capabilities, both superpowers have maintained counterforce doctrines and deployed extensive counterforce arsenals. The nuclear arms competition

---

[97] However, the balance between these costs and benefits will depend on how restrictive the agreement is. For example, agreements that hardly restrain the superpowers' forces will provide smaller benefits in reduced competition but could generate essentially the same compliance problems.

[98] For elaboration, see Chapter Three. For similar points see Robert Jervis, "Security Regimes," *International Organization* 36, no. 2 (Spring 1982): 373–76. One qualification, however, is that buying offense when there is no security dilemma is clearly unnecessary and therefore has the potential to project an especially threatening image.

has been damped by the dominance of retaliatory capabilities, but has nevertheless been more intense than if both countries had adopted more defensive doctrines.

Which specific arms control policies the United States should pursue depends on the details of forces and politics. Nonetheless, putting aside feasibility for the moment, some general guidance is possible. Limiting and reducing counterforce will provide the clearest benefits. Possibly most important, limits on counterforce would provide diplomatic benefits by reducing superpower competition and its possibly negative spiral effects on the superpowers' views of each other's intentions. While the robustness of the superpowers' retaliatory capabilities moderates the dangers of counterforce, the superpower arms race remains a source of unnecessary tension.

In addition, limiting counterforce could make a severe superpower crisis less dangerous by further reducing the already small incentives for launching a massive preemptive attack. Probably far more important, limits on counterforce would make even clearer the futility of military doctrines designed to reduce the costs of an all-out war. Consequently, political and military leaders would be less likely to overestimate their incentives for striking first in a severe crisis.

Ceilings on the size of superpower arsenals and agreements that slowed their modernization would be less important than limits on counterforce but might still be valuable. These agreements provide diplomatic value by constraining deployments that might appear threatening even though they pose no real threat to the superpowers' military capabilities. Limits on counterforce facilitate limits on the modernization of retaliatory capabilities by protecting the ability of deployed systems to retaliate. In many cases, the level at which ceilings are set would not be especially important; the status quo might be chosen if it facilitates agreement.

Finally, although it appears to command strong support across the political spectrum, reducing the size of offenses does not deserve priority. The case for reductions is strongest when viewed as an anti-counterforce measure—specifically, as part of a plan for increasing ICBM survivability. Other arguments for pursuing reductions are weaker. The diplomatic benefits of even large cuts, say on the order of 50 percent, are likely to be smaller than is generally believed. Since these cuts will leave the superpowers with highly redundant retaliatory capabilities, people worried by the sheer size of the superpowers' destructive capabilities should feel little relief. Further, in MAD, smaller forces will appear less threatening only if they pose a reduced threat to the superpowers' retaliatory capabilities. While this is a possible outcome, policies focused specifically on counterforce are more likely to yield success by this measure. Finally, focusing on reductions confuses the debate by incorrectly suggesting that large numbers of weapons are themselves a problem and that disarmament is the long-term goal. In contrast, policies focused on counterforce correctly identify the sources of potential danger.

Although this broad guidance is straightforward, designing an arms control policy is more complicated since sound policy must consider the feasibility of reaching agreements. If the United States is unlikely to achieve the most desirable agreements, then it might be better off pursuing somewhat less desirable agreements that are more easily achieved. The best should not be allowed to be the enemy of the good.

The history of superpower strategic arms control alerts us to the importance of considering feasibility. Although theoretical arguments for limiting counterforce have been prominent since the early 1960s and analysts have developed a plethora of ambitious proposals, the record remains one of modest limitations. The limited test ban treaty did not slow the superpowers' ability to develop more advanced nuclear weapons. The SALT I and II limits on missiles and bombers are generally believed to have essentially codified the superpowers' deployment plans. Neither agreement significantly constrained modernization of offenses; instead, counterforce capabilities were allowed to grow through MIRVing and improvements in the accuracy of ballistic missiles.[99] Nor did either agreement require substantial reductions in the size of the superpowers' offenses.[100] In START, the Reagan administration pursued deep cuts for much of its tenure, but left office without a strategic arms agreement.

The exception to the rule of modest strategic arms limitations is the ABM Treaty, which banned militarily significant deployments of BMD and is of unlimited duration. Even here, however, there is some question as to whether the superpowers would have deployed large BMD forces if the treaty had not been negotiated, since neither superpower had developed BMD that held any prospect of protecting its cities. Assuming a START agreement is achieved, it might count as another exception, since superpower forces would be reduced by approximately 50 percent. We should note, however, that the agreement currently under negotiation would not prevent either superpower from modernizing its strategic nuclear force, allowing the deployment of more lethal counterforce systems. Further, the agreement would not increase the survivability of the silo-based ICBMs that the United States would retain under the agreement.

The failure to achieve more extensive limits during the 1970s and 1980s, which according to arms control theory would have increased U.S. security,

[99] There is a possible exception, however—SALT II in combination with multiple point structure basing proposed by the Carter administration might have reduced the Soviet threat to MX.

[100] For a more extensive review see Carnesale and Haass, "Conclusions," in *Superpower Arms Control*, pp. 342–46. Michael MccGuire, *Military Objectives in Soviet Foreign Policy* (Washington, D.C.: Brookings Institution, 1987), p. 240, disagrees, arguing that SALT II probably resulted in a 40-percent reduction in the planned deployment of MIRVed Soviet ICBMs.

cannot be explained by the standard criteria for judging the feasibility of arms control agreements. These criteria—that an agreement establish rough parity and be adequately verifiable—could have been satisfied by a wide range of more restrictive and probably more desirable agreements.[101]

Instead, superpower arms control has been severely impeded by a variety of domestic and international barriers.[102] Two closely related factors have been especially important in defeating efforts to limit counterforce. First, both superpowers have maintained strategic doctrines that are heavily oriented toward counterforce targeting; neither appears to have given up entirely on the hope of limiting damage if war occurs.

Second, and closely related, at least in the United States, the military has opposed limits on counterforce.[103] The history of nuclear arms control includes many cases in which the U.S. military has resisted limits on future counterforce weapons or has tried to use arms control to maintain its counterforce capability: during SALT I these interests were reflected in opposition to a ban on MIRVs;[104] during SALT II the military was influential in making sure the treaty protected MX by allowing each side to deploy one new type of ICBM;[105] during the formulation of the U.S. position on START the Joint

---

[101] On the political necessity of parity see Michael Krepon, *Strategic Stalemate*, pp. 129–32. On the requirements of verification see Michael Krepon, "The Political Dynamics of Verification and Compliance Debates," and Mark M. Lowenthal and Joel Wit, "The Politics of Verification," both in William C. Potter, ed., *Verification and Arms Control* (Lexington, Mass.: Lexington Books, 1985).

These criteria are themselves contentious. On disputes about parity see Richard K. Betts, "Elusive Equivalence: The Political and Military Meaning of Parity," in Samuel P. Huntington, ed., *The Strategic Imperative* (Cambridge, Mass.: Ballinger, 1982), pp. 101–40. Examining the sources of disagreement about the requirements of verification is James A. Shear, "Explaining the Verification Debate," in Eden and Miller, *Nuclear Arguments*.

[102] Steven E. Miller, "Politics over Promise: Domestic Impediments to Arms Control," *International Security* 8, no. 4 (Spring 1984): 67–90; idem, "The Viability of Nuclear Arms Control: U.S. Domestic and Bilateral Factors," *Bulletin of Peace Proposals* 16, no. 3 (1985): 263–76; and idem, *The Limits of Mutual Restraint*.

[103] Military opposition to limits on counterforce is far from surprising since a variety of organizational considerations provide reinforcing reasons for the military to prefer a counterforce doctrine. See Chapter Eleven for a brief discussion.

[104] Gerard Smith, *Doubletalk: The Story of SALT I* (Garden City, N.Y.: Doubleday, 1980; Lanham, Md.: University Press of America, 1985), pp. 157–70. Smith argues that "in both capitals, political authorities would have to take and sustain extremely difficult positions vis-à-vis their military if MIRVs were to be controlled, positions which could undermine crucial military support for the entire SALT effort. This common military interest in letting MIRV run free went a long way to spoil chances for a MIRV ban" (p. 157; see also pp. 158, 161). See also Greenwood, *Making the MIRV*, on the strong institutional interest in MIRV and the difficulties this created for arms control.

[105] Talbott, *Endgame*, 158–60. The March 1977 proposal, which had the strong support of Secretary of Defense Brown, would have banned MX. However, this proposal was not developed in the standard interagency process. Talbott notes that the JCS were "disgruntled" with the possibility of trading away MX, but also that they conceded that "deep reductions in the Soviet heavy

Chiefs protected their ability to destroy Soviet forces by insisting that cuts in the number of warheads be combined with low limits on the number of launchers;[106] and later in the START negotiations the Joint Chiefs supported a ban on mobile ICBMs in part because Soviet mobiles would be difficult to target.[107] Since military opposition to an agreement is probably sufficient to prevent the broad domestic support required for ratification of arms control agreements, limiting counterforce will require overcoming this potentially critical barrier.

It is possible that the past will not be a good guide to the future. Increased Soviet willingness to make concessions under Gorbachev's leadership and possible changes in Soviet doctrine may help to eliminate barriers to more ambitious agreements. The INF Treaty and Soviet positions in the START and conventional arms control talks suggest that this may be the case.[108] In addition, in the United States wide recognition of improved superpower relations and the end of the Cold War may increase the prospects for achieving ambitious agreements by generating strong pressures for arms control while simultaneously creating doubts about the need to modernize American strategic forces. Nevertheless, the history of strategic arms control strongly suggests that prudent U.S. policy should establish priorities among theoretically desirable agreements.

The United States should give highest priority to protecting the ABM Treaty. It limits counterforce by banning militarily significant deployments of ballistic missile defense, thereby making it more difficult for the superpowers to acquire damage-limitation capabilities.[109] Its diplomatic value is greater than its deterrent value since all foreseeable area defenses can be defeated by retaliatory capabilities.

---

and land-based MIRV force were much more important'' (pp. 61–62). Talbott also recounts that when Defense Department experts realized that provisions designed to stop improvements in the accuracy of Soviet MIRVs might ban the development of U.S. maneuvering reentry vehicles (MARVs), the Department of Defense insisted that the United States retract its provision (pp. 192–93).

[106] Strobe Talbott, *Deadly Gambits: The Reagan Administration and the Stalemate in Nuclear Arms Control* (New York: Alfred A. Knopf, 1984), pp. 254–62.

[107] R. Jeffery Smith, "Proposal to Ban Mobile Missiles Favors Targeting over Arms Control," *Science* 233 (22 August 1986): 831. See also Talbott, *Deadly Gambits*, p. 259. It is interesting to note in this regard that Soviet willingness in SALT II to accept limits on the fractionation of its MIRVs did greatly reduce the threat that the Soviet Union could easily pose to the basing mode the Carter administration planned for MX. If the Soviets believed that the United States would deploy MPS, then they did negotiate away in SALT II much of their ability to destroy U.S. land-based forces. I have been unable to find explanations of this Soviet decision.

[108] See Hardenbergh, ed., *Arms Control Reporter*, for descriptions of these negotiations.

[109] However, by limiting BMD that might protect retaliatory forces the treaty might also preserve the superpowers' abilities to destroy land-based forces, most importantly ICBMs. In concluding in favor of the treaty I have weighed the benefits of forgoing area defenses against the costs of forgoing point defenses.

The treaty deserves priority primarily because it already exists. In general, strategic defenses are not more threatening than offensive counterforce. In other words, if we considered only benefits, the ABM Treaty might not receive special priority among anti-counterforce agreements. However, if correctly handled, the prospects for maintaining the ABM Treaty are better than for severely limiting other types of counterforce. Thus, the United States should direct its policies toward protecting these limits before focusing on additional limits. This is accomplished most obviously by rejecting deployment of BMD as a long-term objective. In addition, arms control agreements, including ceilings, that constrain the superpowers from competing in strategic offenses might also help protect the ABM Treaty. In an environment of intense competition the ABM Treaty seems out of step with U.S. policy and is therefore more vulnerable.[110]

The obvious next objective for arms control is to eliminate the threat that Soviet ICBMs pose to U.S. ICBMs, since this is the major counterforce threat currently facing the United States. However, considering feasibility raises doubts about whether this should be the focus of U.S. arms control efforts. First, an agreement that significantly increases the survivability of current silo-based U.S. ICBMs would require radical restructuring of the Soviet force—eliminating or at least severely limiting MIRVed ICBMs—and is therefore unlikely.[111] In return, the Soviets would probably require changes in U.S. forces that make their silos more survivable, which also seems unlikely.

Second, although arms control is more likely to contribute to the survivability of mobile ICBMs, since reductions of Soviet forces on the scale now planned in START could be valuable in this role, questions remain about this approach. Will a few hundred survivable mobile ICBMs be considered an adequate solution to the ICBM vulnerability problem when a much larger number of silo-based warheads would remain highly vulnerable? If not, then the diplomatic value of the agreement will be reduced. In addition, there are still doubts about whether the United States will proceed with mobile basing; deciding against it would preclude this arms control solution.

Given that ICBM vulnerability does not jeopardize the U.S. ability to maintain a redundant and somewhat diversified retaliatory force, one option is therefore to accept ICBM vulnerability (or get rid of vulnerable ICBMs) and build an arms control regime around the ABM Treaty, which would be sup-

---

[110] Blechman, "Do Negotiated Arms Control Limitations Have a Future?" p. 109, made this point before the treaty was threatened by SDI.

[111] The Bush administration proposed that the superpowers ban mobile MIRVs as the first stage of a restructuring that would eventually eliminate all land-based MIRVed missiles. The Soviets are reported to have rejected this change in the START agreement partly because they have deployed this type of missile and the United States has not, and partly because it failed to constrain American sea-based ballistic missiles. See Michael R. Gordon, "Soviets Rebuffed by Cheney on Plan Curbing Sea Arms," *New York Times*, 16 April 1990, pp. 1, 8, and Andrew Rosenthal, "All the Arms Talk," *New York Times*, 30 April 1990, p. 8.

ported by ceilings on force size and other restraints that would reduce superpower competition. Getting rid of silo-based ICBMs eliminates targets for Soviet counterforce systems, thereby reducing the dangers created by Soviet counterforce and the need to constrain it in an arms control agreement. At a minimum, the United States should not make solving the ICBM vulnerability problem a necessary condition for reaching strategic agreements with the Soviet Union, since other limitations would also be valuable.

Nevertheless, given the continuing consensus on the need to increase ICBM survivability, the United States will probably require arms control to contribute to a solution. Given this situation, and assuming that the superpowers have reached a START agreement, a sound arms control policy would include the following features. First, if the United States decides to deploy mobile ICBMs, there should be insistence on further reduction in Soviet forces only if they are necessary to achieve the desired level of survivability of the mobile basing mode. The United States should be open to the possibility of continuing with an agreement that retains ceilings near START levels and deploying its mobile missiles in a larger mobile or deceptive basing system. Although placing greater demands on the basing mode, this might be preferable if it increases the prospects for maintaining limits on the size of the Soviet force, thereby protecting the long-term survivability of the mobile missiles.

Second, reductions have even less to offer if the United States decides not to deploy a mobile basing mode, but instead to increase the survivability of silo-based ICBMs by agreeing to move away from MIRVed ballistic missiles. In this case, the United States should also try to negotiate limits on increases in the lethality of Soviet MIRVed SLBMs, since they are likely to eventually threaten U.S. silos, and should be willing to trade the Trident II missile to achieve this constraint on Soviet forces. The United States and the Soviet Union would not need to reduce the size of their SLBM forces, however. If the superpowers agree to deploy only single warhead ICBMs they may want smaller ICBM forces, at least partly because such a force is more expensive per warhead than a MIRVed ICBM force. If so, these reductions should emerge out of the effort to limit counter-silo capabilities, and not as a key objective of the negotiations.

Third, if the United States decides to retain much of its current ICBM force, it should consider bans on new ballistic missiles and flight testing. If these restrictions could halt the decline in silo survivability, they would insure approximately as many survivable warheads as current plans for mobile basing.

Finally, the United States should not enlarge its counterforce arsenal in the hope of using these systems as bargaining chips. It already has plenty of counterforce to trade away, and chances are it will not trade its newest counterforce systems.[112] Since the United States will be better off forgoing counterforce

---

[112] For example, although the Reagan administration argued that MX was required as a bar-

even if the Soviet Union maintains its threat to U.S. ICBMs,[113] the risks of this negotiating strategy exceed its benefits.

Should the United States pursue other agreements limiting counterforce? Because large asymmetries in both ASW and air defense make agreements on these systems extremely unlikely, the United States should not pursue constraints on these systems.[114] Instead, the United States should unilaterally forgo strategic ASW and continue modernizing its air-breathing capabilities as necessary to offset improvements in Soviet air defenses. Without limits on Soviet air defenses, negotiated limits on this modernization are ill-advised. Possibly more promising are agreements to limit ASAT capabilities and to ban depressed-trajectory SLBMs, which because of their short warning time would pose an increased threat to the survivability of U.S. bombers. Neither superpower has extensive deployments of these systems, which might increase the prospects for limiting them.[115]

Achieving limits on counterforce as well as other systems will probably require the superpowers to solve the problems that are being created by systems that are especially difficult to monitor, including mobile ICBMs but especially sea-launched cruise missiles (SLCMs). Schemes for limiting SLCMs may be unworkable.[116] While not logically necessary, this could make limits on other systems harder to achieve. Although from a strategic perspective limits on SLCMs are not critical, the superpowers may be unwilling to place ceilings on certain strategic offensive systems while leaving others unconstrained.[117] If so, then SLCMs could be a major barrier to a future strategic

---

gaining chip, it was allowed by their START proposals; similarly, the United States has not tried to trade the D-5 for Soviet counterforce.

[113] Chapter Seven examines this comparison.

[114] Neither superpower has traded away strategic nuclear forces in which it had a clear advantage: Carnesale and Haass, "Conclusions," in *Superpower Arms Control*, p. 330. In addition, achieving limits on ASW and air defenses would be especially difficult since they have important conventional roles.

[115] Along these lines, Bernard Brodie observed that "it is always easier to reach international agreement to keep sharply in check a system of which deployment has not yet or only barely begun rather than to cut back on one that is fully deployed," *War and Politics* (New York: Macmillan, 1975), p. 390.

[116] For a range of views See Stanley R. Sloan, Alva M. Bowen, Jr., and Ronald O'Rourke, "The Implications for Strategic Arms Control of Nuclear Armed Sea Launched Cruise Missiles," (Washington, D.C.: Congressional Research Service, December 1985); Valerie Thomas, "Verification of Limits on Long-Range Nuclear SLCMs," *Science & Global Security* 1, nos. 1–2 (1989): 27–48; Rose E. Gottemoeller, "Finding Solutions to SLCM Arms Control Problems," *International Security* 13, no. 3 (Winter 1988/89): 175–83; and James P. Rubin, "Limiting SLCMs—A Better Way to Start," *Arms Control Today* 19, no. 3 (April 1989): 10–16.

[117] There is, however, a precedent for this type of agreement—SALT I left bombers unconstrained.

Some analysts have argued that there are good reasons for not limiting SLCMs—they are relatively inexpensive, lack a prompt counterforce capability, and are highly survivable. See Schelling and Halperin, *Strategy and Arms Control*, "Preface to the 1985 edition," p. xii, and Edward

agreement. Analyses of mobile missile basing modes show that there are co-operative measures that would enable the United States to monitor Soviet launchers with acceptable uncertainty.[118] Extensive cooperation, including on-site inspection, seems far more likely since the INF Treaty, which provides for extensive cooperative measures. However, monitoring a ceiling on mobiles promises to be more difficult than monitoring a complete ban;[119] and most analysts believe that a strategic arms control agreement should be held to a higher standard than an agreement limiting long-range theater nuclear missiles. In addition, concern about whether an agreement is adequately verifiable would probably increase if the superpowers consider moving to still smaller forces. Developing cooperative measures that make adequate verification possible therefore deserves priority. If these verification problems prove insurmountable, we may find that an important opportunity to ban SLCMs and mobile missiles passed while the Reagan administration pursued infeasible reductions and SDI.

Beyond calling for priorities, the likely difficulty of reaching agreements highlights the importance of unilateral measures. Since the United States would be more secure without a counterforce doctrine, it should not deploy larger numbers of highly lethal ballistic missiles even if constraints on Soviet counterforce cannot be negotiated. As noted above, whatever benefits coun-

---

N. Luttwak, "Ten Questions about SALT II, *Commentary* 68, no. 2 (August 1979): 27–28. See also Sidney D. Drell and Thomas H. Johnson, "Managing Strategic Weapons," *Foreign Affairs* 66, no. 5 (Summer 1988): 1037–39. However, others have pointed to the short-warning-time threat that SLCMs could pose to U.S. command and control—see note 1 in Chapter Seven.

[118] On land-mobile basing see Steve Fetter, "Verifying START," *Public Agenda* 2, no. 1 (Fall/Winter 1989): 1–19; Report of the Defense Policy Panel of the Committee on Armed Services, U.S. House of Representatives, *Breakout, Verification and Force Structure: Dealing with the Full Implications of START* (Washington, D.C.: GPO, 1988); Harry Sauerwein, "Mobile ICBMs and Arms Control," *Survival* (September/October 1981): 215–22, and Louis C. Finch, "Verification of Arms Control Limits on Land-Mobile ICBM Launchers," *Congressional Record* 129, no. 42 (April 7, 1983). On verifying the multiple protective structure basing mode proposed during the Carter administration see Office of Technology Assessment, *MX Missile Basing* (Washington, D.C.: GPO, 1981), pp. 58–59, 320–21; U.S. Congress, *Fiscal Year 1982 Arms Control Impact Statements*, Joint Committee Print, 97th Cong., 1st sess. (1981), pp. 41, 63–67; Paul K. Davis, "Land-Mobile ICBMs: Verification and Breakout," in William C. Potter, ed., *Verification and SALT: The Challenge of Strategic Deception* (Boulder, Colo.: Westview Press, 1980); and Stephen M. Meyer, "Verification and the ICBM Shell-Game," *International Security* 4, no. 2 (Fall 1979): 40–68.

[119] There is a history of U.S. doubts about whether mobiles could be adequately verified. This concern led to a U.S. unilateral statement in SALT I opposing the deployment of mobile missiles: Unilateral Statement 3.B, reprinted in ACDA, *Arms Control and Disarmament Agreements* (August 1980), p. 56. Concerns about verifiability reduced enthusiasm for deceptive mobile basing in some circles of the Carter administration: Strobe Talbott, *Endgame: The Inside Story of SALT* (New York: Harper and Row, 1979), p. 170. And the Reagan administration proposed banning mobile missiles in part because of verification: Gerald M. Boyd, "Reagan Proposes U.S.-Soviet Accord on Mobile Missiles," *New York Times*, 2 November 1985, p. 4.

terforce might provide as a bargaining chip are insufficient to warrant additional counterforce. The United States should probably move in the opposite direction, unilaterally reducing some of the counterforce it has already deployed.

Unfortunately, achieving this unilateral restraint may not be easier than negotiated restraint—the doctrinal and organizational factors that impede negotiations will also tend to block unilateral restraint. Ironically, arms control will be far less necessary if superpower doctrines change.[120] On the other hand, arms control would be most valuable if it could facilitate a shift in the superpowers' nuclear doctrines. Arms control might play such a role if the United States was unwilling to unilaterally reject its counterforce doctrine, but a winning domestic coalition would support this change once the Soviet Union agreed to match it.

The arms control agenda I have outlined may appear less ambitious than many proposals common in the arms control debate, including the reduction proposals developed by the Reagan and Bush administrations. If so, this appearance stems largely from rejecting the conventional wisdom that reducing force size would provide large benefits. In fact, my proposals are quite ambitious—unlike reductions, turning the superpowers away from counterforce will require fundamental changes in their strategic nuclear policies. Such a policy, by combining restraints on counterforce with ceilings, would provide essentially all the benefits arms control can offer.

Thus, policymakers in the field of arms control face a variety of challenges. They must redefine its agenda, shifting the emphasis from reductions to counterforce. This requires linking arms control more explicitly to the debate over the requirements of deterrence, and then winning this debate against those who favor a counterforce doctrine. This will increase the prospects for both negotiated and unilateral restraint. The shift away from reductions also requires accepting that U.S. policy should be directed entirely toward making MAD as safe as possible and not implicitly directed toward a disarmed future. By focusing on how forces and military doctrines can increase the probability of war, and by establishing priorities, this revised arms control agenda holds the greatest promise for increasing U.S. security.

---

[120] Miller, "The Viability of Nuclear Arms Control," p. 266, reaches the same conclusion.

CHAPTER ELEVEN

Conclusions

THE PRECEDING chapters provide a detailed analysis of a wide range of issues and arguments central to U.S. nuclear strategy and force posture. I first explored the theoretical and factual disputes that underlie the debate over strategic nuclear policy, identifying the basic questions and then assessing competing answers. Following chapters then used this foundation to assess the benefits and costs of specific policies. Among its advantages, this type of systematic analysis enables us to understand policy disputes in terms of disagreements over basic questions—instead of the details of specific debates—and to explore more carefully the logic that links these more general positions to policy conclusions. Taken as a whole, the book demonstrates that analysts' positions on basic questions provide a reasonably fine-grained map of where they will stand in the debate over nuclear strategy and forces.[1] Further, we find that there are a relatively small number of basic disputes and, therefore, that focusing on them provides valuable leverage in the policy debate.

While the individual chapters are the best guide to my conclusions on specific questions, this book reaches two broad substantive conclusions. First, the United States should explicitly reject efforts to move from MAD to alternative strategic nuclear worlds. The United States would probably be less secure in any of the three basic alternatives than it is in MAD. Thorough analysis demonstrates that even the best case for the alternatives—perfect (and near-perfect) strategic defenses, U.S. superiority, and disarmament—is insufficient to make any of them clearly preferable to MAD. More likely cases for these alternatives show them to be even less desirable.

Understood broadly, the advantages of MAD reflect the overwhelming advantage that nuclear weapons give to defense (retaliation) over offense (damage limitation). The result is that nuclear weapons essentially eliminate the security dilemma, thereby enabling both superpowers to simultaneously satisfy their requirements for deterrence with high confidence. These advantages of MAD go beyond the ability of nuclear weapons to provide a highly effective deterrent by threatening enormous costs in response to aggression. The United States could threaten the same costs with higher credibility if it regained nu-

---

[1] This said, I should add that most policy issues also contain some specific arguments that do not arise, or are far less prominent, in other policy issues. Further, analysts who start from essentially the same positions on these disputes do not always reach the same conclusions. This need not indicate inconsistency, since they could, for example, place different weights on the various costs and benefits of a given policy.

clear superiority. MAD has the additional advantage of helping to eliminate fundamental causes of war by providing both superpowers with a high degree of security, thereby creating the opportunity to avoid many of the dangers generated by international anarchy and the more specific dangers identified by the spiral model. All else being equal, the United States enjoys greater security when the Soviet Union is more secure.

A number of near term-policy implications follow. Most generally, policies should not be pursued because they might increase the probability of eventually reaching one of these alternatives. Thus, although there *may* be arguments for directing arms control toward reducing the size of superpower forces, enhancing the prospects for disarmament is not one of them. Similarly, even if deploying less-than-near-perfect ballistic missile defense would increase the probability of eventually reaching a world of mutual highly effective defenses, this should not count in its favor; instead, these strategic defenses should be judged more narrowly on the benefits they can provide in MAD. And, although U.S. superiority would probably require combining extensive deployments of offensive counterforce with strategic defense, this does not strengthen the case for pursuing these programs.

Furthermore, the United States should not pursue research and development of ballistic missile defense with an eye toward eventually deploying near-perfect defenses. There are no benefits to keeping this possibility open. Rather, R&D should be pursued solely to deter Soviet withdrawal from the ABM Treaty. Many supporters of the ABM Treaty appear to favor continuing research for both purposes, reflecting their continuing interest in near-perfect defenses. The difference is significant. As the development of BMD technology progresses, pursuing the former objective could lead the United States to conclude that the treaty imposes undesirable constraints, even if the Soviets prefer to continue living within its bounds. In this case, the United States will eventually face a severe tradeoff between continuing to have Soviet BMD constrained and continuing to investigate the feasibility of near-perfect defenses. This tension does not exist if the United States limits its objectives to deterring Soviet withdrawal from the ABM Treaty.

Having concluded that reaching any of these alternative worlds should not be a long-term U.S. objective, understanding the transitions from MAD to them is much less important. Nevertheless, the preceding chapters offer one insight worth highlighting: the policies that are frequently seen as first steps would not increase the probability of eventually reaching the alternative worlds. Achieving the alternatives would require truly fundamental changes in military capabilities and/or superpower relations. Because the supposed first steps would not help bring about these necessary changes, they would not significantly increase the probability of reaching the alternative worlds. For example, disarmament would be possible only following the virtual elimination of superpower hostility and distrust; even large reductions in the size of superpower forces are quite unlikely to increase the probability of such a transformation. Consequently, analysts who remain unconvinced by my arguments about why these worlds are not clearly preferable to MAD still should not support these near-term policies on the grounds that they are first steps out of MAD.

My second broad conclusion is that having committed itself to living in MAD, the United States should reject strategies based on counterforce and adopt a strategy based on a flexible assured destruction capability—that is, one that provides a spectrum of options for attacking Soviet society but little or no capability dedicated to destroying Soviet forces.

The United States should reject its current nuclear doctrine for three basic reasons. First, the United States should not buy counterforce for damage limitation since feasible counterforce is insufficiently effective to risk launching a first strike to reduce the costs of an all-out war.

Second, counterforce is unnecessary for deterrence: it adds little or nothing to the U.S. ability to deter Soviet attacks, including large conventional attacks against U.S. allies. Although proponents have presented a long list of arguments for counterforce, none of them is strong. Many of these arguments are based on the positions presented by the military denial school and therefore suffer the weaknesses of this foundation. For example, arguments for deploying counterforce to favorably shift or to restore the ratio of surviving forces fail because the ratio of forces matters so little in MAD. Other arguments for counterforce are logically flawed. Probably most prominent is the argument that the United States needs counterforce to threaten limited nuclear attacks. Although limited nuclear threats might play an important role in increasing U.S. credibility, counterforce does not enhance these options. The logic supporting limited options calls for preserving Soviet incentives for restrained retaliation. Although this demands options that would leave most of Soviet society unharmed, the ability to destroy Soviet forces offers nothing special. Forces capable of destroying Soviet industrial capabilities and population centers can provide the United States with a wide range of limited options, enabling it to threaten from relatively low costs to near total costs. To increase the variety of its options, the United States might also target Soviet forces, but this does not require the ability to destroy them efficiently or in large numbers. Considering the entire list of arguments, proponents have identified at most scant benefits.

Third, continued U.S. interest in these counterforce policies reflects misunderstandings about the implications of the nuclear revolution, and brings a variety of dangers. Correctly understood, nuclear weapons have created a world of overwhelming defense dominance (of retaliatory capabilities over damage-limitation capabilities) that virtually eliminates first-strike incentives and crisis instability. The United States, however, has not fully accepted the nuclear revolution: it continues to place great importance on the ability to destroy Soviet nuclear forces and has not rejected attempts to limit damage in an all-out war. In a severe crisis, given this view of MAD, the extensive U.S.

counterforce arsenal might encourage a U.S. leader to risk starting a cata-strophic war in the hope of limiting damage, scant and misconceived as these benefits would be. It might also pressure Soviet leaders to preempt based on their belief that the United States might launch a damage limitation attack. Further, even if the United States acquires an extensive counterforce arsenal for reasons other than damage-limitation, Soviet leaders might not appreciate the difference.

In addition, a doctrine that requires an extensive counterforce arsenal could be a source of superpower tensions, generating the political effects predicted by the spiral model. Although in MAD nuclear weapons essentially eliminate the security dilemma, U.S. counterforce can generate negative political con-sequences by suggesting that the United States remains committed to acquir-ing military advantages. In addition, misunderstanding the nuclear revolution leads American analysts to exaggerate the threat that Soviet counterforce poses to U.S. security, which can in turn support exaggerations of Soviet hos-tility. Furthermore, an extensive counterforce arsenal could increase the prob-ability of accidental war, create barriers to valuable arms control agreements, and increase the economic costs of U.S. forces.

Consequently, the United States should revise its doctrine and warplans, explicitly shifting to a doctrine based on a flexible assured destruction capa-bility. The United States should stop acquiring counterforce and should seri-ously consider retiring much of the counterforce it has already deployed. In addition, U.S. arms control policy should give priority to limiting counter-force, not reducing force size per se, and should strengthen the ABM Treaty to avoid a competition in strategic defenses that might look useful for damage limitation.

Further, more attention should be paid to how the United States should em-ploy (and should not employ) nuclear weapons. Thinking through these issues could reduce the probability and scale of nuclear war—especially since the United States will probably have large numbers of counterforce weapons well into the next century. What factors should a U.S. decisionmaker consider in deciding whether to employ nuclear weapons and what type of attack to launch? How should U.S. objectives, the level of the conflict, and information about the adversary's objectives, doctrine, and capabilities influence this cru-cial choice?

As important, how should the decision process be structured? One way to reduce the probability of poor decisions is to convince leaders that thinking in some detail about how to use and not use nuclear weapons deserves their con-sideration well *before* the question ever arises.[2] It may be at least as important,

---

[2] American presidents have tended to show little interest in the nuclear warplans. See Janne E. Nolan, *Guardians of the Arsenal: The Politics of Nuclear Strategy* (New York: Basic Books, 1989).

however, to insure that the president has advisers who are responsible for understanding the full range of issues involved in such a critical decision. Decisions on the use of nuclear weapons are likely to be influenced by who briefs the president, how they describe U.S. options, and their expectations about Soviet reactions. Under the best circumstances, deciding whether and how to employ nuclear weapons promises to be exceedingly difficult. To balance the important perspective of military advisers, political advisers with expertise in nuclear operations and capabilities—including full knowledge of the nuclear warplans and alert procedures—should be included in decisions to use nuclear weapons as well as to move to high levels of alert.[3]

Although these changes in U.S. doctrine do not require technological advances or cooperation with the Soviet Union, a radical shift away from counterforce policies must overcome imposing barriers. First, as we have reviewed in some detail, proponents of counterforce present a wide array of arguments, many of which are influential in the U.S. debate and are incorporated in current U.S. doctrine. The case against counterforce is strong but opponents have been unable to win this debate. This may be partly because traditional military thinking and conventionalized nuclear strategy have an advantage in competing with the logic of the nuclear revolution—which requires us to accept that in MAD deterrence depends on threatening costs, not defeating Soviet forces. Further, some analysts believe that forgoing preparations to reduce the costs of an all-out war is irresponsible or defeatist, even though the costs would remain so high. Opponents of counterforce may also be partly responsible since they have not presented a full analysis of the costs of counterforce nor admitted its potential benefits, limited as they are.

The second major barrier is the U.S. military's organizational interest in counterforce. As discussed in Chapter Seven, the military has often given priority to acquiring counterforce weapons; and, as discussed in Chapter Ten, has often been successful in insuring that they were not traded away in arms control negotiations. This inclination toward counterforce reflects basic organizational interests. Thus, moving away from a counterforce doctrine will require a fundamental reorientation of the military commands responsible for strategic nuclear forces.

We can best understand the depth of the military's inclination toward coun-

---

[3] Richard K. Betts, "Surprise Attack and Preemption," in Graham T. Allison, Albert Carnesale, and Joseph Nye, Jr., eds., *Hawks, Doves & Owls* (New York, W. W. Norton, 1985), pp. 73–74, observes that "to ensure consistency between political aims and military signals" political advisers should be included in crisis decisions, including decisions on changing levels of alert. He holds that military professionals face three problems in these situations: "(1) their professional ethos forbids them to express opinions on political matters; (2) they have a conflict of interest: their primary responsibility—to maximize capability to wage war—can conflict with diplomatic crisis management, which is the responsibility of civilians; and (3) historically, virtually all military leaders have tried to prevent 'meddling' by policy authorities in operational matters."

terforce, and damage limitation in particular, in terms of recent studies that find that militaries tend to prefer offensive strategies.[4] First, militaries prefer offensive strategies because they help increase the size and budget of the organization. Damage limitation requires large, highly sophisticated forces; in contrast, deterrence based upon the ability to retaliate against cities requires a relatively small survivable force that need not be accurate or prompt.

Second, to manage the uncertainty that exists in the external environment, organizations establish "standard scenarios" for which they prepare their capabilities and standard operating procedures.[5] In the special case of militaries, the competitive nature of warfare also encourages plans to deny the adversary its standard scenario.[6] Thus, a doctrine that includes the option of a counterforce first strike would be attractive: it enables the United States to employ its force most effectively against Soviet capabilities, thereby limiting the range of bad outcomes the Soviet military could achieve; and it eliminates the Soviet ability to take the initiative and to fight the war it planned. Along the same lines, in preparation for scenarios in which the Soviets attack first, this logic calls for planning to launch a counterforce second strike before the Soviet weapons reach the United States. This type of plan eliminates uncertainty about which U.S. forces will be available for retaliation and enables the United States to destroy as much of the remaining Soviet force as possible.

Third, military organizations seek autonomy.[7] The alternative to massive counterforce attacks designed for damage limitation is a deterrent strategy based on limited nuclear options and bargaining. Limited options are unattractive because they will necessarily involve civilians in the fighting of a protracted war. Employing a limited option is also unappealing since it decreases the United States' ability to use its forces most effectively—limited attacks forgo the initiative and do not disrupt the adversary's plans.[8]

---

[4] My discussion follows closely the derivation and discussion of these military organizational proclivities in Barry R. Posen, *The Sources of Military Doctrine: France, Britain and Germany between the World Wars* (Ithaca: Cornell University Press, 1984), pp. 34–50. Also evaluating the preference of militaries for the offense are Jack Snyder, "Civil-Military Relations and the Cult of the Offensive, 1914 and 1984," *International Security* 9, no. 1 (Summer 1984): 108–46; idem, *The Ideology of the Offensive: Military Decision Making and the Disasters of 1914* (Ithaca: Cornell University Press, 1984); and Stephen Van Evera, "Causes of War," Chapter 7.

[5] Richard K. Betts, *Soldiers, Statesmen and Cold War Crises* (Cambridge: Harvard University Press, 1977), observes that "military planners and the Joint Chiefs who rely on them usually have a preference for formulaic solutions that reduce problems to manageable terms, clarify responsibilities and calculations of capabilities vis-à-vis objectives, and maximize certainty and efficiency" (p. 157); see also p. 36.

[6] Posen, *The Sources of Military Doctrine*, p. 48.

[7] Morton H. Halperin, *Bureaucratic Politics and Foreign Policy* (Washington, D.C.: Brookings Institution, 1974), pp. 51–54; see also Betts, *Soldiers, Statesmen and Cold War Crises*, pp. 5–12.

[8] These considerations contributed to a lack of enthusiasm among the Joint Chiefs of Staff toward McNamara's call for nuclear options in the early 1960s. See Henry S. Rowen, "The

Fourth, a damage-limitation strategy allows the military to protect its organizational essence, which is attacking the adversary's forces in pursuit of victory.[9] Militaries prefer to defeat the adversary's capabilities, not manipulate its will. Thus, we expect militaries to dislike deterrence strategies, especially those that envision bargaining with limited nuclear options. Comparing how militaries view different strategies, Posen observes that "from specialists in victory, defense turns soldiers into specialists in attrition, and deterrence makes them specialists in slaughter."[10] Former commander of the Strategic Air Command Russell Dougherty observes that "a commander planning deliberate attacks on cities and non-combatants would . . . have a major morale problem on his hands with his command and his combat crews."[11]

Given these strong organizational interests, we expect the U.S. military to remain strongly committed to counterforce. This is not surprising once we recognize that damage limitation may not be literally impossible. If the military sees itself as responsible for achieving the best possible outcome if war occurs, then from its perspective counterforce will continue to make sense. Further, even if it is entirely infeasible, the military might continue to pursue damage limitation. Organizational interests can put blinders on organizations. According to Jack Snyder, "military decision-makers will tend to overestimate the feasibility of an operational plan if a realistic assessment would require forsaking fundamental beliefs or values. Whenever offensive doctrines are inextricably tied to the autonomy, 'essence,' or basic worldview of the military, the cognitive need to see the offensive as possible will be strong."[12] Thus, in light of its organizational interests, we expect that the U.S. military may view counterforce in ways that overestimate its ability to limit damage, or may avoid addressing the issue of feasibility altogether.[13]

Because the U.S. military has extensive influence in determining U.S. force requirements, shifting to a strategy based on a flexible assured destruction capability will probably require an overwhelming consensus on the strength

Evolution of Strategic Nuclear Doctrine," in Laurence Martin, ed., *Strategic Thought in the Nuclear Age* (Baltimore: Johns Hopkins University Press, 1979), pp. 154–55.

[9] On the importance of organizational essence see Halperin, *Bureaucratic Politics and Foreign Policy*, pp. 28–40. Graham T. Allison and Frederick A. Morris, "Armaments and Arms Control: Exploring the Determinants of Military Weapons," *Daedalus* (Summer 1975): 120, note that "Air Force officers supported MIRV because it contributed to their central mission, namely fighting strategic wars, and their special interest, namely destruction of 'time-urgent' military targets."

[10] Posen, *The Sources of Military Doctrine*, p. 50; see also pp. 48–49 on military inclinations to focus on military rather than political factors.

[11] Russell E. Dougherty, "The Psychological Climate of Nuclear Command," in Carter et al., *Managing Nuclear Operations*, p. 423.

[12] Snyder, "Civil-Military Relations," p. 137.

[13] Finding support for this expectation is Lynn Eden, "Oblivion Is Not Enough: How the U.S. Air Force Thinks about Deterrence, Nuclear War, and Nuclear Weapons" (unpublished paper, February 1989).

of the case against counterforce. At a minimum, this will require winning the debate over U.S. nuclear strategy. I hope that by providing a more extensive analysis of counterforce—exploring the problems with superiority, and highlighting the dangers of counterforce in MAD and the very limited benefits that counterforce might provide—this book will contribute to creating such a consensus.

Recent dramatic changes in Soviet military and foreign policy might play an important role in helping to establish this consensus. The Soviet Union now poses a significantly reduced conventional military threat to Western Europe. Probably more important, there appears to be a consensus in the United States and among its Western European allies that Soviet intentions have changed, that the Soviet Union is less interested in challenging their interests. This belief has contributed to increasingly broad acceptance that the Cold War has come to an end.

These changes influence the debate over U.S. nuclear doctrine in two reinforcing ways. First, one of the key missions for U.S. counterforce is deterring conventional and limited nuclear attacks against U.S. allies, most prominently its Western European allies. With the reduction in the Soviet threat, the need to extend deterrence is also reduced. Second, many of the arguments for American counterforce, including extending deterrence, rest on the need to hedge against extremely risky Soviet behavior. The importance of hedging decreases as Soviet objectives become clearer and less threatening. In short, changes in the Soviet Union have further damaged two key rationales for American counterforce, thereby adding to the case against the current American nuclear strategy.

The basic arguments for revising U.S. nuclear doctrine were strong before recent changes in the Soviet Union. These changes, therefore, are best understood as improving the prospects for creating a consensus that American nuclear strategy should be revised along the lines I have outlined, not as being the reason for a new strategy. A less threatening view of the Soviet Union may be helpful in winning the ongoing debate over U.S. strategy and in undermining support for continuing investments in the improvement and expansion of the U.S. counterforce arsenal. The prospects for revising U.S. doctrine may also be increased by Soviet willingness to move away from its counterforce policies and to negotiate arms control agreements that limit both countries' counterforce.

However, in presenting the case for rejecting the current American counterforce doctrine, we should emphasize that it does not hinge on improved superpower relations and a continuation of recent trends in the Soviet Union. The possibility of a reversal in Soviet foreign policy cannot be entirely ruled out. Proponents of maintaining the current U.S. nuclear doctrine can combine this possibility with the fact that the Soviet Union will retain large conventional and nuclear forces to rebuild a case for hedging against future Soviet aggression. This case for counterforce, however, is undermined by the weakness of the arguments that have been used to support U.S. doctrine for over twenty years.

In closing, the good news is that MAD is potentially much safer than the prevailing wisdom suggests and is probably preferable to the basic alternatives. Thus, U.S. policy objectives should be more modest and more achievable than has generally been believed. The bad news is that the superpowers have failed to take advantage of the opportunities created by the nuclear revolution. The overwhelming dominance of retaliatory capabilities provides the United States with the opportunity to maintain high confidence in its ability to deter Soviet attacks while at the same time avoiding the first-strike incentives and exaggerated political conflicts that necessary military capabilities can sometimes generate. Instead of accepting this opportunity, the United States continues emphasizing offensive counterforce and has renewed its interest in deploying highly effective strategic defenses. Clear thinking about nuclear weapons should help redirect U.S. policy in safer directions.

Index

ABM. *See* ballistic missile defense
ABM Treaty. *See* Antiballistic Missile Treaty
Abrahamson, Lt. Gen. James, 106n.11
accidental war, 249–51, 301–3, 318n.9
Adomeit, Hannes, 29n.28, 69n.16, 242n.74
Allison, Graham, 6n.9, 161n.66, 367n.9
Allyn, Bruce J., 162n.66
Almquist, Peter, 38n.53
American Physical Society Study Group, 105n.7
American Security Council, 65n.7, 344n.75
Anderson, J. Edward, 257n.2
Antiballistic Missile Treaty, 16, 87, 90, 255, 284, 286, 298, 305–8, 310–14, 331–32, 346, 353, 355–56, 362; and Standing Consultative Commission, 312
antisatellite capability, 119, 142, 314, 325
antisubmarine warfare, 74n.32, 145n.24, 208, 251–52, 254, 261, 321, 325, 358
anti-tactical ballistic missiles, 313
Arbatov, Alexi, 81n.53
Arbatov, G. A., 84
Arkin, William, 87n.79, 343n.73
Armbruster, Frank, 302n.42
arms control: and bargaining chips, 344–48; and ceilings, 328, 332–35, 356–57; contribution to U.S. military capabilities, 320–25; and cost of war, 339–51; deterrent value of, 318–28; diplomatic value of, 329–37; feasibility of, 353–55; for limiting counterforce, 330–34, 352–60; and lulling effect, 332–34; and nuclear freeze, 327–28; and reductions, 318, 328–29, 335–37, 339–41, 357, 360
Arms Control and Disarmament Agency, 23, 359n.119
arms race stability. *See* robustness of forces
Art, Robert, 27n.21, 73n.28, 105n.8, 107n.13, 182, 343n.73, 345n.78
Aspin, Les, 258n.5, 270, 279n.48, 280n.50
Axelrod, Robert, 183n.35

B-1 bomber, 343
B-2 bomber, 16, 88, 208, 248, 253, 255
Backfire bomber, 348

back-to-MAD capability, 141–44
BAD (Both Are Defended), 103–32; defined, 107. *See also* ballistic missile defense
Baker, John, 147n.30
Balaschak, Mark, 323n.23
Ball, Desmond, 5n.6, 23n.7, 34n.42, 212n.10, 213n.13, 247n.88, 290n.11, 291n.15
ballistic missile defense: and accidental war, 301–3; and allies, 128; and arms control, 297–301; and command and control, 289–92; costs of, 305–10; feasibility of, 104–5; and ICBM survivability, 288–89; and multipolarity, 129–31; near-perfect type, 111–24; perfect type, 107–11; and small attacks, 292–94; and suitcase bombs, 128–29; and uncertainty, 126–27, 294–301
Barash, G. E., 288n.7
bargaining chips, 300n.34, 344–48
Barkenbus, Jack, 315n.3
Barnett, Richard, 166n.4, 181n.30
Barnett, Roger, 31n.30, 218n.22
Barton, John, 6n.9, 166n.4, 171n.10, 181n.30
Bechhoefer, Bernard, 166n.4
Bennett, Andrew, 70nn. 19 and 20
Bennett, Bruce, 257n.2, 267n.23
Beres, Louis Rene, 245n.83
Berman, Robert, 147n.30
Betts, Richard, 13n.1, 38nn. 52 and 53, 40n.55, 41n.65, 56n.95, 151nn. 39 and 40, 153n.45, 155n.52, 201n.64, 208n.3, 248n.92, 282n.56, 301n.38, 309n.55, 354n.101, 365n.3, 366nn. 5 and 7
Bialer, Severyn, 89nn. 87 and 88, 90n.94
Biddle, Steven, 139n.12
Biddle, Tami Davis, 153n.46
Bing, George, 22n.6, 329n.45, 340n.64
Bjorkman, Thomas, 86n.72
Blair, Bruce, 5n.8, 22n.7, 38n.52, 47n.73, 207, 245n.87, 264n.18, 265n.19, 324n.34, 326n.36
Blechman, Barry, 41n.56, 66n.9, 149n.35, 309n.54, 338n.59, 356n.110
Blight, James, 161n.66